PRAISE FOR

THE SLEEPWALKERS

n important book. . . . One of the most impressive and stimulating studies of the period
ver published."
                                        —Max Hastings, *The Sunday Times*

monumental new volume. . . . Revelatory, even revolutionary. . . . Clark has done a master-
ıl job explaining the inexplicable."
                                        —*The Boston Globe*

xcellent. . . . The book is stylishly written as well as superb scholarship. No analysis of the
rigins of the First World War will henceforth be able to bypass this magisterial work."
                                        —Ian Kershaw, BBC History

his compelling examination of the causes of World War I deserves to become the new
tandard one-volume account of that contentious subject."   —*Foreign Affairs*

he centenary of the Great War is nearly upon us, and the first salvoes of a barrage of
ew histories have arrived. Mightiest among them is *The Sleepwalkers*. . . . As spacious
nd convincing a treatment as has yet appeared. . . . Clark's prose is clear and laced with
olor."
                                        —*The Daily Beast*

great book. . . . An amazing narrative history of the crisis and the larger context." —*Slate*

superb account of the causes of the first world war. . . . Clark brilliantly puts this illogical
onflict into context."
                                        —*The Guardian*

he most readable account of the origins of the First World War since Barbara Tuchman's
he Guns of August. The difference is that *The Sleepwalkers* is a lovingly researched work
f the highest scholarship. It is hard to believe we will ever see a better narrative of what
vas perhaps the biggest collective blunder in the history of international relations."
                                        —Niall Ferguson

 breathtakingly good book. . . . Clark's narrative sophistication, his philosophical aware-
ıess, and his almost preternatural command of his sources make *The Sleepwalkers* an
xemplary instance of how to navigate this tricky terrain. It is not only the best book on the
rigins of the First World War that I know but also a brilliant and intellectually bracing
nodel for the writing of history more generally."
                                        —Thomas Laqueur, *The London Review of Books*

 meticulously researched, superbly organized, and handsomely written account."
                                        —*Military History Quarterly*

THE SLEEPWALKERS

ALSO BY CHRISTOPHER CLARK

Iron Kingdom: The Rise and Downfall of Prussia, 1600–1947

Kaiser Wilhelm II: A Life in Power

*The Politics of Conversion: Missionary Protestantism
and the Jews in Prussia, 1728–1947*

THE
SLEEPWALKERS

HOW EUROPE WENT TO WAR IN 1914

CHRISTOPHER CLARK

HARPER ⊙ PERENNIAL

NEW YORK • LONDON • TORONTO • SYDNEY • NEW DELHI • AUCKLAND

HARPER ● PERENNIAL

First published in Great Britain in 2012 by Allen Lane, an imprint of Penguin Books.

First U.S. hardcover published in 2013 by HarperCollins Publishers.

FIRST HARPER PERENNIAL EDITION PUBLISHED 2014.

The Library of Congress has catalogued the hardcover edition as follows:

Clark, Christopher M.
    The sleepwalkers : how Europe went to war in 1914 / Christopher Clark. — First U.S. edition.
        p. cm.
    "First published in Great Britain in 2012 by Allen Lane, an imprint of Penguin Books."
    Includes bibliographical references and index.
    ISBN 978-0-06-114665-7
    1. World War, 1914–1918—Causes.   2. World War, 1914–1918—Diplomatic history.   3. Europe—Politics and government—1871–1918.   I. Title.
    D511.C54 2013
    940.3'11—dc23   2012038473

ISBN 978-0-06-114666-4 (pbk.)

15   16   17   18   OFF/RRD   10   9   8

For Josef and Alexander

Contents

PART THREE
Crisis

List of Illustrations

List of Maps

Acknowledgements

On 12 May 1916, James Joseph O'Brien, grazier, of Tallwood Station in northern New South Wales applied to enlist in the Australian Imperial Force. After training for two months at the Sydney showgrounds, Private O'Brien was assigned to the 35th Battalion of the 3rd Division of the AIF and embarked on the SS *Benalla* for England, where he received further training. On around 18 August 1917, he joined his unit in France, in time to take part in the battles of the Third Ypres campaign.

Jim was my great-uncle. He had been dead for twenty years when my aunt Joan Pratt, née Munro, gave me his wartime journal, a small brown notebook full of packing lists, addresses, instructions and the odd laconic diary entry. Commenting on the battle for Broodseinde Ridge on 4 October 1917, Jim wrote: 'It was a great battle and I have no desire to see another.' This is his account, dated 12 October 1917, of the battle of Passchendaele II:

> We left the details camp (which was close to Ypres) and made for the Passchendaele sector of the line. It took us ten hours to get there and we were tired out after the march. Twenty-five minutes after arriving there (which was 5.25 on the morning of the 12th) we hopped over the bags. All went well until we reached a marsh which gave us great trouble to get through. When we *did* get through, our barrage had shifted ahead about a mile and we had to make pace to catch it. About 11 a.m. we got to our second objective and remained there until 4 p.m., when we had to retreat, [...] It was only the will of God that got me through, for machine gun bullets and shrapnel were flying everywhere.

Jim's active war service came an end at 2 a.m. on 30 May 1918, when, in the words of his journal, he 'stopped a bomb from the Fatherland and got wounded in both legs'. The shell had fallen at his feet, blowing him upwards and killing the men around him.

By the time I knew him, Jim was a wry, frail old man whose memory was on the blink. He was reticent on the subject of his war experience, but I do remember one conversation that took place when I was around nine years old. I asked him whether the men who fought in the war were scared or keen to get into the fight. He replied that some were scared and some were keen. Did the keen ones fight better than the scared ones, I asked. 'No,' said Jim. 'It was the keen ones who shat themselves first.' I was deeply impressed by this reply and puzzled over it – especially the word 'first' – for some time.

The horror of this remote conflict still commands our attention. But its mystery lies elsewhere, in the obscure and convoluted events that made such carnage possible. In exploring these, I have accumulated more intellectual debts than I can possibly repay. Conversations with Daniel Anders, Margaret Lavinia Anderson, Chris Bayly, Tim Blanning, Konstantin Bosch, Richard Bosworth, Annabel Brett, Mark Cornwall, Richard Drayton, Richard Evans, Robert Evans, Niall Ferguson, Isabel V. Hull, Alan Kramer, Günther Kronenbitter, Michael Ledger-Lomas, Dominic Lieven, James Mackenzie, Alois Maderspacher, Mark Migotti, Annika Mombauer, Frank Lorenz Müller, William Mulligan, Paul Munro, Paul Robinson, Ulinka Rublack, James Sheehan, Brendan Simms, Robert Tombs and Adam Tooze have helped me to sharpen arguments. Ira Katznelson provided advice on decision theory; Andrew Preston on adversarial structures in the making of foreign policy; Holger Afflerbach on the Riezler diaries, the Triple Alliance and finer details of German policy in the July Crisis; Keith Jeffery on Henry Wilson; John Röhl on Kaiser Wilhelm II. Hartmut Pogge von Strandmann drew my attention to the little-known but informative memoirs of his relative Basil Strandmann, who was the Russian chargé d'affaires in Belgrade when war broke out in 1914. Keith Neilson shared an unpublished study of the decision-makers at the apex of the British Foreign Office; Bruce Menning allowed me to see his important article, forthcoming in *Journal of Modern History*, on Russian military intelligence; Thomas Otte sent me a pre-publication pdf of his magisterial new study *The Foreign Office Mind* and Jürgen Angelow did the same with his *Der Weg in die Urkatastrophe*; John Keiger and Gerd Krumeich sent offprints and references on French foreign policy; Andreas Rose sent a copy fresh from the press of his *Zwischen Empire und Kontinent*; Zara Steiner, whose books are landmarks in this field, was generous with her time and conversation and shared a dossier of articles and notes. Over the last five years, Samuel R. Williamson, whose classic studies of the international crisis and Austro-Hungarian foreign policy opened several of the lines of enquiry explored in this book, sent unpublished chapters, contacts and references and allowed me to pick his brains on the arcana of Austro-Hungarian policy. The email friendship that resulted has been one of the rewards of working on this book.

Thanks are also due to those who helped me surmount linguistic boundaries: to Miroslav Došen for his help with Serbian printed sources and to Srdjan Jovanović for assistance with archival documents in Belgrade; to Rumen Cholakov for help with Bulgarian secondary texts and to Sergei Podbolotov, unstinting labourer in the vineyard of history, whose wisdom, intelligence and wry humour made my research in Moscow as enjoyable and enlightening as it was productive. Then there are those generous spirits who read part or all or the work in various states of completion: Jonathan Steinberg and John Thompson both read every word and offered insightful comments and suggestions. David Reynolds helped to put fires out in the most challenging chapters. Patrick Higgins read and criticized the first chapter and warned of pitfalls. Amitav Ghosh provided invaluable feedback and advice. For all the errors that remain, I accept responsibility.

I am fortunate in having a wonderful agent in Andrew Wylie, to whom I owe a great deal, and immensely grateful to Simon Winder of Penguin for his encouragement, guidance and enthusiasm, and to Richard Duguid for overseeing the book's production with amiable efficiency. The indefatigable copy-editor Bela Cunha sought out and destroyed all the errors, infelicities, inconsistencies and 'aphids' (superfluous quotation marks) she could find and remained cheerful – just – in the face of my efforts to drive her mad by tampering endlessly with the text. Nina Lübbren, whose grandfather Julius Lübbren was also at Passchendaele in 1917 (on the other side), tolerated my labours from a standpoint of benevolent neutrality. The book is dedicated with love and admiration to our two sons, Josef and Alexander, in the hope that they will never know war.

1. Europe in 1914

Introduction

The European continent was at peace on the morning of Sunday 28 June 1914, when Archduke Franz Ferdinand and his wife Sophie Chotek arrived at Sarajevo railway station. Thirty-seven days later, it was at war. The conflict that began that summer mobilized 65 million troops, claimed three empires, 20 million military and civilian deaths, and 21 million wounded. The horrors of Europe's twentieth century were born of this catastrophe; it was, as the American historian Fritz Stern put it, 'the first calamity of the twentieth century, the calamity from which all other calamities sprang'.[1] The debate over why it happened began before the first shots were fired and has been running ever since. It has spawned an historical literature of unparalleled size, sophistication and moral intensity. For international relations theorists the events of 1914 remain the political crisis *par excellence*, intricate enough to accommodate any number of hypotheses.

The historian who seeks to understand the genesis of the First World War confronts several problems. The first and most obvious is an over-supply of sources. Each of the belligerent states produced official multi-volume editions of diplomatic papers, vast works of collective archival labour. There are treacherous currents in this ocean of sources. Most of the official document editions produced in the interwar period have an apologetic spin. The fifty-seven-volume German publication *Die Grosse Politik*, comprising 15,889 documents organized in 300 subject areas, was not prepared with purely scholarly objectives in mind; it was hoped that the disclosure of the pre-war record would suffice to refute the 'war guilt' thesis enshrined in the terms of the Versailles treaty.[2] For the French government too, the post-war publication of documents was an enterprise of 'essentially political character', as Foreign Minister Jean Louis Barthou put it in May 1934. Its purpose was to 'counter-balance the campaign launched by Germany following the Treaty of Versailles'.[3] In Vienna, as Ludwig Bittner, co-editor of the eight-volume collection *Österreich-Ungarns Aussenpolitik*, pointed out in 1926, the aim was to produce an authoritative source edition before some international body – the League of Nations perhaps? – forced the Austrian government into publication under less auspicious circumstances.[4] The early Soviet documentary publications were motivated in part by the desire to prove that the war had been initiated by the autocratic Tsar and his alliance partner, the bourgeois Raymond Poincaré, in the hope of de-legitimizing French demands for the repayment of pre-war loans.[5] Even in Britain, where *British Documents on the Origins of the War* was launched amid high-minded appeals to disinterested scholarship, the resulting documentary record was not without tendentious omissions that produced a somewhat unbalanced picture of Britain's place in the events preceding the outbreak of war in 1914.[6] In short, the great European documentary editions were, for all their undeniable value to scholars, munitions in a 'world war of documents', as the German military historian Bernhard Schwertfeger remarked in a critical study of 1929.[7]

The memoirs of statesmen, commanders and other key decision-makers, though indispensable to anyone trying to understand what happened on the road to war, are no less problematic. Some are frustratingly reticent on questions of burning interest. To name just a few examples: the *Reflections on the World War* published in 1919 by German Chancellor Theobald von Bethmann Hollweg has virtually nothing to say on the subject of his actions or those of his colleagues during the July Crisis of 1914; Russian Foreign Minister Sergei Sazonov's political memoirs are breezy, pompous, intermittently mendacious and totally uninformative about his own role in key events; French President Raymond Poincaré's ten-volume memoir of his years in power is propagandistic rather than revelatory – there are striking discrepancies between his 'recollections' of events during the crisis and the contemporary jottings in his unpublished diary.[8] The amiable memoirs of British Foreign Secretary Sir Edward Grey are sketchy on the delicate question of the commitments he had made to the Entente powers before August 1914 and the role these played in his handling of the crisis.[9]

When the American historian Bernadotte Everly Schmitt of the University of Chicago travelled to Europe in the late 1920s with letters of introduction to interview former politicians who had played a role in events, he was struck by the apparently total immunity of his interlocutors to self-doubt. (The one exception was Grey, who 'spontaneously remarked' that he had made a tactical error in seeking to negotiate with Vienna through Berlin during the July Crisis, but the misjudgement alluded to was of subordinate importance and the comment reflected a specifically English style of mandarin self-deprecation rather than a genuine concession of responsibility.)[10] There were problems with memory, too. Schmitt tracked down Peter Bark, the former Russian minister of finance, now a London banker. In 1914, Bark had participated in meetings at which decisions of momentous importance were made. Yet when Schmitt met him, Bark insisted that he had 'little recollection of events from that era'.[11] Fortunately, the former minister's own contemporary notes are more informative. When the researcher Luciano Magrini travelled to Belgrade in the autumn of 1937 to interview every surviving figure with a known link to the Sarajevo conspiracy, he found that there were some witnesses who attested to matters of which they could have no knowledge, others who 'remained dumb or gave a false account of what they know', and others again who 'added adornments to their statements or were mainly interested in self-justification'.[12]

There are, moreover, still significant gaps in our knowledge. Many important exchanges between key actors were verbal and are not recorded – they can be reconstructed only from indirect evidence or later testimony. The Serbian organizations linked with the assassination at Sarajevo were extremely secretive and left virtually no paper trail. Dragutin Dimitrijević, head of Serbian military intelligence, a key figure in the plot to assassinate Archduke Franz Ferdinand at Sarajevo, regularly burned his papers. Much remains unknown about the precise content of the earliest discussions between Vienna and Berlin on what should be done in response to the assassinations at Sarajevo. The minutes of the summit meetings that took place between the French and Russian political leaderships in St Petersburg on 20–23 June, documents of potentially enormous importance to understanding the last phase of the crisis, have never been found (the Russian protocols were probably simply lost; the French team entrusted with editing the *Documents Diplomatiques Français* failed to find the French version). The Bolsheviks did publish many key diplomatic documents in an effort to discredit the imperialist machinations of the great powers, but these appeared at irregular intervals in no particular order and were generally focused on specific issues, such as Russian designs on the Bosphorus. Some documents (the exact number is still unknown) were lost in transit during the chaos of the Civil War and the Soviet Union never produced a systematically compiled documentary record to rival the British, French, German and Austrian source editions.[13] The published record on the Russian side remains, to this day, far from complete.

The exceptionally intricate structure of this crisis is another distinctive feature. The Cuban missile crisis was complex enough, yet it involved just two principal protagonists (the USA and the Soviet Union), plus a range of proxies and subordinate players. By contrast, the story of how this war came about must make sense of the multilateral interactions among five autonomous players of equal importance – Germany, Austria-Hungary, France, Russia and Britain – six, if we add Italy, plus various other strategically significant and equally autonomous sovereign actors, such as the Ottoman Empire and the states of the Balkan peninsula, a region of high political tension and instability in the years before the outbreak of war.

A further element of convolution arises from the fact that policy-making processes within the states caught up in the crisis were often far from transparent. One can think of July 1914 as an 'international' crisis, a term that suggests an array of nation-states, conceived as compact, autonomous, discrete entities, like billiard balls on a table. But the sovereign structures that generated policy during the crisis were profoundly disunified. There was uncertainty (and has been ever since among historians) about where exactly the power to shape policy was located within the various executives, and 'policies' – or at least policy-driving initiatives of various kinds – did not necessarily come from the apex of the system; they could emanate from quite peripheral locations in the diplomatic apparatus, from military commanders, from ministerial officials and even from ambassadors, who were often policy-makers in their own right.

The surviving sources thus offer up a chaos of promises, threats, plans and prognostications – and this in turn helps to explain why the outbreak of this war has proved susceptible to such a bewildering variety of interpretations. There is virtually no viewpoint on its origins that cannot be supported from a selection of the available sources. And this helps in turn to explain why the 'WWI origins' literature has assumed such vast dimensions that no single historian (not even a fantasy figure with an easy command of all the necessary languages) could hope to read it in one lifetime – twenty years ago, an overview of the current literature counted 25,000 books and articles.[14] Some accounts have focused on the culpability of one bad-apple state (Germany has been most popular, but not one of the great powers has escaped the ascription of chief responsibility); others have shared the blame around or have looked for faults in the 'system'. There was always enough complexity to keep the argument going. And beyond the debates of the historians, which have tended to turn on questions of culpability or the relationship between individual agency and structural constraint, there is a substantial international relations commentary, in which categories such as deterrence, détente and inadvertence, or universalizable mechanisms such as balancing, bargaining and bandwagoning, occupy centre stage. Though the debate on this subject is now nearly a century old, there is no reason to believe that it has run its course.[15]

But if the debate is old, the subject is still fresh – in fact it is fresher and more relevant now than it was twenty or thirty years ago. The changes in our own world have altered our perspective on the events of 1914. In the 1960s–80s, a kind of period charm accumulated in popular awareness around the events of 1914. It was easy to imagine the disaster of Europe's 'last summer' as an Edwardian costume drama. The effete rituals and gaudy uniforms, the 'ornamentalism' of a world still largely organized around hereditary monarchy had a distancing effect on present-day recollection. They seemed to signal that the protagonists were people from another, vanished world. The presumption stealthily asserted itself that if the actors' hats had gaudy green ostrich feathers on them, then their thoughts and motivations probably did too.[16]

And yet what must strike any twenty-first-century reader who follows the course of the summer crisis of 1914 is its raw modernity. It began with a squad of suicide bombers and a cavalcade of automobiles. Behind the outrage at Sarajevo was an avowedly terrorist organization with a cult of sacrifice, death and revenge; but this organization was extra-territorial, without a clear geographical or political location; it was scattered in cells across political borders, it was unaccountable, its links to any sovereign government were oblique, hidden and certainly very difficult to discern from outside the organization. Indeed, one could even say that July 1914 is less remote from us – less illegible – now than it was in the 1980s. Since the end of the Cold War, a system of global bipolar stability has made way for a more complex and unpredictable array of forces, including declining empires and rising powers – a state of affairs that invites comparison with the Europe of 1914. These shifts in perspective prompt us to rethink the story of how war came to Europe. Accepting this challenge does not mean embracing a vulgar presentism that remakes the past to meet the needs of the present, but rather acknowledging those features of the past of which our changed vantage point can afford us a clearer view.

Among these is the Balkan context of the war's inception. Serbia is one of the blind spots in the historiography of the July Crisis. The assassination at Sarajevo is treated in many accounts as a mere pretext, an event with little bearing on the real forces whose interaction brought about the conflict. In an excellent recent account of the outbreak of war in 1914, the authors declare that 'the killings [at Sarajevo] by themselves caused nothing. It was the use made of this event that brought the nations to war.'[17] The marginalization of the Serbian and thereby of the larger Balkan dimension of the story began during the July Crisis itself, which opened as a response to the murders at Sarajevo, but later changed gear, entering a geopolitical phase in which Serbia and its actions occupied a subordinate place.

Our moral compass has shifted, too. The fact that Serbian-dominated Yugoslavia emerged as one of the victor states of the war seemed implicitly to vindicate the act of the man who pulled the trigger on 28 June – certainly that was the view of the Yugoslav authorities, who marked the spot where he did so with bronze footprints and a plaque celebrating the assassin's 'first steps into Yugoslav freedom'. In an era when the national idea was still full of promise, there was an intuitive sympathy with South Slav nationalism and little affection for the ponderous multinational commonwealth of the Habsburg Empire. The Yugoslav wars of the 1990s have reminded us of the lethality of Balkan nationalism. Since Srebrenica and the siege of Sarajevo, it has become harder to think of Serbia as the mere object or victim of great power politics and easier to conceive of Serbian nationalism as an historical force in its own right. From the perspective of today's European Union we are inclined to look more sympathetically – or at least less contemptuously – than we used to on the vanished imperial patchwork of Habsburg Austria-Hungary.

Lastly, it is perhaps less obvious now that we should dismiss the two killings at Sarajevo as a mere mishap incapable of carrying real causal weight. The attack on the World Trade Center in September 2001 exemplified the way in which a single, symbolic event – however deeply it may be enmeshed in larger historical processes – can change politics irrevocably, rendering old options obsolete and endowing new ones with an unforeseen urgency. Putting Sarajevo and the Balkans back at the centre of the story does not mean demonizing the Serbs or their statesmen, nor does it dispense us from the obligation to understand the forces working on and in those Serbian politicians, officers and activists whose behaviour and decisions helped to determine what kind of consequences the shootings at Sarajevo would have.

This book thus strives to understand the July Crisis of 1914 as a modern event, the most complex of modern times, perhaps of any time so far. It is concerned less with why the war happened than with how it came about. Questions of why and how are logically inseparable, but they lead us in different directions. The question of *how* invites us to look closely at the sequences of interactions that produced certain outcomes. By contrast, the question of *why* invites us to go in search of remote and categorical causes: imperialism, nationalism, armaments, alliances, high finance, ideas of national honour, the mechanics of mobilization. The why approach brings a certain analytical clarity, but it also has a distorting effect, because it creates the illusion of a steadily building causal pressure; the factors pile up on top of each other pushing down on the events; political actors become mere executors of forces long established and beyond their control.

The story this book tells is, by contrast, saturated with agency. The key decision-makers – kings, emperors, foreign ministers, ambassadors, military commanders and a host of lesser officials – walked towards danger in watchful, calculated steps. The outbreak of war was the culmination of chains of decisions made by political actors with conscious objectives, who were capable of a degree of self-reflection, acknowledged a range of options and formed the best judgements they could on the basis of the best information they had to hand. Nationalism, armaments, alliances and finance were all part of the story, but they can be made to carry real explanatory weight only if they can be seen to have shaped the decisions that – in combination – made war break out.

A Bulgarian historian of the Balkan Wars recently observed that 'once we pose the question "why", guilt becomes the focal point'.[18] Questions of guilt and responsibility in the outbreak of war entered this story even before the war had begun. The entire source record is full of ascriptions of blame (this was a world in which aggressive intentions were always assigned to the opponent and defensive intentions to one-self) and the judgement delivered by Article 231 of the Treaty of Versailles has ensured the continuing prominence of the 'war guilt' question. Here, too, the focus on *how* suggests an alternative approach: a journey through the events that is not driven by the need to draw up a charge sheet against this or that state or individual, but aims to identify the decisions that brought war about and to understand the reasoning or emotions behind them. This does not mean excluding questions of responsibility entirely from the discussion – the aim is rather to let the *why* answers grow, as it were, out of the *how* answers, rather than the other way around.

This book tells the story of how war came to continental Europe. It traces the paths to war in a multi-layered narrative encompassing the key decision-centres in Vienna, Berlin, St Petersburg, Paris, London and Belgrade with brief excursions to Rome, Constantinople and Sofia. It is divided into three parts. Part I focuses on the two antagonists, Serbia and Austria-Hungary, whose quarrel ignited the conflict, following their interaction down to the eve of the Sarajevo assassinations. Part II breaks with the narrative approach to ask four questions in four chapters: how did the polarization of Europe into opposed blocs come about? How did the governments of the European states generate foreign policy? How did the Balkans – a peripheral region far from Europe's centres of power and wealth – come to be the theatre of a crisis of such magnitude? How did an international system that seemed to be entering an era of détente produce a general war? Part III opens with the assassinations at Sarajevo and offers a narrative of the July Crisis itself, examining the interactions between the key decision-centres and bringing to light the calculations, misunderstandings and decisions that drove the crisis from one phase to the next.

It is a central argument of this book that the events of July 1914 make sense only when we illuminate the journeys travelled by the key decision-makers. To do this, we need to do more than simply revisit the sequence of international 'crises' that preceded the outbreak of war – we need to understand how those events were experienced and woven into narratives that structured perceptions and motivated behaviour. Why did the men whose decisions took Europe to war behave and see things as they did? How did the sense of fearfulness and foreboding that one finds in so many of the sources connect with the arrogance and swaggering we encounter – often in the very same individuals? Why did such exotic features of the pre-war scene as the Albanian Question and the 'Bulgarian loan' matter so much, and how were they joined up in the heads of those who had political power? When decision-makers discoursed on the international situation or on external threats, were they seeing something real, or projecting their own fears and desires on to their opponents, or both? The aim has been to reconstruct as vividly as possible the highly dynamic 'decision positions' occupied by the key actors before and during the summer of 1914.

Some of the most interesting recent writing on the subject has argued that, far from being inevitable, this war was in fact 'improbable' – at least until it actually happened.[19] From this it would follow that the conflict was not the consequence of a long-run deterioration, but of short-term shocks to the international system. Whether one accepts this view or not, it has the merit of opening the story to an element of contingency. And it is certainly true that while some of the developments I examine in this book seem to point unequivocally in the direction of what actually transpired in 1914, there are other vectors of pre-war change that suggest different, unrealized outcomes. With this in mind, the book aims to show how the pieces of causality were assembled that, once in place, enabled the war to happen, but to do so without over-determining the outcome. I have tried to remain alert to the fact that the people, events and forces described in this book carried in them the seeds of other, perhaps less terrible, futures.

PART I

Roads to Sarajevo

I

Serbian Ghosts

MURDER IN BELGRADE

Shortly after two o'clock on the morning of 11 June 1903, twenty-eight officers of the Serbian army approached the main entrance of the royal palace in Belgrade.* After an exchange of fire, the sentries standing guard before the building were arrested and disarmed. With keys taken from the duty captain, the conspirators broke into the reception hall and made for the royal bedchamber, hurrying up stairways and along corridors. Finding the king's apartments barred by a pair of heavy oaken doors, the conspirators blew them open with a carton of dynamite. The charge was so strong that the doors were torn from their hinges and thrown across the antechamber inside, killing the royal adjutant behind them. The blast also fused the palace electrics, so that the building was plunged into darkness. Unperturbed, the intruders discovered some candles in a nearby room and entered the royal apartment. By the time they reached the bedroom, King Alexandar and Queen Draga were no longer to be found. But the queen's French novel was splayed face-down on the bedside table. Someone touched the sheets and felt that the bed was still warm – it seemed they had only recently left. Having searched the bedchamber in vain, the intruders combed through the palace with candles and drawn revolvers.

While the officers strode from room to room, firing at cabinets, tapestries, sofas and other potential hiding places, King Alexandar and Queen Draga huddled upstairs in a tiny annexe adjoining the bedchamber where the queen's maids usually ironed and darned her clothes. For

---

* Today the former palace houses the Belgrade City Assembly on Dragoslava Jovanovića.

nearly two hours, the search continued. The king took advantage of this interlude to dress as quietly as he could in a pair of trousers and a red silk shirt; he had no wish to be found naked by his enemies. The queen managed to cover herself in a petticoat, white silk stays and a single yellow stocking.

Across Belgrade, other victims were found and killed: the queen's two brothers, widely suspected of harbouring designs on the Serbian throne, were induced to leave their sister's home in Belgrade and 'taken to a guard-house close to the Palace, where they were insulted and barbarously stabbed'.[1] Assassins also broke into the apartments of the prime minister, Dimitrije Cincar-Marković, and the minister of war, Milovan Pavlović. Both were slain; twenty-five rounds were fired into Pavlović, who had concealed himself in a wooden chest. Interior Minister Belimir Theodorović was shot and mistakenly left for dead but later recovered from his wounds; other ministers were placed under arrest.

Back at the palace, the king's loyal first adjutant, Lazar Petrović, who had been disarmed and seized after an exchange of fire, was led through the darkened halls by the assassins and forced to call out to the king from every door. Returning to the royal chamber for a second search, the conspirators at last found a concealed entry behind the drapery. When one of the assailants proposed to cut the wall open with an axe, Petrović saw that the game was up and agreed to ask the king to come out. From behind the panelling, the king enquired who was calling, to which his adjutant responded: 'I am, your Laza, open the door to your officers!' The king replied: 'Can I trust the oath of my officers?' The conspirators replied in the affirmative. According to one account, the king, flabby, bespectacled and incongruously dressed in his red silk shirt, emerged with his arms around the queen. The couple were cut down in a hail of shots at point-blank range. Petrović, who drew a concealed revolver in a final hopeless bid to protect his master (or so it was later claimed), was also killed. An orgy of gratuitous violence followed. The corpses were stabbed with swords, torn with a bayonet, partially disembowelled and hacked with an axe until they were mutilated beyond recognition, according to the later testimony of the king's traumatized Italian barber, who was ordered to collect the bodies and dress them for burial. The body of the queen was hoisted to the railing of the bedroom window and tossed, virtually naked and slimy with gore, into the gardens. It was reported that as the assassins attempted to do the same with Alexandar, one of his hands closed momentarily around the railing. An officer hacked through the fist with a sabre and the body fell, with a sprinkle of severed digits, to the earth. By the time the assassins had gathered in the gardens to have a smoke and inspect the results of their handiwork, it had begun to rain.[2]

The events of 11 June 1903 marked a new departure in Serbian political history. The Obrenović dynasty that had ruled Serbia throughout most of the country's brief life as a modern independent state was no more. Within hours of the assassination, the conspirators announced the termination of the Obrenović line and the succession to the throne of Petar Karadjordjević, currently living in Swiss exile.

Why was there such a brutal reckoning with the Obrenović dynasty? Monarchy had never established a stable institutional existence in Serbia. The root of the problem lay partly in the coexistence of rival dynastic families. Two great clans, the Obrenović and the Karadjordjević,

Petar I Karadjordjević

had distinguished themselves in the struggle to liberate Serbia from Ottoman control. The swarthy former cattleherd 'Black George' (Serbian: 'Kara Djordje') Petrović, founder of the Karadjordjević line, led an uprising in 1804 that succeeded for some years in driving the Ottomans out of Serbia, but fled into Austrian exile in 1813 when the Ottomans mounted a counter-offensive. Two years later, a second uprising unfolded under the leadership of Miloš Obrenović, a supple political operator who succeeded in negotiating the recognition of a Serbian Principality with the Ottoman authorities. When Karadjordjević returned to Serbia from exile, he was assassinated on the orders of Obrenović and with the connivance of the Ottomans. Having dispatched his main political rival, Obrenović was granted the title of Prince of Serbia. Members of the Obrenović clan ruled Serbia during most of its existence as a principality within the Ottoman Empire (1817–78).

The pairing of rival dynasties, an exposed location between the Ottoman and the Austrian empires and a markedly undeferential political culture dominated by peasant smallholders: these factors in combination ensured that monarchy remained an embattled institution. It is striking how few of the nineteenth-century Serbian regents died on the throne of natural causes. The principality's founder, Prince Miloš Obrenović, was a brutal autocrat whose reign was scarred by frequent rebellions. In the summer of 1839, Miloš abdicated in favour of his eldest son, Milan, who was so ill with the measles that he was still unaware of his elevation when he died thirteen days later. The reign of the younger son, Mihailo, came to a premature halt when he was deposed by a rebellion in 1842, making way for the installation of a Karadjordjević – none other than Alexandar, the son of 'Black George'. But in 1858, Alexandar, too, was forced to abdicate, to be succeeded again by Mihailo, who returned to the throne in 1860. Mihailo was no more popular during his second reign than he had been during the first; eight years later he was assassinated, together with a female cousin, in a plot that may have been supported by the Karadjordjević clan.

The long reign of Mihailo's successor, Prince Milan Obrenović (1868–89), provided a degree of political continuity. In 1882, four years after the Congress of Berlin had accorded Serbia the status of an independent state, Milan proclaimed it a kingdom and himself king. But high levels of political turbulence remained a problem. In 1883, the government's efforts to decommission the firearms of peasant militias in north-eastern Serbia triggered a major provincial uprising, the Timok rebellion. Milan responded with brutal reprisals against the rebels and a witch-hunt against senior political figures in Belgrade suspected of having fomented the unrest.

Serbian political culture was transformed in the early 1880s by the emergence of political parties of the modern type with newspapers, caucuses, manifestos, campaign strategies and local committees. To this formidable new force in public life the king responded with autocratic measures. When elections in 1883 produced a hostile majority in the Serbian parliament (known as the Skupština), the king refused to appoint a government recruited from the dominant Radical Party, choosing instead to assemble a cabinet of bureaucrats. The Skupština was opened by decree and then closed again by decree ten minutes later. A disastrous war against Bulgaria in 1885 – the result of royal executive decisions made without any consultation either with ministers or with parliament – and an acrimonious and scandalous divorce from his wife, Queen Nathalie, further undermined the monarch's standing. When Milan abdicated in 1889 (in the hope, among other things, of marrying the pretty young wife of his personal secretary), his departure seemed long overdue.

The regency put in place to manage Serbian affairs during the minority of Milan's son, Crown Prince Alexandar, lasted four years. In 1893, at the age of only sixteen, Alexandar overthrew the regency in a bizarre coup d'état: the cabinet ministers were invited to dinner and cordially informed in the course of a toast that they were all under arrest; the young king announced that he intended to arrogate to himself 'full royal power'; key ministerial buildings and the telegraph administration had already been occupied by the military.[3] The citizens of Belgrade awoke on the following morning to find the city plastered with posters announcing that Alexandar had seized power.

In reality, ex-King Milan was still managing events from behind the scenes. It was Milan who had set up the regency and it was Milan who engineered the coup on behalf of his son. In a grotesque family manoeuvre for which it is hard to find any contemporary European parallel, the abdicated father served as chief adviser to the royal son. During the years 1897–1900, this arrangement was formalized in the 'Milan–Alexander duarchy'. 'King Father Milan' was appointed supreme commander of the Serbian army, the first civilian ever to hold this office.

During Alexandar's reign, the history of the Obrenović dynasty entered its terminal phase. Supported from the sidelines by his father, Alexandar quickly squandered the hopeful goodwill that often attends the inauguration of a new regime. He ignored the relatively liberal provisions of the Serbian constitution, imposing instead a form of neo-absolutist rule: secret ballots were eliminated, press freedoms were rescinded, newspapers were closed down. When the leadership of the Radical Party protested, they found themselves excluded from the exercise of power. Alexandar abolished, imposed and suspended constitutions in the manner of a tinpot dictator. He showed no respect for the independence of the judiciary, and even plotted against the lives of senior politicians. The spectacle of the king and King Father Milan recklessly operating the levers of the state in tandem – not to mention Queen Mother Nathalie, who remained an important figure behind the scenes, despite the breakdown of her marriage with Milan – had a devastating impact on the standing of the dynasty.

Alexandar's decision to marry the disreputable widow of an obscure engineer did nothing to improve the situation. He had met Draga Mašin in 1897, when she was serving as a maid of honour to his mother. Draga was ten years older than the king, unpopular with Belgrade society, widely believed to be infertile and well known for her allegedly numerous sexual liaisons. During a heated meeting of the Crown Council, when ministers attempted in vain to dissuade the king from marrying Mašin, the interior minister Djordje Genčić came up with a powerful argument: 'Sire, you cannot marry her. She has been everybody's mistress – mine included.' The minister's reward for his candour was a hard slap across the face – Genčić would later join the ranks of the regicide conspiracy.[4] There were similar encounters with other senior officials.[5] At one rather overwrought cabinet meeting, the acting prime minister even proposed placing the king under palace arrest or having him bundled out of the country by force in order to prevent the union from being solemnized.[6] So intense was the opposition to Mašin among the political classes that the king found it impossible for a time to recruit suitable candidates into senior posts; the news of Alexandar and Draga's engagement alone was enough to trigger the resignation of the entire cabinet and the king was obliged to make do with an eclectic 'wedding cabinet' of little-known figures.

The controversy over the marriage also strained the relationship

King Alexandar and Queen Draga *c.* 1900

between the king and his father. Milan was so outraged at the prospect of Draga's becoming his daughter-in-law that he resigned his post as commander-in-chief of the army. In a letter written to his son in June 1900, he declared that Alexandar was 'pushing Serbia into an abyss' and closed with a forthright warning: 'I shall be the first to cheer the government which shall drive you from the country, after such a folly on your part.'[7] Alexandar went ahead just the same with his plan (he and Draga were married on 23 June 1900 in Belgrade) and exploited the opportunity created by his father's resignation to reinforce his own control over the officer corps. There was a purge of Milan's friends (and Draga's enemies) from senior military and civil service posts; the King Father was kept under constant surveillance, then encouraged to leave Serbia and later prevented from returning. It was something of a relief to the royal couple when Milan, who had settled in Austria, died in January 1901.

There was a brief revival in the monarch's popularity late in 1900, when an announcement by the palace that the queen was expecting a child prompted a wave of public sympathy. But the outrage was correspondingly intense in April 1901 when it was revealed that Draga's pregnancy had been a ruse designed to placate public opinion (rumours spread in the capital of a foiled plan to establish a 'suppositious infant' as heir to the Serbian throne). Ignoring these ill omens, Alexandar launched a propaganda cult around his queen, celebrating her birthday with lavish public events and naming regiments, schools and even villages after her. At the same time, his constitutional manipulations became bolder. On one famous occasion in March 1903, the king suspended the Serbian constitution in the middle of the night while repressive new press and association laws were hurried on to the statute books, and then reinstated it just forty-five minutes later.

By the spring of 1903, Alexandar and Draga had united most of Serbian society against them. The Radical Party, which had won an absolute majority of Skupština seats in the elections of July 1901, resented the king's autocratic manipulations. Among the powerful mercantile and banking families (especially those involved in the export of livestock and foodstuffs) there were many who saw the pro-Vienna bias of Obrenović foreign policy as locking the Serbian economy into an Austrian monopoly and depriving the country's capitalists of access to world markets.[8] On 6 April 1903, a demonstration in Belgrade decrying the king's constitutional manipulations was brutally dispersed by police and gendarmes, who killed eighteen and wounded about fifty others.[9] Over one hundred people – including a number of army officers – were arrested and imprisoned, though most were freed after a few days.

At the epicentre of the deepening opposition to the crown was the Serbian army. By the turn of the twentieth century, the army was one of the most dynamic institutions in Serbian society. In a still largely rural and underperforming economy, where careers offering upward mobility were hard to come by, an officer commission was a privileged route to status and influence. This pre-eminence had been reinforced by King Milan, who lavished funding on the military, expanding the officer corps while cutting back the state's already meagre expenditure on higher education. But the fat years came to an abrupt end after the King Father's departure in 1900: Alexandar pruned back the military budget, officers' salaries were allowed to fall months into arrears, and a policy of court favouritism ensured that friends or relatives of the king and his wife were promoted to key posts over the heads of their colleagues. These resentments were sharpened by the widespread belief – despite official denials – that the king, having failed to generate a biological heir, was planning to designate Queen Draga's brother Nikodije Lunjevica as successor to the Serbian throne.[10]

During the summer of 1901, a military conspiracy crystallized around a gifted young lieutenant of the Serbian army who would play an important role in the events of July 1914. Later known as 'Apis', because his heavy build reminded his admirers of the broad-shouldered bull-god of ancient Egypt, Dragutin Dimitrijević had been appointed to a post on the General Staff immediately after his graduation from the Serbian Military Academy, a sure sign of the great esteem in which he was held by his superiors. Dimitrijević was made for the world of political conspiracy. Obsessively secretive, utterly dedicated to his military and political work, ruthless in his methods and icily composed in moments of crisis, Apis was not a man who could have held sway over a great popular movement. But he did possess in abundance the capacity, within small groups and private circles, to win and groom disciples, to confer a sense of importance upon his following, to silence doubts and to motivate extreme action.[11] One collaborator described him as 'a secret force at whose disposal I have to place myself, though my reason gives me no grounds for doing so'. Another of the regicides puzzled over the reasons for Apis's influence: neither his intelligence, nor his eloquence, nor the force of his ideas seemed sufficient to account for it; 'yet he was the only one among us who solely by his presence was able to turn my thoughts into his stream and with a few words spoken in the most ordinary manner could make out of me an obedient executor of his will'.[12] The milieu in which Dimitrijević deployed these gifts was emphatically masculine. Women were a marginal presence in his adult life; he never showed any sexual interest in them. His natural habitat, and the scene of all his intrigues, was the smoke-filled, men-only world of the Belgrade coffee-houses – a space at once private and public, where conversations could be seen without necessarily being heard. The best-known surviving photograph of him depicts the burly moustachioed intriguer with two associates in a characteristically conspiratorial pose.

Dimitrijević originally planned to kill the royal couple at a ball in central Belgrade on 11 September (the queen's birthday). In a plan that seems lifted from the pages of an Ian Fleming novel, two officers were assigned to mount an attack on the Danube power plant that supplied Belgrade with electricity, while another was to disable the smaller station serving the building where the ball was in progress. Once the lights were shut off, the four assassins in attendance at the ball planned to set fire to the curtains, sound the fire alarms and liquidate the king and his wife by forcing them to ingest poison (this method was chosen in order to circumvent a possible search for firearms). The poison was successfully tested on a cat, but in every other respect the plan was a failure. The power plant turned out to be too heavily guarded and the queen decided in any case not to attend the ball.[13]

Undeterred by this and other failed attempts, the conspirators worked hard over the next two years at expanding the scope of the coup. Over one hundred officers were recruited, including many younger military men. By the end of 1901 there were also contacts with civilian political leaders, among them the former interior minister Djordje Genčić, he who had been slapped for his candid objections to the king's marriage plans. In the autumn of 1902, the conspiracy was given formal expression in a secret oath. Drawn up by Dimitrijević-Apis, it was refreshingly straightforward about the object of the enterprise: 'Anticipating certain collapse of the state [. . .] and blaming for this primarily the king and his paramour Draga Mašin, we swear that we shall murder them and to that effect affix our signatures.'[14]

By the spring of 1903, when the plot encompassed between 120 and 150 conspirators, the plan to kill the royal couple inside their own palace was mature. Carrying it out required extensive preparation, however, because the king and his wife, falling prey to an entirely justified paranoia, stepped up their security arrangements. The king never appeared in town except in the company of a crowd of attendants; Draga was so terrified of an attack that she had at one point confined herself to the palace for six weeks. Guard details in and around the building were doubled. The rumours of an impending coup were so widespread that the London *Times* of 27 April 1903 could cite a 'confidential' Belgrade source to the effect that 'there exists a military conspiracy against the throne of such an extent that neither King nor Government dare take steps to crush it'.[15]

The recruitment of key insiders, including officers from the Palace Guard and the king's own aide-de-camp, provided the assassins with a means of picking their way past the successive lines of sentries and gaining access to the inner sanctum. The date of the attack was chosen just three days in advance, when it was known that all the key conspirators

Assassination of the Obrenović, from *Le Petit Journal*, 28 June 1903

would be in place and on duty at their respective posts. It was agreed that the thing must be done in the greatest possible haste and then be made known immediately, in order to forestall an intervention by the police, or by regiments remaining loyal to the king.[16] The desire to advertise the success of the enterprise as soon as it was accomplished may help to explain the decision to toss the royal corpses from the bedroom balcony. Apis joined the killing squad that broke into the palace, but he missed the final act of the drama; he was shot and seriously wounded in an exchange of fire with guards inside the main entrance. He collapsed on the spot, lost consciousness and only narrowly escaped bleeding to death.

'IRRESPONSIBLE ELEMENTS'

'Town quiet people generally seem unmoved,' noted Sir George Bonham, the British minister in Belgrade, in a lapidary dispatch to London on the evening of 11 June.[17] The Serbian 'revolution', Bonham reported, had been 'hailed with open satisfaction' by the inhabitants of the capital; the day following the murders was 'kept as a holiday and the streets decorated with flags'. There was 'an entire absence of decent regret'.[18] The 'most striking feature' of the Serbian tragedy, declared Sir Francis Plunkett, Bonham's colleague in Vienna, was 'the extraordinary calmness with which the execution of such an atrocious crime has been accepted'.[19]

Hostile observers saw in this equanimity of mood evidence of the heartlessness of a nation by long tradition inured to violence and regicide. In reality, the citizens of Belgrade had good reason to welcome the assassinations. The conspirators immediately turned power over to an all-party provisional government. Parliament was swiftly reconvened. Petar Karadjordjević was recalled from his Swiss exile and elected king by the parliament. The emphatically democratic constitution of 1888 – now renamed the Constitution of 1903 – was reinstated with some minor modifications. The age-old problem of the rivalry between two Serbian dynasties was suddenly a thing of the past. The fact that Karadjordjević, who had spent much of his life in France and Switzerland, was an aficionado of John Stuart Mill – in his younger years, he had even translated Mill's *On Liberty* into Serbian – was encouraging to those with liberal instincts.

Even more reassuring was Petar's proclamation to the people, delivered shortly after his return from exile, that he intended to reign as 'the truly constitutional king of Serbia'.[20] The kingdom now became a genuinely parliamentary polity, in which the monarch reigned but did not govern. The murder during the coup of the repressive prime minister Cincar-Marković – a favourite of Alexandar – was a clear signal that political power would henceforth depend upon popular support and party networks, rather than on the goodwill of the crown. Political parties could go about their work without fear of reprisals. The press was at last free of the censorship that had been the norm under the Obrenović rulers. The prospect beckoned of a national political life more responsive to popular needs and more in tune with public opinion. Serbia stood on the threshold of a new epoch in its political existence.[21]

But if the coup of 1903 resolved some old issues, it also created new problems that would weigh heavily on the events of 1914. Above all, the conspiratorial network that had come together to murder the royal family did not simply melt away, but remained an important force in Serbian politics and public life. The provisional revolutionary government formed on the day after the assassinations included four

conspirators (among them the ministers of war, public works and economics) and six party politicians. Apis, still recovering from his wounds,
was formally thanked for what he had done by the Skupština and
became a national hero. The fact that the new regime depended for its
existence on the bloody work of the conspirators, combined with fear
of what the network might still be capable of, made open criticism difficult. One minister in the new government confided to a newspaper
correspondent ten days after the event that he found the actions of the
assassins 'deplorable' but was 'unable to characterise them openly in
such terms owing to the feeling which it might create in the army, on the
support of which both throne and Government depend'.[22]

The regicide network was especially influential at court. 'So far', the
British envoy Wilfred Thesiger reported from Belgrade in November
1905, the conspirator officers 'have formed his Majesty's most important and even sole support'; their removal would leave the crown
'without any party whose devotion or even friendship could be relied
on'.[23] It was thus hardly surprising that when King Petar looked in the
winter of 1905 for a companion to accompany his son, Crown Prince
Djordje, on a journey across Europe, he should choose none other than
Apis, fresh from a long convalescence and still carrying three of the bullets that had entered his body on the night of the assassinations. The
chief architect of the regicide was thus charged with seeing the next
Karadjordjević king through to the end of his education as prince. In the
event, Djordje never became king; he disqualified himself from the Serbian succession in 1909 by kicking his valet to death.[24]

The Austrian minister in Belgrade could thus report with only slight
exaggeration that the king remained, even after his election by the
parliament, the 'prisoner' of those who had brought him into power.[25]
'The King is a nullity,' one senior official at the Austrian Foreign Office
concluded at the end of November. 'The whole show is run by the people
of 11 June.'[26] The conspirators used this leverage to secure for themselves the most desirable military and government posts. The newly
appointed royal adjutants were all conspirators, as were the ordnance
officers and the chief of the postal department in the ministry of war,
and the conspirators were able to influence military appointments,
including senior command positions. Using their privileged access to the
monarch, they also exercised an influence over political questions of
national importance.[27]

The machinations of the regicides did not go unchallenged. There was external pressure on the new government to detach itself from the network, especially from Britain, which withdrew its minister plenipotentiary and left the legation in the hands of the chargé d'affaires, Thesiger. As late as autumn 1905, many symbolically important Belgrade functions – especially events at court – were still being boycotted by representatives of the European great powers. Within the army itself, a military 'counter-conspiracy' concentrated in the fortress town of Niš emerged under the leadership of Captain Milan Novaković, who produced a manifesto calling for the dismissal from the service of sixty-eight named prominent regicides. Novaković was swiftly arrested and after a spirited defence of his actions, he and his accomplices were tried, found guilty and sentenced to varying periods of imprisonment by a military court. When he left prison two years later, Novaković resumed his public attacks on the regicides and was incarcerated again. In September 1907, he and a male relative perished in mysterious circumstances during an alleged escape attempt, a scandal that triggered outrage in parliament and the liberal press.[28] The question of the relationship between the army and the civilian authorities thus remained unresolved after the assassinations of 1903, a state of affairs that would shape Serbia's handling of events in 1914.

The man who shouldered the lion's share of the responsibility for managing this challenging constellation was the Radical leader, Nikola Pašić. Pašić, a Zurich-trained engineering graduate, was the kingdom's dominant statesman after the regicide. During the years 1904–18, he headed ten cabinets for a total of nine years. As the man who stood at the apex of Serbian politics before, during and after the Sarajevo assassinations in 1914, Pašić would be one of the key players in the crisis that preceded the outbreak of the First World War.

This was surely one of the most remarkable political careers in modern European history, not just on account of its longevity – Pašić was active in Serbian politics for over forty years – but also because of the alternation of moments of giddy triumph with situations of extreme peril. Though he was nominally an engineer, politics consumed his entire existence – this is one of the reasons why he remained unmarried until the age of forty-five.[29] From the beginning, he was deeply committed to the struggle for Serbian independence from foreign sovereignty. In 1875, when there was a revolt against Turkish rule in Bosnia, the young Pašić travelled there as correspondent for the irredentist newspaper *Narodno Oslobodjenje* (National Liberation) in order to send dispatches from the front line of the Serbian national struggle. In the early 1880s, he oversaw the modernization of the Radical Party, which would remain the single most powerful force in Serbian politics until the outbreak of the First World War.

The Radicals embodied an eclectic politics that combined liberal constitutional ideas with calls for Serbian expansion and the territorial unification of all the Serbs of the Balkan peninsula. The popular base of the party – and the key to its enduring electoral success – was the small-holding peasantry that made up the bulk of the country's population. As a party of peasants, the Radicals embraced a variety of populism that linked them to pan-Slavist groups in Russia. They were suspicious of the professional army, not only because they resented the fiscal burdens imposed to maintain it, but also because they remained wedded to the peasant militia as the best and most natural form of armed organization. During the Timok rebellion of 1883, the Radicals sided with the arms-bearing peasants against the government and the suppression of the uprising was followed by reprisals against Radical leaders. Pašić was among those who came under suspicion; he fled into exile just in time to escape arrest and was sentenced to death *in absentia*. During his years in exile he established enduring contacts in St Petersburg and became the darling of pan-Slav circles; thereafter his policy was always closely linked with Russian policy.[30] After Milan's abdication in 1889, Pašić, whose exile had established him as a hero of the Radical movement, was pardoned. He returned to Belgrade amid popular adulation to be elected president of the Skupština and then mayor of the capital city. But his first tenure as prime minister (February 1891–August 1892) ended with his resignation in protest at the continuing extra-constitutional manipulations of Milan and the Regents.

In 1893, following his coup against the regency, Alexandar dispatched Pašić to St Petersburg as Serbian envoy extraordinary. The aim was to placate Pašić's political ambition while at the same time removing him from Belgrade. Pašić worked hard to build a deeper Russian-Serbian relationship, making no secret of his belief that the future national emancipation of Serbia would ultimately depend on Russian assistance.[31] But this work was disrupted by the re-entry into Belgrade politics of King Father Milan. Radicals were hounded and purged from the civil service, and Pašić was recalled. In the years of the Milan–Alexandar reign, Pašić was closely watched and kept at arm's length from power. In 1898, he was sentenced to nine months in prison on the pretext that he had insulted Milan in a party publication. Pašić was still in prison in 1899 when the country was shaken by a botched attempt on the King Father's life. Once again, the Radicals were suspected of complicity in the plot, though their link with the young Bosnian who fired the shot was and remains unclear. King Alexandar demanded that Pašić be executed on suspicion of complicity in the assassination attempt, but the Radical leader's life was saved, ironically enough in view of later developments, by the urgent representations of the Austro-Hungarian government. In a ruse characteristic of Alexandar's reign, Pašić was informed that he would be executed along with a dozen of his Radical colleagues unless he signed an admission of moral co-responsibility for the assassination attempt. Unaware that his life had already been saved by Vienna's intervention, Pašić consented; the document was published and he emerged from prison under popular suspicion that he had incriminated his party in order to save his own skin. He was biologically alive, but, for the moment at least, politically dead. During the troubled final years of Alexandar's reign, he withdrew almost entirely from public life.

The change of regime inaugurated a golden age in Pašić's political career. He and his party were now the dominant force in Serbian public life. Power suited this man who struggled so long to obtain it, and he quickly grew into the role of a father of his nation. Pašić was disliked by the Belgrade intellectual elite, but he enjoyed an immense pre-eminence among the peasantry. He spoke with the heavy, rustic dialect of Zaječar, found funny by people in Belgrade. His diction was halting, full of asides and interjections that lent themselves to anecdote. On being told that the famous satirical writer Branislav Nušić had protested against the annexation of Bosnia and Herzegovina in 1908 by leading a demonstration through town and then riding his horse into the ministry of foreign affairs, Pašić is said to have responded: 'Errr . . . you see . . . I knew he was good at writing books, but, hmmm . . ., that he could ride so well, that I did not know . . .'[32] Pašić was a poor speaker, but an excellent communicator, especially to the peasants who formed the overwhelming majority of the Serbian electorate. In their eyes, Pašić's unsophisticated speech and slow-burning wit, not to mention his luxuriant, patriarchal beard, were marks of an almost supernatural prudence, foresight and wisdom. Among his friends and supporters, he went by the appellation 'Baja' – a word that denotes a man of stature who is not only respected, but also loved by his contemporaries.[33]

A death sentence, long years of exile, the paranoia of a life under constant surveillance – all this left a deep imprint upon Pašić's practice and outlook as a politician. He acquired habits of caution, secrecy and obliqueness. Many years later, a former secretary would recall that he tended not to commit ideas and decisions to paper, or even, indeed, to the spoken word. He was in the habit of regularly burning his papers, both official and private. He developed a tendency to affect passivity in situations of potential conflict, a disinclination to show his hand until the last moment. He was pragmatic to the point where in the eyes of his opponents he seemed totally devoid of principle. All this was interwoven with an intense sensitivity to public opinion, a need to feel attuned to the Serb nation in whose cause he had suffered and worked.[34] Pašić was informed of the regicide plot in advance and maintained its secrecy, but refused to be drawn into active involvement. When the details of the planned operation were passed to him on the day before the assault on the palace, his very characteristic reaction was to take his family by train to the Adriatic coast, then under Austrian rule, and wait out the consequences.

Pašić understood that his success would depend upon securing his own and the government's independence, while at the same time establishing a stable and durable relationship with the army and the regicide network within it. It was not simply a question of the one-hundred-odd men who had actually taken part in the plot, but of the many younger officers – their numbers were steadily growing – who saw in the conspirators the incarnation of a Serbian national will. The issue was complicated by the fact that Pašić's most formidable political opponents, the Independent Radicals, a breakaway faction that had split from his own party in 1901, were willing to collaborate with the regicides if it helped them to undermine the Pašić government.

Pašić dealt intelligently with this delicate situation. He made personal overtures to individual conspirators with a view to disrupting the formation of an anti-government coalition. Despite protests from Radical Party colleagues, he backed a generous funding package for the army that made up some of the ground lost since the departure of King

Father Milan; he publicly acknowledged the legitimacy of the coup of 1903 (a matter of great symbolic importance to the conspirators) and opposed efforts to bring the regicides to trial. At the same time, however, he worked steadily towards curtailing their presence in public life. When it became known that the conspirators were planning to hold a celebratory dance on the first anniversary of the killings, Pašić (then foreign minister) intervened to have the festivity postponed to 15 June, the anniversary of the new king's election. During 1905, when the political influence of the regicides was a matter frequently raised in press and parliament, Pašić warned the Skupština of the threat posed to the democratic order by 'non-responsible actors' operating outside the structures of constitutional authority – a line that played well with the Radical rank and file, who detested what they saw as the praetorian spirit of the officer corps. In 1906, he skilfully exploited the issue of the renewal of normal relations with Great Britain in order to secure the pensioning off of a number of senior regicide officers.[35]

These deft manoeuvres had an ambivalent effect. The most prominent regicides were removed from exposed positions and the influence of their network on national politics was diminished in the short term. On the other hand, Pašić could do little to halt its growth within the army and among sympathetic civilians, the so-called *zaveritelji* – converts after the act to the cause of the conspiracy – who were prone to even more extreme views than the original accomplices.[36] Most importantly of all, the removal of the most senior regicides from public life left the indefatigable Apis in a position of uncontested dominance within the network. Apis was always a central figure at anniversary celebrations of the regicide, at which officer conspirators met to drink beer and make merry in the Kolarac restaurant in a small park next to the National Theatre in central Belgrade, and he did more than any other conspirator to recruit a core of ultra-nationalist officers prepared to support the struggle for the union of all Serbs by any available means.

MENTAL MAPS

Underpinning the idea of the 'unification of all Serbs' was a mental image of Serbia that bore little relation to the political map of the Balkans at the turn of the twentieth century. Its most influential political expression was a secret memorandum drawn up by the Serbian interior minister Ilija Garašanin for Prince Alexandar Karadjordjević in 1844. Known after its publication in 1906 as *Načertanije* (from the Old Serbian *náčrt*, 'draft'), Garašanin's proposal sketched out a 'Programme for the National and Foreign Policy of Serbia'. It would be difficult to overstate the influence of this document on generations of Serb politicians and patriots; in time it became the Magna Carta of Serb nationalism.* Garašanin opened his memorandum with the observation that Serbia is 'small, but must not remain in this condition'.[37] The first commandment of Serbian policy, he argued, must be the 'principle of national unity'; by which he meant the unification of all Serbs within the boundaries of a Serbian state: 'Where a Serb dwells, that is Serbia.' The historical template for this expansive vision of Serbian statehood was the medieval empire of Stepan Dušan, a vast swathe of territory encompassing most of the present-day Serbian republic, along with the entirety of present-day Albania, most of Macedonia, and all of Central and Northern Greece, but not Bosnia, interestingly enough.

Tsar Dušan's empire had supposedly collapsed after a defeat at the hands of the Turks on Kosovo Field on 28 June 1389. But this setback, Garašanin argued, had not undermined the Serbian state's legitimacy; it had merely interrupted its historical existence. The 'restoration' of a Greater Serbia unifying all Serbs was thus no innovation, but the expression of an ancient historical right. 'They cannot accuse [us] of seeking something new, unfounded, of constituting a revolution or an upheaval, but rather everyone must acknowledge that it is politically necessary, that it was founded in very ancient times and has its roots in the former political and national life of the Serbs.'[38] Garašanin's argument thus exhibited that dramatic foreshortening of historical time that can sometimes be observed in the discourses of integral nationalism; it rested, moreover, upon the fiction that Tsar Dušan's sprawling, multi-ethnic, composite, medieval polity could be conflated with the modern idea of a culturally and linguistically homogenous nation-state. Serb patriots saw no inconsistency here, since they argued that virtually all the

---

* The author of the text on which *Načertanije* was based was the Czech František Zach, whose template envisaged a federal organization of the South Slav peoples. But where Zach had written 'South Slav', Garašanin substituted 'Serb' or 'Serbian'. This and other changes transformed Zach's cosmopolitan vision into a more narrowly focused Serbian nationalist manifesto.

inhabitants of these lands were essentially Serbs. Vuk Karadžić, the architect of the modern Serbo-Croat literary language and author of a famous nationalist tract, *Srbi svi i svuda* ('Serbs all and everywhere', published in 1836), spoke of a nation of 5 million Serbs speaking the 'Serbian language' and scattered from Bosnia and Herzegovina to the Banat of Temesvar (eastern Hungary, now in western Romania), the Bačka (a region extending from northern Serbia into southern Hungary), Croatia, Dalmatia and the Adriatic coast from Trieste to northern Albania. Of course there were some in these lands, Karadžić conceded (he was referring in particular to the Croats), 'who still find it difficult to call themselves Serbs, but it seems likely that they will gradually become used to it'.[39]

The unification programme committed the Serbian polity, as Garašanin knew, to a long struggle with the two great land empires, the Ottoman and the Austrian, whose dominions encroached on the Greater Serbia of the nationalist imagination. In 1844, the Ottoman Empire still controlled most of the Balkan peninsula. 'Serbia must constantly strive to break stone after stone out of the façade of the Turkish State and absorb them into itself, so that it can use this good material on the good old foundations of the Serbian Empire to build and establish a great new Serbian state.'[40] Austria, too, was destined to be a foe.[41] In Hungary, Croatia-Slavonia and Istria-Dalmatia there were Serbs (not to mention many Croats who had not yet embraced Serbdom) supposedly awaiting liberation from Habsburg rule and unification under the umbrella of the Belgrade state.

Until 1918, when many of its objectives were met, Garašanin's memorandum remained the key policy blueprint for Serbia's rulers, while its precepts were broadcast to the population at large through a drip-feed of nationalist propaganda partly coordinated from Belgrade and partly driven by patriot networks within the press.[42] The Greater Serbian vision was not just a question of government policy, however, or even of propaganda. It was woven deeply into the culture and identity of the Serbs. The memory of Dušan's empire resonated within the extraordinarily vivid tradition of Serbian popular epic songs. These were long ballads, often sung to the melancholy accompaniment of the one-stringed gusla, in which singers and listeners relived the great archetypal moments of Serbian history. In villages and markets across the Serbian lands, these songs established a remarkably intimate linkage between poetry, history and identity. An early observer of this was the German historian Leopold von Ranke, who noted in his history of Serbia, published in 1829, that 'the history of the nation, developed by its poetry, has through it been converted into a national property, and is thus preserved in the memory of the people'.[43]

What was preserved above all within this tradition was the memory of the Serbian struggle against alien rule. A recurring preoccupation was the defeat of the Serbs at the hands of the Turks at Kosovo Field on 28 June 1389. Embroidered over the centuries, this rather indecisive medieval battle burgeoned into a symbolic set-piece between Serbdom and its infidel foe. Around it twined a chronicle peopled not only by shining heroes who had united the Serbs in their time of trouble, but also by treacherous villains who had withheld their support from the common cause, or had betrayed the Serbs to their enemies. The mythical pantheon included the celebrated assassin Miloš Obilić, of whom the songs tell that he infiltrated Turkish headquarters on the day of the battle and cut the Sultan's throat, before being captured and beheaded by Ottoman guards. Assassination, martyrdom, victimhood and the thirst for revenge on behalf of the dead were central themes.[44]

An imagined Serbia, projected on to a mythical past, came to brilliant life within this song-culture. Observing performances of epic songs among the Bosnian Serbs during the anti-Turkish uprising of 1875, the British archaeologist Sir Arthur Evans marvelled at their capacity to 'make the Bosnian Serb forget the narrower traditions of his [. . .] kingdom in these more glorious legends', to merge his experience with that of his 'brothers' in all Serbian lands and thereby 'override the cant of geographers and diplomatists'.[45] It is true that this culture of oral epic entered an era of gradual decline in the nineteenth century, as it began to be displaced by popular print. But the British diplomat Sir Charles Eliot heard the epics performed by travelling players at markets in the valley of the river Drina when he made a journey through Serbia in 1897. 'These rhapsodies,' he noted, 'are sung in a monotonous chant to the accompaniment of a single-stringed guitar, but with such genuine feeling and expression that the whole effect is not unpleasing.'[46] In any case, the immensely influential printed collections of Serbian epic poetry compiled and published by Vuk Karadžić ensured that they remained in circulation among the growing literary elite. Moreover, the epic corpus continued to grow. *The Mountain Wreath*, a classic of the genre

published in 1847 by the Prince-Bishop of Montenegro, Petar II
Petrović-Njegos, glorified the mythical tyrant-slayer and national mar-
tyr Miloš Obilić and called for the renewal of the struggle against alien
rule. *The Mountain Wreath* entered the Serb national canon and has
stayed there ever since.[47]

The commitment to the redemption of 'lost' Serbian lands, coupled
with the predicaments of an exposed location between two land empires,
endowed the foreign policy of the Serbian state with a number of distinctive features. The first of these was an indeterminacy of geographical
focus. The commitment in principle to a Greater Serbia was one thing,
but where exactly should the process of redemption begin? In the Vojvodina, within the Kingdom of Hungary? In Ottoman Kosovo, known as
'Old Serbia'? In Bosnia, which had never been part of Dušan's empire
but contained a substantial population of Serbs? Or in Macedonia to
the south, still under Ottoman rule? The mismatch between the visionary objective of 'unification' and the meagre financial and military
resources available to the Serbian state meant that Belgrade policy-makers had no choice but to respond opportunistically to rapidly changing
conditions on the Balkan peninsula. As a result, the orientation of Serbian foreign policy between 1844 and 1914 swung like a compass needle
from one point on the state's periphery to another. The logic of these
oscillations was as often as not reactive. In 1848, when Serbs in the
Vojvodina rose up against the Magyarizing policies of the Hungarian
revolutionary government, Garašanin assisted them with supplies
and volunteer forces from the principality of Serbia. In 1875, all eyes
were on Herzegovina, where the Serbs had risen in revolt against the
Ottomans – among those who rushed to the scene of that struggle were
Pašić and the military commander and future king Petar Karadjordjević,
who fought there under an alias. After 1903, following an abortive local
uprising against the Turks, there was intensified interest in liberating
the Serbs of Ottoman Macedonia. In 1908, when the Austrians formally
annexed Bosnia and Herzegovina (having held them under military
occupation since 1878), the annexed areas shot to the top of the agenda.
In 1912 and 1913, however, Macedonia was once again the first priority.

Serbian foreign policy had to struggle with the discrepancy between
the visionary nationalism that suffused the country's political culture
and the complex ethnopolitical realities of the Balkans. Kosovo was at
the centre of the Serbian mythscape, but it was not, in ethnic terms, an

unequivocally Serbian territory. Muslim Albanian speakers had been in the majority there since at least the eighteenth century.[48] Many of the Serbs Vuk Karadžić counted in Dalmatia and Istria were in fact Croats, who had no wish to join a greater Serbian state. Bosnia, which had historically never been part of Serbia, contained many Serbs (they constituted 43 per cent of the population of Bosnia and Herzegovina in 1878, when the two provinces were occupied by Austria-Hungary) but it also contained Catholic Croats (about 20 per cent) and Bosnian Muslims (about 33 per cent). (The survival of a substantial Muslim minority was one of the distinctive features of Bosnia – in Serbia itself, the Muslim communities had for the most part been harassed into emigration, deported or killed during the long struggle for independence.)[49]

Even more complicated was the case of Macedonia. Superimposed on to a present-day political map of the Balkans, the geographical region known as Macedonia encompasses, in addition to the former Yugoslav Republic of the same name, border areas along the southern Serbian and eastern Albanian periphery, a large chunk of south-western Bulgaria, and a huge swathe of northern Greece.[50] The precise historical boundaries of Macedonia remain controversial today (witness the still smouldering conflict between Athens and Skopje over the use of the name 'Macedonia' for the Skopje Republic) as does the question of whether and to what extent this region possessed a distinctive cultural, linguistic or national identity (to this day, the existence of a Macedonian language is acknowledged by linguists everywhere in the world except Serbia, Bulgaria and Greece).[51] In 1897, when Sir Charles Eliot travelled through Serbia, he was surprised to find that his Serbian companions 'would not allow that there were any Bulgarians in Macedonia', but rather 'insisted that the Slavonic inhabitants of that country were all Serbs'.[52] Sixteen years later, when the Carnegie Foundation dispatched a commission to the area to investigate atrocities committed in the course of the Second Balkan War, they found it impossible to establish a local consensus on the ethnicity of the people living in Macedonia, so polarized was the atmosphere in which these issues were discussed, even at the universities. The report the commission published in that year included not one, but two ethnic maps of the region, reflecting the view from Belgrade and the view from Sofia respectively. In one, western and northern Macedonia pullulated with unliberated Serbs awaiting unification with their motherland, in the other, the region appeared as the heartland of the Bulgarian zone of settlement.[53] During the last decades of the nineteenth century, the Serbs, the Greeks and the Bulgarians all ran highly active propaganda agencies inside Macedonia, whose purpose was to proselytize the local Slavs to their respective national causes.

The mismatch between national visions and ethnic realities made it highly likely that the realization of Serbian objectives would be a violent process, not only at the regional level, where the interests of greater and lesser powers were engaged, but also in the towns and villages of the contested areas. Some statesmen met this challenge by trying to package Serbian national objectives within a more generous 'Serbo-Croat' political vision encompassing the idea of multi-ethnic collaboration. Among them was Nikola Pašić, who wrote at length in the 1890s about the need for Serbs and Croats to unite in a world where small nations were bound to go under. Underlying this rhetoric, however, were the assumptions, first, that Serbs and Croats were in essence the same people and, second, that the Serbs would have to lead this process because they were a more authentically Slavic people than the Catholic Croats, who had so long been exposed to 'the influence of foreign culture'.[54]

Serbia could ill afford to pursue these objectives before the eyes of the world. A degree of clandestinity was thus pre-programmed into the pursuit of 'liberty' for Serbs who were still the subjects of neighbouring states or empires. Garašanin articulated this imperative in 1848 during the uprising in the Vojvodina. 'The Vojvodina Serbs,' he wrote, 'expect from all Serbdom a helping hand, so they can triumph over their traditional enemy. [. . .] But because of political factors, we cannot aid them publicly. It only remains for us to aid them in secret.'[55] This preference for covert operations can also be observed in Macedonia. Following an abortive Macedonian insurrection against the Turks in August 1903, the new Karadjordjević regime began to operate an active policy in the region. Committees were established to promote Serb guerrilla activity in Macedonia, and there were meetings in Belgrade to recruit and supply bands of fighters. Confronted by the Ottoman minister in Belgrade, the Serbian foreign minister Kaljević denied any involvement by the government and protested that the meetings were in any case not illegal, since they had been convened 'not for the raising of bands, but merely for collecting funds and expressing sympathy for co-religionists beyond the border'.[56]

The regicides were deeply involved in this cross-border activity. The conspirator officers and their fellow travellers within the army convened an informal national committee in Belgrade, coordinated the campaign and commanded many of the volunteer units. These were not, strictly speaking, units of the Serbian army proper, but the fact that volunteer officers were immediately granted leave by the army suggested a generous measure of official backing.[57] Militia activity steadily expanded in scope, and there were numerous violent skirmishes between Serb *četniks* (guerrillas) and bands of Bulgarian volunteers. In February 1907, the British government requested that Belgrade put a stop to this activity, which appeared likely to trigger a war between Serbia and Bulgaria. Once again, Belgrade disclaimed responsibility, denying that it was funding četnik activity and declaring that it 'could not prevent [its people] from defending themselves against foreign bands'. But the plausibility of this posture was undermined by the government's continuing support for the struggle – in November 1906, the Skupština had already voted 300,000 dinars for aid to Serbs suffering in Old Serbia and Macedonia, and this was followed by a 'secret credit' for 'extraordinary expenses and the defence of national interests'.[58]

Irredentism of this kind was fraught with risk. It was easy to send guerrilla chiefs into the field, but difficult to control them once they were there. By the winter of 1907, it was clear that a number of the četnik bands were operating in Macedonia independently of any supervision; only with some difficulty did an emissary from Belgrade succeed in re-imposing control. The 'Macedonian imbroglio' thus delivered an equivocal lesson, with fateful implications for the events of 1914. On the one hand, the devolution of command functions to activist cells dominated by members of the conspirator network carried the danger that control over Serb national policy might pass from the political centre to irresponsible elements on the periphery. On the other hand, the diplomacy of 1906–7 demonstrated that the fuzzy, informal relationship between the Serbian government and the networks entrusted with delivering irredentist policy could be exploited to deflect political responsibility from Belgrade and maximize the government's room for manoeuvre. The Belgrade political elite became accustomed to a kind of doublethink founded on the intermittent pretence that the foreign policy of official Serbia and the work of national liberation beyond the frontiers of the state were separate phenomena.

SEPARATION

'Agreement and harmony with Austria are a political impossibility for Serbia,' wrote Garašanin in 1844.[59] Until 1903, the potential for open conflict between Belgrade and Vienna was limited. The two countries shared a long frontier that was, from Belgrade's perspective, more or less indefensible. The Serbian capital, handsomely situated on the confluence of the rivers Danube and Sava, was only a short drive from the border with Austria-Hungary. Serbian exports went mainly to the empire and a large proportion of its imports were sourced there. The imperatives of geography were reinforced by Russia's policy in the region. At the Congress of Berlin in 1878, Russia had helped to carve a large Bulgarian entity out of Ottoman Europe, in the expectation that Bulgaria would remain a Russian client. Since it was foreseeable that Bulgaria and Serbia would one day be rivals for territory in Macedonia, Prince (later King) Milan sought to balance this threat by seeking a closer relationship with Vienna. Russia's support for Sofia thus pushed Serbia into the arms of Vienna. As long as Russia continued to play its Balkan policy with Bulgarian cards, relations between Vienna and Belgrade were likely to remain harmonious.

In June 1881, Austria-Hungary and Serbia agreed a commercial treaty. Three weeks later, it was supplemented by a secret convention, negotiated and signed by Prince Milan himself, which stipulated that Austria-Hungary would not only assist Serbia in its efforts to secure elevation to the status of a kingdom but would also support Serbian claims to territorial annexations in Macedonia. Serbia, for its part, agreed not to undermine the monarchy's position in Bosnia and Herzegovina. Article II stated that Serbia 'would not permit any political, religious or other intrigue to be directed from her territory against the Austro-Hungarian monarchy, including Bosnia, Herzegovina and the Sanjak of Novi Pazar'. Milan reinforced these agreements with a personal engagement in writing not to enter into 'any kind of treaty' with a third state without first consulting Vienna.[60]

These agreements were, to be sure, a fragile foundation for good Austro-Serbian relations: they had no anchorage in the sentimental life of the Serbian public, which was deeply anti-Austrian; they symbolized a relationship of economic dependency which was increasingly unacceptable to Serbian nationalist opinion; and they depended on the cooperation of an erratic and increasingly unpopular Serbian monarch. But as long as Milan Obrenović remained on the throne, they at least ensured that Serbia would not side with Russia against Austria, and that the sharp end of Belgrade's foreign policy would stay pointed in the direction of Macedonia and the coming contest with Bulgaria, rather than at Bosnia and Herzegovina.[61] A new trade treaty was signed in 1892 and the Secret Convention was renewed for ten years in 1889; it was allowed to expire thereafter, though it continued to be the operative platform for Serbian policy vis-à-vis Vienna.

The change of dynasty in 1903 signalled a major realignment. Austria was quick to recognize the Karadjordjević coup, partly because Petar had assured the Austrians beforehand that it was his intention to keep Serbia on an Austrophile course.[62] But it was soon evident that Serbia's new leaders planned to push towards greater economic and political independence. During 1905–6, a crisis unfolded in which trade policy, armaments orders, high finance and geopolitics were closely intertwined. Vienna pursued a threefold objective: to secure a commercial treaty with Serbia, to ensure that Serbian armaments orders would continue to be placed with Austrian firms, and to contract a major loan to Belgrade.[63]

The failure to achieve agreement on any of these questions produced a drastic cooling of relations between the two neighbours, and the outcome was an unmitigated disaster for Vienna. The Serbian armaments orders went to the French firm Schneider-Creusot instead of to the Austrian rival, Škoda of Bohemia. The Austrians reacted by closing the border to Serbian pork, triggering a customs conflict that came to be known as the 'pig war' (1906–9). But this was a counter-productive measure, since Serbia quickly found other export markets (especially in Germany, France and Belgium) and at last began to build slaughterhouses on a substantial scale, thus emancipating itself from its long-standing dependence on Austro-Hungarian processing facilities. Finally, Belgrade secured a major loan again not from Vienna, but from Paris (offered in return for the placement of armaments orders with French firms).

It is worth pausing for a moment to consider the larger significance of this French loan. Like all the emergent Balkan states, Serbia was an inveterate borrower, totally dependent on international credit, most of which was used to finance military expansion and infrastructural projects. Throughout the reign of King Milan, the Austrians remained willing lenders to Belgrade. But since these loans outran the debtor state's financial resources, they had to be hypothecated against various pledges: for each loan some definite revenue was pledged, or some railway property mortgaged. It was agreed that pledged revenues from railways, stamp and liquor taxes should be paid into a special treasury controlled jointly by the representatives of the Serbian government and the bondholders. This arrangement kept the Serbian state afloat during the 1880s and 90s, but did nothing to restrain the financial profligacy of the Belgrade government, which had managed to accumulate an indebtedness of over 350 million francs by 1895. With bankruptcy looming, Belgrade negotiated a new loan through which almost all of the old debts were consolidated at a lower rate of interest. The pledged revenues were placed under a separate administration run partly by the representatives of the creditors.

In other words, fragile debtors like Serbia (the same applied to the other Balkan states and to the Ottoman Empire) could secure loans on reasonable terms only if they agreed to concessions of fiscal control that amounted to the partial hypothecation of sovereign state functions. For this reason among others, international loans were a political issue of the highest importance, inextricably wound up with diplomacy and power politics. French international lending in particular was highly politicized. Paris vetoed loans to governments whose policies were deemed unfriendly to French interests; it facilitated loans in return for economic or political concessions; on occasion it reluctantly conceded a loan to unreliable but strategically important clients in order to prevent them from seeking relief elsewhere. It pursued potential clients aggressively – in Serbia's case the government were given to understand in the summer of 1905 that if they did not give France first refusal on the loan, the Paris money markets would be closed altogether to Serbia.[64] Acknowledging this nexus between strategy and finance, the French foreign ministry merged its commercial and political divisions in 1907.[65]

Seen against this background, the Serbian loan of 1906 was an important turning point. French financial relations with Belgrade became, in the words of an early American analyst of pre-war high finance, 'more intimate and dominant'.[66] The French came to own more than three quarters of all Serbian debt.[67] These were vast commitments for the Serbian state – repayment schedules extended forwards to 1967 (in fact Belgrade defaulted on the greater part of its obligations after

1918). The lion's share of this money went into military purchases (especially fast-firing artillery), most of which were transacted in France, much to the annoyance not just of Austrian, but also of British diplomats and armaments suppliers. The loan of 1906 also enabled Serbia to resist Vienna's commercial pressure and to wage a protracted tariff war. 'The undoubtedly successful issue of Mr Pašić's resistance to [Austrian] demands,' the British envoy in Belgrade reported in 1906, 'marks a distinct step in the economic and political emancipation of Servia.'[68]

These successes in the field of high finance should not distract us from the parlous condition of the Serbian economy as a whole. This had much less to do with Austrian tariff policy than with a process of economic decline that was deeply rooted in the country's history and agrarian structure. The emergence and subsequent expansion of Serbia were accompanied by a process of drastic de-urbanization, as the mainly Muslim towns were depopulated through decades of harassment and deportations.[69] What replaced the relatively urbanized and cosmopolitan imperial structures of the Ottoman periphery was a society and an economy entirely dominated by smallholding Christian peasants, a consequence in part of the absence of a home-grown Serbian aristocracy and in part of the ruling dynasty's efforts to prevent the emergence of such a ruling class by blocking the consolidation of latifundial estates.[70] While the cities shrank, the population grew at an awesome rate; hundreds of thousands of hectares of marginal land were opened up for exploitation by young families, loosening social constraints on marriage and fertility. But this rampant growth in the production of people did nothing to reverse the cycle of underperformance and decline that gripped the Serbian economy between the middle of the nineteenth century and the outbreak of the First World War in 1914.[71] Per capita output in farming fell by 27.5 per cent between the early 1870s and 1910–12, partly because the expansion of arable land led to large-scale deforestation and thus to a decline in the pasture lands needed to sustain large-scale pig-husbandry, traditionally the most profitable and efficient arm of Serbian agricultural production. By the 1880s, the beautiful forested wilderness of the Šumadija – perfect pasture land for swine – had all but disappeared.[72]

This record might have mattered less if there had been marked growth in the commercial and industrial sectors, but here, too, the picture was bleak, even by Balkan standards. The rural population had poor access to markets and there was not much in the way of starter industries, such as the textiles mills that helped to drive industrial growth in neighbouring Bulgaria.[73] Under these conditions, Serbian economic development depended upon inward investment – the first effort to pack and export plum jam on an industrial basis was launched by employees of a Budapest fruit-processing company; the silk and wine booms of the late nineteenth century were likewise triggered by foreign entrepreneurs. But inward investment remained sluggish, in part because foreign firms were put off by the xenophobia, corrupt officials and underdeveloped business ethics they encountered when they attempted to set up operations in Serbia. Even in areas where it was government policy to encourage investment, the harassment of foreign businesses by local authorities remained a serious problem.[74]

Investment in Serbia's human capital was just as unimpressive: in 1900, there were still only four teaching colleges for all Serbia, half of all elementary-school teachers had no pedagogical training, most school classes were not held in buildings designed for the purpose and only around one third of children actually attended school. All these shortcomings reflected the cultural preferences of a rural population that cared little for education and saw schools as alien institutions imposed by the government. In 1905, pressed to ratify a new revenue source, the peasant-dominated assembly of the Skupština chose to tax school books rather than home distillation. The result was a strikingly low rate of literacy, ranging from 27 per cent in the northern districts of the kingdom to only 12 per cent in the south-east.[75]

This grim landscape of 'growth without development' bears on our story in a number of ways. It meant that Serbian society remained unusually homogeneous both in socioeconomic and cultural terms. The bond between urban life and the folkways of peasant oral culture, with its powerful mythical narratives, was never severed. Even Belgrade – where the literacy rate in 1900 was only 21 per cent – remained a city of rural immigrants, a world of 'peasant urbanites' deeply influenced by the culture and kinship structures of traditional rural society.[76] In this environment, the development of modern consciousness was experienced not as an evolution from a previous way of understanding the world, but rather as a dissonant overlayering of modern attitudes on to a way of being that was still enchanted by traditional beliefs and values.[77]

This highly distinctive economic and cultural conjuncture helps to explain several salient features of pre-war Serbia. In an economy so lacking in opportunities for ambitious and talented young men, the army remained the biggest show in town. And this in turn helps to account for the fragility of the civilian authorities in the face of challenges from the military command structure – a crucial factor in the crisis that engulfed Serbia in the summer of 1914. However, it was also true that the partisan warfare of irregular militias and guerrilla bands which was such a central theme in the story of Serbia's emergence as an independent nation owed its durability to the persistence of a peasant culture that remained wary of the regular army. For a government confronted with an increasingly arrogant military culture and lacking the organic connection with a large and prosperous educated class that underpinned other nineteenth-century parliamentary systems, nationalism represented the single most potent political instrument and cultural force. The almost universal enthusiasm for the annexation of yet unredeemed Serb lands drew not only on the mythical passions embedded in popular culture, but also on the land-hunger of a peasantry whose plots were growing smaller and less productive. Under these conditions, the argument – however dubious – that Serbia's economic woes were the fault of Vienna's punitive tariffs and the stranglehold of Austrian and Hungarian capital could not fail to meet with the most enthusiastic approbation. These constraints also fed Belgrade's obsession with securing an outlet to the sea that would supposedly enable it to break out of backwardness. The relative weakness of commercial and industrial development ensured that Serbia's rulers remained dependent upon international finance for the military expenditures they required in order to pursue an active foreign policy. And this in turn helps to explain the deepening integration of Serbia into France's web of alliances after 1905, which was rooted in both financial and geopolitical imperatives.

ESCALATION

After 1903, the attention of Serbian nationalists was focused mainly on the three-way struggle between Serbs, Bulgarians and Turks unfolding in Macedonia. All this changed in 1908 with the annexation of Bosnia and Herzegovina by Austria-Hungary. Since these two formally

Ottoman provinces had been under Austrian occupation for thirty years and there had never been any question of an alteration of this arrangement, it might seem that the nominal change from occupation to outright annexation ought to have been a matter of indifference. The Serbian public took a different view. The announcement created an 'unparalleled outburst of resentment and national enthusiasm', both in Belgrade and in the provinces. There were 'many meetings', at which speakers 'clamoured for war against Austria'.[78] More than 20,000 people attended an anti-Austrian rally at the National Theatre in Belgrade, where Ljuba Davidović, leader of the Independent Radicals, gave a speech declaring that Serbians must fight the annexation to the death. 'We will struggle until we are victorious, but if we are defeated, we will be defeated knowing that we gave our greatest effort, and that we have the respect not only of all Serbs but also of the whole Slavic race.'[79] A few days later, the impetuous Crown Prince Djordje delivered a speech before an audience of about 10,000 in the capital city, in which he proposed to lead the Serbian people in an armed crusade to retrieve the annexed provinces: 'I am extremely proud to be a soldier and I would be proud to be the one who leads you, the Serbian people, in this desperate struggle for life and death, for our nation and our honour.'[80] Even Nikola Pašić, leader of the Serbian Radical Party, who was at this time not a serving minister and thus freer to speak his mind, argued that if the annexation could not be reversed, Serbia must prepare for a war of liberation.[81] The Russian liberal Pavel Miliukov, who visited Serbia in 1908, was shocked by the intensity of the public emotion. The anticipation of war with Austria, he recalled, became 'a readiness to fight, and victory seemed both easy and certain'. These views were universal and so unquestioned that 'to get into an argument over [them] would have been totally useless'.[82]

The mental maps that informed elite and popular understandings of Serbia's policy and purpose were once again in evidence. The only way to understand the intensity of the feeling aroused in Serbia by the annexation, the British minister in Belgrade explained in a report of 27 April 1909, was to recall that

> Every patriotic Servian who takes any interest or active part in politics, thinks of the Servian nation not as merely including the subjects of King Peter, but as consisting of all those who are akin to them in race and

language. He looks forward, consequently, to the eventual creation of a Greater Servia, which shall bring into one fold all the different sections of the nation, at present divided under Austrian, Hungarian and Turkish dominion. [...] From his point of view, Bosnia is both geographically and ethnographically the heart of Great Servia.[83]

In an almost contemporary tract on the crisis, the celebrated ethnographer Jovan Cvijic, Nikola Pašić's most influential adviser on the nationality question, observed that 'it [was] plain that Bosnia and Herzegovina, by . . . their central position in the ethnographical mass of the Serbo-Croat race, . . . hold the key to the Serb problem. Without them, there can be no Great Serb state'.[84] From the perspective of pan-Serb publicists, Bosnia-Herzegovina belonged to the 'Serb lands under foreign domination' – its population was 'entirely Servian in race and language', consisting of Serbs, Serbo-Croats and 'Serb-Mohammedans', except, of course, for the minority of 'temporary inhabitants' and 'exploiters' installed by the Austrians over the previous thirty years.[85]

Powered by this wave of outrage, a new mass organization sprang up to pursue nationalist objectives. Known as the Serbian National Defence (Srpska Narodna Odbrana), it recruited thousands of members dispersed across more than 220 committees in towns and villages of Serbia and a network of auxiliaries within Bosnia and Herzegovina.[86] The irredentist campaign that had been gaining momentum in Macedonia was now directed at the annexed provinces: Narodna Odbrana organized guerrilla bands, recruited volunteers, established espionage networks within Bosnia and lobbied the government for a more aggressive national policy. Veterans from the fighting in Macedonia, such as Major Voja Tankosić, a close associate of Apis, were deployed to the Bosnian frontier, where they trained thousands of new recruits for the coming struggle there. It looked for a time as if Serbia was on the point of launching a suicidal assault on its neighbour.[87]

The leaders in Belgrade at first encouraged the agitation, but they were also quick to see that Serbia stood no chance of reversing the annexation. The key to this sobering of the mood was Russia, which did little to encourage Serbian resistance. This was hardly surprising, since it was the Russian foreign minister Alexander Izvolsky who had proposed the annexation – in principle at least – to his Austrian counterpart Alois Aehrenthal. Izvolsky had even warned the Serbian foreign minister

Milovan Milovanović in advance of the impending annexation. At a meeting at Marienbad, where Izvolsky was taking the waters, the Russian foreign minister had informed his Serbian counterpart that although St Petersburg considered the Balkan states to be 'children of Russia', neither Russia herself, nor any of the other great powers would do anything to contest the annexation. (Izvolsky omitted to mention to his Serbian interlocutor the fact that he himself had proposed the annexation of the provinces to the Austrians as part of a deal to secure better access for Russian warships to the Turkish Straits.) The Serbian minister in St Petersburg was later warned that Belgrade should under no circumstances mobilize against Austria, 'because no one would be able to help us, the whole world wants peace'.[88]

Foreign Minister Milovanović, a moderate politician who had been critical of Pašić's handling of the Austro-Serbian crisis of 1905–6 and was shocked to find him advocating war in 1908, was placed in an extremely delicate position. Having conferred directly with Izvolsky, he could see that there was no mileage in the idea of rallying the European powers against the annexation. But he also had to rein in the nationalist hysteria in Serbia, while at the same time unifying the Skupština and the political elite behind a moderate 'national' policy – two objectives that were virtually irreconcilable, since the Serbian public would construe any hint of a concession to Vienna's standpoint as a 'betrayal' of the national interest.[89] His difficulties were compounded by the hostility between the Radicals and their former party comrades the Independent Radicals, who expounded an uncompromising brand of pan-Serb nationalism. Factional rivalries within the Radical leadership, such as that between the 'Pašić group' and the 'court Radicals' around Milovanović, deepened the confusion and uncertainty. Behind the scenes, Milovanović worked hard to pursue a moderate policy focused on securing limited territorial compensation for Serbia, and endured without complaint the vilification of the pan-Serb press. In public, however, he adopted an intransigent rhetoric bound to rouse enthusiasm at home and provoke outrage in the Austrian newspapers. 'The Serbian national programme,' he announced to rapturous applause in a speech before the Skupština in October 1908, 'demands that Bosnia and Herzegovina be emancipated;' by interfering with the realization of this plan, he declared, Austria-Hungary had made it inevitable that 'one day in the near or distant future, Serbia and all of Serbdom will fight it in a struggle for life or death'.[90]

Milovanović's predicament illuminates the stresses to which Serbian policy-makers were exposed in this era. This intelligent and cautious man understood very clearly the limitations imposed by Serbia's location and condition. In the winter of 1908–9, all the powers urged Belgrade to step down and accept the inevitable.[91] But he also knew that no responsible minister could afford openly to disavow the national programme of Serbian unification. And in any case, Milovanović was himself a fervent and sincere proponent of that programme. Serbia, he had once said, could never afford to abandon the cause of Serbdom. 'From a Serbian standpoint, there is no difference between Serbian state interests and the interests of other Serbs.'[92] Here again were the projections of the Serbian mental map, on which political and ethnic imperatives were merged. The crucial point was this: moderates like Milovanović and even Pašić (who eventually climbed down from his calls for war) differed fundamentally from the extreme nationalists only on the matter of *how* to manage the predicaments facing the state. They could not afford (and did not wish) to disavow the nationalist programme as such. Domestically, then, the extremists were always at a rhetorical advantage, since it was they who set the terms of the debate. In such an environment, moderates would find it difficult to make themselves heard, unless they adopted the language of the extremists. And this in turn made it difficult for external observers to discern any variation in the positions adopted across the political elite, which could deceptively appear to form a solid front of unanimity. The dangerous dynamics of this political culture would haunt Belgrade in June and July 1914.

In the event, Austria-Hungary of course prevailed and Belgrade was forced formally to renounce its claims on 31 March 1909. With great difficulty, the government managed to calm the agitation. Belgrade promised Vienna that it would disarm and break up its 'volunteers and bands'.[93] Srpska Narodna Odbrana was divested of its insurrectionary and war-waging functions and transformed – outwardly at least – into a peaceful pan-Serbian propaganda and information agency operating in close association with a range of other nationalist associations, such as the Soko gymnastic societies and groups like Prosveta and Prirednik, whose task was to reinforce Serbian cultural identity through literature, public education and youth work.

Serbia may have failed to reverse the annexation or secure the territorial concessions that Milovanović had demanded as compensation, but there were two important changes. First, the crisis inaugurated a period of closer collaboration between Belgrade and the two friendly great powers. The link to St Petersburg was strengthened by the arrival of the new Russian minister, Baron Nikolai Hartwig, a vehement pan-Slav and Serbophile, who would play a central role in Belgrade political life until his sudden death just before the outbreak of war in 1914. The financial and political ties to France were also reinforced – manifested in a huge loan from Paris for the purpose of expanding the Serbian army and improving its striking power.

Secondly, the rage and disappointment of 1908–9 had a radicalizing effect on the nationalist groups. Though they were temporarily demoralized by the government's capitulation on the annexation question, they did not renounce their ambitions. A gulf opened up between the government and the nationalist milieu. Bogdan Radenković, a civilian national activist in Macedonia, where the struggle against the Bulgarians continued, met with officer veterans of the Macedonian front, some of them conspirators of 1903, to discuss the creation of a new secret entity. The result was the formation on 3 March 1911 in a Belgrade apartment of Ujedinjenje ili smrt! ('Union or death!'), popularly known as the 'Black Hand'. Apis, now Professor of Tactics at the Military Academy, was among the seven men – five officer-regicides and two civilians – present at that founding meeting; he brought with him the network of younger regicides and fellow travellers over which he now exercised unchallenged leadership.[94] The constitution of Ujedinjenje ili smrt! opened with the unsurprising declaration that the aim of the new association was the 'unification of Serbdom'. Further articles stated that the members must strive to influence the government to adopt the idea that Serbia was the 'Piedmont' of the Serbs, and indeed of all the South Slav peoples – the journal founded to expound the ideals of Ujedinjenje ili smrt! duly bore the title *Pijemont*. The new movement assumed an encompassing and hegemonic concept of Serbdom – Black Hand propaganda did not acknowledge the separate identity of Bosnian Muslims and flatly denied the existence of Croats.[95] In order to prepare Serbdom for what would surely be a violent struggle for unity, the society would undertake revolutionary work in all territories inhabited by Serbs. Out-side the borders of the Serbian state, the society would also combat by all means available the enemies of the Serbian idea.[96]

In their work for the 'national cause' these men increasingly saw themselves as enemies of the democratic parliamentary system in Serbia and especially of the Radical Party, whose leaders they denounced as traitors to the nation.[97] Within Ujedinjenje ili smrt! the old hatred of the Serbian military for the Radical Party lived on. There were also affinities with proto-fascist ideology: the objective was not merely a change in the sovereign personnel of the state – that had been achieved in 1903, without any appreciable benefits to the Serbian nation – but rather a thoroughgoing renovation of Serbian politics and society, a 'regenera-tion of our degenerate race'.[98]

The movement thrived on a cult of secrecy. Members were inducted by means of a ceremony devised by Jovanović-Čupa, a member of the founding council and a freemason. New recruits swore an oath before a hooded figure in a darkened room pledging absolute obedience to the organization on pain of death.

> I [name], in joining the organisation Union or Death, swear by the sun that warms me, by the earth that nourishes me, before God, by the blood of my ancestors, on my honour and on my life, that I will from this moment until my death be faithful to the laws of this organisation, and that I will always be ready to make any sacrifice for it.
>
> I swear before God, on my honour and on my life, that I will execute all missions and commands without question.
>
> I swear before God, on my honour and my life, that I will take all the secrets of this organisation into my grave with me.
>
> May God and my comrades in the organisation be my judges if, know-ingly or not, I should ever violate this oath.[99]

Little was kept in the way of records – there was no central register of members, but a loose network of cells, none of which possessed an over-view of the organization's extent or activities. As a result, uncertainty remains about the size of the organization. By the end of 1911, the num-ber of members had risen to around 2,000–2,500; it grew dramatically during the Balkan Wars, but a retrospective estimate deriving from a defector-turned-informant of 100,000–150,000 is certainly inflated.[100]

Whatever the precise numbers, the Black Hand spread quickly into the structures of official Serbia, reaching out from their base within the military to infiltrate the cadres of Serbian border guards and customs officers, especially along the Serbian–Bosnian frontier. There were also numerous recruits among the espionage agents still working in Bosnia for the Narodna Odbrana, despite the ostensible shut-down of 1909. Among their activities was the maintenance of a terrorist training camp, at which recruits were instructed in marksmanship, bomb-throwing, bridge-blowing and espionage.[101]

Here was a set-up made to measure for the seasoned conspirator Apis. The cult of secrecy suited his temperament. So did the organization's official insignia, a circular logo bearing a skull, crossbones, a knife, a phial of poison and a bomb. Asked later why he and his colleagues had adopted these symbols, Apis replied that, for him, 'those emblems [did] not have such a frightening or negative look'. After all, it was the task of all nationally minded Serbs 'to save Serbdom with bombs, knives and rifles'. 'In my work in [Macedonia],' he recalled, 'poison was used and all guerrillas carried it both as a means of attack and to save someone if he fell into enemy hands. That is why such emblems entered the organisation's seal and it was a sign that these people were prepared to die.'[102]

There was a paradoxically public quality to the clandestinity of the Black Hand.[103] Loose talk soon ensured that the government and the press were aware of the movement's existence and there is even some evidence that Prince Alexandar, successor to the throne after the abdication of his older brother Djordje, was informed in advance of the new foundation and was supportive of its activities. (The prince was one of a small circle of sponsors who helped to finance the foundation of *Pijemont*.) Recruitment processes were informal and often semi-public; recruiters had merely to mention the patriotic work of the organization and many officers joined without further ado.[104] There were dinners and banquets in the Belgrade cafés, where Apis would preside over a long table thronged with nationalist students.[105] When the commandant of Belgrade, Miloš Bozanović, asked his subordinate, Major Kostić, for information about the Black Hand, Kostić was incredulous: 'Don't you know? It is public knowledge. They are talking about it in the cafés and public houses.' Perhaps all this was inevitable in a city like Belgrade where everyone knew everyone, and where social life took place in coffee-houses, rather than in private homes. But the spectacular secrecy of the Black Hand presumably also filled an emotional need, for what was the point of belonging to a secret organization if nobody knew that you did? To be seen wining and dining with other conspirators at the regular table conferred a sense of importance; it also created a thrilling sense of collusion among those who were formally outside the network, but in the know – and this was important for a movement that claimed to represent the silent majority of the Serbian nation.

But if its existence was a matter of general knowledge, there was plenty of room for uncertainty about its aims. Like many Radical Party leaders, Pašić viewed the Black Hand as a movement primarily dedicated to the overthrow of the Serbian state from within – he appears to have seen its ultra-nationalism as mere camouflage for domestic subversion. This misreading made its way into many of the diplomatic reports. The usually well informed Austrian minister in Belgrade reported in November 1911, for example, that the Black Hand's claim to be a patriotic group operating outside Serbia in order to unite all Serbs was 'really only a cover; its real purpose is to intervene in internal affairs'.[106] This misapprehension would continue to befuddle the Austrian authorities during the crisis of July 1914.

Within Bosnia and Herzegovina, the networks of Ujedinjenje ili smrt! and Narodna Odbrana became interwoven with local groups of pan-Serb activists, of which the most important was Mlada Bosna ('Young Bosnia'). Mlada Bosna was not a unified organization, but rather an aggregation of groups and cells of revolutionary youth operating across the province from around 1904; its focus was less narrowly Serbian than that of the Black Hand or of Narodna Odbrana.[107] Since they were operating under the eyes of the Austrian police, the Young Bosnians adopted a decentred, flexible structure based on small 'circles' (kruzki), linked only by designated intermediaries. Young Bosnia's great hour arrived in 1910, when one of their number launched a suicide attack on the Austrian governor of Bosnia. On 3 June 1910, on the occasion of the opening of the Bosnian parliament, Bogdan Žerajić, a Serbian student from Herzegovina, fired five shots at Governor Marijan Varešanin. When all his bullets went wide, Žerajić emptied the sixth and last round into his own head. He was buried anonymously in a section of Sarajevo cemetery reserved for criminals and suicides, but his grave soon became a shrine for the Serb underground movement and his deed was celebrated by the nationalist press in Belgrade.[108]

No one did more to exalt Žerajić's reputation than his fellow Young Bosnian Vladimir Gačinović. Gačinović had left Bosnia to attend high school in Belgrade, staying on to complete one term at the university there, before winning a government scholarship to the University of Vienna. In 1911 he had joined both Ujedinjenje ili smrt! and Narodna Odbrana; after his return to Sarajevo, he established a network of activist cells in the city. But Gačinović was best known for a tract he wrote celebrating the life and death of Žerajić. *The Death of a Hero* described the suicide shooter as 'a man of action, of strength, of life and virtue, a type such as opens an epoch' and closed with an incendiary challenge: 'Young Serbs, will you produce such men?' Gačinović 's pamphlet circulated widely as contraband in Bosnia and became one of the key cult texts of the pan-Serbian terrorist milieu, blending as it did the themes of assassination and sacrifice in a manner reminiscent of the Kosovo epics.[109] Žerajić's attack marked the beginning of the systematic use of political terrorism against the political elite of the Habsburg Empire; there were seven further similar incidents and more than a dozen other abortive plots were detected in the South Slav provinces of the empire during the three years between Žerajić's death and the fatal shots of 28 June 1914 in Sarajevo.[110]

THREE TURKISH WARS

At the end of September 1911, only six months after the foundation of Ujedinjenje ili smrt!, Italy launched an invasion of Libya. This unprovoked attack on one of the integral provinces of the Ottoman Empire triggered a cascade of opportunist attacks on Ottoman-controlled territory in the Balkans. A loose coalition of Balkan states – Serbia, Montenegro, Bulgaria and Greece – mounted parallel assaults on Ottoman territory, thereby starting the First Balkan War (October 1912–May 1913). The result was a momentous victory for the Balkan allies over the Ottoman forces, who were driven out of Albania, Macedonia and Thrace. In the Second Balkan War (June–July 1913), the belligerents fought over the spoils of the first: Serbia, Greece, Montenegro and Romania fought Bulgaria for territories in Macedonia, Thrace and the Dobrudja.

The impact of these two wars is discussed in more detail in chapter 5. For the moment, it suffices to note that their most conspicuous beneficiary was Serbia, which acquired central Vardar, including Ohrid, Bitola, Kosovo, Štip and Kočani, plus the eastern half of the Sanjak of Novi Pazar (the western half fell to Montenegro). The kingdom's territorial extent increased from 18,650 to 33,891 square miles and its population grew by more than one and a half million. The acquisition of Kosovo, the mythscape of Serbian national poetry, was a cause for great rejoicing, and since the kingdom now shared a border with Montenegro to the west, there was the prospect that Serbia might, through a political union with its neighbour, secure a permanent access to the Adriatic coast. Moreover, Serbia's conduct of the war appeared to show that the years of military investment financed by French loans (there was another big one from a consortium of French banks in September 1913) had not been in vain. Three hundred thousand troops had been put into the field within three weeks of the first mobilization order. The Serbian army was now, as one foreign observer noted, 'a factor to be reckoned with', and Serbia itself a major regional power.[111] Dayrell Crackanthorpe, the British minister in Belgrade, reported on the mood of public elation: 'Serbia feels that she has, so to speak, attained her majority and [...] can pursue a national policy of her own.' The kingdom's political elites were currently 'passing through a phase of extreme self-satisfaction'; everywhere in the press and in public debate, Serbian successes in the field were contrasted with 'the failures of Austrian diplomacy'.[112]

For many of those in the territories newly conquered by Belgrade, the imposition of Serbian rule brought harassment and oppression. The freedom of association, assembly and the press guaranteed under the Serbian constitution of 1903 (Articles 24, 25 and 22) were not introduced into the new territories; nor was Article 13 revoking the death penalty for political crimes. The inhabitants of the new areas were denied active or passive voting rights. In other words, the conquered areas acquired, for the moment, the character of a colony. The government justified these decisions on the grounds that the cultural level of the new territories was so low that granting them freedom would endanger the country. In reality the chief concern was to keep the non-Serbs who constituted the majority in many areas out of national politics. Opposition newspapers such as *Radičke Novine* and *Pravda* were quick to point out that the 'new Serbs' had actually enjoyed better political rights under the Turks than they did under Serbian administration.[113]

On the Serbian side, this was a war in two kinds, fought not only by regular army units, but also, as so often in the past, by partisan bands, *comitatjis*, and other freelance fighters. In the newly conquered areas, the collusion between official authorities and informal groups had appalling consequences. There was much arbitrary destruction of Turkish buildings, such as schools, baths and mosques. British consuls managed to limit the damage in some instances by persuading the local Serbian military commanders that this or that building dated back to the empire of Stepan Dušan and was thus a part of the Serbian national patrimony; this ruse succeeded, for example, in the case of the beautiful sixteenth-century Turkish bridge in Macedonian Skopje (Üsküb).[114]

In October and November 1913, the British vice-consuls in Skopje and Monastir reported systematic intimidation, arbitrary detentions, beatings, rapes, village-burnings and massacres by the Serbs in the annexed areas.[115] 'It is already abundantly evident,' Vice-Consul Greig of Monastir reported, 'that Moslems under Servian rule have nothing whatsoever to expect but periodical massacre, certain exploitation and final ruin.' Eleven days later, he filed a further report warning that the 'Bulgarian and especially the Moslem populations in the districts of Perlepe, Krchevo and Krushevo [were] in danger of extermination by the very frequent and barbarous massacres and pillage to which they are subjected by Servian bands'.[116] By the end of the month, 'pillages, murder and outrages of other kinds by bands of Servian comitajis and persons in league with them' had created conditions of near-anarchy.[117] Albanians and other Muslims, Bulgars, Vlachs and Jews, the vice-consul reported in December, dreaded the prospect of subjection to 'a penniless state' that seemed bent on 'draining every community of its means of existence to an extent unknown in the blackest days of the Turkish regime'.[118] From Bitola in the south, near the Greek border, the British vice-consul reported that the old municipal officials had been replaced by a new cohort of corrupt 'Servian ex-propagandists' whose ringleaders were '(1) an ex-barber, spy and Serbian agent [. . .] and (2) a local Serboman of unmentionable profession called Maxim'. 'Nothing,' Greig concluded, 'could be more favourable to the enemies of Servia than the reign of terror set up by this clique.'[119]

What is interesting about these reports is not merely their disturbing content, but the scepticism with which they were received by the British minister Crackanthorpe, a man of pronounced Serbophile sentiment. Crackanthorpe, whose most important source on the events unfolding in the annexed areas was 'a Servian officer of his acquaintance',[120] accepted the official denials of the Belgrade government at face value and tried to mute the impact of Greig's dispatches from Monastir by suggesting to the Foreign Office that the vice-consul was the dupe of hysterical refugees and their tall tales. Already, one might argue, the events unfolding in the Balkans were being viewed through the geopolitical lens of the alliance system, in which Serbia figured as a friendly state locked in a gallant struggle with fearsome neighbouring Austria-Hungary. It was only the cumulative detail of the reports emerging from the annexed areas, combined with corroborating accounts from Romanian, Swiss and French officials that persuaded the British Foreign Office that the news of Macedonian atrocities should not be dismissed as Austrian propaganda.

In the meantime, the Serbian government showed no interest whatsoever in preventing further outrages or in instigating an investigation of those that had already occurred. When Pašić was alerted to the events in Bitola by the British, he simply replied that he did not know the prefect there personally and therefore could not comment. His offer to send a commissioner to the south to explore the matter further never materialized. Informed by the Serbian minister in Constantinople of complaints from a delegation of senior Muslim dignitaries, he declared that these stories stemmed from emigrants who had exaggerated their sufferings in order to secure a warmer welcome among their new compatriots.[121] When the Carnegie Commission – composed of a hand-picked international team of experts selected for their impartiality – arrived in the Balkans to conduct their famous investigation of the atrocities committed in the contested areas, they received virtually no assistance from Belgrade.[122]

The wars seemed for a time to have resolved the tensions within the executive structure in Belgrade. For a brief interval, the covert networks, the regular army, the partisan bands and the cabinet ministers pulled together in the national cause. Apis was sent to conduct covert operations for the army in Macedonia before the Serbian invasion in 1912; in its work negotiating with Albanian chieftains in 1913, the Black Hand essentially functioned as an arm of the foreign ministry in Belgrade. The pacification of the newly conquered areas in the south involved not just regular army units but also volunteer bands affiliated with Black Hand operatives such as Voja Tankosić, a former regicide conspirator who had overseen the murder of Queen Draga's two brothers.[123] It was a mark of the Black Hand's enhanced prestige that Apis was promoted to lieutenant-colonel in January 1913 and appointed chief of the General Staff's intelligence division in August, a role that placed him in control of the extensive network of Serbian Narodna Odbrana agents inside Austria-Hungary.[124]

The mood of unity began to dissipate as soon as the Balkan Wars were over, when disputes over the management of the newly acquired areas triggered a catastrophic deterioration in civil–military relations. On one side were the ministry of war, the Serbian army and various fellow travellers from the ranks of the Independent Radical opposition; on the other side were the Radical Party leaders who made up most of the rest of the cabinet.[125] The dispute centred on the character of the administration to be introduced in the new lands. The Pašić cabinet intended to install a system of interim civil administration by decree. The army, by contrast, favoured a continuation of military rule. Buoyed up by its recent successes, the military leadership refused to cede control in the annexed zone. It was a matter not just of power, but also of policy, for the hardliners took the view that only a firm and illiberal administration would be suited to the consolidation of Serbian control in areas of mixed ethnicity. When the Radical minister of the interior Stojan Protić issued a Priority Decree in April 1914 formally subordinating the army to the civil authorities, a fully fledged crisis broke out. Officers in the new areas refused to comply with the decree, the military party linked arms with the Independent Radical opposition in the Skupština, just as the conspirators had done after 1903. There was even talk of an impending coup, to be coordinated by Apis, who would lead troops of the Belgrade garrison to the royal palace, force King Petar to abdicate in favour of his son Prince Alexandar and assassinate the Radical members of the cabinet.[126]

By the end of May 1914, the situation in Belgrade was so finely balanced that it required the intervention of foreign powers to prevent the collapse of the Pašić government. In a highly unusual move, the Russian minister in Belgrade declared publicly that Russia's Balkan policies required Pašić's retention in office. The French backed him up by hinting that a post-Pašić government dominated by Independents and members of the military party might no longer receive the lavish Parisian financial backing that had sustained state investment in Serbia since 1905. It was an imperfect repeat of 1899, when the wily Radical leader had been saved from execution by the intervention of the Austrian minister. Outmanoeuvred, Apis retired from the fray.[127] With the threat of an immediate takeover temporarily averted, Pašić looked to the coming elections in June 1914 to consolidate his position.

There was nothing in these opaque political struggles to comfort the observers of Serbian affairs in Vienna. As Dayrell Crackanthorpe pointed out in March 1914, both the 'more moderate and prudent section of opinion' represented in the Radical cabinet and the 'military party' influenced by the Black Hand believed in the more or less imminent dissolution of Austria-Hungary and the succession of Serbia to the vast lands of the empire that still awaited pan-Serbian redemption. The difference was one of method: while the military party believed in a 'war of aggression when the moment arrives and the country is prepared', the moderates took the view that 'the signal for the disruption of the Austro-Hungarian Empire will come, not from without, but from within the Empire' and thus favoured a posture of preparedness for all eventualities. In institutional terms, moreover, the fabric of moderate official Serbia and the hardline irredentist networks remained deeply intertwined. The senior echelons of the military and its intelligence service, with its system of agents in Bosnia and Herzegovina, the customs service, parts of the interior ministry and other government organs were deeply infiltrated by the networks, just as the networks were infiltrated by the state.

THE CONSPIRACY

Reconstructing the details of the plot to assassinate Archduke Franz Ferdinand in Sarajevo is difficult. The assassins themselves made every effort to cover the tracks that linked them to Belgrade. Many of the surviving participants refused to speak of their involvement; others played down their roles or covered their tracks with obfuscating speculations, producing a chaos of conflicting testimony. The plot itself produced no surviving documentation: virtually all those who took part were habituated to a milieu that was obsessed with secrecy. The collusion between the Serbian state and the networks implicated in the plot was by design furtive and informal – there was no real paper trail. The historiography of the conspiracy has therefore had to make do with a dubious combination of post-war recollections, depositions and affidavits made under conditions of duress, claims allegedly based on sources that have since been destroyed, and scraps of documentary evidence, most of them related only obliquely to the planning and implementation of the plot. Yet so much hangs on the background to this plot that historians have pored with forensic intensity over nearly every detail. It is thus possible to chart a line of maximum plausibility through the chaos of the sources and the tendentious distortions of much of the secondary literature.

Apis was the principal architect behind the plot, but the idea itself probably originated from his associate Rade Malobabić, a Serb born in Austria-Hungary who had worked for some years with the Narodna Odbrana as a spy, collecting information on Austrian fortifications and troop movements and bringing it to the Serbian frontier officers who doubled as Black Hand operatives and, through them, to Serbian military intelligence.[128] Malobabić was a super-agent, a man of extraordinary dedication and cunning who knew the borderlands well and repeatedly evaded capture by the Austrian authorities. He is reported on one occasion to have swum across the virtually frozen Drina, from which he emerged covered in shards of ice, in order to report to his handlers on the Serbian side of the border.[129] It was probably Malobabić who first informed Apis of the impending visit to Sarajevo by Franz Ferdinand, heir apparent to the Austrian throne, in June 1914.[130]

Exactly why Apis pressed for the assassination of the archduke is difficult to establish, since he left no straightforward account of his motivations. In early 1914, the hostility of the local activists in Bosnia was focused primarily on the person of Oskar Potiorek, the Austrian governor of Bosnia, a successor to Varešanin, whom Žerajić had failed to kill in June 1910. In turning their efforts towards Archduke Franz Ferdinand, Apis raised the political stakes. The assassination of a governor would stir things up, but it might easily be construed as a local affair, motivated by issues of regional governance. By contrast, an assault on the heir to the Habsburg throne, at a time when the reigning

Emperor was well into his eighty-third year, was bound to be seen as an attack on the empire's very existence.

It should be emphasized that the archduke was not targeted on account of any alleged hostility to the Slavic minorities in the Austro-Hungarian Empire, but, on the contrary, because, to borrow the words of his assassin, Gavrilo Princip, 'as future Sovereign he would have prevented our union by carrying through certain reforms'.[131] Princip was alluding to the archduke's reputed support for structural reforms of the monarchy that would assign more autonomy to the Slavic lands. Many within the Serbian irredentist milieu recognized this idea as a potentially catastrophic threat to the reunificationist project. If the Habsburg monarchy were to transform itself successfully into a tripartite entity governed from Vienna along federal lines, with Zagreb, for example, as a capital with the same status as Budapest, there was the danger that Serbia would forfeit its vanguard role as the Piedmont of the South Slavs.[132] The targeting of the archduke thus exemplified one abiding strand in the logic of terrorist movements, namely that reformers and moderates are more to be feared than outright enemies and hardliners.

The men selected to carry out the assassination of the archduke had all been formed in the world of the irredentist networks. It was the former *comitatji* Voja Tankosić who recruited the three Bosnian Serb youths who formed the core of the assassination unit that would be sent to Sarajevo. Trifko Grabež, Nedeljko Čabrinović and Gavrilo Princip were all nineteen years of age when Tankosić enrolled them in the conspiracy. They were good friends who spent much time in each other's company. Grabež was the son of an orthodox priest in Pale, about twelve miles to the east of Sarajevo, who had travelled to Belgrade to continue his high school education. Čabrinović had left school at the age of fourteen and subsequently drifted to Belgrade, where he found work as a print-setter for a firm specializing in anarchist literature. Princip, like Grabež, had left Sarajevo in order to attend school in Belgrade. All three were from poor families and unhappy households. Grabež and Čabrinović had suffered under and rebelled against the male authority figures in their own early lives. During his trial, Čabrinović told the court that his father had mistreated him at home because he made such poor progress at his school in Sarajevo; the boy was eventually expelled for slapping one of his teachers in the face. The tensions at home were aggravated by the fact that Čabrinović senior worked as a police informer for the hated Austrians – a stigma that the boy hoped to slough off through his engagement in the national cause. Grabež too had been thrown out of his grammar school in Tuzla for punching one of his professors.[133] Money was scarce – only Princip had a regular income, in the form of a very modest allowance from his parents, but this was usually shared out among the friends or lent to impecunious acquaintances.[134] Čabrinović later recalled that on arriving in Belgrade, he had for some days carried all his possessions around with him in a small suitcase, presumably because he had nowhere to stay.[135] Unsurprisingly, the boys were not in the best of health. Princip in particular was thin and sickly; he was probably already tubercular. Illness had forced him to leave school early in Sarajevo. The protocol of his trial describes him as 'a small fragile youth'.[136]

These boys had little in the way of bad habits. They were made of that sombre, youthful stuff, rich in ideals but poor in experience, that modern terrorist movements feed upon. Alcohol was not to their taste. Although they were heterosexual by romantic inclination, they did not seek the society of young women. They read nationalist poetry and irredentist

Young Gavrilo Princip

Nedeljko Čabrinović

newspapers and pamphlets. The boys dwelt at length on the suffering of the Serbian nation, for which they blamed everyone but the Serbs themselves, and felt the slights and humiliations of the least of their countrymen as if they were their own. A recurring theme was the economic degradation of their Bosnian countryfolk by the Austrian authorities (a complaint that overlooked the fact that Bosnia was in fact more industrialized and more prosperous in terms of per capita income than most of the Serbian heartland).[137] Sacrifice was a central preoccupation, almost an obsession. Princip had even found the time to learn by heart the entirety of *The Mountain Wreath*, Petrović-Njegos's stirring epic celebration of the selfless tyrannicide Miloš Obilić.[138] Princip stated to the court during his trial that in the days before the assassination, it had been his habit to go to the grave of the suicide assassin Bogdan Žerajić: 'I often spent whole nights there, thinking about our situation, about our miserable conditions and about [Žerajić], and so it was that I resolved to carry out the assassination.'[139] Čabrinović, too, reported that he had made his way to Žerajić's grave as soon as he had arrived in Sarajevo. Finding it neglected, he had laid flowers on it (a footnote to the Austrian trial transcript noted snidely that these blooms were stolen from other graves nearby). It was during these sojourns at Žerajić's resting place, Čabrinović declared, that he formed the intention to die as Žerajić had done. 'I knew in any case that I would not live long. The thought of suicide was always with me; I was indifferent to everything.'[140]

This loitering at the grave of a suicide is interesting and suggestive because it speaks to that fascination with the figure of the suicide assassin that was so central to the Kosovo myth, and more broadly to the self-awareness of the pan-Serbian milieu, whose journals, diaries and correspondence are shot through with tropes of sacrifice. Even the attack itself was supposed to deliver an encoded reference to Žerajić's earlier act, for Princip had originally planned to take up his post exactly where Žerajić had stood, on the Emperor Bridge: 'I wanted to shoot from the same spot as the deceased Žerajić.'[141]

For all of the assassins, Belgrade was the crucible that radicalized their politics and aligned them with the cause of Serb unification. In a telling passage of the court protocol, Čabrinović recalled how in 1912, when he had become too ill to continue working in Serbia and decided to return home, he had gone to the Belgrade office of the Narodna Odbrana, where he had been told that a Bosnian Serb could always get money for the journey back to Sarajevo. He was met at the office by a certain Major Vasić, secretary of the local association of the NO, who gave him money and patriotic texts, confiscated his book of Maupassant short stories on the ground that these were unworthy of a young Serb patriot, and urged him always to be 'a good Serb'.[142] Meetings of this kind were crucial to the formation of these young men, whose relations with male figures of authority had been so strained. Within the nationalist networks, there were older men prepared not just to help them with money and advice, but also to show them affection and respect, to provide them with a sense – so conspicuously lacking in their experience hitherto – that their lives were meaningful, that they belonged to an historical moment, that they were part of a great and flourishing enterprise.

This grooming by older men of younger men for induction into the networks was a crucial element in the success of the irredentist movement. When he returned from Belgrade to Sarajevo, Čabrinović found it impossible to fit back into his old socialist milieu; sensing that his outlook on the world had changed, the party comrades denounced him as a Serbian agitator and spy and expelled him from the party. By the time he returned to Belgrade in 1913, Čabrinović was no longer a revolutionary leftist, but an 'anarchist with nationalism mixed in'.[143] Princip passed through this energized environment as well: having left Sarajevo in May 1912 in order to complete his secondary education in Belgrade, he too crossed the path of the indefatigable Major Vasić. When the First Balkan War broke out, Vasić helped him make his way to the Turkish border to sign up as a volunteer fighter, but the local commander – who happened, incidentally, to be Voja Tankosić – turned him down at the border on the grounds that he was 'too weak and small'.

At least as important as the contact with activists like Vasić, or with the written propaganda of the Narodna Odbrana was the coffee-house social milieu that provided a sense of belonging for young Bosnian Serbs hanging out in Belgrade. Čabrinović frequented the Acorn Garland, the Green Garland and the Little Goldfish, where, he later recalled, he heard 'all manner of talk' and mixed with 'students, typesetters' and 'partisans', but especially with Bosnian Serbs. The young men ate, smoked and talked of politics or debated the contents of newspaper reports.[144] It was in the Acorn Garland and the Green Garland that Čabrinović and Princip first considered the possibility of assassinating the heir to the Austrian throne; the senior Black Hand operative who provided the young men with Browning pistols and boxes of ammunition, was likewise 'a popular figure on the Belgrade coffee-house circuit'.[145] The prevalent political mood in these places was ultra-nationalist and anti-Austrian. There is a revealing passage in the court transcript in which the judge asked Princip where Grabež had acquired his ultra-nationalist political views. Princip replied artlessly: 'After he [Grabež] came to Belgrade, he too took up the same principles.' Seizing on the implication, the judge pressed further: 'So coming to Belgrade is enough, in other words, to ensure that someone will be instilled with the same ideas as yourself?'[146] But Princip, seeing that he was being drawn out of cover, refused to comment further.

Once planning for the assassination began in earnest, care was taken to ensure that there was no ostensible link between the assassins' cell and the authorities in Belgrade. The assassins' handler was a man called Milan Ciganović, a Bosnian Serb and Black Hand member who had fought with the partisans against the Bulgarians under Tankosić and was now an employee of the Serbian state railways. Ciganović reported

Milan Ciganović

to Tankosić, who in turn reported to Apis. All orders were passed by word of mouth.

Training for the assassination took place in the Serbian capital. Princip had already received instruction in shooting at the Partisan Academy and was the best shot of the three. On 27 May they were provided with the weapons they would use. Four revolvers and six small bombs, weighing less than two and a half pounds each, from the Serbian State Arsenal at Kragujevac. They were also issued with poison in the form of small flasks of cyanide swaddled in cotton. Their instructions were to shoot themselves as soon as the assassination had been carried out or, failing that, to take their lives by swallowing cyanide. Here was a further precaution against an indiscretion or a forced confession that might incriminate Belgrade. Moreover it suited the boys, who were exalted at the idea of throwing away their lives and saw their deed as an act of martyrdom.

The three assassins entered Bosnia with the help of the Black Hand network and its connections in the Serbian customs service. Čabrinović crossed at the border post in Mali Zvornik on 30 May with the assistance of agents from the Black Hand's 'underground railway' – schoolteachers, a border guard, the secretary to a town mayor and so on – and made his way to Tuzla, where he waited for his friends to show up. Princip and Grabež were guided by Serbian border officials to the crossing point at Lješnica and shown on 31 May to a wooded island on the river Drina that ran at that point between Serbian and Bosnian territory. This hiding place, much used by smugglers, concealed them from the notice of the Austrian border police. After nightfall on the following day they were led into Austrian territory by a part-time smuggler working in the service of the underground railway.

Although they took great care to avoid being seen by Austrian police or officials, the three assassins were extremely indiscreet in their dealings with fellow Serbs. Princip and Grabež, for example, were taken by a schoolteacher working for the underground railway to the home of a Bosnian Serb farmer by the name of Mitar Kerović. Having drunk too many glasses of plum brandy en route, the teacher tried to impress the peasants: 'Do you know who these people are? They're going to Sarajevo to throw bombs and kill the Archduke who is going to come there.'[147] Succumbing to boyish bravado (they had crossed the Drina now and were on their native soil) Princip joined in, brandishing his revolver and showing his hosts how the bombs were operated. For this folly, the Kerović family – illiterate, apolitical individuals with only a very dim grasp of what the boys were up to – would pay a terrible price. Nedjo Kerović, who gave the boys a lift to Tuzla in his cart, was later found guilty of treason and being an accessory to murder and sentenced to death (commuted to twenty years in prison). His father, Mitar, was sentenced to life imprisonment. Their testimony at the trial of the assassins in October 1914 provided some of the rare moments of bleak humour in the proceedings. Asked his age by the presiding judge, Nedjo Kerović, himself the father of five children, replied that he didn't rightly know, they should ask his father. When Kerović senior was asked how much he had had to drink on the night when the boys arrived, he replied: 'When I drink, I don't keep count; I just drink as much as I can.'[148]

The boys were joined in Sarajevo by another four-man cell, recruited by the Bosnian Serb and Black Hand member Danilo Ilić. At twenty-three years of age, Ilić was the oldest of them all. He had been trained as a schoolteacher on an Austrian government scholarship, but had resigned after falling ill. He was a member of Young Bosnia and a personal friend of Gačinović , the troubadour of Žerajić. Like the others, Ilić had been to Belgrade in 1913, where he had passed through the usual coffee shops, been recruited to the Black Hand and had won the confidence of Apis, before returning in March 1914 to Sarajevo, where he worked as a proof-reader and editor of a local paper.

Ilić's first recruit for the assassination brigade was the revolutionary leftist Muslim carpenter Muhamed Mehmedbašić, a native of Herzegovina. The two men knew each other well. In January 1914, they had met in France with Voja Tankosić to plan an attempt on the life of Potiorek. The plan failed. On his way home in the train, Mehmedbašić had panicked at the sight of uniformed policemen and flushed his phial of poison down the toilet (the dagger he was supposed to dip in it was tossed from a window). The other two Sarajevan recruits were Cvijetko Popović, an academically brilliant eighteen-year-old high-school student, and Vaso Čubrilović, brother of the young schoolteacher who had led the boys to the house of the Kerović family. At seventeen years of age, Čubrilović, another schoolroom rebel, was the youngest of the crew. He had never met Ilić before the cell was put together and the two local boys did not meet Princip, Mehmedbašić, Čabrinović and Grabež until after the assassination.[149]

Ilić's choice of collaborators – a man with a proven record of ineptitude in carrying out high-risk assignments and two completely inexperienced schoolboys – seems bizarre at first glance, but there was method in the madness. The real purpose of the Sarajevan second cell was to cover the tracks of the conspiracy. In this connection, Mehmedbašić was an inspired choice, because he was a willing, if incompetent, assassin, and thus useful backup for the Belgrade cell, but not a Serb. As Black Hand members, Ilić and Princip could be depended upon (in theory) to take their own lives, or at least remain silent after the event. The Sarajevo boys would be unable to testify, for the simple reason that they knew nothing about the larger background to the plot. The impression would thus emerge that this was a purely local undertaking, with no links to Belgrade.

NIKOLA PAŠIĆ REACTS

How much did Nikola Pašić know of the plot to kill Franz Ferdinand, and what steps did he take to prevent it? It is virtually certain that Pašić was informed of the plan in some detail. There are several indications of this, but the most eloquent testimony is that of Ljuba Jovanović, minister of education in the Pašić government. Jovanović recalled (in a memoir fragment published in 1924 but probably written much earlier) that Pašić had told the Serbian cabinet 'at the end of May or the beginning of June' that 'there were people who were preparing to go to Sarajevo to kill Franz Ferdinand'. The entire cabinet, including Pašić, agreed that the prime minister should issue instructions to the frontier authorities along the Drina to prevent a crossing.[150] Other documents and scraps of testimony, compounded by Pašić's own strange and obfuscating behaviour after 1918, further reinforce the case for Pašić's foreknowledge of the plot.[151] But *how* did he know? His informant was probably – though this supposition rests on indirect evidence – none other than the Serbian Railways employee and Black Hand agent Milan Ciganović, who was, it would appear, a personal agent of the prime minister himself, charged with keeping an eye on the activities of the secret society. If this was so, then Pašić possessed detailed and timely knowledge, not only of the plot, but of the persons and organization behind it.[152]

The three Sarajevo-bound assassins who entered Bosnia at the end of May left virtually no trace in the Serbian official records. In any case they were not the only ones moving weapons illegally across the border in the summer of 1914. Reports from the Serbian border authorities during the first half of June reveal a dense web of covert cross-border activity. On 4 June, the district chief of Podrinje at Sabac alerted the minister of the interior, Protić, to a plan by officers working with the border control 'to transfer a certain quantity of bombs and weapons using some of our people in Bosnia'. The district chief had considered impounding the weapons, but as these were in a suitcase that was already on the Bosnian side of the border, he feared that an attempt to retrieve it might incriminate or expose the operations of the frontier forces. Further enquiries revealed that the agent who was supposed to take charge of the weapons on the Bosnian side was none other than Rade Malobabić.[153]

What was alarming about these operations, one local official complained, was not simply that they were conducted without the knowledge of the relevant civilian authorities, but that they were undertaken 'publicly and in broad daylight'. And since the perpetrators were 'public officials', the impression might easily arise 'that we welcomed such actions'. Pašić and Interior Minister Protić saw the point. If it is true that Pašić already knew at this time of the plot's existence, we would expect him to have done whatever was possible to shut down activities that might incriminate the Belgrade government. On 10 June, word indeed went out to the civilian authorities of the border districts that 'all such activities should be prevented'.[154]

Whether the *civilian* commanders in the affected areas were in any position to interdict the operations of the Border Guards was another question. When Raiko Stepanović, a sergeant of the Border Guards who had smuggled a suitcase full of guns and bombs across the border, was summoned to give an account of himself to the district chief, he simply refused to appear.[155] Following a meeting of the cabinet in mid-June, an order went out to the civilian authorities demanding an official enquiry on the illegal passage of arms and persons into Bosnia and a curt note was sent to the captain of the 4 Border Guards on 16 June 'recommending' that he 'cease this traffic of arms, munitions and other explosives from Serbia into Bosnia'. There was no reply. It later emerged that military commanders on the border were under strict orders to forward such civilian interventions unanswered to their superior officers.[156]

In other words, the Serbian border was no longer under the control of the government in Belgrade. When Minister of War Stepanović wrote to the chief of the General Staff asking for a statement clarifying the official position of the military on covert operations in Bosnia, the query was passed first to the head of the operations department, who claimed to know nothing of these matters, and subsequently to the head of Military Intelligence, none other than Apis himself. In a long, impertinent and thoroughly disingenuous reply to the head of the operations department, Apis defended the record and reputation of agent Malobabić and insisted that any guns passed to his hands were purely for the self-defence of Serbian agents working in Bosnia. Of bombs he claimed to know nothing whatsoever (three years later he would in fact state on oath that he had personally entrusted Malobabić with supplying and coordinating the assassination of Franz Ferdinand).[157] If a security risk arose on the border, he declared, this was not on account of the discreet and necessary operations of the military but because of the insolence of civilian operatives who claimed the right to police the border. In short, the fault lay with the civilians for attempting to interfere with sensitive military operations beyond their competence or understanding.[158] This reply was forwarded to Putnik, the chief of the Serbian General Staff, who summarized and endorsed it in a letter of 23 June to the minister of war. The fissure between the structures of civilian authority and a military command substantially infiltrated by the Black Hand now ran all the way from the banks of the Drina to the ministerial quarter in Belgrade.

Rattled by the resolute tone of the reply from Apis and the chief of the General Staff, Pašić took the step on 24 June of ordering a full investigation into the activities of the frontier guards. He had learned from 'many sources', he wrote in a top secret letter to the minister of war, that 'the officers' were engaged in work that was not only dangerous, but treasonable, 'because it aims at the creation of conflict between Serbia and Austria-Hungary'.

All our allies and friends of Serbia, if they knew what our officers and sergeants are doing, would not only abandon us, they would stand on the side of Austria-Hungary and allow her to punish her restless and disloyal neighbour, who prepares revolts and assassinations on her territory. The life interests of Serbia impose on her the obligation to be aware of everything that could provoke an armed conflict with Austria-Hungary at a time when peace is necessary for us to recuperate and prepare for the future events that lie ahead.[159]

The letter closed with an order that a 'severe investigation' be launched to establish exactly how many officers were guilty of such 'reckless and wanton' activity with a view to the 'extirpation and suppression' of the offending groups.

In a sense, of course, this was locking the stable door after the horse had bolted, since the boys had crossed the border at the end of May. Over two weeks had passed by the time Pašić acted to close the borders and nearly four by the time he was ready to launch an investigation of the perpetrators behind the plot. It is difficult to ascertain why the prime minister was so slow to act on the news of the conspiracy. He must have known that instructions to the frontier guards were bound to be fruitless, given that so many of them were affiliated with Ujedinjenje ili smrt!. Perhaps he feared the consequences of antagonizing his powerful enemy, Apis. It is striking that, despite the calls for a 'severe investigation', Apis remained in post as head of Serbian Military Intelligence throughout the crisis – he was not dismissed or even suspended from duties pending the outcome of the investigation. We should recall in this connection the extremity of the political crisis that had paralysed Serbia during May 1914. Pašić prevailed in that struggle, but only by a whisker, and only with the assistance of the ambassadors of the two great powers with most influence in Serbian affairs. There is thus some doubt as to whether he possessed the means to close down Apis's activities, even if he were inclined to do so. Perhaps Pašić even feared that an open confrontation might trigger his own assassination by Black Hand agents, though this seems unlikely, given the fact that he had already survived the May crisis unscathed. On the other hand, it is worth remembering that the Serbian prime minister remained, despite everything, the most powerful man in the country, a statesman of unparalleled skill at the head of a mass party whose delegates still dominated the national legislature. It is more probable that Pašić reverted during these weeks to the habits of long years at the turbulent apex of Serbian political life: keep your head down, don't rock the boat, let conflicts resolve themselves, wait out the storm.

Nevertheless, Pašić still had one important card in his hand: he could have foiled the conspiracy at little risk to himself by warning Vienna confidentially of the plot to kill the archduke. Heated controversy surrounds the question of whether such a warning was given. The evidentiary situation is especially difficult on this issue, because it was in no one's interest in retrospect to acknowledge that a formal warning had been offered or received. Pašić himself expressly denied that he had attempted to warn Vienna in an interview granted to the Hungarian newspaper *Az Est* on 7 July 1914.[160] He could hardly do otherwise, since avowing foreknowledge would have exposed him and his colleagues to the charge that they were accessories to the conspiracy. Apologists for Serbia in the post-war years were bound to follow the same line, because their argument for Belgrade's innocence of co-responsibility in the outbreak of war rested on the thesis that the Serbian government was entirely ignorant of any plot. The Austrian authorities were also unlikely to acknowledge a warning, because it would raise the question of why better measures had not been taken to protect the heir apparent's life – on 2 July, the semi-official Viennese newspaper *Fremdenblatt* issued a statement denying that there was any truth in the rumour that the Austrian Foreign Office had received any prior notification of the impending outrage.[161]

There is nonetheless powerful evidence that a warning of sorts was given. The most unimpeachable source is the French under-secretary for foreign affairs, Abel Ferry, who recorded in his office diary on 1 July that he had just received a visit by the Serbian minister to Paris, Milenko Vesnić, an old friend. In the course of their conversation, Vesnić stated among other things that the Serbian government had 'warned the Austrian Government that it had got wind of the plot'.[162] Among those who confirm this is the Serbian military attaché in Vienna, who told the Italian historian Magrini in 1915 that Pašić had sent a telegram to the Serbian legation in Vienna stating that 'owing to an information leak, the Serbian Government had grounds to suspect that a plot was being hatched against the life of the Archduke on the occasion of his journey to Bosnia' and that the Austro-Hungarian government would be well advised to postpone the visit.[163]

It is possible to reconstruct from recollections and the testimony of third persons what Jovan Jovanović, the Serbian minister in Vienna, did next. He met with Leon Biliński, joint Austro-Hungarian finance minister, at noon on 21 June in order to issue the Austrian government with a warning against the likely consequences if the archduke were to visit

Bosnia. But the warning was delivered only in the most oblique terms. A visit by the heir apparent on the anniversary of the Kosovo defeat, Jovanović suggested, would surely be regarded as a provocation. Among the young Serbs serving in the Austro-Hungarian forces 'there might be one who would put a ball-cartridge in his rifle or revolver in place of a blank cartridge . . .' Biliński, unimpressed by these auguries, 'showed no sign of attaching any importance to the communication' and merely replied: 'let us hope nothing does happen'.[164] Biliński refused in later years to speak with journalists or historians about this episode, protesting that a veil of oblivion should be drawn over these dark moments in recent history. It is clear that he was disinclined at the time to take the warning seriously – it was couched in such general terms that it might even be construed as a gesture of mere intimidation, an unwarranted attempt by the Serbian minister to intervene in the internal affairs of the monarchy by implying vague threats against its most senior personnel. Biliński thus saw no reason to pass the message on to the Austrian foreign minister, Count Berchtold.

In short: a warning of sorts was sent, but not one that was adequate to the situation. In retrospect, it has the look of a covering manoeuvre. Jovanović could have issued a more specific and forthright warning by providing the Austrians with the best information to hand in Belgrade. Pašić, too, could have informed the Austrians directly of the danger, rather than via Jovanović. He could have launched a real investigation of the conspiracy and risked his own office rather than the peace and security of his nation. But there were, as ever, constraints and complications. Jovanović, for one thing, was not just a member of the Serbian diplomatic service, but also a senior pan-Serb activist with the classical career profile of an ultra-nationalist. He was a former *comitadji* who had been involved in fomenting unrest in Bosnia after the annexation of 1908 and was even rumoured to have commanded guerrilla bands. He also happened to be, in the summer of 1914, the Black Hand's candidate for foreign minister in the event that the Pašić government were to be chased from power.[165] Indeed the Serbian envoy's pan-Serb views were so notorious that Vienna had made it known to Belgrade that his replacement by a less hostile figure would not be unwelcome. This is one of the reasons why Jovanović chose to approach Biliński rather than Count Berchtold, who held him in very poor regard.[166]

Pašić, too, was acting from complex motivations. On the one hand there was his concern – widely shared within the Radical leadership – about how the networks affiliated with Ujedinjenje ili smrt! might respond to what they would certainly perceive as a gross betrayal.[167] He may have hoped that the attempt in Sarajevo would fail. Most important of all, surely, was his awareness of how deeply the structures of the state and the very logic of its historical existence were interwoven with the irredentist networks. Pašić might regret their excesses, but he could not openly disavow them. Indeed, there was danger in even acknowledging publicly an awareness of their activities. This was not just a question of the legacy of Serbian national consolidation, which had always depended upon the collaboration of state agencies with voluntarist networks capable of infiltrating neighbouring states. It also touched upon the future. Serbia had needed the nationalist networks in the past and would depend on them again when the moment came, as Pašić knew it some day would, to redeem Bosnia and Herzegovina for Serbdom.

Everything we know about this subtle, interesting man suggests that he understood that Serbia needed peace above all if it were to rebuild its strength after the bloodshed of the Balkan Wars. The integration of the newly annexed areas – in itself a violent and traumatic process – had only just begun. Forced elections were looming.[168] But it is a characteristic of the most skilful politicians that they are capable of reasoning simultaneously at different levels of conditionality. Pašić wanted peace, but he also believed – he had never concealed it – that the final historical phase of Serbian expansion would in all probability not be achieved without war. Only a major European conflict in which the great powers were engaged would suffice to dislodge the formidable obstacles that stood in the way of Serbian 'reunification'.

Perhaps Pašić recalled the warning Charles Hardinge, permanent under-secretary at the Foreign Office in London, had offered Grujic, the Serbian minister in London, during the annexation crisis of 1908–9. Hardinge had cautioned the minister in January 1909 that support from Russia and the Entente powers would be forthcoming only if Serbia were to be attacked by Austria-Hungary; if Serbia itself took the initiative, help was out of the question.[169] That Pašić may have been thinking along these lines is suggested by an exchange between the Serbian prime minister and the Russian Tsar in the early spring of 1914, in which Pašić pressed upon the Tsar his need for Russian help in the event of an Aus-tro-Hungarian attack.[170] Such a scenario would fail, of course, if the world were to construe the assassination plot itself as an act of Serbian aggression; but Pašić was certain that the Austrians would be unable to establish any connection between the assassination (if it were to suc-ceed) and the government of Serbia because, in his own mind, no such linkage existed.[171] An attack from Austria-Hungary must therefore surely trigger support from Russia and her allies; Serbia would not stand alone.[172] This was not, in Pašić's view, primarily a question of Russia's attachment to Serbia, but rather the logical consequence of the imperatives governing Russian policy in the Balkans.[173] So strong was Pašić's reputed trust in this redemptive mechanism that even *Pijemont* occasionally ridiculed him for his 'great belief in Russia'.[174] Reports received by Pašić in mid-June from the Serbian minister in St Petersburg that Russia had restructured its eastern frontier in order to deploy much larger forces for an 'offensive against the west' may well have reinforced the plausibility of this line of thought.[175]

This is not to say that Pašić consciously sought a broader conflict, or that the idea of provoking an Austrian attack motivated his behaviour in any direct sense. But perhaps the inkling that war was the historically necessary crucible of Serbian nationhood diminished his sense of urgency when the opportunity arose to stop the assassins before it was too late. These thoughts and scenarios must have circled in his mind as he reflected – with ponderous slowness – on how to handle the situation created by the news of the Sarajevo plot.

The legacy of Serbian history and in particular of the kingdom's devel-opment since 1903 weighed heavily on Belgrade in the summer of 1914. This was still a raw and fragile democracy in which the civilian deci-sion-makers were on the defensive – the struggle for power between the praetorian, conspiratorial networks born with the regicide of 1903, and the Radical leaders who controlled parliament was still unresolved. The irredentist milieu had emerged triumphant from the two Balkan Wars more determined than ever to press ahead. The deep interpenetration of state and non-official irredentist agencies at home and beyond the national borders made a nonsense of efforts to police their activities. These features of the political culture pressed hard on the men who governed the country, but they were also an incalculable burden on its relations with the Austro-Hungarian Empire. 'For anyone who is not a Serb,' the sometime Serbian minister in Berlin, Miloš Bogičević, later observed, 'it is difficult to find one's way among the different national organisations aiming to realise the Greater Serbian ideal.'[176] This opacity in the structure of the movements and of their relationship with state agencies rendered the task of untangling official and unofficial forms of irredentism virtually impossible, even for a seasoned foreign observer of the Belgrade scene. This, too, would be a perilous burden in July 1914.

From Nikola Pašić's perspective, the pressures mounting up in the summer of that year – financial and military exhaustion after two bitter wars, the threat of a military putsch in the newly annexed territories, the failure to foil an assassination plot against a powerful and unforgiving neighbour – must have seemed intolerable. But the man who would have to steer this complex and unstable polity through the crisis triggered by the events of 28 June 1914 was himself a product of its political culture: secretive, even furtive, cautious to the point of lassitude. These were the attributes Pašić had acquired over more than three decades in Serbian public life. They had helped him to survive in the small, turbulent world of Belgrade politics. But they were dangerously ill-adapted to the crisis that would engulf Serbia after the terrorists had accomplished their mission in Sarajevo.

2

The Empire without Qualities

CONFLICT AND EQUILIBRIUM

Two military disasters defined the trajectory of the Habsburg Empire in the last half-century of its existence. At Solferino in 1859, French and Piedmontese forces prevailed over an army of 100,000 Austrian troops, opening the way to the creation of a new Italian nation-state. At Königgrätz in 1866, the Prussians destroyed an Austrian army of 240,000, ejecting the empire from the emergent German nation-state. The cumulative impact of these shocks transformed the inner life of the Austrian lands.

Shaken by military defeat, the neo-absolutist Austrian Empire metamorphosed into the Austro-Hungarian Empire. Under the Compromise hammered out in 1867, power was shared out between the two dominant nationalities, the Germans in the west and the Hungarians in the east. What emerged was a unique polity, like an egg with two yolks, in which the Kingdom of Hungary and a territory centred on the Austrian lands and often called Cisleithania (meaning 'the lands on this side of the River Leithe') lived side by side within the translucent envelope of a Habsburg dual monarchy. Each of the two entities had its own parliament, but there was no common prime minister and no common cabinet. Only foreign affairs, defence and defence-related aspects of finance were handled by 'joint ministers' who were answerable directly to the Emperor. Matters of interest to the empire as a whole could not be discussed in common parliamentary session, because to do so would have implied that the Kingdom of Hungary was merely the subordinate part of some larger imperial entity. Instead, an exchange of views had to take place between the 'delegations', groups of thirty deputies from each parliament, who met alternately in Vienna and Budapest.

The dualist compromise had many enemies at the time and has had many critics since. In the eyes of hardline Magyar nationalists, it was a sell-out that denied the Hungarians the full national independence that was their due. Some claimed that Austria was still exploiting the Kingdom of Hungary as an agrarian colony. Vienna's refusal to relinquish control over the armed forces and create a separate and equal Hungarian army was especially contentious – a constitutional crisis over this question paralysed the empire's political life in 1905.[1] On the other hand, Austrian Germans argued that the Hungarians were freeloading on the more advanced economy of the Austrian lands, and ought to pay a higher share of the empire's running costs. Conflict was programmed into the system, because the Compromise required that the two imperial 'halves' renegotiate every ten years the customs union by which revenues and taxation were shared out between them. The demands of the Hungarians became bolder with every review of the union.[2] And there was little in the Compromise to recommend it to the political elites of the other national minorities, who had in effect been placed under the tutelage of the two 'master races'. The first post-Compromise Hungarian prime minister, Gyula Andrássy, captured this aspect of the settlement when he commented to his Austrian counterpart: 'You look after your Slavs and we'll look after ours.'[3] The last decades before the outbreak of war were increasingly dominated by the struggle for national rights among the empire's eleven official nationalities – Germans, Hungarians, Czechs, Slovaks, Slovenes, Croats, Serbs, Romanians, Ruthenians, Poles and Italians.

How these challenges were met varied between the two imperial halves. The Hungarians dealt with the nationalities problem mainly by behaving as if it didn't exist. The kingdom's electoral franchise extended to only 6 per cent of the population because it was pegged to a property qualification that favoured the Magyars, who made up the bulk of the wealthier strata of the population. The result was that Magyar deputies, though they represented only 48.1 per cent of the population, controlled over 90 per cent of the parliamentary seats. The 3 million Romanians of Transylvania, the largest of the kingdom's national minorities, comprised 15.4 per cent of the population, but held only five of the Hungarian parliament's 400-odd seats.[4] From the late 1870s, moreover, the Hungarian government pursued a campaign of aggressive 'Magyarization'. Education laws imposed the use of the Magyar language on all state and faith schools, even those catering to children of kindergarten age. Teachers were required to be fluent in Magyar and could be dismissed if they were found to be 'hostile to the [Hungarian] state'. This degradation of language rights was underwritten by harsh measures against ethnic minority activists.[5] Serbs from the Vojvodina in the south of the kingdom, Slovaks from the northern counties and Romanians from the Grand Duchy of Transylvania did occasionally collaborate in pursuit of minority objectives, but with little effect, since they could muster only a small number of mandates.

In Cisleithania, by contrast, successive administrations tampered endlessly with the system in order to accommodate minority demands. Franchise reforms in 1882 and 1907 (when virtually universal male suffrage was introduced) went some way towards levelling the political playing field. But these democratizing measures merely heightened the potential for national conflict, especially over the sensitive question of language use in public institutions such as schools, courts and administrative bodies.

Nowhere were the frictions generated by nationalist politics more in evidence than in the Cisleithanian parliament, which met from 1883 in a handsome neo-classical building on Vienna's Ringstrasse. In this 516-seat legislature, the largest in Europe, the familiar spectrum of party-political ideological diversity was cross-cut by national affiliations producing a panoply of splinter groups and grouplets. Among the thirty-odd parties that held mandates after the 1907 elections, for example, were twenty-eight Czech Agrarians, eighteen Young Czechs (Radical nationalists), seventeen Czech Conservatives, seven Old Czechs (moderate nationalists), two Czech-Progressives (Realist tendency), one 'wild' (independent) Czech and nine Czech National Socialists. The Poles, the Germans, the Italians and even the Slovenes and the Ruthenes were similarly divided along ideological lines.

Since there was no official language in Cisleithania (by contrast with the Kingdom of Hungary), there was no single official language of parliamentary procedure. German, Czech, Polish, Ruthenian, Croat, Serbian, Slovenian, Italian, Romanian and Russian were all permitted. But no interpreters were provided, and there was no facility for recording or monitoring the content of speeches that were not in German, unless the deputy in question himself chose to supply the house with a translated text of his speech. Deputies from even the most insignificant factions could thus block unwelcome initiatives by delivering long speeches in a language that only a handful of their colleagues understood. Whether they were actually addressing the issues raised by the current motion, or simply reciting long poems in their own national idiom, was difficult to ascertain. The Czechs in particular were renowned for the baroque extravagance of their filibustering.[6] The Cisleithanian parliament became a celebrated tourist attraction, especially in winter, when Viennese pleasure-seekers crowded into the heated visitors' galleries. By contrast with the city's theatres and opera houses, a Berlin journalist wrily observed, entry to parliamentary sessions was free.*

So intense did the national conflict become that in 1912–14 multiple parliamentary crises crippled the legislative life of the monarchy: the Bohemian Diet had become so obstreperous by 1913 that the Austrian prime minister, Count Karl Stürgkh, dissolved it, installing in its place an imperial commission tasked to govern the province. Czech protests against this measure brought the Cisleithanian parliament to its knees in March 1914. On 16 March, Stürgkh dismissed this assembly too – it was still in suspension when Austria-Hungary declared war on Serbia in July, so that Cisleithania was in effect being run under a kind of administrative absolutism when the war broke out. Things were not much better in Hungary: in 1912, following protests in Zagreb and other South Slav cities against an unpopular governor, the Croatian Diet and constitution were suspended; in Budapest itself, the last pre-war years witnessed the advent of a parliamentary absolutism focused on protecting Magyar hegemony against the challenge posed by minority national opposition and the demand for franchise reform.[7]

These spectacular symptoms of dysfunctionality might appear to support the view that the Austro-Hungarian Empire was a moribund polity, whose disappearance from the political map was merely a matter of time: an argument deployed by hostile contemporaries to suggest that the empire's efforts to defend its integrity during the last years before the outbreak of war were in some sense illegitimate.[8] In reality, the roots of Austria-Hungary's political turbulence went less deep than appearances suggested. There was, to be sure, intermittent

---

* Among those who came to watch the antics of the deputies was the young drifter Adolf Hitler. Between February 1908 and the summer of 1909, when Czech obstructionism was at its height, he was often to be found in the visitors' gallery. He would later claim that the experience had 'cured' him of his youthful admiration for the parliamentary system.

ethnic conflict – riots in Ljubljana in 1908 for example, or periodic Czech–German brawls in Prague – but it never came close to the levels of violence experienced in the contemporary Russian Empire, or in twentieth-century Belfast. As for the turbulence of the Cisleithanian parliament, it was a chronic ailment, rather than a terminal disease. The business of government could always be carried on temporarily under the emergency powers provided under Clause 14 of the 1867 Constitution. To a certain extent, moreover, different kinds of political conflict cancelled each other out. The conflict between socialists, liberals, clerical conservatives and other political groupings after 1907 was a boon to the Austrian part of the monarchy, because it cut across the national camps and thereby undermined the virulence of nationalism as a political principle. Balancing the complex array of forces that resulted to sustain a working majority was a complex task requiring tact, flexibility and strategic imagination, but the careers of the last three Austrian prime ministers before 1914, Beck, Bienerth and Stürgkh, showed – despite intermittent breakdowns in the system – that it could be done.[9]

The Habsburg lands passed during the last pre-war decade through a phase of strong economic growth with a corresponding rise in general prosperity – an important point of contrast with the contemporary Ottoman Empire, but also with another classic collapsing polity, the Soviet Union of the 1980s. Free markets and competition across the empire's vast customs union stimulated technical progress and the introduction of new products. The sheer size and diversity of the double monarchy meant that new industrial plants benefited from sophisticated networks of cooperating industries underpinned by an effective transport infrastructure and a high-quality service and support sector. The salutary economic effects were particularly evident in the Kingdom of Hungary. In the 1840s, Hungary really had been the larder of the Austrian Empire – 90 per cent of its exports to Austria consisted of agricultural products. But by the years 1909–13, Hungarian industrial exports had risen to 44 per cent, while the constantly growing demand for cheap foodstuffs of the Austro-Bohemian industrial region ensured that the Hungarian agricultural sector survived in the best of health, protected by the Habsburg common market from Romanian, Russian and American competition.[10] For the monarchy as a whole, most economic historians agree that the period 1887–1913 saw an 'industrial revolution', or a take-off into self-sustaining growth, with the usual indices of expansion: pig-iron consumption increased fourfold between 1881 and 1911, railroad coverage did the same between 1870 and 1900, and infant mortality decreased, while elementary schooling figures surpassed those in Germany, France, Italy and Russia.[11] In the last years before the war, Austria-Hungary, and Hungary in particular (with an average annual growth of 4.8 per cent), was one of the fastest-growing economies in Europe.[12]

Even a critical observer like the *Times* correspondent Henry Wickham Steed, a long-time resident of Vienna, recognized in 1913 that 'the "race struggle" in Austria' was in essence a conflict for shares of patronage within the existing system:

> The essence of the language struggle is that it is a struggle for bureaucratic influence. Similarly, the demands for new Universities or High Schools put forward by Czechs, Ruthenes, Slovenes, and Italians but resisted by the Germans, Poles, or other races, as the case may be, are demands for the creation of new machines to turn out potential officials whom the political influence of Parliamentary parties may then be trusted to hoist into bureaucratic appointments.[13]

There was, moreover, slow but unmistakable progress towards a more accommodating policy on national rights (at least in Cisleithania). The equality of all the subject nationalities and languages in Cisleithania was formally recognized in the Basic Law of 1867, and a body of case law accumulated to provide solutions for problems the drafters of the Compromise had not foreseen, such as language provisions for Czech minorities in German areas of Bohemia. Throughout the last peacetime years of the empire's existence, the Cisleithanian authorities continued to adjust the system in response to national minority demands. The Galician Compromise agreed in the Galician Diet in Lemberg (today Lviv) on 28 January 1914, for example, assured a fixed proportion of the mandates in an enlarged regional legislature to the under-represented Ruthenes (Ukrainians) and promised the imminent establishment of a Ukrainian university.[14] Even the Hungarian administration was showing signs of a change of heart by the beginning of 1914, as the international climate worsened. The South Slavs of Croatia-Slavonia were promised the abolition of extraordinary powers and a guarantee of freedom of the press, while a message went out to

Transylvania that the Budapest government intended to meet many of the demands of the Romanian majority in that region. The Russian foreign minister, Sergei Sazonov, was so impressed by the thought that these measures might stabilize Habsburg rule in the Romanian areas that he proposed to Tsar Nicholas II in January 1914 granting similar concessions to the millions of Poles in western Russia.[15]

These case-by-case adjustments to specific demands suggested that the system might eventually produce a comprehensive mesh of guarantees for nationality rights within an agreed framework.[16] And there were signs that the administration was getting better at responding to the material demands of the regions.[17] It was the state, of course, that performed this role, not the beleaguered parliaments of the Habsburg lands. The proliferation of school boards, town councils, county commissions, mayoral elections and the like ensured that the state intersected with the life of the citizenry in a more intimate and consistent way than the political parties or the legislative assemblies.[18] It was not (or not primarily) an apparatus of repression, but a vibrant entity commanding strong attachments, a broker among manifold social, economic and cultural interests.[19] The Habsburg bureaucracy was costly to maintain – expenditure for the domestic administration rose by 366 per cent during the years 1890–1911.[20] But most inhabitants of the empire associated the Habsburg state with the benefits of orderly government: public education, welfare, sanitation, the rule of law and the maintenance of a sophisticated infrastructure.[21] These features of the Habsburg polity loomed large in memory after the monarchy's extinction. In the late 1920s, when the writer (and engineering graduate) Robert Musil looked back on the Austro-Hungarian Empire in the last peaceful year of its existence, the picture that formed before his mind's eye was one of 'white, broad, prosperous streets [. . .] that stretched like rivers of order, like ribbons of bright military serge, embracing the lands with the paper-white arm of administration'.[22]

Finally, most minority activists acknowledged the value of the Habsburg commonwealth as a system of collective security. The bitterness of conflicts *between* minority nationalities – Croats and Serbs in Croatia-Slavonia, for example, or Poles and Ruthenians in Galicia – and the many areas of ethnically mixed settlement suggested that the creation of new and separate national entities might cause more problems than it resolved.[23] And how, in any case, would such fledgeling nation-states fare without the protective carapace of the empire? In 1848, the Czech nationalist historian František Palacky had warned that disbanding the Habsburg Empire, far from liberating the Czechs, would merely provide the basis for 'Russian universal monarchy'. 'I am impelled by natural as well as historical causes to seek [in Vienna] the centre called to secure and to protect for my people peace, freedom and justice.'[24] In 1891, Prince Charles Schwarzenberg advanced the same argument when he asked the Young Czech nationalist Edward Grégr: 'If you and yours hate this state, ... what will you do with your country, which is too small to stand alone? Will you give it to Germany, or to Russia, for you have no other choice if you abandon the Austrian union.'[25] Before 1914, radical nationalists seeking full separation from the empire were still a small minority. In many areas, nationalist political groups were counterbalanced by networks of associations – veterans' clubs, religious and charitable groups, associations of *bersaglieri* (sharp-shooters) – nurturing various forms of Habsburg patriotism.[26]

The venerability and permanence of the monarchy were personified in the imperturbable, bewhiskered figure of Emperor Franz Joseph. His had been a life abnormally rich in private tragedy. The Emperor's son Rudolf had killed himself in a double suicide with his mistress at the family hunting lodge, his wife Elisabeth ('Sissi') had been stabbed to death by an Italian anarchist on the banks of Lake Geneva, his brother Maximilian had been executed by Mexican insurgents at Queretaro and his favourite niece had burned to death when a cigarette set fire to her dress. The Emperor had borne these blows with a glacial stoicism. In public life, he projected a persona 'demonic', as the satirist Karl Kraus put it, in its 'unpersonality'. His stylized commentary on virtually every official ceremony – 'It was nice, we were quite pleased' – was a house-hold phrase across the lands of the monarchy.[27] The Emperor demonstrated considerable skill in managing the complex machinery of his state, balancing opposed forces in order to maintain all within an equilibrium of well-tempered dissatisfaction and involving himself closely in all phases of constitutional reform.[28] Yet by 1914 he had become a force for inertia. In the last two years before the war, he backed the autocratic Magyar premier István Tisza against minority demands for Hungarian franchise reform. As long as the Kingdom of Hungary continued to deliver the funds and votes Vienna needed, Franz Joseph was prepared to accept the hegemony of the Magyar elite, notwithstanding its disregard for the interests of the national minorities in the lands of the kingdom.[29] There were signs that he was drifting out of touch with contemporary life: 'The powerfully surging life of our times,' wrote the Austrian German politician Joseph Maria Baernreither in 1913, when Franz Joseph was eighty-three, 'scarcely reaches the ear of our emperor as distant rustling. He is denied any real participation in this life. He no longer understands the times, and the times pass on regardless.'[30]

Nevertheless: the Emperor remained the focus of powerful political and emotional attachments. It was widely recognized that his popularity was anchored outside of his constitutional role, in broadly shared popular emotions.[31] By 1914, he had been on the throne for longer than most of his subjects had been alive. He seemed, in the words of Joseph Roth's masterpiece *The Radetzky March*, 'coffered up in an icy and everlasting old age, like armour of an awe-inspiring crystal'.[32] He made regular appearances in the dreams of his subjects. His sky-blue eyes continued to gaze out from portraits across tens of thousands of taverns, schoolrooms, offices and railway waiting rooms, while the daily newspapers marvelled at the supple and elastic stride with which the old man leapt from his carriage on state occasions. Prosperous and relatively well administered, the empire, like its elderly sovereign, exhibited a curious stability amid turmoil. Crises came and went without appearing to threaten the existence of the system as such. The situation was always, as the Viennese journalist Karl Kraus quipped, 'desperate, but not serious'.

A special and anomalous case was Bosnia-Herzegovina, which the Austrians 'occupied' under Ottoman suzerainty in 1878 on the authorization of the Treaty of Berlin and formally annexed thirty years later. Late nineteenth-century Bosnia was a heavily forested, mountainous land bounded by peaks of over 2,000 metres in the south and by valley of the river Save in the north. Herzegovina consisted mainly of a wild, high karst plateau crossed by swift watercourses and closed in by mountain chains – a land of harsh terrain and virtually non-existent infrastructure. The condition of these two Balkan provinces under Habsburg rule has long been the subject of controversy. The young Bosnian Serb terrorists who travelled to Sarajevo in the summer of 1914 to kill the heir to the Austrian throne defended their actions by reference to the oppression of their brothers in Bosnia and Herzegovina, and historians have sometimes suggested that the Austrians themselves were to blame for driving the Bosnian Serbs into the arms of Belgrade by a combination of oppression and misgovernment.

Is this right? There were widespread protests during the early years of the occupation, especially against conscription. But this was nothing new – the provinces had experienced chronic turbulence under Ottoman rule; what was exceptional was the relative serenity of the period from the mid-1880s down to 1914.[33] The condition of the peasantry after 1878 was a sore point. The Austrians chose not to abolish the Ottoman *agaluk* estate system, on which about 90,000 Bosnian serfs or *kmets* were still working in 1914, and some historians have seen this as evidence of a 'divide and rule' policy designed to press down the mainly Serb peasantry while currying favour with the Croats and Muslims in the towns. But this is a retrospective projection. Cultural and institutional conservatism, not a philosophy of colonial domination, underpinned Austrian governance in the new provinces. 'Gradualism and continuity' characterized Austrian rule in all areas of Bosnia-Herzegovina where they encountered traditional institutions.[34] Where possible, the laws and institutions inherited from the Ottoman era were harmonized and clarified, rather than discarded out of hand. But the Habsburg administration did facilitate the emancipation of subject peasants by means of a one-off payment; over 40,000 Bosnian *kmets* purchased their autonomy in this way between the occupation and the outbreak of war in 1914. In any case, the Serbian *kmets* who remained within the old estate system on the eve of the First World War were not especially badly off by the standards of early twentieth-century peasant Europe; they were probably more prosperous than their counterparts in Dalmatia or southern Italy.

The Austrian administration also did much to increase the productivity of agriculture and industry in Bosnia-Herzegovina. They set up model farms, including a vineyard and a fish-farm, introduced rudimentary agronomic training for country schoolteachers and even established an agricultural college in Ilidze, at a time when no such institution existed in neighbouring Serbia. If the uptake of new methods was still relatively slow, this had more to do with the resistance of the peasantry to innovation than with Austrian negligence. There was also a massive influx of investment capital. A road and railway network appeared, including some of the best mountain roads in Europe. These infrastructural projects served a partly military purpose, to be sure, but there was also massive investment across a range of sectors, including mining, metallurgy, forestry and chemicals production. The pace of industrialization peaked during the administration of Count Benjamin Kállay (1882–1903) and the consequence was a surge in industrial output (12.4 per cent per annum on average over the period 1881–1913) without precedent elsewhere in the Balkan lands.[35] In short, the Habsburg administration treated the new provinces as a showcase whose purpose was to 'demonstrate the humanity and efficiency of Habsburg rule'; by 1914, Bosnia-Herzegovina had been developed to a level comparable with the rest of the double monarchy.[36]

The worst blemish on the record of the Austrian administration in Bosnia-Herzegovina was the appallingly low rate of literacy and school attendance, which was worse even than Serbia's.[37] But this was not the consequence of an Austrian policy of mass stultification. The Austrians

2. Bosnia-Herzegovina 1914

built primary schools – nearly 200 of them – not to mention three high schools, a teacher training college and a technical institute. It was not a stellar effort, but it was not outright neglect either. The problem lay partly in getting peasants to send their children to school.[38] Only in 1909, after the formal annexation of the provinces, was compulsory primary education introduced.

All was not sweetness and light in Bosnia-Herzegovina, to be sure. The Habsburg administration bore down hard on anything that smelled like nationalist mobilization against the empire, sometimes with a heavy and undiscriminating hand. In 1913, Oskar Potiorek, military governor of Bosnia-Herzegovina, suspended most of the Bosnian constitution of 1910, tightened government controls of the school system, banned the circulation of newspapers from Serbia and closed down many Bosnian Serb cultural organizations, though this was, it should be pointed out, in response to an escalation in Serbian ultra-nationalist militancy.[39] Another vexing factor was the political frustration of Serbs and Croats just across the border to the west and north in Croatia-Slavonia, and to the east in the Vojvodina, both ruled from Budapest under the restrictive Hungarian franchise. But all in all, this was a relatively fair and efficient administration informed by a pragmatic respect for the diverse traditions of the national groups in the provinces. Theodore Roosevelt was not too far off the mark when he observed, during a visit to the White House by two senior Austrian politicians in June 1904, that the Habsburg monarchy had 'understood how to treat the different nations and religions in this country on an equal footing and how thereby to achieve such great successes'; he added, perhaps unhappily, that he believed the US administration in the Philippines could learn a lot from the Austrian example.[40] Visitors, too, were struck by the even-handedness of the Habsburg regime: there was a tone of 'mutual respect and mutual toleration' among the ethno-religious groups, one American journalist observed in 1902; the courts were 'wisely and honestly administered' and 'justice [was] awarded to every citizen, regardless of his religion or social position'.[41]

Evaluating the condition and prospects of the Austro-Hungarian Empire on the eve of the First World War confronts us in an acute way with the problem of temporal perspective. The collapse of the empire amid war and defeat in 1918 impressed itself upon the retrospective view of the Habsburg lands, overshadowing the scene with auguries of imminent and ineluctable decline. The Czech national activist Edvard Beneš was a case in point. During the First World War, Beneš became the organizer of a secret Czech pro-independence movement; in 1918, he was one of the founding fathers of the new Czechoslovak nation-state. But in a study of the 'Austrian Problem and the Czech Question' published in 1908, he had expressed confidence in the future of the Habsburg commonwealth. 'People have spoken of the dissolution of Austria. I do not believe in it at all. The historic and economic ties which bind the Austrian nations to one another are too strong to let such a thing happen.'[42] A particularly striking example is the sometime *Times* correspondent (later editor) Henry Wickham Steed. In 1954, Steed declared in a letter to the *Times Literary Supplement* that when he had left the Austro-Hungarian Empire in 1913, 'it was with the feeling that I was escaping from a doomed edifice'. His words confirmed what was then the widely held view. Back in 1913, however, he had seen things differently. Though he was an outspoken critic of many features of Habsburg governance, he wrote in that year that he had been unable during ten years of 'constant observation and experience' to perceive 'any sufficient reason' why the Habsburg monarchy 'should not retain its rightful place in the European Community'. 'Its internal crises,' he concluded, 'are often crises of growth rather than crises of decay.'[43] It was only during the First World War that Steed became a propagandist for the dismemberment of the Austro-Hungarian state and an ardent defender of the post-war settlement in Central Europe. For the 1927 English translation of Tomáš Masaryk's Czech nationalist memoir *The Making of a State*, Steed supplied a foreword in which he declared that the name 'Austria' was synonymous with 'every device that could kill the soul of a people, corrupt it with a modicum of material well-being, deprive it of freedom of conscience and of thought, undermine its sturdiness, sap its steadfastness and turn it from the pursuit of its ideal'.[44]

Such reversals of polarity could occur in the other direction too. The Hungarian scholar Oszkár Jászi – one of the most profound experts on the Habsburg Empire – was sharply critical of the dualist system. In 1929, he concluded an ambitious study of the monarchy's dissolution with the observation that 'the World War was not the cause, but only the final liquidation of the deep hatred and distrust of the various nations'.[45] And yet in 1949, after a further world war and a calamitous period of dictatorship and genocide in his home country, Jászi, who had lived in

American exile since 1919, struck a different note. In the old Habsburg monarchy, he wrote, 'the rule of law was tolerably secure; individual liberties were more and more recognised; political rights continuously extended; the principle of national autonomy growingly respected. The free flow of persons and goods extended its benefits to the remotest parts of the monarchy'.[46] While the euphoria of national independence disposed some who had once been loyal Habsburg citizens to impugn the old dual monarchy, others who were vigorous dissenters before 1914 later fell prey to nostalgia. In 1939, reflecting on the collapse of the monarchy, the Hungarian writer Mihály Babits wrote: 'we now regret the loss and weep for the return of what we once hated. We are independent, but instead of feeling joy we can only tremble.'[47]

THE CHESS PLAYERS

After the ejection of the Austrians from Italy in 1859 and Germany in 1866, the Balkan region became by default the pre-eminent focus of Austro-Hungarian foreign policy. Unfortunately, this narrowing of geo-political range happened to coincide with an era of growing volatility across the Balkan peninsula. The underlying problem was the waning of Ottoman authority in south-eastern Europe, which created a zone of tension between the two great powers with a strategic interest in the region.[48] Both Russia and Austria-Hungary felt historically entitled to exercise hegemony in those areas from which the Ottomans withdrew. The House of Habsburg had traditionally been the guardian of Europe's eastern gate against the Turks. In Russia, the ideology of pan-Slavism asserted a natural commonality of interest between the emergent Slavic (especially Orthodox) nations of the Balkan peninsula and the patron power in St Petersburg. Ottoman retreat also raised questions about future control of the Turkish Straits, an issue of acute strategic import-ance to Russian policy-makers. At the same time, ambitious new Balkan states emerged with conflicting interests and objectives of their own. Across this turbulent terrain, Austria and Russia manoeuvred like chess players hoping with each move to cancel out or diminish the opponent's advantage.

Until 1908, cooperation, self-restraint and the demarcation of informal spheres of influence ensured that the dangers implicit in this state of affairs were contained.[49] In the revised Three Emperors' League treaty of 1881 between Russia, Austria-Hungary and Germany, Russia undertook to 'respect' the Austro-Hungarian occupation of Bosnia-Herzegovina authorized in 1878 at the Treaty of Berlin and the three signatories agreed to 'take account' of each other's 'interests in the Balkan Peninsula'.[50] Further Austro-Russian understandings in 1897 and 1903 reaffirmed the joint commitment to the Balkan status quo.

The complexity of Balkan politics was such, however, that maintaining good relations with the rival great power was not enough to ensure tranquillity. The lesser beasts of the peninsula also had to be placated and tamed. And the most important of these, from Vienna's standpoint, was the Kingdom of Serbia. During the long reign of the Austrophile Milan Obrenović, Serbia remained a docile partner in Vienna's designs, acquiescing in the empire's claim to regional hegemony. Vienna, in return, supported Belgrade's bid for elevation to the status of kingdom in 1882 and promised diplomatic support in the event that Serbia should seek to expand southwards into Ottoman Macedonia. As the Austro-Hungarian foreign minister, Gustav Count Kálnoky von Köröspatak, informed his Russian counterpart in the summer of 1883, good relations with Serbia were the keystone of the empire's Balkan policy.[51]

Though friendly, King Milan of Serbia could be an exasperating partner. In 1885 the king created a commotion in Vienna by proposing to abdicate, send his son to school in Austria and allow the empire to annex his kingdom. The Austrians were having none of this nonsense. At a meeting in Vienna the dejected monarch was reminded of his kingly duties and sent back to Belgrade. 'A flourishing and independent Serbia,' Kálnoky explained to the Austrian prime minister, 'suits our intentions [. . .] better than the possession of an unruly province.'[52] On 14 November, however, only four months after appearing to lose his will to rule, Milan suddenly and unexpectedly invaded neighbouring Bulgaria, Russia's client state. The resulting conflict was shortlived, because the Serbian army was easily beaten back by the Bulgarians, but assiduous great power diplomacy was required to prevent this unexpected démarche from ruffling the feathers of the Austro-Russian détente.

The son proved even more erratic than the father: Alexandar boasted intemperately of Austro-Hungarian support for his kingdom and declared publicly in 1899 that 'the enemies of Serbia are the enemies of

Austria-Hungary' – a *faux pas* that raised eyebrows in St Petersburg and caused considerable embarrassment in Vienna. But he was also tempted by the advantages of a Russophile policy; by 1902, after the death of King Father Milan, King Alexandar was energetically suing for Russian support; he even declared to a journalist in St Petersburg that the Habsburg monarchy was 'the arch enemy of Serbia'.[53] There was thus little regret in Vienna at the news of Alexandar's premature death, although the politicians there were as shocked as everyone else by the brutality with which he and his line were exterminated.

Only gradually did it become clear to the Austrians that the regicide of June 1903 marked a real break. The foreign ministry in Vienna hastened to establish good relations with the usurper Petar Karadjordjević, whom they optimistically viewed as Austrophile in temperament. Austria-Hungary became the first foreign state to recognize formally the new Serbian regime. But it soon became clear that the foundations no longer existed for a harmonious relationship between the two neighbours. The management of political affairs passed into the hands of men openly hostile to the dual monarchy and the policy-makers in Vienna studied with growing concern the nationalist expectorations of the Belgrade press, now freed from governmental restraints. In September 1903, Konstantin Dumba the Austrian minister in Belgrade reported that relations between the two countries were 'as bad as possible'. Vienna rediscovered its moral outrage at the regicide and joined the British in imposing sanctions on the Karadjordjević court. Hoping to profit from this loosening of the Austro-Serbian bond, the Russians moved in, assuring the Belgrade government that Serbia's future lay in the west, on the Adriatic coastline, and urging them not to renew their long-standing commercial treaty with Vienna.[54]

At the end of 1905, these tensions broke out into open conflict with the discovery in Vienna that Serbia and Bulgaria had signed a 'secret' customs union. Vienna's demand early in 1906 that Belgrade repudiate the union proved counter-productive; among other things, it transformed the Bulgarian union, which had been a matter of indifference to most Serbs, into the fetish (for a time at least) of Serbian national opinion.[55] The general outlines of the 1906 crisis are set out in chapter 1, but one further point should be borne in mind, namely that what worried the politicians in Vienna was less the negligible commercial significance of the union with Bulgaria than the political logic underlying it. What if the Serbo-Bulgarian customs union were merely the first step in the direction of a 'league' of Balkan states hostile to Austria-Hungary and receptive to promptings from St Petersburg?

It is easy to write this off as Austrian paranoia, but in reality, the policy-makers in Vienna were not far off the mark: the Serbian-Bulgarian customs agreement *was* in fact the third of a sequence of secret alliances between Serbia and Bulgaria, of which the first two were already clearly anti-Austrian in orientation. A Treaty of Friendship and a Treaty of Alliance had already been signed in Belgrade on 12 May 1904 in circumstances of the strictest secrecy. Dumba had done his utmost to find out what was going on between the Bulgarian delegates visiting the city and their Serbian interlocutors, but though his suspicions were raised, he had failed to penetrate the curtain of confidentiality surrounding the negotiations. Vienna's fear of Russian involvement, it turned out, was well founded. St Petersburg was indeed – notwithstanding the Austro-Russian détente and the immense effort of a disastrous war with Japan – working towards the creation of a Balkan alliance. A key figure in the negotiations was the Bulgarian diplomat Dimitar Rizov, some-time agent of the Russian Asiatic Department. On 15 September 1904 at eleven o'clock in the morning, the Russian ambassadors in Belgrade and Sofia were simultaneously (and secretly) presented with copies of the Serbian-Bulgarian Treaty of Alliance by the foreign ministers of Serbia and Bulgaria respectively.[56]

One difficult feature of Austro-Hungarian Balkan policy was the deepening interpenetration of foreign and domestic issues.[57] For obvious reasons, domestic and international politics were most likely to become entangled in the case of those minorities for whom there existed an independent 'motherland' outside the boundaries of the empire. The Czechs, Slovenes, Poles, Slovaks and Croats of the Habsburg lands possessed no such sovereign external nation-state. The 3 million Romanians in the Duchy of Transylvania, on the other hand, did. Thanks to the intricacies of the dualist system, there was little Vienna could do to prevent oppressive Hungarian cultural policies from alienating the neighbouring kingdom of Romania, a political partner of great strategic value in the region. Yet it proved possible, at least until around 1910, to insulate Austro-Romanian relations from the impact of domestic tensions, mainly because the government of Romania, an ally of Austria and Germany, made no effort to foment or exploit ethnic discord in Transylvania.

The same could not be said, however, of the Serbs and the Kingdom of Serbia after 1903. Just over 40 per cent of the population of Bosnia-Herzegovina were Serbs, and there were large areas of Serbian settlement in the Vojvodina in southern Hungary and smaller ones in Croatia-Slavonia. After the regicide of 1903, Belgrade stepped up the pace of irredentist activity within the empire, focusing in particular on Bosnia-Herzegovina. In February 1906, the Austrian military attaché in Belgrade, Pomiankowski, summarized the problem in a letter to the chief of the General Staff. It was certain, Pomiankowski declared, that Serbia would number among the empire's enemies in the event of a future military conflict. The problem was less the attitude of the government as such than the ultra-nationalist orientation of the political culture as a whole: even if a 'sensible' government were at the helm, Pomiankowski warned, it would be in no position to prevent the 'all-powerful radical chauvinists' from launching 'an adventure'. More dangerous, however, than Serbia's 'open enmity and its miserable army' was the 'fifth-column work of the [Serbian] Radicals in peacetime, which systematically poisons the attitude of our South Slav population and could, if the worst came to the worst, create very serious difficulties for our army'.[58]

The 'chauvinist' irredentism of the Serbian state, or more precisely, of the most influential political forces within it, came to occupy a central place in Vienna's assessments of the relationship with Belgrade. The official instructions composed in the summer of 1907 by Foreign Minister Count Alois von Aehrenthal for the new Austrian envoy to Serbia convey a sense of how relations had deteriorated since the regicide. Under King Milan, Aehrenthal recalled, the Serbian crown had been strong enough to counteract any 'public Bosnian agitation', but since the events of July 1903, everything had changed. It was not just that King Petar was politically too weak to oppose the forces of chauvinist nationalism, but rather that he had himself begun to exploit the national movement in order to consolidate his position. One of the 'foremost tasks' of the new Austrian minister in Belgrade would therefore be the close observation and analysis of Serbian nationalist activity. When the opportunity arose, the minister was to inform King Petar and Prime

Minister Pašić that he was fully acquainted with the scope and character of pan-Serb nationalist activity; the leaders in Belgrade should be left in no doubt that Austria-Hungary regarded its occupation of Bosnia-Herzegovina as 'definitive'. Above all, the minister was not to be put off by the usual official denials:

> It is to be expected that they will respond to your well-meant warnings with the time-honoured cliché that the Serbian politicians always roll out when they are reproached with their furtive machinations vis-à-vis the occupied provinces: 'The Serbian Government strives to maintain correct and blameless relations, but is in no position to hold back the sentiment of the nation, which demands action etc. etc.'[59]

Aehrenthal's official instruction captures the salient features of Vienna's attitude to Belgrade: a belief in the primordial power of Serbian nationalism, a visceral distrust of the leading statesmen, and a deepening anxiety over the future of Bosnia, concealed behind a pose of lofty and invulnerable superiority.

The scene was thus set for the annexation of Bosnia and Herzegovina in 1908. There had never been any doubt, either in Austria or in the chancelleries of the other great powers, that Vienna regarded the occupation of 1878 as permanent. In one of the secret articles of the renewed Three Emperors' Alliance of 1881, Austria-Hungary had explicitly asserted the 'right to annex these provinces at whatever moment she shall deem opportune', and this claim was repeated at intervals in Austro-Russian diplomatic agreements. Nor was it contested in principle by Russia, though St Petersburg reserved the right to impose conditions when the moment for such a change of status arrived. The advantages to Austria-Hungary of a formal annexation were obvious enough. It would remove any doubt about the future of the provinces – a matter of some urgency, since the occupation statute agreed at the Congress of Berlin was due to expire in 1908. It would allow Bosnia and Herzegovina to be integrated more fully into the political fabric of the empire, through the establishment, for example, of a provincial parliament. It would create a more stable environment for inward investment. More importantly, it would signal to Belgrade (and to the Serbs in Bosnia-Herzegovina) the permanence of Austria-Hungary's possession and thus, in theory at least, remove one incentive for further agitation.

Aehrenthal, who became foreign minister in October 1906, also had other reasons for pressing ahead. Until around the turn of the century, he had been a staunch supporter of the dualist system. But his faith in the Compromise was shaken in 1905 by the bitter infighting between the Austrian and Hungarian political elites over the administration of the joint armed forces. By 1907, he had come to favour a tripartite solution to the monarchy's problems; the two dominant power-centres within the monarchy would be supplemented by a third entity incorporating the South Slavs (above all Croats, Slovenes and Serbs). This was a programme with a considerable following among the South Slav elites, especially the Croats, who resented being divided between Cisleithania, the Kingdom of Hungary and the province of Croatia-Slavonia, ruled from Budapest. Only if Bosnia-Herzegovina were fully annexed to the empire would it be possible eventually to incorporate it into the structure of a reformed trialist monarchy. And this in turn – such was Aehrenthal's devout hope – would provide an internal counterweight to the irredentist activities of Belgrade. Far from being the 'Piedmont' of South Slavdom in the Balkans, Serbia would become the severed limb of a vast, Croat-dominated South Slav entity within the empire.[60]

The clinching argument for annexation was the Young Turk revolution that broke out in Ottoman Macedonia in the summer of 1908. The Young Turks forced the Sultan in Constantinople to proclaim a constitution and the establishment of a parliament. They planned to subject the Ottoman imperial system to a root-and-branch reform. Rumours circulated to the effect that the new Turkish leadership would shortly call general elections throughout the Ottoman Empire, including the areas occupied by Austria-Hungary, which currently possessed no representative organs of their own. What if the new Turkish administration, its legitimacy and confidence enhanced by the revolution, were to demand the return of its lost western salient and to woo its inhabitants with the promise of constitutional reform?[61] Hoping to capitalize on these uncertainties, an opportunist Muslim–Serb coalition emerged in Bosnia calling for autonomy under Turkish suzerainty.[62] There was now the danger that an ethnic alliance within the province might join forces with the Turks to push the Austrians out.

In order to forestall any such complications, Aehrenthal moved quickly to prepare the ground for annexation. The Ottomans were bought out of their nominal sovereignty with a handsome indemnity. Much more important were the Russians, upon whose acquiescence the whole project depended. Aehrenthal was a firm believer in the importance of good relations with Russia – as Austrian ambassador in St Petersburg during the years 1899–1906, he had helped to consolidate the Austro-Russian rapprochement. Securing the agreement of the Russian foreign minister, Alexandr Izvolsky, was easy. The Russians had no objection to the formalization of Austria-Hungary's status in Bosnia-Herzegovina, provided St Petersburg received something in return. Indeed it was Izvolsky, with the support of Tsar Nicholas II, who proposed that the annexation of Bosnia-Herzegovina be exchanged for Austrian support for improved Russian access to the Turkish Straits. On 16 September 1908, Izvolsky and Aehrenthal clarifed the terms of the deal at Schloss Buchlau, the Moravian estate of Leopold von Berchtold, Austro-Hungarian ambassador in St Petersburg. In a sense, therefore, the annexation of 1908 was born out of the spirit of the Austro-Russian Balkan entente. There was, moreover, a neat symmetry about the exchange, since Izvolsky and Aehrenthal were essentially after the same thing: gains that would be secured through secret negotiations at the expense of the Ottoman Empire and in contravention of the Treaty of Berlin.[63]

Despite these preparations, Aehrenthal's announcement of the annexation on 5 October 1908 triggered a major European crisis. Izvolsky denied having reached any agreement with Aehrenthal. He subsequently even denied that he had been advised in advance of Aehrenthal's intentions, and demanded that an international conference be convened to clarify the status of Bosnia-Herzegovina.[64] The resulting crisis dragged on for months as Serbia, Russia and Austria mobilized and counter-mobilized and Aehrenthal continued to evade Izvolsky's call for a conference that had not been foreseen in the agreement at Buchlau. The issue was resolved only by the 'St Petersburg note' of March 1909, in which the Germans demanded that the Russians at last recognize the annexation and urge Serbia to do likewise. If they did not, Chancellor Bülow warned, then things would 'take their course'. This formulation hinted not just at the possibility of an Austrian war on Serbia, but, more importantly, at the possibility that the Germans would release the documents proving Izvolsky's complicity in the original annexation deal. Izvolsky immediately backed down.

Aehrenthal has traditionally carried the lion's share of the responsibility for the annexation crisis. Is this fair? To be sure, the Austrian foreign minister's manoeuvres lacked diplomatic transparency. He chose to operate with the tools of the old diplomacy: confidential meetings, the exchange of pledges, and secret bilateral agreements, rather than attempting to resolve the annexation issue through an international conference involving all the signatories of the Treaty of Berlin. This preference for furtive arrangements made it easier for Izvolsky to claim that he, and by extension Russia, had been hoodwinked by the 'slippery' Austrian minister. Yet the evidence suggests that the crisis took the course that it did because Izvolsky lied in the most extravagant fashion in order to save his job and reputation. The Russian foreign minister had made two serious errors of judgement. He had assumed, firstly, that London would support his demand for the opening of the Turkish Straits to Russian warships. He had also grossly underestimated the impact of the annexation on Russian nationalist opinion. According to one account, he was initially perfectly calm when news of the annexation reached him in Paris on 8 October 1908. It was only during his stay in London a few days later, when the British proved uncooperative and he got wind of the press response in St Petersburg, that he realized his error, panicked, and began to construct himself as Aehrenthal's dupe.[65]

Whatever the rights and wrongs of Aehrenthal's policy, the Bosnian annexation crisis was a turning point in Balkan geopolitics. It devastated what remained of Austro-Russian readiness to collaborate on resolving Balkan questions; from this moment onwards, it would be much more difficult to contain the negative energies generated by conflicts among the Balkan states. It also alienated Austria's neighbour and ally, the Kingdom of Italy. There had long been latent tensions between the two states – Italian minority rights in Dalmatia and Croatia-Slavonia and power-political rivalry in the Adriatic were the two most important bones of contention – but the annexation crisis prompted calls for Italian compensation and kindled Italian resentments to a new pitch of intensity. In the last years before the outbreak of war, it became increasingly difficult to reconcile Italian and Austrian objectives on the Balkan Adriatic coast.[66] The Germans were initially noncommittal on the annexation question, but they soon rallied energetically to Austria-Hungary's support, and this, too, was an ambivalent development. It had the desired effect of dissuading the Russian government from attempting to extract further capital out of the annexation crisis, but in the longer run, it reinforced the sense in both St Petersburg and London that Austria was the satellite of Berlin – a perception that would play a dangerous role in the crisis of 1914.

In Russia, the impact of the crisis was especially deep and lasting. Defeat in the war with Japan in 1904–5 had shut off the prospect of far eastern expansion for the foreseeable future. The Anglo-Russian Convention signed by Izvolsky and the British ambassador Sir Arthur Nicolson on 31 August 1907 had established the limits of Russian influence in Persia, Afghanistan and Tibet. The Balkans remained (for the moment) the only arena in which Russia could still pursue a policy focused on projecting imperial power.[67] Intense public emotions were invested in Russia's status as protector of the lesser Slavic peoples, and underlying these in the minds of the key decision-makers was a deepening preoccupation with the question of access to the Turkish Straits. Misled by Izvolsky and fired up by chauvinist popular emotion, the Russian government and public opinion interpreted the annexation as a brutal betrayal of the understanding between the two powers, an unforgivable humiliation and an unacceptable provocation in a sphere of vital interest. In the years that followed the Bosnian crisis, the Russians launched a programme of military investment so substantial that it triggered a European arms race.[68] There were also signs of a deeper Russian political involvement with Serbia. In the autumn of 1909, the Russian foreign ministry appointed Nikolai Hartwig, a 'fiery fanatic in the old slavophile tradition', to the Russian embassy in Belgrade. Once in office, Hartwig, an energetic and intelligent envoy, worked hard to push Belgrade into taking up a more assertive position against Vienna. Indeed, he pushed so hard in this direction that he sometimes exceeded the instructions of his managers in St Petersburg.[69]

LIES AND FORGERIES

The annexation crisis also further poisoned relations between Vienna and Belgrade. As so often, the situation was exacerbated by political conditions inside the dual monarchy. For several years, the Austro-Hungarian authorities had been observing the activities of the Serbo-Croat coalition, a political faction that emerged within the Croatian Diet at Agram (today, Zagreb), capital of Hungarian-ruled Croatia-Slavonia, in 1905. After the diet elections of 1906, the coalition secured control of the

Agram administration, embraced a 'Yugoslav' agenda seeking a closer union of the South Slav peoples within the empire, and fought long battles with the Hungarian authorities over such ticklish issues as the requirement that all state railway officials should be able to speak Magyar. There was nothing especially unusual about this constellation; what worried the Austrians was the suspicion that some or all of the deputies of the coalition might be operating as a fifth column for Belgrade.[70]

During the crisis of 1908–9, these apprehensions escalated to the point of paranoia. In March 1909, just as Russia was backing down from a confrontation over Bosnia, the Habsburg administration launched an astonishingly inept judicial assault on the Serbo-Croat coalition, charging fifty-three mainly Serb activists with treason for plotting to detach the South Slav lands from Austria-Hungary and join them to Serbia. At around the same time, the Vienna-based historian and writer Dr Heinrich Friedjung published an article in the *Neue Freie Presse* accusing three prominent coalition politicians of receiving subsidies from Belgrade in return for treasonous activity on behalf of the Kingdom of Serbia. Friedjung claimed to have been shown confidential government documents demonstrating beyond doubt the truth of these charges.

The treason trial at Agram dragged on from 3 March until 5 November 1909 and quickly collapsed into an unmitigated public relations disaster for the government. The court heard 276 witnesses for the prosecution, but none who had been nominated by the defence. All thirty-one convictions handed down in Agram were subsequently quashed on appeal in Vienna. At the same time, a chain of libel trials against Friedjung and the editor of the *Reichspost*, which had reprinted his claims, revealed further embarrassing manipulations. The 'secret documents' on which the good doctor had based his charges turned out to be forgeries passed to the Austrian legation in Belgrade by a shady Serbian double agent, and supplied in turn to Friedjung by the foreign ministry in Vienna. The unfortunate Friedjung, whose excellent reputation as an historian had been shamefully misused, apologized and withdrew his accusations. But the tireless Czech national activist and advocate for the accused, Tomáš Masaryk, continued to pursue the matter at the highest level, searching far and wide (including in Belgrade) for new evidence and claiming in various public forums that the Austrian ambassador in Belgrade had knowingly procured the forgeries on Count Aehrenthal's behalf.[71]

It is highly unlikely that the authorities in Vienna knew from the outset that the documents were inauthentic. Paranoia probably engendered credulity; the Austrians were primed to believe what they feared to find. But the Agram and Friedjung trials imposed a lasting burden on relations between Vienna and Belgrade. Particularly awkward was the fact that the scandal soon began to focus on the Austrian representative in Serbia, Johann Count Forgách von Ghymes and Gács, with far-reaching consequences for the diplomatic relationship between the two countries. Throughout 1910 and 1911, the Masaryk campaign continued to produce new and embarrassing 'revelations' of Austrian perfidy (not all of which were true). The Serbian press rejoiced and there were loud demands for Forgách's recall from Belgrade.[72] But Forgách, who had long since ceased to take any pleasure whatsoever in his posting, vigorously (and probably truthfully) denied all charges and Aehrenthal, who was himself under attack, felt unable to remove the embattled envoy for as long as this might imply an acknowledgement from Vienna that the Austrian authorities had deliberately deceived the public. 'The situation is not pleasant for me,' Forgách wrote in a private letter to the Foreign Office section chief in Vienna in November 1910, 'but I will survive the Belgrade newspaper storms – as I have survived so much else – provided the government here behaves in a halfway decent fashion.'[73]

What especially infuriated Forgách was the continuing involvement of senior Serbian officials – foremost among them the Foreign Office section chief Miroslav Spalajković – in the campaign to discredit him. Spalajković provided Masaryk with evidence against the Austrian government; he was even called as an expert witness on behalf of the Serbo-Croat coalition during the Friedjung trials. Having helped to explode the credibility of the forged documents, Spalajković went a step further and asserted that Forgách had *deliberately* secured them, in the hope of trumping up charges against the Serbo-Croat coalition. In the winter of 1910–11, the Dutch envoy in Belgrade, Vredenburch, reported that Spalajković continued to disseminate rumours against the Austrian representative across the diplomatic community.[74] To make matters worse, Spalajković and his wife were constantly to be seen in the company of Hartwig, the new Russian minister; indeed it was said that the couple virtually lived at the Russian mission.[75] Forgách became unhealthily obsessed with the man he called 'our deadly enemy'; an exchange of curt letters between the envoy and the official further poisoned relations between them, and by April 1911 Forgách had ordered all personnel at the Austrian legation in Belgrade to avoid contact of any kind with Spalajković. 'This constantly overwrought man,' he informed Aehrenthal, 'is in some respects not entirely sane. Since the annexation, his hatred for the [Austro-Hungarian] Monarchy has developed almost into a mental illness.'[76]

Forgách's position in Belgrade had clearly become untenable, and he was recalled in the summer of 1911. But the scandal of the Agram–Friedjung trials and their aftermath in the Serbian capital are worth recalling, because they involved individuals who would figure prominently in the events of 1914. Miroslav Spalajković was a very senior foreign policy official with a long-standing interest in Bosnia-Herzegovina – his wife was a Bosnian and he had composed a doctoral thesis at the University of Paris in 1897 arguing that, as the two provinces remained autonomous legal entities under Ottoman suzerainty, their annexation by Austria-Hungary could never be legitimate.[77] He subsequently served as the Serbian minister in Sofia, where he played an important role – in collusion with the Russians – in forging the Serbian-Bulgarian alliance at the centre of the Balkan League that launched the First Balkan War in 1912. During his posting at Sofia he remained Nikolai Hartwig's most intimate friend, visiting him in Belgrade 'up to twenty times a month'.[78] He was subsequently transferred to the even more important legation in St Petersburg. Here his task would be to interpret the intentions of the Tsar and his ministers to the Serbian government in Belgrade as the crisis of July 1914 unfolded. Forgách, too, who left his posting as a staunch Serbophobe, remained on the scene as one of the leading figures in a cohort of officials who helped shape the policies of the Austro-Hungarian foreign ministry after the sudden death of Aehrenthal from leukaemia in 1912.[79] And we should not forget the bitter personal animosity between Izvolsky and Aehrenthal, which was rightly identified by the Vienna quality press in the aftermath of the Bosnian crisis as an impediment to the improvement of relations between Austria-Hungary and Russia.[80] It is a curious feature of the July Crisis of 1914 that so many of the key actors in it had known each other for so long. Beneath the surface of many of the key transactions lurked personal antipathies and long-remembered injuries.

*

The Serbian problem was not a matter that the Austrians could handle in isolation. It was embedded within a complex of interlocked questions. First there was the pressing issue of Serbia's relationship with Russia, which was closer after the annexation crisis than it had been before. Vienna was deeply suspicious of the Russian minister Hartwig, whose Austrophobia, pan-Slavism and growing influence in Belgrade augured ill for the future. Hartwig, the French minister in Sofia reported, was 'the archetype of the true Muzhik', a partisan of the 'old Russian Turkish policy' who was prepared to 'sacrifice the Far East for the Balkans'.[81] Hartwig established relations of extraordinary intimacy with Prime Minister Nikola Pašić. The two men met almost daily – 'your beard is consulting with our beard', the officials of the Serbian foreign ministry would comment to the junior diplomats of the Russian mission. 'No one,' a Russian staffer commented, 'believed that secrets were possible in relation to the political goals shared by [Russia and Serbia].'[82] The Russian minister was greeted everywhere in Belgrade like a conquering hero: 'people just needed to see his characteristic head and he would get standing ovations'.[83]

Vienna could in theory offset Serbian hostility by seeking better relations with Bulgaria. But pursuing this option also entailed difficulties. Since there was still a bitter dispute over the border between Bulgaria and Romania, cosying up to Sofia brought the risk of alienating Bucharest. A hostile Bucharest was extremely undesirable because of the huge Romanian minority in Hungarian Transylvania. If Romania were to turn away from Vienna towards St Petersburg, the minority issue might well become a question of regional security. Hungarian diplomats and political leaders in particular warned that 'Greater Romania' posed as serious a threat to the dual monarchy as 'Greater Serbia'.

A further concern was the little principality of Montenegro on the Adriatic coast. This picturesque, impoverished kingdom provided the backdrop for Franz Lehár's The Merry Widow, where it appeared thinly disguised as the 'Grand Duchy of Pontevedro' (the German libretto gave the game away by explicitly stating that the singers should wear 'Montenegrin national costume').[84] Montenegro was the smallest of the Balkan states, with a population of only 250,000 scattered across a beautiful but unforgiving terrain of black peaks and plunging ravines. This was a country where the king, dressed in a splendid uniform of gold, silver, red and blue, could be seen smoking at dusk in front of his palace, hoping to chat with a passer-by. When the Prague journalist Egon Erwin Kisch travelled by foot from Cetinje, then the capital of Montenegro, to the beautiful port city of Rijeka (now in Croatia) in the summer of 1913, he was disconcerted to hear gunshots ringing out across the valleys. He wondered at first whether a Balkan war had broken out, but his guard assured him that it was just the Montenegrin youth with their Russian rifles shooting small fish in the fast-flowing mountain streams.[85]

Though poor and tiny, Montenegro was not unimportant. Its mountain guns on the Lovčen heights overlooked the indefensible Austrian harbour facilities at Cattaro on the Adriatic, to the vexation of Habsburg naval planners. Nikola, the reigning prince since 1861 and thus the third-longest-serving European monarch after Queen Victoria and Franz Joseph, was extraordinarily ambitious. He had succeeded in doubling the territory of his kingdom at the Berlin Congress of 1878, expanded it again during the annexation crisis of 1908, and thereafter had his eye on a piece of northern Albania. He elevated himself to the status of king in 1910. He also married off his female offspring with quite extraordinary skill. King Petar Karadjordjević of Serbia was his son-in-law (though his Montenegrin wife had died by the time Petar was crowned); another of Nikola's daughters, Elena, married Victor Emmanuel III of Italy (king from 1900); two others married Russian archdukes in St Petersburg, where they became prominent figures in Russian high society. Nikola exploited his strategically sensitive position in order to attract funding from powerful foreign sponsors, most importantly Russia. In 1904, he demonstrated his solidarity with the great Slav ally by solemnly declaring war on Japan. The Russians reciprocated with military subsidies and a military mission whose task was the 'reorganisation of the Montenegrin army'.[86]

Italy, linked through its royal house with Montenegro, was a further complication. Italy had been a member of the Triple Alliance with Austria and Germany since May 1882 and renewed its membership in 1891, 1902 and 1912. But public sentiment on the question of relations with Austria was deeply divided. Broadly speaking, liberal, secular, nationalist Italy tended to favour a policy of confrontation with Austrians, especially in the Adriatic, which Italian nationalists regarded as a natural avenue for the consolidation of Italian influence. Catholic, clerical, conservative Italy tended by contrast to favour a policy of rap-prochement and collaboration with Vienna. Reflecting these divided loyalties, Rome operated an elaborate, multi-layered and often contra-dictory diplomacy. In 1900 and 1902, the Italian government signed secret agreements with France that cancelled out most of its treaty obli-gations to Vienna and Berlin. From 1904, moreover, the Italians made it increasingly clear that they viewed Austro-Hungarian policy in the Bal-kans as impinging on their interests in the area. Montenegro was seen as a promising field for the expansion of Italian commercial and cul-tural influence in the Balkans and Foreign Minister Tomaso Tittoni cultivated very friendly relations with Belgrade and Sofia.[87]

The Italians reacted sharply to the annexation of Bosnia in 1908, less because they objected in principle to the Austrian move than because Aehrenthal refused to compensate Rome with the foundation of an Ital-ian university in the mainly Italian-speaking Habsburg port of Trieste.[88] In October 1909, King Victor Emmanuel III broke ranks with the Triple Alliance to sign a secret agreement with Tsar Nicholas II. The 'Racco-nigi Bargain', as it later became known, stipulated that Italy and Russia would not conclude agreements on the 'European East' without each other's consent and that the two powers pledged 'to regard with benev-olence, the one Russia's interests in the matter of the Straits, the other Italian interests in Tripoli and Cyrenaica'.[89] The agreement was less momentous than it seemed, for the Italians soon after signed an under-standing with Vienna that largely cancelled out the pledges of Racconigi, but it signalled Rome's determination to pursue a more assertive and independent policy.

The likeliest apple of future Austro-Italian discord in the Balkans was Albania, still locked within the Ottoman Empire, which both Italy and Austria viewed as falling within their sphere of influence. Since the 1850s, Austria had, through its vice-consulate in Skutari, exercised a kind of religious protectorate over the Catholics in the north of the country. But the Italians, too, took a strong interest in Albania with its long Adriatic coastline. By the turn of the century, Rome and Vienna had agreed that they would support Albanian independence in the event of a collapse of Ottoman power in the region. The question of how exactly influence would be shared between the two Adriatic powers remained unresolved.

DECEPTIVE CALM

In March 1909, Serbia formally pledged that it would desist from further covert operations against Austrian territory and maintain good neighbourly relations with the empire. In 1910, Vienna and Belgrade even agreed, after much wrangling, a trade treaty ending the Austro-Serbian commercial conflict. A 24 per cent rise in Serbian imports during that year bore witness to improving economic conditions. Austro-Hungarian goods began to reappear on the shelves of shops in Belgrade, and by 1912, the dual monarchy was once again the main buyer and supplier of Serbia.[90] At meetings between Pašić and the Austrian representative, there were assurances of goodwill on both sides. But a deep awkwardness had settled over the two states' relations that seemed impossible to dispel. Although there was talk of an official visit by King Petar to Vienna, it never materialized. On the initially genuine pretext of the monarch's ill health, the Serbian government moved the visit from Vienna to Budapest, then postponed it, and then, in April 1911, put it off indefinitely. Yet, to the chagrin of the Austrians, there was a highly successful royal trip to Paris in the winter of 1911. The French visit was deemed so important that the Serbian envoy in Paris returned to Belgrade to help prepare it. An earlier plan to combine the journey to France with stops in Vienna and Rome was jettisoned. Petar arrived in Paris on 16 November and was accommodated in the court of the Quay d'Orsay, where he was welcomed by the president of the republic and presented with a gold medal, fashioned especially for the occasion, commemorating the king's service, as a young Serbian exile and volunteer, in the French war of 1870 against Prussia. At a state dinner on the same evening – and to the intense annoyance of the Austrians – President Fallières opened his speech by hailing Petar as 'the King of all the Serbs' (including, implicitly, those living within the Austro-Hungarian Empire) and 'the man who was going to lead his country and people into freedom'. 'Visibly excited', Petar replied that he and his fellow Serbs would count on France in their fight for freedom.[91]

Behind the scenes, moreover, the work to redeem Bosnia-Herzegovina for Serbdom continued. Narodna Odbrana, ostensibly converted into a purely cultural organization, soon resumed its former activities; its branch organizations proliferated after 1909 and spilled over into

Bosnia-Herzegovina. The Austrians monitored – as far as they were able – the espionage activity of Serbian agents crossing the border. A characteristic example was a certain Dragomir Djordjević, a reserve lieutenant in the Serbian army who combined his cultural work as an 'actor' in Bosnia with the management of a covert network of Serb informants; he was spotted returning to Serbia for weapons training in October 1910.[92] Austrian representatives in Serbia were also aware from an early stage of the existence of Ujedinjenje ili smrt!, though they were at first unsure of what they should make of this mysterious new-comer to the Belgrade scene. In a report filed on 12 November 1911, the new minister in Belgrade (Forgách's successor), Stephan von Ugron zu Abránfalva, notified Vienna of the existence of 'an association sup-posedly existing in officer circles' that was currently the subject of press comment in Serbia. At this point, 'nothing positive' was known about the group, save that it called itself the Black Hand and was chiefly con-cerned with regaining the influence over national politics that the army had enjoyed in the Obrenović era.

Further reports from Ugron and the Austrian military attaché Otto Gellinek fleshed out the picture somewhat. Apis was now identified as the dominant figure in the new network and a more elaborate picture emerged of its objectives: 'The programme of the movement consists in the removal of all personalities in the country who stand in the way of the Greater-Serbian idea' and the enthronement of a leader 'who will be ready to lead the fight for the unification of all Serbs'.[93] Press rumours to the effect that the Black Hand had drawn up a hit-list of politicians to be assassinated in the event of a coup against the current Radical government, nourished by the mysterious murders of two prominent opposition politicians in the autumn of 1911, were later discounted as false. It appeared, Gellinek reported on 22 November 1911, that the conspirators planned to use legal means to remove the 'inner enemies of Serbdom', in order then to 'turn with unified force against its external foes'.[94]

The Austrians initially viewed these developments with surprising equanimity. It was virtually impossible, Gellinek observed, to keep any organization in Serbia secret for long 'because for every five conspir-ators, there is one informant'. Conspiracies were nothing new in Serbia, after all; the matter was therefore of little importance.[95] But the attitude of the Austrian observers changed as they began to grasp the extent of the Black Hand's influence over parts of the state apparatus. In

December 1911, the military attaché reported that the Serbian minister of war had called off an investigation into the movement 'because there would otherwise be difficulties of far-reaching significance'. Early in February 1912, he observed that the network had acquired semi-official character; it appeared that the government was 'fully informed on all members [of the Black Hand] and on their activity'; the fact that Minister of War Stepanović, a protector of the organization, remained in office was a sign of its growing political influence.[96]

A complex picture emerged that would shape Austrian behaviour in the summer of 1914. It was clear on the one hand that Unity or Death! was a subversive network genuinely opposed to and feared by the current civilian authorities in the Kingdom of Serbia. But it was also the case that the great-Serbian objectives of the network were widely condoned and supported, both by elements of the civilian leadership and by the broader public in Serbia. More importantly, there were times when the movement and the administration appeared to operate in tandem. In February 1912, Ugron warned that the Serbian authorities might collaborate with 'an enthusiastic military-patriotic movement', provided its energies could be turned outwards against Serbia's external foes and away from subversive activity within the kingdom itself.[97] The irredentist organ *Pijemont* openly espoused anti-Habsburg ultra-nationalist objectives – by defining itself thus in terms of 'national' goals, Ugron noted, the Black Hand made it difficult for the Serbian civilian authorites to take action against it.[98] In short, the Austrians grasped both the extent of Black Hand influence and the complexity of the constraints preventing the Pašić government from taking action to counter it.

The outlines of this analysis remained in place until the summer of 1914. The Austrians followed as closely as they could the dramatic growth of the network during the Balkan Wars of 1912 and 1913. In January 1914, attention focused on the trial of a regicide officer by the name of Vemić, who had been notorious in 1903 for carrying about with him in a suitcase a desiccated flap of flesh that he had cut from one of Queen Draga's breasts as a trophy of the night of 11 June. In October 1913, during the Second Balkan War, Vemić shot dead a Serbian recruit for being too slow to follow an order and was tried by a military tribunal. His acquittal by a court staffed entirely by senior officers triggered uproar in parts of the Belgrade press and Vemić was called for a retrial before the Serbian Supreme Court. But his sentence – a mere ten months of imprisonment – was cut short by a royal pardon, extracted by the military leadership from the king at the end of December 1913.[99] The officer corps is 'a politically decisive factor in today's Serbia', Gellinek noted in May 1914. This growth in the 'praetorian element' in Serbian public life in turn represented an enhanced threat to Austria-Hungary, since 'the officer corps is also the bastion of the great-Serbian, extreme Austrophobe tendency'.[100]

The most enigmatic ingredient in the mix was Nikola Pašić, the 'uncrowned king of Serbia'. Pašić held his fire during the political storms of 1913–14 and refused to allow himself to be provoked into a direct confrontation with the officer corps. 'With his customary agility', Gellinek observed on 21 May 1914, the prime minister sidestepped hostile interpellations in the Skupština by insisting that the Serbian government and the Serbian officer corps were in 'the fullest agreement' on all important questions.[101] In a report filed on 21 June – a week before the assassinations at Sarajevo – Gellinek summed up the situation in four points. The crown had fallen into the hands of the conspirators and was largely powerless. The army continued to pursue its own objectives in domestic and foreign policy. The Russian minister, Nikolai Hartwig, remained an exceptionally influential figure in Belgrade. But none of this meant that Pašić should be written off as a factor in Serbian politics; on the contrary, the founder and leader for three decades of the 'extreme russophile' Radical Party still occupied, despite everything, an 'omnipotent position'.[102]

Yet establishing direct communications with Nikola Pašić proved extraordinarily difficult. A curious episode from the autumn of 1913 illustrates the point. On 3 October, Pašić paid a pre-scheduled visit to Vienna. The trip was timely, because Vienna and Belgrade were locked in a confrontation over the Serbian occupation of parts of northern Albania. On 1 October, a letter warning Belgrade that the Serbs must quit Albania had elicited a noncommittal reply. Accompanied by his ambassador, Pašić attended meetings with various Austrian ministers, including a lunch with the Austrian foreign minister, Berchtold; the Hungarian prime minister, István Tisza; Forgách; Biliński and others. Yet at no point was there a thorough discussion of the issue at hand. Biliński, joint finance minister with special responsibility for

Bosnia-Herzegovina, recalled in his memoirs that Pašić was an exceptionally evasive interlocutor. Full of 'fire and phrases', he parried questions from his Austrian interlocutors with waffling assurances that 'all would be well'. Biliński also faulted Berchtold for failing to press the Serbian statesman harder. 'Small in appearance, with a flowing patriarchal beard, fanatical eyes and a modest bearing', Pašić perplexed the Austrian foreign minister with his combination of graceful joviality and wilful obfuscation.[103] At the first meeting between them, before lunch, Berchtold was so disarmed by the warmth of Pašić's overtures that when they came next to the topic of Albania, he omitted to press home the gravity of Austria's objections to the Serbian occupation. Sometime during the afternoon following their meeting, Berchtold suddenly remembered that he had 'forgotten' to inform Pašić of Vienna's strong views on the matter. It was agreed that he would broach the Albanian Question with the Serbian leader that evening when the two men were both expected to attend the opera. But when the foreign minister arrived a little late to take his seat in the royal box, he found that Pašić had already retired to his hotel, where he was supposedly in bed fast asleep. The Serbian prime minister left Vienna early next morning without any further meeting having taken place. Berchtold went back to his desk and spent the small hours writing a letter that was taken round to the hotel by courier so that it reached Pašić as he was leaving the city. But since it was scrawled in German script (not to mention Berchtold's notoriously inscrutable hand) Pašić was unable to read it. Even when the letter was deciphered in Belgrade, Pašić supposedly found it difficult to see what Berchtold was getting at.[104] And the people at the Austrian Foreign Office had no idea either, because Berchtold had not thought to preserve a rough copy of the text. This comedy of errors – assuming that Biliński's recollection a decade later can be trusted – is no doubt in part an indictment of Austrian disarray, perhaps also of Berchtold's almost painfully courteous diffidence and reserve, but it also hints at Pašić's famous elusiveness.[105] Above all, it conveys a sense of the paralysing awkwardness that had settled over Austro-Serbian relations by the eve of the First World War.

What emerged from Austrian Serbia-watching in the last years, months and weeks before the assassination was a fairly nuanced account of the destabilizing forces at work in the neighbouring state. This was a hostile and therefore a tendentious and one-sided picture, to be sure.

Austrian observations of events in Serbia were embedded in a matrix of negative attitudes – rooted partly in experience and partly in long-standing stereotypes – about Serbian political culture and the prominent actors within it. Bad faith, deceitfulness, unreliability, evasiveness, violence and excitability were recurring themes in the envoy reports from Belgrade. Conspicuously absent was a thorough analysis of the operational relationship between the Austrophobe groups within Serbia and irredentist terrorism within the Habsburg lands. It is possible that the fiasco of the Agram–Friedjung trials put brakes on Austrian intelligence-gathering after 1909, just as the Iran-Contra scandals of the Ronald Reagan presidency in the 1980s led to a temporary scaling down of covert intelligence activity by US agencies.[106] The Austrians recognized that Narodna Odbrana aimed at the subversion of Habsburg rule in Bosnia and ran networks of activists in the Habsburg lands. They presumed that the roots of all Serbian irredentist activity within the empire led back to the pan-Serbian propaganda of the Belgrade-based patriotic networks. But the precise nature of the links and the relationship between Narodna Odbrana and the Black Hand were poorly understood. Nevertheless: the key points of reference that would shape Austrian thought and action after the events at Sarajevo were all in place by the spring of 1914.

HAWKS AND DOVES

The Balkan Wars destroyed Austria's security position on the Balkan peninsula and created a bigger and stronger Serbia. The kingdom's territory expanded by over 80 per cent. During the Second Balkan War, the Serbian armed forces under their supreme commander General Putnik displayed impressive discipline and initiative. The Habsburg government had often adopted a dismissive tone in its discussions of the military threat posed by Belgrade. In a telling metaphor, Aehrenthal had once described Serbia as a 'rascally boy' pinching apples from the Austrian orchard. Such levity was no longer possible. A General Staff report of 9 November 1912 expressed surprise at the dramatic growth in Serbia's striking power. Improvements to the railway network underway since the beginning of the year, the modernization of weaponry and equipment and the massive increase in the number of front-line units, all financed by French loans, had transformed Serbia into a formidable combatant.[107] It was very likely, moreover, that Serbia's military strength would increase with time; 1.6 million people lived in the new territories conquered by Serbia during the two Balkan Wars. In a report of October 1913, the Belgrade military attaché Otto Gellinek observed that while there was no cause for immediate alarm, no one should underestimate the kingdom's military prowess. It would henceforth be necessary when calculating the monarchy's defence needs to match all Serbian front-line units man-for-man with Austrian troops.[108]

The question of how to respond to the deteriorating security situation in the Balkans divided the key decision-makers in Vienna. Should Austria-Hungary seek some sort of accommodation with Serbia, or contain it by diplomatic means? Should Vienna strive to mend the ruined entente with St Petersburg? Or did the solution lie in military conflict? It was difficult to extract unequivocal answers from the multilayered networks of the Austro-Hungarian state. Foreign policy in the empire did not emanate from a compact executive cell at the apex of the system. It emerged from interactions across an archipelago of power-centres whose relationships with each other were partly informal and in constant flux. The General Staff was one such centre, the Military Chancellery of the heir to the throne another. The Foreign Office on the Ballhausplatz was obviously a key player, though it really functioned as a framework within which competing policy groups jostled for influence. The dualist constitution required that the Hungarian prime minister be consulted on questions of imperial foreign policy and the intimate connection between domestic and foreign problems ensured that other ministers and senior officials also laid claim to a role in resolving specific issues: Leon Biliński, for example, the joint minister of finance with responsibility for the administration of Bosnia-Herzegovina, or even his theoretical subordinate Governor Potiorek, the *Landeschef* of Bosnia, whose views did not always accord with those of the minister. So open was the texture of this system that even quite junior figures – diplomats, for example, or section heads within the foreign ministry – might seek to shape imperial policy by submitting unsolicited memoranda that could on occasion play an important role in focusing attitudes within the policy-making elite. Presiding over it all was the Emperor, whose power to approve or block the initiatives of his ministers and advisers remained unchallenged. But his was a passive rather than a proactive role – he responded to, and mediated between, initiatives generated by the loosely assembled power-centres of the political elite.[109]

Against the background of this strikingly polycratic system, three figures emerge as especially influential: the chief of the Austrian General Staff, Fieldmarshal Lieutenant Franz Baron Conrad von Hötzendorf; the heir to the Habsburg throne, Archduke Franz Ferdinand of Austria-Este; and the joint foreign minister from 1912, Count Leopold von Berchtold.

Conrad von Hötzendorf was one of the most intriguing figures to hold high military office in early twentieth-century Europe. He was fifty-four years old when he was appointed chief of the General Staff in 1906 and remained throughout his career a steadfast advocate of war against the monarchy's enemies. In his views on the empire's external relations, Conrad was relentlessly aggressive. Yet he also entertained deep and sincere doubts about his fitness for office and often toyed with

Count Leopold Berchtold

Conrad von Hötzendorf

the idea of resigning. He was shy in elegant company and relished the solitude of walks in the mountains, where he produced melancholy pencil sketches of steep slopes shrouded in dark conifers. His tendency to self-doubt was reinforced by periodic bouts of severe depression, especially after the death of his wife in 1905. He sought an escape from this turmoil in his relationship with Gina von Reininghaus, the wife of a Viennese industrialist.

Conrad's pursuit of this potentially scandalous liaison casts a vivid light on his personality. It began at a Vienna dinner party in 1907, when the two happened to be seated together. A week or so later, Conrad presented himself at the Reininghaus villa in the Operngasse and announced to his hostess: 'I am terribly in love with you and have only one thought in my head: that you should become my wife.' Taken aback, Gina replied that this was completely out of the question; she was bound by a 'sevenfold commitment' in the form of a husband and six children. 'Nevertheless,' Conrad persevered, 'I shall never rest – this wish will be my guiding star.'[110] A day or so later, an adjutant popped by to inform Reininghaus that, in view of the staff chief's fragile mental state, she should think twice before depriving him of hope. Conrad himself made a further appearance eight days later, at which he declared that if she were to turn him down definitively, he would resign his post as chief of the General Staff and disappear from public life. They reached an agreement: Reininghaus would remain for the foreseeable future with her husband and children. But should it appear opportune at some point to separate from her husband, she would keep Conrad in mind. The staff chief's bold gambit – a triumphant application of the cult of the offensive to the art of courting – had paid off.

Gina was to remain with her husband for another eight years. Exactly when she and Conrad started an affair is not known. Gina's husband, Hans von Reininghaus, was in any case a complacent cuckold – the wealthy businessman had other women to divert himself with and the connection with Conrad provided welcome access to lucrative military supply contracts. In the meanwhile, Conrad visited his beloved whenever he could. He also wrote love letters, sometimes several a day. But since it was impossible to post them to his intended without risking a scandal, he collated them in an album bearing the title 'Diary of my Sufferings'. Apart from scraps of news, the theme was consistent: she was his sole joy, only the thought of her could lift him from the abyss of despair, his destiny was in her hands, and so on. In all, he accumulated over 3,000 letters between 1907 and 1915, some stretching to sixty pages in length. Gina became aware of the album's existence only after his death.[111]

It would be difficult to overstate the importance of this relationship; it was at the centre of Conrad's life throughout the years from 1907 to the outbreak of war, eclipsing all other concerns, including the military and political questions that came to his desk. Its obsessive quality may help to explain some features of Conrad's professional demeanour – his willingness, for example, to risk his professional standing by associating himself with extreme positions, and his relative immunity from the fear of being exposed or discredited. He even came to see war as a means of gaining possession of Gina. Only as a victorious war-hero, Conrad believed, would he be able to sweep aside the social obstacles and the scandal attaching to a marriage with a prominent divorcée. He fantasized in a letter to Gina about returning from a 'Balkan war' draped in the laurels of triumph, throwing caution to the winds and making her his wife.[112] Photographs taken of him during these years show a man fastidiously concerned with maintaining a manly, dapper and youthful outward appearance. Among his private papers, now deposited in the Haus-, Hof- und Staatsarchiv in Vienna, can be found advertisements for anti-wrinkle creams cut from the pages of the daily press. In short, Conrad exemplified a brittle, rather overwrought form of European masculinity that was in some respects characteristic of the *fin-de-siècle*.

Conrad approached the geopolitical predicaments of the Habsburg monarchy with the same monomaniacal fixity he brought to his love life. Even in the context of the pre-1914 European military commanders he stands out as unusually aggressive. His answer to virtually every diplomatic challenge was 'war'; in this there was virtually no change between 1906 and 1914. Conrad repeatedly counselled preventive wars against Serbia, Montenegro, Russia, Romania and even Italy, Austria's disloyal ally and Balkan rival.[113] He made no secret of these convictions, but rather broadcast them openly through journals such as the *Militärische Rundschau* that were known to be close to the General Staff.[114] He was proud of the immobility of his opinions, which he saw as an indication of manly solidity and steadfastness. 'I am advocating here the position I have always maintained' was a favourite phrase in the letters and reports he sent to ministers and colleagues. Moreover, he favoured an abrasive, carping and self-righteous style of communication that irritated his colleagues and superiors. In 1912, when their affair was an established fact, Gina advised Conrad that he might get on better with the Emperor if he spoke mildly with the old man and avoided 'the method of cudgel-blows'.[115]

There were many potential enemies on Conrad's horizon, but Serbia became his chief preoccupation. In a memorandum composed at the end of 1907 he called for the invasion and annexation of Serbia, which he described as 'a constant breeding ground for those aspirations and machinations that aim at the separation of the South Slav areas [of the Empire]'.[116] During 1908–9, when the annexation crisis was at its height, he called repeatedly for preventive war against Belgrade. 'It is a crime,' he told Gina von Reininghaus in the spring of 1909, 'that nothing is being done. War against Serbia could have saved the monarchy. In a few years we shall atone bitterly for this omission, and I shall be chosen to bear the entire responsibility and drain the chalice to its dregs.'[117] He called for war against Serbia again during the Balkan War crisis of 1912–13. During the twelve months between 1 January 1913 and 1 January 1914, he counselled a Serbian war no fewer than twenty-five times.[118] Underlying this single-minded pursuit of conflict was a social Darwinist philosophy in which struggle and the competition for primacy were seen as unavoidable and necessary facts of the political life between states. Conrad's was not yet a racist outlook (though there were certainly many younger Habsburg officers who envisaged a coming clash between the Germanic and the Slavic peoples), but rather a bleak Hobbesian vision of eternal strife between states bound to pursue their own security at the cost of all else.[119]

Until the outbreak of the Balkan Wars, Conrad's interventions were higher in volume than in impact. The immutability of his views itself undermined their credibility among the civilian leadership. Emperor Franz Joseph flatly rejected his calls for preventive war against Serbia in 1908. Aehrenthal, too, remained impervious to his arguments and grew increasingly impatient at the staff chief's efforts to intervene in the policy-making process. By October 1911, when Conrad pushed hard for war with Italy, Aehrenthal had had enough and filed a formal complaint with the Emperor. Conrad, Aehrenthal wrote, had created a 'war party' within the General Staff. If this development were left unchecked, it would 'paralyse the Monarchy's capacity for political action'.[120] The conflict came to a head during a stormy audience with the Emperor on 15 November. Fed up with the obstreperous staff chief, Emperor Franz Joseph summoned him to Schönbrunn for a dressing down: 'These incessant attacks on Aehrenthal, these pinpricks, I forbid them,' he told Conrad. 'These ever-recurring reproaches regarding Italy and the Balkans are directed at *Me*. Policy – it is *I* who make it! My policy is a policy of peace. Everyone must learn to live with that.'[121] It is worth emphasizing this clash between the Habsburg Emperor and his chief of staff. A collision of this kind would have been unthinkable under Conrad's predecessors.[122] It was a sign that the constituent bits of the Habsburg command structure were drifting apart, acquiring a partial autonomy that gravely complicated the process of decision-making. Completely undaunted by the Emperor's reproaches, Conrad busied himself preparing a trenchant reply, but Franz Joseph dismissed him from his post before he had the chance to present it. His removal was officially announced on 2 December 1911.[123]

The most consistent and influential opponent of Conrad and his war

Franz Ferdinand, Archduke of Austria-Este

policy was Franz Ferdinand, heir to the Habsburg throne, the man whose death at Sarajevo would precipitate the July Crisis of 1914. Franz Ferdinand occupied a complex but crucial position within the Habsburg leadership structure. At court, he was an isolated figure. His relations with the Emperor were not warm. His nomination as heir to the throne had come about only because the Emperor's son, Crown Prince Rudolf, had committed suicide in January 1889. The memory of this gifted and brooding prince doubtless overshadowed the Emperor's relationship with the abrasive and temperamental man who replaced him. Not until five years after his son's death was the Emperor prepared to appoint Franz Ferdinand his presumptive successor and only two years later, in 1896, did the archduke become the definitive heir to the throne. But even then, the Emperor's meetings with his nephew tended to be conducted in a tone of wounding condescension and it was said that the archduke went to imperial audiences trembling like a schoolboy on his way to the headmaster's office.

The scandal of Franz Ferdinand's marriage to the Czech noblewoman

Sophie Chotek in July 1900 was a further burden on his relationship with the Emperor. This was a marriage of love contracted against the wishes of the Emperor and the Habsburg royal family. Though descended from an elevated Bohemian lineage, Countess Sophie Chotek von Chotkova and Wognin did not meet the exacting genealogical criteria of the House of Habsburg. Franz Ferdinand had to wage a long campaign, enlisting the support of archbishops and ministers and ultimately of Kaiser Wilhelm II of Germany and Pope Leo XIII, in order to secure permission for the union. Franz Joseph eventually gave in, but he remained unreconciled to the marriage until the couple's violent death in 1914.[124] His heir was obliged to swear an oath excluding the as yet unborn children of his marriage from the line of succession to the Habsburg throne. After the wedding, the couple continued to endure the slights of a Habsburg court protocol that regulated nearly every facet of dynastic public life: Sophie, forbidden ever to carry the title archduchess, was styled first princess and later Duchess of Hohenberg. She was not permitted to join her husband in the royal box at the opera, sit near him at gala dinners, or accompany him in the splendid royal carriage with its golden wheels. Her chief tormentor was the Emperor's chamberlain, Prince Montenuovo, himself the illegitimate offspring of one of Napoleon's wives, who enforced the rules of etiquette at every opportunity with exquisite precision.

After 1906, when the Emperor appointed his nephew inspector-general of the army, Franz Ferdinand compensated for the long years of isolation at court by building a power base of his own within the rickety executive structure of the double monarchy. In addition to securing a number of key appointments (Aehrenthal and Conrad, among others), the archduke expanded the activities of his Military Chancellery, which was housed near his residence in the Lower Belvedere. Under the energetic supervision of a gifted head of personal staff, Major Alexander Brosch von Aarenau, the Military Chancellery was reorganized along ministerial lines; its ostensibly military information channels served as a cover for political data-gathering and a network of friendly journalists managed from the Belvedere promulgated the archduke's ideas, pummelled political opponents and attempted to shape public debates. Processing over 10,000 pieces of correspondence per year, the Chancellery matured into an imperial think-tank, a power-centre within the system that some saw as a 'shadow government'.[125] Like all think-tanks, this one had its axes to grind. An internal study of its operations concluded that its chief political objective was to hinder any 'possible mishaps' that could accelerate the 'national-federal fragmentation' of the Habsburg Empire.[126]

At the heart of this concern about political fragmentation was a deep-seated hostility to the Hungarian elites who controlled the eastern half of the Austro-Hungarian Empire.[127] The archduke and his advisers were outspoken critics of the dualist political system forged in the aftermath of Austria's defeat at the hands of Prussia in 1866. This arrangement had, in Franz Ferdinand's eyes, one fatal flaw: it concentrated power in the hands of an arrogant and politically disloyal Magyar elite, while at the same time marginalizing and alienating the other nine official Habsburg nationalities. Once installed with his staff at the Lower Belvedere, Captain Brosch von Aarenau built up a network of disaffected non-Magyar intellectuals and experts and the Military Chancellery became a clearing house for Slav and Romanian opposition to the oppressive minority policies of the Kingdom of Hungary.[128]

The archduke made no secret of the fact that he intended to restructure the imperial system after his accession to the throne. The key objective was to break or diminish the Hungarian hegemony in the eastern part of the monarchy. For a time, Franz Ferdinand favoured strengthening the Slavic element in the monarchy by creating a Croat- (and thus Catholic-) dominated 'Yugoslavia' within the empire. It was his association with this idea that so aroused the hatred of his orthodox Serbian enemies. By 1914, however, it appears he had dropped this plan in favour of a far-reaching transformation by which the empire would become a 'United States of Great Austria', comprising fifteen member states, many of which would have Slav majorities.[129]

By diminishing the status of the Hungarians, the archduke and his advisers hoped to reinforce the authority of the Habsburg dynasty while at same time rekindling the loyalties of the lesser nationalities. Whatever one thought of this programme, and obviously Hungarians didn't think much of it, it did identify the archduke as a man of radical intentions whose accession to the throne would bring an end to the habit of muddling through that seemed to paralyse Austrian policy in the last decades before 1914. It also placed the heir to the throne in direct political opposition to the reigning sovereign. The Emperor refused to countenance any tampering with the dualist Compromise of 1867, which he regarded as the most enduring achievement of his own early years in office.

Franz Ferdinand's domestic reform programme also had far-reaching implications for his views on foreign policy. He believed that the current structural weakness of the monarchy and the need for radical internal reform categorically ruled out an external policy focused on confrontation. Franz Ferdinand was thus adamantly opposed to the aggressive adventurism of Conrad. There was an irony in this, since it was Franz Ferdinand, in his role as chief inspector, who had hoisted Conrad into his General Staff post, promoting him over the heads of many formally better qualified officers – it was perhaps for this reason that the archduke was widely, and wrongly, seen as the head of the Austrian war party. The two men did agree on some questions: the egalitarian handling of the nationalities, for example, and the pensioning-off of elderly senior officers who seemed likely to disappoint in the event of war.[130] Franz Ferdinand also liked Conrad personally, in part because the latter adopted a respectful and sympathetic attitude to his wife (the heir to the throne tended in general to judge people by how they treated the awkward fact of his marriage and Conrad, for obvious reasons, was inclined to indulge the archduke's unorthodox love-match). But in the sphere of security and diplomacy their views were worlds apart.

Conrad saw the army exclusively as an instrument of modern warfare and was fully committed to its modernization and preparation for the real conditions of the next major conflict; for Franz Ferdinand, by contrast, the army was above all a safeguard for domestic stability. Franz Ferdinand was a navalist determined to consolidate Austrian dominance in the Adriatic through the construction of a fleet of dreadnoughts; Conrad saw the navy as a drain on resources that would be better invested in the military: 'the most beautiful naval victory', he told the archduke, 'would not compensate for a defeat on land'.[131] By contrast with Conrad, Franz Ferdinand opposed the annexation of Bosnia. 'In view of our desolate domestic situation,' he told Aehrenthal in August 1908, 'I am as a matter of principle against all such power-plays.'[132] In mid-October, perturbed by the furious Serbian response to the annexation in Serbia he warned Aehrenthal not to let the crisis come to a war: 'We would gain nothing from that and it rather looks as if these Balkan toads, egged on by England and perhaps Italy, want to goad us to a precipitate military step.'[133] It was all very well to give the

Serbs and Montenegrins a drubbing, he confided to Brosch, but of what use were these 'cheap laurels' if they landed the empire with a general European escalation and 'a fight on two or three fronts' that it was incapable of sustaining? Conrad, he warned, must be restrained. An open break came in December 1911, when Conrad demanded that Austria-Hungary seize the opportunity created by the Libyan War to attack Italy. It was largely because Franz Ferdinand abandoned him that Conrad was dismissed by the Emperor in December 1911.[134]

Franz Ferdinand's most influential ally was the new Habsburg foreign minister, Leopold Count Berchtold von und zu Ungarschitz, Fratting und Pullitz. Berchtold was a nobleman of immense wealth and fastidious taste, an urbane, patrician representative of that landed class that still held sway in the upper reaches of the Austro-Hungarian administration. By temperament cautious, even fearful, he was not an instinctive politician. His true passions were for the arts, literature and horse racing, all of which he pursued as vigorously as his wealth allowed. His willingness to follow a diplomatic career had more to do with personal loyalty to the Emperor and to Foreign Minister Aehrenthal than with an appetite for personal power or renown. The reluctance he professed when invited to accept posts of increasing seniority and responsibility was unquestionably genuine.

After transferring from the civil service to the Foreign Office, Berchtold served at the embassies in Paris and London before taking up a post at St Petersburg in 1903. There he became a close friend and ally of Aehrenthal, who had been ambassador to Russia since 1899. The St Petersburg posting appealed to Berchtold because he was an enthusiastic supporter of the Austro-Russian entente. He believed that harmonious relations with Russia, founded on cooperation in areas of potential conflict such as the Balkans, were crucial both to the empire's security and to European peace. He derived great professional satisfaction from the fact that he was able, as Aehrenthal's colleague in St Petersburg, to play a role in the consolidation of good relations between the two powers. When Aehrenthal departed for Vienna, Berchtold gladly accepted the ambassadorial post, confident in the knowledge that his own views of the Austro-Russian relationship were entirely in step with those of the new minister in Vienna.[135]

It was a shock, therefore, to find himself on the front line when Austro-Russian relations took a drastic turn for the worse in 1908. The first eighteen months of Berchtold's new posting had been relatively harmonious, despite signs that Izvolsky was drifting away from the entente with Austria towards a continental strategy founded on the new Anglo-Russian Convention of 1907.[136] But the Bosnian annexation crisis destroyed any prospect of further collaboration with the Russian foreign minister and undermined the policy of détente in whose name Berchtold had accepted office. Berchtold deeply regretted Aehrenthal's willingness to risk Russian goodwill for the sake of Austro-Hungarian prestige. In a letter to the minister of 19 November 1908, Berchtold offered an implicit critique of his former mentor's policy. In light of the 'pathological escalation of pan-Slav-influenced Russian national sentiment', he wrote, the further continuation of 'the active Balkan policy inaugurated by us' would inevitably have 'a further negative impact on our relationship with Russia'. Recent events had made his work in St Petersburg 'extremely difficult'. Another man would perhaps be able to find the charisma and warmth to restore good relations, 'but for someone of my modest capabilities, this seems the equivalent of squaring the circle'. He closed with a request to be recalled from his post once the situation returned to normal.[137]

Berchtold would remain in St Petersburg until April 1911, but his posting had become a burden to him. The conspicuous display of wealth that was characteristic of social life among the oligarchs of early twentieth-century St Petersburg had begun to pall. In January 1910, he attended an immense ball at the palace of Countess Thekla Orlov-Davidov – a building designed by Boulanger on the model of Versailles – where the ballrooms and galleries were decked out with thousands of fresh flowers that had been shipped through the northern winter in a special train at huge expense from greenhouses on the French Riviera. Even for this wealthy art connoisseur and racing enthusiast, such profligacy was hard to stomach.[138] It was with a sense of deep relief that Berchtold left St Petersburg and returned to his estate in Buchlau. The spell of recuperation was to last only ten months. On 19 February 1912, the Emperor summoned him to Vienna and appointed him Aehrenthal's successor as minister of foreign affairs.

Berchtold brought to his new office a sincere desire to repair relations with Russia; indeed, it was the belief that he would be able to achieve this that prompted the Emperor to appoint him.[139] The quest for détente was supported by the new Austrian ambassador to

St Petersburg, Count Duglas Thurn, and Berchtold soon found that he had a powerful ally in the person of Franz Ferdinand, who immediately latched on to the new foreign minister, showering advice on him, assuring him that he would be much better than his 'frightful predecessors, Goluchowski and Aehrenthal', and supporting the policy of détente in the Balkans.[140] For the moment, it was unclear what could be done to improve matters with Russia: Nikolai Hartwig was encouraging Serbian ultra-nationalism, including irredentist agitation within the Habsburg monarchy; most importantly, and unbeknown to the Austrians, Russian agents were already working hard to build a Balkan League against Turkey and Austria. Nevertheless, the new administration in the Joint Foreign Office was willing to embark on an exchange of views. His policy, Berchtold announced in an address to the Hungarian delegation on 30 April 1912, would be a 'policy of stability and peace, the conservation of what exists, and the avoidance of entanglements and shocks'.[141]

The Balkan Wars would test this commitment to breaking point. The chief bone of contention was Albania. The Austrians remained committed to the creation of an independent Albania, which, it was hoped, might in time become an Austrian satellite. The Serbian government, on the other hand, was determined to secure a swathe of territory connecting the country's heartland with the Adriatic coast. During the Balkan conflicts of 1912 and 1913, successive Serbian assaults on northern Albania triggered a sequence of international crises. The result was a marked deterioration in Austro-Serbian relations. Austria's willingness to meet Serbian demands (or even to take them seriously) withered away and Serbia, its confidence heightened by the acquisition of new lands in the south and south-east, became an increasingly threatening presence.

Austrian hostility to Belgrade's triumphant progress was reinforced from the autumn of 1913 by dark tidings from the areas conquered by Serbian forces. From Austrian Consul-General Jehlitschka in Skopje came reports in October 1913 of atrocities against the local inhabitants. One such spoke of the destruction of ten small villages whose entire population had been exterminated. The men were first forced to come out of the village and shot in lines; the houses were then set on fire, and when the women and children fled from the flames, they were killed with bayonets. In general, the consul-general reported, it was the officers who shot the men; the killing of the women and children was left to the enlisted men. Another source described the behaviour of Serbian troops after the taking of Gostivar, one of the towns in an area where there had been an Albanian uprising against the Serbian invaders. Some 300 Gostivar Muslims who had played no role in the uprising were arrested and taken out of the town during the night in groups of twenty to thirty to be beaten and stabbed to death with rifle butts and bayonets (gunshots would have woken the sleeping inhabitants of the town), before being thrown into a large open grave that had been dug beforehand for that purpose. These were not spontaneous acts of brutality, Jehlitschka concluded, but rather 'a cold-blooded and systematic elimination or annihilation operation that appeared to have been carried out on orders from above'.[142]

Such reports, which accord, as we have seen, with those of the British officials in the area, inevitably affected the mood and attitude of the political leadership in Vienna. In May 1914, the Serbian envoy in Vienna, Jovanović, reported that even the French ambassador had complained to him about the behaviour of the Serbs in the new provinces; similar complaints were forthcoming from Greek, Turkish, Bulgarian and Albanian colleagues, and it was to be feared that the damage to Serbia's reputation could have 'very bad consequences'.[143] The glib denials of Pašić and his ministers reinforced the impression that the government was either itself behind the atrocities or unwilling to do anything to prevent or investigate them. The Austro-Hungarian minister in Belgrade was amused to see leader articles in the Viennese press advising the Serbian government to go easy on the minorities and win them over by a policy of conciliation. Such advice, he observed in a letter to Berchtold, might well be heeded in 'civilised states'. But Serbia was a state where 'murder and killing have been raised to a system'.[144] The impact of these reports on Austrian policy is difficult to measure – they were hardly surprising to those in Vienna who already subscribed to a grossly stereotypical view of Serbia and its citizens. At the very least, they underscored in Vienna's eyes the political illegitimacy of Serbian territorial expansion.

Nevertheless: a war between Austria and Serbia did not appear likely in the spring and summer of 1914. The mood in Belgrade was relatively calm in the spring of that year, reflecting the exhaustion and sense of satiation that followed the Balkan Wars. The instability of the newly conquered areas and the civil–military crisis that racked Serbia during

May gave grounds to suspect that the Belgrade government would be focusing mainly on tasks of domestic consolidation for the foreseeable future. In a report sent on 24 May 1914, the Austro-Hungarian minister in Belgrade, Baron Giesl, observed that although Serbian troop numbers along the Albanian border remained high, there seemed little reason to fear further incursions.[145] And three weeks later, on 16 June, a dispatch from Gellinek, the military attaché in Belgrade, struck a similarly placid note. It was true that officers on holiday had been recalled, reservists asked not to leave their current addresses and the army was being kept at a heightened state of readiness. But there were no signs of aggressive intentions towards either Austria-Hungary or Albania.[146] All was quiet on the southern front.

Nor was there any indication that the Austrians themselves had war in mind. Early in June, Berchtold instructed a senior Foreign Office section chief, Baron Franz Matscheko, to prepare a secret position statement outlining the empire's key concerns in the Balkans and proposing remedies. The 'Matscheko memorandum', which was drawn up in consultation with Forgách and Berchtold and passed to the foreign minister's desk on 24 June, is the clearest picture we have of Vienna's thinking in the summer of 1914. It is not a cheerful document. Matscheko notes only two positive Balkan developments: signs of a rapprochement between Austria-Hungary and Bulgaria, which had finally 'awakened from the Russian hypnosis', and the creation of an independent Albania.[147] But Albania was not exactly a model of successful state-building: levels of domestic turbulence and lawlessness were high, and there was general agreement among Albanians that order would not be achieved without external help.[148] And almost everything else was negative. Serbia, enlarged and strengthened by the two Balkan Wars, represented a greater threat than ever before, Romanian public opinion had shifted in Russia's favour, raising the question of when Romania would break formally with the Triple Alliance to align itself with Russia. Austria was confronted at every turn by a Russian policy – supported by Paris – that was 'in the last resort aggressive and directed against the *status quo*'. For now that Turkey-in-Europe had been destroyed, the only purpose behind a Russian-sponsored Balkan League could be the ultimate dismemberment of the Austro-Hungarian Empire itself, whose lands Russia would one day feed to its hungry satellites.

What was the remedy? The memorandum focused on four key

diplomatic objectives. First, the Germans must be brought into line with Austrian Balkan policy – Berlin had consistently failed to understand the gravity of the challenges Vienna faced on the Balkan peninsula and would have to be educated towards a more supportive attitude. Secondly, Romania should be pressed to declare where its allegiances lay. The Russians had been courting Bucharest in the hope of gaining a new salient against Austria-Hungary. If the Romanians intended to align themselves with the Entente, Vienna needed to know as soon as possible, so that arrangements could be made for the defence of Transylvania and the rest of eastern Hungary. Thirdly, an effort should be made to expedite the conclusion of an alliance with Bulgaria to counter the effects of the deepening relationship between Russia and Belgrade. Finally, efforts should be made to woo Serbia away from a policy of confrontation using economic concessions, though Matscheko was sceptical about whether it would be possible by this means to overcome Belgrade's hostility.

There was an edgy note of paranoia in the Matscheko memorandum, a weird combination of shrillness and fatalism that many Austrian contemporaries would have recognized as characteristic of the mood and cultural style of early twentieth-century Vienna. But there was no hint in it whatsoever that Vienna regarded war – whether of the limited or the more general variety – as imminent, necessary or desirable. On the contrary, the focus was firmly on diplomatic methods and objectives, in accordance with Vienna's self-image as the exponent of a 'conservative policy of peace'.[149]

Conrad, on the other hand, who had been recalled to the post of chief of staff in December 1912, remained robotically committed to a war policy. But his authority was on the wane. In May 1913, it was discovered that Colonel Alfred Redl, former chief of military counter-intelligence and chief of staff of 8th Army Corps in Prague, had been routinely passing top-level Austrian military secrets to St Petersburg, including entire mobilization schedules, the outlines of which were forwarded in turn by the Russians to Belgrade. The scandal shed an unflattering light on Conrad's skills as a military administrator, to say the least, for all appointments at this level were his responsibility. Redl was a flamboyant homosexual whose indiscreet and expensive liaisons made him an easy target for the blackmail specialists of Russian intelligence. How, one might ask, had this escaped the notice of Conrad, the man who had been responsible for monitoring Redl's progress since 1906? It was widely noted that Conrad took little interest in this aspect of his work and had only a sketchy acquaintance with many of the most senior military appointees. He compounded his error by having the disgraced colonel pressed to commit suicide with a pistol handed to him in a hotel room. Redl turned the pistol on himself, an ugly dénouement that offended the devoutly Catholic heir to the throne and – more to the point – deprived the General Staff of the opportunity to extract from Redl a full account of what had been passed to St Petersburg and how.

This may have been Conrad's precise intention, for it emerged that the persons involved in trafficking Austrian military secrets included a staff officer of South Slav heritage by the name of Čedomil Jandrić, who happened to be a close friend of Conrad's son, Kurt. Čedomil and Kurt had been classmates at the Military Academy and often went out drinking and merrymaking together. Evidence emerged to suggest that Jandrić, together with the Italian mistress of Hötzendorf junior (in this respect, at least, Kurt was a chip off the old block) and various other friends from their circle had been involved in selling military secrets to the Italians, most of which were then passed by the Italians to St Petersburg. Kurt von Hötzendorf may himself have been directly implicated in espionage activity for the Russians, if the claims of Colonel Mikhail Alekseevich Svechin, who was then military intelligence chief for the St Petersburg military district, are to be believed. Svechin later recalled that the Austrian agents supplying Russia with high-quality military intelligence included the chief of staff's son, who, it was claimed, had stolen into his father's study and removed General Staff war-planning documents for copying. The impact of these bizarre entanglements on Conrad can easily be imagined. The full extent of Kurt von Hötzendorf's culpability (if indeed he was himself an agent) was not revealed at the time, but at a high-ranking meeting chaired by Conrad in Vienna during May 1913, it was announced that the young man had been found guilty of withholding important information about his compromised associates. Having urged the meeting to mete out the severest possible penalty, Conrad became dizzy, surrendered the chair and was obliged briefly to leave the room.[150] For all his arrogance, the staff chief was profoundly demoralized by the Redl disaster, so much so that he was uncharacteristically quiet during the summer months of 1913.[151]

Franz Ferdinand was still the most formidable obstacle to a

war policy. The heir to the throne worked harder than anyone else to neutralize the impact of Conrad's counsels on the leading decision-makers. In early February 1913, barely six weeks after Conrad's recall to office, Franz Ferdinand reminded him during a meeting at Schönbrunn Palace that 'it [was] the duty of the government to preserve peace'. Conrad replied, with his usual candour: 'But certainly not at any price.'[152] Franz Ferdinand repeatedly warned Berchtold not to heed the arguments of the chief of the General Staff and sent his aide Colonel Carl Bardolff to Conrad with a stern instruction not to 'drive' the foreign minister 'to an action'. The archduke, Conrad was informed, would countenance 'under no circumstances a war with Russia'; he wanted 'not a single plum-tree, not a single sheep from Serbia, nothing was further from his mind'.[153] Relations between the two men grew increasingly fractious. In the autumn of 1913, the hostility between them broke into the open. Franz Ferdinand sharply reprimanded the chief of the General Staff before a gathering of senior officers for changing the dispositions of the manoeuvres without consulting him. Only the mediation of Franz Ferdinand's former staff chief Brosch von Aarenau prevented Conrad from resigning. It was only a matter of time before Conrad would be forced from office. 'Since the Redl case,' one of the archduke's aides recalled, 'the Chief was a dead man [. . .] it was just a question of setting a date for the funeral.'[154] After further angry exchanges at the Bosnian summer manoeuvres of 1914, Franz Ferdinand resolved to be rid of his troublesome chief of staff. Had the archduke survived his visit to Sarajevo, Conrad would have been dismissed from his post. The hawks would have lost their most resolute and consistent spokesman.

In the meanwhile, there were signs of improvement – on the surface at least – in diplomatic relations with Belgrade. The Austro-Hungarian government owned a 51 per cent share of the Oriental Railway Company, an international concern operating on an initially Turkish concession in Macedonia. Now that most of its track had passed under Serbian control, Vienna and Belgrade needed to agree on who owned the track, who should be responsible for the cost of repairing war damage and how and whether work on it should continue. Since Belgrade insisted on full Serbian ownership, negotiations began in spring 1914 to agree a price and conditions of transfer. The discussions were complex, difficult and occasionally rancorous, especially when arbitrary interventions by Pašić on minor points disrupted the flow of negotiations, but they received some positive coverage in the Austrian and Serbian press, and they were still underway when the archduke travelled to Sarajevo.[155] A further encouraging development was an agreement at the end of May 1914, after months of official wrangling, to exchange a small number of prisoners held by both states on charges of espionage. These were modest but hopeful indications that Austria-Hungary and Serbia might in time learn to live as good neighbours.

PART II

One Continent Divided

3

The Polarization of Europe, 1887–1907

If you compare a diagram of the alliances among the European great powers in 1887 with a similar map for the year 1907, you see the outlines of a transformation. The first diagram reveals a multi-polar system, in which a plurality of forces and interests balance each other in precarious equilibrium. Britain and France were rivals in Africa and South Asia; Britain confronted Russia in Persia and Central Asia. France was determined to reverse the verdict of the German victory of 1870. Conflicting interests in the Balkans gave rise to tensions between Russia and Austria-Hungary. Italy and Austria were rivals in the Adriatic and quarrelled intermittently over the status of Italophone communities within the Austro-Hungarian Empire, while there were tensions between Italy and France over the latter's policy in northern Africa. All these pressures were held in check by the patchwork of the 1887 system. The Triple Alliance between Germany, Austria and Italy (20 May 1882) prevented the tensions between Rome and Vienna from breaking into open conflict. The defensive Reinsurance Treaty between Germany and Russia (18 June 1887) contained articles deterring either power from seeking its fortunes in war with another continental state and insulated the Russo-German relationship against the fallout from Austro-Russian tensions.* The Russo-German link also ensured that France would be unable to build an anti-German coalition with Russia. And Britain was loosely tied into the continental system through the Mediterranean Agreement of 1887 with Italy and Austria – an exchange of notes rather

* Under the terms of the Reinsurance Treaty, both powers agreed to observe neutrality should either country be involved in a war with a third country; but they also agreed that neutrality would not apply if Germany attacked France or Russia attacked Austria-Hungary.

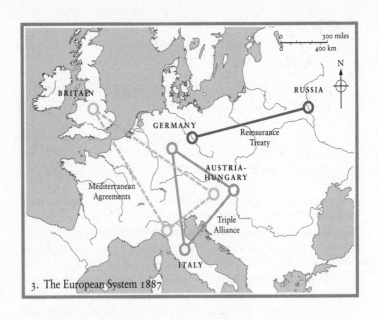

3. The European System 1887

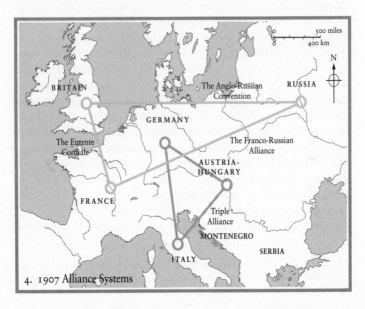

4. 1907 Alliance Systems

than a treaty – whose purpose was to thwart French challenges in the Mediterranean and Russian ones in the Balkans or the Turkish Straits.

Move forward twenty years to a diagram of the European alliances in 1907, and the picture has changed utterly. You see a bipolar Europe organized around two alliance systems. The Triple Alliance is still in place (though Italy's loyalty to it is increasingly questionable). France and Russia are conjoined in the Franco-Russian Alliance (drafted in 1892 and ratified in 1894), which stipulates that if any member of the Triple Alliance should mobilize, the two signatories will 'at the first news of this event and without any previous agreement being necessary' mobilize immediately the whole of their forces and deploy them 'with such speed that Germany shall be forced to fight simultaneously on the East and on the West'.[1] Britain is linked to the Franco-Russian Alliance through the Entente Cordiale with France (1904) and the Anglo-Russian Convention of 1907. It will be some years before these loose alignments tauten into the coalitions that will fight the First World War in Europe, but the profiles of two armed camps are already clearly visible.

The polarization of Europe's geopolitical system was a crucial precondition for the war that broke out in 1914. It is almost impossible to see how a crisis in Austro-Serbian relations, however grave, could have dragged the Europe of 1887 into a continental war. The bifurcation into two alliance blocs did not *cause* the war; indeed it did as much to mute as to escalate conflict in the pre-war years. Yet without the two blocs, the war could not have broken out in the way that it did. The bipolar system structured the environment in which the crucial decisions were made. To understand how that polarization came about, it is necessary to answer four interlinked questions. Why did Russia and France form an alliance against Germany in the 1890s? Why did Britain opt to throw in its lot with that alliance? What role did Germany play in bringing about its own encirclement by a hostile coalition? And to what extent can the structural transformation of the alliance system account for the events that brought war to Europe and the world in 1914?

DANGEROUS LIAISON: THE FRANCO-RUSSIAN ALLIANCE

The roots of the Franco-Russian Alliance lie in the situation created in Europe by the formation of the German Empire in 1870. For centuries, the German centre of Europe had been fragmented and weak; now it was united and strong. The war of 1870 placed the relationship between Germany and France on a permanently difficult footing. The sheer scale of the German victory over France – a victory most contemporaries had not predicted – traumatized the French elites, triggering a crisis that reached deep into French culture, while the annexation of Alsace-Lorraine – strongly advocated by the military and reluctantly accepted by German chancellor Otto von Bismarck – imposed a lasting burden on Franco-German relations.[2] Alsace-Lorraine became the holy grail of the French cult of *revanche*, providing the focus for successive waves of chauvinist agitation. The lost provinces were never the sole driving force behind French policy. Yet they periodically inflamed public opinion and exerted a stealthy pressure on the policy-makers in Paris. Even without the annexation, however, the very existence of the new German Empire would have transformed the relationship with France, whose security had traditionally been underwritten by the political fragmentation of German Europe.[3] After 1871, France was bound to seek every possible opportunity to contain the new and formidable power on its eastern border. A lasting enmity between France and Germany was thus to some extent programmed into the European international system.[4] It is hard to overstate the world-historical impact of this transformation. Relations among the European states would henceforth be driven by a new and unfamiliar dynamic.

Given the size and potential military capacity of the new German Empire, the chief objective of French policy had to be to contain Germany by forming an anti-German alliance. The most attractive candidate for such a partnership, despite its very different political system, was Russia. As J. B. Eustis, the former American ambassador to Paris, observed in 1897, France 'had one of two courses open, either to be self-reliant and independent, falling back upon her own resources to brave every peril [...], or to seek to make an alliance with Russia, the only power accessible to her'.[5] If this should happen, Germany would face the threat of a potentially hostile alliance on two separate fronts.[6]

Berlin could prevent this only by attaching Russia to an alliance system of its own. This was the rationale underpinning the Three Emperors' League signed by Germany with Austria and Russia in 1873. But any alliance system incorporating both Russia and Austria-Hungary was necessarily unstable, given the two powers' overlapping Balkan interests. Should it prove impossible to contain those tensions, Germany would be forced to choose between Austria-Hungary and Russia. If Germany chose Austria-Hungary, the barrier to a Franco-Russian partnership would fall away. The German chancellor Otto von Bismarck, chief architect of the empire and the principal author of its foreign policy until his departure from office in March 1890, was fully aware of the problem and fashioned his policy accordingly. His objective, as he declared in the summer of 1877, was to create 'an overall political situation in which all powers, except France, need us and are kept by virtue of their mutual relations as far as possible from forming coalitions against us'.[7] Bismarck adopted a double-edged policy that aimed, on the one hand, to avoid direct confrontations between Germany and other major powers and, on the other, to exploit the discord among the other powers whenever possible for Germany's advantage.

Bismarck pursued these objectives with considerable success. He reduced the risk of British alienation by staying out of the rush for colonial possessions in Africa and the Pacific. He maintained a posture of scrupulous disinterest in Balkan affairs, declaring in a famous speech to the Reichstag in December 1876 that the Balkan Question was not worth 'the healthy bones of one Pomeranian musketeer'.[8] When Russia's war on the Ottoman Empire in 1877–8 triggered a major international crisis, Bismarck used the Berlin Congress to persuade the powers that Germany was capable of acting as the disinterested guardian of continental peace. By mediating in the conflict over the post-war territorial settlement without seeking any direct reward for Germany, the chancellor aimed to demonstrate that European peace and German security were in effect one and the same thing.[9] In 1887, the heyday of the Bismarckian alliance system, Germany was tied by agreements of one kind or another to virtually every continental power. The Triple Alliance with Austria and Italy and the Reinsurance Treaty with Russia ensured that France remained frozen out and unable to found an anti-German coalition. The Mediterranean Agreement between Britain, Italy and Austria, settled through Bismarck's mediation, even linked Berlin indirectly (via the Triple Alliance) with London.

There were, however, limits to what Bismarckian diplomacy could achieve, especially in regard to Russia, whose Balkan commitments were difficult to accommodate within the fragile fabric of the Three Emperors' Alliance. The Bulgarian crisis of the mid-1880s is a case in point. In 1885, a Bulgarian irredentist movement seized control of neighbouring Ottoman-ruled Eastern Roumelia and announced the creation of a Greater Bulgaria.[10] The Russian government opposed the annexation because it brought the Bulgarians worryingly close to the Bosphorus and Constantinople, the strategic apple of Russia's eye. By contrast, the British government, irritated by recent Russian provocations in Central Asia, ordered its consuls to recognize the new Bulgarian regime. Then King Milan of Serbia stirred things up by invading Bulgaria in November 1885. The Serbs were thrown back, and Austria had to intervene to prevent the Bulgarians from occupying Belgrade. In the compromise peace that followed, the Russians succeeded in blocking outright recognition of Greater Bulgaria, but were obliged to accept a form of personal union between the northern and southern (Ottoman) parts of the country. Further Russian interventions, including the kidnapping, intimidation and forced abdication of the Bulgarian prince, failed to bring the Bulgarian government into obedience to St Petersburg. In the spring of 1887, it seemed entirely possible that the Russians might invade Bulgaria and impose a puppet government, a move that Austria-Hungary and Britain were bound to oppose. The Russians ultimately decided against the incalculable risks of a war for Bulgaria, but a wave of intense anti-German feeling surged through the Russian press and public, because the pan-Slav press now viewed Germany as the guardian of Austria's Balkan interests and the chief impediment to the exercise of Russia's custodianship over the Balkan Slavs.

There was a lesson in all of this for Berlin. The Balkan problem remained. The Bulgarian crisis highlighted for a moment the immense danger latent in the instabilities of that region, namely that the activities of an unimportant lesser state might one day inveigle two great powers into a course of action tending towards war. How could this challenge be met? Bismarck's answer, once again, was to seek good relations with

Russia and thereby mute conflicts of interest, keep St Petersburg away from Paris and exercise a moderating influence in the Balkans. The chancellor patched up relations with the Russian Empire by agreeing the Reinsurance Treaty of 1887 with the moderate and pro-German Russian foreign minister Nikolai Giers. Under the terms of this agreement, Berlin promised to support Russian objectives in the Turkish Straits and to remain neutral in the event of a war between Russia and a third power, except, of course, in the case of an unprovoked Russian attack upon Austria-Hungary, whereupon Germany would observe its treaty obligations under the Dual Alliance to aid the dual monarchy.

Not everyone in Berlin was persuaded of the wisdom of this course. Given the aggressive tone of the Russian press and the increasingly confrontational flavour of German–Russian relations, many were sceptical of the value of the Reinsurance Treaty. Even Bismarck's son, Herbert, secretary of state for the Foreign Office, doubted the value of the latest treaty with Russia. 'If the worst came to the worst', Bismarck Junior confided to his brother, the Reinsurance Treaty might 'keep the Russians off our necks for 6–8 weeks'.[11] Others, particularly within the military, succumbed to a mood of paranoia and began calling for a preventive war on the Russia Empire. An anti-Bismarck faction emerged within the senior echelons of the administration, driven by, among other things, a growing frustration with the baroque complexity and inner contradictions of the chancellor's diplomacy. Why, the critics asked, should the Germans undertake to protect Austria-Hungary against Russia and Russia against Austria-Hungary? No other power behaved like this; why should Germany always be hedging and balancing, why should it alone among the great powers be denied the right to an independent policy founded upon its own interest? In the eyes of the anti-Bismarck *fronde*, the chancellor's remarkable web of transcontinental commitments looked less like a system than a creaking Heath-Robinsonian contraption, a flimsy joist-work of 'plasters and patches' designed to avoid the pressing choices that confronted the German Empire in an increasingly dangerous world.[12] It was in response to this current of feeling that Bismarck's successor, Chancellor Leo von Caprivi, allowed the Reinsurance Treaty with Russia to lapse in the spring of 1890.

With the non-renewal of the Reinsurance Treaty between Germany and Russia, the door was open for a Franco-Russian rapprochement. But there were still many obstacles. The autocrat Alexander III was an unpalatable political partner for the republican French political elite – and the converse was equally true. It was also doubtful whether Russia would gain much from an alliance with France. After all, in a serious conflict with Germany, the Russians would probably in any case be able to count on French support; why should they sacrifice their freedom of action in order to secure it? Were war to break out between Russia and Germany, it was virtually inconceivable that the French government would simply stand aside. At the very least, the Germans would be obliged to maintain a substantial defensive force on the French frontier, a measure that would reduce the pressure on the Russian front – and these advantages could be had without the inconvenience of a formal treaty. Although France and Russia shared an interest in opposing the imperial designs of Britain, their spheres of influence on the imperial periphery were too far apart to permit close cooperation. The French were not in a good position to support Russian objectives in the Balkans, and it seemed doubtful that Russia would ever gain from supporting French objectives in, say, North Africa. On some questions, Russian and French interests were diametrically opposed: it was French policy, for example, to block Russian designs on the Turkish Straits that might ultimately compromise French influence in the Eastern Mediterranean – this was an area where common interests grouped France with Britain, rather than Russia.[13]

It was also difficult to see why the Russians should compromise their good relations with Germany. There were periodic tensions between the two empires, most importantly over the question of German tariffs on Russian grain imports, but little in the way of direct clashes of interest. Russia's arguments with Berlin arose for the most part from the Balkan rivalry with Vienna. And the very fact of German power seemed an argument for tethering the two neighbours together, especially in the sphere of Balkan policy, where it was hoped that a good understanding between St Petersburg and Berlin might have a restraining effect on Vienna. This was the formula that had intermittently worked in the era of the Three Emperors' Leagues. German neutrality was thus potentially more useful to Russia than French support. The Russians had long recognized this – this is why they had chosen to base their continental security policy on pacts with Germany in the first place. And this was why Tsar Alexander III, though he felt no personal sympathy for

Germany or the Germans, had turned a deaf ear to the raging of the press and pushed ahead with the Reinsurance Treaty in 1887.

Why, then, did the Russians welcome French overtures in the early 1890s? The Germans certainly facilitated the reorientation of Russian policy by declining to renew the treaty, despite the offer of improved terms from the pro-German Russian foreign minister, Nikolai Giers. The modest German army bill of June 1890, which increased the peace-time strength of the armed forces by 18,574 men, also played a part inasmuch as, coming on the heels of non-renewal, it generated a sense of threat in St Petersburg. The departure of Bismarck and the increasing political prominence of the excitable Kaiser Wilhelm II, whom Tsar Alexander described as a 'rascally young fop', raised unsettling questions about the future orientation of German foreign policy.[14] The prospect of large French loans on good terms was also attractive. But the crucial catalyst lay elsewhere, in Russian fears that Britain was about to join the Triple Alliance.

The early 1890s were the highpoint of pre-war Anglo-German rapprochement. The Heligoland–Zanzibar Treaty of 1 July 1890, by which the British and the Germans exchanged or ceded various African territories and Germany acquired the tiny North Sea island of Heligoland, triggered alarm in St Petersburg. Russian anxiety surged in the summer of 1891, when the renewal of the Triple Alliance and a visit by the German Kaiser to London prompted Germanophile effusions in the British press. Britain, trumpeted the *Morning Post*, had in effect 'joined the Triple, or rather the Quadruple Alliance'; England and Germany, the *Standard* observed on 11 July 1891, were 'friends and allies of ancient standing' and future threats to European peace would be met 'by the union of England's naval strength with the military strength of Germany'.[15] Press cuttings of this stripe fattened the dispatches of the French and Russian ambassadors in London. It seemed that England, Russia's rival in the Far East and Central Asia, was about to join forces with her powerful western neighbour and, by extension, with Austria, her rival on the Balkan peninsula. The result, as the French ambassador in St Petersburg warned, would be a 'continental rapprochement between the Cabinets of London and Berlin' with potentially disastrous consequences for Russia.[16]

The apparently deepening intimacy between Britain and Germany threatened to fuse Russia's Balkan predicament with the tensions generated by its bitter global rivalry with Britain – a rivalry that was played out in multiple theatres: Afghanistan, Persia, China, and the Turkish Straits. To balance against this perceived threat, the Russians put aside their reservations and openly pursued an arrangement with France. In a letter of 19 August 1891 to his ambassador in Paris, Giers, who had earlier pressed for renewal of the Reinsurance Treaty with Germany, set out the thinking behind the quest for an arrangement with France: it was the renewal of the Triple Alliance in combination with the 'more or less probable adhesion of Great Britain to the political aims that this alliance pursues', that had motivated Russia and France to seek 'an exchange of ideas to define the attitude [. . .] of our respective governments'.[17] The Definition of Understanding signed between the two states in the summer of 1891 duly incorporated Giers's reference to the threat posed by British accession to the Triple Alliance. A Franco-Russian military convention followed on 18 August 1892 and two years later the two countries signed the fully-fledged alliance of 1894.

Two points about this sequence of events deserve emphasis. The first is that the motives for forming this alliance were complex. While the desire to contain Germany was the key factor for Paris, the Russians were more concerned with blocking Austria-Hungary in the Balkans. But both powers were also deeply concerned at what they saw as a growing intimacy between Britain and the Triple Alliance. For the Russians in particular, whose foreign policy was at this time moderately Germanophile, it was the global confrontation with the British Empire that topped the agenda, not hostility to Berlin. There was, to be sure, a vein of vivid Germanophobia in parts of the Russian leadership – Nikolai Giers was horrified to be told by Tsar Alexander III that if a war were to break out between Russia and Austria, the aim of the Franco-Russian Alliance would be to 'destroy' Germany in its current form and replace it with 'a number of small weak states'.[18] But on the whole, Russian hostility to Germany was still primarily a function of Germany's relationship with Austria and of its supposedly deepening link with Britain. As late as 1900, supplementary military provisions were added to the Franco-Russian treaty, stipulating that if an Anglo-Russian war broke out, France would move 100,000 men to the Channel coast, while if an Anglo-French war broke out, Russia would move troops to the Indian frontier along railways that Russia promised to improve with the aid of French finance.[19]

Secondly, it is worth noting the novel quality of the Franco-Russian Alliance of 1894. By contrast with the earlier alliances of the European system, such as the Dual and Triple Alliances and the League of the Three Emperors, this one came into life as a military convention, whose terms stipulated the combined deployment of land forces against a common enemy (a naval convention was added in 1912).[20] The aim was no longer to 'manage adversarial relations' *between* alliance partners, but to meet and balance the threat from a competing coalition. In this sense, the Franco-Russian Alliance marked a 'turning-point in the prelude to the Great War'.[21]

The formation of the Franco-Russian Alliance did not in itself make a clash with Germany inevitable, or even likely. The alliance soon acquired an anchorage in the popular culture of both countries, through the festivities associated with royal and naval visits, through postcards, menus, cartoons and merchandising.[22] But the divergences in French and Russian interests remained an obstacle to close collaboration: throughout the 1890s, French foreign ministers took the view that since the Russians were unwilling to fight for the return of Alsace-Lorraine, the alliance with St Petersburg should impose only minimal obligations on France.[23] The Russians, for their part, had no intention of allowing the alliance to alienate them from Germany; on the contrary, they saw it as placing them in a better position to maintain good relations with Berlin. As Vladimir Lamzdorf, chief assistant to the Russian foreign minister, put it in 1895, the purpose of the alliance was to consolidate Russia's independence of action and to guarantee France's survival, while at the same time restraining her anti-German ambitions.[24] During the first decade of the alliance, Russian policy-makers – chief among them the Tsar – were preoccupied not with Central or south-eastern Europe, but with the economic and political penetration of northern China. More importantly, the shared suspicion of *Britain* that had helped to bring about the Franco-Russian Alliance also prevented it – for a time at least – from acquiring an exclusively anti-German orientation. Russia's interest in securing informal control over Manchuria brought St Petersburg into conflict with British China policy and ensured that relations with London would remain far more tense for the foreseeable future than those with Berlin.

THE JUDGEMENT OF PARIS

For France, too, there were difficult decisions to be made about how to balance the imperatives generated by rivalry with Britain with those arising from relations with Germany. During the first four years of the Franco-Russian Alliance, the French foreign minister Gabriel Hanotaux adopted a firmly anti-British policy. Egged on by the leader articles of the French colonialist press, Hanotaux mounted a direct challenge to the British presence in Egypt, a policy that culminated in the surreal 'Fashoda incident' of 1898, when a French expeditionary force made an epic journey across Africa to stake a claim to the Upper Nile, while British troops marched south from occupied Egypt to meet the French at Fashoda, a ruined Egyptian outpost in the Sudanese marshes. The resulting political crisis took both powers to the threshold of war in the summer of 1898. Only when the French backed down did the danger of a conflict pass.

French policy vis-à-vis Germany had to take account of the priorities imposed by this colonial struggle with Great Britain. In a confidential memorandum of June 1892, Hanotaux noted that current French policy permitted only very limited collaboration with Berlin. The problem with this approach was that it left open the possibility of an understanding between Germany and Britain – the very prospect that had helped to motivate the formation of the Franco-Russian Alliance. One way of avoiding Anglo-German collusion, Hanotaux speculated, might be to seek a broader Franco-German-Russian understanding. This in turn would enable Paris to secure German support against Britain in Egypt and thereby destroy 'the harmony that has existed for so long between Germany and England'. The resulting link with the eastern neighbour would, of course, be temporary and instrumental: a lasting conciliation with Germany would be possible, Hanotaux wrote, only if Berlin were willing to cede permanently the provinces annexed in 1870.[25]

The same choices faced Hanotaux's successor, Théophile Delcassé, who came to office in the summer of 1898. Like most politically active Frenchmen, Delcassé was profoundly suspicious of Germany and constantly revisited this issue in his political writings and utterances. His ardour for the lost provinces was so intense that the members of his

Théophile Delcassé

family dared not mention the names 'Alsace' and 'Lorraine' in his presence; 'we had the confused feeling that it was too sensitive to be spoken
of', his daughter later recalled.[26] But as an imperial power bent on
expanding its influence on multiple fronts, France faced other predicaments that could on occasion eclipse the confrontation with Germany.
In 1893, as colonial under-secretary, it was Delcassé who had pressed
for the deployment of French colonial forces to challenge Britain on the
Upper Nile.[27] When he came to office at the height of the Fashoda crisis,
his first step was to back down in the hope of securing concessions from
London in southern Sudan. But when London simply refused to budge,
Delcassé swung back to an anti-British stance and attempted (just as
Hanotaux had done) to challenge the British occupation of Egypt. His
ultimate goal was the French acquisition of Morocco.[28]

In order to heighten the pressure on Britain, Delcassé tried, exactly as
Hanotaux had foreseen, to bring the Germans into a consortium with
France and Russia. During the autumn, winter and spring of 1899–
1900, the political weather seemed auspicious for such an enterprise: in
conversations with the French ambassador in Berlin, the new German

chancellor Bernhard von Bülow hinted at shared Franco-German interests outside Europe. It was well known in Paris that the German press
(like the French) was hostile to Britain's war on the Boer Republic.
Reports of wrathful anti-British outbursts on that subject by the German Kaiser gave further cause for optimism. In January 1900, leader
articles inspired by Delcassé's press office urged Germany to join forces
with France on the Egyptian question, pointing out that Germany too
would benefit from the neutralization of the Suez Canal, and that the
combined naval forces of the continental powers would be sufficient to
ensure British respect for any international settlement. In the diplomatic
community, it was common knowledge that these articles hailed from
the office of Delcassé and expressed the official policy of the French
ministry of foreign affairs.[29]

While he waited for a German response, Delcassé prepared his colleagues in Paris, with characteristic impetuosity, for a war with Britain
that might well be global in scope. 'Some suggest a landing in England,'
he told the French cabinet on 28 February 1900, 'others an expedition
to Egypt; yet others advocate an attack on Burma by troops from Indo-
China which would coincide with a Russian march on India.'[30] It was
agreed that an enlarged meeting of the Conseil Supérieur de la Guerre
should be convened to consider the question of where exactly France
should mount an assault on the British Empire. Britain represented a
threat to world peace, Delcassé declared, and it was time, as he remarked
to a journalist in March 1900, to take a stand 'for the good of civilisation'.[31] The British, he claimed, were working on all fronts to alienate
Italy and Spain from France; they had their own beady eyes on Morocco
(in later years, Delcassé became preoccupied with *American* plans to
seize Morocco[32]). For a time, the visceral distrust usually directed at
Berlin was refocused on London.

These extraordinary deliberations came to nothing, because the Germans refused to play along with Delcassé's plan for a continental league
against Britain. From Berlin came the vexing proposal that the British
government should be consulted before any demands were addressed to
London. There was, it seemed, a gaping discrepancy between the Kaiser's anti-English verbal outbursts and the hesitant course of his foreign
policy: 'He *says* "I detest the English . . .",' Delcassé complained, 'but he
paralyses everything.'[33] The real deal-breaker was Berlin's demand for
something in return: on 15 March 1900, the French ambassador in

Berlin reported that the Germans would continue negotiations on the formation of an anti-British coalition only on the preliminary condition that France, Russia and Germany should undertake to 'guarantee the status quo as it affected their European possessions'. This was a coded request for the affirmation by France of German sovereignty in Alsace and Lorraine.[34]

The response from Berlin prompted a deep and lasting reorientation in Delcassé's thinking. From this moment, the French foreign minister abandoned any thought of Franco-German collaboration.[35] The project of a joint démarche on Egypt was unceremoniously dropped. Instead, Delcassé gravitated, via a series of intermediate positions, towards the notion that French objectives could be achieved in *collaboration* with Britain, by means of an imperial barter: the consolidation of British control over Egypt would be exchanged for British acquiescence in French control over Morocco. This arrangement had the advantage that it would prevent the dreaded (though in reality very unlikely) prospect of an Anglo-German joint initiative in Morocco.[36] By 1903, the French foreign minister had come to believe that a Morocco–Egypt exchange should serve as the foundation for an encompassing entente with Britain.

This reorientation had profound implications for Franco-German relations, for the decision to appease rather than to oppose Britain facilitated a more forceful articulation of the anti-German potential in French foreign policy. We can see this clearly in the changes in Delcassé's approach to the acquisition of Morocco. In an earlier incarnation of his programme, Delcassé had envisaged using an Egyptian challenge to pressure Britain into acquiescence on Morocco and buying off the other interested powers with concessions. Spain would receive lands in northern Morocco, Italy would be offered French support for Italian ambitions in Libya, and the Germans would be compensated with territories from French Central Africa. The new post-1900 Morocco policy was different in two important respects: it was to be accomplished, firstly, in concert with Britain. More importantly, Delcassé now planned to seize Morocco, a country whose independence had been guaranteed under an international treaty, without compensating or even consulting the German government. By adopting this provocative programme and holding to it over the protests of his French colleagues, Delcassé laid a diplomatic tripwire in North Africa that would be activated in the Moroccan crisis of 1905.

THE END OF BRITISH NEUTRALITY

In a speech to the House of Commons of 9 February 1871, only three weeks after the proclamation of the German Empire in the Hall of Mirrors at Versailles, the Conservative statesman Benjamin Disraeli reflected on the world-historical meaning of the Franco-Prussian War. It was, he told the members of the House, 'no common war', like the war between Prussia and Austria in 1866, or the French wars over Italy, or even the Crimean War. 'The war represents the German revolution, a greater political event than the French Revolution of last century.' There was not a single diplomatic tradition, he added, which had not been swept away. 'The balance of power has been entirely destroyed, and the country which suffers more and feels the effects of this change most, is England.'[37]

Disraeli's words have often been cited as a prescient vision of the coming conflict with Germany. But to read the speech this way – through the lens of 1914 and 1939 – is to misapprehend his intentions. What mattered most to the British statesman in the aftermath of the Franco-Prussian War was not the rise of Germany, but the untethering of Britain's old enemy Russia from the settlement imposed on her after the Crimean War (1853–6). Under the terms laid down by the governments of Britain and France in the Treaty of Paris of 1856, the waters of the Black Sea were 'formally and in perpetuity interdicted' to ships of war either of the powers possessing its coasts or of any other power.[38] The purpose of the treaty was to prevent Russia from threatening the Eastern Mediterranean or disrupting the British land and sea routes to India. But the political foundations of the 1856 treaty were destroyed by the defeat of France. The new French Republic broke with the Crimean settlement, renouncing its opposition to a Russian militarization of the Black Sea. Knowing that Great Britain alone could not enforce the Black Sea clauses, Russia now pressed ahead with the building of a Black Sea battlefleet. On 12 December 1870, news reached London that Russia had 'repudiated' the Peace of 1856 and was constructing a 'new Sebastopol' – an arsenal and a port for ships of war – in the town of Poti on the eastern coast of the Black Sea, only a few miles away from the Turkish frontier.[39]

It seemed that a new era of Russian expansionism was dawning, and it was this prospect that captured Disraeli's attention in the speech of

9 February 1871. For 200 years, Disraeli observed, Russia had pursued a policy of 'legitimate' expansion as it 'found its way to the coast'. But the militarization of the Black Sea appeared to herald a new and unsettling phase of Russian aggression, focused on the desire to acquire Constantinople and control of the Turkish Straits. Since Russia had 'no moral claim to Constantinople' and 'no political necessity to go there', Disraeli declared, this was 'not a legitimate, but a disturbing policy'. Russia was not the only threat on Disraeli's horizon – he was also concerned at the growing power and belligerence of the United States – but the important point is that when he spoke of the 'German revolution' he was not referring to the threat posed by the new Germany, but rather to the global and imperial consequences of the recent war between Germany and France, a war which had 'dislocated' the 'whole machinery of States'.[40]

Disraeli's speech announced a theme that would remain central to British foreign policy until 1914. During the years 1894–1905, it was Russia, not Germany, that posed 'the most significant long-term threat' to British interests.[41] The China Question that exercised British policy-makers in those years is a case in point.[42] In China, as in the Balkans, the underlying motor of change was the retreating power of an ancient empire. During the early 1890s, Russian penetration into northern China triggered a cascade of local and regional conflicts that culminated in the Sino-Japanese War of 1894–5.[43] Victorious Japan emerged as a rival with Russia for influence in northern China. China's defeat, in the meanwhile, inaugurated a race for concessions by the great powers hoping to exploit the further decay of the Chinese state. The negative energies generated by the race for China in turn heightened tensions in Europe.[44]

The core of the problem, from Britain's perspective, was the growth of Russian power and influence. In China, which in terms of its trade potential was infinitely more important to Britain than Africa, Russia posed a direct threat to British interests. The problem became even more acute after the international intervention to suppress the Boxer Rebellion (1898–1901), when the Russians capitalized on their role in the intervention to reinforce their position in northern China.[45] Yet, in view of the Russian Empire's geographical location and the preponderance of its land forces, it was hard to see how its penetration of East Asia could be resisted. A new Great Game was opening up that Russia seemed likely to win.[46] India was another vulnerable frontier: British policy-makers observed with alarm that the steady penetration of the Russian railway system into Central Asia meant that Russia enjoyed 'better military access' to the subcontinent than Britain itself.[47]

Since Russia appeared to be pursuing an anti-British policy in Central Asia and the Far East, and France was a rival and challenger of Britain in Africa, the Franco-Russian Alliance appeared from London's perspective to be a chiefly anti-British device. The problem was particularly pressing during the Boer War, when the deployment of substantial troop contingents in South Africa left northern India exposed. In August 1901, a report by the Intelligence Department of the War Office on the 'Military Needs of the Empire in a War with France and Russia' concluded that the Indian army was in no position to defend its key strongpoints against a Russian attack.[48] To make matters worse, Russian diplomats were not merely (in British eyes) hostile, expansionist and ruthless, but also prone to underhandedness and false dealing. 'The lying is unprecedented even in the annals of Russian diplomacy,' Lord George Hamilton, secretary of state for India, reported in March 1901, during negotiations towards a settlement in China. 'Russia's diplomacy, as you know, is one long and manifold lie,' George Curzon, Viceroy of India, told the Earl of Selborne, First Lord of the Admiralty, in 1903.[49]

British policy-makers responded to the Russian threat by pursuing a two-track policy. The first involved rapprochement with Japan and France, the second the quest for a power-sharing agreement with Russia itself that would take the pressure off Britain's imperial periphery. In the aftermath of the Sino-Japanese War of 1894–5, Britain and Japan shared a common interest in opposing further Russian expansion. Japan was Britain's 'natural ally' in the Far East, as Foreign Secretary Kimberley put it in a letter of May 1895 to the British minister in Tokyo.[50] The threat posed to Russia's Chinese frontier by Japan's formidable land forces – 200,000 Japanese troops had entered Manchuria by the end of 1895 – would offset the vulnerability of the British imperial periphery in northern India. The swiftly growing Japanese fleet would provide a further 'counterpoise to the Russians' and thereby relieve the strain on Britain's overstretched fleets.[51] In 1901, after a long period of cautious rapprochement, discussions began with a view to a formal alliance – first a naval defence pact, later the more encompassing agreement signed in London on 30 January 1902. Renewed (with expanded terms) in

1905 and in 1911, the Anglo-Japanese Alliance became a fixture in the international system of the pre-war world.

The same logic underlay the British decision to seek an understanding with France. Already in 1896, Lord Salisbury had found that concessions to France along the Mekong valley in the borderlands between British Burma and French Indochina produced the welcome side effect of drawing the French in and temporarily loosening the cohesion of the Franco-Russian Alliance.[52] The Entente Cordiale of 1904 was, by the same token, not primarily an anti-German agreement (at least not from Whitehall's perspective) but one that was intended to mute colonial tensions with France, while at the same time generating some measure of indirect leverage on Russia. Delcassé had encouraged this speculation by suggesting that if an Entente were to come into being, France would exercise a restraining influence on Russia and even make it clear to St Petersburg that French support would not be forthcoming if Russia were to pick a fight with Britain.[53] There was thus good reason to hope, as Lord Lansdowne put it, that 'a good understanding with France would not improbably be the precursor of a better understanding with Russia'.[54]

The last point is important. At the same time as they balanced against Russia with Japan, British policy-makers strove to meet the Russian challenge by tethering St Petersburg to an imperial power-sharing agreement. There was no contradiction in this. As Sir Thomas Sanderson, permanent under-secretary at the Foreign Office, observed in a letter to the British ambassador at St Petersburg in May 1902, the Japanese alliance was useful precisely because 'until [the Russians] see that we can take our pigs to other markets, we are not likely to bring them to book'; it would thus tend 'to promote rather than discourage [Britain's] chance of some definite understanding'.[55] British security reviews continued to envisage catastrophic scenarios in Central Asia: the Russians, the British cabinet was told in December 1901, were capable of pouring 200,000 troops into Transcaspia and the Herat. In order to prevail against such a force, the British garrison in India would have to be increased permanently by between 50,000 and 100,000 men, at huge cost to the government – this at a time when the best financial advice called for drastic cuts in expenditure.[56] And the 'frenzied pace' of Russian railway building to the Afghan frontier suggested that the situation was swiftly developing to Britain's disadvantage.[57]

These concerns were further amplified by the outbreak of war between Russia and Japan in February 1904. The fact that Russian forces at sea and on land performed rather poorly against their Japanese adversaries at first did nothing whatsoever to mute British anxieties. What if, as Viscount Kitchener warned, the Russians were tempted to offset their losses against Japan by threatening India? In this event, India would require massive reinforcements – by February 1905, the projected figure was 211,824 troops, according to government of India estimates.[58] The attendant rise in expenditure would be enormous – Kitchener estimated that countering 'the menacing advance of Russia' would cost '£20 million plus an annual charge of another £1.5 million'.[59] This was a matter of some consequence for the Liberal government that came to power in 1905 promising to cut military costs and expand domestic programmes. And if Britain could no longer afford to defend the north-western frontier of India by force, then it followed that a non-military means must be found of securing India against a Russian assault.

Japan's victory over Russia in 1905 clinched the argument in favour of an agreement. Given the magnitude of the Russian defeat and the wave of domestic turbulence that paralysed the country, the claim that the threat from Russia justified immense investment in Indian defence no longer seemed so compelling.[60] The new foreign secretary, Edward Grey, came to office in December 1905 determined to 'see Russia re-established in the councils of Europe, and I hope on better terms with us than she has been yet'.[61] In May 1906, Grey succeeded in having the option of Indian reinforcements placed on the back burner.

One aspect of this entangled tale of imperial readjustments deserves particular emphasis: neither the Entente Cordiale with France nor the Convention with Russia was conceived by British policy-makers primarily as an anti-German device. Inasmuch as Germany figured in British designs, it was mostly as a subordinate function of tensions with France and Russia. The German government excited resentment and anger above all whenever it appeared to make common cause with Russia and France against Britain – as in the spring of 1895, for example, when Germany joined its two great power neighbours in pressuring Tokyo to return to China territory conquered during the Sino-Japanese War, or in 1897, when the Germans unexpectedly seized a Chinese bridgehead at Kiaochow (Jiaozhou) on the Shantung peninsula – a move that London (rightly) believed had been secretly approved and encouraged by the Russians. In both cases, German actions were read against the background of perceived French and Russian designs against Britain. In the Chinese theatre, as elsewhere, Germany was a diplomatic irritant rather than an existential threat. 'Anglo-German antagonism' was not, in other words, the primary determinant of British policy; indeed, until around 1904–5, it was more often than not the function of other more pressing concerns.[62]

BELATED EMPIRE: GERMANY

The primary aim of German foreign policy in the Bismarck era was to prevent the emergence of a hostile coalition of great powers. For as long as it continued, the tension between the world empires made this objective relatively easy to accomplish. French rivalry with Britain intermittently distracted Paris from its hostility towards Germany; Russia's hostility to Britain deflected Russian attention from the Balkans and thus helped to stave off an Austro-Russian clash. As a mainly continental power, Germany, so long as it did not itself aspire to found a global empire, could stay out of the great struggles over Africa, Central Asia and China. And as long as Britain, France and Russia remained imperial rivals, Berlin would always be able to play the margins between them. This state of affairs enhanced the empire's security and created a certain wriggle room for the policy-makers in Berlin.

But the Bismarck strategy also exacted a cost. It required that Germany always punch under its weight, abstain from the imperial feeding frenzies in Africa, Asia and elsewhere and remain on the sidelines when other powers quarrelled over global power shares. It also required that Berlin enter into contradictory commitments to neighbouring powers. The consequence was a sense of national paralysis that played badly with the electors whose votes determined the composition of the German national parliament. The idea of colonial possessions – imagined as eldorados with cheap labour and raw materials and burgeoning native or settler populations to buy national exports – was as bewitching to the German middle classes as to those of the established European empires.

It should be noted that even modest German efforts to overleap the power-political constraints on imperial expansion met with sturdy resistance from the established world powers. In this connection, it is worth recalling an obvious but important difference between the belated German Empire and its world-imperial rivals. As the possessors of vast portions of the earth's inhabited surface with a military presence along extended imperial peripheries, Britain, France and Russia controlled tokens that could be exchanged and bargained over at relatively little cost to the metropolis. Britain could offer France concessions in the Mekong delta; Russia could offer Britain a demarcation of zones of influence in Persia; France could offer Italy access to coveted territories in northern Africa. Germany could not credibly make such offers, because it was always in the position of a parvenu with nothing to trade, pushing to gain a place at an already crowded table. Its attempts to secure a share of the meagre portions that remained usually met with firm resistance from the established club.

In 1884–5, for example, when the German government attempted to placate imperialist appetites by approving the acquisition of a modest suite of colonial possessions, it met with a dismissive response from Britain. In 1883, the Bremen merchant Heinrich Vogelsang had purchased land along the Angra Pequeña coast in today's southern Namibia. In the following year, Bismarck officially asked the British government whether it intended to lay claim to the area. From London came a terse reply stating that Britain was unwilling to allow any other country to establish itself anywhere in the region between Portuguese Angola and the British Cape Colony. Berlin responded with two probing questions: on what was the British claim based? And would the British authorities undertake to protect German settlers in the area?[63] Months passed before Whitehall deigned to send a reply. Bismarck was irritated by this condescending style, but he needn't have taken it personally – London adopted exactly the same brusque and haughty manner when dealing with the Americans over the Venezuelan boundary dispute in 1895–6.[64] Then, when the Germans went ahead regardless and announced their formal acquisition of the area, the British government promptly countered with a claim of its own. Temperatures in Berlin rose. It was intolerable, Bismarck fumed, that Britain should demand the privilege of an 'African Monroe Doctrine'.[65] The chancellor stepped up the political pressure. His son Herbert was sent to London to head negotiations. The British, distracted by more serious challenges (Russian designs on

Afghanistan, African tensions with France), eventually gave in and the crisis passed, but this was a salutary reminder of how little room remained at the table for the latest of Europe's great powers.

It was partly in order to escape from the self-imposed constraints of Bismarckian policy that Germany abandoned the Reinsurance Treaty with Russia in 1890. The changing of the guard in that year – the departure of Bismarck, the appointment of Leo von Caprivi to the chancellorship and the emergence of Kaiser Wilhelm II as a key player in imperial politics – inaugurated a new phase in German external relations. The 'new course' of the early 1890s was initially less a matter of concerted intention than of irresolution and drift. The vacuum created by Bismarck's sudden departure remained unfilled. The initiative passed to Friedrich von Holstein, chief of the foreign ministry's political department. Holstein's policy was to reinforce ties with Austria-Hungary while balancing possible Balkan risks through an agreement with London, though he did not favour a fully-fledged alliance with Britain. The idea at the core of his thinking was independence. A Germany allied to Britain risked becoming London's fall-guy on the continent – the memory of the Seven Years War, when Frederick of Prussia, as Britain's ally, had found himself encircled by a mighty continental coalition, was important here. It was crucial, as Holstein's close associate Bernhard von Bülow put it in March 1890, that Germany 'should not become dependent on any foreign power'.[66] The price for an agreement with Britain would be the renunciation by Germany of colonial acquisitions, but this was a price Caprivi was happy to pay.

The policy of the free hand looked innocuous enough, but it carried very considerable risks. In the summer of 1891, the Germans learned that their Italian ally was engaged in secret talks with France, in the hope of securing French support for future Italian acquisitions in northern Africa. At the same time, news reached Berlin of an official visit by a French flotilla to the Russian port of Kronstadt, where French officers were greeted with jubilation by the Russian press and public. The Franco-Russian Military Convention that followed in 1892 revealed that even the appearance of close collaboration with Britain carried the risk of heightening Germany's exposure on the continent without providing compensatory security benefits. And, most alarming of all, the deepening intimacy between France and Russia did not seem to pressure Britain into seeking closer relations with Germany; on the contrary, it prompted British policy-makers to begin considering the merits of appeasement, first of France and later of Russia. The fact that the French flotilla paid a symbolic visit to Portsmouth on its way home from Russia in 1891 also had a sobering effect on the mood in Berlin.[67]

Was Germany strong enough to make her way without the support of powerful allies? Caprivi's answer to this question was to expand the empire's defensive capacity. The passage of the army bill of 1893 brought the strength of the army to 552,000 – 150,000 more than a decade before – and military expenditure in that year reached double the 1886 figure. Yet these increases were not integrated with a larger political strategy; their purpose was to achieve deterrence.

The diplomatic implications of this quest for military self-reliance were a matter of contention among the key policy-makers in Berlin. Given the virtual impossibility of better relations with France, should Germany persist in seeking a deal with Britain, or did salvation lie in improved relations with Russia? The pursuit of both options produced frustrating results. The German policy-makers had high hopes of the Russo-German Trade Treaty concluded in the spring of 1894. Ratified by the Reichstag over the vehement protests of the German farming lobby, the treaty was a landmark in commercial relations that brought immense economic benefit to both countries. But it did nothing to loosen Russian attachment to the French alliance; on the contrary, the Russians viewed the treaty as a vindication of their policy and an indication of what could be achieved when the Germans were held in a diplomatically inferior position.[68]

The British option was no less difficult. The main reason for this is simply that Caprivi's policy of the 'free hand' freed London's hand much more than it did Berlin's. The conclusion of the Franco-Russian Alliance allowed Britain to oscillate between the continental camps and reduced the incentive to look for a firm understanding with Berlin. Only at times of crisis on the imperial periphery did London actively seek closer ties, but these did not and could not ever amount to the offer of a fully-fledged alliance on terms that Berlin could reasonably be expected to accept. In 1901, for example, with British forces tied down in South Africa and the Russians piling on the pressure in China, Foreign Secretary Lansdowne was so keen to secure German support against Russia that he circulated to cabinet a draft proposal for a secret treaty of alliance with Germany that would under certain conditions have committed

Britain and Germany to wage war on Russia in support of Japan. Tentative feelers were put out to Berlin, but the Germans were reluctant to be drawn into any kind of anti-Russian combination, for fear that this would leave them perilously exposed in a continental conflict in which the support of the British navy would carry little weight.[69] The question that worried Bülow was: what could the British offer the Germans that would offset the heightened French and Russian enmity that a German alliance with Britain would inevitably bring in its wake? This was the structural problem that always haunted efforts to formalize an Anglo-German rapprochement.

A further and more obvious problem was that Berlin's efforts to pursue German interests outside Europe inevitably met with protest from Britain. When the Turkish Sultan Abdul Hamid entrusted the Deutsche Bahn-Gesellschaft with the construction of a branch line of the Anatolian Railway to Konya, in the direction of Baghdad, there were loud complaints from the British government which saw in the German-financed project an 'unauthorised penetration into the English sphere', because it would diminish the profitability of the British-financed Smyrna Railway – in this, as in many other disputes, British policy-makers proceeded from the assumption that whereas British imperial interests were 'vital' and 'essential', German ones were a mere 'luxury', the energetic pursuit of which must be construed as a provocation by other powers.[70] The dispute over the Anglo-Congolese Treaty of 12 May 1894, by which Britain acquired a 25-kilometre-wide corridor of land linking Uganda with Rhodesia, was a further case in point. This treaty, essentially designed to obstruct French designs on the Upper Nile, also had the effect of abutting German South-east Africa with a cordon of British territory. Only under concerted German pressure did London eventually back down. This outcome produced jubilation in a German press desperate for signs of national self-assertion. It also reinforced the belief among German policy-makers that standing up to Britain was the only way to secure German interests.[71]

Anglo-German tension peaked during the Transvaal crisis of 1894–5. There had long been local problems between the British-controlled Cape Colony and the neighbouring Boer South African Republic, also known as the Transvaal. Although the independence of the Transvaal was internationally recognized (including by Britain), Cecil Rhodes, the dominant figure in the Cape Colony, pressed for annexation of the northern neighbour, lured by the vast gold deposits discovered there in the 1880s. Since German settlers played a prominent role in the Transvaal economy and Germans owned one-fifth of all foreign capital invested there, the Berlin government took an interest in maintaining the Republic's independence. In 1894, Berlin's involvement in plans to build a German-financed railway linking the landlocked Transvaal with Delagoa Bay in Portuguese Mozambique triggered protests from London. While the British government considered acquiring control of the offending railway through the annexation of Delagoa Bay and rejected any arrangement that would dilute their political and economic dominance in the region, the Germans insisted on the continuing political and economic independence of the Transvaal.[72] There was further friction in the autumn of 1895, when the British ambassador in Berlin, Sir Edward Malet, spoke of the Transvaal as a trouble spot in Anglo-German relations and hinted darkly at the possibility of war between the two countries if Germany refused to back down.

The German government were thus in an ill humour when an abortive British attack on the Transvaal in December 1895 triggered an international crisis. The British government had not formally sanctioned Dr Leander Starr Jameson's raid on the Republic, though at least one British government minister (Joseph Chamberlain) had prior knowledge of it. And the raid itself was a fiasco: Jameson's men were quickly defeated and captured by troops of the Transvaal Republic. In Berlin, as in Paris and St Petersburg, it was universally believed, despite official denials from Whitehall, that London was behind the attempted invasion. Determined to signal its indignation, the German government dispatched a personal telegram from the Kaiser to Paul Kruger, president of the Transvaal Republic. The 'Kruger telegram', as it came to be known, wished the president a happy new year, and congratulated him on having defended 'the independence of his country against external attack' without 'appealing for the help of friendly powers'.[73]

This mildly worded message produced a torrent of outrage in the British press and a corresponding wave of jubilation in Germany, where it was welcomed as a sign that something was finally being done to stand up for German interests overseas. But the Kruger telegram was little more than gesture politics. Germany quickly withdrew from the confrontation with Great Britain over southern Africa. It lacked the means to project its will, or even to secure the respect due to an equal partner in such conflicts of interest. Berlin ultimately accepted a compromise agreement, which in return for nugatory British concessions excluded Germany from further involvement in the political future of southern Africa.[74] To the disgust of the German nationalist press, the German government refused to intervene on behalf of the Transvaal before or during the Boer War of 1899–1902 that resulted in the Transvaal's defeat and its conversion into a British colony.

The 1890s were thus a period of deepening German isolation. A commitment from Britain remained elusive and the Franco-Russian Alliance seemed to narrow considerably the room for movement on the continent. Yet Germany's statesmen were extraordinarily slow to see the scale of the problem, mainly because they believed that the continuing tension between the world empires was in itself a guarantee that these would never combine against Germany. Far from countering their isolation through a policy of rapprochement, German policy-makers raised the quest for self-reliance to the status of a guiding principle.[75] The most consequential manifestation of this development was the decision to build a large navy.

In the mid-1890s, after a long period of stagnation and relative decline, naval construction and strategy came to occupy a central place in German security and foreign policy.[76] Public opinion played a role here – in Germany, as in Britain, big ships were the fetish of the quality press and its educated middle-class readers.[77] The immensely fashionable 'navalism' of the American writer Alfred Thayer Mahan also played a part. Mahan foretold in *The Influence of Sea Power upon History* (1890) a struggle for global power that would be decided by vast fleets of heavy battleships and cruisers. Kaiser Wilhelm II, who supported the naval programme, was a keen nautical hobbyist and an avid reader of Mahan; in the sketchbooks of the young Wilhelm we find many battleships – lovingly pencilled floating fortresses bristling with enormous guns. But the international dimension was also crucial: it was above all the sequence of peripheral clashes with Britain that triggered the decision to acquire a more formidable naval weapon. After the Transvaal episode, the Kaiser became obsessed with the need for ships, to the point where he began to see virtually every international crisis as a lesson in the primacy of naval power.[78]

The Kaiser's deepening personal preoccupation with naval matters coincided with a bitter factional struggle within the uppermost ranks of the German naval administration. The chief of the naval cabinet, Admiral Baron Gustav von Senden Bibran, and his ambitious protégé Alfred von Tirpitz pressed for the construction on a grand scale of large battleships. On the other side of the fight was the cautious Admiral Friedrich Hollmann, secretary of state for the navy and the man with responsibility for drafting naval bills for the Reichstag. Hollmann remained committed to the construction of a force of fast cruisers of the type favoured by the still-fashionable French *jeune école*. Whereas Tirpitz saw German naval strategy in terms of a future struggle for parity with Great Britain in waters close to home, Hollmann envisaged a more flexible, long-distance weapon that would be used to press German claims and protect German interests on the periphery. Between 1893 and 1896, Tirpitz and his allies waged a guerrilla campaign against Hollmann, openly questioning his competence and bombarding the Kaiser with memoranda outlining their own strategy proposals. After oscillating for a while between the two camps, Wilhelm II withdrew his support from Hollmann in 1897 and appointed Tirpitz in his place.[79] On 26 March 1898, following an intense propaganda campaign, the Reichstag passed a new navy bill. In place of the eclectic and unfocused proposals of the early and mid-1890s, Admiral von Tirpitz's Imperial Naval Office installed a massive long-term construction programme that would dominate German defence expenditure until 1912. Its ultimate objective was to enable Germany to confront the British navy on equal terms.[80]

Germany's decision to embark on an ambitious naval programme has occupied a commanding position in the literature on the origins of the First World War. Viewed with hindsight, it might appear to foreshadow, or even perhaps to explain, the conflict that broke out in 1914. Wasn't the decision to challenge British naval hegemony a needless provocation that permanently soured relations between the two states and deepened the polarization of the European system?

There are many criticisms one can make of German naval strategy, the most serious being that it was not embedded in a broader policy concept, beyond the quest for a free hand in world affairs. But the new naval programme was neither an outrageous nor an unwarranted move. The Germans had ample reason to believe that they would not be taken seriously unless they acquired a credible naval weapon. It should not be forgotten that the British were accustomed to using a rather masterful tone in their communications with the Germans. In March 1897, for example, a meeting took place between the assistant under-secretary at the British Foreign Office, Sir Francis Bertie, known as 'the Bull' for his aggressive manner, and the chargé d'affaires and acting German ambassador in London, Baron Hermann von Eckardstein. In the course of their discussion, Eckardstein, a notorious Anglophile who dressed in the manner of Edward VII and loved to be seen about the London clubs, touched on the question of German interests in southern Africa. Bertie's response came as a shock. Should the Germans lay so much as a finger on the Transvaal, Bertie declared, the British government would not stop at any step, 'even the ultimate' (an unmistakable reference to war), to 'repel any German intervention'. 'Should it come to a war with Germany,' he went on, 'the entire English nation would be behind it, and a blockade of Hamburg and Bremen and the annihilation of German commerce on the high seas would be child's play for the English fleet.'[81]

German naval policy has to be seen against this background of friction and threat. Of course, there can be no doubt about the anti-English orientation of the new weapon – Tirpitz himself made this abundantly clear: the memorandum setting out his fleet plan to the Kaiser in June 1897 began with the lapidary observation that: 'For Germany, the most dangerous naval enemy at the present time is England,' and the same assertion cropped up in various forms throughout the draft proposals and memoranda of later years.[82] But there was nothing surprising about this: armaments programmes usually measure themselves against the most formidable potential opponent; until the signing of the Entente Cordiale in 1904, the programmatic documents of the French naval strategists of the *jeune école* had envisioned the systematic use – in the event of war – of fast, well armed cruisers to attack commercial shipping and force the British Isles into starvation and submission. As late as 1898, this prospect had seemed real enough in British naval circles to generate panic over the need for extra cruisers and the consolidation of domestic food supplies.[83]

In any case, it was not the building of German ships after 1898 that propelled Britain into closer relations with France and Russia. The decisions to enter into an Entente with France and to seek an arrangement with Russia came about primarily as a consequence of pressures on the imperial periphery. British policy-makers were less obsessed with, and less alarmed by, German naval building than is often supposed.[84] British naval strategy was never focused solely on Germany, but on the need to remain dominant in a world of great naval powers – including France, Russia and the United States. Nor did German naval construction have the mesmerizing effect on British strategists that has sometimes been claimed for it.[85] In 1905, the director of British naval intelligence could confidently describe Britain's naval preponderance over Germany as 'overwhelming'.[86] In October 1906, Charles Hardinge, permanent under-secretary at the Foreign Office, acknowledged that Germany posed no immediate naval threat to Britain. In the following year, Admiral Sir A. K. Wilson remarked in a report on current Admiralty war plans that an Anglo-German conflict was unlikely, that neither power was in a position to do the other any 'vital injury' and that 'it was difficult to see how such a conflict could arise'. Foreign Secretary Edward Grey was also sanguine: 'We shall have seven dreadnoughts afloat before they have one,' he observed in November 1907. 'In 1910, they will have four to our seven, but between now and then there is plenty of time to lay down new ones if they do so.'[87] Even the First Sea Lord Sir John ('Jackie') Fisher wrote to King Edward VII in 1907 boasting of Britain's superiority over the Germans: 'England has 7 dreadnoughts and 3 invincibles, while Germany [has] not yet begun one!' There was good reason for such confidence, because the Germans lost the naval race hands down: whereas the number of German battle-ships rose from thirteen to sixteen in the years 1898–1905, the British battle fleet rose from twenty-nine to forty-four ships. Tirpitz had aimed at achieving a ratio of one German battleship to every 1.5 British, but he never got close. In 1913, the German naval command formally and unilaterally renounced the Anglo-German arms race, Tirpitz declaring that he was satisfied with the ratios demanded Britain. By 1914, Britain's lead was once again increasing. The naval scares that periodically swept through the British press and political circles were real enough, but they were driven in large part by campaigns launched by the navalists to fend off demands for funding from the cash-starved British army.[88]

There was thus a gross discrepancy between the rhetorical storm kicked up by Tirpitz and his colleagues to justify naval expenditure and the relatively meagre results achieved. German naval construction was intended to provide support for what had come to be known by 1900 as *Weltpolitik* – meaning literally 'global policy'. The term denoted a foreign policy focused on extending Germany's influence as a global power and thereby aligning it with the other big players on the world scene. 'Phenomenal masses of land will be partitioned in all corners of the world in the course of the next decades,' the historian and publicist Hans Delbrück warned in an important essay of 1897. 'And the nationality that remains empty-handed will be excluded for a generation to come from the ranks of those great peoples that define the contours of the human spirit.'[89] In a popular and influential speech of 6 December 1897, the secretary of state for foreign affairs, Bernhard von Bülow, articulated the ebullient new mood. 'The times when the German left the earth to one of his neighbours, the sea to the other, and reserved for himself the heavens where pure philosophy reigns – these times are over,' he announced. 'We don't want to put anyone in the shadow, but we too demand our place in the sun.'[90]

For a time, the word *Weltpolitik* seemed to capture the mood of the German middle classes and the national-minded quality press. The word resonated because it bundled together so many contemporary aspirations. *Weltpolitik* meant the quest to expand foreign export markets (at a time of declining export growth); it meant escaping from the constraints of the continental alliance system to operate on a broader world arena. It expressed the appetite for genuinely national projects that would help knit together the disparate regions of the German Empire and reflected the almost universal conviction that Germany, a late arrival at the imperial feast, would have to play catch-up if it wished to earn the respect of the other great powers. Yet, while it connoted all these things, *Weltpolitik* never acquired a stable or precise meaning.[91] Even Bernhard von Bülow, widely credited with establishing *Weltpolitik* as the guiding principle of German foreign policy, never produced a definitive account of what it was. His contradictory utterances on the subject suggest that it was little more than the old policy of the 'free hand' with a larger navy and more menacing mood music. 'We are supposed to be pursuing *Weltpolitk*,' the former chief of the General Staff General Alfred von Waldersee noted grumpily in his diary in January 1900. 'If only I knew what that was supposed to be.'[92]

The concrete achievements of *Weltpolitik* after 1897 were correspondingly modest, especially if we measure them against the imperial predations of the United States in the same years: while Germany secured the Mariana and Caroline islands, a segment of Samoa and the small bridgehead at Kiaochow on the Chinese coast, the United States waged war against Spain over Cuba and in the process acquired the Philippines, Puerto Rico and Guam in 1898, formalized its possession of Hawaii in the same year, fought a horrific colonial war in the Philippines (1899–1902) that cost between half a million and 750,000 Filipino lives; acquired some of the Samoan islands in 1899 and subsequently built a canal across the Central American Isthmus under the protection of a Canal Zone under its own control, in accordance with its secretary of state's express view that it was 'practically sovereign' on the continent of South America.[93] When Bülow wrote to Kaiser Wilhelm II in exultant tones that 'this gain will stimulate people and navy to follow Your Majesty further along the path which leads to world power, greatness and eternal glory', he was referring to Germany's acquisition of the economically and strategically worthless Caroline Islands![94] Small wonder that some historians have concluded that Germany's *Weltpolitik* was designed above all with domestic consumers in mind: as a means of strengthening national solidarity, saddling the national parliament with long-term budgetary commitments, muting the appeal of dissident political creeds such as social democracy and thereby consolidating the dominance of the existing industrial and political elites.[95]

Perhaps the most remarkable shortcoming of German policy in the years around 1900 was the failure to see how swiftly the international environment was changing to Germany's disadvantage. The policymakers in Berlin remained confident in the first years of the twentieth century that the global tension between the British Empire and Russia would continue to guarantee a certain freedom of manoeuvre for Germany. In the short term, they focused on maintaining good relations with St Petersburg. In the longer run, they believed, the burden of opposing Russia and the growth of the German fleet would force Britain to seek better relations with Berlin.

THE GREAT TURNING POINT?

On the night of 8–9 February 1904, Admiral Togo Heiachiro's fleet attacked and sank Russian battleships at anchor off Port Arthur on the Chinese coast, thereby starting the Russo-Japanese War. The Japanese began the conflict, but it was the Russians who had provoked it. For the past decade, the Tsar and his most powerful advisers had been mesmerized by the prospect of acquiring a vast East Asian empire. The Russians had steadily pushed forward into northern China, the Liao-dong peninsula and northern Korea, encroaching on the Japanese sphere of interest. They used the Boxer Rebellion of 1898–1901 (itself in part the consequence of Russian incursions into China) as a pretext for sending 177,000 troops to Manchuria, supposedly to protect its railways. After the rebellion subsided, Russia ignored demands from the other powers for the withdrawal of its troops. By early 1903, it was clear that they intended to occupy Manchuria indefinitely. Repeated requests from the Japanese for a formal demarcation of Russian and Japanese spheres of influence in Manchuria and Korea respectively received short shrift in St Petersburg.

Strengthened by their alliance of 1902 with Britain, the Japanese felt confident enough to take matters into their own hands. The war that followed brought defeat for Russia on a scale that no one had foreseen. Two of the three Russian fleets were destroyed (the third, the Black Sea Fleet, was saved, ironically enough, by the restrictions still preventing Russian warships from passing the Turkish Straits). Russian forces were overrun and defeated in Manchuria in 1904, the Japanese besieged Port Arthur, and the army sent to relieve it was forced to retreat from the area. In January 1905, after a long and bitter fight, Port Arthur surrendered. Two months later, a Japanese army numbering 270,000 men routed a slightly larger Russian force near Mukden in Manchuria. While these disasters were unfolding, a wave of inter-ethnic violence, massive strikes, political protests and uprisings swept across the Russian Empire, exposing the inner fragility of the Tsarist autocracy; at one point, an army of nearly 300,000 – larger than the force facing the Japanese in Manchuria – had to be stationed in Poland to restore order.

The impact of the Russo-Japanese conflict was both profound and ambivalent. In the short term, the war seemed to offer Germany unexpected opportunities to break through the constraints imposed by the Franco-Russian Alliance and the Anglo-French Entente. In the longer term, however, it had precisely the opposite effect: it produced a tightening of the alliance system that refocused formerly peripheral tensions on to the continent of Europe and drastically reduced Germany's freedom of movement. Since both these aspects bear on the events of 1914, it is worth looking briefly at each in turn.

By the summer of 1904, Germany's diplomatic position was

substantially worse than it had been when Bismarck left office in 1890. German political leaders made light of these developments, mainly because they believed that tensions between Britain and the continental powers would keep the door to a German-British rapprochement permanently open. Against this background, the news of the Anglo-French Entente came as a serious blow. In a letter to Bülow of April 1904, Kaiser Wilhelm informed the chancellor that the Entente gave him 'much food for thought', because the fact that England and France no longer had to fear anything from each other meant that their 'need to take account of our position becomes ever less pressing'.[96]

How could Germany extricate itself from this unhappy state of affairs? Two options presented themselves. The first was to commit the Reich to an arrangement with Russia and thereby weaken or neutralize the Franco-Russian Alliance. The second was to find some means of weakening the new entente between Britain and France. The Russo-Japanese War provided the opportunity to test both options. The German Kaiser had been calling for some time – without success – for a diplomatic approach to the Russians and he quickly spotted the advantages to be reaped from Russia's predicament. In a letter of February 1904 to the Tsar, he pointed out that the French were supplying the Japanese with raw materials and thus hardly behaving as reliable allies.[97] In June he told Nicholas that he believed France's entente with Britain, an ally of Japan, was 'preventing the French from coming to your aid!' Other letters made sympathetic noises about the ill fortune of the Russian army and expressed confidence in future successes.[98] The Germans also provided more practical help, such as the coaling of Russian battleships from German stations en route to the East. These overtures culminated in two formal offers of alliance. The first, presented on 30 October 1904, proposed an alliance stipulating that each of the two signatories would come to the other's aid in the event of either being attacked in Europe or anywhere else in the world. But Tsar Nicholas was unwilling to enter into a formal agreement before consulting his French ally. Since it was inconceivable that the French would agree, this was tantamount to rejecting the proposal.

By the summer of 1905, however, Russia's domestic and military position had worsened drastically. When the Kaiser renewed his approaches to Nicholas, he found the Tsar more inclined to consider a German offer. In the summer of 1905, the royal yacht *Hohenzollern* made its way towards the small fishing village of Björkö in the Gulf of Finland for a rendezvous with the Tsar's *Polar Star*. The two boats moored alongside each other on 23 July and the Tsar came aboard for dinner. Confidential discussions followed, during which Wilhelm played – with considerable success – on the Tsar's anxieties about British designs against Russia and the unreliability of the French, who had now thrown in their lot with Britain. The overwrought Nicholas burst into tears, embraced his German cousin and signed on the dotted line. But the draft treaty that resulted did not survive the scrutiny of the Tsar's officials in St Petersburg. It was impossible, they pointed out, to reconcile a commitment to Berlin with the French alliance that still constituted the bedrock of Russian security. Reports from Paris confirmed that the French would never tolerate any alteration of the terms of the alliance for the sake of Russo-German rapprochement. The Tsar remained favourably disposed to an agreement of some kind with Germany, but under pressure from his political and economic advisers he gradually dropped the idea. The eastern road out of German isolation was thus closed off, at least for the foreseeable future.

At the same time, the German leadership looked for ways of pushing open the door that had recently been shut by the Anglo-French Entente. As part of the comprehensive settlement of outstanding colonial disputes negotiated through the Entente Cordiale, the British had agreed to recognize Morocco as standing within the French sphere of influence, in return for French recognition of British primacy in Egypt. Determined to capitalize on this arrangement while the British commitment was still fresh, the French government sent a diplomatic mission to Fez with a view to arranging the consolidation of French control in Morocco in January 1905.

Given the terms of the Anglo-French agreement, there was nothing especially surprising in the bid to consolidate French power in Morocco. But the French foreign minister chose to endow the policy with a pointedly anti-German spin. Potential disagreements with Spain had been resolved through the exchange of territory, and the North African agreement of 1902 with Italy ensured that Rome would be acquiescent. British agreement was built into the terms of the Entente. But the Germans were offered nothing. Berlin was not even informed in advance of French intentions. This was a departure from Delcassé's own earlier policy, which had foreseen that German assent would be negotiated in return for territorial compensation 'in other parts of Africa where she may have ambitions'.[99] In opting to freeze the Germans out, Delcassé built an entirely unnecessary element of provocation into his North African policy and exposed himself to the criticism of his French colleagues: even Paul Revoil, Delcassé's closest collaborator in the Moroccan question, lamented the minister's intransigence; the 'great misfortune', Revoil protested, was that Delcassé found it 'repugnant to have talks with Germany. "The Germans are swindlers", he says. But, in heaven's name, I'm not asking for an exchange of romantic words or lovers' rings but for a business discussion!'[100] Even Eugène Étienne, leader of the French Colonial Party, viewed Delcassé's refusal to negotiate with the Germans over Morocco as 'the height of imprudence'.[101]

The German Foreign Office, for its part, had long been watching French moves in Morocco with suspicion and was determined not to allow the French government to act unilaterally in a manner that would damage German interests in the area. The German viewpoint was legitimate in legal terms: an international agreement of 1881 had formally recognized Morocco as an area whose status could only be altered multilaterally, by international treaty. The ultimate objective of German policy, however, was not to uphold international law, but rather to test the strength of the Entente. Reports from London had given the Germans reason to suppose that the British government would not feel bound to intervene in a dispute over Morocco between France and a third power.[102] It was hoped that this in turn would remind the French – in the Kaiser's quaint formulation – that 'a navy has no wheels', and thereby soften their opposition to an understanding of some kind with Germany.[103] In this sense, the Moroccan initiative can be seen as a western version of the approaches made to Russia during 1904–5.

Early in January 1905 a French delegation travelled to Fez in the Moroccan interior to demand control over the Moroccan army and police; the Sultan refused. On 31 March 1905, Kaiser Wilhelm II made a surprise visit to the city of Tangier. Amid delirious cheers from the population of the city, who saw in the German sovereign a welcome counterweight to the French, Wilhelm rode to the German legation, gave the cold shoulder to the third secretary of the French legation, who had welcomed him to Morocco 'in the name of M. Delcassé', and made a speech in which he asserted that German commercial and economic interests, together with the independence and integrity of Morocco, should be maintained.[104] After scarcely two hours in the city, he returned to his ship and sailed off.

In the short term, this spectacular exercise in gesture politics was a great success. The landing prompted outrage in France, but the British showed no interest in intervening and after a phase of mutual threats and brinkmanship, the French government opted to pursue a peaceful resolution. Théophile Delcassé was dismissed and his policy of provocation temporarily discredited; his responsibilities were assumed by the new and inexperienced French premier Maurice Rouvier, who proposed bilateral negotiations over the future of Morocco. But the Germans, unwisely in retrospect, tried to press their advantage, turning down Rouvier's proposal and insisting instead that the dispute be resolved at an international conference, as required under the terms of the treaty of 1881. The request was eventually granted, but the German triumph was shortlived. At the conference that convened in the Spanish port town of Algeciras in January 1906, the quasi-independence of Morocco was confirmed in general terms, but the German negotiators failed to gain any support from the other great powers (except for the Austrians) for their further proposals regarding the internationalization of the Moroccan police and financial institutions. Britain, Italy and Spain, who had all been bought off through compensation deals and Russia, which had been promised a further French loan in return for its support, sided firmly with France. The Russian delegates travelled to Algeciras with instructions to support 'energetically' every French proposal.[105] The uselessness of the Triple Alliance was revealed for all to see. It was, it turned out, a gross error to seek the multilateral resolution of an issue that had already been resolved by France bilaterally with most of the interested powers. The German policy-makers had bungled. On 5 April 1906, Chancellor Bernhard von Bülow, chief architect of the German policy on Morocco, turned white and collapsed in the Reichstag shortly after making a speech on the outcome of Algeciras. He was to remain in convalescence until October.[106]

The efforts of the German government to probe eastern and western options as a means of overcoming German isolation were thus a resounding failure. The Anglo-French Entente was strengthened rather than weakened by the German challenge to France in Morocco.[107] In the east too, the opportunities created for Germany by the Russo-Japanese War turned out to be illusory. The eastern option was shut off for the foreseeable future in the summer of 1907, when Britain and Russia signed a treaty resolving all their disputes over Persia, Afghanistan and Tibet.

The Convention of 1907 was not driven by hostility towards, or fear of, Germany. It was rather the other way around: since Russia posed the greater threat to Britain across a greater range of vulnerable points, it was Russia that must be appeased and Germany that must be opposed. This had been the dominant British thinking on a rapprochement with Russia since before the turn of the century and it remained valid after the Convention was signed. In March 1909, Sir Charles Hardinge put the matter succinctly. 'We have no pending questions with Germany except that of naval construction,' he told Sir Arthur Nicolson, who would soon succeed him, 'while our whole future in Asia is bound up with maintaining the best and most friendly relations with Russia. We cannot afford to sacrifice in any way our entente with Russia, even for the sake of a reduced naval programme.'[108] The same point can be made for the Russian decision-makers who agreed the Convention: this was not, for them, a policy directed against Germany, but rather a retrenching move designed to secure breathing space for domestic consolidation or (depending on whom you asked) greater freedom of external action. Of particular interest was the link between a deal over Persia and the prospect of British support for improved Russian access to the Turkish Straits. For Izvolsky and his ambassador in London, Count Benckendorff, the Straits question was 'the core of the Convention' and the key to securing favourable revision of Russian access rights at a 'suitable time' in the near future.[109]

In other words: while the new international system that emerged from 1907 chiefly disadvantaged Germany, we should not assume that this outcome faithfully reflected the designs that brought it about. Only in the case of France can one speak of a policy that consistently assigned a high priority to containing Germany. It makes more sense to think of this array of agreements as the European consequence of world-historical transitions – the Sino-Japanese War and the emergence of Japan as a regional power, the fiscal burdens imposed by African conflicts and the Great Game in Central Asia, the retreat of Ottoman power in Africa and south-western Europe, and the rise of the China Question, meaning not just the great-power competition there but also the high levels of Chinese domestic turbulence that resulted. Germany's 'restlessness' and its parvenu importuning were part of the picture, but they were perceived within a field of vision that encompassed broader concerns. The once widely held view that Germany caused its own isolation through its egregious international behaviour is not borne out by a broader analysis of the processes by which the realignments of this era were brought about.[110]

In fact the causal relationship between antagonism to Germany and the new alliance system ran to some extent in the other direction: it was not that antagonism to Germany caused its isolation, but rather that the new system itself channelled and intensified hostility towards the German Empire. In Russia's case, for example, the victory of Japan in the East and the provisional settlement of the imperial quarrel with Britain in Central Asia inevitably refocused foreign policy on the sole remaining theatre in which it could still pursue an imperial vision – the Balkans, an area where conflict with Austria-Hungary and, by extension, Germany was going to be difficult to avoid. The old factional divide within the Russian foreign policy community between 'Asianists' and 'Europeanists' was resolved in the latter's favour. Under Izvolsky and Sazonov, Europeanists, who tended to distrust Germany and to favour good relations with Britain and France, always occupied a majority of the key positions.[111] The Anglo-French Entente likewise neutralized the anti-British sentiment that before 1904 had intermittently diluted the Germanophobia of French statesmen.

PAINTING THE DEVIL ON THE WALL

Particularly striking is the case of Britain. It is astonishing how aggressively a number of key British policy-makers responded to the German challenge to French penetration of Morocco. On 22 April 1905, Foreign Secretary Lord Lansdowne informed the English ambassador in Paris that he believed the Germans might seek a port on the West African coast in compensation for the French seizure of Morocco and that England was prepared to join with France 'in offering strong opposition to this proposal'.[112] The British ambassador in Paris was none other than Sir Francis 'the Bull' Bertie, Viscount of Thame, the former parliamentary under-secretary who had browbeaten the German chargé d'affaires Eckardstein with threats of war over the Transvaal. In passing Lansdowne's message of support to Delcassé, who had heard nothing of

German designs on a Moorish port, Bertie used much firmer language, conveying the sense of a categorical and unconditional support for French measures: 'The Government of His Britannic Majesty,' the French Foreign Office was told, 'considers that the conduct of Germany in the Moroccan question is most unreasonable in view of the attitude of M. Delcassé, and it desires to accord to His Excellency all the support in its power.'[113] In a private conversation with Delcassé, Bertie stiffened the foreign minister's back with belligerent talk; a day or so later the foreign minister informed a close associate that France's position was now impregnable, using language that recalled Bertie's earlier threats to Eckardstein:

> [Germany] knows that she would have England against her. I repeat that England would back us to the hilt and not sign peace without us. Do you think that the Emperor Wilhelm can calmly envisage the prospect of seeing his battle fleet destroyed, his naval commerce ruined and his ports bombarded by the English fleet?[114]

There were militant signals from other parts of the British decision-making establishment as well. General Grierson, director of military operations, accompanied by his deputy, made a personal inspection tour of the Franco-Belgian borderlands in March 1905 in order to appraise conditions for the landing of a British expeditionary force. In April, the First Sea Lord, Sir John 'Jackie' Fisher, who had been 'longing to have a go' at the Germans since the beginning of the crisis, went so far as to propose that the British navy deploy to the Kiel Canal and land an expeditionary force on the coast of Schleswig-Holstein.[115] These strikingly belligerent responses had nothing to do with the rights or wrongs of the position adopted by Germany vis-à-vis the French penetration of Morocco; they resulted from the apprehension that Germany was testing the strength of the new Entente, which was founded, after all, on an agreement to exchange British dominance in Egypt for French dominance in Morocco.

The accession of Sir Edward Grey to the office of foreign secretary in December 1905 consolidated the influence of an emergent anti-German faction within the British Foreign Office. Grey's associates and subordinates supplied him with a steady stream of memos and minutes warning of the threat posed by Berlin.[116] Dissenting voices within the Foreign Office were marginalized. Dispatches from British envoys in Germany that went against the grain of the dominant view, like those filed by Lascelles, De Salis and Goschen in Berlin, were plastered with sceptical marginalia when they reached London. By contrast, the reports of Sir Fairfax Cartwright in Munich and later Vienna, which never failed to put the maximum negative spin on contemporary developments in Germany and Austria, were welcomed with accolades: 'An excellent and valuable report in all respects', 'Most interesting and well worth reading', 'An interesting and suggestive despatch', 'A most able despatch', 'Mr Cartwright is a shrewd observer', 'a thoughtful review of the situation', and so on.[117]

In the 'official mind' of British foreign policy, the history of Anglo-German relations was reconceived as a black record of German provocations. The Foreign Office junior clerk G. S. Spicer came to believe that Germany had been pursuing 'a line consistently unfriendly to the interests of Great Britain' since the days of Bismarck.[118] Looking back in later years, Grey was inclined to view the two decades between 1884 and his instalment in office as an era of fundamentally misguided concessions to an implacable foe.[119] 'Vague and undefined schemes of Teutonic expansion' were imputed to the German leadership.[120] The Germans were accused of seeking to establish a dictatorship over the continent, of 'deliberately aiming at world predominance', of wanting, as Bertie put it in the practical language of an Eton boy, to 'push us into the water and steal our clothes'.[121] In November 1909, Sir Charles Hardinge described Germany as 'the only aggressive Power in Europe'.[122] Repeated, mantra-like, at every possible opportunity in dispatches, letters and departmental minutes, such assertions merged to form a new virtual reality, a way of making sense of the world.

Why did these people become so hostile to Germany? Did the Germans behave 'worse' than the other powers, bullying and pushing in situations where other powers found a more emollient and biddable modus operandi? It is difficult, of course, in an environment where subjective impressions counted for so much and the norms of acceptable behaviour were so variable, to determine exactly how 'provocative' specific styles and initiatives were. Was the Kruger telegram more provocative than the baldly worded Grover Cleveland message, sent by Washington at around the same time to discourage British incursions into Venezuela? Was the seizure of Kiaochow more provocative than the American acquisition of the Canal Zone or the creation of a Russian protectorate over Mongolia? Was Germany's blundering pursuit of a diplomatic triumph at Agadir more provocative than the unilateral measures by which France broke with the Franco-German Morocco Agreement in 1911 (see chapter 4)? Perhaps these are the wrong questions to ask. The Germanophobes were rarely very specific about their case against the Germans. They spoke in general terms of the vaunting ambition and bullying 'demeanour' of Germany, the unpredictability of the Kaiser and the threat German military prowess posed to the European balance of power, but they were coy about identifying actual German offences against good international practice.

The fullest account of British grievances can be found in a famous Memorandum on the Present State of British Relations with France and Germany composed by Eyre Crowe, then senior clerk in the Western Department at the Foreign Office, in January 1907. Crowe was one of the most extraordinary figures in the British foreign-policy world. His father had worked for the British consular service, but his mother and his wife were both German, and Crowe himself, born in Leipzig, was seventeen and not yet fluent in English when he first visited England to cram for the Foreign Office entrance exam. Throughout his life, he spoke English with what contemporaries described as a 'guttural' accent – one subordinate recalled being dressed down with the words 'what you have wr-r-ritten on this r-r-report is utter r-r-rot'. The perception that Crowe, though admirably efficient and industrious in his handling of departmental business, remained irredeemably Germanic in style and attitude ensured that he never ascended as far through the ranks of the service as his talent warranted. Despite or perhaps in part because of these personal attributes, Crowe became one of Whitehall's most implacable opponents of a rapprochement with Germany.

The memorandum of 1 January 1907 opened with a brief overview of the recent Moroccan crisis. Crowe endowed the narrative with the contours of a Boy's Own morality tale. The German bully had threatened France in the hope of 'nipping in the bud' her 'young friendship' with Britain. But the bully had underestimated the pluck and loyalty of France's British pal; he 'miscalculated the strength of British feeling and the character of His Majesty's ministers'. Like most bullies, this one was a coward, and the prospect of an 'Anglo-French coalition in arms' was enough to see him off. But before he retreated, the bully further disgraced himself by crudely currying favour with the British friend, 'painting in attractive colours a policy of cooperation with Germany'. How ought Britain to respond to this unlovely posturing? As the pre-eminent world power, Crowe argued, Britain was bound by what amounted to a 'law of nature' to resist any state that aspired to establish a coalition opposed to British hegemony. Yet this was exactly what German policy intended to do. Germany's ultimate objective was 'German hegemony, at first in Europe and eventually in the world'. But whereas British hegemony was welcomed and enjoyed by all and envied and feared by none on account of its political liberality and the freedom of its commerce, the vociferations of the Kaiser and the pan-German press showed that German hegemony would amount to a 'political dictator-ship' that would be 'the wreckage of the liberties of Europe'.

Of course Crowe could not and did not object in principle to the growth in German power and influence. The problem lay in the abrasive and provocative way in which Germany pursued its objectives. But of what exactly did Germany's provocations consist? They included such enormities as 'dubious proceedings' in Zanzibar, and the seizure of the Cameroons at a time when London had already announced its intention to grant the inhabitants of that country a British protectorate. Every-where they looked – or so it seemed to Crowe – the British found themselves stumbling over the Germans. The list of outrages continued, from German financial support for the Transvaal Republic, to com-plaints at London's conduct of the South African war, to vexatious meddling in the Yangtze Valley region, 'then considered to be practically a British preserve'. And to make matters worse, there was the 'some-what unsavoury business' of German efforts to influence the international press, from New York, to St Petersburg, Vienna, Madrid, Lisbon, Rome, Cairo and even London, 'where the German Embassy entertains confi-dential and largely unsuspected relations with a number of respectable and widely read papers'.[123]

There is much one could say about this fascinating document, which Grey circulated as recommended reading to Prime Minister Sir Henry Campbell-Bannerman and other senior ministers. First there is Crowe's almost comical tendency to view the wars, protectorates, occupations and annexations of imperial Britain as a natural and desirable state of affairs, and the comparatively ineffectual manoeuvres of the Germans as gratuitous and outrageous breaches of the peace. How impossible of the Germans to pester Britain on the Samoa question when London was on the point of 'submitting' its quarrel with the Transvaal 'to the arbitrament of war'! Then there was the tendency to see the long arm of German policy behind every inter-imperial conflict; thus, it was the Germans who 'fomented' Britain's 'troubles with Russia in Central Asia' and 'carefully encouraged' the European opposition to Britain's occupation of Egypt. Wherever there was friction between Britain and its imperial rivals, the Germans were supposedly pulling strings in the background. As for German press manipulations from Cairo to London, there was more than a pinch of paranoia in Crowe's handling of this issue: German press work paled into insignificance beside the much larger and better-financed subsidy operations run by St Petersburg and Paris.

Perhaps the offensive incidents were ultimately of secondary importance; the core of the argument was Crowe's nightmarish psychogram of the German nation-state, imagined as a composite person conniving to gain concessions by 'offensive bluster and persistent nagging', a 'professional blackmailer', 'bullying and offending' at every turn, manifesting a 'heedless disregard of the suceptibilities of other people'. Whether there was any underlying plan behind all the bluster, or whether it was 'no more than the expression of a vague, confused, and unpractical statesmanship, not fully realizing its own drift' made little difference. The upshot was the same: only the firmest discipline would teach the Germans good behaviour. The French too, Crowe recalled, had once been very annoying, gratuitously challenging Britain at every turn. But Britain's adamant refusal to yield an inch of ground on Egypt and the Sudan, followed by the threat of war over Fashoda, had put an end to all that. Now Britain and France were the best of friends. It followed that only the most 'unbending determination' to uphold 'British rights and interests in every part of the globe' would win 'the respect of the German government and the German nation'. This was not a scenario that left much room to accommodate the rising power of Europe's youngest empire.

Lurking beneath these apprehensions, though only indirectly alluded to in Crowe's text, was the spectacle of Germany's titanic economic growth. In 1862, when Bismarck had become minister-president of Prussia, the manufacturing regions of the German states accounted, with 4.9 per cent, for the fifth-largest share of world industrial production – Britain, with 19.9 per cent, was well ahead in first place. In 1880–1900 Germany rose to third place behind the United States and Britain. By 1913, it was behind the United States, but ahead of Britain. In other words, during the years 1860–1913, the German share of world industrial production increased fourfold, while the British sank by a third. Even more impressive was Germany's expanding share of world trade. In 1880, Britain controlled 22.4 per cent of world trade; the Germans, though in second place, were well behind with 10.3 per cent. By 1913, however, Germany, with 12.3 per cent, was hard on the heels of Britain, whose share had shrunk to 14.2 per cent. Everywhere one looked, one saw the contours of an economic miracle: between 1895 and 1913, German industrial output shot up by 150 per cent, metal production by 300 per cent, coal production by 200 per cent. By 1913, the German economy generated and consumed 20 per cent more electricity than Britain, France and Italy combined.[124] In Britain, the words 'Made in Germany' came to carry strong connotations of threat, not because German commercial or industrial practice was more aggressive or expansionist than anyone else's, but because they hinted at the limits of British global dominance.[125]

German economic power underscored the political anxieties of the great-power executives, just as Chinese economic power does today. Yet there was nothing inevitable about the ascendancy of Germanophobe attitudes in British foreign policy.[126] They were not universal, even within the upper reaches of the Foreign Office itself, and they were even less prevalent across the rest of the political elite. Hard work behind the scenes was needed to lever Bertie, Nicolson and Hardinge into the senior posts from which they were able to shape the tone and course of British policy. Bertie owed his rapid ascent after years of frustration in low-level positions to his energetic politicking with the private secretary to King Edward VII. Hardinge, too, was a seasoned courtier and intriguer, who pushed Bertie's candidacy for the Paris ambassadorship in 1905. Hardinge employed his connections at court to 'override' a 'certain amount of obstruction at the top of the F.O.'.[127] Bertie and Hardinge in turn cooperated in levering Arthur Nicolson into senior ambassadorial posts, despite the fact that his wife was said to shun society and to 'dress like a housemaid'.[128] British policy could have taken a different course: had Grey and his associates failed to secure so many influential posts, less intransigent voices, such as those of Goschen and Lascelles or of the parliamentary under-secretary Edmond Fitzmaurice, who deplored the 'anti-German virus' afflicting his colleagues, might have found a wider hearing. Instead, the Grey group gradually tightened their grip on British policy, setting the terms under which relations with Germany were viewed and understood.

The 'invention', as Keith Wilson has put it,[129] of Germany as the key threat to Britain reflected and consolidated a broader structural shift. The polycentric world of the 'great games' in Africa, China, Persia, Tibet and Afghanistan, a world in which policy-makers often felt they were lurching from crisis to crisis and reacting to remote challenges rather than setting the agenda, was making way for a simpler cosmos in which one enemy dominated the scene. This was not the *cause* of Britain's alignment with Russia and France, but rather its consequence. For the restructuring of the alliance system facilitated – indeed it necessitated – the refocusing of British anxieties and paranoia, which were riding high in the years around the Boer War.[130] British foreign policy – like American foreign policy in the twentieth century[131] – had always depended on scenarios of threat and invasion as focusing devices. In the mid-nineteenth century, French invasion scares had periodically galvanized the political elites; by the 1890s, France had been displaced in the British political and public imagination by Russia, whose Cossack hordes would soon be invading India and Essex.[132] Now it was Germany's turn. The target was new, but the mechanisms were familiar.

In retrospect, it is tempting to discern in the upheavals of 1904–7 the birth of the Triple Entente that would wage war in 1914. That was certainly how it looked to the French diplomat Maurice Paléologue, who published his diaries of these years three decades later under the title *A Great Turning Point*. Recomposed to incorporate the wisdom of hindsight, Paléologue's 'diaries' endowed French policy-makers (and especially Paléologue himself) with an almost supernatural foreknowledge of the war to come.[133] In this respect they exemplify a distortion of perception that is common to the post-war 'memoirs' of many pre-war statesmen. The immense denouement of 1914 seems to us to command the horizons of the preceding decade. Yet the reality is that it does so only in our eyes, which is to say: in retrospect.

It was still far from clear in 1907 that the new alliances would take Europe to war. The weakness of Russia after the disaster of 1905 obliged the policy-makers in St Petersburg in the first instance to seek good relations with Germany, and it was widely accepted in St Petersburg, for the time being at least, that Russia's domestic fragility ruled out any form of international adventurism.[134] It was hard to imagine the circumstances in which France might be willing to chance its arm for the Russians in the Balkans and even harder to imagine Russians marching to Berlin for the sake of Alsace and Lorraine. In 1909, Paris underscored its independence by signing an accord on Morocco with Germany, a 'striking instance of the crossing of lines' between the alliance blocs.[135] Then, in November 1910, Russian and German leaders met in Potsdam and Berlin to reconcile German and Russian interests in Turkey and Persia. There was no question of loosening the Franco-Russian bond, to be sure, but this was a significant gesture in the direction of détente.[136] As for the Anglo-Russian Convention of 1907, it may have muted the tensions between Russia and Britain but it did not remove their cause, and right through until 1914 there were voices in the Foreign Office warning of the Russian threat to Britain's far-flung empire.

In short: the future was not foreordained. The Triple Entente that went to war in 1914 still lay beyond the mental horizons of most statesmen. The great turning point of 1904–7 helps to explain the emergence of the *structures* within which a continental war became possible. But it cannot explain the specific reasons why that conflict arose. In order to do that, we need to examine how decision-making processes shaped policy outcomes and how the loose network of the continental alliances became interlocked with conflicts unfolding on the Balkan peninsula.

4

The Many Voices of European Foreign Policy

In a cartoon published in the late 1890s, a French artist depicted the crisis brewing over China on the eve of the Boxer Uprising. Watched warily by Britain and Russia, Germany makes to carve out a slice identified as 'Kiao-Tschaou' from a pie called 'China', while France offers her Russian ally moral support and Japan looks on. Behind them all, a Qing official throws up his hands in despair, but is powerless to intervene. As so often in such images, the powers are represented as individual persons: Britain, Germany and Russia by caricatures of their respective sovereigns, France by 'Marianne', the personification of the Republic, and Japan and China by stereotypical exotic figures. Personifying states as individuals was part of the shorthand of European political caricature, but it also reflects a deep habit of thought: the tendency to conceptualize states as composite individuals governed by compact executive agencies animated by an indivisible will.

Yet even a very cursory look at the governments of early twentieth-century Europe reveals that the executive structures from which policies emerged were far from unified. Policy-making was not the prerogative of single sovereign individuals. Initiatives with a bearing on the course of a country's policy could and did emanate from quite peripheral locations in the political structure. Factional alignments, functional frictions within government, economic or financial constraints and the volatile chemistry of public opinion all exerted a constantly varying pressure on decision-making processes. As the power to shape decisions shifted from one node in the executive structure to another, there were corresponding oscillations in the tone and orientation of policy. This chaos of competing voices is crucial to understanding the periodic agitations of the European system during the last pre-war years. It also helps to

'The Scramble for China', by Henri Meyer, *Le Petit Journal*, 1898

explain why the July Crisis of 1914 became the most complex and opaque political crisis of modern times.

SOVEREIGN DECISION-MAKERS

Early twentieth-century Europe was a continent of monarchies. Of the six most important powers, five were monarchies of one kind or another; only one (France) was a republic. The relatively new nation-states of the Balkan peninsula – Greece, Serbia, Montenegro, Bulgaria, Romania and Albania – were all monarchies. The Europe of fast cruisers, radio-telegraph, and electric cigar-lighters still carried at its heart this ancient, glittering institution yoking large and complex states to the vagaries of human biology. The European executives were still centred on the thrones and the men or women who sat on them. Ministers in Germany, Austria-Hungary and Russia were imperial appointees. The three emperors had unlimited access to state papers. They also exercised formal authority over their respective armed forces. Dynastic institutions and networks structured the communications between states. Ambassadors presented their credentials to the sovereign in person and direct communications and meetings between monarchs continued to take place throughout the pre-war years; indeed they acquired a heightened importance, creating a parallel plane of interaction whose relationship to official diplomacy was sometimes difficult to ascertain.

Monarchs were symbolic as well as political actors, and in this role they could capture and focus collective emotions and associations. When Parisian onlookers gawped at Edward VII sprawled in a chair outside his hotel smoking a cigar, they felt they were looking at England in the form of a very fat, fashionable and confident man. His triumphant ascent in Parisian public opinion in 1903 helped smooth the path to the Entente signed with France in the following year. Even the mild-mannered despot Nicholas II was greeted like a conquering hero by the French when he visited Paris in 1896, despite his autocratic political philosophy and negligible charisma, because he was seen as the personification of the Franco-Russian Alliance.[1] And who embodied the most unsettling aspects of German foreign policy – its vacillations, lack of focus and frustrated ambition – better than the febrile, tactless, panic-prone, overbearing Kaiser Wilhelm, the man who dared to advise

Wilhelm II and Nicholas II wearing the uniforms of each other's countries

Wilhelm II

Edward VII in his uniform as colonel of the
Austrian 12th Hussars

Edvard Grieg on how to conduct *Peer Gynt*?[2] Whether or not the Kaiser actually made German policy, he certainly symbolized it for Germany's opponents.

At the core of the monarchical club that reigned over pre-war Europe was the trio of imperial cousins: Tsar Nicholas II, Kaiser Wilhelm II and George V. By the turn of the twentieth century, the genealogical web of Europe's reigning families had thickened almost to the point of fusion. Kaiser Wilhelm II and King George V were both grandsons of Queen Victoria. Tsar Nicholas II's wife, Alexandra of Hesse-Darmstadt, was Victoria's granddaughter. The mothers of George V and Nicholas II were sisters from the house of Denmark. Kaiser Wilhelm and Tsar Nicholas II were both great-great grandsons of Tsar Paul I. The Kaiser's great-aunt, Charlotte of Prussia, was the Tsar's grandmother. Viewed from this perspective, the outbreak of war in 1914 looks rather like the culmination of a family feud.

Assessing how much influence these monarchs wielded over or within their respective executives is difficult. Britain, Germany and Russia represented three very different kinds of monarchy. Russia's was, in theory at least, an autocracy in which the parliamentary and constitutional restraints on the monarch's authority were weak. Edward VII and George V were constitutional and parliamentary monarchs with no direct access to the levers of power. Kaiser Wilhelm II was something in between – in Germany, a constitutional and parliamentary system was grafted on to elements of the old Prussian military monarchy that had survived the process of national unification. But the formal structures of governance were not necessarily the most significant determinants of monarchical influence. Other important variables included the determination, competence and intellectual grasp of the monarch himself, the ability of ministers to block unwelcome initiatives and the extent of agreement between monarchs and their governments.

One of the most striking features of the influence wielded by the sovereigns on the formulation of foreign policy is its variation over time. Edward VII, who presided over the diplomatic realignments of 1904–7, had strong views on foreign policy and prided himself on being well informed. His attitudes were those of an imperialist 'jingo'; he was infuriated by Liberal opposition to the Afghan War of 1878–9, for example, and told the colonial administrator Sir Henry Bartle Frere: 'If I had my way I should not be content until we had taken the whole of Afghanistan and kept it.'[3] He was overjoyed at the news of the raid against the Transvaal Republic in 1895, supportive of Cecil Rhodes's involvement in it, and infuriated by the Kaiser's Kruger telegram. Throughout his adult life he maintained a determined hostility to Germany. The roots of this antipathy appear to have lain partly in his opposition to his mother, Queen Victoria, whom he regarded as excessively friendly to Prussia, and partly in his fear and loathing of Baron Stockmar, the unsmiling Germanic pedagogue appointed by Victoria and Albert to hold the young Edward to a regime of unstinting study. The Prussian-Danish War of 1864 was a formative episode in his early political life – Edward's sympathies in that conflict rested firmly with the Danish relatives of his new bride.[4] After his accession to the throne, Edward was an important sponsor of the anti-German group of policy-makers around Sir Francis Bertie.[5]

The king's influence reached its height in 1903, when an official visit to Paris – 'the most important royal visit in modern history', as it has been called – paved the road towards the Entente between the two imperial rivals. Relations between the two western empires were still soured at this time by French outrage over the Boer War. The visit, which had been organized on Edward's own initiative, was a public relations triumph and did much to clear the air.[6] After the Entente had been signed, Edward continued to work towards an agreement with Russia, even though, like many of his countrymen, he detested the tsarist political system and remained suspicious of the designs that Russia had on Persia, Afghanistan and northern India. In 1906, when he heard that the Russian foreign minister Izvolsky was in Paris, he rushed south from Scotland in the hope that a meeting could be set up. Izvolsky responded in kind and made the journey to London, where the two men met for talks that – according to Charles Hardinge – 'helped materially to smooth the path of the negotiations then in progress for an agreement with Russia'.[7] In both these instances, the king was not deploying executive powers as such, but acting as a kind of supernumerary ambassador. He could do this because his priorities accorded closely with those of the liberal imperialist faction at Whitehall, whose dominance in foreign policy he had himself helped to reinforce.

George V was a very different case. Until his accession in 1910, he took little interest in foreign affairs and had acquired only the sketchiest sense of Britain's relations with other powers. The Austrian ambassador

Count Mensdorff was delighted with the new king, who seemed, by contrast with his father, to be innocent of strong biases for or against any foreign state.[8] If Mensdorff hoped the changing of the guard would produce an attenuation of the anti-German theme in British policy, he was soon to be disappointed. In foreign policy, the new monarch's seeming neutrality merely meant that policy remained firmly in the hands of the liberal imperialists around Grey. George never acquired a political network to rival his father's, refrained from backstairs intrigue and avoided expounding policy without the explicit permission of his ministers.[9] He was in more or less constant communication with Edward Grey and granted the foreign secretary frequent audiences whenever he was in London. He was scrupulous about seeking Grey's approval for the content of political conversations with foreign representatives – especially his German relatives.[10] George's accession to the throne thus resulted in a sharp decline in the crown's influence on the general orientation of foreign policy, even though the two monarchs wielded identical constitutional powers.

Even within the highly authoritarian setting of the Russian autocracy, the influence of the Tsar over foreign policy was subject to narrow constraints and waxed and waned over time. Like George V, the new Tsar was a blank sheet of paper when he came to the throne in 1894. He had not created a political network of his own before the accession and his deference to his father ensured that he refrained from expressing a view on government policy. As an adolescent, he had shown little aptitude for the study of affairs of state. Konstantin Pobedonostsev, the conservative jurist drafted in to give the teenage Nicky a master class on the inner workings of the tsarist state, later recalled: 'I could only observe that he was completely absorbed in picking his nose.'[11] Even after he mounted the throne, extreme shyness and terror at the prospect of having to wield real authority prevented him in the early years from imposing his political preferences – insofar as he had them – on the government. He lacked, moreover, the kind of executive support he would have needed to shape the course of policy in a consistent way. He possessed, for example, no personal secretariat and no personal secretary. He could – and did – insist on being informed of even quite minor ministerial decisions, but in a state as vast as Russia's, this merely meant that the monarch was engulfed in trivia while matters of real import fell by the wayside.[12]

The Tsar was nonetheless able, especially from around 1900, to impart a certain direction to Russian foreign policy. By the late 1890s, Russia was deeply involved in the economic penetration of China. Not everyone in the administration was happy with the Far Eastern policy. Some resented the immense cost of the infrastructural and military commitments involved. Others, such as the minister of war, General Aleksei A. Kuropatkin, viewed the Far East as a distraction from more pressing concerns on the western periphery, especially the Balkans and the Turkish Straits. But at this time Nicholas II still firmly believed that the future of Russia lay in Siberia and the Far East and ensured that the exponents of the Eastern policy prevailed over their opponents. Despite some initial misgivings, he supported the policy of seizing the Chinese bridgehead at Port Arthur (today Lüshun) on the Liaodong peninsula in 1898. In Korea, Nicholas came to support a policy of Russian penetration that placed St Petersburg on a collision course with Tokyo.

Nicholas's interventions took the form of informal alignments, rather than of executive decisions. He was closely associated, for example, with the aristocratic entrepreneurs who ran the vast Yalu river timber concession in Korea. The Yalu timber magnate A. M. Bezobrazov, a former officer of the elite Chevaliers Guards, used his personal connection with the Tsar to establish the Yalu as a platform for extending Russian informal empire on the Korean peninsula. In 1901, the finance minister Sergei Witte reported that Bezobrazov was with the Tsar 'no less than two times a week – for hours at a time' advising him on Far Eastern policy.[13] Ministers were exasperated by the presence at court of these influential outsiders, but there was little they could do to curb their influence. These informal links in turn drew the Tsar into an ever more aggressive vision of Russian policy in the region. 'I do not want to seize Korea,' Nicholas told Prince Henry of Prussia in 1901, 'but under no circumstances can I allow Japan to become firmly established there. That would be a *casus belli*.'[14]

Nicholas further tightened his control over policy by appointing a Viceroy of the Far East with full responsibility not only for civil and military matters but also for relations with Tokyo. The holder of this office, Admiral E. I. Alekseev, was subject directly to the Tsar and thus immune from ministerial supervision. The appointment had been engineered by the clique around Bezobrazov, who saw it as a means of bypassing the relatively cautious Far Eastern policy of the foreign ministry. As a consequence, Russia operated what were in effect two parallel official and non-official imperial policies, enabling Nicholas II to pick between options and play the factions off against each other.[15] Admiral Alekseev had no experience or understanding of diplomatic forms and exhibited an abrasive and intransigent style that was bound to alienate and anger his Japanese interlocutors. Whether Nicholas II ever consciously adopted a policy of war with Japan is doubtful, but he certainly carried the lion's share of responsibility for the war that broke out in 1904, and thus also for the disasters that followed.[16]

On the eve of the Russo-Japanese War, then, one could say that the Tsar's influence was up, while that of his ministers was down. But this state of affairs was shortlived, because the catastrophic outcome of the Tsar's policy sharply diminished his ability to set the agenda. As the news of successive defeats sank in and social unrest engulfed Russia, a group of ministers led by Sergei Witte pushed through reforms designed to unify government. Power was concentrated in a Council of Ministers, headed for the first time by a 'chairman' or prime minister. Under Witte and his successor, P. A. Stolypin (1906–11), the executive was shielded to some extent against arbitrary interventions by the monarch. Stolypin in particular, a man of immense determination, intelligence, charisma and tireless industry, managed to assert his personal authority over most of the ministers, achieving a level of coherence in government that had been unknown before 1905. During the Stolypin years, Nicholas seemed 'curiously absent from political activity'.[17]

The Tsar did not acquiesce for long in this arrangement. Even while Stolypin was in power, Nicholas found ways of circumventing his control by making deals with individual ministers behind the premier's back. Among them was Foreign Minister Izvolsky, whose mishandling of negotiations with his Austria-Hungarian counterpart triggered the Bosnian annexation crisis of 1908–9. In return for Vienna's diplomatic support over Russian access to the Turkish Straits, Izvolsky approved the Austrian annexation of Bosnia-Herzegovina. Neither Prime Minister Stolypin nor his ministerial colleagues had been informed in advance of this daring enterprise, which was cleared directly with Tsar Nicholas himself. By the time of Stolypin's assassination by terrorists in the autumn of 1911, Nicholas was systematically undercutting his authority by supporting his political opponents. Confronted with a ministerial bloc that threatened to confine his freedom of action, Nicholas withdrew his support and intrigued against the men he had himself placed in power. Witte fell victim to this autocratic behaviour in 1906; Stolypin would have done so if he had not been killed, and his successor, the mild-mannered Vladimir Kokovtsov, was removed from office in February 1914 because he too had revealed himself a devotee of the idea of 'united government'. I return below to the implications of these machinations for the course of Russian foreign policy – for the moment, the key point is that the years 1911–14 saw a decline in united government and the reassertion of autocratic power.[18]

Yet this autocratic power was *not* deployed in support of a consistent policy vision. It was used in a negative way, to safeguard the autonomy and power of the monarch by breaking any political formations that looked as if they might secure the initiative. The consequence of autocratic intervention was thus not the imposition of the Tsar's will as such, but rather a lasting uncertainty about who had the power to do what – a state of affairs that nourished factional strife and critically undermined the consistency of Russian decision-making.

Of the three imperial cousins, Wilhelm II was and remains the most controversial. The extent of his power within the German executive is still hotly disputed.[19] The Kaiser certainly came to the throne *intending* to be the author of his country's foreign policy. 'The Foreign Office? Why, I am the Foreign Office!' he once exclaimed.[20] 'I am the sole master of German policy,' he remarked in a letter to the Prince of Wales (the future Edward VII), 'and my country must follow me wherever I go.'[21] Wilhelm took a personal interest in the appointment of ambassadors and occasionally backed personal favourites against the advice of the chancellor and the Foreign Office. To a greater extent than either of his two imperial cousins, he regarded the meetings and correspondence with fellow dynasts that were part of the regular traffic between monarchies as a unique diplomatic resource to be exploited in his country's interest.[22] Like Nicholas II, Wilhelm frequently – especially in the early years of his reign – bypassed his responsible ministers by consulting with 'favourites', encouraged factional strife in order to undermine the unity of government, and expounded views that had not been cleared with the relevant ministers or were at odds with the prevailing policy.

It was in this last area – the unauthorized exposition of unsanctioned political views – that the Kaiser achieved the most hostile notice, both from contemporaries and from historians.[23] There can be no doubt about the bizarre tone and content of many of the Kaiser's personal communications in telegrams, letters, marginal comments, conversations, interviews and speeches on foreign and domestic political themes. Their exceptional volume alone is remarkable: the Kaiser spoke, wrote, telegraphed, scribbled and ranted more or less continuously during the thirty years of his reign, and a huge portion of these articulations was recorded and preserved for posterity. Some of them were tasteless or inappropriate. Two examples, both of them linked with the United States, will serve to illustrate the point. On 4 April 1906, Kaiser Wilhelm II was a dinner guest at the US embassy in Berlin. During a lively conversation with his American hosts, the Kaiser spoke of the necessity of securing more space for the rapidly growing German population, which had counted around 40 million at the time of his accession, he told the ambassador, but was now around 60 million. This was a good thing in itself, but the question of nutrition was going to become acute in the next twenty years. On the other hand, large portions of France appeared to be under-populated and in need of development; perhaps one should ask the French government whether they would mind pulling their border back westwards to accommodate the surfeit of Germans? These inane burblings (which we can presume were offered in jest) were earnestly recorded by one of his interlocutors and forwarded to Washington with the next diplomatic bag.[24] The other example stems from November 1908, when there was widespread press speculation over a possible war between the United States and Japan. Agitated by this prospect and keen to ingratiate himself with the Atlantic power, the Kaiser fired off a letter to President Roosevelt offering him – this time in all seriousness – a Prussian army corps to be stationed on the Californian coast.[25]

How exactly did such utterances connect with the world of actual policy outcomes? Any foreign minister or ambassador in a modern democracy who indulged in such grossly inappropriate communications would be sacked on the spot. But how much did such sovereign gaffes matter in the larger scheme of things? The extreme inconsistency of the Kaiser's utterances makes an assessment of their impact difficult. Had Wilhelm pursued a clear and consistent policy vision, we could simply measure intentions against outcomes, but his intentions were always equivocal and the focus of his attention was always shifting. In the late 1890s, the Kaiser became enthusiastic about a project to create a 'New Germany' (*Neudeutschland*) in Brazil and 'demanded impatiently' that migration to that region be encouraged and increased as quickly as possible – needless to say, absolutely nothing came of this. In 1899, he informed Cecil Rhodes that it was his intention to secure 'Mesopotamia' as a German colony. In 1900, at the time of the Boxer Rebellion, we find him proposing that the Germans should send an entire army corps to China with a view to partitioning the country. In 1903, he was once again declaring 'Latin America is our target!' and urging the Admiralty staff – who apparently had nothing better to do – to prepare invasion plans for Cuba, Puerto Rico and New York, invasion plans that were a complete waste of time, since (among other things) the General Staff never agreed to provide the necessary troops.[26]

The Kaiser picked up ideas, enthused over them, grew bored or discouraged, and dropped them again. He was angry with the Russian Tsar one week, but infatuated with him the next.[27] There were endless alliance projects: for an alliance *with* Russia and France *against* Japan and Britain; *with* Russia, Britain and France *against* the USA; *with* China and America *against* Japan and the Triple Entente, or *with* Japan *and* the USA against the Entente, and so on.[28] In the autumn of 1896, at a time when relations between Britain and Germany had cooled following tensions over the status of the Transvaal, the Kaiser proposed a continental league with France and Russia for the joint defence of colonial possessions against Britain. At virtually the same time, however, he played with the notion of eliminating any cause of conflict with Britain by simply doing away with all the German colonies except East Africa. But by the spring of 1897, Wilhelm had dropped this idea and was proposing that Germany should enter into a closer relationship with France.[29]

Wilhelm wasn't content to fire off notes and marginalia to his ministers, he also broached his ideas directly to the representatives of foreign powers. Sometimes his interventions opposed the direction of official policy, sometimes they endorsed it; sometimes they overshot the mark to arrive at a grossly overdrawn parody of the official view. In 1890, when the Foreign Office was cooling relations with the French, Wilhelm was warming them up again; he did the same thing during the Moroccan crisis of 1905 – while the Foreign Office stepped up the pressure on Paris, Wilhelm assured various foreign generals and journalists and a former French minister that he sought reconciliation with France and had no intention of risking war over Morocco. In March, on the eve of his departure for Tangier, the Kaiser delivered a speech in Bremen in which he announced that the lessons of history had taught him 'never to strive after an empty power over the world'. The German Empire he added, would have to earn 'the most absolute trust as a calm, honest and peaceful neighbour'. A number of senior political figures – especially among the hawks within the military command – believed that this speech spiked the guns of official policy on Morocco.[30]

In January 1904, the Kaiser found himself seated next to King Leopold of the Belgians (who had come to Berlin to celebrate Wilhelm's birthday) at a gala dinner and used the occasion to inform Leopold that he expected Belgium to side with Germany in the event of a war with France. Should the Belgian king opt to stand with Germany, Wilhelm promised, the Belgians would gain new territories in northern France, and Wilhelm would reward the Belgian king with 'the crown of old Burgundy'. When Leopold, taken aback, replied that his ministers and the Belgian parliament would hardly accept such a fanciful and audacious plan, Wilhelm retorted that he could not respect a monarch who felt himself to be responsible to ministers and deputies, rather than to the Lord God. If the Belgian king were not more forthcoming, the Kaiser would be obliged to proceed 'on purely strategic principles' – in other words, to invade and occupy Belgium. Leopold is said to have been so upset by these remarks that, when rising from his seat at the end of the meal, he put his helmet on the wrong way round.[31]

It was precisely because of episodes like this that Wilhelm's ministers sought to keep him at one remove from the actual decision-making process. It is an extraordinary fact that the most important foreign policy decision of Wilhelm's reign – not to renew the Reinsurance Treaty with Russia in 1890 – was made without the Kaiser's involvement or prior knowledge.[32] In the summer of 1905, Chancellor Bernhard von Bülow entrusted Wilhelm with the task of putting an alliance proposal to Nicholas II off the Finnish coast at Björkö, only to find on the Kaiser's return that Wilhelm had dared to make an alteration in the draft of the treaty. The chancellor's response was to tender his resignation. Terrified at the prospect of being abandoned by his most powerful official, Wilhelm immediately backed down; Bülow agreed to remain in office and the treaty amendment was withdrawn.[33]

The Kaiser constantly complained of being kept out of the loop, of being denied access to important diplomatic documents. He was par-ticularly upset when foreign policy officials insisted on vetting his personal correspondence with foreign heads of state. There was quite a fuss, for example, when the German ambassador in Washington, Speck von Sternburg, refused to pass on a letter from Wilhelm to President Roosevelt in 1908, in which the Kaiser expressed his profound admir-ation for the American president. It was not the political content of the letter that worried the diplomats, but rather the effusiveness and imma-turity of its tone. It was surely unacceptable, one official remarked, that the sovereign of the German Empire should write to the president of the United States 'as an infatuated schoolboy might write to a pretty seamstress'.[34]

These were disturbing utterances, to be sure. In an environment where governments were constantly puzzling over each other's inten-tions, they were even potentially dangerous. Nevertheless, we should bear three points in mind. The first is that in such encounters, the Kaiser was performing a role of leadership and control that he was incapable of exercising in practice. Secondly, these rhetorical menaces were always associated with imagined scenarios in which Germany was the *attacked* party. Wilhelm's indecent proposal to Leopold of the Belgians was not conceived as an offensive venture, but as part of a German response to a French attack. What was bizarre about his reflections on the possible need in a future conflict to breach Belgian neutrality is not the *idea* of the breach as such – the option of a Belgian invasion was discussed and weighed up by the French and British General Staffs as well – but the context in which it was broached and the identity of the two interlocu-tors. It was one of this Kaiser's many peculiarities that he was completely unable to calibrate his behaviour to the contexts in which his high office obliged him to operate. Too often he spoke not like a monarch, but like an over-excited teenager giving free rein to his current preoccupations. He was an extreme exemplar of that Edwardian social category, the club bore who is forever explaining some pet project to the man in the next chair. Small wonder that the prospect of being buttonholed by the Kaiser over lunch or dinner, when escape was impossible, struck fear into the hearts of so many European royals.

Wilhelm's interventions greatly exercised the men of the German for-eign ministry, but they did little to shape the course of German policy. Indeed it may in part have been a deepening sense of impotence and disconnection from the real levers of power that fired up Wilhelm's recurring fantasies about future world wars between Japan and the USA, invasions of Puerto Rico, global jihad against the British Empire, a German protectorate over China and so on. These were the blue-sky scenarios of an inveterate geopolitical fantasist, not policies as such. And whenever a real conflict seemed imminent, Wilhelm pulled in his horns and quickly found reasons why Germany could not possibly go to war. When tensions with France reached a peak at the end of 1905, Wilhelm took fright and informed Chancellor Bülow that socialist agitation at home absolutely ruled out any offensive action abroad; in the following year, rattled by the news that King Edward VII had just paid an unscheduled visit to the fallen French foreign minister Théophile Delcassé, he warned the chancellor that Germany's artillery and navy were in no condition to hold out in a conflict.[35] Wilhelm could talk tough, but when trouble loomed he tended to turn and run for cover. He would do exactly that during the July Crisis of 1914. 'It is a curious thing,' Jules Cambon, French ambassador in Berlin, observed in a letter to a senior official at the French foreign ministry in May 1912, 'to see how this man, so sudden, so reckless and impulsive in words, is full of caution and patience in action.'[36]

An overview of the early twentieth-century monarchs suggests a fluctuating and ultimately relatively modest impact on actual policy outcomes. Emperor Franz Joseph of Austria-Hungary read vast quantities of dispatches and met with his foreign ministers regularly. Yet for all his stupendous work as the 'first bureaucrat' of his empire, Franz Joseph, like Nicholas II, found it impossible to master the oceans of information that came to his desk. Little effort was made to ensure that he apportioned his time in accordance with the relative importance of the issues arising.[37] Austro-Hungarian foreign policy was shaped not by the executive fiats of the Emperor, but by the interaction of factions and lobbies within and around the ministry. Italy's Victor Emanuel III (r. 1900–1946) worked much less hard than Franz Joseph – he spent most of his time in Piedmont or on his estates at Castelporziano and, though he did make an effort to get through some diplomatic dispatches, he also spent around three hours a day reading newspapers and meticulously listing the errors he found in them. The Italian king cultivated close relations with his foreign ministers and he certainly supported the momentous decision to seize Libya in 1911, but direct interventions were few and far between.[38] Nicholas II could favour this or that faction or minister and thereby undermine the cohesion of government, but was unable to set the agenda, especially after the fiasco of the Russo-Japanese War. Wilhelm II was more energetic than Nicholas, but his ministers were also better able than their Russian colleagues to shield the policy-making process against interventions from above. Wilhelm's initiatives were in any case too disparate and ill coordinated to provide any kind of alternative operational platform.

Whether or not they intervened aggressively in the political process, the continental monarchs nonetheless remained, by virtue of their very existence, an unsettling factor in international relations. The presence in only partially democratized systems of sovereigns who were the putative focal points of their respective executives with access to all state papers and personnel and with ultimate responsibility for every executive decision created ambiguity. A purely dynastic foreign policy, in which monarchs met each other to resolve great affairs of state, was obviously no longer apposite – the futile meeting at Björkö proved that. Yet the temptation to view the monarch as the helmsman and personification of the executive remained strong among diplomats, statesmen and especially the monarchs themselves. Their presence created a persistent uncertainty about where exactly the pivot of the decision-making process rested. In this sense, kings and emperors could become a source of obfuscation in international relations. The resulting lack of clarity dogged efforts to establish secure and transparent relations between states.

Monarchical structures also shrouded the power relations within each executive. In Italy, for example, it was unclear who actually commanded the army – the king, the minister of war or the chief of the General Staff. The Italian staff chief did his best to keep civilians out of his discussions with his German and Austrian counterparts, and civilian officials reciprocated by shutting the officers out of the political loop – with the result, for example, that the chief of Italy's General Staff was not even informed of the stipulations of the Triple Alliance defining the conditions under which Italy might be called upon to fight a war on behalf of its allies.[39]

In a situation like this – and we can find analogous conditions in all the continental monarchies – the king or emperor was the sole point at which separate chains of command converged. If he failed to perform an integrating function, if the crown failed to compensate for the insufficiencies, as it were, of the constitution, the system remained unresolved, potentially incoherent. And the continental monarchs often did fail in this role, or rather they refused to perform it in the first place, because they hoped by dealing separately with key functionaries within the executive to preserve what remained of their own initiative and preeminence within the system. And this in turn had a malign effect on decision-making processes. In an environment where the decision reached by a responsible minister could be overridden or undermined by a colleague or rival, ministers often found it hard to determine 'how their activities fitted into the larger picture'.[40] The resulting ambient confusion encouraged ministers, officials, military commanders and policy experts to think of themselves as entitled to press their cases in debate, but not as personally responsible for policy outcomes. At the same time, the pressure to secure the favour of the monarch stimulated an atmosphere of competition and sycophancy that militated against the kinds of interdepartmental consultation that might have produced a more balanced approach to decision-making. The consequence was a culture of factionalism and rhetorical excess that would bear dangerous fruit in July 1914.

WHO GOVERNED IN ST PETERSBURG?

If the monarchs didn't determine the course of foreign policy, who did? The obvious answer must surely be: the foreign ministers. These men oversaw the activities of the diplomatic corps and the foreign ministries, read and replied to the most important foreign dispatches and were responsible for explaining and justifying policy to parliament and the public. In reality, however, the power of the foreign ministers to shape policy fluctuated at least as much and varied at least as widely across the European powers as did the political traction of the sovereigns. Their influence depended upon a range of factors: the power and favour of other ministers, especially prime ministers, the attitude and behaviour of the monarch, the willingness of senior foreign ministerial functionaries and ambassadors to follow the minister's lead and the level of factional instability within the system.

In Russia, the foreign minister and his family occupied private apartments in the ministry, a vast, dark red edifice on the great square facing the Winter Palace, so that his social life and those of his wife and children, were interwoven with the work of the ministry.[41] His capacity to shape policy was determined by the dynamics of a political system whose parameters were redefined in the aftermath of the Russo-Japanese War and the 1905 Revolution. A group of powerful ministers moved to establish a more concentrated decision-making structure that would enable the executive to balance domestic and foreign imperatives and to impose discipline on the most senior officials. How exactly this should be achieved was a matter of controversy. The most energetic and talented of the reformers was Sergei Witte, an expert on finance and economic policy who had resigned from the government in 1903 because he opposed its forward policy in Korea. Witte wanted a 'cabinet' headed by a 'prime minister' with the power not only to discipline his fellow ministers, but also to control their access to the Tsar. The more conservative sometime finance minister Vladimir Kokovtsov* viewed these proposals as an assault on the principle of tsarist autocracy, which he took to be the only form of government suitable to Russian conditions. A compromise was struck: a cabinet of sorts was created in the form of the Council of Ministers, and its chairman or prime minister was granted the power to dismiss an uncooperative minister. But the 'right of individual report' – in other words, the right of ministers to present their views to the Tsar independently of the chairman of the council – was retained.

What resulted was a somewhat unresolved arrangement in which everything depended on the balance of initiative between the successive chairmen, their ministers and the Tsar. If the chairman was forceful and strong, he might hope to impose his will on the ministers. But if a confident minister managed to secure the support of the Tsar, he might be able to break with his colleagues and go his own way. With the appointment of Pyotr Stolypin as Chairman of the Council of Ministers in the summer of 1906, the new system acquired a charismatic and dominant leader. And the new foreign minister, Alexander Izvolsky, looked like the kind of politician who would be able to make the new arrangement

---

* Kokovtsov resigned as minister of finance in 1905 but resumed the office in November 1905 and retained it until February 1914. From 1911, he was both minister of finance and prime minister.

Pyotr Stolypin

work. He saw himself as a man of the 'new politics' and promptly established foreign ministry liaison posts to manage relations with the Duma. The tone of his dealings with the Tsar was respectful, but less deferential than that of his predecessors. He was committed to the reform and modernization of the ministry and he was an outspoken enthusiast for 'unified government'.[42] Most importantly of all, he agreed with most of his colleagues in the Council of Ministers on the desirability of the settlement with Britain.

It soon emerged, however, that Izvolsky's vision of Russian foreign policy diverged from that of his colleagues in key ways. Stolypin and Kokovtsov saw the Anglo-Russian Convention as securing the opportunity to withdraw from the adventurism of the years before the Russo-Japanese War and concentrate on the tasks of domestic consolidation and economic growth. For Izvolsky, however, the agreement with England was a licence to pursue a more assertive policy. Izvolsky believed that the cordial relations inaugurated by the Convention would allow him to secure London's acceptance of free access by Russian warships to the Turkish Straits. This was not just wishful thinking: the

British foreign secretary Sir Edward Grey had explicitly encouraged Izvolsky to think along these lines. In a conversation with the Russian ambassador in London in March 1907, Grey had declared that 'if permanent good relations were to be established' between the two countries, 'England would no longer make it a settled object of its policy to maintain the existing arrangement' in the Straits.[43]

It was against this background that Izvolsky launched in 1908 his ill-fated negotiations with Aehrenthal, in which he promised Russian approval for the annexation of Bosnia-Herzegovina in return for Austrian support for a revision of the Straits settlement. The agreement with Aehrenthal was supposed to be the first step towards a comprehensive revision. This démarche was undertaken with the support of the Tsar; indeed it may have been Nicholas II who pushed Izvolsky into offering the Austrians a deal. Having been an ardent exponent of Far Eastern expansion before 1904, the Tsar was now focusing his attention on the Straits: 'the thought of taking the Dardanelles and Constantinople', one Russian politician recalled, 'was constantly on his mind'.[44] Rather than risking rejection from Stolypin, Kokovtsov and the other ministers, Izvolsky exploited the right of individual report. It was the highpoint of the foreign minister's political independence – an independence acquired by playing the margins between the different power centres in the system. But the triumph was shortlived. Since there was no deal to be had in London, the Straits policy failed. Izvolsky was disgraced in the eyes of Russian public opinion and returned to face the ire of Stolypin and Kokovtsov.

In the short term, then, the débâcle of the Bosnian annexation crisis (like the débâcle of the Japanese war) led to a reassertion of the collective authority of the Council of Ministers. The Tsar lost the initiative, at least for the moment. Izvolsky was forced to back down and to submit to the discipline of 'united government'. Stolypin, on the other hand, now reached the peak of his power. Conservative supporters of the autocracy began to view him with alarm as an over-mighty 'lord' or 'Grand Vizier' who had usurped the powers of his imperial master. The choice of Sergei Sazonov to replace Izvolsky in September 1910 appeared to reinforce Stolypin's dominance. Sazonov was a relatively junior diplomat, had little experience in senior chancellery posts within the ministry of foreign affairs and lacked aristocratic and imperial connections. He had little knowledge of St Petersburg politics and scarcely any influence in government circles. His chief qualifications for office, critical outsiders noted, were a reputation for 'mediocrity and obedience' and the fact that he was Stolypin's brother-in law.[45]

After the débâcle of Izvolsky's policy and his departure from office, Russian foreign policy thus bore the imprint not of the foreign minister, but of the prime minister, Chairman Pyotr Stolypin, whose view was that Russia needed peace at all costs and should pursue a policy of conciliation on every front. The consequence was a period of pronounced rapprochement with Berlin, despite the recent tensions over Bosnia. In November 1910, a visit by Nicholas II and Sazonov to Potsdam set in train discussions culminating in an agreement marking a highpoint in Russo-German détente.[46]

Stolypin's assassination at first did little to change the orientation of policy. In the immediate aftermath of his patron's death, Sazonov struggled to find his own voice. But Sazonov's weakness, in combination with Stolypin's death, in turn amplified a further potential instability within the system; the most experienced and confident Russian agents abroad were free to play a more independent role. Two ministers in particular, N. V. Charykov in Constantinople and Nikolai Hartwig in Belgrade, sensing a loosening of control from St Petersburg, embarked on potentially hazardous independent initiatives in order to capitalize on the worsening political situation in the Balkans.[47] In the meanwhile, the Russian ambassador to France was none other than the former foreign minister, Alexander Izvolsky, whose determination to shape policy – on the Balkans especially – remained undiminished after his transfer back into the diplomatic service. Izvolsky hatched his own intrigues in Paris, all the while 'hectoring Sazonov through the diplomatic pouch'.[48]

Sazonov's eclipse was not permanent. With time, he began to make his own way in Balkan policy, exploiting the political weakness of Kokovtsov, Stolypin's successor as Chairman of the Council of Ministers. The key point is that the influences shaping policy in Russia were constantly changing. Power flowed through the system, concentrating at different points: the monarch, the foreign minister, the prime minister, the ambassadors. Indeed we can speak of a kind of 'hydraulics of power', in which the waxing of one node in the system produced the waning of others. And the adversarial dynamic within the system was further energized by the tension between opposed policy options. Russian liberal nationalists and pan-Slavs were likely to favour a forward policy on the Turkish Straits and a posture of solidarity with the Slavic 'little brothers' on the Balkan peninsula. Conservatives, by contrast, tended to be acutely aware of Russia's inner political and financial weakness and the dangers – as Kokovtsov put it – of pursuing 'an active foreign policy at the expense of the peasant's stomach'; they therefore favoured a policy of peace at all costs.[49]

When the significance of the Bosnian annexation crisis was debated in the Duma in the spring of 1909, for example, the conservative interests represented in the Council of the United Nobility argued that the annexation had in no way damaged Russian interests or security and that Russia should adopt a policy of complete non-interference in Balkan affairs, while seeking reconciliation with Berlin. The real enemy, they argued, was Britain, which was trying to push Russia into a war with Germany in order to consolidate British control of world markets. Against this position, the pro-French and pro-British liberals of the Constitutional Democrat (Cadet) Party called for the transformation of the Triple Entente into a Triple Alliance that would enable Russia to project power in the Balkan region and arrest the decline of its great power status.[50] This was one of the central problems confronting all the foreign policy executives (and those who try to understand them today): the 'national interest' was not an objective imperative pressing in upon government from the world outside, but the projection of particular interests within the political elite itself.[51]

WHO GOVERNED IN PARIS?

In France, there was a different but broadly analogous dynamic. To a much greater extent than in Russia, the foreign ministry, or the Quai d'Orsay as it was known on account of its location, enjoyed formidable power and autonomy. It was a socially cohesive and relatively stable organization with a high sense of its own calling. A dense network of family connections reinforced the ministry's *esprit de corps*: the brothers Jules and Paul Cambon were the ambassadors to Berlin and London respectively, the ambassador to St Petersburg in 1914, Maurice Paléologue, was Jules and Paul's brother-in-law, and there were other dynasties – the Herbettes, the de Margeries, and the de Courcels, to name just a few. The ministry of foreign affairs protected its independence through habits of secrecy. Sensitive information was only rarely released to cabinet ministers. It was not unusual for senior functionaries to withhold information from the most senior politicians, even from the president of the Republic himself. In January 1895, for example, during the tenure of Foreign Minister Gabriel Hanotaux, President Casimir Périer resigned after only six months in office, protesting that the ministry of foreign affairs had failed to keep him informed even of the most important developments. Policy documents were treated as arcana. Raymond Poincaré was informed of the details of the Franco-Russian Alliance only when he became premier and foreign minister in 1912.[52]

But the relative independence of the ministry did not necessarily confer power and autonomy upon the minister. French foreign ministers tended to be weak, weaker indeed than their own ministerial staff. One reason for this was the relatively rapid turnover of ministers, a consequence of the perennially high levels of political turbulence in pre-war France. Between 1 January 1913 and the outbreak of war, for example,

Joseph Caillaux

there were no fewer than six different foreign ministers. Ministerial office was a more transitory and less important stage in the life cycle of French politicians than in Britain, Germany or Austria-Hungary. And in the absence of any code of cabinet solidarity, the energies and ambition of ministers tended to be consumed in the bitter factional strife that was part of the everyday life of government in the Third Republic.

Of course, there were exceptions to this rule. If a minister stayed in power for long enough and possessed sufficient determination and industry, he could certainly imprint his personality upon the workings of the ministry. Théophile Delcassé is a good example. He remained in office for a staggering seven years (from June 1898 until June 1905) and established his mastery over the ministry not only through tireless work, but also by ignoring his permanent officials in Paris and cultivating a network of like-minded ambassadors and functionaries from across the organization. In France, as elsewhere in Europe, the waxing and waning of specific offices within the system produced adjustments in the distribution of power. Under a forceful minister like Delcassé, the power-share of the senior civil service functionaries known collectively as the Centrale tended to shrink, while the ambassadors, freed from the constraints imposed by the centre, flourished, just as Izvolsky and Hartwig did during the early years of Sazonov. Delcassé's long spell in office saw the emergence of an inner cabinet of senior ambassadors around the Cambon brothers (London and Berlin) and Camille Barrère (Rome). The ambassadors met regularly in Paris to discuss policy and lobby key officials. They communicated with the minister through private letters, bypassing the functionaries of the Centrale.

The senior ambassadors developed an extraordinarily elevated sense of their own importance, especially if we measure it against the professional ethos of today's ambassadors. Paul Cambon is a characteristic example: he remarked in a letter of 1901 that the whole of French diplomatic history amounted to little more than a long list of attempts by agents abroad to achieve something in the face of resistance from Paris. When he disagreed with his official instructions from the capital, he not infrequently burned them. During a tense conversation with Justin de Selves, minister of foreign affairs from June 1911 until January 1912, Cambon somewhat tactlessly informed de Selves that he considered himself the minister's equal.[53] This claim looks less bizarre if we bear in mind that between 1898, when he became ambassador to London, and the

Paul Cambon

summer of 1914, Cambon saw nine ministers enter and leave office – two of them did so twice. Cambon did not regard himself as a subordinate employee of the government, but as a servant of France whose expertise entitled him to a major role in the policy-making process.

Underpinning Cambon's exalted sense of self was the belief – shared by many of the senior ambassadors – that one did not merely represent France, one *personified* it. Though he was ambassador in London from 1898 until 1920, Cambon spoke not a word of English. During his meetings with Edward Grey (who spoke no French), he insisted that every utterance be translated into French, including easily recognized words such as 'yes'.[54] He firmly believed – like many members of the French elite – that French was the only language capable of articulating rational thought and he objected to the foundation of French schools in Britain on the eccentric grounds that French people raised in Britain tended to end up mentally retarded.[55] Cambon and Delcassé established a close working relationship whose fruit was the Entente Cordiale of 1904. It was Cambon, more than anyone else, who laid the groundwork for the Entente, working hard from 1901 to persuade his British interlocutors to settle over Morocco, while at the same time urging Delcassé to relinquish France's putative claims on Egypt.[56]

Things changed after Delcassé's departure at the height of the first Moroccan crisis. His successors were less forceful and authoritative figures. Maurice Rouvier and Léon Bourgeois occupied the minister's post for only ten and seven months respectively; Stéphen Pichon had a longer spell, from October 1906 to March 1911, but he abhorred regular hard work and was often absent from his desk in the Quai d'Orsay. The result was a steady rise in the influence of the Centrale.[57] By 1911, two factional groupings had coalesced within the world of French foreign affairs. On the one side were the old ambassadors and their allies within the administration, who tended to favour détente with Germany and a pragmatic, open-ended approach to France's foreign relations. On the other were the 'Young Turks', as Jules Cambon called them, of the Centrale.

The ambassadors wielded the authority of age and the experience acquired over long years in the field. The men of the Centrale, on the other hand, possessed formidable institutional and structural advantages. They could issue press releases, they controlled the transmission of official documents, and above all, they had access to the *cabinet noir* within the ministerial office – a small but important department responsible for opening letters and intercepting and deciphering diplomatic traffic. And just as in Russia, these structural and adversarial divisions coincided with divergent views of external relations. The agitations of the internal struggle for influence could thus have a direct impact on the orientation of policy.

French policy on the Morocco question is a case in point. After the Franco-German clash over Morocco in 1905 and the German débâcle at Algeciras in the following year, Paris and Berlin struggled to find an accord that would put the Moroccan conflict behind them. On the French side, opinions were divided on how German claims vis-à-vis Morocco ought to be handled. Should Paris seek to accommodate German interests in Morocco, or should it proceed as if German rights in the territory simply did not exist? The most outspoken exponent of the first view was Jules Cambon, brother of Paul and French ambassador to Berlin. Cambon had several reasons for seeking détente with Germany. The Germans, he argued, had a right to speak up for the interests of their industrialists and investors abroad. He also formed the view that the most senior German policy-makers – from the Kaiser and his close friend Count Philipp zu Eulenburg, to the chancellor Bernhard von Bülow, the German foreign secretary Heinrich von Tschirschky and his successor Wilhelm von Schoen – were sincerely desirous of better relations with Paris. It was France, he argued, with its factionalized politics and its perfervid nationalist press, that was chiefly responsible for the misunderstandings that had arisen between the two neighbouring powers. The fruit of Cambon's efforts was the Franco-German Accord of 9 February 1909, which excluded Berlin from any political initiative in Morocco, while affirming the value of Franco-German cooperation in the economic sphere.[58]

On the other side of the argument were the men of the Centrale who opposed concessions of any kind. From behind the scenes, key officials such as the maniacally Germanophobe Maurice Herbette, head of communications at the Quai d'Orsay from 1907 to 1911, used his extensive newspaper contacts to sabotage negotiations by leaking potentially controversial conciliatory proposals to the French press before they had been seen by the Germans, and even by stirring up jingoist press campaigns against Cambon himself.[59] Herbette was an excellent example of an official who managed to imprint his own outlook on French policy-making. In a memorandum of 1908 that resembles Eyre Crowe's famous British Foreign Office memorandum of the previous year (except for the fact that whereas Crowe's document fills twenty-five pages of print, Herbette's stretches to an astonishing 300 pages of chaotic manuscript), Herbette painted the recent history of Franco-German relations in the darkest colours as a catalogue of malign ruses, 'insinuations' and menaces. The Germans, he wrote, were insincere, suspicious, disloyal, duplicitous. Their efforts to conciliate were cunning ploys designed to trick and isolate France; their representations on behalf of their interests abroad were mere provocations; their foreign policy a repellent alternaton of 'menaces and promises'. France, he concluded, bore absolutely none of the responsibility for the poor state of relations between the two states, her handling of Germany had always been unimpeachably 'conciliatory and dignified': 'an impartial examination of the documents proves that France and its governments cannot in any way be made responsible for this situation'. Like Crowe's memorandum of the previous year, Herbette's memorandum was focused on the ascription of reprehensible motives and 'symptoms' rather than on naming actual transgressions.[60] There is no evidence that Herbette ever changed his views on Germany. He and other intransigent officials within the Centrale were a formidable obstacle to détente with Berlin.

With the collapse of the government at the beginning of March 1911 and Pichon's fall from office, the influence of the Centrale reached an all-time high. Pichon's successor as foreign minister was the conscientious but completely inexperienced Jean Cruppi, a former magistrate whose main qualification for the foreign affairs portfolio was that so many individuals better suited for the post had already turned it down – an indication of the low regard in which ministerial posts were held. During Cruppi's short period at the ministry – he took office on 2 March 1911 and was out by 27 June – the Centrale seized effective control over policy. Under pressure from the political and commercial director at the Quai d'Orsay, Cruppi agreed to terminate all economic links with Germany in Morocco, an unequivocal repudiation of the 1909 accord. A sequence of unilateral initiatives followed – negotiations for the joint Franco-German management of a railway from Fez to Tangier were broken off without notice and a new financial agreement with Morocco was drafted in which there was no mention whatsoever of German participation. Cambon was horrified: the French, he warned, were conducting their relations with Germany in an 'esprit de chicane'.[61]

Finally, in deciding, without consulting other interested countries, to deploy a substantial force of French metropolitan troops to the Moroccan city of Fez in the spring of 1911 on the pretext of repressing a local uprising and protecting French colonists, Paris broke comprehensively both with the Act of Algeciras and with the Franco-German Accord of 1909. The claim that this deployment was needed to protect the European community in Fez was bogus; the rebellion had occurred deep in the Moroccan interior and the danger to Europeans was remote. The Sultan's appeal for assistance from Paris had in fact been formulated by the French consul and was passed to him for signature after Paris had already decided to intervene.[62] We return below to the Agadir crisis that followed these steps – for the moment the crucial point is that it was not the French government as such that generated the forward policy in Morocco, but the hawks of the Quai d'Orsay, whose influence over policy was unrivalled in the spring and early summer of 1911.[63] Here, as in Russia, the flux of power from one part of the executive to another produced rapid shifts in the tone and direction of policy.

WHO GOVERNED IN BERLIN?

In Germany, too, foreign policy was shaped by the interaction between power-centres within the system. But there were some structural differences. The most important was that, within the complex federal structure created to house the German Empire founded in 1871, the role of foreign minister was largely absorbed in the office of the imperial chancellor. This pivotal post was in fact a composite, in which a range of different offices were linked in personal union. The chancellor of the German Empire was usually also both the minister-president and the foreign minister of Prussia, the dominant federal state, whose territory encompassed about three-fifths of the citizens and territory of the new empire. There was no imperial foreign minister, just an imperial state secretary for foreign affairs, who was the direct subordinate of the chancellor. And the chancellor's intimate link with the making of foreign policy was physically manifested in the fact that his private apartments were accommodated in the small and crowded palace at Wilhelmstrasse 76, where the German Foreign Office was also at home.

This was the system that had allowed Otto von Bismarck to dominate the unique constitutional structure he had helped to create in the aftermath of the German Wars of Unification and single-handedly to manage its external affairs. Bismarck's departure in the early spring of 1890 left a power vacuum that no one could fill.[64] Leo von Caprivi, the first post-Bismarckian chancellor and Prussian foreign minister, had no experience in foreign affairs. Caprivi's epoch-making decision not to renew the Reinsurance Treaty was in fact driven by a faction within the German Foreign Office which had secretly opposed the Bismarckian line for some time. Led by Friedrich von Holstein, director of the political department at the Foreign Office, a highly intelligent, hyper-articulate, privately malicious and socially reclusive individual who aroused admiration but not much affection in his fellows, this faction had little difficulty in winning over the new chancellor. Just as in France, in other words, the weakness of the foreign minister (or in this case, chancellor) meant that the initiative slipped towards the permanent officials of the Wilhelmstrasse, the Berlin equivalent of the Centrale. This state of affairs continued under Caprivi's successor, Prince Chlodwig von Hohenlohe-Schillingsfürst, who occupied the chancellorship in the years 1894–9. It was Holstein, not the chancellor or the imperial foreign secretary, who determined the shape of German foreign policy in the early and mid-1890s.

Holstein could do this in part because he had excellent ties both with the responsible politicians and with the coterie of advisers around Kaiser Wilhelm II.[65] These were the years when Wilhelm was most energetically throwing his weight about, determined to become 'his own Bismarck' and to establish his own 'personal rule' over the cumbersome German system. He failed in this objective, but his antics did paradoxically produce a concentration of executive power, by virtue of the fact that the most senior politicians and officials clubbed together to ward off sovereign threats to the integrity of the decision-making process. Friedrich von Holstein, Count Philipp zu Eulenburg, the Kaiser's intimate friend and influential adviser, and even the ineffectual chancellor Hohenlohe became adept at 'managing the Kaiser'.[66] They did so mainly by not taking him too seriously. In a letter of February 1897 to Eulenburg, Holstein observed that this was the 'third policy programme' he had seen from the sovereign in three months. Eulenburg told him to take it easy: the Kaiser's projects were not 'programmes', he assured Holstein, but whimsical 'marginal jottings' of limited import for the conduct of policy. The chancellor, too, was unconcerned. 'It seems that His Majesty is recommending another new programme,' Hohenlohe wrote, 'but I don't take it too tragically; I've seen too many programmes come and go.'[67]

It was Eulenburg and Holstein who placed the career diplomat Bernhard von Bülow on the road to the chancellorship. Already as imperial foreign secretary under Chancellor Hohenlohe (1897–1900), Bülow had been able, with the help of his friends, to secure control of German policy. His position was even stronger after 1900, when the Kaiser, acting on Eulenburg's advice, appointed Bülow to the chancellorship. More than any chancellor before him, Bülow deployed all the arts of the seasoned courtier to draw Wilhelm into his confidence. Despite internal rivalries and suspicions, the Bülow–Holstein–Eulenburg troika for a time kept a remarkably tight hold on policy-making.[68] The system worked well as long as three conditions were satisfied: (i) the partners were in agreement on their ultimate objectives, (ii) their policies were successful, and (iii) the Kaiser remained quiescent.

During the Morocco crisis of 1905–6, all three of these preconditions lapsed. First, Holstein and Bülow found themselves in disagreement on German aims in Morocco (Bülow wanted compensation; Holstein hoped, unrealistically, to explode the Anglo-French Entente). Then it became clear at the conference of Algeciras in 1906, where the German delegation found itself isolated and outmanoeuvred by France, that the Morocco policy had been disastrously mishandled. One consequence of this fiasco was that the Kaiser, who had always been sceptical of the Moroccan démarche, disassociated himself from his chancellor and re-emerged as a threat to the policy-making process.[69]

It was the inverse of what happened at around the same time in Russia, where the débâcle of the Tsar's East Asia policy weakened the sovereign's position and set the scene for the assertion of cabinet responsibility. In Germany, by contrast, the failure of the senior officials temporarily restored the Kaiser's freedom of movement. In January 1906, when the office of foreign secretary suddenly fell vacant (because its previous incumbent had died of overwork), Wilhelm II imposed a replacement of his own choice, disregarding Bulow's advice. It was widely understood that Heinrich von Tschirschky, a close associate of the Kaiser who had often accompanied him on his travels, had been appointed to replace the Bülow–Holstein policy with something more conciliatory. By early 1907, there was talk of feuding between the 'Bülow camp' and the 'Tschirschky circle'.

In the final years of his chancellorship, which lasted until 1909, Bülow fought ruthlessly to regain his former supremacy. He tried, as Bismarck had done in the 1880s, to build a new parliamentary bloc defined by loyalty to his own person, in the hope of rendering himself politically indispensable to the Kaiser. He helped to engineer the shattering scandal of the 'Daily Telegraph Affair' (November 1908) in which jejune remarks by Wilhelm in an interview published in a British newspaper triggered a wave of protest from a German public tired of the Kaiser's public indiscretions. Bülow was even indirectly involved in the chain of press campaigns in 1907–8 that exposed homosexuals within the Kaiser's intimate circle – including Eulenburg, the chancellor's erstwhile friend and ally, now reviled by Bülow, who was himself probably homosexual, as a potential rival for the Kaiser's favour.[70] Despite these extravagant manoeuvres, Bülow never regained his earlier influence over foreign policy.[71] The appointment of Theobald von Bethmann Hollweg to the chancellorship on 14 July 1909 brought a degree of stabilization. Bethmann may have lacked a background in foreign affairs, but he was a steady, moderate and formidable figure who quickly asserted his authority over the ministers and imperial secretaries.[72] It helped that after the shock and humiliation of the *Daily Telegraph* and Eulenburg scandals, the Kaiser was less inclined than in earlier years to challenge the authority of his ministers in public.

THE TROUBLED SUPREMACY OF
SIR EDWARD GREY

Britain presents a rather different picture. Unlike Stolypin and Koko-vtsov or their German colleagues Bülow and Bethmann Hollweg, the British foreign secretary, Sir Edward Grey, had no reason to fear unwanted interventions by the sovereign. George V was perfectly happy to be led by his foreign secretary in international matters. And Grey also enjoyed the unstinting support of his prime minister, Herbert Asquith. Nor did he have to contend, as his French colleagues did, with over-mighty functionaries in his own Foreign Office. Grey's continuity in office alone assured him a more consistent influence over policy than most of his French colleagues ever enjoyed. While Edward Grey remained in control of the Foreign Office for the years between December 1905 and December 1916, the same period in France saw fifteen ministers of foreign affairs come and go. Moreover, Grey's arrival at the Foreign Office consolidated the influence of a network of senior officials who broadly shared his view of British foreign policy. Grey was without doubt the most powerful foreign minister of pre-war Europe.

Like most of his nineteenth-century predecessors, Sir Edward Grey was born into the top tier of British society. He was the descendant of a distinguished line of Whig grandees – his great grand-uncle was the Earl Grey of the 1832 Reform Bill and eponym of the popular scented tea. Of all the politicians who walked the European political stage before 1914, Grey is one of the most baffling. His aloof and lofty style did not go down well with the rank and file of the Liberal Party. He had long been a Liberal MP, yet he believed that foreign policy was too import-ant to be subjected to the agitations of parliamentary debate. He was a foreign secretary who knew little of the world outside Britain, had never shown much interest in travelling, spoke no foreign languages and felt

Sir Edward Grey

ill at ease in the company of foreigners. He was a Liberal politician whose vision of policy was opposed by most Liberals and supported by most Conservatives. He became the most powerful member of the faction known as 'the liberal imperialists', yet he appears to have cared little for the British Empire – his views on foreign policy and national security were tightly focused on the European continent.

There was a curious dissonance between Grey's persona – private and public – and his modus operandi in politics. As a young man, he had shown little sign of intellectual curiosity, political ambition or drive. He idled away his years at Balliol College, Oxford, where he spent most of his time becoming Varsity champion in real tennis, before graduating with a third in Jurisprudence, a subject he had chosen because it was reputed to be easy. His first (unpaid) political post was fixed up through Whig family connections. As an adult, Grey always cultivated the image of a man for whom politics was a wearisome duty, rather than a vocation. When parliament was dissolved in 1895 following a Liberal defeat in a key vote, Grey, who was then serving as an MP and parliamentary under-secretary of state for foreign affairs, professed to feel no regrets.

'I shall never be in office again and the days of my stay in the House of Commons are probably numbered. We [he and his wife Dorothy] are both very relieved.'[73] Grey was a passionate naturalist, birdwatcher and fisherman. By the turn of the century, he was already well known as the author of a justly celebrated essay on fly-fishing. Even as foreign secretary, he was apt to leave his desk at the earliest opportunity for country jaunts and disliked being recalled to London any sooner than was absolutely necessary. Some of those who worked with Grey, such as the diplomat Cecil Spring-Rice, felt that the country excursions were getting out of hand and that the foreign secretary would be well advised to 'spare some time from his ducks to learn French'.[74] Colleagues found it difficult to discern political motivation in Grey; he struck them as 'devoid of personal ambition, aloof and unapproachable'.[75]

And yet Grey did develop a deep appetite for power and a readiness to deploy conspiratorial methods in order to obtain and hold on to it. His accession to the post of foreign secretary was the fruit of careful planning with his trusted friends and fellow liberal imperialists, Herbert Asquith and R. B. Haldane. In the 'Relugas Compact', a plot hatched at Grey's fishing lodge in the Scottish hamlet of that name, the three men agreed to push aside the Liberal leader Sir Henry Campbell-Bannerman and establish themselves in key cabinet posts. Secretiveness and a preference for discreet, behind-the-scenes dealing remained a hallmark of his style as foreign secretary. The posture of gentlemanly diffidence belied an intuitive feel for the methods and tactics of adversarial politics.

Grey quickly secured unchallenged control over the policy-making process, ensuring that British policy focused primarily on the 'German threat'. It would be going too far, of course, to view this reorientation of British policy as a function solely of Edward Grey's power. Grey was not the puppet-master; the men of the new policy – Bertie, Hardinge, Nicolson, Mallet, Tyrrell and so on – were not manipulated or controlled by him, but worked alongside him as the members of a loose coalition driven by shared sentiments. Indeed, Grey was quite dependent on some of these collaborators – many of his decisions and memoranda, for example, were modelled closely on reports from Hardinge.[76] The ascendancy of the Grey group was eased by recent structural reforms to the Foreign Office whose object had not been to reinforce the authority of the foreign secretary, but rather to parcel influence out more widely across a range of senior officials.[77] Nevertheless, the energy and vigilance with which Grey maintained his ascendancy are impressive. It helped, of course, that he enjoyed the firm support of his former co-conspirator Herbert Asquith, prime minister from 1908 until 1916. The backing of a large part of the Conservative bloc in the House of Commons was another important asset – and Grey proved adept at maintaining his cross-party appeal.

But Grey's plenitude of power and consistency of vision did not entirely protect British policy-making from the agitations characteristic of the European executives. The anti-German position adopted by the Grey group did not enjoy wide support outside the Foreign Office. It was not even backed by the majority of the British cabinet. The Liberal government, and the Liberal movement more generally, were polarized by the tension between liberal imperialist and radical elements. Many of the leading radicals, and they included some of the most venerable figures in the party, deplored the foreign secretary's policy of alignment with Russia. They accused Grey and his associates of adopting a pose towards Germany that was unnecessarily provocative. They doubted whether the advantages of appeasing Russia outweighed the potential benefits of friendship with the German Empire. They worried whether the creation of a Triple Entente might not pressure Germany into adopting an ever more aggressive stance and they pressed for détente with Berlin. A further problem was the complexion of British public opinion, especially within the cultural and political elite, which, despite intermittent Anglo-German 'press wars', was drifting into a more pro-German mood during the last few years before the outbreak of war.[78] Antagonism to Germany coexisted across the British elites with multi-layered cultural ties and a deep admiration of the country's cultural, economic and scientific achievements.[79]

Grey met these challenges by shielding the policy-making process from the scrutiny of unfriendly eyes. Documents emanating from his desk were often marked 'For Limited Circulation Only'; a typical annotation from his private secretary reads 'Sir E. Grey thinks this circulation sufficient'. Consultations on important policy decisions – notably regarding the deepening commitment to France – were confined to trusted contacts within the administration. Cabinet was not informed, for example, of the discussions between France and Britain in December 1905 and May 1906, in which military representatives of both countries agreed in principle the form that a British military intervention in support of France would take in the event of war. This mode of proceeding suited Grey's elitist understanding of politics and his avowed view of the Entente, which was that it should be cultivated 'in a loyal and generous spirit' ensuring that any pitfalls arising would 'strengthen' rather than weaken the 'Agreement', and that the gradual advance into a deepening commitment should always be insulated from 'party controversy'.[80] In other words, Grey ran a double-track policy. In public, he repeatedly denied that Britain was under any obligation to come to France's aid. London's hands remained absolutely free. Pressed by hostile colleagues, he could always say that the interlinked mobilization scenarios of the military were mere contingency plans. By means of these complex manoeuvres, Grey was able to impart a remarkable inner consistency to the management of British foreign policy.

Yet it is easy to see how this state of affairs – driven by the shifting balance of power between factions within the British government and the political elite – gave rise to confusion. To those French interlocutors who dealt directly with the foreign secretary and his associates, it was clear that 'Sir Grey', as some of them quaintly called him, would stand by France in the event of a war, notwithstanding the official insistence on the non-binding character of the Entente. But to the Germans, who were not privy to these conversations, it looked very much as if Britain might stand aside from the continental coalition, especially if the Franco-Russian Alliance took the initiative against Germany, rather than the other way around.

THE AGADIR CRISIS OF 1911

The fluctuation of power across different points in the decision-making structures amplified the complexity and unpredictabilty of interactions in the European international system, especially in those moments of political crisis when two or more executives interacted with each other in an atmosphere of heightened pressure and threat. We can observe this effect with particular clarity in the quarrel that broke out between Germany and France over Morocco in the summer of 1911. The Franco-German Moroccan Agreement of 1909 broke down, as we have seen, following a sequence of steps undertaken by the Quai d'Orsay, culminating in the dispatch of a large French force to the Sultanate in April 1911. On 5 June 1911, alarmed at the prospect of a unilateral French seizure of power in Morocco, the Spanish government deployed troops to occupy Larache and Ksar-el-Kebir in northern and north-western Morocco. A German intervention was now inevitable, and the gunboat *Panther*, an unimpressive craft that was two years overdue for scrapping, duly dropped anchor off the Moroccan coast on 1 July 1911.

There is something very odd about the Agadir crisis. It was allowed to escalate to the point where it seemed that a western-European war was imminent, yet the positions advanced by the opposing parties were not irreconcilable and eventually provided the basis for an enduring settlement. Why did the escalation happen? Part of the reason lay in the intransigence of the Quai d'Orsay. It was the Centrale that seized and held the initiative in the early phase of the crisis. The position of the permanent officials was strengthened by the fact that Foreign Minister Jean Cruppi left office on 27 June, a few days before the *Panther* arrived off Agadir. His successor Justin de Selves – a default candidate like Cruppi – immediately fell under the thrall of the *chef du cabinet* at the French foreign ministry, Maurice Herbette. As chief of communications between 1907 and 1911, Herbette had built up an extensive network of newspaper contacts and he worked hard during the Agadir crisis to discredit the very idea of talks with Germany. It was partly a consequence of the intransigence of Herbette and other powerful permanent officials that it was not until the end of July 1911 that the French ambassador in Berlin was even instructed to commence talks with Berlin about how Germany might be compensated for the consolidation of French exclusive dominion in Morocco.

This conciliatory move was itself only possible because Ambassador Jules Cambon appealed from his Berlin posting over the head of his foreign minister to the energetic and outspoken premier Joseph Caillaux, who had taken office on 27 June, just before the crisis broke. The son of a finance minister, the celebrated Eugène Caillaux who had paid off the French indemnity to Germany so swiftly after 1870, Joseph Caillaux was an economic liberal and fiscal modernizer who viewed foreign affairs with the pragmatic eyes of a businessman. He saw no reason why German commercial interests in Morocco should not be treated on exactly the same footing as those of other nationalities and he was critical of the mercantilist style of economic strategy that had become a hallmark of European imperialism.[81] The cabinet was split between Caillaux, who favoured a conciliatory policy on Morocco, and Justin de Selves, who functioned as a mouthpiece for the hawks at the Quai d'Orsay. De Selves was under pressure from his ministry to send French cruisers to Agadir, a move that might have triggered a serious escalation. After Caillaux vetoed this option, the hawks began to organize against him and Jules Cambon. Press releases were used to discredit the champions of conciliation. Caillaux became so exasperated at Maurice Herbette's efforts to sabotage his policy that he summoned him to his office and told him, fitting the action to the words: 'I will break you like this pencil'.[82] Caillaux was eventually able to achieve an agreement with Germany, but only by conducting confidential and unofficial talks with Berlin (through the German embassy in Paris, through Jules Cambon in Berlin and through the mediation of a businessman called Fondère) that successfully circumvented the minister and his officials.[83] The result was that by the beginning of August, Caillaux had secretly accepted a compensation deal with Berlin to which his foreign minister Justin de Selves remained adamantly opposed.[84]

This backstairs diplomacy helped the premier to bypass the Germanophobe hawks of the French foreign ministry, but it brought its own additional risks. In the first week of August 1911, a brief breakdown in communications led to an entirely unnecessary escalation, including threats to dispatch French and British warships to Agadir, even though Caillaux and his German counterpart were at that point in fact both willing to compromise.[85] Caillaux blamed his mediator Fondère for the misunderstanding, but there would have been no need for a go-between like Fondère or for Caillaux's backstairs dealing, had it not been for the fact that the officials of the ministry were conspiring to throw him out of office and wreck negotiations for an understanding with Germany. Inevitably, this also meant that Caillaux was sometimes forced to backtrack on his commitments, because his ministerial colleagues refused to accept the assurances he had made to Berlin. And these complex manoeuvres heightened the uncertainty in Berlin about how French moves should be read: it was a matter of weighing contradictory trends against each other, as one junior German diplomat did when he reported that 'despite the screaming in the press and the chauvinism of the army', Caillaux's policy would probably prevail.[86]

As for German policy during the crisis, it was formulated not by

Chancellor Bethmann Hollweg, and certainly not by the Kaiser, who was completely uninterested in Morocco, but by the energetic Swabian imperial state secretary for foreign affairs, Alfred von Kiderlen-Wächter. Kiderlen had been involved in drawing up the Franco-German Agreement on Morocco of February 1909 and it was natural that he should play a leading role in formulating Germany's response to the French troop deployment. In a manner characteristic of the upper reaches of the German executive, the foreign secretary seized personal control of the Morocco policy-thread, managing communications with Paris and keeping the chancellor at arm's length from the developing crisis.[87] Kiderlen had no interest in securing a German share of Morocco, but he was determined not to allow France unilaterally to impose exclusive control there. He hoped, by mirroring French moves with a sequence of incremental German gestures of protest, to secure an acknowledgement of German rights and some form of territorial compensation in the French Congo. He had good reason to believe that this objective could be secured without conflict, for in May 1911, Joseph Caillaux, then finance minister, had assured German diplomats in Paris that 'France would be prepared, if we [the Germans] recognized its vital interest in Morocco, to make concessions to us elsewhere.'[88] After Caillaux's accession to the office of premier in June, therefore, Kiderlen assumed that this would be France's policy. He rejected plans to send two ships to Agadir; he believed that the *Panther*, which was not equipped to organize an effective landing and had no instructions to attempt one, would suffice for a symbolic demonstration.[89]

The subsequent evolution of the crisis revealed that Kiderlen had grossly misjudged the French response. He also seriously mismanaged the German domestic environment. Kiderlen's personal relations with Kaiser Wilhelm II were not especially cordial and the Emperor was as sceptical of the administration's policy on North Africa in 1911 as he had been in 1905.[90] In order to bolster himself against possible opposition from this quarter, Kiderlen marshalled the support of German ultra-nationalist politicians and publicists. But he was unable, once the press campaign got underway, to control its tone or content. As a consequence, a German policy that aimed consistently to keep the crisis below the threshold of armed confrontation unfolded against the background of thunderous nationalist press agitation that rang alarm bells in Paris and London. Banner headlines in the ultra-nationalist papers shrieking 'West Morocco to Germany!' were grist to the mills of the hawks in Paris. They also worried the Kaiser, who issued such sharp criticisms of the foreign secretary's policy that on 17 July Kiderlen tendered his resignation – only through Chancellor Bethmann's mediation was it possible to save the policy and keep Kiderlen in office.[91]

On 4 November 1911, a Franco-German treaty at last defined the terms of an agreement. Morocco became an exclusively French protectorate, German business interests were assured of respectful treatment and parts of the French Congo were conceded to Germany. But the 1911 Moroccan crisis had exposed the perilous incoherence of French diplomacy. An internal disciplinary committee convened on 18 November 1911 to investigate the actions of Maurice Herbette revealed the elaborate machinations of the permanent officials in Paris. Caillaux, too, was discredited. He and his cabinet were associated in the public eye with a treaty that many French nationalists thought had conceded too much to the Germans, which is remarkable, given that it conceded less than Delcassé had envisaged offering in exchange for Morocco in the late 1890s. Revelations of the premier's secret negotiations with the Germans (acquired as decrypts by the *cabinet noir* and tactically leaked to the press by the Centrale) sealed his fate and Caillaux fell from office on 21 January 1912, having occupied the premiership for only seven months.

In Germany, too, the treaty of November 1911 was denounced – for granting the Germans too little. Kiderlen was partly to blame for this – there was a gaping discrepancy between what Germany could expect to achieve by challenging the French over Morocco and the glittering prizes – a 'German West Morocco', for example – held out to the public by the ultra-nationalist press whose agitation Kiderlen had briefly and unwisely encouraged. By doing this, the foreign secretary contributed to the deepening alienation between the government and those who claimed to be its 'natural supporters' on the far right. Yet this faustian pact with the nationalist media had only been necessary because Kiderlen had no other means of ensuring that the sovereign would not compromise his own control of the policy-making process.

Perhaps the most important consequence of German policy oscillation during the crisis was a growing tendency in Paris to misread German actions as driven by a policy of bluff. When he read the files of the Quai d'Orsai in the first months of 1912, the new incoming premier and foreign minister, Raymond Poincaré, was struck by the alternation of toughness and concessions in German policy: 'whenever we have adopted a conciliatory approach to Germany', Poincaré observed, 'she has abused it; on the other hand, on each occasion when we have have shown firmness, she has yielded'. From this he drew the ominous conclusion that Germany understood 'only the language of force'.[92]

Britain's involvement in the crisis, too, bore the imprint of deep divisions within the executive structure. The reaction of the Liberal cabinet in London was initially cautious, since it was felt that France was largely responsible for triggering the crisis and should be urged to give ground. On 19 July, the cabinet even authorized Grey to inform Paris that there were circumstances under which Britain might accept a German presence in Morocco. The French government angrily replied that British acquiescence on this point would amount to a breach in the Anglo-French agreement of 1904.[93] At the same time, the anti-Germans around Grey adopted a robustly pro-French position. Nicolson, Buchanan, Haldane and Grey himself talked up the threat posed by Germany and revived the notion that what was at stake was the maintenance of the Entente. On 19 July, the secretary of state for war Richard Haldane asked the director of military operations Sir Henry Wilson to delay his departure for the continent so that he could spend a morning assessing prospective troop strengths in the event of a conflict on the Franco-German frontier.[94] When Justin de Selves expressed surprise at the extent of German demands for compensation in the Congo, Sir Francis Bertie wrote to Grey from Paris of the 'excessive' requirements of the Germans, which 'are known by them to be impossible of acceptance and are intended to reconcile the French to the establishment of Germany on the Moroccan coast'[95] – this was a misreading of the German position, and it was calculated to strike fear into the British navalists, for whom the establishment of a German stronghold on the Atlantic would have been unacceptable.

It was the prospect of a German Atlantic port that enabled Grey to secure cabinet approval for a private warning to the German ambassador on 21 July that if Germany meant to land at Agadir, Britain would be obliged to defend her interests there – by which Grey meant the deployment of British warships.[96] On the same day, the Grey group raised the temperature yet further: on the evening of 21 July 1911, the Chancellor of the Exchequer David Lloyd George delivered a speech at

the Mansion House issuing a sharp warning to Berlin. It was imperative, Lloyd George said, that Britain should maintain 'her place and her
prestige among the Great Powers of the world'. British power had more
than once 'redeemed' continental nations from 'overwhelming disaster
and even from national extinction'. If Britain were to be forced to
choose between peace on the one hand and the surrender of her international pre-eminence on the other, 'then I say emphatically that peace
at that price would be a humiliation intolerable for a great nation like
ours to endure'.[97] In the days that followed, Grey stoked the fires of a
naval panic in London, warning Lloyd George and Churchill that the
British fleet was in danger of imminent attack and informing Reginald
McKenna, First Lord of the Admiralty, that the German fleet was mobilized and ready to strike – in reality, the High Seas Fleet was scattered
and the Germans had no intention of concentrating it.[98]

The Mansion House speech was no spontaneous outburst; it was a
gambit carefully planned by Grey, Asquith and Lloyd George. Just as
Caillaux bypassed his Foreign Office in order to impose his own dovish
agenda on the negotiations with Berlin, so the anti-Germans around
Grey bypassed the dovish radicals in the Liberal cabinet in order to
deliver a harsh and potentially provocative message to the Germans.
Lloyd George had not cleared the sensitive passages of his speech with
the cabinet, only with Prime Minister Asquith and Foreign Secretary
Grey.[99] The speech was all the more important for the fact that it
signalled Lloyd George's defection from the camp of the dove radicals
to that of the liberal imperialists. His words caused consternation in
Berlin, where it was felt that the British government was needlessly
disrupting the passage of Franco-German negotiations. 'Who is Lloyd
George to lay down the law to Germany and to stop a quick Franco-
German settlement?' Arthur Zimmermann, under-secretary of state
for foreign affairs, asked the British ambassador in Berlin.[100]

Lloyd George's words also shocked those British cabinet ministers
who had not signed up to Grey's programme. Viscount Morley, secretary of state for India, denounced the speech – and Grey's subsequent
defence of it in conversation with the German ambassador in London –
as an 'unwarranted and unfortunate provocation to Germany'. The
Lord Chancellor, Lord Loreburn, was appalled to find Britain so aggressively backing France in a dispute in which (as it seemed to Loreburn)
Paris was by no means clear of blame. He entreated Grey to disavow the

speech and to make it clear that Britain had no intention of interfering in the negotiations between France and Germany.[101]

The Grey group prevailed. At a meeting of the Committee of Imperial Defence convened on 23 August 1911, it was agreed that should a Franco-German war break out, Britain would mount a rapid continental intervention, including the transshipment of a British Expeditionary Force. Asquith, Grey, Haldane, Lloyd George and the service chiefs were present, but key radicals, including Morley, Crewe, Harcourt and Esher, were either not informed or not invited. The weeks that followed were filled (to the horror of the radicals) with enthusiastic planning for war. Even Asquith recoiled from the extensive 'military conversations' designed to coordinate mobilization plans and strategy with the French in September 1911, but Grey refused to have them stopped.[102] To a greater extent than either of the two original quarrelling parties, Britain was willing to consider the possibility of a drastic escalation.[103] While the French had made no war preparations, even at the height of the crisis, Bethmann remarked in a letter to the German ambassador in London, 'Britain seems to have been ready to strike every day.'[104] The Austrian foreign minister Count Aehrenthal came to a similar conclusion, noting on 3 August that England had for a moment seemed ready to use the Moroccan quarrel as a pretext for a full-on 'reckoning' with its German rival.[105] The contrast with Russia's relatively reserved and conciliatory position was particularly striking.[106] Only after this British reaction did Vienna abandon the policy of neutrality it had hitherto adopted on the Morocco question.[107]

The battle between the hawks and the doves was not yet over. Just as the officials of the French foreign ministry wrought their revenge upon Caillaux and the hapless Justin de Selves, toppling them from office in January 1912, so in Britain the radical Liberal sceptics renewed their assault on the policy pursued by Grey. Among the ministers there were many who had never appreciated the depth of Grey's commitments to France before Agadir. In December 1911, there was a backbench revolt against Grey. Part of the ill-feeling against him arose from a frustration at the secretiveness of his tactics – why had no one been told about the undertakings the government was supposedly making on behalf of the British people? Arthur Ponsonby and Noel Buxton, both prominent Liberal anti-Grey activists, demanded that a committee be formed to improve Anglo-German relations. The backlash against the foreign secretary swept through virtually the entire liberal press. But whereas the die-hards in Paris did succeed in discrediting both Caillaux and his conciliatory approach, the 'pro-German' lobby in Britain failed to dislodge Grey or his policy.

There were three reasons for this: the first was that British ministers were inherently less vulnerable to this kind of campaigning, thanks to the robust partisan structure of British parliamentary politics; then there was the fact that if Grey's policy were comprehensively disavowed, he himself might resign, taking Lloyd George, Haldane and possibly Churchill with him – this would be the end of the Liberals in government, a sobering thought for the Liberal non-interventionists. No less important was the support of the parliamentary Conservatives for Grey's policy of military entente with France. One of the things that helped the foreign secretary to weather the storms of the Agadir crisis was the secret assurance of support from Arthur Balfour, leader of the Conservative Party until November 1911.[108] This dependence on the parliamentary opposition would prove something of a liability in the summer of 1914, when a looming crisis over Ireland raised questions about the continuation of Conservative support.

But if the essentials of Grey's *ententiste* policy remained in place, the fact that he had to defend his position against such vociferous and influential domestic opposition nonetheless prevented him from articulating his commitments as unequivocally as he might have wished. After Agadir, Grey had to walk a tightrope between French demands that he make a clearer commitment and the insistence of the non-interventionists in cabinet (who were, after all, still in the majority) that he do no such thing. In two cabinet resolutions of November 1911, fifteen of his fellow cabinet ministers called Grey to order, demanding that he desist from sponsoring high-level military discussions between Britain and France without their prior knowledge and approval. In January 1912, there was talk among the non-interventionists led by Loreburn of agreeing a cabinet statement to the effect that Britain was 'not under any obligation, direct or indirect, express or implied, to support France against Germany by force of arms'. Grey and his people were spared this blow only by Loreburn's illness and retirement.[109]

The need to balance such concerted opposition from inside his government with a policy focused on maintaining the entente as a security device produced a baffling ambiguity in British diplomatic signalling.

On the one hand, British military commanders had always been accorded a certain discretion in their dealings with their French colleagues; their assurances of British military support in the event of a conflict with Germany helped to harden the French position.[110] These initiatives were not sanctioned by Cabinet, let alone by the British parliament. During the Agadir crisis of 1911, the new DMO, Major General Henry Wilson, was sent to Paris for discussions with the French General Staff aimed at agreeing a schedule for an Anglo-French joint mobilization against Germany. The resulting Wilson–Dubail memorandum of 21 July 1911 (General Auguste Dubail was at that time the French General Staff chief) stipulated that by day fifteen of mobilization, six British infantry divisions, one cavalry division, and two mounted brigades (encompassing 150,000 men and 67,000 horses) would be deployed on the French left flank.[111] The decision in the early months of 1912 to neutralize German naval expansion by coordinating Anglo-French naval strategy strengthened the presumption that something like a defensive alliance was coming into existence.

On the other hand, the famous Grey–Cambon letters of 22–23 November 1912, 'extorted', as Morley later put it, from Grey by his non-interventionist opponents, made it clear that the Entente was anything but an alliance, for they asserted the freedom of both partners to act independently, even if one of the parties were to be attacked by a third power. Was there an obligation to support France, or was there not? It was all very well for Grey to declare in public that these were mere contingency plans with no binding force. In private, the foreign secretary acknowledged that he viewed the Anglo-French military conversations as 'committing us to cooperation with France', so long as her actions were 'non-provocative and reasonable'. When the permanent under-secretary for foreign affairs, Sir Arthur Nicolson, insisted to Grey at the beginning of August 1914 that 'you have over and over again promised M. Cambon that if Germany was the aggressor you would stand by France', Grey merely replied: 'Yes, but he has nothing in writing.'[112]

Anglo-French diplomacy thus came to be marked at the highest level – on the British side – by a kind of doublethink. It was understood that Grey must tailor his public statements and even his official communications to the expectations of the non-interventionists in cabinet and among the broader public. Yet, when Paul Cambon listened to his anti-German friends in London, or to Bertie in Paris, he heard what he wanted to hear. This was a difficult arrangement for the French to live with, to say the least. As the July Crisis of 1914 reached its climax, it would cost the decision-makers in Paris, the French ambassador in London and indeed Grey himself a few moments of high anxiety. More importantly, uncertainty about the British commitment forced French strategists to compensate in the east for their weaknesses in the west by committing ever more strongly to militarizing the alliance with Russia.[113] The French government, Baron Guillaume, the Belgian minister in Paris, noted in the spring of 1913, was obliged to 'tighten more and more its alliance with Russia, because it is aware that Britain's friendship for it is less and less solid and effective'.[114] For Germany too the irresolution of British policy was a source of confusion and vexation. On the one hand, Grey was obliged to maintain the appearance of an open door to Berlin in order to placate the non-interventionists. Yet he also felt obliged from time to time to administer harsh warnings to the Germans, lest they come to the conclusion that France had been comprehensively abandoned and could be attacked without fear of a British response. The result of this system of mixed messaging, a consequence of the mutability of power relations within the European executives, was a perennial uncertainty about British intentions that would unsettle the policy-makers in Berlin throughout the July Crisis.

SOLDIERS AND CIVILIANS

'The situation [in Europe] is extraordinary,' Colonel Edward House reported to American President Woodrow Wilson after a trip to Europe in May 1914. 'It is militarism run stark mad.'[115] House's views may have been shaped in part by a personal experience: he was a 'political colonel' of the American type. He had been appointed to that rank in the Texas militia in return for political services there. But when Colonel House visited Berlin, the Germans took him to be a military man and always sat him with the generals at dinner. His views on the prevalence of militarism may have owed something to this unfortunate misunderstanding.[116] Be that as it may, there is no doubt that, viewed from across the Atlantic, pre-war Europe presented a curious spectacle. Senior statesmen, emperors and kings attended public occasions wearing military uniform; elaborate military reviews were an integral part of the public ceremonial of power; immense illuminated naval displays drew huge crowds and filled the pages of the illustrated journals; conscript armies grew in size until they became male microcosms of the nation; the cult of military display entered the public and the private life of even the smallest communities. In what ways did this 'militarism' shape the decisions that led Europe to war in 1914? Did the roots of the July Crisis lie, as some historians have argued, in an abdication of responsibility by civilian politicians and a usurpation of political power by the generals?

There was without doubt a struggle between the soldiers and the civilians within the pre-war executives: it was a struggle for money. Defence expenditure accounted for a substantial share of government spending. Military commanders keen to improve equipment, training and infrastructure had to contend (as they do today) with civilian politicians for access to government resources. Conversely, ministers of finance and their political allies fought to impose restraint in the name of fiscal rigour or domestic consolidation. Who prevailed in these contests depended on the structure of the institutional environment and the prevailing domestic and international political constellation.

Until 1908, the chaotic structure of the Russian military command made it difficult for the generals to lobby government effectively. But the balance began to shift from 1908, when reforms to the military administration created a more concentrated executive structure, establishing the minister of war as the pre-eminent defence official with the exclusive right to report to the Tsar on military matters.[117] From 1909, a rivalry of epic bitterness evolved between the new war minister Vladimir Sukhomlinov (who was still in post in July 1914) and the strong-willed conservative finance minister, Vladimir Kokovtsov. Backed by the powerful premier Pyotr Stolypin, Kokovtsov, a champion of fiscal responsibility and domestic economic development, routinely blocked or curtailed Sukhomlinov's draft budgets. Professional friction swiftly deepened into lively personal hatred.[118] Sukhomlinov thought Kokovtsov 'narrow, verbose and self-seeking'; Kokovtsov accused the minister of war (with more justice) of incompetence, irresponsibility and corruption.[119]

Kokovtsov's German equivalent was Adolf Wermuth, treasury minister in 1909–11, who, with the support of Chancellor Bethmann Hollweg, worked hard to rebalance the Reich budget and cut public debt. Wermuth was critical of overspending under Tirpitz and often complained of the naval secretary's irresponsibility, just as Kokovtsov complained of Sukhomlinov's profligate handling of military funding.[120] The treasury minister's motto was: 'no expenditures without revenues'.[121] There was also perennial tension between the chief of staff and the minister of war, since the former's demands for increased funding were often rejected or opposed by the latter.[122] A recent study has even suggested that the famous memorandum of 1905 in which the chief of the General Staff Alfred von Schlieffen sketched the outlines of a massive westward offensive, was not a 'war plan' as such but a plea for more government money – among other things, Schlieffen's sketch envisaged the deployment of eighty-one divisions, more than the German army when mobilized actually possessed at the time.[123] The question of military finance was complicated in Germany by the fact that the federal constitution assigned direct taxation revenues to the member states, rather than to the Reich government. The devolved structure of the German Empire placed a fiscal limit on Reich defence expenditure that had no direct counterpart in Britain, France or Russia.[124]

Nevertheless, the conflict over resources was muted in Germany by the fact that military budgets were submitted to the parliament only at five-yearly intervals – a system known as the *Quinquennat*. Because senior military figures valued the *Quinquennat* as a means of protecting the army from constant parliamentary interference, they were reluctant to jeopardize it by requesting large extra-budgetary credits. This system worked as a powerful incentive for self-restraint. As the Prussian minister of war Karl von Einem observed in June 1906, the *Quinquennat* was a cumbersome arrangement, but it was useful nonetheless, because 'the savage and persistent agitation against the existence of the army which arises with every military expansion would only become all the more dangerous if it were a yearly occurrence'.[125] Even in 1911, when the *Quinquennat* came up for renewal and Chief of Staff Moltke and War Minister Heeringen joined forces in pressing for substantial growth, the opposition of Treasury Minister Wermuth and Chancellor Bethmann Hollweg ensured that the resulting increase in the strength of the peacetime army was very modest (10,000 men).[126]

We can discern analogous tensions in every European executive. In Britain, the Liberals campaigned (and won an absolute majority) in

1906 on the promise to cut back the vast military expenditure of the Boer War years under the slogan 'Peace, Retrenchment and Reform'. Budgetary constraints were a significant factor in the decision to seek an understanding with France and Russia. One consequence was that, while British naval budgets continued to soar (British naval spending was three times the German figure in 1904 and still more than double in 1913), army expenditure remained static throughout the pre-war years, forcing War Minister Haldane to focus on efficiency savings and reorganization rather than expansion.[127] In Austria-Hungary, the tumultuous domestic politics of dualism virtually paralysed the monarchy's military development after the turn of the century, as autonomist groups within the Hungarian parliament fought to starve the monarchy's joint army of Hungarian tax revenues and recruits. In this environment, proposals for increased military allocations were worn down in endless legislative feuding, and the Habsburg military languished in a condition, as the Austrian staff chief put it, of 'persistent stagnation'. This was one reason why, as late as 1912, Austria-Hungary spent only 2.6 per cent of its net national product on defence – a smaller proportion than any other European power and certainly far below what its economy could afford (the figures for Russia, France and Germany in that year were 4.5, 4.0 and 3.8 per cent respectively).[128]

In France, the 'Dreyfus affair' of the 1890s had destroyed the civil–military consensus of the Third Republic and placed the senior echelons of the army, viewed as a bastion of clerical and reactionary attitudes, under a cloud of public suspicion, especially in the eyes of the republican and anticlerical left. In the wake of the scandal, three successive Radical governments pursued a programme of aggressive 'republicanizing' military reform, especially under prime ministers Émile Combes (1903–5) and Georges Clemenceau (1906–9). Government control over the army was tightened, the civilian-minded ministry of war grew stronger vis-à-vis the regular army commanders and the period of service was reduced in March 1905 – against the advice of the military experts – from three years to two with a view to transforming the politically suspect 'praetorian guard' of the Dreyfus years into a 'citizen army' of civilian reservists for national defence in wartime.

Only in the last pre-war years did the tide begin to turn in favour of the French military. In France, as earlier in Russia, the army leadership was streamlined in 1911 and the chief of the General Staff, Joseph

Joffre, was designated as the official responsible for military planning in peacetime and the command of the main army at war. The 'long and painful story' of the struggle to secure increased funds continued, but in 1912–14, the pro-military attitude of the Poincaré government and then of the Poincaré presidency, reinforced by complex realignments in French politics and opinion, created an environment more conducive to rearmament.[129] By 1913 it was politically feasible to press for a return to a three-year training regime, albeit over the protests of Finance Minister Louis-Lucien Klotz, who argued that the reinforcement of border fortifications would be cheaper and more effective.[130] In Germany, too, the souring of the mood after Agadir encouraged Minister of War Josias von Heeringen and Chief of Staff Helmuth von Moltke to press harder for army growth. From his position in the Reich Treasury Office, Adolf Wermuth fought a robust rearguard action against higher expenditures, but resigned in March 1912, after it became clear that his policy no longer enjoyed broad governmental support. The fiscal rigorism of the Wermuth era was renounced, and the exponents of military expenditure gradually gained the upper hand over their naval rivals. After a long period of relative stagnation, the army bill of 3 July 1913 took German military expenditure to unprecedented heights.[131]

In Russia, Vladimir Kokovtsov, who remained finance minister and succeeded Pyotr Stolypin as premier after the latter's assassination, found it harder and harder to fight off the relentless lobbying and back-stairs intrigues of War Minister Sukhomlinov. The feud between the two men came to a head at an important ministerial meeting in the spring of 1913, when Sukhomlinov ambushed the premier with a major budget-ary proposal on which everyone at the table had been briefed except Kokovtsov himself. The support of the sovereign was crucial to this shift in the balance of power. 'In your conflicts with Sukhomlinov you are always right,' Nicholas II told Kokovtsov in October 1912. 'But I want you to understand my attitude: I have been supporting Sukhom-linov not because I have no confidence in you, but because I cannot refuse to agree to military appropriations.'[132]

Did this massive transfer of resources entail a transfer of power, or at least of political influence? An answer to this question has to take account of the diverse conditions prevailing in the various states. The country where we encounter the firmest regime of civilian control is without doubt France. In December 1911, when Joffre outlined his new strategic plan, focused on a massive offensive deployment across the Franco-German border, the Radical prime minister Joseph Caillaux curtly informed the staff chief that decision-making was ultimately the responsibility of the civilian authorities.[133] The task of the CGS, Caillaux frequently pointed out, was merely to advise his political masters on the matters that fell within his expertise. The switch to increased military expenditure and the decision to invest in Joffre's offensive deployment in 1912–14 emanated not from the military, but from the politicians, under the leadership of the hawkish but in constitutional terms emphatically civilian Raymond Poincaré.

The situation in Russia was quite different. Here, the presence of the Tsar as the focal point of the autocratic system made it possible for individual ministers to carve out a certain relative autonomy. War Minister Vladimir Sukhomlinov is a characteristic example. At the time of his appointment in 1909, a struggle was raging in St Petersburg over parliamentary control of the army. An influential group of deputies was attempting to assert the Duma's right of oversight over defence policy. Sukhomlinov was brought in to see off the Duma, prevent the infiltration of 'civilian attitudes' into military decision-making and protect the Tsar's prerogative, a role that earned him the hatred of public opinion, but assured him strong support from the throne.[134] This backing from the sovereign enabled the war minister to formulate a security policy dramatically at variance with official Russian commitments to the alliance with France.

Rather than meeting French demands for a swift offensive strike against Germany in the first phase of mobilization, Sukhomlinov's Reorganization of 1910 shifted the focus of Russian deployments away from the western border zones in the Polish salient to locations in the Russian interior. The aim was to achieve a better balance between unit strengths and population density and to create a force that could be deployed, if necessary, to an eastern theatre of operations. The extreme west was to be abandoned to the enemy in the first phase of hostilities, pending a massive combined counter-offensive by the Russian armies.[135] It does not seem that any effort was made to square this innovation with the ministry of foreign affairs. French military experts were initially horrified at the new plan, which they saw as depriving the Franco-Russian Alliance of the military initiative against Germany. The Russians did ultimately address these French concerns, but it is remarkable nonetheless that Sukhomlinov possessed sufficient independence to devise and implement a policy that appeared to run against the grain of the alliance with France, the centrepiece of Russian foreign policy.[136]

Armed with the support of the Tsar, Sukhomlinov was also able to undermine the authority of Prime Minister Kokovtsov, not just by challenging him over military budgeting, but also by building a hostile bloc in the Council of Ministers. And this in turn furnished him with a platform from which he could expound his views on Russia's security situation. In a series of key meetings in the fourth week of November 1912, Sukhomlinov expounded the view that war was inevitable, 'and it would be more profitable for us to begin it as soon as possible'; a war, he argued, 'would bring [Russia] nothing but good'. These bizarre and deluded claims astonished the cautious Kokovtsov.[137] But Sukhomlinov was able to do this only because he had the support of other civilian ministers, Rukhlov, Maklakov, Shcheglovitov, and most importantly the powerful A. V. Krivoshein, minister of agriculture and a confidant of the Tsar. In the last months of 1912, a 'war party' emerged within the Council of Ministers, led by Sukhomlinov and Krivoshein.[138]

In Germany, too, the praetorian character of the system assured the military a certain freedom of manoeuvre. Key figures such as the chief of staff could clearly acquire intermittent leverage on decision-making, especially at moments of heightened tension.[139] Establishing what military commanders said is easy enough; ascertaining the weight of their counsels in government decision-making is much less straightforward, especially in an environment where the absence of a collegial decision-making organ like the Russian Council of Ministers removed the need for open conflict between military and civilian office-holders.

One way of understanding the interaction between military and civilian policy-making is to examine the relationship between the official diplomatic apparatus of ambassadors, ministers and legation secretaries and the parallel network – overseen by the General Staff and the Admiralty – of the military and naval attachés, whose perspective on events sometimes diverged from that of the official diplomatic networks. To take just one example: in October 1911, Wilhelm Widenmann, the German naval attaché in London, sent an alarming report to Berlin. British naval officers, Widenmann wrote, were now openly admitting that England had 'mobilised its entire fleet' during the summer months of the Agadir crisis. England, it seemed, had 'merely been waiting for a signal from France to fall upon Germany'. To make matters worse, the new First Sea Lord was the 'unscrupulous, ambitious and unreliable demagogue' Winston Churchill. Germany must therefore steel itself for the possibility of an unprovoked attack, in the manner of the British annihilation of the Danish fleet at Copenhagen in 1807. Further naval rearmament was essential, for 'only one thing impresses in England: a firm goal and the indomitable will to accomplish it'.[140] These dispatches were passed to Wilhelm II, who covered them in delighted annotations – 'correct', 'correct', 'excellent' and so on. There was nothing especially remarkable in any of this – Widenmann was reacting in part to what he had observed in London, but his underlying purpose was to prevent the General Staff back in Berlin from using the Agadir crisis to challenge the financial pre-eminence of the navy.[141]

The significance of the Widenmann reports lay less in their content or the Kaiser's reactions than in the response they elicited from the chancellor and the foreign secretary. Irritated by this para-diplomatic panic-mongering, Bethmann Hollweg requested the German ambassador in London, Count Metternich, to file a counter-dispatch refuting Widenmann's arguments. Metternich responded with a report that nuanced Widenmann's claims. While it was true that 'all England' had been 'prepared for war' in the summer of 1911, this did not imply a readiness for aggressive action. To be sure, there were many younger naval officers to whom a war would 'not be unwelcome', but this was an attitude common to the military functionaries of other countries. In any case, Metternich observed – and here was the sting – in England, such questions were decided not by army or naval officers, nor by ministers of war, nor by the First Sea Lord, but rather by a cabinet composed of responsible ministers. 'Over here,' Metternich announced, 'fleet and army are regarded as the most important instruments of policy, as means to an end, but not as determinants of the course of policy.' In any case, the English were now keen to put the tensions of the summer behind them. Instead of putting all of its eggs in the armaments basket, therefore, the German government should seek an improvement in its relations with London.[142]

This time, the Kaiser was less happy: 'wrong', 'rubbish', 'unbelievable hogwash!', 'scaredy-cat' screamed the scribbles on the margins of the document. 'I don't agree with the judgement of the Ambassador! The Naval Attaché is right!'[143] The odd thing about this pair of conflicting dispatches is that both of them went on to shape policy: the Kaiser used the Widenmann report as a pretext for demanding a further naval law, while Bethmann persisted with the policy of détente recommended by Metternich. In Germany, as one senior commander later observed, 'the Kaiser made one policy, the Chancellor another [and] the General Staff came up with its own answers'.[144]

It looks, at first glance, as if we can draw a line between democratic, parliamentary Britain and France on the one hand, where civilian decision-makers called the shots, and the more authoritarian constitutions of Russia, Austria and Germany, where, despite variations in the degree of parliamentarization, military personnel could compete with their civilian colleagues on an equal or superior footing for political influence, thanks to their privileged access to the sovereign. But the reality was more complex than this dichotomy would allow. In France, the restructuring of the military after 1911 produced an extraordinary concentration of authority in the hands of Chief of Staff Joffre, to the extent that he wielded greater power over the armed forces than his aristocratic, militarist German counterpart, Helmuth von Moltke; what is more, the new French measures secured for the army almost complete autonomy within the state – though this autonomy depended, unlike that of the German army, upon the cooperation and support of the relevant civilian ministers.[145]

In Britain, too, the deepening of the entente with France was driven by military, rather than civilian negotiations and agreements. We have already seen how eagerly key military figures in Britain proffered support to France during the first Moroccan crisis in 1905–6. And it is far from clear that the leading British military commanders saw themselves as compliant servants of their political masters. Wilson was not simply acting on instructions; he had his own views on Britain's military role in a future continental war and consistently pressed for a military confrontation. Like his continental colleagues, Wilson despised civilian politicians, believing them entirely incapable of understanding military affairs. Sir Edward Grey, he wrote in his diary, was an 'ignorant, vain and weak man, quite unfit to be the foreign minister of any country larger than Portugal'. As for the rest of the Liberal cabinet, they were no more than 'dirty, ignorant curs'. The whole idea of civilian government of the army was 'vicious in theory and hopeless in practice'.[146]

Conservative in his politics, Wilson intrigued energetically against a Liberal political leadership he despised, siphoning information from the Foreign Office through his close associate Permanent Under-secretary Sir Arthur Nicolson and passing it to his allies in the Conservative Party. In Major General Henry Wilson, Britain possessed 'its own version' of Austria-Hungary's Conrad and Serbia's Apis.[147] The significance of the military discussions with France lay not just in the pressure they exerted on the civilian leadership, but also in the fact that they seemed, by virtue of their very existence, to imply a moral obligation to fight with France in the event of a war with Germany. The militarization of the Entente thus exposed the widening discrepancy between British military planning and an official diplomatic stance for which the commitments associated with the term 'alliance' were still anathema.

Something analogous took place in the context of the French alliance with Russia. The efforts of the French military commanders to undo the effects of Sukhomlinov's 1910 deployment plan led to a deepening interdependence of military planning in the two allied states – a process managed by the military, but sanctioned by the civilian leadership. But even as the civilians licensed this process, they could not prevent it from shifting the parameters within which political decisions could be made. When the French insisted at the annual Franco-Russian joint General Staff meetings that the Russians spend vast amounts of borrowed money to upgrade their westward strategic railways, the effect was to push the balance of power in St Petersburg away from Kokovtsov towards his adversaries in the Russian military command. Kokovtsov was probably right when he accused the military command of exploiting inter-service ties within the alliance in order to strengthen their own leverage within the Russian political system.[148]

Conversely, the demands of the Russians on their French allies had potentially far-reaching consequences for French domestic politics. In 1914, when the Russians warned that any reduction in the period of national military service would undermine the value of France as an ally, they locked the country's leading statesmen into supporting a measure (the recently adopted Three Year Law) which was controversial with the French electorate. Even the most technical details of operational planning could provide gunpowder for political explosions.[149] In France, a small group of key policy-makers went to great pains to conceal the extent and nature of the strategic commitments of the alliance from those (mainly Radicals and Radical Socialists) who might object on political grounds. The need for discretion became especially acute in early 1914, when Poincaré cooperated with the military in concealing the essentially offensive character of French strategic planning from a cabinet, a chamber and a public increasingly committed to a *défenciste* approach. So secretive was Poincaré in his handling of these issues that he and Joffre even withheld the details of the new French deployment plans from the minister of war, Adolphe Messimy.[150] By the spring of 1914, the French commitment to a coordinated Franco-Russian military strategy had become a potentially disuptive force in politics, because it obliged France to hold fast to a form of military planning and preparation whose public legitimacy was in question. How long Poincaré could have continued this balancing act we shall never know, because the outbreak of war in the summer of 1914 made the question obsolete.

We can thus speak of two reciprocal processes – one in which a generous measure of initiative was ceded to a constitutionally subordinate military leadership, and another in which a praetorian military enjoying relative independence in constitutional terms was contained, steered or deflected by the statesmen. Moltke's demands for preventive war were blocked by the Kaiser and by the civilian leaders, just as Conrad's were by the Emperor, Archduke Franz Ferdinand and Leopold von Berchtold.[151] Kokovtsov was, for a time at least, strikingly successful in blocking the war minister's more ambitious initiatives. At the end of 1913, when Sukhomlinov tried to have Kokovtsov – as prime minister and minister of finance – excluded entirely from deliberations on military budgeting, the Council of Ministers recognized that the imperious war minister had gone too far and turned down the request.[152] In Russia, Germany and Austria, Britain and France, military policy remained ultimately subordinate to the political and strategic objectives of the civilian leaderships.[153]

Nevertheless: unanswered questions about the balance of power between civilian and military factions and their respective influence on decision-making continued to befog relations between the great power executives. The European powers all assumed the existence of a hawkish military faction within each prospective opponent's government and worked hard to establish how much influence it wielded. In a conversation with Count Pourtalès, the German ambassador in St Petersburg, at the beginning of February 1913, when Austro-Russian tensions over the Balkans were riding high, Foreign Minister Sazonov acknowledged that the Austro-Hungarian foreign minister, whom he remembered from his St Petersburg days, was a man of peaceable intentions and outlook. But was he strong enough to resist the pressure from the chief of the General Staff, General Conrad von Hötzendorf, whose belligerent schemes were well known to Russian military intelligence? And even if Berchtold was still, for the moment, in control, might not power slip into the hands of the military as the dual monarchy grew weaker and looked for increasingly radical solutions?[154] There was an element of projection in these speculations. Sazonov, who observed at first hand the power struggle between Sukhomlinov and Kokovtsov and had recently seen the staff chief push Russia to the brink of war with Austria-Hungary, knew better than most how labile the relationship between military and civilian decision-makers could be. In a subtle analysis of the mood in St Petersburg in March 1914, Pourtalès discerned a kind of equilibrium between belligerent and pacific elements: 'Just as there are no personalities of whom one can say that they have *both* the desire *and* the influence to plunge Russia into a military adventure, so we lack men whose position and influence are strong enough to awaken confidence that they will be able to steer Russia on a peaceful course over a period of years ...'[155] Kokovtsov's analysis of the same problem was less sanguine. It seemed to him that the Tsar spent more and more of his time in the company of 'military circles' whose 'simplistic views' were 'gathering more and more force'.[156]

The intrinsic difficulty of interpreting such relationships from an external vantage point was heightened by the fact that civilian politicians were not averse to exploiting (or even inventing) the existence of a 'war party' to lend weight to their own arguments: thus, during the Haldane mission of 1912, the Germans encouraged the British to believe that the Berlin government was split between a dove and a hawk faction and that British concessions would strengthen Chancellor Bethmann Hollweg against belligerent elements in Berlin. They adopted the same tactic in May 1914, arguing (through a series of 'inspired' press articles) that the continuation of Anglo-Russian naval talks would merely strengthen the hand of the militarists against the moderate civilian leadership.[157] Here, as in other areas of inter-governmental communication, the mutability of civil-military relations within the respective systems was amplified by misperceptions and misrepresentations.

THE PRESS AND PUBLIC OPINION

'Most of the conflicts the world has seen in the past ten decades,' the German chancellor Bernhard von Bülow declared before the German parliament in March 1909, 'have not been called forth by princely ambition or ministerial conspiracy but through the passionate agitation of public opinion, which through the press and parliament has swept along the executive.'[158] Was there any truth in Bülow's claim? Did the power to shape foreign policy lie beyond the chancelleries and ministries in the world of the lobby groups and political print?

One thing is beyond doubt: the last decades before the outbreak of the war saw a dramatic expansion of the political public sphere and broader public discussion of issues linked to international relations. In Germany, an array of nationalist pressure groups emerged, dedicated to channelling popular sentiment and lobbying government. The consequence was a transformation in the substance and style of political critique, which became more demagogic and more diffuse and extreme in its objectives, so that governments often found themselves on the defensive, parrying charges that they had not been assertive enough in the pursuit of national aims.[159] In Italy, too, we can discern the beginnings of a more assertive and demanding political public: under the influence of the ultra-nationalist Enrico Corradini and the demagogue Giovanni Papini, Italy's first nationalist party, the Associazione Nazionalista Italiana, was founded in 1910; through its parliamentary deputies and its newspaper, *L'Idea Nazionale*, it demanded the immediate 'repatriation' of the Italian-populated territories along the Adriatic coast of the Austro-Hungarian Empire and was prepared to endorse war if no other means sufficed. By 1911, even more moderate papers, such as *La Tribuna* of Rome and *La Stampa* of Turin, were employing nationalist journalists.[160] Here, even more than in Germany, there was ample potential for friction with a government obliged to balance conflicting priorities.[161] In Russia, too, the last decades of the nineteenth century saw the emergence of a mass press – by 1913, the *Russkoe Slovo*, Moscow's best-selling daily paper, was selling up to 800,000 copies per day. Although censorship was still operating, the authorities permitted fairly free discussion of foreign affairs (as long as they did not directly criticize the Tsar or his ministers) and many of the most important dailies engaged retired diplomats to write on foreign policy.[162] In the aftermath of the Bosnian crisis, moreover, Russian public opinion grew more assertive – especially on Balkan issues – and more anti-governmental.[163] In Britain, too, a burgeoning mass press fed its readers on a rich diet of jingoism, xenophobia, security scares and war fever. During the Boer War, the *Daily Mail* sold one million copies per day; in 1907, it was still averaging between 850,000 and 900,000.

Monarchs, ministers and senior officials thus had good reason to take the press seriously. In parliamentary systems, positive publicity might be expected to translate into votes, while negative coverage supplied grist for the mills of the opposition. In more authoritarian systems, public support was an indispensable ersatz for democratic legitimacy. Some monarchs and statesmen were positively obsessive about the press and spent hours each day poring through cuttings. Wilhelm II was an extreme case, but his sensitivity to public criticism was not in itself unusual.[164] 'If we lose the confidence of public opinion in our foreign policy,' Tsar Alexander III had told Foreign Minister Lamzdorf, 'then all is lost.'[165] It is hard to find anyone in the executives of early twentieth-century Europe who did not acknowledge the importance of the press for the making of foreign policy. But were they swept along by it?

An ambivalence underlay the preoccupation with published opinion. On the one hand, ministers, officials and monarchs believed in and sometimes even feared the press as a mirror and channel for public sentiments and attitudes. All the foreign ministers knew what it was like to be exposed to a hostile domestic press campaign over which they had no control – Grey was the butt of the Liberal press in 1911, Kiderlen-Wächter was attacked in the nationalist papers after the Agadir crisis, the Kaiser was ridiculed for many reasons – among them for his supposedly timid and irresolute view of foreign policy. French politicians suspected of softness towards Germany could be hounded, like Joseph Caillaux, from office. In January 1914, Sazonov and his ministry were denounced for 'pusillanimity' by the Russian nationalist press.[166] Fear of negative publicity was one reason for the secretiveness of so many of the foreign ministries. As Charles Hardinge observed in a letter to Nicolson, then British ambassador in St Petersburg, in 1908, Edward Grey's policy of rapprochement with Russia was difficult to sell to the British public: 'We have had to suppress the truth and resort to subterfuge at times to meet hostile public opinion . . .'[167] In St Petersburg, the memory of the publicity storm that had ruined Izvolsky remained fresh throughout the pre-war years.[168]

Most policy-makers took an intelligent and differentiated view of the press. They saw that it was volatile – subject to short-term agitations and frenzies that quickly subsided. They understood that public sentiment was driven by contrary impulses, that the demands it made on government were seldom realistic; they saw, to paraphrase Theodore Roosevelt, that public opinion usually combined 'the unbridled tongue with the unready hand'.[169] Public opinion was frenetic and panic-prone, but it was also highly mutable – witness the way in which the established Anglophobia of the French press melted away during Edward VII's visit to Paris in 1903: as the king drove with his entourage from the Porte Dauphine railway station down the Champs Élysées, there were shouts of 'Vive Fashoda!', 'Vivent les Boers!' and 'Vive Jeanne d'Arc!', not to mention hostile headlines and insulting caricatures. Yet within a few days, the king won over his hosts with endearing speeches and charming remarks that were quickly taken up by the main newspapers.[170] In Serbia, the wave of national outrage stirred by Austria's interdiction of the customs union with Bulgaria in 1906 soon died away as Serbian citizens woke up to the fact that the terms of the commercial treaty on offer from Austria-Hungary were in fact better for Serbian consumers than membership of the union with Sofia.[171] There were sharp fluctuations in public sentiment in Germany during the Agadir crisis of 1911; at the beginning of September a peace demonstration in Berlin attracted 100,000 people, yet only a few weeks later, the mood was less emollient, as reflected in the decision at the Social Democratic Party's Jena Congress to reject calls for a general strike in the event of war.[172] As late as the spring and summer of 1914, the French envoy in Belgrade noted sharp fluctuations in Serbian press coverage of relations with Austria-Hungary: whereas there had been energetic campaigns against Vienna in March and April, the first week of June brought an unexpected mood of détente and concilation on both sides of the Austro-Serbian border.[173]

As for those aggressive ultra-nationalist organizations whose voices could be heard in all the European capitals, most of them represented small, extremist constituencies. It was a striking feature of the most belligerent ultra-nationalist lobbies that their leaderships were undermined by constant infighting and schisms – the Pan-German League was riven by factional strife; even the much larger and more moderate Naval League suffered in the years 1905–8 from an internal 'civil war' between pro-governmental and oppositional groups. The Union of the Russian People, a chauvinist, anti Semitic, ultra-nationalist organization founded in August 1906, with some 900 offices across the cities and towns of Russia, collapsed in 1908–9 after severe infighting into an array of smaller and mutually hostile groups.[174]

It remained unclear how the public opinion within articulate elites with direct access to the press related to the attitudes prevailing among the masses of the population. War scares and jingo campaigns made good newspaper copy, but how socially deep were they? It was a grave mistake, the German consul-general in Moscow warned in December 1912, to assume that the belligerence and Germanophobia of the Russian 'war party' and the Slavophile press were characteristic of the mood in the country, for these circles entertained only 'the loosest connection with the actual tendencies of Russian life'. The problem with German newspaper coverage of these issues, the consul argued, was that it tended to be written by journalists with little experience of Russia and a very narrow range of elite social contacts.[175] In May 1913, the Belgian minister in Paris, Baron Guillaume, acknowledged the efflorescence of 'a certain chauvinism' in France. It could be observed not just in the nationalist papers, but also in the theatres, reviews and café-concerts, where numerous performances offered jingoist fare that was 'calculated to over-excite spirits'. But, he added, 'the true people of France do not approve of these manifestations . . .'[176]

All the governments, with the exception of Britain, maintained press offices whose purpose was both to monitor and, where possible, to shape press coverage of issues touching on security and international relations. In Britain, the foreign secretary appears to have felt little need to convince (or even inform) the public of the merits of his policies and there were no official efforts to influence the press; many of the major newspapers received handsome subsidies, but these came from private or party-political sources, rather than from government. This did not, of course, prevent a dense network of informal relationships from developing between Whitehall officials and key journalists.[177] The picture in Italy was rather different. Giovanni Giolitti, prime minister (for the fourth time) in 1911–14, made regular payments to at least thirty journalists in return for supportive coverage of his policies.[178] The Russian foreign ministry acquired a press department in 1906, and from 1910 Sazonov orchestrated regular tea-time meetings at the ministry with the most important editors and Duma leaders.[179] Relations between the Russian diplomats and some favoured newspapers were so close, one journalist reported in 1911, that the ministry of foreign affairs in St Petersburg 'often seemed a mere branch office of the *Novoye Vremya*'. The newspaper's editor, Jegorov, was often to be seen in the ministry's press bureau, and Nelidov, chief of the bureau and himself a former journalist, was a frequent visitor to the paper's editorial offices.[180] In France, the relationship between diplomats and journalists was especially intimate: nearly half of the foreign ministers of the Third Republic were former writers or journalists and the 'lines of communication' between foreign ministers and the press were 'almost always open'.[181] In December 1912, when he was prime minister of France, Raymond Poincaré even launched a new journal, *La Politique Étrangère*, to promote his views on foreign policy across the French political elite.

Semi-official newspapers and 'inspired' articles planted in the domestic press to test the climate of opinion were familiar tools of continental diplomacy. Inspired journalism masqueraded as the autonomous expression of an independent press, but its effectiveness depended precisely on the suspicion among readers that it emanated from the seat of power. It was universally understood in Serbia, for example, that *Samouprava* represented the views of the government; the *Norddeutsche Allgemeine Zeitung* was considered the official organ of the German Foreign Office; in Russia, the government made its views known through its own semi-official journal, *Rossiya*, but also ran occasional inspired campaigns in other more popular papers, like *Novoye Vremya*.[182] The French foreign ministry, like the German, disbursed cash to journalists from a secret fund and maintained close ties with *Le Temps* and the *Agence Havas*, while using the less serious-minded *Le Matin* to launch 'trial balloons'.[183]

Interventions of this kind could go wrong. Once it was known that a particular newspaper often carried inspired pieces, there was the risk that indiscreet, tendentious or erroneous reports by the same paper would be mistaken for intentional signals from the government, as happened, for example, in February 1913, when *Le Temps* ran an article based on *unauthorized* leaks from an unnamed source disclosing some of the details of recent government deliberations on French rearmament – furious official denials followed.[184] Russian foreign minister Izvolsky's efforts in 1908 to 'prepare [Russian] public opinion and the press' for the news that Russia had approved the Austrian annexation of Bosnia-Herzegovina proved totally inadequate to the force of the public response.[185] And in 1914, *Novoye Vremya*, despite its previously intimate relationship with the ministry of foreign affairs, turned against Sazonov, accusing him of excessive timidity in the defence of Russian interests, possibly because it was now under the influence of the ministry of war.[186] In the aftermath of the Friedjung Affair of 1909, when Austrian foreign minister Aehrenthal threw his weight behind a press campaign based on false allegations of treason against prominent Serbian politicians, the government was forced to sacrifice the head of the foreign ministry's Literary Bureau; his successor was sacked amid a storm of press and parliamentary criticism over the bungled 'Prochaska affair' of the winter of 1912, when allegations of Serbian mistreatment of an Austrian consular official were likewise found to be bogus.[187]

Official manipulations of the press also took place across national borders. Early in 1905, the Russians were distributing around £8,000 a month to the Parisian press, in the hope of stimulating public support for a massive French loan. The French government subsidized pro-French newspapers in Italy (and Spain during the conference at Algeciras), and during the Russo-Japanese and Balkan Wars the Russians handed out huge bribes to French journalists.[188] The Germans maintained a very modest fund for supporting friendly journalists in St Petersburg and plied newspaper editors in London with subsidies in the hope, mostly disappointed, of obtaining more positive coverage of Germany.[189]

Inspired leader articles might also be formulated for the eyes of a foreign government. During the Morocco crisis of 1905, for example, Théophile Delcassé used thinly disguised press releases divulging the details of British military planning in order to intimidate the Germans. Here the inspired press functioned as a form of deniable, sub-diplomatic international communication that could achieve a deterrent or motivating effect without binding anyone to a specific commitment; had Delcassé himself issued a more explicit threat, he would have placed the British Foreign Office in an impossible position. In February 1912, the French ambassador in St Petersburg, Georges Louis, dispatched the translation of an article in the *Novoye Vremya* with a covering letter noting that it reflected 'very accurately the opinion of Russian military circles'.[190] In this case the inspired press enabled discrete organizations within the administration – here the ministry of war – to broadcast their views without officially compromising the government. But it did sometimes occur that different ministries briefed the press in opposed directions, as in March 1914 when the *Birzheviia Vedomosti* (Stock Exchange News) published a leader piece, widely assumed to have been 'inspired' by Sukhomlinov, announcing that Russia was 'ready for war' and had 'abandoned' the idea of a purely defensive strategy. Sazonov responded with a conciliatory counter-piece in the semi-official *Rossiya*. This was a classic case of parallel signalling – Sukhomlinov was reassuring the French of Russia's readiness and determination to fulfil its alliance obligations, while Sazonov's response was intended for the German (and possibly British) foreign offices.

An article published in the *Kölnische Zeitung* at around the same time attributing aggressive intentions to St Petersburg on account of the most recent hike in Russian military expenditure was almost certainly planted by the German foreign ministry in the hope of eliciting a clarifying Russian response.[191] In areas where the European powers competed for local influence, the use of subsidized press organs to win friends and discredit the machinations of one's opponents was commonplace. The Germans worried about the immense influence of 'English money' on the Russian press, and German envoys in Constantinople frequently complained of the dominance of the French-language press, whose subsidized leader-writers did 'everything possible to incite [hostility] against us'.[192]

In these contexts, the press was the *instrument* of foreign policy, not its determinant. But this did not prevent policy-makers from taking the press seriously as an index of opinion. In the spring of 1912, Jules Cambon worried lest the chauvinism of the French press heighten the risk of conflict: 'I wish that those Frenchmen whose profession it is to create or represent opinion would [exercise restraint] and that they would not amuse themselves in playing with fire by speaking of inevitable war. There is is nothing inevitable in this world . . .'[193] Six months later, with the First Balkan War underway and pan-Slav feeling rising high in parts of the Russian press, the Russian ambassador in Berlin feared – or at least claimed to fear – that the 'state of mind of the population of his country [might] dominate the conduct of his government'.[194]

Ministers and diplomats who were confident about the capacity of their own governments to shield the policy-making process from the vicissitudes of domestic published opinion often doubted the ability of foreign governments to do the same. In the aftermath of the Agadir crisis of 1911, the German military leadership feared that nationalist agitation and reviving confidence in France might pressure an otherwise peaceable government in Paris into launching a surprise atack on Germany.[195] The fear that an essentially peaceable German leadership would be swept into a war on her neighbours by chauvinistic opinion leaders at home was in turn a frequently recurring theme in French policy discussions.[196] The Russian government, in particular, was widely seen as susceptible to pressure from the public sphere – especially when this took the form of agitation on Balkan issues – and there was some truth in this view, as the course of the July Crisis would show. But the Russians also viewed the parliamentary western governments as acutely vulnerable to public pressure, precisely because they were democratically constituted, and the British encouraged this inference by suggesting, as Grey habitually did, that 'the course of the English government in [. . .] a crisis must depend on the view taken by English public opinion'.[197] Statesmen frequently hid behind the claim that they were acting under the constraints imposed by opinion in their own country: in 1908–9, the French cautioned the Russians against starting a war over the Balkans, for example, on the grounds that this region was not important to the French public; Izvolsky got his own back in 1911, when he urged Paris – without forgetting to remind his French interlocutors of their earlier advice – to settle with the Germans on the grounds that 'Russia would have difficulty making its public opinion accept a war over Morocco'.[198] The Serbian ambassador in Vienna claimed in November 1912 that Prime Minister Nikola Pašić had no choice but to pursue an irredentist policy on behalf of his country – if instead he attempted to conciliate Austria, the 'war party' in Belgrade would sweep him from power and replace him with one of their own number, and Sazonov justified the Serbian leader's belligerent public postures by reference to the 'somewhat overwrought' quality of Serbian opinion.[199]

Sazonov's claim to the German ambassador Pourtalès in November 1912 that concern for public opinion obliged him to defend Serbia's interests against Austria-Hungary was entirely characteristic. He used the same argument to persuade the Romanians not to initiate a conflict with Bulgaria in January 1913: 'be very careful! If you wage war with Bulgaria, I will not be able to resist an over-excited public opinion.'[200] In reality, Sazonov had little respect for newspaper editors and leader-writers and believed that he understood Russian opinion better than the newspapers did. He was quite prepared, when necessary, to sail against the tide of press commentary, all the while exploiting jingoist campaigns at home to persuade the representatives of other powers that he was under pressure to take certain measures.[201] The readers of dispatches often saw through these evasions: when reports reached Kaiser Wilhelm in 1908 and 1909 informing him that pro-Slav public opinion might push the Russian government into action over Bosnia-Herzegovina, he scribbled the word 'Bluff' in the margins.[202] Nevertheless: the wide-spread assumption that *foreign* governments were under pressure to align themselves with their own domestic opinion meant that press reports were the bread and butter of diplomatic dispatches. Sheaves of newspaper cuttings and translations fattened the files flowing into foreign ministries from every European legation.

The efforts of all governments by one means or another to shape published opinion enhanced the importance of press monitoring, because it opened up the possibility that the press might provide the key, if not to public opinion, then at least to the opinion and intentions of the government. Thus Grey saw in the anti-British press campaigns of the Agadir crisis in September 1911 a tactical manoeuvre by the German government designed to mobilize support for further naval bills in the coming Reichstag elections, while the Austrian ambassador accused the Russian foreign minister of encouraging negative coverage of Austro-Russian efforts towards détente after the Bosnian crisis.[203] Diplomats constantly sifted through the press looking for the inspired pieces that might provide the key to the thinking of this or that ministry. But since most governments used a range of organs, it was often difficult to know for sure whether a specific article was inspired or not. In May 1910, for example, when the French newspaper *Le Temps* published an article sharply criticizing the latest Russian troop deployment plans, the Russian foreign ministry assumed (wrongly as it happened, in this case) that the piece was officially inspired and forwarded a protest to Paris.[204] It was a mistake, the German ambassador in Paris wrote, always to assume that the views expressed in *Le Temps* reflected those of the ministry of foreign affairs or of the government – its editor, André Tardieu, had sometimes fallen out with the authorities on account of his heterodox declarations on matters of national interest.[205] In January 1914, the Belgian minister in Paris warned his government that while the big political leaders in *Le Temps* were generally the work of Tardieu, they were usually inspired by the Russian ambassador, Izvolsky.[206] This haze of uncertainty meant not only that embassy officials had to be vigilant in trawling the press, but also that adverse published comment on foreign governments could give rise on occasion to feuds, in which two foreign ministries skirmished through the pages of the inspired press, in the process stirring public emotions in ways that could be difficult to control. The British and the German foreign offices were typical in the tendency of each to overstate the extent to which public opinion was controlled by the other government.[207]

Press feuds could also spring up spontaneously, without government involvement. It was widely acknowledged by the governments that slanging-matches between chauvinistic newspaper editors could escalate to the point where they threatened to poison the atmosphere of international relations. At a meeting that took place at Reval in June 1908 between Tsar Nicholas II, King Edward VII and Charles Hardinge, the Tsar confided to Hardinge that the 'liberty' of the Russian press had caused him and his government 'considerable embarrassment', since 'every incident that occurred in any distant province of the empire, such as an earthquake or thunderstorms, was at once put down to Germany's account, and serious complaints had recently been made to him and the government of the unfriendly tone of the Russian press'. But the Tsar confessed that he felt unable to remedy this state of affairs except by an occasional official communiqué to the press and 'this had generally but slight effect'. He 'wished very much that the press would turn their attention to internal rather than foreign affairs'.[208]

Between 1896, when the British newspapers responded with outrage to the Kaiser's Kruger telegram and 1911 when the British and German papers clashed over events in Morocco, there were repeated press wars between Britain and Germany. Efforts by the two governments to achieve 'press disarmament' in 1906 and 1907 by exchanging delegations of senior journalists were largely ineffective.[209] Press wars were possible because the newspapers in each state frequently reported on the attitudes adopted by foreign newspapers on questions of national interest; it was not uncommon for entire articles to be reprinted or paraphrased. Thus Tatishchev, the Russian military plenipotentiary in Berlin, could report to Tsar Nicholas II in February 1913 that pan-Slavist articles in *Novoye Vremya* were making a 'distressing impression' in Germany.[210] International press relations were especially tense between Austria and Serbia, where the major papers watched their counterparts across the border with eagle eyes (or were supplied with cuttings and translations by the respective foreign ministries) and where complaints about press coverage on the other side of the border were a stock theme – this problem would play a prominent role in the diplomacy of the July Crisis in 1914.

It is questionable, nonetheless, whether the European press was becoming steadily more bellicose in the years before 1914. Recent research on the German newspapers suggests a more complex picture. A study of German press coverage during a sequence of major pre-war crises (Morocco, Bosnia, Agadir, the Balkans, etc.) discerned an increasingly polarized view of international relations and a declining confidence in diplomatic solutions. But there were also periods of quiescence in between, and the era of the Anglo-German press wars came to an abrupt halt in 1912 – the last two pre-war years were a period, by contrast, of 'unusual harmony and peacefulness'.[211] Even Friedrich von Bernhardi, whose *Germany and the Next War* (1911) is often cited as an example of the increasing bellicosity of German opinion, opened his appallingly aggressive tract with a long passage lamenting the 'pacifism' of his compatriots.[212] Nor did chauvinism always speak with one voice. In Britain, anti-Russian sentiment was still a powerful public force in the last few years before the outbreak of war, notwithstanding the Anglo-Russian Convention of 1907. In the winter of 1911–12, as the Agadir crisis was subsiding, the rank and file of the Liberal Party accused Grey of seeking an excessive intimacy with Russia at the expense of a more cooperative relationship with Germany. The public meetings convened up and down the country at the end of January 1912 to demand an Anglo-German understanding were driven in part by hostility to Russia, whose machinations were seen as threatening British interests at numerous points along the imperial periphery.[213]

Politicians often spoke, or complained, of opinion as an external force pressing on government. In doing so, they implied that opinion – whether public or published – was something outside government, like a fog pressing on the window panes of ministerial offices, something that policy-makers could choose to exclude from their own sphere of action. And by opinion, they mostly meant the public approval or rejection of their own persons and policies. But there is something deeper than opinion, something we could call mentality – a fabric of 'unspoken assumptions', as James Joll called it, that shaped the attitudes and behaviour of statesmen, legislators and publicists alike.[214] In this domain, we can perhaps discern a deepening readiness for war across Europe, particularly within the educated elites. This did not take the form of bloodthirsty calls for violence against another state, but rather of a 'defensive patriotism'[215] that encompassed the possibility of war without necessarily welcoming it, a viewpoint underpinned by the conviction that conflict was a 'natural' feature of international politics. 'The idea of a prolonged peace is an idle dream,' wrote Viscount Esher, a promoter of the Anglo-French Entente and a close friend and adviser of Edward VII, in 1910. Two years later, he told an audience of Cambridge undergraduates not to underestimate the 'poetic and romantic aspects of the clash of arms', warning that to do so would be to 'display enfeebled spirit and an impoverished imagination'.[216] War, Henry Spenser Wilkinson, the Chichele Professor of Military History at Oxford, observed in his inaugural lecture, was 'one of the modes of human intercourse'. This fatalistic acceptance of war's inevitability was held in place by a loose assemblage of arguments and attitudes – some argued from Darwinian or Huxleyite principles that in view of their energy and ambition, England and Germany were bound to come to blows, notwithstanding their close racial kinship; others claimed that turmoil was a natural feature of highly developed civilizations with their sophisticated armaments; yet others hailed war as therapeutic, as 'beneficial to society and a force for social advance'.[217]

Underpinning the reception of such views in both Britain and Germany was a 'sacrificial ideology' nourished, in turn, by the positive depictions of military conflict to be found in newspapers and the books read by boys of school age.[218] A pamphlet penned by a belligerent clergyman from New Zealand and published by the National Service League urged every schoolboy to recall that he 'stands between his mother and his sisters, his sweetheart and girl friends and all the women he meets and sees and the inconceivable infamy of alien invasion'.[219] Even the Scouting movement, founded in 1908, possessed from its inception – notwithstanding its celebration of woodlore, campfires and outdoor adventure – a 'strong military identification which was emphasised throughout the pre-war period'.[220] In Russia, the years following the Russo-Japanese War witnessed a 'military renaissance' driven by the desire for military reform: in 1910, 572 new titles on military subjects were published. Most of these were not warmongering tracts, but political interventions in the debate over how the reform of the Russian military should be linked to broader processes of social change that would orient society towards the sacrifices demanded by a major war effort.[221]

These developments, which had their counterparts in all the European states, help to explain the readiness of the legislatures to accept the financial burden of increased armaments expenditure during the pre-war period. In France, the support of the Chamber of Deputies, after heated controversy, for the new three-year military service law in 1913 reflected the revived 'prestige of war' in a public sphere that had tended since the Dreyfus affair to exhibit a strong anti-militarist ethos, though we should not forget that Radical deputies supported this law in part because for the first time it would be financed by a progressive property tax.[222] In Germany, too, Bethmann Hollweg managed to secure centre-right support for the massive army bill of 1913; for the separate bill to fund these measures, he was able to capture a centre-left coalition, though only because he was willing to raise part of the money by levying a new tax on the property-owning classes. In both cases, arguments for heightened military preparedness had to be admixed with other socio-political incentives in order to secure the support needed to drive these huge bills through parliament. In Russia, by contrast, the enthusiasm of the political elite for armaments was such after 1908 that the Duma approved allocations even faster than the military commanders could work out what to do with them; here it was the Octobrist bloc in the Duma, not the ministers, who initially drove the campaign for Russian army expansion.[223] In Britain, too, the prevalent mood of defensive patriotism left its mark on the legislature: whereas in 1902 only three MPs supported the National Service League, by 1912 the figure had risen to 180.[224]

The press entered into the calculations of policy-makers in many different ways. It was never under their control, and they were never under its control. We should speak rather of a reciprocity between public opinion and public life, a process of constant interaction, in which policy-makers sought intermittently to guide opinion in a congenial direction, but were careful to shield their own autonomy and to protect the integrity of decision-making processes. On the other hand, statesmen continued to view the foreign press as an indicator not just of public opinion but of official views and intentions, and this meant that uncertainties about who was inspiring or licensing which utterances could further complicate communications between states. More fundamental – and more difficult to measure – were the shifts in mentality that articulated themselves not in the calls of chauvinists for firmness or confrontation, but in a deep and widespread readiness to accept war, conceived as a certainty imposed by the nature of international relations. The weight of this accumulated readiness would manifest itself during the July Crisis of 1914 not in the form of aggressive programmatic statements, but through the eloquent silence of those civilian leaders who, in a better world, might have been expected to point out that a war between great powers would be the very worst of things.

THE FLUIDITY OF POWER

Even if we were to assume that the foreign policies of the pre-war European powers were formulated and managed by compact executives animated by a unified and coherent purpose, reconstructing the relations among them would still be a daunting task, given that no relationship between any two powers can be fully understood without reference to relations with all of the others. But in the Europe of 1903–14, the reality was even more complex than the 'international' model would suggest. The chaotic interventions of monarchs, ambiguous relationships between civil and military, adversarial competition among key politicians in systems characterized by low levels of ministerial or cabinet solidarity, compounded by the agitations of a critical mass press against a background of intermittent crisis and heightened tension over security issues made this a period of unprecedented uncertainty in international relations. The policy oscillations and mixed signalling that resulted made it difficult, not just for historians, but for the statesmen of the last pre-war years to read the international environment.

It would be a mistake to push this observation too far. All complex political executives, even authoritarian ones, are subject to inner tensions and oscillations.[225] The literature on twentieth-century US foreign relations dwells at length on intra-governmental power struggles and intrigues. In a brilliant study of the US entry into the Vietnam War, Andrew Preston shows that while Presidents Lyndon B. Johnson and John F. Kennedy were reluctant to wage war and the State Department was largely opposed to intervention, the smaller and more nimble National Security Council, which strongly favoured war and operated beyond congressional oversight, narrowed down the president's options on Vietnam until war was virtually unavoidable.[226]

Yet the situation in pre-First World War Europe was different (and worse) in one important respect. For all the tensions that may evolve within it, the American executive is actually – in constitutional terms – a very tightly focused organization in which responsibility for executive decisions in foreign policy ultimately falls unambiguously upon the president. This was not the case for the pre-war European governments. There were perennial doubts about whether Grey had the right to commit himself as he did without consulting the cabinet or Parliament; indeed, these doubts were so pressing that they prevented him from making a clear and unequivocal statement of his intentions. The situation was even fuzzier in France, where the balance of initiative between the ministry of foreign affairs, the cabinet and the presidency remained unresolved, and even the masterful and determined Poincaré faced efforts to shut him out of the decision-making process altogether in the spring of 1914. In Austria-Hungary, and to a lesser extent in Russia, the power to shape foreign policy flowed around a loose human circuitry within the hivelike structure of the political elite, concentrating at different parts of the system, depending upon who formed the more effective and determined alignments. In these cases, as in Germany, the presence of an 'all-highest' sovereign did not clarify, but rather blurred the power relations within the system.

It is not a question, as in the Cuban Missile Crisis, of reconstructing the ratiocinations of two superpowers sifting through their options, but of understanding sustained rapid-fire interactions between executive structures with a relatively poor understanding of each other's intentions, operating with low levels of confidence and trust (even within the respective alliances) and with high levels of hostility and paranoia. The volatility inherent in such a constellation was heightened by the fluidity of power within each executive and its tendency to migrate from one node in the system to another. It may be true that dissent and polemics within the diplomatic services could have a salutary effect, in that they raised questions and objections that might have been suppressed in a more disciplined policy environment.[227] But the risks surely outweighed the benefits: when hawks dominated the signalling process on both sides of a potentially conflictual interaction, as happened in the Agadir crisis and would happen again after 28 June 1914, swift and unpredictable escalations could be the result.

5

Balkan Entanglements

The First World War was the Third Balkan War before it became the First World War. How was this possible? Conflicts and crises on the south-eastern periphery, where the Ottoman Empire abutted Christian Europe, were nothing new. The European system had always accommodated them without endangering the peace of the continent as a whole. But the last years before 1914 saw fundamental change. In the autumn of 1911, Italy launched a war of conquest on an African province of the Ottoman Empire, triggering a chain of opportunist assaults on Ottoman territories across the Balkans. The system of geopolitical balances that had enabled local conflicts to be contained was swept away. In the aftermath of the two Balkan Wars of 1912 and 1913, Austria-Hungary faced a new and threatening situation on its south-eastern periphery, while the retreat of Ottoman power raised strategic questions that Russian diplomats and policy-makers found it impossible to ignore. The two continental alliance blocs were drawn deeper into the antipathies of a region that was entering a period of unprecedented volatility. In the process, the conflicts of the Balkan theatre became tightly intertwined with the geopolitics of the European system, creating a set of escalatory mechanisms that would enable a conflict of Balkan inception to engulf the continent within five weeks in the summer of 1914.

AIR STRIKES ON LIBYA

Early on the morning of 5 January 1912, George Frederick Abbott was woken in his tent in the Libyan desert by shouting and gunfire. Running out into the sunshine, he saw the Arab and Turkish soldiers of his

encampment staring at something in the sky. It was an Italian mono-
plane flying at 2,000 feet, its wings touched by the rays of the morning
sun. Heedless of the rifle-fire from the camp, the plane sailed off grace-
fully to the south-west. The Italian invasion of Libya was in its fourth
month. Turcophile by sentiment, Abbott had joined the Ottoman forces
there as a British observer with the intention of writing a history of the
campaign. He noted that the Arabs, 'beyond letting off their guns',
appeared unimpressed by the flying machine: 'They have an enormous
capacity for taking new things as a matter of course.' When the plane
returned a day later, it bombarded the encampment with bundles of
proclamations, which fluttered in the sunlight 'like so many flakes of toy
snow'. The Arabs, Abbott recalled, 'left off firing and, stooping, picked
up the sheets eagerly, in the hope that they might be bank-notes.'[1]

Abbott's Ottoman companions were lucky to be bombarded only
with verbose Italian war propaganda in antiquated Arabic. Elsewhere,
the gross technological imbalance between the Italian armed forces and
the Ottoman subjects whose provinces they were invading had more
lethal effects. Before many major actions in the Libyan War, aeroplanes
went up in reconnaissance, signalling the enemy's position and strength,
so that the Italians could shell the Turkish guns from field batteries or
from ironclads moored offshore. This was the first war to see aerial
bombardments. In February 1912, an Ottoman retreat between the
Zanzur oasis and Gargaresch to the south-east of Tripoli became a rout
when the Italian dirigible *P3* dropped bombs among the retiring troops.[2]
Dirigibles could carry up to 250 bombs charged with high explosive.
Bombs were dropped in small numbers from aeroplanes too, though
this was an awkward business, since the aviator had somehow to steer
the machine while gripping the bomb between his knees and using his
free hand to insert the fuse, before aiming it at the troops below.[3]

The military searchlight, though a less new technology (the Royal
Navy had used searchlights against Egyptian forces in Alexandria as
early as 1882) was another high-tech weapon that figured prominently
in contemporary accounts of the Libyan War. It was probably of even
greater tactical significance than the planes and dirigibles, since its use
prevented the Ottoman forces from mounting night attacks, or at least
made these far more costly in casualties. The British observer Ernest
Bennett recalled picking his way with a small group of Arab fighters
along a coastal path towards their bivouac at Bir Terin, when the party

were suddenly pinpointed by the searchlight of an Italian cruiser: 'The sight of the poor Arabs silhouetted against the electric rays saddened me. Searchlights, Maxims, batteries, warships, aeroplanes – the odds seemed so terrible!'[4]

The cascade of wars that brought mayhem to the Balkans began in Africa. It was the Italian attack on Libya in 1911 that flashed the green light for the all-out Balkan assault on the Ottoman periphery. Unlike Egypt (now British) and Morocco (now effectively French), the three *vilayets* later known as Libya were integral provinces of the Ottoman Empire. The totally unprovoked Italian attack on these last Ottoman African possessions 'broke the ice', as one contemporary British observer put it, for the Balkan states.[5] There had been talk for some years of a joint campaign to drive the Turks out of the Balkans, but nothing in the way of practical measures. Only after Italy's assault were the Balkan states emboldened to take up arms. Looking back on these events in 1924, Miroslav Spalajković, the former political head of the Serbian foreign ministry in Belgrade, recalled that it was the Italian attack on Tripoli that had inaugurated the process that had led to the war: 'all subsequent events are nothing more than the evolution of that first aggression'.[6]

Italian diplomacy had been trying to secure an Italian sphere of interest in North Africa since before the turn of the century. In the summer of 1902, under the terms of the Prinetti–Barrère Accord, Rome and Paris had secretly agreed that in the event of a major redistribution of territory, France would take Morocco, while Italy would be granted a free hand in Libya. The agreement ratified a process of rapprochement with France, the arch-rival in northern Africa, that had been underway since 1898.[7] A note from London in March 1902 helpfully promised that Britain would ensure that 'any alteration in the status of Libya would be in conformity with Italian interests'. These agreements exemplify a policy of concessions that was designed to loosen the hold of the Triple Alliance on Italy, its most unreliable component. It was in keeping with this approach that Tsar Nicholas II agreed the 'Racconigi Bargain' of 1909 with King Victor Emmanuel III, in which Russia acknowledged Italy's special interest in Libya in return for Italian support for Russian policy on access to the Turkish Straits.[8]

Selling a policy of invasion and annexation to the politically active part of the Italian public was not difficult. Colonialism was on the march in Italy, as it was elsewhere, and the 'memory' of Roman Africa, when Libya had been the bread basket of the empire, assured Tripolitania a central place on the kingdom's colonial horizons. In 1908, the modest Ufficio Coloniale in Rome was expanded and upgraded to the Direzione Centrale degli Affari Coloniali, a sign of the growing weight of African concerns within government.[9] From 1909 onwards, the nationalist Enrico Corradini, supported by the nationalist organ *L'Idea Nazionale*, campaigned energetically for an imperialist enterprise focused on Libya; by the spring of 1911 he was openly demanding a policy of invasion and seizure.[10] It was widely believed within the political elite that Italy needed somewhere 'fruitful' in which to plant her departing emigrants. Even the socialists were susceptible to these arguments, though they tended to shroud them in the language of economic necessity.[11]

Until the summer of 1911, however, Italy's leading statesmen remained faithful to the country's ancient axiom that Italy must not provoke the break-up of the Ottoman Empire. As late as the summer of 1911, Prime Minister Giovanni Giolitti was still firmly rejecting calls to adopt a more aggressive position vis-à-vis Constantinople on a range of issues relating to the governance of Ottoman Albania.[12] It was the French intervention in Morocco that changed everything. The Italian foreign ministry believed it had excellent grounds for demanding a *quid pro quo* in Libya. In view of France's 'radical modification' of the situation in the Mediterranean, it would now be impossible, an Italian foreign ministry senior official pointed out, to 'justify' a policy of continuing inaction 'before public opinion'.[13]

It was Britain, France and Russia, the powers of the Entente, rather than Italy's allies within the Triple Alliance, that encouraged Rome to take action. In early July 1911, the Italians mentioned to the British government the 'vexations' supposedly visited upon Italian subjects in Tripoli by the Ottoman authorities (it was standard practice for European powers to legitimate their predations with the claim that their presence was needed to protect their nationals from ill-treatment). On 28 July, when the question of an actual intervention was raised with the foreign secretary by the Italian ambassador in London, Marquis Guiglielmo Imperiali, Grey's reaction was astonishingly favourable. Grey 'desired to sympathise with Italy', he told the ambassador, 'in view of the very good relations between us'. If the Italians were receiving unfair treatment in Tripoli and 'should the hand of Italy be forced', Grey undertook to 'express to the Turks the opinion that, in face of the unfair treatment meted out to Italians, the Turkish government could not expect anything else'.[14] Unsurprisingly, the Italians read these obfuscating formulations as a green light for an attack on Libya.[15] And Grey remained faithful to this line: on 19 September, he instructed Permanent Under-secretary of State Sir Arthur Nicolson that it was 'most important' that neither England nor France obstruct Italy in her designs.[16] Italian enquiries in St Petersburg produced an even more accommodating response. The Italian ambassador to St Petersburg was told that Russia would not complain if Italy acquired Libya; indeed St Petersburg urged Italy to act in a 'prompt and resolute manner'.[17]

There was thus intensive prior discussion with the Entente states. By contrast, Italy treated its allies in the Triple Alliance with cavalier disregard. On 14 September, Giolitti and the Marquis di San Giuliano, Italy's foreign minister, met in Rome to agree that a military action should be launched as swiftly as possible, so that it would be under way 'before the Austrian and German governments [were aware] of it'.[18] This reticence was well advised for the Germans had no wish to see their Italian ally go to war against their Ottoman friends and were already doing what they could to achieve a peaceful resolution of the issues outstanding between Rome and Constantinople. The German ambassador in the Ottoman capital even warned his Italian colleague that an Italian occupation of Libya might bring down the Young Turk regime and trigger a sequence of disorders that would reopen the entire Eastern Question.[19] The Austrian foreign minister Count Aehrenthal repeatedly urged restraint on the Italians, warning them that precipitous action in Libya could have undesirable consequences on the Balkan peninsula and reminding them that they themselves had always proclaimed that the stability and integrity of the Ottoman Empire were in Italy's best interests.[20]

San Giuliano was fully aware of the contradictions in Italy's policy and cognizant of the 'undesirable consequences' that worried the Austrians. In a long report of 28 July 1911 to the king and prime minister, the foreign minister weighed up the arguments for and against an invasion. He acknowledged the 'probability' that the damage inflicted on the prestige of the Ottoman Empire would 'induce the Balkan peoples to action against it and hasten a crisis that might [...] almost force

Austria to act in the Balkans'.[21] The train of thought underlying these prescient comments was not solicitude for the security of the Austro-Hungarian Empire as such, but rather apprehension at the possibility that a wave of upheavals might favour Austrian Balkan interests at Italy's expense – especially in Albania, which was viewed in many quarters as yet another future Italian colony.[22] Yet these Balkan dangers were balanced in San Giuliano's mind by the thought that time might be running out for an Italian venture in northern Africa:

> If political causes do not weaken or dissolve the Ottoman Empire, it, within two or three years, will have a powerful fleet that would render more difficult for us and perhaps even impossible an enterprise against Tripoli . . .[23]

The most striking feature of this last argument is the total absence of any foundation for it. The Ottoman government was, to be sure, striving to upgrade its obsolete fleet; an order had been placed for one modern battleship from England and another was in preparation for a purchase from Brazil. But these modest efforts were dwarfed by Italian naval construction plans, not to mention the current strength of the Italian fleet, and there was no reason to suppose that they would ever unsettle Italy's comfortable naval superiority over the Ottomans in the eastern Mediterranean.[24] San Giuliano's argument was thus founded less in the facts of the naval balance of power than in a kind of temporal claustrophobia that we find at work in the reasoning of many European statesmen of this era – a sense that time was running out, that in an environment where assets were waning and threats were growing, any delay was sure to bring severe penalties.

So it was that, after a sequence of minor naval skirmishes, the signal to stand by rang out on 3 October 1911 across a squadron of Italian warships moored before Tripoli harbour. An Italian commander on board one of the ships recalled 'a rush of gunners to guns, of carriers to ammunition rooms, of signalmen to the speaking-tubes'. Ammunition lifts raised to the batteries the white shells, tipped with red, which were laid out in neat lines behind each gun. At exactly 3.13 in the afternoon the *Benedetto Brin* fired the first shell at the Red Fort that stood on the spit of land enclosing Tripoli harbour. It was the signal for a gigantic volley that 'boomed across the sea in clouds of white smoke'.[25] The city of Tripoli fell after perfunctory resistance and was occupied by 1,700 Italian marines only forty-eight hours after the commencement of hostilities.

The occupations of Tobruk, Derna, Benghazi and Homs followed over the next few weeks. In the following months, Italian troops, 20,000 at first, later increasing to 100,000, descended on the thinly defended *vilayet* of Tripolitania.

The 'rapid liquidation' San Giuliano had hoped for did not come about. The Italians found it difficult to break into the interior of the country and for the first six months of the war remained confined to their coastal bridgeheads. An Italian decree of 5 November formally announcing the 'annexation' of Tripolitania and Cyrenaica was a gesture intended to pre-empt premature mediation by the other powers, not a faithful reflection of the military situation. In a succession of naval actions off the Lebanese coast in January and February 1912, the Italians destroyed the Ottoman naval presence at Beirut and eliminated the only remaining threat to Italian naval dominance in the southern Mediterranean. But the land war dragged on amid hair-raising reports of Italian atrocities against the Arab population. Despite their technological inferiority, the Ottoman defenders and their auxiliaries inflicted bruising defeats on the invaders. A series of concentric Turco-Arab attacks on the Italian perimeter around Tripoli during the first month of the war broke through the lines at various points, destroying some units and exacting high casualties, while armed 'rebels' inside the perimeter harassed the defending forces from behind.[26] Throughout the conflict, small skirmishes, ambushes and guerrilla warfare impeded movement between the main coastal strongholds or into the interior. It would take the Italians twenty years to 'pacify' the Libyan hinterland.

San Giuliano had seen that the invasion and seizure of Libya might have a disinhibiting effect on the Christian states of the Balkan peninsula. If this outcome was probable after the initial invasion, it became inevitable when Italy attempted to break the stalemate on land by taking the sea war into Ottoman home waters. On 18 April 1912, Italian gunboats bombarded the two outer forts guarding the entrance to the Turkish Straits. The gun crews fired 346 shells from moorings seven miles off shore, killing one soldier and one horse, and damaging a barrack. It was a symbolic demonstration, rather than a real blow at the enemy's military strength. The Turks responded, predictably enough, by closing the Straits to neutral commerce.

Ten days later, there was a further naval attack on the Dodecanese Islands at the southern end of the Aegean Sea; between 28 April and

21 May 1912, the Italians seized control of thirteen islands, whose Greek natives greeted them as heroes and liberators. After a lull, the Italians stepped up the pressure in July, sending eight submarines into the Straits. Once again, there was talk of a Turkish closure, though on this occasion Constantinople agreed under Russian pressure merely to narrow the width of the channel by laying mines. In October 1912, the Italian government threatened to launch a major naval campaign in the Aegean if the Ottoman government did not agree to conclude a peace. Under pressure from the great powers – and especially Russia and Austria, who were concerned, respectively, by the disruption to shipping and the growing danger of Balkan complications – the Turks finally caved in and signed a secret peace treaty on 15 October stipulating the autonomy of Tripolitania and Cyrenaica. An Imperial *Ferman* (decree) of the same date announced the withdrawal of Ottoman direct rule from the lost provinces. Three days later, this arrangement was publicly confirmed in the Treaty of Lausanne.[27]

The Italo-Turkish War, today largely forgotten, disturbed the European and international system in significant ways. The Libyan struggle against the Italian occupation was one of the crucial early catalysts in the emergence of modern Arab nationalism.[28] It was the powers of the Entente that had encouraged Italy to this bold act of unprovoked predation, while Italy's partners in the Triple Alliance reluctantly acquiesced.[29] There was something revelatory in this constellation. The interventions of the powers exposed the weakness, indeed the incoherence, of the Triple Alliance. The repeated warnings from Austria and Berlin that Italy's action would unsettle the entire Balkan peninsula in dangerous and unpredictable ways were ignored. Italy, it seemed, was an ally in name only.

There was as yet no overt hint of Italy's later defection to the Entente. Italian foreign policy still played a complex and ambiguous game in which contradictory commitments were precariously balanced. The traditional rivalry with France over northern Africa still seethed below the surface. Sensational naval incidents, such as the impounding by Italian naval craft of French steamers suspected of carrying Turkish arms and military personnel ensured that the war stirred mutual bitterness and paranoia between Italy and its long-resented Latin *sorellastra* (stepsister).[30] Nonetheless, the war confirmed an insight of great importance to Paris and London, namely that Italy was, for the moment, a more valuable asset to the Entente inside the Triple Alliance than outside it. In a letter of January 1912 to premier Raymond Poincaré, Paul Cambon noted that Italy was 'more burdensome than useful as an ally':

> Against Austria she harbours a latent hostility that nothing can disarm and, as regards France, we have reasons to think that in the event of a conflict, she would remain neutral or more likely would await events before taking part. It is thus unnecessary for us to attach her more closely to us . . .[31]

Underlying the disarray of the Triple Alliance was a development of even more fundamental importance. In mounting her assault on Libya, Italy had the more or less reluctant support of most of Europe. This in itself was a noteworthy state of affairs, for it revealed how comprehensively the pro-Ottoman European coalition had dissolved. In the 1850s, a concert of powers had emerged to contain Russian predations against the Ottoman Empire – the result was the Crimean War. This grouping had reconstituted itself in different form after the Russo-Turkish War at the Conference of Berlin in 1878 and had regrouped during the Bulgarian crises of the mid-1880s. It was now nowhere to be seen. In the opening phase of the Italian war, the Ottoman Empire had sought an English alliance, but London, reluctant to alienate Italy, did not respond. The two Balkan Wars that followed then broke the concert beyond repair.[32]

A transition of profound significance was taking place: Britain was gradually withdrawing from its century-long commitment to bottle the Russians into the Black Sea by sustaining the integrity of the Ottoman Empire. To be sure, British suspicion of Russia was still too intense to permit a complete relaxation of vigilance on the Straits. Grey refused in 1908 to accede to Izvolsky's request for a loosening of the restrictions on Russian access to the Turkish Straits, notwithstanding the Anglo-Russian Convention signed in the previous year. Right up until 1914, the Ottoman fleet on the Bosphorus was still commanded by a Briton, Admiral Sir Arthur Henry Limpus. But the gradual loosening of the British commitment to the Ottoman system created by degrees a geopolitical vacuum, into which Germany equally gradually slipped.[33] In 1887, Bismarck had assured the Russian ambassador in Berlin that Germany had no objection to seeing the Russians 'masters of the Straits, possessors of the entrance to the Bosphorus and of Constantinople itself'.[34] But after the departure of Bismarck in 1890 and the slackening of the traditional tie to Russia, Germany's leaders sought closer links with Constantinople. Kaiser Wilhelm II made lavishly publicized journeys to the Ottoman Empire in October 1889 and again in October 1898, and from the 1890s German finance was deeply involved in Ottoman railway construction, first in the form of the Anatolian Railway, later in the famous Baghdad Railway, begun in 1903, which was supposed on completion to connect Berlin via Constantinople to Ottoman Iraq.

A structural continuity underlay this Anglo-German changing of the guard. The problem of the Straits – which is another way of describing the problem of containing Russian power in the eastern Mediterranean – would remain one of the constants of the modern European system (if we leave aside the brief interlude of 1915–17, when France and Britain sought to bind St Petersburg to the wartime coalition by promising Constantinople and the Turkish Straits to Russia). It was still in evidence after 1945, when Turkey was shielded against potential Soviet aggression by her alliance with the United States. This critical strategic commitment has meant that Turkey, though it remains excluded from the EU, has been a member of NATO since 1952. The gradual replacement of Britain by Germany as the guardian of the Straits at *this* particular juncture was of momentous importance, because it happened to coincide with the sundering of Europe into two alliance blocs. The question of the Turkish Straits, which had once helped to unify the European concert, was now ever more deeply implicated in the antagonisms of a bipolar system.

BALKAN HELTER-SKELTER

By the time the Ottomans sued for peace with Italy in the autumn of 1912, the preparations for a major Balkan conflict were already well underway. On 28 September 1911, the day Italy delivered its ultimatum to Constantinople, the Serbian foreign minister warned that if the Italo-Turkish War were to be protracted, it would inevitably bring Balkan repercussions.[35] Almost as soon as the Italian declaration of war became known in October 1911, arrangements were put in train for a meeting between representatives of the Serbian and Bulgarian governments to discuss a joint military venture.[36] A first Serbian draft of a treaty of alliance with Bulgaria spelling out the provisions for an offensive war against Turkey was complete by November 1911. The defensive Serbo-Bulgarian alliance signed in March 1912 was followed by an openly offensive one in May, just as Italy was seizing the Dodecanese. The Serbo-Bulgarian accords were focused mainly on military objectives against Ottoman south-eastern Europe, but they also foresaw the possibility of combined action against Austria-Hungary.[37] Around the Serbo-Bulgarian core, a secret Balkan League now coalesced whose purpose was to expel the Turks from the peninsula. The peace negotiations between Italy and the Ottoman Empire were still dragging on when the League states began mobilizing for a general Balkan War. Hostilities opened on 8 October 1912 with a Montenegrin attack on Ottoman positions. On 18 October 1912, just as the peace of Lausanne was being signed, King Petar I issued a royal declaration announcing that he had 'by the grace of God ordered [his] brave army to join in the Holy War to free our brethren and to ensure a better future'.[38]

The war that broke out in the Balkans in October 1912 had been foreseen by nearly everyone. What astonished contemporary observers was the swiftness and scope of the victories secured by the Balkan League states. Battles flared up across the peninsula as Serbian, Bulgarian, Greek and Montenegrin armies advanced on the Ottoman strongholds. Geography dictated that the fulcrum of the Bulgarian war would be in Eastern Thrace, whose broad undulating plains narrow into the isthmus at the end of which Constantinople stands. Into this area the Bulgarians poured nearly 300,000 men – approximately 15 per cent of the country's total male population (in all, just over 30 per cent of Bulgarian males were mobilized during the First Balkan War).[39] At Kirk-Kilisse (Lozengrad), a battle raged for three days along a thirty-six-mile front stretching eastward from the Ottoman fortress of Edirne (Adrianople). Led by the exceptionally energetic Dimitriev, who was known as 'Napoleon' on account both of his small stature and his preference for leading from the heat of battle, the Bulgarian infantry attacked with great determination and ferocity. When the Ottomans fell back in disarray, the Bulgarians followed through mud and heavy rain until they reached country for which they lacked good maps or reconnaissance – their commanders had never expected them to get this far. The Bulgarian onslaught broke at last on the Chataldja line of fortifications, only twenty miles from Constantinople. Here, on 17 November 1912, with the capital city at their backs, the Ottomans held the line, deploying accurate artillery fire to inflict appalling casualties on the advancing lines of infantry, and repelling wave after wave of assaults. This was as close as the Bulgarians would ever get to Constantinople.

While the Bulgarians pushed into Thrace, the Serbian 1st Army advanced south into northern Macedonia with around 132,000 men. On 22 October, earlier than they expected, they encountered an Ottoman force encamped around the town of Kumanovo. On the following day, a battle broke out along a ten-mile front under cold driving rain. After two days of fighting the Serbs inflicted a crushing defeat on the Ottomans. There was no immediate follow-up, but the Serbian army drove on southwards and in three days of sporadic but heavy fighting around the town of Prilep, again under the autumn rain, the Serbs once more drove the Ottoman troops from their positions. At the request of their Bulgarian allies, who were anxious to secure Salonika before the Greeks got their hands on it and had no further troops to spare, the Serbian command ordered the 1st Army on 8 November to advance on Bitola, a picturesque town on the river Dragor in south-western Macedonia. Here the Ottomans had halted and consolidated their position, placing their artillery on the Oblakov heights overlooking the main approach from the north. Heavy artillery fire from the heights initially held the Serbs back. Only after the Oblakov ridge was stormed and taken on 17 November did the tide of the battle turn decisively in the Serbs' favour. Firing with impressive skill from high ground, the Serbian artillery destroyed the Ottoman batteries defending the town, opening the way for an infantry assault that would turn the Ottoman flank. This was the last stand of the Ottomans in Macedonia. And in the meanwhile, the Serbian 3rd Army had advanced westwards into northern Albania, where they supported the Montenegrin army in besieging the fortified city of Scutari.

From the beginning of the conflict, the Greeks had focused their attention single-mindedly on securing Salonika, the largest city of Macedonia and the key strategic port of the region. Leaving the Macedonian strongholds on their left flank to the Serbs and Bulgarians, the Greek Army of Thessaly marched to the north-east, overrunning Ottoman positions on the Sarantaporos pass and Yannitsa on 22 October and

5. The Balkans: In 1912

6. The Balkans: Ceasefire Lines After the First Balkan War

7. The Balkans: After the Second Balkan War

2 November. The road to Salonika was now open. An almost comical interlude followed. During the first week of November, Greek units began surrounding the city. The Bulgarians, realizing that the Greeks were about to take this coveted prize, ordered their own 7th Rila Division to race southwards in the hope of pre-empting a Greek occupation, a deployment that forced them to leave Bitola to the Serbs. As they approached the city, messengers were sent ahead urging the Ottoman commander to surrender to the Bulgarian army under favourable terms. From the commander came the forlorn reply: 'I have only one Thessaloniki, which I have already surrendered' – the Greeks had got there first. Having initially refused the Bulgarians entry, the Greek command eventually agreed to let 15,000 Bulgarians co-occupy the city with 25,000 Greek troops. In a parallel campaign waged in the Epirus, or southern Albania, the Greeks became bogged down in a siege of the well-fortified Ottoman positions around Yanina. The fighting dragged on in some areas, but the scale of the allies' success was extraordinary: in only six weeks, they had conquered nearly half of all European Turkey. By 3 December 1912, when an armistice was signed, the only points of

continuing Ottoman resistance west of the Chataldja line were Adrianople, Yanina and Scutari, all of which were still under siege.

As the squabbling over Salonika suggests, the First Balkan War contained the seeds of a second conflict over the territorial spoils from the first. In the treaty founding their alliance in March 1912, Serbia and Bulgaria had agreed a clear plan of partition: the Bulgarians were to get southern Macedonia, including the towns of Ohrid, Prilep and Bitola. Serbia was assigned Kosovo – heartland of the Serbian mythscape – and the Sanjak of Novi Pazar. Northern Macedonia, including the important town of Skopje, was assigned to a 'disputed zone' – if the two parties failed to reach an agreement, they both undertook to accept the arbitration of the Russian Tsar. The Bulgarians were pleased with this agreement – especially as they expected the Russians to rule in their favour.[40]

The Serbs, by contrast, were far from happy. Many in the political elite felt that the March alliance, which had been negotiated by the moderate prime minister Milovan Milovanović, had given too much away. Among the critics were the chief of the General Staff Radomir Putnik and the Radical Party leader Nikola Pašić. 'In my opinion,' Pašić later commented, 'we conceded too much, or better said, we abandoned some Serbian areas which we should never have dared to abandon, even if we were left without an agreement.'[41] A few months later, in July 1912, Milovanović died unexpectedly, removing one of the chief exponents of moderation in Serbian foreign policy. Six weeks after his death, the ardent nationalist Pašić took office as prime minister and minister for foreign affairs.

The first unequivocal sign that the Serbian government intended to breach the terms of the treaty with Bulgaria came even before the First Balkan War had broken out. On 15 September 1912, Pašić had dispatched a confidential circular to the Serbian delegations to the European powers, in which he referred to 'Old Serbia' and defined this area as encompassing Prilep, Kičevo and Ohrid, areas that had been promised in March to Bulgaria. As the war got underway, Serbian designs on Macedonia were temporarily overshadowed by the advance into northern Albania, which distracted the leadership with the bewitching prospect of a port on the Adriatic. This was the old problem of Serbian national 'unification': that it could potentially involve expansion in a number of different directions, forcing decision-makers to choose between options. As soon as it became clear, however, that Austria-Hungary had no intention of allowing the Serbs to acquire a swathe of Albania and the prospect of an Adriatic port receded from view, the leaders in Belgrade began to broach publicly the idea of revising the terms of the treaty with Bulgaria in Serbia's favour. A particular fetish was Monastir, which the Serbs had taken, after repeated charges and heavy losses, 'with the bayonet'.[42] Alarmed, the Bulgarians sent requests for clarification, which Pašić handled with his usual evasiveness; 'all differences could and would be settled easily', he assured the Bulgarians, yet at the same time there was talk behind the scenes of annexing not just Prilep and Bitola from the Bulgarian zone but also the hotly coveted city of Skopje in the 'disputed zone'.[43] Tempers were raised further by news of Serbian mistreatment of Bulgars in the 'liberated lands'. It didn't help that the heir to the throne, Prince Alexandar, had walked about various Macedonian towns during a tour of the conquered areas engaging local Bulgars in the following formulaic dialogue:

'What are you?'
    'Bulgarian.'
    'You are not Bulgarian. Fuck your father.'[44]

It looked for some months as if a conflict might be avoided, because both Belgrade and Sofia agreed at the end of April 1913 to submit the Macedonian dispute to Russian arbitration. Anxious to bring the issue to a resolution, Sofia sent Dimitar Rizov, the Bulgarian diplomat who had assisted at the birth of the Serbian-Bulgarian Treaty of Alliance in 1904 (see chapter 2), to Belgrade to lay out the basis for an amicable settlement.[45] Known as an exponent of Serbo-Bulgarian collaboration, Rizov was the right man to secure a deal, if any was to be had. But his conversations with the Serbian government convinced him that Belgrade had absolutely no intention of relinquishing any of the lands and strongholds that it currently held within the 'Bulgarian zone'. He was particularly shocked at the influence wielded by the Russian minister. Hartwig's weight in Serbian affairs was such, he reported to the Bulgarian prime minister, 'that his [diplomatic] colleagues privately call him "the Regent", for, in reality, he fulfils the functions of the ailing Serbian king'.[46] On 28 May, one day after Rizov's departure from Belgrade, Pašić at last went public with his annexation policy, declaring before the

Skupština that Serbia would keep all the lands it had fought so hard to acquire.

Further conflict over Macedonia was now inevitable. In the last week of May 1913, large contingents of Serbian troops were moved to forward positions along the Bulgarian frontier and the railways were temporarily closed to civilian traffic.[47] On 30 June, Pašić was once again before the Skupština, defending his Macedonia policy against extreme nationalist deputies who argued that Serbia should simply have seized the captured provinces outright. Just as the debate was warming up, a messenger arrived to inform the prime minister that Bulgarian forces had attacked Serbian positions in the contested areas at two o'clock that morning. There had been no declaration of war. The Skupština erupted in uproar and Pašić left the session to coordinate the government's preparations for a counter-offensive.

In the Inter-Allied War that followed, Serbia, Greece, Turkey and Romania joined forces to tear chunks of territory out of the flanks of Bulgaria. Bulgarian forces entering Macedonia were checked by the Serbs on the river Bregalnica in early July. Then well dug-in Bulgarian troops around Kalimantsi in north-eastern Macedonia repelled a Serbian counter-attack on 15–18 July and prevented the Serbs from invading western Bulgaria. While the Serbian front stagnated, the Greeks attacked from the south in a campaign that culminated in the bloody but inconclusive Battle of Kresna Gorge. At the same time, a Romanian assault in the east, which brought Romanian troops to within seven miles of Sofia, forced the Bulgarian government to sue for an armistice. In the Peace of Bucharest concluded on 10 August 1913, Bulgaria, after stupendous bloodletting, lost most of the territories it had acquired in the first war.

THE WOBBLER

Russian policy on the Balkan events evolved in the shadow of the Bosnian annexation crisis of 1908–9. The Russians forgot (or never learned of) the role Izvolsky had played in proposing the exchange of Bosnia-Herzegovina for Austrian diplomatic support on the Straits question. The broader international context – the refusal of Britain, for example, to support the Russian bid for access to the Turkish Straits – was likewise elided from memory. Stripped down to serve the ends of nationalist and pan-Slavist propaganda, the Bosnian annexation was remembered as an infamous chapter in the history of Austrian perfidy, made worse by Germany's intervention in defence of its ally in March 1909. It was a 'humiliation' the like of which Russia must never again be made to endure. But the Bosnian débâcle also revealed the extent of Russia's isolation in Balkan matters, for neither Britain nor France had shown much zeal in helping St Petersburg to extricate itself from the mess that Izvolsky had helped to create. In future, it was clear, a way would have to be found of applying pressure in the region without alienating Russia's western partners.

The most striking feature of Russian Balkan policy in 1911–12 was the weakness of central control and coordination. Stolypin's assassination on 18 September 1911 plunged the system into disarray. The premier had been dead for just ten days when the Italian government issued its ultimatum to the Ottoman government. The new premier, Vladimir Kokovtsov, was still finding his feet. Sazonov was abroad between March and December 1911, convalescing from a serious illness. In his absence, Assistant Foreign Minister Neratov struggled to stay abreast of developments. The reins of ministerial control slackened. The result was a fracturing of Russian policy into parallel and mutually incompatible elements. On the one hand, the Russian ambassador to Constantinople, N. V. Charykov, attempted to exploit the Ottoman Empire's predicament in order to negotiate improved conditions for Russian shipping in the Turkish Straits.[48] As the Libyan crisis unfolded, Charykov proposed to the Ottoman government that Russia guarantee Turkish possession of Constantinople along with a defensible Thracian hinterland. In return, the Ottoman government would grant the Russians free passage for warships through the Dardanelles and the Bosphorus.[49]

At the very same time, Nikolai Hartwig, minister in Belgrade, pursued a very different line. Hartwig had been trained within the Asiatic Department of the Russian foreign ministry, a sub-culture characterized by a preference for assertive positions and ruthless methods.[50] Since his arrival in the Serbian capital in the autumn of 1909, he had been the champion of an active Russian policy on the Balkan peninsula. He had made no effort to conceal his Austrophobe and pan-Slav views. Andrey Toshev, the Bulgarian minister in the Serbian capital, was doubtless exaggerating when he claimed that 'step by step [Hartwig] took into his own hands the actual direction of the [Serbian] kingdom', but there is no question that Hartwig occupied a position of unrivalled influence in Belgrade's political life.[51] Hartwig's popularity at the court of Tsar Nicholas II and the general lack of vigorous control or scrutiny from St Petersburg meant that, as the chargé d'affaires at the Russian mission in Belgrade ruefully noted, he was relatively free to elaborate his own extreme views, even when these conflicted with the official signals emanating from the ministry. He had 'secured such a position that he could give the Serbs his own version of the steps Russia was about to take'.[52]

While Charykov explored the possibility of a lasting rapprochement with Constantinople, Hartwig pushed the Serbs to form an offensive alliance with Bulgaria against the Ottoman Empire. He was in an excellent position to coordinate these efforts, since his old friend Miroslav Spalajković, who had virtually lived at the Russian mission during the scandal of the Friedjung trial, had accepted a posting as the Serbian minister in Sofia, where he helped to smooth the path towards a Serbo-Bulgarian treaty. In addition to pressing his arguments upon the Serbian government, Hartwig plied Assistant Minister Neratov with letters insisting that the formation of a Balkan League against the Ottomans (and, by implication, Austria-Hungary) was the only way to secure Russian interests in the region. 'The present moment is such,' he told Neratov on 6 October 1911, three days after the Italian shelling of Tripoli, 'that both states [Serbia and Bulgaria] would be committing the greatest offence against Russia and Slavdom if they showed even the slightest vacillation.'[53]

Sazonov thus faced a choice between irreconcilable options when he returned from his convalescence abroad at the end of 1911. He elected to disavow Charykov. The Ottoman government were told to disregard the ambassador's overtures and Charykov was recalled from his post a few months later.[54] Sazonov claimed that he was punishing his ambassador for disregarding his instructions, jumping over 'all the barriers' set by St Petersburg and thereby 'making a mess of things'.[55] But this was a smokescreen: Charykov had secured Assistant Minister Neratov's backing for his proposals, and he was certainly not the only Russian envoy making policy on the trot – Hartwig was a far worse offender in this respect. Sazonov's real reason for disavowing the ambassador to Constantinople was his concern that the moment was not yet ripe for a renewed Russian initiative on the Straits.[56] In December 1911, on his way back from his convalescence in Switzerland, Sazonov had learned from Izvolsky and from the Russian ambassador to London, Count Benckendorff, that pressing the Straits question directly would place relations with France and Britain under strain. British attitudes were a particular concern, because the winter of 1911–12 saw the re-emergence of tensions over the Anglo-Russian settlement in Persia. The worse these tensions became, the less likely it was that Britain would adopt a benevolent view of Russian objectives in the Straits question. Meanwhile, Russia's lukewarm support for France's Moroccan adventure in the spring and summer of 1911 had loosened the link to Paris. The French government was in any case reluctant to see the Russians gain improved access to the Eastern Mediterranean, which they regarded as their own sphere of interest. Most importantly of all, the immense scale of French investment in the Ottoman Empire made Paris deeply suspicious of any Russian initiative that looked likely to compromise its financial health. At a time when the bonds holding the Entente together appeared relatively weak, potentially divisive proposals on an area of such strategic importance as the Turkish Straits were inopportune. For the moment, in other words, Sazonov was obliged to prioritize the cohesion of the Entente over Russian interest in improved access to the Straits.

At the same time as he disassociated himself from Charykov's initiative, Sazonov supported Hartwig's pro-Serbian and leaguist policy on

Sergei Sazonov

the Balkans, as a means both of countering Austrian designs and applying indirect pressure to the Ottomans. But the Russian foreign minister was careful to avoid challenging the Ottomans in a way that might alienate the western Entente partners. The desire to exploit the opportunities opening up on the Bosphorus had to be balanced against the risks of acting alone. He encouraged the Italians in their hit-and-run raids on the Dardanelles, even though these were likely to trigger a Turkish closure of the waterway that would severely disrupt Russian commercial traffic. Sazonov told the British and the French that his aim was to draw Italy into a Balkan partnership; as he told Sir George Buchanan, the British ambassador in St Petersburg, he saw in the Italians 'a valuable counterpoise to Austria'; in reality he hoped that the Italian raids might at some point offer the Russians an excuse for demanding that their own warships be granted access.[57] It was essential, Sazonov told Izvolsky at the beginning of October 1912, that Russia not 'present herself as rallying and unifying opposition to Turkey'.[58]

Sazonov also supported and sponsored the emergence of the Balkan League. He had been an exponent of League policy since coming to office and claimed to be inspired by the vision of half a million bayonets forming a rampart between the central powers and the Balkan states.[59] His motives in sponsoring the formation of the Serbo-Bulgarian alliance treaty of March 1912 were both anti-Austrian and anti-Turkish. The treaty stated that the signatories would 'come to each other's assistance with all of their forces' in the event of 'any Great Power attempting to annex, occupy or temporarily to invade' any formerly Turkish Balkan territory – a clear, if implicit, reference to Austria, which was suspected of harbouring designs on the Sanjak of Novi Pazar.[60]

Sazonov knew perfectly well that the Balkan peninsula was likely to become highly unstable in the aftermath of the Libyan War. It was essential, he believed, that Russia remain in control of any resulting conflict. The terms of the Serbo-Bulgarian treaty accordingly assigned to Russia a coordinating and arbitrating role in any post-conflict settlement. A secret protocol stipulated that the signatories were to advise Russia in advance of their intention to wage war; if the two states disagreed on whether or when to commence an attack (on Turkey), a Russian veto would be binding. If an agreement over the partitioning of conquered territory proved elusive, the issue must be submitted to arbitration by Russia: the decision of Russia was binding for both parties to the treaty.[61]

The alliance thus looked likely to serve as a valuable tool for the pursuit of Russian interests.[62] Yet some doubts remained. Past experience suggested that the Balkan League Russia had helped to create might not prove obedient to the promptings of St Petersburg. Disagreement on this point had led in October and November 1911 to a bitter feud between Hartwig, who favoured an aggressive Balkan League policy, and A. V. Nekliudov, the Russian minister in Sofia, who worried that the resulting alliance would slip out of Russian control. Nekliudov had a point: what if the two signatory states did in fact agree on the feasibility and timing of an attack? In that case, the Russian treaty veto would be meaningless (this is indeed what happened). And what if the two signatories recruited other neighbouring states – Montenegro and Greece, for example – to their coalition without consulting St Petersburg? This, too, happened: Russia was informed of, but not consulted about, the secret military articles attached to the alliance; St Petersburg's objections to the inclusion of Montenegro and Greece were disregarded. The League threatened to slip out of control even before it had come fully into being.[63]

When the Balkan tiger leapt out of its cage in October 1912, Sazonov made demonstrative but largely gestural efforts to restrain it. The Russian ambassador in London was informed, on the one hand, that he should not consent to any proposals that involved Russia collaborating with Austria.[64] At the same time, the League states were warned that they could not count on Russian assistance.[65] These admonitions must have sounded strange to Serbian and Bulgarian ears, given the encouragement both states had received from Russia to make common cause against the Turks. Milenko Vesnić, the Serbian envoy to France, recalled a meeting with Sazonov in Paris in October 1912, just as the war was beginning. Speaking before a group of French officials at the Quai d'Orsay, Sazonov told Vesnić that he believed the Serbian mobilization had been an 'ill-conceived démarche' and that it was crucial that the war be contained and brought to a swift close. Irritated but undaunted, Vesnić reminded Sazonov that the Russian foreign ministry had had 'full knowledge of the agreement struck between Serbia and Bulgaria'. Embarrassed – French officials were present! – Sazonov replied that this was true, but that it applied only to the first treaty, which was 'merely defensive' – a dubious assertion, to say the least.[66] Russian diplomacy was playing two roles – instigator and peacekeeper – at the same time.

Sazonov told Sofia that he did not object to a Balkan war as such, but was concerned about timing: a Balkan war might trigger broader consequences, and Russia was not yet militarily ready to risk a general conflagration.[67] The confusion generated by Sazonov's own ambivalent messaging was compounded by the enthusiastic warmongering of Hartwig and the Russian military attaché in Sofia, who both encouraged their respective interlocutors to believe that if things did go wrong, Russia would not leave the Balkan 'little brothers' to fend for themselves. It was reported that Nekliudov, the Russian minister in Sofia, 'wept' for joy when the Serbo-Bulgarian mobilizations were announced.[68]

But what if Russian Balkan policy, instead of furthering Russian designs on the Straits, were to place them at risk? The political leadership in St Petersburg could live with the idea that the Straits would remain for the time being under the relatively weak custodianship of the Ottomans, but the notion that another power might put down a root on the banks of the Bosphorus was utterly unacceptable. In October 1912, the unexpectedly rapid advance of the Bulgarian armies on the Chataldja line in eastern Thrace – the last great defensive works before the Ottoman capital – alarmed Sazonov and his colleagues. How should Russia respond if the Bulgarians, whose wilful king was known to aspire to the ancient crown of Byzantium, were to seize and occupy Constantinople? In that event, Sazonov told Buchanan, 'Russia would be obliged to warn them off,' for, he added rather disengenuously, 'though Russia had no desire to establish herself at Constantinople she could not allow any other power to take possession of it'.[69] In a letter to Nekliudov that was copied to the legations at Paris, London, Constantinople and Belgrade, Sazonov deployed the familiar argument that a Bulgarian seizure of Constantinople would turn Russian public opinion against Sofia.[70] An ominous warning was issued to the Bulgarian minister in St Petersburg: 'Do not enter Constantinople under any circumstances because you will otherwise complicate your affairs too gravely.'[71] Only the blood-soaked collapse of the Bulgarian advance on the Chataldja line of fortifications saved Sazonov from having to intervene in a manner that might have unsettled the allied powers.

These manoeuvres were performed against a background of mounting press agitation in Russia. Russian newspaper editors were electrified by the news of the struggle unfolding between the Balkan states and the ancestral enemy on the Bosphorus. No other issue possessed comparable power to trigger excitement, solidarity, indignation and anger in the Russian urban public. 'If the Slavs and the Greeks prove victorious,' *Novoye Vremya* asked at the end of October 1912, 'where is the iron hand that will [. . .] snatch from them the fruits of victories that they will have purchased with their blood?'[72] Assessing the impact of these currents on Sazonov is difficult. The Russian foreign minister resented the press's interest in the details of his policy and affected an attitude of contempt towards journalists and their opinions. On the other hand, he appears to have been highly sensitive to press critique. On one occasion, he convened a press conference to complain at the hostile treatment he had received from journalists. In a circular of 31 October to Russia's ambassadors to the great powers, Sazonov declared that he had no intention of allowing nationalist voices in the Russian press to influence his handling of policy. But he went on to suggest that envoys might consider using reports of press agitation to 'incline [foreign] cabinets to the idea of the necessity of taking into account the difficulty of our position'[73] – in other words, while he denied that the press was a force in his own decision-making, he saw that adverse newspaper coverage could be exploited abroad to secure a certain room for manoeuvre in diplomatic negotiations. Few documents better evoke the complexity of the relationship between key decision-makers and the press.

Improvisation and frenetic vacillation remained a hallmark of Sazonov's policy during the First Balkan War. At the end of October he solemnly announced his support for Austria's policy of maintaining the territorial status quo on the Balkan peninsula. But then, on 8 November, Sazonov informed the Italian government that Serbian access to the Adriatic Sea was an absolute necessity, adding portentously: 'It is dangerous to ignore facts.' Yet only three days later he told Hartwig that the creation of an independent *Albanian* state on the Adriatic coast was an 'inevitable necessity', adding once again: 'To ignore facts is dangerous.'[74] Hartwig was ordered to warn Pašić that if the Serbs pushed too hard, Russia might be forced to stand aside and leave them to their own devices – a task the Russian minister performed under protest and with undisguised distaste. Copies of this message were forwarded by Sazonov to London and Paris.[75] And yet by 17 November, he was arguing once again for a Serbian corridor to the coast.[76] Notes were dispatched to Paris and London declaring that Russia might be obliged to intervene militarily against Austria-Hungary if the latter attacked Serbia; the two allied governments were asked to express their views.[77] 'Sazonov is so continually changing his ground,' the British ambassador George Buchanan wrote from St Petersburg in November 1912, 'that it is difficult to follow the successive phases of pessimism and optimism through which he passes.'[78] 'I have more than once reproached Sazonov with inconsistency and with frequent changes of front,' Buchanan reported two months later. But to be fair, he went on, the Russian minister 'was not a free agent' – he was obliged above all to take account of the views of the Tsar, who had recently fallen under the influence of the military party in St Petersburg.[79] Robert Vansittart, former third secretary in Paris and Tehran, now serving in the Foreign Office in London, summed up the problem succinctly: 'M. Sazonov is a sad wobbler.'[80]

THE BALKAN WINTER CRISIS OF 1912–13

While Sazonov wobbled, there were signs of a hardening of attitudes on the Balkans across the Russian leadership. The decision to announce a trial mobilization on 30 September 1912, just as the Balkan states were mobilizing, suggested that Russia intended to cover its Balkan diplomacy with military actions intended to intimidate Vienna. The Austrian General Staff reported that 50–60,000 Russian reservists had been called up in the Warsaw district of the Polish salient (adjoining Austrian Galicia) and that 170,000 further call-ups were expected, creating a massive concentration of Russian troops along the Austro-Hungarian border. When quizzed on these measures, Sazonov claimed to have had no knowledge of them; Sukhomlinov, by contrast, maintained that the foreign minister had been fully informed.[81] Whether Sazonov was party to the decision or not (and both scenarios are equally plausible), the trial mobilization – and the decision to go ahead with it even as the Balkan War broke out – marked a departure from the caution that had previously restrained Russia's policy. Russian thinking had begun to embrace a strategy of 'real power' in which diplomatic efforts were underwritten by the threat of military force. 'We can probably rely on the real support of France and England,' Sazonov commented in a letter of 10 October 1912 to Kokovtsov, 'only insofar as both of these states acknowledge the extent of our readiness to take possible risks.'[82] Only the fullest measure of military readiness, he told Izvolsky in a paradoxical ratiocination characteristic of his policy in the last years before the outbreak of war, would enable Russia to apply 'peaceful pressure' in pursuit of its aims.[83]

The move towards a more assertive Russian Balkan policy also marked a shift in the balance of power between Kokovtsov and Sukhomlinov. In the course of the negotiations over the 1913 military budget in October–November 1912, it became clear that the Tsar was no longer willing to support Kokovtsov in his calls for restraint on military expenditure. At a sequence of meetings on 31 October–2 November, the Council of Ministers agreed a supplementary military credit of 66.8 million roubles. The originator of this move was not Sukhomlinov, but Sazonov, who had written to Kokovtsov on 23 October saying that he intended to raise the army's readiness for a confrontation with Austria-Hungary or Turkey. Kokovtsov had no choice but to forward the letter to Sukhomlinov, who then formally requested the credit. This was a crucial step in the undermining of Kokovtsov's position: the premier was powerless to overrule an initiative backed both by the foreign minister and the minister of war, and supported from behind the scenes by the Tsar.[84] After 5 November, when the Tsar authorized an order postponing the homeward rotation of the senior class of Russian conscripts, the number of reservists on extended duty rose to around 400,000.[85] Frontier troop strengths – according to information passed by St Petersburg to the French – were now only a little short of the wartime level, and these steps were flanked by other Russian measures: the deployment of some units to forward positions near the Galician border with Austria, arms requisitions and the retention of rolling stock. The aim was to ensure, as Chief of Staff Zhilinsky told the French military attaché, that 'we can [. . .] adjust to any eventuality'.[86]

The decisive step in the direction of a further escalation came in the fourth week of November 1912, when Minister of War Sukhomlinov and members of the military command nearly succeeded in persuading the Tsar to issue orders for a partial mobilization against Austria-Hungary. Kokovtsov recalled being told on 22 November that the Tsar wished to see him and Sazonov on the following morning. When they arrived, they found to their horror that a military conference had already resolved to issue mobilization orders for the Kiev and Warsaw military districts, which adjoined Austro-Hungarian territory. Sukhomlinov, it seemed, had wanted to mobilize on the previous day, but the Tsar had delayed the order so as to consult the relevant ministers first. Outraged at these high-handed manoeuvres by the military, Kokovtsov pointed out the idiocy of the proposed measure. Above all, a partial mobilization against Austria made no sense whatsoever, since Germany was obliged to assist Austria if it were attacked. And what about France? Since there had been no consultation with Paris, a sudden mobilization might well leave Russia facing the consequences of its folly alone. Then there was the constitutional issue: Sukhomlinov, Kokovtsov argued, had no right even to broach such a policy with the Tsar without first consulting the minister of foreign affairs. Nicholas II backed down and agreed to cancel the war minister's orders.[87] On this occasion, Sazonov joined premier Vladimir Kokovtsov in denouncing the proposal as politically senseless, strategically unfeasible and highly dangerous. It was one of the last gasps of 'united government' in Imperial Russia.

Yet the fact remains that during the winter crisis of 1912–13, Sazonov supported a policy of confrontation with Austria, a policy ensuring that the Russo-Austrian frontier remained 'at the diplomatic storm centre'.[88] There was a brief change of heart after the stand-off of 23 November between the civilians and the military command over the mobilization question, but the mood in St Petersburg remained belligerent. In mid-December, War Minister Sukhomlinov proposed to the Council of Ministers a raft of measures: the reinforcement of frontier cavalry units in the Kiev and Warsaw military districts, a call-up of reservists for training to bring frontier units to war strength, the transport of horses to the frontier areas, the reinforcement of military guards and a ban on the export of horses. Had all of these measures been carried out, they might well have pushed the winter crisis over the threshold to war – a pan-European escalation would have been certain, given that Paris was at this time urging the Russians to step up their measures against Austria and had promised its support in the event of a military conflict involving Germany. But this was going too far for Sazonov, and once again he joined Kokovtsov in rejecting Sukhomlinov's proposal. This time, the proponents of peace secured only a partial victory: the call-up of infantry reservists and the ban on horse exports were rejected as too inflammatory, but the other measures went ahead, with predictably unsettling effects on the mood in Vienna.[89]

In the light of what had passed before, Sazonov's offer in the last week of December 1912 to stand down a portion of the Russian reinforcements along the Galician frontier, but only on the condition that Vienna stood its forces down first, looked like a further act of intimidation rather than a genuine effort to achieve de-escalation and disengagement.[90] When the Austrians failed to comply, St Petersburg stepped up the threat once more, hinting at the possibility of a further extension of the senior conscript class by means of a public announcement that would have triggered a general war panic. Sazonov even told the British ambassador George Buchanan at the beginning of January 1913 that he had a 'project for mobilising on the Austrian frontier' and was planning to bring up more troops. There was renewed talk (by Sazonov this time, not just Sukhomlinov) of a mobilization of the Kiev military district and a Russian ultimatum to Vienna.[91]

The resulting Austro-Russian armed stalemate was politically and financially painful for both sides: in Vienna, the border confrontation imposed disastrous burdens on the monarchy's fragile finances. It also raised questions about the loyalty of Czech, South Slav and other national minority reservists, many of whom stood to lose their civilian jobs if the state of high alert continued. On the Russian side, too, there were doubts about the political reliability of the frontier units – insubordination among the reservists recalled for duty threatened to spread to the peacetime army and officers along the Galician front were demanding either war right now or the standing down of the reserves. The finance ministry and its chief, Vladimir Kokovtsov, also complained of the financial burden imposed by the retention of the reservists, although generally speaking, financial concerns appear to have played a less prominent role in St Petersburg, where the army was wallowing in money, than they did in Vienna, where ministers feared the total collapse of financial control.[92] Kokovtsov succeeded in tilting the balance back in favour of de-escalation and persuaded the Tsar not to go ahead with further potentially provocative measures.

In the event, it was the Austrians who took the first step backwards, gradually reducing their frontier troop strengths from the end of January. In February and March, Berchtold followed up with concessions to Belgrade. On 21 February, Franz Joseph proposed a substantial reduction in Galician company strengths and Nicholas II in return agreed to propose the release of the senior conscript class. De-escalation became official in the second week of March, with major and publicly announced troop reductions on both sides of the border.[93]

The Balkan winter crisis of 1912–13 had passed, to general relief. But it changed in a lasting way the contours of politics in Vienna and St Petersburg. Austrian policy-makers became accustomed to a more militarized style of diplomacy.[94] In St Petersburg, a Russian war party emerged. Among its most intransigent members were the Grand Dukes Nikolai Nikolaievich and Pyotr Nikolaievich, both senior military commanders and both married to Montenegrin princesses. 'All the pacifism of the emperor,' wrote the Belgian minister in St Petersburg at the beginning of 1913, 'cannot silence those [at court] who proclaim the impossibility of recoiling ever again before Austria.'[95] Belligerent views gained ground, not just because the Tsar (intermittently) and senior military or naval commanders supported them, but also because they were also espoused by an influential coterie of civilian ministers, of whom the most important was the minister of agriculture, Alexander Krivoshein.

Krivoshein was one of the most dynamic and interesting figures on the Russian political scene. He was the consummate political networker: intelligent, sophisticated, shrewd and possessed of an uncanny gift for making the right friends.[96] As a young man, he was notorious for his skill in befriending the sons of powerful ministers who subsequently helped him find attractive posts. In 1905, he infiltrated the circle associated with the Tsar's secretary D. Trepov (the autumn of 1905 was the only time the Tsar used the services of a private secretary). By 1906, though he still lacked any permanent official post, Krivoshein was already being received by the sovereign.[97] He was also immensely rich, having married into the Morozov family, heirs to a vast textiles empire, an alliance that also assured him close relations with Moscow's industrial elite.

Krivoshein's politics were forged by his early experience of Russian Poland – he was born and grew up in Warsaw. The region was a breeding ground for nationalist Russian officials. Russian bureaucrats in the Polish western *gubernias* felt, in the words of one senior functionary, 'like a besieged camp, their thoughts always drifting towards national authority'.[98] The western salient became one of the footholds of the Duma nationalists after 1905. Foreign policy was not initially among Krivoshein's specialities. He was an agrarian and administrative modernizer in the style of Stolypin. He found communication with foreigners difficult,

Alexander V. Krivoshein

because, unlike most members of his class in Russia, he spoke neither German nor French fluently. Nevertheless: as his political star ascended, he acquired the appetite to wield influence in this, the most prestigious domain of government activity. Moreover, his appointment as minister of land-tenure regulation and agriculture in May 1908 involved a stronger geopolitical dimension than its title suggested. Krivoshein's ministry was involved in promoting Russian settlement in the Far East and he thus took an active interest in security questions relating to the frontier between the Russian Far East and Chinese inner Manchuria.[99] Like many eastern-oriented politicians, Krivoshein favoured the maintenance of good relations with Germany. He did not share Izvolsky's apocalyptic view of the Austrian annexation of Bosnia-Herzegovina and resisted the foreign minister's calls for 'revenge' against the powers of the Triple Alliance.[100]

During the last few years before the summer of 1914, however, Krivoshein underwent a transition. Stolypin, who had been a powerful mentor, was dead. United government was in disarray. Krivoshein began more intensively to cultivate nationalist circles in the Duma and the public sphere. During the Balkan winter crisis of 1912–13, he supported

Sukhomlinov's forward policy in the Balkans, on the grounds that it was time to 'stop cringing before the Germans' and place one's trust instead in the Russian people and their age-old love for their homeland.[101] In the spring of 1913, he led a high-volume campaign to revise the terms of Russia's current tariff treaty with Germany. The treaty had been negotiated with the Germans by Sergei Witte and Kokovtsov in 1904; by 1913, the view was widespread in the Russian political classes that the treaty allowed 'the cunning, cold German industrialist' to collect 'tribute' from the 'simple-minded Russian worker of the soil'.[102] The campaign, a clear disavowal of Kokovtsov's agrarian policy, stirred feuding between the German and Russian press. Krivoshein's son later recalled that as the controversy heated up and relations with Germany cooled, Krivoshein became a favourite at the French embassy, where he was often seen with his new circle of French friends.[103]

Krivoshein's deepening enthusiasm for a firm foreign policy also reflected the aspiration (important for Izvolsky and Sazonov, too) to find issues that would forge bonds between society and government. Krivoshein and his ministry stood out among government and official circles for their close collaboration with the *zemstvos* (elected organs of local government) and a range of civil-society-based organizations. In July 1913, he opened an agricultural exhibition in Kiev with a short address that became famous as the 'we and they' speech. In it he declared that Russia would attain well-being only when there was no longer a harmful division between 'us', the government, and 'them', society. In short: Krivoshein represented a formidable compound of technocratic modernism, populism, agrarian sectoralism, parliamentary authority and increasingly hawkish views in external affairs. By 1913, he was undoubtedly the best-connected and most powerful civilian minister. No wonder Kokovtsov spoke despairingly of his own 'isolation' and 'complete helplessness' in the face of a ministerial party that was clearly determined to drive him from office.[104]

BULGARIA OR SERBIA?

There was one strategic choice that Sazonov and his colleagues would eventually be forced to confront. Should Russia support Bulgaria or Serbia? Of the two countries, Bulgaria was clearly the more strategically important. Its location on the Black Sea and Bosphorus coasts made it an important partner. The defeat of Ottoman forces in the Russo-Turkish War of 1877–8 had created the conditions for the emergence, under Russian custodianship, of a self-governing Bulgarian state under the nominal suzerainty of the Ottoman Porte. Bulgaria was thus historically a client state of St Petersburg. But Sofia never became the obedient satellite that the Russians had wished for. Russophile and 'western' political factions competed for control of foreign policy (as indeed they still do today) and the leadership exploited the country's strategically sensitive location by transferring their allegiances from one power to another.

After the accession to the throne of Ferdinand of Saxe-Coburg and Gotha-Koháry, who ruled Bulgaria, first as prince regnant (*knjaz*) and later as king (tsar) from 1885 until 1918, these oscillations became more frequent. Ferdinand manoeuvred between Russophile and Germanophile ministerial factions.[105] The Bulgarian monarch 'always made it a rule not to commit himself to any definite line of action', Sir George Buchanan later recalled. 'An opportunist inspired solely by regard for his own personal interests, he preferred to [. . .] coquet first with one and then with another of the powers . . .'.[106] The Bosnian annexation crisis of 1908–9 brought a cooling of relations with St Petersburg, because Ferdinand temporarily aligned himself with Vienna, exploiting the moment to throw aside the Treaty of Berlin (which had defined Bulgaria as an autonomous principality of the Ottoman Empire), declare Bulgarian unity and independence, and proclaim himself Tsar of the Bulgars at a lavish ceremony at Turnovo, the country's ancient capital. Izvolsky was appalled at this disloyalty and warned that the Bulgarians would soon pay a price for betraying their friends. It was a passing irritation: when negotiations between Sofia and Constantinople over recognition of the kingdom's independence broke down and the Ottomans began concentrating troops on the Bulgarian border, Sofia appealed to St Petersburg for help and all was forgiven. The Russians brokered an independence agreement with Constantinople and Bulgaria became for a time a loyal regional partner of the Entente.[107]

Yet even the most Bulgarophile policy-makers in St Petersburg recognized that relations with Sofia had to take Serbian interests into account, especially after the Bosnian annexation crisis, which had created a wave of pro-Serbian feeling in Russian public opinion. In December 1909, anxious to rebuild a forward position on the Balkan peninsula, the

Russian ministry of war drafted a secret convention that envisaged joint Russo-Bulgarian operations against the Habsburg Empire, Romania or Turkey and promised the entirety of Macedonia and the Dobrudja (a disputed zone along the border with Romania) to Bulgaria. But the convention was shelved on Izvolsky's instructions because it was deemed too injurious to Serbian interests. With Hartwig in Belgrade goading the Serbs against Austria-Hungary and agitating on their behalf in St Petersburg, the irreconcilability of the Serbian and Bulgarian options became increasingly obvious.

In March 1910, delegations from Sofia *and* Belgrade visited St Petersburg within two weeks of each other for high-level talks. The Bulgarians pressed their Russian interlocutors to abandon Serbia and commit clearly to Sofia – only on this basis would a stable coalition of Balkan states emerge. It was impossible, the Bulgarian premier Malinov told Izvolsky, for the Russians to create a Great Bulgaria and a Great Serbia at the same time:

> Once you decide to go with us for the sake of your own interests, we will easily settle the Macedonian question with the Serbs. As soon as this is understood in Belgrade – and you must make it clear in order to be understood – the Serbs will become much more conciliatory.[108]

No sooner had the Bulgarians left than King Petar, who was much more popular at the Tsar's court than the wily Ferdinand, arrived to press the Serbian case. He received crucial assurances: Russia no longer intended to grant Bulgaria the status of a privileged client. The long-standing Russian commitment to support the Bulgarian claim to Macedonia would remain officially in place, but behind the scenes Izvolsky promised that he would find ways of 'satisfying the interests and rights of Serbia'. Above all – this was news that electrified the foreign ministry in Belgrade – Russia now accepted that a part of Macedonia must fall to Serbia.[109]

One of the attractions of the Balkan League policy in Russian eyes was precisely that it enabled the inconsistency between the options to be bridged, at least for the moment. Once the Serbo-Bulgarian alliance of March 1912 found what appeared to be a mutually acceptable solution to the problem of Macedonia, it was possible to imagine that the League might prove a durable instrument of Russian policy on the peninsula. The provision for Russian arbitration in the disputed zone seemed to protect Russia's special role on the peninsula while creating a mechanism by which the Slavic patron could contain and channel the conflict between its clients.

The unexpectedly rapid advance of the Bulgarian armies on Constantinople caused panic in St Petersburg. Sazonov had urged Sofia to be 'wise' and prudent enough to 'stop at the right moment'; his alarm was deepened by the bizarre suspicion that the French were urging the Bulgarians to seize the Ottoman capital.[110] But the mood calmed after the collapse of the Bulgarian advance and in the aftermath of the war, St Petersburg focused on mediating a settlement between the two victor states under the terms set out in the treaty of March 1912. But Serbia refused to vacate the territories it had seized and Bulgaria refused to relinquish its claim to those areas. Mediation was virtually impossible: the Bulgarians claimed that any mediation must take place on the basis of the treaty of March 1912, whereas the Serbian government took the view that events on the ground had rendered the treaty null and void. The Balkan states were, as Tsar Nicholas put it, like 'well-behaved youngsters' who had 'grown up to become stubborn hooligans'.[111]

Sazonov gravitated at first towards Bulgaria and blamed Serbia, reasonably enough, for refusing to vacate the conquered areas. But by the end of March 1913, the Russian foreign minister had swung back to Belgrade and was urging Sofia to make concessions. When he learned that the Bulgarians were about to recall their ambassador in Belgrade, Andrey Toshev, Sazonov flew into a rage and accused the Bulgarians of acting under the instructions of Vienna; thanks to their 'impertinence towards Russia and Slavdom', the Bulgarians were throwing themselves 'into ruin'.[112] The Bulgarians agreed not to recall Ambassador Toshev and the quarrel was patched up, but there was a lasting Russian reorientation away from Sofia. It helped that the Bulgarians were the ones to commence hostilities on 29 June, since Sazonov had repeatedly warned that whoever started the next war was going to pay a heavy price. (Yet the Russians had a hand in this, too, since Hartwig had instructed Nikola Pašić under no circumstances to take the initiative, but to wait for a Bulgarian attack.)

At the same time, there was a shift in Russian policy vis-à-vis Romania. During the First Balkan War, Sazonov had interceded with Bucharest to ensure that there was no opportunist Romanian assault on Bulgarian territory – he was referring to the Dobrudja, the border region claimed by both states. In the early summer of 1913, by contrast, when the Serbo-Bulgarian agreement on Macedonia broke down, Sazonov let it be known in Bucharest that Russia would *not* take action if Romania intervened against the aggressor in a Serbo-Bulgarian war.[113] This was the firmest step against Bulgaria hitherto; it made the Russian position unprecedentedly clear.

St Petersburg's adoption of a more exclusively pro-Serbian position was reinforced by financial developments. In the aftermath of the Second Balkan War, the belligerent states were, as the Carnegie Foundation's inquiry into the cause and conduct of the Balkan wars put it, in the condition of 'beggars [who] are seeking to borrow money to pay their debts and build up again their military and productive forces'.[114] None was in a more parlous condition than Bulgaria, which had just fought a war against four opponents at devastating human and economic cost (Bulgaria suffered 93,000 casualties in the second war – more than its four opponents combined).[115] Under the new liberal premier Vasil Radoslavov, who entered office at the head of a coalition on 17 July 1913, the Bulgarian government put out requests for a massive credit. Vienna was the first to respond, with a small advance of 30 million francs, at the end of October, but this amount was not even enough to enable the Bulgarian government to continue servicing its debts. Despite assurances that Sofia would assign the Dardanelles in perpetuity to the Russian sphere of influence, St Petersburg was unwilling to help out. Sazonov took the view that Russia must withhold any financial assistance to Sofia for as long as the Radoslavov government, which he viewed as hostile to Russia, remained in power. Russia was in any case in no condition to issue credits on the scale required by Sofia, even if it had wished to do so. More important, therefore, was the pressure applied to France, which still had access to substantial reservoirs of finance capital, to follow the Russian line and withhold support from Sofia.[116]

Not that the French needed much persuading. They had been channelling politically motivated finance into Belgrade since the Austro-Serbian 'pig war'. International lending was an established and highly effective instrument of French diplomacy. André de Panafieu, the French minister in Sofia, captured the relationship between money and foreign policy when he observed in a dispatch of 20 January 1914 that as long as Sofia remained on friendly terms with Vienna, it would always be easy to think of reasons to turn down a Bulgarian loan.[117] Yet it was also clear to Sazonov that pushing the policy too far might prove counter-productive. When the new Russian minister, Alexander Savinsky, was sent to Sofia in January 1914, his mission was to prevent Bulgaria from drifting towards the Germanic powers.[118] From the Russian chargé d'affaires in Sofia came warnings that blocking the loan would simply mean that Bulgaria would wind up using German money to buy Austrian weapons.[119] Under the pressure of these arguments, forcefully conveyed to Paris by Izvolsky, the Quai d'Orsay began in February to consider a Bulgarian loan, but under onerous terms, including the requirement that the money must be used to purchase only French armaments and munitions.[120]

Predictably, perhaps, it was the Germans who came to the rescue. By mid-March, the German government had agreed to support a Bulgarian loan backed by German banks. This did not reflect some long-laid German plan to draw Bulgaria into the clutches of the Triple Alliance – during the summer the Germans also offered large loans under generous conditions to Serbia.[121] It just happened that whereas the Serbs already had a strong line of credit and had no intention of accepting any offer that might cast doubt on the strength of their commitment to the Entente, the Bulgarians were desperate. Once they learned of the negotiations going on between Berlin and Sofia, the Russian and French governments responded with last-ditch efforts to prevent the loan from going ahead. Savinsky placed inspired articles in the Bulgarian Russophile press and constantly urged Sazonov to step up the pressure on Sofia.[122] And then, at the last moment, the French bank Périer & Cie, specialists in loans to Latin America and the East, appeared on the scene with a counter-offer: 500 million francs at 5 per cent. The Périer offer, which had almost certainly been brokered by the Russians through Izvolsky in Paris, stipulated that the loan would be secured with a Russian guarantee – in the event of default, Russia undertook to take over the Bulgarian obligations. The aim was to combine a very large credit with an element of political dependency that would reinforce the influence of the Entente in the Balkans; the plan was to persuade the Bulgarians to accept the loan and then pressure them at a later date into changing their government.[123] But the Périer offer was finalized too late (16 June 1914), to turn the game around and it was the German loan that ultimately won out, after tortuous negotiations to secure improved terms.[124] Amid scenes of uproar, the German finance package was passed, if that is the right word, by the Bulgarian Sobranje (the national parliament) on 16 July. In reality the bill was neither read, nor discussed, nor formally voted. At the close of the meeting, the government simply announced that it had been passed by the House. The opposition reacted by accusing the government of selling the country and 'hurling books and inkstands at the heads of the ministers'. Prime Minister Radoslavov was seen calling for order and brandishing a revolver.[125] The loan had become a dangerous tool wielded by the alliance blocs. This weaponization of international credit was nothing new, but its deployment in this instance locked Bulgaria into the policy of the Triple Alliance, just as Serbia had been integrated into the political system of the Entente.

What was happening in the Balkans was nothing less than the reversal of the old pattern of allegiances. In the past Russia had backed Bulgaria, while Austria-Hungary looked to Belgrade and Bucharest. By 1914, this arrangement had been turned inside out. Romania, too, was part of this process. By the early summer of 1913, Sazonov was inviting the government in Bucharest to help itself to a piece of Bulgaria in the event of a Serbo-Bulgarian war. The time was ripe for such an overture, because the Romanians resented what they saw as Vienna's flirtations with Sofia; King Carol of Romania also resented Austrian opposition to the Treaty of Bucharest, which he saw as his personal diplomatic achievement.[126] The deepening rapprochement between St Petersburg and Bucharest was formalized on 14 June 1914 when the Tsar visited King Carol at Constanţa, on Romania's Black Sea coast. It was an occasion heavy with symbolic freight. The only foreign representative to receive a decoration from the hands of the Tsar was the French minister to Romania, Camille Blondel, who had, as it happened, only recently been awarded a high decoration by King Petar of Serbia. Present at the festivities was Ottokar Czernin, the Austro-Hungarian minister to Bucharest, who interpreted the day as the public consummation of Romania's 'realignment towards the Triple Entente'.[127]

The consequence was a further drastic diminution of Austria-Hungary's political influence on the peninsula. Romanian irredentism would now be deflected away from Bessarabia, where it conflicted with Russian interests, and oriented towards Transylvania, where it would threaten the integrity of the Habsburg monarchy. There were, of course, limits to Romania's willingness to be coopted to Russian objectives. When Sazonov asked the Romanian premier and foreign minister Ion Brătianu what attitude Romania would adopt 'in the event of an armed conflict between Russia and Austria-Hungary, *if Russia should find itself obliged by circumstances to commence hostilities*', the Romanian statesman, 'visibly shocked' by Sazonov's question, gave an 'evasive reply'. When pressed further, however, Brătianu conceded that Romania and St Petersburg had a common interest in preventing 'any weakening of Serbia'. That was enough for Sazonov. The Russo-Romanian rapprochement thus constituted, as a French ministerial report observed, 'a new means for Russia of applying pressure to Austria'.[128] But perhaps the most striking feature of this restructuring of Balkan geopolitics was how quickly it came about. This was not a phenomenon of the *longue durée*, which would have taken years to undo, but rather a short-term adjustment to rapid changes in the geopolitical environment. In November 1913, Sazonov had told the Belgian minister in St Petersburg that he believed the current Bulgarian reorientation towards Vienna was likely to be shortlived – it was the work of one particular parliamentary faction, supported by the mercurial King Ferdinand, 'for whom we have not one atom of respect'.[129] Given time, the new Balkan alignment might just as quickly have made way for further adjustments and new systems. What matters is that this particular pattern of alignments was still in place in the summer of 1914.

Serbia was now Russia's salient in the Balkans. There was nothing necessary or natural about this state of affairs. In 1909, Aehrenthal had railed against Russia's 'mad claim' to act as protectress of Serbia, even in situations where no Serbian question touching on the interests of the powers had arisen. He had a point. Russia's claim to act on behalf of its orthodox Balkan 'children' was nothing more than a populist justification for a policy designed to weaken Austria-Hungary, win popularity at home and secure hegemony on the Balkan hinterland to the Turkish Straits. The doctrine of pan-Slavism may have been popular with the Russian nationalist press, but it was no more legitimate as a platform for political action than Hitler's concept of *Lebensraum*. Nor was it in any sense a coherent foundation for policy, since the Bulgarians, too, were orthodox Slavs and the Romanians, though orthodox, were not Slavs. Russia's commitment to Serbia was driven by power-politics, not by the diffuse energies of pan-Slavism. It created a dangerous asymmetry in relations between the two Balkan great powers, for Austria-Hungary possessed no comparable salient on the periphery of the Russian Empire.

It is difficult to quantify, but impossible to deny, the galvanizing effect of the Russian commitment on the Serbian kingdom. In February 1914, Pašić returned from his visit to Russia 'completely intoxicated and touched to the depth of his soul' by the favour shown to him by the Russian Tsar:

> In every word of your tsar [Pašić told Hartwig], I felt the particular benevolence of His Imperial Majesty for Serbia; for us this was a valuable reward for our unalterable veneration for Russia, whose advice in all matters of foreign policy I have unswervingly followed. The good will of the tsar is in our eyes also a guarantee for a bright future for Serbia, which, without the powerful moral help of Russia would be in no position to overcome the difficulties which the neighbouring monarchy, always hostile to Serbia, creates for us at every turn.[130]

The dispatches from Spalajković in St Petersburg conveyed a similarly exultant confidence in the strength of Russian support. The Tsar 'declared his sympathies for Serbia', Spalajković reported after a meeting with the Russian sovereign on 21 January 1914, 'and assured me that this was true of all the Russian nation and especially of that part that has the influence to make decisions'.[131] The 'entire Russian press is pro-Serb', he announced on 27 March. Criticism of the Serbs in the Bulgarian press received extremely hostile attention in the Russian papers. 'Once it was the Bulgarians who had influence over the Russian press, now it's our turn,' he declared. Only one paper, *Rech*, was less friendly; in recent months it had published reports criticizing the behaviour of the Serbian government in the newly conquered areas of Macedonia.[132] But these negative reports appeared to have no effect on the official Russian view of the new provinces, which was reassuringly rosy. According to Spalajković, who had spoken with Sazonov's deputy, Neratov, the Russian foreign ministry was very impressed by how well the Serbs were performing in the annexed territories, speaking blithely of how they were building roads and restoring buildings 'so that in a very short time it was impossible to recognise them' – there was no mention of expulsions or massacres here.[133]

M. Descos, the French envoy in Belgrade, registered the new mood of confidence in the kingdom. Reporting on a speech by Pašić to the

Skupština, he noted that the key to the government's current 'policy of peace' was to secure for Serbia an opportunity to 'fortify her army and cultivate her alliance and seek to draw the best part possible from new events as they arise'. It was noteworthy that 'M. Pašić, who is usually so modest, seems to want to arrogate to himself a certain authority in Balkan affairs – perhaps he thinks the moment has come for Serbia to take a leadership role.' On the other hand, Descos added, the Serbian leader lives 'in such close contact with the Russian minister that it is difficult to distinguish the latter from those [Serbian] statesmen whose ideas dominate the issue'.[134] Assured of the deepening identity of Serbian and Russian interests, the leaders in Belgrade in turn became increasingly ready to accept the promptings of St Petersburg. At the end of 1912, for example, the Russian ambassador in Vienna complained to St Petersburg that the Serbian minister seemed excessively friendly in his dealings with the Austrians. The result was a note from the Russian foreign ministry to Pašić urging that the Serbs avoid 'all too open discussions' with the Austrians, lest these give rise to 'the rumour of a special [Serbian] agreement with Vienna'. Pašić responded by sending his representative a telegram consistingly solely of the words 'Be careful' and composed in the presence of Hartwig.[135] 'They will of course follow our instructions,' Hartwig assured Sazonov in his New Year's letter of January 1914.[136]

AUSTRIA'S TROUBLES

'The actual beginning of the great Balkan war,' the *Times* correspondent Wickham Steed reported from Vienna on 17 October 1912, 'is felt here to be a moment of historical solemnity. Whatever its course, it must radically change the situation'.[137] For no other great power did the conflict unfolding in the Balkans pose problems of such urgency and magnitude. The unexpectedly swift victories of the League states confronted Austria-Hungary with a skein of interwoven issues. First, there was the fact that Austria's Balkan policy was irreparably ruined. Vienna's axiom, that one must always maintain Turkey as the key ordering force in the region, was now irrelevant. Rapid improvisation was called for. The 'status quo conservatism' of the summer of 1912 had to be abandoned; in its place a new programme emerged focused on managing the changes underway in the Balkans so as to minimize the damage to Austro-Hungarian interests. Serbian territorial conquests were acceptable, but they must be accompanied by assurances of Serbia's good behaviour in future, preferably through some form of institutionalized economic cooperation (Vienna was prepared to settle this on a much more generous basis than under the old customs union and a mission was dispatched to Belgrade to propose terms).[138] On the other hand, Serbia must not under any circumstances be permitted to push its frontiers to the Adriatic coast. The reasoning behind this was that a Serbian port might in time come under the control of a foreign power (namely Russia). This apprehension sounds far-fetched, but it gained plausibility from Hartwig's reputation as the vehemently Austrophobe uncrowned 'king of Belgrade'.

Vienna also insisted – in keeping with its established policy – that Albania must be founded and maintained as an independent state. Publicized under the slogan 'the Balkans for the Balkan peoples', this policy offered back-up for the interdiction of a Serbian land-grab on the Adriatic, since any port that Belgrade acquired would of necessity lie in the midst of Albanian-inhabited country.[139] The announcement of this policy prompted cries of protest from pro-Belgrade elements within the monarchy – at a meeting of the Bosnian Diet at Sarajevo in November 1912, Serb deputies adopted a resolution to the effect that 'the sacrifices and victories' of the Serbian armies 'justified the "restoration" of Albania to Serbia' and expressed bitterness at the fact that the Austro-Hungarian monarchy continued to contest the 'autonomous rights' of its South Slavs while advocating the cause of the 'uncultured Albanians'.[140] To the European powers, however, the Berchtold programme looked like a moderate response to the dramatic changes unfolding in the Balkans. Even Sazonov eventually fell in behind the consensus in favour of Albanian independence.

The wild card in the pack was Serbia. By the end of October 1912, the Serbian armies were already pushing towards the coast, cutting down savagely all resistance from the Albanians in their path. A series of minor provocations further soured relations: the Serbs intercepted Austrian consular mail and disrupted other consular communications, and there were reports that consuls had been arrested or abducted. Was the Austro-Hungarian consul in Mitrovitza, for example, placed under four-day house arrest by the Serbian army for his own protection, as the

Serbian authorities claimed, or 'so that he would not witness the "removal" of the local Albanian population', as the consul himself maintained? In the midst of all the panic, the Austro-Hungarian foreign ministry made another attempt to spin the news in its favour. When it proved impossible to make contact with Oskar Prochaska, the Austro-Hungarian consul in Prizren, rumours circulated in Vienna that he had been abducted and castrated by his Serbian captors. The ministry investigated and discovered that while he had indeed been illegally detained (on trumped-up charges of encouraging Turkish resistance), the rumour of castration was false. Instead of quashing the rumour, the ministry allowed it to persist for a week or two in order to extract the maximum in propaganda capital from the alleged outrage. Prochaska turned up a few weeks later with his sexual parts still attached. The trick backfired, and there was much adverse comment. The Prochaska affair was a modest but inept exercise in media manipulation that provided further ammunition for those who claimed that Austria always argued with forged documents and false accusations.[141]

For a time it seemed that the Albanian Question might ignite a broader European conflict. By the middle of November 1912, Montenegrin and Serbian forces occupied a swathe of northern Albania, including Alessio (Lezhë), and the harbour cities San Giovanni di Medua (Medva) and Durazzo (Durrës). A largely Montenegrin force lay in siege around the city of Scutari (Shkodër), home to 30,000 Albanians. The invasion threatened to create *faits accomplis* that would undermine Vienna's policy. Berchtold continued to insist on the creation of an independent Albania and the removal of the occupying forces. But the Montenegrins and Serbians refused to relinquish their Albanian footholds. Vienna was determined, if it became absolutely necessary, to dislodge the invaders by force. But the Russian trial mobilization and raised Russian troop strengths in the border areas adjoining Austria-Hungary suggested that St Petersburg might also be willing to support its clients by military means. On 22 November, King Nikola of Montenegro informed the Austrian minister in Cetinje that 'if the Monarchy tries to drive me out with force, I will fight to the last goat and the last cartridge'.[142]

The Albanian Question continued to unsettle European politics throughout the winter and spring of 1912–13. On 17 December 1912, the issue was raised at the first meeting of the conference of great power ambassadors convened in London under the chairmanship of Edward Grey to resolve the issues arising from the Balkan War. The ambassadors agreed that a neutral, autonomous Albanian state should be established under the joint guarantee of the powers. Sazonov – after some wobbling – accepted the case for Albanian autonomy. But drawing the frontiers of the new state proved a contentious business. The Russians demanded that the towns of Prizren, Peć, Dibra, Djakovica and Scutari be assigned to their Serbo-Montenegrin clients, while Austria wished to see them incorporated in the new Albania. Vienna eventually mollified St Petersburg by approving the concession to Serbia of most of the contested areas along the Albanian border – a policy initially driven not by Berchtold, but by his ambassador in London, Count Mensdorff, who, together with his Russian colleague, Count Benckendorff, did much to reconcile opposing standpoints during the conference.[143] By March 1913, the issue of the Albanian–Serbian border was – in theory, at least – largely resolved.

Yet the situation remained tense, because over 100,000 Serbian troops remained in Albania. Only on 11 April did the Belgrade government announce that it would withdraw its troops from the country. International attention now focused on the Montenegrins, who were still besieging Scutari and refused to move. King Nikola declared that he might be willing to climb down if the great powers mounted a direct attack on Montenegrin territory and thereby provided him with the pretext for an 'honourable withdrawal' – whether he was in earnest or simply thumbing his nose at the international community was impossible to say.[144] On the night of 22–23 April, Essad Pasha Toptani, the Albanian-born commandant of Scutari, capitulated and withdrew his garrison from the city. Montenegrin flags were hoisted over the town and its fortress and there was exultation across Montenegro and Serbia. According to the Dutch minister in Belgrade, the news of the fall of Scutari met with 'indescribable jubilation' in the Serbian capital; the city was hung with flags, all businesses were closed and a crowd of 20,000 revellers raised ovations outside the Russian embassy.[145]

When further joint notes from London demanding Montenegro's withdrawal were ignored, it was agreed that the next meeting of the Ambassadors' Conference (scheduled for 5 May) would resolve a joint response by the powers. The Austrians began in the meantime to prepare for a unilateral action against the Montenegrin invaders, should diplomacy fail. How the Russians would respond to Austrian military action was unclear. By late January 1913, the Russian court and foreign office were wearying of the impetuous Montenegrin king. Nikola may have believed that he was acting in the Slavic interest and thus merited Russia's wholehearted support – in reality, the foreign ministry in St Petersburg viewed him as a loose cannon, whose chief objective was to burnish his domestic reputation.[146] In April 1913, the foreign ministry in St Petersburg took the highly unusual step of issuing a declaration publicly disavowing Nikola and his designs on Scutari. In it, Sazonov (who was not named but acknowledged authorship) rebuked the press for its ignorant handling of the issues and stated that Nikola had no right to Scutari, which was a 'purely Albanian' town.[147] Russia was thus prepared to accept a joint initiative by the powers. But as the Scutari crisis came to a head, Sazonov also warned that Russian popular opinion might force him to intervene militarily if the Austrians acted on their own. 'The political outlook,' Buchanan reported from St Petersburg, 'is blacker than at any other period of the crisis.'[148]

After months of international nailbiting, the problem suddenly went away. On 4 May, the day before the ambassadors were to meet in London, King Nikola announced that he was placing 'the destiny of the city of Scutari in the hands of the powers'. The city was subsequently assigned to the Albanian state. A peace treaty signed in London on 30 May 1913 brought the First Balkan War formally to a close. On 29 July, at the fifty-fourth session of the conference, the ambassadors confirmed that Albania would become an independent sovereign state, notwithstanding the fact that nearly half of all Albanian-settled areas (notably Kosovo) lay outside the boundaries agreed in London.[149]

The ink was scarcely dry on the Peace of London when war broke out again in the Balkans, this time over the distribution of the spoils from the first conflict. The Treaty of Bucharest of 10 August 1913 assigned to Serbia new areas in south-eastern Macedonia, thereby confirming an increase in the kingdom's territorial extent – compared with the pre-1912 status quo – by close to 100 per cent and an enlargement of its population by just over 64 per cent. Confusion broke out in Vienna about how to respond to the new situation. Berchtold was still attempting to regain political control amid a cacophony of competing policy proposals when reports reached Vienna during the summer of 1913 of renewed unrest on the Albanian–Serbian frontier. Despite repeated rebukes and warnings, Belgrade still refused to evacuate its troops from certain areas on the Albanian side of the border agreed at the London conference. Their ostensible purpose was to protect Serbia from Albanian banditry; the reality was that the misbehaviour of the Serbian troops was itself the main reason for the trouble along the border. In July, Vienna requested a withdrawal, but to no avail. Then a concert of great powers, coordinated by Edward Grey, presented a collective demand for evacuation, but that, too, failed to have an effect. France and Russia blocked a further collective protest in early September; when individual protests were presented to Belgrade by Austria, Germany and Britain, the response was an announcement from the acting foreign minister, Miroslav Spalajković, denying that there were any Serbian troops in the contested area, followed somewhat inconsistently by a statement some days later that the troops in question had now been withdrawn behind the Drin river line. But this still left Serbian troops well inside the London boundary. Reports on 17 September that Belgrade was about to establish customs offices in several of the invaded areas caused further consternation in Vienna.[150]

This arduous sequence of cat-and-mouse encounters between Vienna and Belgrade helps explain why Austrian decision-makers gradually lost confidence in the efficacy of the standard diplomatic procedures in handling interest conflicts with Serbia. When Albanians near the frontier responded to Serbian provocations (the denial, for example, in contravention of the London agreement, of access to major Albanian market towns across the Serbian border) with a resumption of guerrilla activity, Serbian units pushed back even further into Albanian territory. The Serbian minister in Vienna, Jovanović, provoked alarm when he stated in an interview with a Viennese newspaper on 26 September that in view of the difficulty of finding any constituted Albanian body which could be made responsible for border disturbances, Serbia might be 'forced to take measures on her own account'. Pašić compounded the problem on 30 September by announcing that Serbia intended, 'for its own protection' to occupy 'strategic points' inside Albanian territory.[151] An Austrian note to the Pašić government on 1 October requesting clarification elicited an evasive reply.

Pašić's brief visit to Vienna on 3 October did nothing to improve the situation. Berchtold, disarmed by the Serbian leader's warm and affable manner, missed the opportunity to convey to him the seriousness of the situation in Austrian eyes. Pašić assured representatives of the press in Vienna that 'he took a favourable view of future relations between Serbia and the Dual Monarchy' but he also spoke unsettlingly of the need for 'boundary changes' on the Albanian frontier.[152] Announcements from Belgrade that Serbia had no intention of 'defying Europe' to seize Albanian territory, were reassuring, as were friendly noises from a senior foreign official in Belgrade who received the Austrian chargé d'affaires Ritter von Storck, 'as warmly as if Pašić had just signed a defensive alliance in Vienna'.[153] Yet attempts to enquire as to the precise state of policy on Albania met with courteous evasions. And at the same time, the advance of Serbian troops into Albania continued. On 9 October, when the Austrian chargé d'affaires insisted on seeing Pašić to discuss the matter, he found the premier once again in a most jovial mood, but still talking of a 'provisional' Serbian occupation of Albanian territory.[154] This was followed on 15 October by announcements in the semi-official newspaper *Samouprava* to the effect that Serbia did after all intend to occupy 'strategic points' in Albania.[155] After a further Austrian warning met with a defiant response, an ultimatum was presented to Belgrade on 17 October. Serbia was given eight days to vacate Albanian territory. If it failed to do so, Austria-Hungary would deploy 'proper means to ensure the realization of its demands'.[156]

The ultimatum was a success. In the autumn of 1913 the great powers were in agreement that Serbia's demands for a chunk of Albania were illegitimate. Even Foreign Minister Sazonov in St Petersburg cleared his throat, conceded that 'Serbia had been more to blame than was generally supposed in the events which led up to the recent ultimatum' and urged Belgrade to yield.[157] Two days after receiving the ultimatum, Pašić announced that Serbian troops would be withdrawn. By 26 October they had vacated the disputed areas.

The October 1913 stand-off with Serbia established several precedents for Austrian handling of the crisis that blew up between the two states after Sarajevo. The first and most obvious was that it seemed to demonstrate the efficacy of an ultimatum. The Austrian note of 17 October received wide support in the press and the news that the Serbs had at last withdrawn their troops from Albania was greeted with euphoria in Vienna. Berchtold had been reviled for his supposed timidity during the Scutari crisis – now he was the man of the hour. The Serbian management of communications with Vienna also left a troubling impression: a sly civility verging on geniality masked a policy of carefully dosed provocations and non-compliance. There was a clash here not just of interests, but also of policy styles. Belgrade, it seemed, would retreat only as far as Vienna pushed, accepting with equanimity any humiliations that might result; when the Austrians relaxed, the probing and provocations would resume. The axiom that Serbia would only ever ultimately understand force acquired more weight.

For Austria-Hungary, the Balkan Wars changed everything. Above all, they revealed how isolated Vienna was and how little understanding there was at the foreign chancelleries for its view of Balkan events. St Petersburg's hostility to the empire and its utter disregard for Vienna's interests in the region could be taken for granted. More worrying was the indifference of the other powers. The reluctance of the international community to see that Austria faced genuine security threats on its southern periphery and had the right to counteract them reflected a broader shift in attitudes. The western powers had traditionally viewed Austria as the fulcrum of stability in central and eastern Europe and thus as a power that must be preserved at all costs. But by 1913, this maxim no longer appeared so compelling. It was undermined by the tendency – which swiftly gained ground among the Entente states after 1907 – to think of Europe in terms of alliance blocs, rather than as a continental geopolitical ecosystem in which every power had a role to play. The anti-Austrian animus of much political reportage in Britain and France during the last pre-war years reinforced this tendency by spreading the view that Austria-Hungary was an anachronistic and doomed entity, or, as the Serbian papers put it, the 'second sick man of Europe' (after the Ottoman Empire, to which this epithet was more commonly applied).[158]

Particularly alarming was the lukewarm nature of German support. Berlin firmly endorsed a policy of confrontation with Serbia in October 1913 – at a time when support could be offered at little risk of a broader conflict – but its record was otherwise patchy. In February 1913, when troop strengths on both sides of the Galician border were so elevated that war seemed imminent, even the military urged caution. Moltke wrote to his colleague Conrad von Hötzendorf, assuring him that while Germany would not hesitate to support Austria-Hungary against a Russian attack, 'it would be difficult to legitimate German intervention in a war provoked by Austria, for which there would be no understanding in the German people'.[159]

One of Vienna's chief concerns was the attitude of the German Kaiser, Wilhelm II. Far from urging his government to solidarity with the Austrians, Wilhelm forbade the Foreign Office in Berlin to participate in any action that 'might impede the Bulgars-Serbs-Greeks in their victorious progress'.[160] The Balkan Wars, he argued, were part of a world-historical development that was going to drive Islam back out of Europe. If one allowed the Balkan states to consolidate themselves at the expense of Turkey, this would create the basis for a stable array of entities that in due course might form a confederation of some kind, the 'United States of the Balkans'. Nothing could be better suited to the preservation of the peace, the buffering of Austro-Russian tensions and the emergence of a new regional market for German exports.[161] And Wilhelm continued to expatiate in this vein. During the crisis of November 1912 over Serbian access to the Adriatic, Wilhelm explicitly rejected the notion that the German government had any obligation to support Vienna against Belgrade. To be sure, the current changes on the peninsula were 'uncomfortable' for Vienna, but he would 'under no circumstances consider marching against Paris and Moscow for the sake of Albania and Durazzo'. On 9 November, he even proposed to the Foreign Office that it should urge Vienna to place Albania under the suzerainty of a Serbian prince.[162]

There was little comfort in these quixotic speculations for the harassed decision-makers in Vienna. At a secret conference with his friend Archduke Franz Ferdinand on 22 November 1912, Wilhelm did express his readiness to support Austria's position on the Serbian troop presence in Albania, even at the risk of war with Russia, but only if it were certain that neither Britain nor France would intervene; an isolated Russia, he added, would be extremely unlikely to risk such a conflict.[163] Yet even these mildly encouraging signals were cancelled out three days later by official messages from Bethmann Hollweg and Kiderlen-Wächter to the effect that Germany would seek a multilateral solution.[164] In February 1913, when the Balkan winter crisis was at its height, Wilhelm wrote a letter to Franz Ferdinand urging that he seek a negotiated de-escalation with Russia on the grounds that the matters at issue were not important enough to justify a continuation of the current armed stand-off.[165] On 18 October, when the Albanian crisis was seething,

Wilhelm conceded in a conversation with Conrad that the situation might 'finally' have arrived 'in which a great power can no longer look on but must reach for the sword'. Yet only ten days later, he was telling the Austrian ambassador in Berlin that Vienna should mollify Belgrade by bribing the leadership with large cash gifts ('from the king downwards they can all be had for money'), military exchange programmes and improved terms of trade.[166] In December 1913, Wilhelm assured the Austrian envoy in Munich that 'a few millions' would suffice to buy Berchtold a firm foothold in Belgrade.[167]

In a report dispatched on 25 April 1914, Fritz Count Szapáry, a foreign ministry high-flyer and specialist in Austro-German relations now serving as minister in St Petersburg, painted a bleak picture of recent German Balkan policy. The solid German backing that had helped to bring the Bosnian annexation crisis to a close in March 1909 was a thing of the past, Szapáry declared. What had replaced it was – Szapáry quoted the mealy-mouthed jargon of the decision-makers in Berlin – a 'conflict-free dialogue directed towards the consolidation of economic-cultural activity zones'. All of Berlin's forward positions vis-à-vis Russia had been abandoned, and Berlin took no steps whatsoever without first consulting St Petersburg. During the Balkan Wars, Germany had compromised the Austrian position by joining the chorus of support for *déinteressement*, pressing Vienna to accept Serbian conquests and provocations. It all amounted to the wholesale 'sacrifice of Austria-Hungary's Balkan interests'. This was a rather histrionic view of the matter, coloured by Szapáry's Hungarian apprehensions at Russia's deepening support for Romania, but it captured a widely felt mood of frustration at the failure of Berlin to deliver any real leverage on the Balkan peninsula. Especially galling was the haste with which Berlin had endorsed the Treaty of Bucharest, thereby depriving Austria of the opportunity to better the position of Bulgaria, which the Austrians, but not the Germans, viewed as a potential counterweight to Serbian power.[168]

This sense of isolation, coupled with the repeated provocations of 1912–13, in turn heightened the readiness in Vienna to resort to unilateral measures. There were signs that the resistance to militant solutions among the key decision-makers in Vienna was waning. The most conspicuous sign of the change in mood was the decision to recall Conrad at the height of the Russian mobilization scare. 'You must again become

Chief of the General Staff,' the Emperor wearily informed the general at an audience on 7 December 1912.[169] After his reinstatement Conrad continued, of course, to counsel war, but that was nothing new. More worrying was the diminishing resistance to extreme measures among the other key actors. During the autumn of 1912, nearly everyone (including the Hungarian prime minister Tisza) at one point or another favoured a policy of confrontation backed up by the threat of military action. A notable exception was Franz Ferdinand, who warned Berchtold in a forceful letter of 12 October against allowing the monarchy to be dragged into Conrad's 'witches' kitchen of war'. There was also Russia to think of, and Bulgaria, and the Germans, who would presumably shrink from any high-risk démarche. As for Belgrade, Franz Ferdinand added, the only people there who sought a conflict were the regicide war party (the party that, unbeknown to him, would slay him eight months later). He did not, he concluded, believe there 'existed any necessity' for war. The pressure to wage it came exclusively from those servants of the Austro-Hungarian crown who 'consciously or unconsciously worked to damage the monarchy'.[170] And yet, on 11 December 1912, during a meeting of senior officials with the Emperor at Schönbrunn palace, even Franz Ferdinand broke with his accustomed support for peace at any price to advocate a military confrontation with Serbia.

This was a momentary lapse, to be sure: as soon as he heard the contrary arguments of Berchtold and the civilian ministers, the heir apparent immediately backed away from his earlier view and expressed his support for Berchtold's diplomatic solution. Four months later, it was Berchtold's turn to break ranks. At a meeting of the Joint Ministerial Council on 2 May 1913, exasperated by the renewed Montenegrin attack on Scutari, Berchtold for the first time accepted the case for mobilization against Montenegro. This was not, of course, tantamount to calling for a European or even a local war, since Montenegro was by this time totally isolated – even the Serbs had withdrawn their support.[171] Berchtold hoped that a mobilization alone would suffice to dislodge the invaders from Albania and believed it highly unlikely that Russia would intervene. As it happened, even mobilization proved unnecessary; Nikola climbed down before the ultimatum was presented.[172] Nevertheless, the resolute tone of that meeting heralded a more belligerent attitude in Vienna. In September–October 1913, after the second Serbian invasion of northern Albania, with Conrad begging as usual for war, Berchtold again agreed in general terms with a policy of confrontation, as did, unusually, Franz Joseph. At this point, Franz Ferdinand and Tisza (for widely differing reasons) remained the only doves among the senior decision-makers. And the success of the ultimatum in securing the withdrawal of Serbian troops from Albania was itself seen as vindicating a more militant style of diplomacy.[173]

This militancy of attitude coincided with a growing awareness of the extent to which economic constraints were starting to limit Austria-Hungary's strategic options. The partial mobilizations of the Balkan War crises had imposed immense financial strains on the monarchy. The extra costs for 1912–13 came to 390 million crowns, as much as the entire yearly budget for the Austro-Hungarian army, a serious matter at a time when the monarchy's economy was entering a recession.[174] In this connection we should recall that Austria-Hungary spent very little on its army: of the great powers, only Italy spent less. It called up a smaller percentage of its population each year (0.27 per cent) than France (0.63 per cent) or Germany (0.46 per cent). The years 1906–12 had been boom years for the empire's economy, but very little of this wealth had been siphoned into the military budgets. The Empire fielded fewer infantry battalions in 1912 than it had in 1866, when its armies had faced the Prussians and the Italians at Königgrätz and Custoza, despite a twofold increase in population over the same period. Dualism was one reason for this – the Hungarians consistently blocked military growth;[175] the pressure to placate the nationalities with expensive infrastructural projects was another block on military investment. To make matters worse, mobilizations in summer and/or early autumn gravely disrupted the agrarian economy, because they removed a large portion of the rural workforce from harvest work.[176] In 1912–13, the critics of the government could argue, peacetime mobilizations had incurred huge costs and disrupted the economy without doing much to enhance the empire's security. Tactical mobilizations, it seemed, were an instrument that the monarchy could no longer afford to deploy. But if that was the case, then the government's flexibility in handling crises on the Balkan periphery must be gravely diminished. Without the intermediate option of purely tactical mobilizations, the decision-making process would inevitably become less nuanced. It would be a matter of peace or war.

THE BALKANIZATION OF THE FRANCO-RUSSIAN ALLIANCE

In the summer of 1912, it was not at all clear that France would support Russia in a purely Balkan conflict. The terms of the Franco-Russian military convention of 1893–4 were ambiguous on this point. Article 2 stipulated that in the event of a general mobilization by *any one* of the powers of the Triple Alliance, France and Russia would simultaneously and immediately mobilize the totality of their forces and deploy as quickly as possible to their frontiers, without the need for any prior agreement.[177] This seemed to imply that a Balkan crisis severe enough to trigger an Austrian mobilization might under certain circumstances automatically bring about a joint Franco-Russian counter-mobilization, which was in turn certain to trigger a German counter-mobilization, since Articles 1 and 2 of the Austro-German Dual Alliance of 1879 required that the signatories assist each other in the event of either of them being attacked by Russia or a power supported by Russia. Here was a mechanism that looked, on the face of it, capable of escalating a Balkan crisis into a continental war, all the more so as it made no distinction between a partial and a full Austrian mobilization.

Confusingly, Article 1 of the Franco-Russian military convention envisaged an obligation to intervene only in the following circumstances: (a) an attack by Germany on France *or* (b) an attack on Russia either by Germany or by Austria-Hungary supported by Germany. This article set the bar for a French military intervention much higher than Article 2. The dissonance in the text reflected the asymmetrical needs that had given rise to the treaty in the first place. For France, the alliance and the military convention attached to it were a means of countering and containing Germany. For Russia, the central concern was Austria-Hungary – try as they might, the French negotiators were unable to persuade their Russian counterparts to renounce the link asserted in Article 2 between an Austro-Hungarian and a French general mobilization. And this, in turn, effectively placed a trigger in the hands of the Russians, who – on paper at least – were free at any time to instigate a continental war in support of their Balkan objectives.[178]

But alliances, like constitutions, are at best only an approximate guide to political realities. The policy-makers in Paris recognized the risks implicit in Article 2 and were quick to assert a restrictive interpretation of French obligations. In 1897, for example, during the Thirty Days' War between Greece and the Ottoman Empire, Foreign Minister Gabriel Hanotaux informed St Petersburg that France would not regard an Austro-Hungarian intervention as a *casus foederis* (case stipulated by treaty).[179] And we have seen how reluctant France was to be drawn into the Bosnian annexation crisis of 1908–9, a crisis in which it refused to recognize an authentic threat to either French or Russian 'vital interests'.[180] In 1911, at the urging of the French, the terms of the military convention were altered. The obligation to render immediate mutual assistance remained in place for the case of a *German* general mobilization; in the case of an Austrian total or partial mobilization, however, it was decided that Russia and France would agree an appropriate course of action.[181]

In 1912, this trend was suddenly thrown into reverse, in what would prove one of the most important policy adjustments of the pre-war. Having sought for some years to insulate France from the consequences of Balkan shocks, the government in Paris now extended the French commitment to include the possibility of an armed intervention in a purely Balkan crisis. The principal agent behind the change of course was Raymond Poincaré, prime minister and minister of foreign affairs from 14 January 1912 until 21 January 1913, and thereafter president of the Republic. On the day following his appointment, Poincaré publicly declared that he would 'maintain the most upright relations with Russia' and 'conduct the foreign policy of France in the fullest agreement with her ally'.[182] It was highly unusual for incoming French foreign ministers to make programmatic statements of this kind. In a series of conversations with Alexander Izvolsky in Paris, Poincaré reassured the Russians that they could count on French support in the event of a war arising from an Austro-Serbian quarrel.[183] The French government, he informed Izvolsky in November 1912, had no reason to fear a 'lack of support on [France's] part'.[184]

Tracing the evolution of this train of thought is not easy. Poincaré's visceral preoccupation with the threat posed by Germany was one driving factor. He had been ten years old when the Germans overran his native Lorraine in 1870, forcing his family to flee. His home town, Bar-le-Duc, was occupied by the Germans for three years, pending the payment of the French indemnity. This did not mean that Poincaré was a *revanchiste* in the mould of Boulanger, but he remained deeply suspicious of the Germans; their efforts to achieve détente with Russia and France were dismissed as snares and delusions. Salvation, Poincaré believed, lay solely in the fortification of the Franco-Russian Alliance, the keystone of French security.[185] He also wanted to prevent a relapse into the chaos of the Agadir crisis, when parallel policy threads had created confusion. Personality played a role here: he loved clarity and he pursued his objectives with remarkable consistency. Critics saw in this determined pursuit of clearly defined objectives evidence of a regrettable lack of flexibility. Poincaré's 'stiffness' (*raideur*), Paul Cambon argued, reflected his 'inexperience of diplomacy and the intellectual structure of the man of law'.[186] His brother Jules spoke of a 'mind in which everything is numbered, classed and recorded, as in a file'.[187]

But Poincaré was not alone in wishing to endow French security policy with a more aggressive orientation. His rise to high office took place against the background of a shift in the tone of French politics after Agadir that historians have called the 'Nationalist Revival'. Republican politicians had tended after the Dreyfus affair to adopt a *défenciste* approach to French security policy marked by an emphasis on border fortifications, heavy artillery and brief training stints for an army conceptualized as the 'nation-in-arms'. By contrast, the years after Agadir saw France return to a policy that took account of the professional interests of the army, accepted the need for longer training periods and a more concentrated amd efficient command structure and envisaged an unequivocally offensive approach to the next war.[188] At the same time, the pacifist and anti-militarist popular mood that had prevailed in 1905 made way for a more belligerent attitude. Not all of France was inundated by the nationalist wave – it was predominantly young, intelligent Parisians who embraced the new bellicism – but the restoration of military strength became one of the regenerating creeds of Republican politics.[189]

It was probably the Italian attack on Libya and the incipient collapse of Ottoman power in Europe that prompted Poincaré to incorporate the Balkans into his strategic thinking. As early as March 1912, he had told Izvolsky that the long-standing distinction between local Balkan crises on the one hand and issues of broader geopolitical significance, 'no longer had any practical importance'. Given the current system of European alliances, it was difficult to imagine 'an event in the Balkans that would not affect the general equilibrium of Europe'. 'Any armed collision between Russia and Austria-Hungary on account of Balkan affairs would constitute a *casus foederis* for the Austro-German alliance; and this in turn would entail the activation of the Franco-Russian Alliance.'[190]

Was Poincaré aware of the risks entailed in supporting Russian policy in the Balkans? A conversation between the French premier and the foreign minister Sazonov during a visit to St Petersburg in August 1912 is illuminating on this point. Poincaré knew that the Serbs and the Bulgarians had signed a treaty, because Izvolsky had informed him of it in April, but he had no idea of what the treaty contained.[191] When the French foreign ministry had asked St Petersburg for clarification, there had been no reply (Sazonov later claimed that he had delayed sending the text to Poincaré for fear that parts of it might be leaked to the French press).[192] During an interview with the foreign minister in St Petersburg in August, Poincaré asked the question again. Sazonov produced the text in Russian and translated it for the French prime minister. The details came as something of a shock, especially the stipulations regarding simultaneous mobilizations against Turkey and, if necessary, Austria, not to mention the reference to the partition of lands still lying deep inside Ottoman Macedonia and – perhaps most disturbingly – the role assigned to Russia as the arbiter in all future disputes, a role, Poincaré observed, that 'appears in every line of the convention'. The notes he jotted down after the meeting convey something of his discomfiture:

> It seems that the treaty contains the seeds not only of a war against Turkey but of a war against Austria. Moreover, it establishes the hegemony of Russia over the Slav kingdoms, since Russia is identified as the arbiter in all questions. I remark to M. Sazonov that this convention does not correspond in the least to the information that I had been given about it, that, if the truth be told, it is a convention of war, and that it not only reveals the ulterior motives of the Serbs and the Bulgarians, but also gives reason to fear that their hopes are being encouraged by Russia . . . [193]

Poincaré was not alone in taking fright at the scale of Russian involvement in Balkan politics. Jean Doulcet, a counsellor at the French embassy in St Petersburg, also noted at around the same time that the Balkan agreements were in effect 'treaties of partition'; Russian support for them suggested that 'the Russians are prepared to take no account whatsoever of Austria and to proceed toward the liquidation of Turkey without concerning themselves with her [i.e. Austria's] interests'.[194]

At this point, one might have expected Poincaré to begin entertaining doubts about the wisdom of supporting St Petersburg in the Balkans. But his discovery of how deeply the Russians had already ensconced themselves in the turbulent affairs of the peninsula seems to have had the opposite effect. Perhaps it was simply a matter of recognizing that in view of the general complexion of Russian policy, a future Balkan conflict was not just likely, but virtually certain, and therefore needed to be incorporated into the horizons of the alliance. A further factor was Poincaré's belief, shared by parts of the French military, that a war of Balkan origin was the scenario most likely to trigger full Russian participation in a joint campaign against Germany. An Austro-Serbian war would – so Poincaré's military advisers told him – tie down between one half and two-thirds of Austrian forces, releasing large contingents of Russian troops for service against Germany, thereby forcing Germany to deploy more of its troops to the east and taking some of the pressure off the French army in the west.[195]

Whatever the reasons for his change of course, by the autumn of 1912 Poincaré was firmly supporting a Russian armed intervention in the Balkans. In a conversation with Izvolsky in the second week of September, when the First Balkan War was in sight but had not yet begun, the French prime minister told the Russian ambassador that the destruction of Bulgaria by Turkey, or an attack by Austria-Hungary on Serbia might 'force Russia to give up its passive role'. Should it be necessary for Russia to mount a military intervention against Austria-Hungary, and should this trigger an intervention by Germany (which was inevitable, given the terms of the Dual Alliance), 'the French government would recognise this in advance as a *casus foederis* and would not hesitate for one moment to fulfil the obligations which it has incurred in respect of Russia'.[196] Six weeks later, with the war well underway, Izvolsky reported to Sazonov that Poincaré was 'not afraid' of the idea that it might prove necessary to 'initiate a war under certain circumstances' and that he was certain the states of the Triple Entente would prevail. This confidence, Izvolsky added, was based on a detailed analysis by the French General Staff that had recently come to the prime minister's desk.[197]

Indeed, Poincaré anticipated his obligations so energetically that there were moments when he appeared in danger of jumping the Russian gun. On 4 November 1912, one month into the First Balkan War, he wrote to Sazonov proposing that Russia join with France and England in pre-emptively opposing an Austrian intervention in the conflict.[198] So unexpected was this overture that Izvolsky wrote to Sazonov explaining it. Until recently, the ambassador pointed out, the French government had not wished to be drawn into what it saw as purely Balkan concerns. But recently there had been a change of view. Paris now recognized that 'any territorial conquest by Austria-Hungary would constitute a breach of the European equilibrium and *would affect France's vital interests*' (here was an unmistakable inversion of the language the French had used in justifying their lack of interest in the Bosnian annexation crisis). Poincaré's proactive approach to Balkan affairs, Izvolsky concluded, signified a 'new outlook' at the French ministry of foreign affairs. He advised the foreign ministry in St Petersburg to take advantage of it immediately and secure the backing of both France and England for the future.[199]

By mid-November, Sazonov did indeed anticipate the possibility of an Austrian attack on Serbia (or at least on the Serbian forces in Albania) and wished to know how London and Paris would react to an armed response by Russia. Grey's answer was characteristically evasive: the question, he replied, was academic and 'one could not give a decision about a hypothetical contingency which has not arisen'.[200] Poincaré's response, by contrast, was to demand clarity from Sazonov: what exactly, he asked, did the Russian government intend? This must be set out clearly – otherwise, by 'taking the initiative, the French government would run the risk of embracing a position which would either fall short of or exceed the intentions of its ally'. The Russians should not doubt that France would support them in the event of a Balkan crisis: 'if Russia goes to war, France will do the same, because we know that in this matter, Germany will back Austria'.[201] In a conversation with the Italian ambassador in Paris only a few days later, Poincaré confirmed that 'should the Austro-Serbian conflict lead to a general war, Russia could count entirely on the armed support of France'.[202]

In his memoirs, Poincaré vehemently denied having made these assurances.[203] And Izvolsky is admittedly not an entirely disinterested witness. This was the man whose mismanagement of the Bosnian annexation crisis had ruined his career in St Petersburg, a diplomat who had left high office under a cloud and remained obsessed with the supposed perfidy of Aehrenthal and Austria. Might he not have lied in order to strengthen the resolve of his colleague (and former subordinate) Sazonov, in Balkan affairs? Might he not – as Poincaré himself later suggested – have overstated the French prime minister's commitment in order to magnify his own role in consolidating the alliance?

These are plausible suppositions, but the evidence suggests that they are wrong. For example: Poincaré's claim, reported by Izvolsky on 12 September, that the French military was confident of victory in the event of the continental escalation of a war begun in the Balkans, is corroborated by a gung-ho General Staff memorandum of 2 September, a document of which Izvolsky could have had no independent knowledge; this suggests at the very least that the conversation in question really did take place.[204] Poincaré's uneasiness, recorded by Izvolsky on 17 November, about overleaping the Russians rings true – Poincaré would confide exactly the same doubts to his diary during the July Crisis of 1914. And there are supporting witnesses, such as the former premier and minister of foreign affairs Alexandre Ribot, a brilliant jurist and political scientist who met with Poincaré on several occasions during the autumn of 1912. In a private note dated 31 October 1912, Ribot recorded: 'Poincaré believes that Serbia will not evacuate Üsküb and that if Austria intervenes, Russia will not be able not to intervene. Germany and France will be obliged by their treaties to enter the scene. The Council of Ministers has deliberated on this and has decided that France ought to hold to its commitments.'[205]

Poincaré's change of course elicited a mixed response among the most senior policy-makers and functionaries. His distrust of Germany and his views on the *casus foederis* resonated positively with an influential *Sciences-po* trained subculture at the foreign ministry, for whom sympathy with the Slavic nations and hostility to Germany were axiomatic. And there was also wide support in the senior echelons of the military. In his memorandum of 2 September 1912 (the one Poincaré cited in his conversations with the Russian ambassador), Colonel Vignal of the 2nd Bureau of the French General Staff instructed the prime minister that *a war begun in the Balkans* would ensure the best conditions for an Entente victory. Since the Austrians would be tied down in a struggle with the South Slavs, Germany would be obliged to decant substantial forces from its westward offensive to defend the east against Russia. Under these circumstances, 'the Triple Entente would have the greatest chances of success and could achieve a victory that would permit it to redraw the map of Europe, despite Austria's local Balkan successes'.[206]

Others were more critical of the new orientation. The ambassador to London, Paul Cambon, was appalled at the confrontational stance Poincaré adopted towards Austria-Hungary during the opening weeks of the First Balkan War. On 5 November 1912, during a visit to Paris, Paul wrote to his brother Jules complaining of an article in *Le Temps*, patently inspired by Poincaré, that challenged Austria directly, upbraiding Vienna in a manner 'without nuance, without patience, without caution'. Paul went on to report a conversation with Poincaré on the evening of Saturday, 2 November. Cambon had ventured to suggest that France might consider allowing Austria to take a part of the Sanjak of Novi Pazar, a mere 'pile of rocks', in return for an assurance of her disinterest in any other Balkan territory. The prime minister's reply surprised him: 'it would be impossible to let [Austria], a power that had not waged war, that had no right etc., to acquire an advantage; that would stir up opinion in France and would constitute a setback for the Triple Entente!' France, Poincaré went on, 'which had done so much since the beginning of this war' – here Cambon inserted an exclamation mark in brackets – 'would be obliged also to demand advantages, an island in the Aegean Sea, for example . . .' On the following morning (Sunday, 3 November) Cambon, who had clearly spent the night worrying about this conversation, went to see Poincaré in order to set out his objections. The Sanjak was not worth a conflict, he told the prime minister; an Aegean island would cause more trouble than it was worth. Cambon was also sceptical of Poincaré's claim to be acting under the pressure of 'opinion'. Contrary to Poincaré's assertion, French public opinion was 'indifferent' to such questions – it was important, Cambon warned, that the government not itself stir up 'a current of opinion that would render a solution impossible'. Poincaré was having none of this and shut the discussion down:

'I have submitted my views to the Government in the Council [of Ministers]' Poincaré replied drily. 'It has approved them, there is a decision by the Cabinet, we cannot go back on it.'

'How do you mean we cannot go back on it?' I replied. 'Except for

2 or 3 ministers, the members of Cabinet know nothing of external policy and the conversation can always remain open on questions of this kind.'

'There is a decision by the government,' he replied very drily, 'it is useless to press the matter.'[207]

What is interesting about this exchange is not the subject matter as such, because far from taking or demanding a piece of the Sanjak, Austria withdrew its troops from the area and left it to the neighbouring states, Serbia and Montenegro. The issue passed and was forgotten. Far more significant is the sense conveyed by Poincaré's remarks of France's deep and direct involvement in the Balkan troubles, most strikingly conveyed in the prime minister's bizarre notion that leaving a piece of the Sanjak to Austria would oblige Paris to seek compensation in the form of 'an island on the Aegean'. And even more ominous was the sense, conveyed not only by Cambon's letter but also in the note by Ribot, that French Balkan policy was no longer being improvised in response to new situations, but rather laid down in hard-and-fast commitments, in 'decisions' on which there could be 'no going back'.

PARIS FORCES THE PACE

In a letter of 19 December 1912, Colonel Ignatiev, the Russian military attaché in Paris, reported a long and revealing conversation with Alexandre Millerand, the French minister of war. Millerand raised the question of the Austrian troop reinforcements on the Serbian and Galician frontiers:

MILLERAND: What do you think is the objective of the Austrian mobilisation?

ME [i.e. Ignatiev]: Predictions are difficult on this question, but undoubtedly the Austrian preparations vis-à-vis Russia thus far have been defensive in character.

MILLERAND: Fine, but don't you think the occupation of Serbia* was a direct summons [*vyzov*] to you to wage war?

* Millerand's meaning here is uncertain, since there was no Austrian 'occupation' of Serbia in 1912: he is probably referring to the annexation of Bosnia, in which case, the term reported here may be Ignatiev's rather than Millerand's.

ME: I cannot answer this question, but I know that we have no desire for a European war, or to take any steps that could provoke a European conflagration.

MILLERAND: So, you'll have to leave Serbia on her own? That of course is your business. But it should be understood that this is not on account of our fault. We are ready [*My gotovy*].[208]

Ignatiev reported that Millerand seemed 'perturbed' and even 'annoyed' by his noncommittal responses to the minister's questions. It was not, the French minister insisted, merely a question of Albania, or the Serbs or Durazzo, but of 'Austrian hegemony on the entire Balkan peninsula' – a matter about which the Russian government could surely ill afford to remain complacent.[209]

There is something remarkable in these utterances by the French minister of war, a respected socialist politician and a stranger to foreign affairs, whose career had been focused on old-age pensions, education and the conditions of labour rather than on geopolitical questions. Yet by 1912 Millerand, a close friend of Poincaré, whom he had known at school, had become one of the leaders of the French national revival. Widely admired for his tenacity, industry and intense patriotism, he sought not only to build military morale and reinforce the autonomy of the army command, but also to instil the French public with martial spirit.[210] His words to Ignatiev reflected an attitude that was widespread within the French leadership during the Balkan winter crisis of 1912–13. 'General Castelnau,' Ignatiev reported, 'twice told me that he personally is ready for war and even that he would like a war.' Indeed, the French government as a whole was 'in full readiness to support us against Austria and Germany, not only by diplomatic means but, if needed, by force of arms'. The reason for this readiness lay, Ignatiev believed, in French confidence that a Balkan war would produce the most advantageous starting point for a broader conflict, since it would oblige Germany to focus its military measures on Russia, 'leaving the French in the rear'.[211] Indeed, so enthusiastic were the messages coming from Paris in November and December 1912 that Sazonov himself informally urged the French to calm down.[212]

The coordinating will behind this policy was Poincaré. There had been many foreign ministers and many premiers who had come and gone without leaving much impression on French foreign policy. But

Poincaré was an exception. He used the combination of the premiership and the ministerial post in foreign affairs to ward off unwelcome influences. He turned up often and early at work, an unequivocal signal of serious intentions in the leisurely French foreign ministry of those days. He insisted on reading and annotating dossiers and on opening his own mail; it was rumoured that he sometimes wrote his own dispatches. He had little patience with the self-importance of the ambassadors, who tended, he grumpily observed in January 1914, to adopt too easily the point of view of the government to which they were accredited.[213] In order to ensure that the Quai d'Orsay did not get out of hand, Poincaré created an inner cabinet of trusted and loyal advisers, just as Delcassé had done at the turn of the century.

In January 1913, Poincaré was elected president of the Republic, becoming the first man ever to jump straight from the office of premier to that of the head of state. Oddly enough, this implied, in theory, a diminution in his capacity to shape the formulation of foreign policy, for by custom and precedent the presidential office tended, despite its formidable prerogatives, not to be an important seat of power. Elected by the two houses of parliament, he was expected to act as the 'pinboy in the bowling alley', picking up fallen cabinets as the chamber knocked them down.[214] But the former premier had no intention of letting the reins slip from his hands; even before his election, Poincaré had made it clear that he intended to exploit to the full the constitutional instruments with which the presidency was furnished – his knowledge and deep understanding of constitutional law ensured that he would do this with a certain bravura. In 1912, he had even published a textbook on political science, in which he argued that the powers of the president – the right to dissolve the chambers of parliament, for example – were a crucial stabilizing factor in the constitution and that the president should properly play a pre-eminent role in international affairs.[215]

Once elected to the presidency of the Republic, Poincaré deployed his indirect influence on the choice of candidates to ensure that his successors in the foreign ministry were either weak and inexperienced or shared Poincaré's strategic and diplomatic vision, or, best of all, a combination of all three. Charles Jonnart, who succeeded Poincaré until March 1913, was a case in point: he was a former governor-general of Algeria who knew next to nothing of external relations and depended upon Poincaré's protégé Maurice Paléologue, chief of the political department, for the day-to-day running of affairs.[216] 'I still command Jonnart,' Poincaré confided to his diary on 26 January 1913. 'I go to the Quai d'Orsay every morning.'[217]

While the French leadership extended the remit of the alliance to cover Russia in the event of possible Balkan incidents, important changes also took place in the provisions associated with the Franco-Russian military convention. The French military command had been alarmed by Sukhomlinov's deployment plan of 1910, which shifted the Russian areas of concentration back out of the Polish salient hundreds of miles to the east, thereby lengthening the projected mobilization times for a westward attack and undermining the presumption of simultaneity that was enshrined in the text of the convention.[218] At the annual Franco-Russian General Staff talks of 1911, the French delegates pressed their Russian colleagues on this question. The reply from the Russian staff chief Yakov Zhilinsky was not especially confidence-inspiring. He promised that the Russian armed forces would make every effort to commence their attack as soon as possible after day 15 of mobilization. But he also conceded that it would take until 1913 and 1914 to finish stocking the army with field artillery and machine guns.[219]

The question of how fast and how many men Russia would mobilize in the event of the *casus foederis*, and in what direction it would deploy them, dominated the Franco-Russian inter-staff discussions in the summers of 1912 and 1913. In the conversations of July 1912, the French CGS, Joseph Joffre, requested that the Russians double-track all their railway lines to the East Prussian and Galician frontiers. Some strategically important lines were even to be quadrupled to allow faster transit of large troop numbers. The Franco-Russian Naval Convention of July 1912, which provided for closer cooperation and coordination of the two navies, was another fruit of these efforts. And there was a gradual improvement in the Russian assurances – whereas Zhilinsky promised in 1912 to attack Germany with 800,000 men by day 15, in the following year he felt able, once the improvements were put in place, to shave a further two days off the schedule.[220] The direction of mobilization was another area of concern. The protocols of the inter-staff discussions record the tireless efforts of the French staff officers to keep the Russians focused on Germany rather than Austria as the principal opponent. For while the French were willing to acknowledge the legitimacy of a Balkan *casus belli*, the entire military purpose of the alliance (from

France's perspective) would be defeated if the Russians deployed the bulk of their military might against the Habsburg Empire and left the French to deal on their own with a massive German attack in the west. When this issue was raised at the 1912 meeting, Zhilinsky objected that the Russians also had other threats to think about: the Austrians, too, had been improving their strategic railways and it was out of the question, given the sensitivity of the region for national morale, that the Russians should risk a defeat in the Balkans. Sweden was another potential threat, and then there was Turkey. But Joffre insisted that the 'destruction of Germany's forces' – *l'anéantissement des forces de l'Allemagne* – would in effect resolve all the other problems facing the alliance; it was essential to concentrate on this objective 'at any price'.[221] A note prepared afterwards by the General Staff summarizing the result of the discussions duly recorded that 'the Russian command recognises Germany as the principal adversary'.[222]

Poincaré did what he could to expedite this powering up of the Russian end of the alliance. When, before leaving for St Petersburg in August 1912, he asked Joffre what issues he should be raising with his hosts – the French staff chief 'pointed to the railways improvement and mentioned nothing else'.[223] Once in the Russian capital, the French premier conscientiously importuned all his interlocutors on the railways question: 'I make him [Tsar Nicholas II] aware of our interest in the improvements requested by our General Staff'; 'I explain to him [Sazonov] the necessity of doubling and quadrupling the routes', and so on.[224] Poincaré's notes even offer a glimpse of the power struggle unfolding within the Russian administration between Kokovtsov and the military command. The Russian premier was sceptical of plans for a forward policy in the Balkans and, as a man of finance, he was unenthusiastic about the prospect of spending huge amounts of borrowed money on railways of dubious commercial value. When he responded to Poincaré's promptings with the observation that the Russians were currently 'studying' the question of railway improvements, Poincaré insisted that 'this study is very urgent, because it is probable that it will be on the German frontier [of Russia] that the outcome of the war will be decided'. What Kokovtsov thought of this bland presumption of an imminent war can readily be imagined. Poincaré recorded only that his colleague seemed 'irritated' by the notion that the Russian army command had enlisted the support of the French government in order to secure military allocations without having to consult the minister of finance (i.e. Kokovtsov himself) directly.[225] At every opportunity, Poincaré helped to step up the pressure on the Russians to re-arm.[226]

The French practised at home what they preached to the Russians. The appointment of Joseph Joffre as chief of the General Staff in July 1911, at the height of the Agadir crisis, placed French strategy in the hands of a man committed to the theory of the 'offensive school'. French strategists had tended to adopt a defensive approach to the prospect of a confrontation with Germany: campaign plans XV (1903) and XVI (1909) both envisaged defensive deployments in the first phase, followed by a decisive counter-stroke once the enemy's intentions were known, rather in the manner of the Sukhomlinov deployment plan of 1910. But Joffre altered campaign plan XVI to allow for an aggressive thrust through Alsace into German territory, in the belief that 'the offensive alone made it possible to break the will of the adversary'. He also worked much more proactively with France's alliance and Entente partners than his predecessors had done. Joffre was the driving force on the French side at the inter-staff meetings of 1911, 1912 and 1913; his partnership with his Russian counterpart Zhilinsky was crucial to their success. There were also intense discussions with the English military commanders, and especially with Henry Wilson. Joffre was the first French strategist to integrate the British Expeditionary Force into his dispositions – his revisions to Plan XVI included detailed stipulations on the concentration of British troops along the Belgian border.[227]

In Joffre, Poincaré found a fitting military partner for his own strategic concept. There were points of disagreement, to be sure. One of the most revealing concerned the question of Belgian neutrality. Leaked German documents and other military intelligence suggested that in the event of war the Germans would attack France through neutral Belgium. On 21 February 1912, when Poincaré, newly installed as premier, convened an informal meeting at the Quai d'Orsay to review French defence arrangements, Joffre advocated a pre-emptive strike through Belgian territory. This, he argued, was the only way to offset French numerical inferiority vis-à-vis Germany. The British would surely understand the need for such a measure, and recent signs of coolness between Belgium and Germany suggested that it might even be possible to arrive at an understanding with Belgium beforehand. But Poincaré flatly refused to consider Joffre's case, on the grounds that an invasion of

Belgium would risk alienating British public opinion and make it impossible for Edward Grey to deliver on his promises to Paris. It was a striking demonstration of the primacy of civilian over military authority in the French Republic, but also of Poincaré's foresight and brilliance in combining a highly aggressive understanding of the *casus foederis* in the east with a strategically defensive approach on the French frontier. That was how Paris solved a conundrum that faced several of the belligerents of 1914, namely the 'paradoxical requirement that a defensive war open aggressively'.[228]

The hardening of commitments continued after Poincaré ascended to the presidency of the Republic. The appointment of Théophile Delcassé as ambassador to St Petersburg in the spring of 1913 was an unmistakable signal. Delcassé's was to be a short posting – he made it clear from the outset that he intended to stay in St Petersburg only until the 1914 French elections. Nevertheless, the choice of this eminent, long-serving former foreign minister who had fallen from office at the height of the first Moroccan crisis left little doubt as to the orientation of French policy. With Delcassé in St Petersburg and Izvolsky in Paris, both parties to the alliance were represented by ambassadors with a strong personal animus against Germany. Delcassé had grown even more Germanophobic in recent years – when he met with Jules Cambon on his way to the east via Berlin, it was noted that he refused to step out of his train so that he could avoid touching German soil with the sole of his shoe.[229] The new ambassador was known for his expertise in the area of strategic railways (as foreign minister at the turn of the century, Delcassé had pressed the Russian government to build them against the British empire!).[230] Small wonder that the Russian press welcomed the news of his appointment, noting that his 'combative temperament' would be an asset to the Triple Entente.[231] Poincaré's letter of introduction to the Tsar announced that the new ambassador's objective would be 'to tighten further the bonds of the Franco-Russian alliance', and there followed the inevitable reminder of the importance of reinforcing with the greatest possible speed the Russian strategic routes to the empire's western frontiers.[232] Ignatiev reported that Delcassé had been authorized by the French government 'to propose to us whatever loan we need for this purpose'.[233]

Delcassé worked as hard as ever during his brief posting (23 March 1913 to 30 January 1914), indeed he was so busy that he was rarely seen in St Petersburg society. At his very first audience with the Tsar, only a day after his arrival, he stressed the importance of 'completing the network of railways, in conformity with the wishes of the Chief of Staff' and took the unusual step of requesting directly that the requisite funds be provided by Kokovtsov.[234] Throughout his time in St Petersburg, Delcassé scarcely ever met with anyone except Sazonov and Kokovtsov – even the British ambassador found it difficult to arrange a meeting with him. 'I run the whole of Russian foreign policy,' he boasted to his French colleagues. 'The people around here haven't the slightest clue.'[235] Delcassé oversaw the negotiations that bore fruit in a massive new French loan: 2,500 million francs, to be issued on the French capital market by private Russian railways companies over a five-year period in yearly instalments of 500 million, on condition that the strategic railways in the western salient were strengthened in the manner envisaged at the joint staff discussions of 1913.[236] Maurice Paléologue, Delcassé's successor at the St Petersburg embassy from January 1914, was a man in the same mould who intended to combine strategic reinforcement with a firmer approach to foreign policy questions.

POINCARÉ UNDER PRESSURE

Throughout the first eighteen months of his presidency (until the outbreak of war), Poincaré reinforced the offensive orientation of French military planning. He supported the campaign for the Three Year Law, passed by the French Chamber and Senate in the summer of 1913, which raised the French standing army to around 700,000 men, reducing the gap in troop numbers between France and Germany to just 50,000 and demonstrating to the Russians that the French were serious about playing their part in the joint effort against the 'principal adversary'.[237] By choosing compliant prime ministers, taking control of the Higher Council of War and deploying to maximum effect his powers under the *secteur réservé* pertaining to the president's right to shape decisions in the field of foreign and military policy, Poincaré became one of the strongest presidents the Third Republic would ever see.[238]

There was a public dimension to all of this activism. The chauvinism of government propaganda since the formation of the Poincaré–Millerand–Delcassé ministry was a recurring theme in the dispatches of

the Belgian minister in Paris, Baron Guillaume. Guillaume was particularly struck by the rhetorical vehemence of the campaign in support of
the Three Year Law, which, having helped to secure Poincaré his election
to the presidency of the Republic, now continued apace, 'heedless of the
dangers to which it gives birth'.[239] 'It was Mssrs. Poincaré, Delcassé and
Millerand,' Guillaume observed in January 1914, 'who invented and
pursued the nationalist, jingoistic and chauvinist politics' whose renaissance was now such a marked feature of public life in France. He saw in
this 'the greatest peril for peace in today's Europe'.[240] Poincaré was not
just a Parisian grandee, the Belgian minister wrote in May 1914, but a
truly national politician who worked extremely hard and with great skill
to build his support base in the provinces. He was an excellent orator
who frequently travelled the length and breadth of France, gave numerous speeches and was acclaimed in every town he visited.[241]

Notwithstanding these provincial successes, the intrinsic volatility of
the French political system ensured that Poincaré's position in Paris
remained fragile. Among other things, the revolving door of French
ministerial office continued to turn and Poincaré's pet foreign minister,
Charles Jonnart, fell from office after only two months. Under his successor, the languid Stéphen Pichon, the mechanisms examined in chapter
4 began once more to make themselves felt: Pichon aligned himself with
the dominant ambassadors and their allies within the Centrale. The
consequence was a temporary drift back in the direction of a more
conciliatory – or at least a less intransigent – approach to Berlin. When
Pichon fell from office with the Barthou government in December 1913,
Poincaré looked for a straw man to replace him. The new prime and
foreign minister, Gaston Doumergue, had to agree before taking office
that he would maintain the Three Year Law and Poincaré's foreign policy. The president hoped that Doumergue, who lacked any experience
whatsoever in external relations, would be obliged to defer to him on all
important matters. But this tactic backfired, for while Doumergue was
a staunch supporter of the Russian alliance, he also worked against
Poincaré, installing the latter's arch-rival Joseph Caillaux as minister
of finance and gradually shutting the president out of foreign policy
discussions.[242]

Poincaré still had powerful and unscrupulous enemies. How vulnerable he was to their political machinations had become clear in May
1913, when a cabinet crisis broke out over the discovery of diplomatic

intercepts exposing secret negotiations between the president and officials of the Catholic Church. In the spring of 1913, Poincaré and Pichon had entered into these talks in the hope of securing the election of a successor to the papal throne who would support France. This might seem harmless enough, given France's interest in consolidating its influence over its religious protectorates in the Levant. But contacts of this kind between a senior politician of the Republic and the Catholic Church were matters of the greatest delicacy in pre-1914 France, where anticlericalism was the default setting of the political culture. The discussions were kept absolutely secret in order to deny the Radicals and their allies ammunition for an anticlerical campaign. But in April and May 1913, the Sûreté at the ministry of the interior intercepted and deciphered three telegrams from the Italian ambassador in Paris referring to negotiations between Poincaré, Pichon and the Vatican. On 6 May, Louis-Lucien Klotz, the minister of the interior, produced the telegrams at a meeting of the cabinet. In the ensuing uproar, Pichon threatened to resign if the interception and leaking of telegrams continued. The interceptions were stopped, but the damage had been done, since this sensitive material could potentially be exploited in future by unscrupulous hands to smear Poincaré as a 'clerical' unfit for public office.

There was a further, personal, aspect to the problem: Poincaré had married his wife Henriette – a double divorcée – in a strictly civil ceremony, as was expected of senior office-holders in the Republic. But in May 1913, after it became known that Henriette's first two husbands were dead, he agreed under pressure from his wife and in deference to the wishes of his much loved and recently deceased mother to solemnize their union with a religious ceremony. Here again was a decision with the potential to scandalize anticlerical opinion. The ceremony was conducted in the strictest secrecy, but Poincaré lived thereafter in fear of an anticlerical campaign that would devastate his popularity. He was spied and informed upon, he confided to a colleague, even within the walls of the Élysée, where 'police agents, servants, ushers, visitors, more than a hundred people each day, have their eyes on me, observe all my gestures and broadcast them more or less exactly'.[243] So concerned was he at this prospect that he went to great lengths to buy off the leading Radicals. To the huge chagrin of the Cambon brothers, he even offered the London embassy to the Anglophile Radical leader and Poincaré-baiter Georges Clemenceau (who refused it).[244] Anxiety about behind-the-scenes intrigue and hostile revelations continued to dog the president until the outbreak of war.

In other words: Poincaré remained vulnerable. And it even seemed that the moment for the man and his policies might be passing. The wave of nationalist *élan* on whose crest he had entered high office in the aftermath of Agadir was already ebbing by early 1914, making way for a new and complex alignment of forces.[245] Poincaré was 'more and more hated' by the socialist and unified radicals, and his rivals Clemenceau and Caillaux never missed any opportunity to attack and goad him.[246] Most worrying of all was the prospect that a new oppositional formation might force the repeal of the Three Year Law and thereby loosen the joist-work of the Franco-Russian Alliance.[247] In a country distinguished – especially after the Dreyfus affair – by strong currents of anti-militarist feeling, the extension of service was an extremely controversial measure. The results of the tumultuous general elections of 26 April and 10 May 1914 were difficult to read, but they suggested that majority support for the Three Year Law hung by a thread. Following the fall of the Doumergue government on 2 June 1914, Poincaré had to find a political combination that would save the law. After several false starts – including the collapse of one government on the day of its first appearance in parliament, an event with few historical precedents[248] – Poincaré reached out to the ex-socialist René Viviani, who formed a new cabinet on 12 June, in which ten of the seventeen ministers supported three-year service. When the new government won a majority in the Chamber on 16 June, it seemed that the crisis had passed. The Three Year Law was safe, at least for the moment. But who could say how long it would survive?

International developments gave further reason for concern. During 1913 and 1914, the policy-makers in Paris became increasingly aware of the growth of Russian power. French military observers reported that the Russian army had made huge advances since the setbacks of the Japanese war; the Russian soldier was 'first class, tough, well trained, disciplined and devoted' and the Russian army was expected to prevail against its 'eventual enemies'.[249] French financial experts corroborated this view of Russia's prospects. One keen student of the Russian economy was M. de Verneuil, a syndic of the brokers at the Paris Stock Exchange with the power to veto the admission of securities to the Paris Bourse. Verneuil had long been involved in Russo-French business ventures when he travelled to St Petersburg to discuss the terms of the new French loan with premier Kokovtsov. In a letter of 7 July 1913, he reported his impressions to Foreign Minister Pichon. Verneuil had already formed a very favourable opinion of Russian economic progress, he wrote, but his recent visit to the Russian capital had convinced him that the reality was far more impressive:

> There is something truly fantastic in preparation, whose symptoms must strike the mind of even the most informed observers. I have the very clear impression that in the next thirty years, we are going to see in Russia a prodigious economic growth which will equal – if it does not surpass it – the colossal movement that took place in the United States during the last quarter of the XIXth century.[250]

Verneuil was not alone: in 1914, the reports of the French military attaché in St Petersburg, General de Laguiche, evoked a Russian 'colossus' supplied with 'inexhaustible resources', armed with 'first-class' soldiers and wielding a 'limitless power'. After attending the spring manoeuvres of that year, Laguiche positively bubbled over with enthusiasm: 'the more I go, the more I admire this material, the Russian man is superior to any I know. There's a source of strength and power there that I have never encountered in any other army.'[251] Press reporting tended to reinforce this impression. In November 1913, *Le Temps* ran an article in which the paper's Russian correspondent Charles Rivet declared that

> We cannot admire too much this great Russian [military] effort. It is produced without creating the slightest trouble of inconvenience to the prosperity of the country. [. . .] whereas in France, new military expenses posed a budgetary problem, Russia has no need to go in search of a new source of revenues. [. . .] In this arms race, Russia is thus better placed than anyone to sustain the competition. The development of its population is accompanied by a growth in wealth; the circumstances permit it to confront – even over the long term – the constant expansion of military contingents and expenses. It will never be obliged to propose slowing this growth, nor, for that matter, are Russia's military leaders at all disposed to do so.[252]

Among those who subscribed to this starry-eyed vision of Russia was Poincaré himself.[253]

All this was, on the face of it, good news for the Franco-Russian Alliance. But in Paris it also gave rise to nagging doubts. What if Russia became so wealthy and so powerful that it ceased to depend for its security on the promise of French aid? At the very least, such headlong growth would surely tilt the balance of power within the alliance to Paris's disadvantage, for, as General de Laguiche observed in February 1914, 'the less need Russia has of other nations, the more she will be able to free herself from our pressure'.[254] This mood of apprehension seems risible to us in retrospect: it was founded on an absurd overestimation of Russian economic progress and military strength.[255] But these false futures were real enough to the people who perceived them; together with other factors in a rapidly changing environment, they suggested that the instruments currently available to contain Germany might not be around for very much longer.

In the last weeks of June 1914, rather to his own surprise, Poincaré was still in control. His policy was secure – at least until the current government fell. René Viviani was a highly effective parliamentary politician, but a complete novice in foreign affairs. It would be easy, should a crisis arise, for the president to steer policy. The offensive military strategy and the commitment to the Balkan *casus foederis* remained intact. But in the medium and longer term, Poincaré's future and that of his policy looked rather uncertain. This combination of strength in the present and vulnerability over the longer term would inform his handling of the crisis that broke out after Gavril Princip fired his fatal shots on 28 June in Sarajevo. Like so many of the decision-makers caught up in those events, Poincaré would feel that he was working against the clock.

6

Last Chances: Détente and Danger, 1912–1914

'Since I have been at the Foreign Office,' Arthur Nicolson wrote early in May 1914, 'I have not seen such calm waters.'[1] Nicolson's remark draws our attention to one of the most curious features of the last two pre-war years, namely that even as the stockpiling of arms continued to gain momentum and the attitudes of some military and civilian leaders grew more militant, the European international system as a whole displayed a surprising capacity for crisis management and détente. Does this mean that a general war was growing *less* probable in the last year and a half before it broke out? Or did the phenomenon of détente merely cloak the reality of a deepening structural antagonism between the alliance blocs? And if the latter is true, how did the processes implicated in détente interact with those pieces of causality that would enable a general war to break out in 1914?

THE LIMITS OF DÉTENTE

In the summer of 1912, the German Kaiser and the Russian Tsar, accompanied by an entourage of senior statesmen, met for informal conversations at Baltic Port (Paldiski), a Russian naval facility on the Pakri peninsula in what is today north-western Estonia. The meeting, planned as the reciprocation of a visit by the Tsar to Potsdam in 1910, went extraordinarily well. While the monarchs walked, dined and inspected troops, the statesmen got together for amicable, wide-ranging discussions. Kokovtsov and Bethmann Hollweg – who met for the first time at Baltic Port – felt an immediate sympathy for each other. These were two restrained, conservative individuals of decidedly moderate views. In a calm and candid conversation, the two prime ministers dwelt on the armaments policies of the two powers. Each assured the other of the essentially defensive nature of his intentions and the two men agreed that the current surge in military expenditures was deeply to be regretted for the unsettling effect it had on public opinion. It was to be hoped, Bethmann remarked, 'that all countries would have so many interests in common as to make them view armaments as a measure of prevention, without allowing them to be actually applied'.[2]

Bethmann's conversations with Foreign Minister Sazonov ranged over a wider range of subjects, but were marked by the same striving for conciliatory language. On the subject of the deepening instability on the Balkan peninsula, Sazonov assured Bethmann that Russia's 'mission' vis-à-vis the Christian Slavic states was historically complete and thus obsolete. Russia, Sazonov claimed, had no intention of exploiting the Ottoman Empire's current difficulties. Bethmann declared that although Germany was sometimes accused of wishing to interfere with the inner workings of the Entente, nothing could be further from his mind. On the other hand, he saw no reason why Germany should not cultivate

Count Vladimir Kokovtsov

friendly relations with the Entente powers. 'How does it look with Austria?' Sazonov asked towards the end of the interview. Bethmann assured him that there could be no question of an aggressive Austrian Balkan policy. 'So there will be no encouragement [by Germany] of Austria?' Sazonov asked, to which Bethmann replied that Berlin had no intention whatsoever of supporting a policy of adventurism in Vienna. Both men agreed before parting that it would be an excellent idea to make these summit meetings a 'fixed institution' to be repeated as a matter of course every two years.[3]

Amazingly enough, even the Kaiser was on his best behaviour at Baltic Port. The Tsar always dreaded meetings with his talkative German cousin – he was reluctant to speak his own mind, because, as Kokovtsov observed, 'he feared the expansiveness of the German Emperor, so foreign to his own nature'.[4] In a note composed in advance of the visit, the German ambassador in St Petersburg, Count Pourtalès, urged that the Kaiser be told to avoid tendentious conversation topics and adopt a 'listening attitude' wherever possible, so that the Tsar would be able to get a word in edgeways.[5] For the most part, Wilhelm showed admirable self-restraint. There were a few small slips: after the first lunch on board the Tsar's yacht *Standart*, the Kaiser drew Sazonov apart and spoke to him ('at him' might be a more appropriate locution) for over an hour in detail about his relationship with his parents, who, he claimed, had never loved him. Sazonov saw this as a shocking illustration of the German Emperor's 'marked tendency to overshoot the boundaries of the reserve and dignity' that one would expect of someone in such an elevated position.[6] On the second day of the trip, during a visit in crippling heat to the ruined fortifications constructed around the port by Peter the Great, Wilhelm again forgot his instructions and buttonholed Kokovtsov on one his latest hobby-horses, the importance of establishing a pan-European oil trust that would be able to compete with American Standard Oil. The conversation, Kokovtsov recalled, 'became extremely animated and went beyond the limits set by court etiquette'.

> The sun was scorching. The tsar did not want to interrupt our conversation, but behind Emperor Wilhelm's back he made signs of impatience to me. The Kaiser, however, continued to answer my arguments with increasing fervour. Finally the Tsar seemed to lose all patience, approached us, and began to listen to our conversation, whereupon Emperor Wilhelm

turned to him with the following words (in French): 'Your Chairman of the Council does not sympathise with my ideas, and I do not want to permit him to remain unconvinced. I want you to allow me to prove my point with data collected at Berlin, and when I am ready I should like to have your permission to resume this conversation with him.'[7]

It is worth picturing this scene – the glare of the sunlight on the broken stone of the old fort, Kokovtsov sweltering in his jacket, the Kaiser red-faced, his moustaches trembling as he warmed to his theme, gesticulating, oblivious to the discomfort of his companions, and behind him the Tsar, trying desperately to end the ordeal and get the party out of the sun. Whether Wilhelm ever sent Kokovtsov the 'data collected at Berlin' on oil consortia is unknown but may be doubted – his bursts of enthuasiasm tended to be as short as they were intense. No wonder the German Kaiser was a figure of terror on the royal circuit.

Wilhelm's passing lapses did nothing to dent the good cheer of the two parties and the summit ended in an unexpectedly high mood. An official joint communiqué released to the press on 6 July declared that the meeting had 'borne an especially warm character', that it constituted new proof of the 'relations of friendship' obtaining between the two monarchs and confirmed the 'firm resolution' of both powers to maintain the 'venerable traditions existing between them'.[8]

Baltic Port was the high-water mark of Russo-German détente in the last years before the outbreak of war in 1914.[9] Yet there were exceedingly narrow limits to what was achieved there. The conversations, though friendly, produced no decisions of substance. The official communiqué released to the press confined itself to waffly generalizations and explicitly stated that the meeting had neither generated 'new agreements' nor effected 'any change whatsoever in the grouping of the Powers, whose value for the maintenance of equilibrium and peace had been proven'.[10] The assurances offered by Bethmann and Sazonov on the Balkan situation concealed a dangerous inconsistency: whereas the Germans did in fact urge restraint on the Austrians, sowing doubts in Vienna about the firmness of Berlin's commitment to the alliance, the Russians were and would continue doing the opposite with their Balkan clients. Sazonov's assurances to Bethmann that Russia had no intention of exploiting the difficulties confronting the Ottoman Empire and that her 'historic mission' on the peninsula was now a thing of the past were misleading, to say the least. If this was to be the basis for a Russo-German understanding, it was a fragile foundation indeed. And even the restrained formulae of the Baltic Port communiqué were enough to trigger spasms of paranoia in London and Paris. Both before and after the meeting, the ministry of foreign affairs in St Petersburg issued firm assurances to London and Paris that their commitment to the 'triple entente' was stronger than ever. In a sense then, the tentative performances of rapprochement at Baltic Port revealed how elusive a truly multilateral détente was likely to be.

Analogous structural and political constraints stood in the way of a lasting détente between Germany and Britain. The Haldane mission of February 1912, when Germany and Britain failed to come to an agreement on naval armaments limitation, is a case in point. The original architect of the mission was Bethmann. His aim was to secure an understanding with Britain that would enable international (especially colonial) questions to be resolved collaboratively rather than through competition and confrontation. The chancellor saw in Admiral Tirpitz's ambitious naval construction programme the chief obstacle to such an understanding. But the Kaiser's personal support for the naval programme and the disjointed, praetorian structure of the German executive meant that oblique manoeuvres were needed to dislodge the current policy. In order to weaken Tirpitz's grip, Bethmann aligned himself with the Admiralty in its long-standing campaign against the Imperial Naval Office (the Admiralty was critical of Tirpitz's concentration on ship numbers rather than the education and training of naval personnel). He encouraged the army, which had long been starved of funds while the naval budgets ballooned, to insist on refurbishment and expansion.[11] And of course he briefed Metternich, the German ambassador in London, to provide him with the ammunition he would need to persuade the Kaiser that curbing naval growth might have a more persuasive effect on London than the current policy of strength and challenge. In short, Bethmann assiduously worked the various switches in the system in the hope of weaning Reich defence policy off its addiction to naval growth.

Like Joseph Caillaux during the Agadir crisis, Bethmann made use of a non-state go-between, the Hamburg-based shipping magnate Albert Ballin, who played a crucial role in opening up a channel of communication. Like many senior figures in the commercial and banking sector,

Ballin believed utterly in the civilizational value of international trade and the criminal stupidity of a European war. Through his contacts with the British banker Sir Ernest Cassel, Ballin was able to bring to Berlin a message conveying British interest in principle in seeking a bilateral understanding on issues arising from naval armaments and colonial questions. In February 1912, Lord Haldane, the secretary of state for war, travelled to Berlin to sound out the possibilities.

Why did the Haldane mission fail? The answer is not simply German intransigence over the scale and pace of naval construction, because Bethmann and – albeit reluctantly – Kaiser Wilhelm II were willing to make concessions on that front.[12] The real sticking-point was Berlin's insistence on something tangible in return, namely an undertaking of British neutrality in the event of a war between Germany and another continental power. Why were the British so unwilling to grant what was asked? The argument that they were bound by the terms of their obligations to France is flawed, because Bethmann was willing to limit the proposed neutrality agreement to cases in which Germany 'cannot be said to be the aggressor', and expressly conceded that any agreement reached would have 'no application insofar as it may not be reconcilable with existing agreements which the high contracting parties have already made'.[13] The true reason for British reticence lay rather in an understandable disinclination to give away something for nothing: Britain was winning the naval arms race hands down and enjoyed unchallenged superiority. Bethmann and Wilhelm wanted a neutrality agreement in exchange for recognizing that superiority as a permanent state of affairs. But why should Britain trade for an asset it already possessed?[14] In sum: it was not ships as such that prevented an agreement, but rather the irreconcilability of perceived interests on both sides.[15]

Haldane returned from Berlin shaking his head at the confusion he had observed there: it was clear even to an outsider that Bethmann had not succeeded in rallying the Kaiser and the Reich Naval Office behind his policy. But in Britain, too, powerful interests were ranged against the mission's success.[16] From the start, it was understood in London as a purely exploratory enterprise. Haldane was obliged to travel to Berlin under the cover of an educational enquiry (he was then chairing the Royal Commission on London University) and he possessed, in the words of a British draft note to the German government, 'no authority to make any agreement or to bind any of his colleagues'.[17] The mission,

Haldane himself reassured Jules Cambon, was about *détente*, not *entente*.[18] In Paris, Bertie worked hard to sabotage the agreement by tipping off Poincaré and goading the Quai d'Orsay to apply pressure to London.[19] It is telling, moreover, that the man entrusted with providing Haldane with documentation and advice during the talks was none other than Sir Arthur Nicolson, a man who had always believed that any concession to Germany risked antagonizing the Russians, whose benevolence was essential to British security. Nicolson made no secret of his hostility to the Haldane venture. 'I do not myself see,' he told Sir Francis Bertie, the British ambassador to Paris, in February 1912, 'why we should abandon the excellent position in which we have been placed, and step down to be involved in endeavours to entangle us in some so-called "understandings" which would undoubtedly, if not actually, impair our relations with France and Russia.'[20] The ambassador agreed: the Haldane mission was a 'foolish move' undertaken merely to silence the 'Grey-must-go radicals'.[21] From the outset, then, there was no realistic chance that the mission would succeed.[22] To the great relief of Nicolson and Bertie, Grey refused to consider a 'neutrality clause' and the Haldane talks collapsed. Ambassador Goschen wrote from Berlin to congratulate Nicolson: 'You have been foremost in this good work.'[23]

As Nicolson's remarks suggest, the growth of détente was constrained – at least in Britain – by bloc thinking, which was still accepted as providing the indispensable foundation for national security. Détente might offer a supplement to bloc strategy, but could not supersede it. Sir Edward Grey had put it elegantly in a speech to the House of Commons in November 1911: 'One does not make new friendships worth having by deserting old ones. New friendships by all means let us make, but not at the expense of the ones we have.'[24]

Precisely because so little had been invested in the Haldane mission, its collapse was easily digested and the post-Agadir Anglo-German détente continued. Only in the light of later events did the failure to achieve a naval agreement come to appear historically significant. In the autumn of 1912, as the Balkan crisis broke, the German foreign secretary Kiderlen-Wächter proposed to Goschen, the British ambassador in Berlin, that the two countries coordinate their response with a view to preventing the powers from falling into two hostile camps. Grey, for his part, let Bethmann know that he desired 'intimate political co-operation' with Germany.[25] Britain and Germany joined in sponsoring the Ambassadors' Conference that met in London between December 1912 and July 1913. The two powers helped to broker compromise solutions to the thorniest problems arising from the First Balkan War, and they urged restraint on their respective bloc partners, Russia and Austria.[26]

Ulterior motives were in play, of course. Foreign Secretary Jagow, who picked up the policy thread when Kiderlen died suddenly in December 1912, hoped that continued Balkan collaboration would counteract British dependence on the Entente powers by opening London's eyes to the aggressiveness of Russian policy in the region. Grey hoped that the Germans would continue reining in the Austrians and thereby prevent Balkan regional conflicts from threatening European peace. But neither side was prepared to make any substantial change to their respective bloc strategies. The Anglo-German 'Balkan détente' worked in large part because it was so tightly focused on an area (the Balkan peninsula) where neither of the two states had fundamental interests at stake. It also depended on Austria and Russia's willingness not to go to war. It was a flimsy thing without substantive content that could survive only for as long as there was no serious threat to peace.

We might thus say that the potential for détente was circumscribed by the resilience of the alliance blocs. This is true enough, except insomuch as it implies that the alliance blocs were solid and immovable fixtures of the international system. But it is worth noting how fragile and flux-prone many of the key decision-makers felt the alliance system was. The Austrians intermittently feared that the Germans were on the point of settling their differences with Russia and leaving their Habsburg allies in the lurch, and there was some justification for this concern, for the evidence suggests that Germany's policy of restraint vis-à-vis Vienna over the period 1910–13 merely emboldened the Russians in the Balkans without yielding an offsetting security benefit.[27] Poincaré saw in the vacuous meeting at Baltic Port the ominous herald of a Russo-German partnership in the Balkans and on the Straits. In the spring of 1913, there was even irritation in Paris at the current 'flirtation' between the courts of St James and Berlin, King George V being suspected of seeking warmer relations with Germany.[28] For Sir George Buchanan, the British ambassador in St Petersburg, the slightest evidence of a thaw between Vienna and St Petersburg sufficed to conjure up the horrifying prospect that Russia would abandon the Entente and join forces with

Germany and Austria, as it had done in the days of the Three Emperors' Leagues of the 1870s and 1880s.

In the case of British relations with Russia, apprehension at the prospect of losing a powerful friend was underscored by the fear of gaining a powerful enemy. During the last three years before the outbreak of war, the old geopolitical tensions between Russia and Britain were coming back to the fore. There were problems all along the Sino-Central-Asian frontier, from Tibet and Outer Mongolia to Turkestan and Afghanistan, but the most urgent issue was Persia. By the summer of 1912, armed Russian penetration of northern Persia was raising questions about whether the Anglo-Russian Convention could be continued in its current form. As early as November 1911, Grey warned Count Benckendorff, the Russian ambassador in London, that he might soon be forced to issue public 'disavowals' of Russian activity in Persia and that Russia was placing the future of the Convention at risk.[29] And this was an issue that attracted interest not just in the Foreign Office, but in cabinet, parliament and the press. When Sazonov and Grey met at Balmoral in September 1912 for talks focused mainly on the Persian question, there were public demonstrations against the Russian minister. Fear for Britain's imperial future combined with the traditional Russophobia of the liberal movement and the British press to form a potent mix. And these concerns remained acute during 1913 and early 1914. In letters of February and March 1914 to Ambassador Buchanan in St Petersburg, Grey commented angrily on Russian plans to construct a strategic railway across Persia and all the way to the Indian frontier. The Russians had begun to push aside British trading interests in Persia, even within the zone allotted to Britain under the terms of the Convention. The situation along the Chinese frontier was hardly more encouraging: in 1912–13, dispatches from British agents reported that the Russians were fomenting 'unusual military activity' between Mongolia and Tibet; shipments of Russian rifles had been detected passing through Urga to Lhasa and Russian Buriat 'monks' were training the Tibetan army, just as the Russians pushed forward into Chinese Turkestan to establish fortified positions only 150 miles from the British garrison at Srinagar.[30] Russia, it appeared, was waiting for the next opportunity to invade India.[31]

These perceived threats produced fine cracks in the policy fabric of the Foreign Office. In Grey's eyes, the vexatious behaviour of the Russians enhanced the value of the Anglo-German Balkan détente. It was impossible not to be struck by how easily British and German diplomats were working together, just at the moment when Sazonov's opportunist Balkan zig-zagging was exasperating Russia's British partners. And Grey was supported in these reflections by his long-serving private secretary, William Tyrrell, the man who saw more of the foreign secretary than any other colleague. Tyrrell had earlier favoured 'the anti-German policy', but he later became 'a convinced advocate of an understanding'.[32] The attractiveness of this option was doubtless reinforced by the awareness that since Germany had lost the naval race, the chief threat posed by Berlin had 'lost its sting'.[33] The return to a more flexible policy promised both to mute the Russophobe arguments of the radical opposition and to spike the guns of the 'Grey-must-go' brigade, who saw in the foreign secretary's hostility to Berlin a needless threat to British independence and European peace.

But this option remained chimerical for as long as the risks of losing Russian allegiance did not seem to be offset by the benefits of closer collaboration with Germany. Until that tipping point was reached – and this did not appear imminent in 1913–14 – the argument for appeasing Russia and opposing Germany continued to carry great weight. Russia was a much more dangerous foe in 1913 than she had been in 1900, especially if one viewed it through the lenses of the British policy-makers who, like their French colleagues, subscribed to an extraordinarily exaggerated assessment of Russian power. Throughout the years between the Russo-Japanese War and the July Crisis of 1914, and despite much evidence to the contrary, British military attachés and experts presented what seems in retrospect an absurdly positive image of Russian military prowess.[34] In an entirely typical report filed in September 1909, General Sir Ian Hamilton, who as former military attaché to the Japanese forces in Manchuria had witnessed the Russian army in action, reported that immense improvements had been made during the interim. Thanks to an 'extraordinary advance' in 'fire and move' tactics, Russian troops could now be described as 'better fighters and keener soldiers than the Germans'. Since Hamilton had also attended German manoeuvres, his words were treated with respect.[35]

In the minds of some of the key policy-makers in London, the Russian threat still eclipsed that posed by Germany. 'What our people fear,' a senior Foreign Office functionary admitted at the beginning of December 1912, when the first Albanian crisis was at its height, 'is that

Germany will go to St Petersburg and propose holding Austria in, if Russia will leave the Entente. This is the real danger of the situation, not a conflict of the powers. We are sincerely afraid lest out of the hurly burly of the crisis Russia should emerge on the side of the [Triple] Alliance'.[36] In Nicolson's eyes, the security of Britain and its world empire still rested on the Anglo-Russian Convention, which he wished to see elaborated (along with the French entente) into a fully fledged alliance. It was 'far more disadvantageous to have an unfriendly France and Russia than an unfriendly Germany'.[37] 'It is absolutely essential to us to keep on the best terms with Russia,' he wrote in May 1914, 'as were we to have an unfriendly or even an indifferent Russia, we should find ourselves in great difficulties in certain localities where we are unfortunately not in a position to defend ourselves.'[38] Even the slightest gesture in the direction of a rapprochement with Berlin risked compromising London's reputation for reliability, and once this was gone, there was the danger that Russia would simply abandon Britain and revert to the role of imperial rival. Underlying Nicolson's view was the conviction – widely shared in London during the last pre-war years – that the awesome expansion of Russian economic power and military strength would soon place it in a position of relative independence, rendering Britain dispensable.

From this it followed that Russia's loyalty must be bought at virtually any price. Nicolson was appalled at the role played by Sazonov in sponsoring the Serbo-Bulgarian alliance against Turkey, and more generally by Russia's egging on of the Serbian government, but these were minor annoyances compared with the catastrophe of a Russian defection. British diplomats were thus in some respects more comfortable with a situation of managed tension in the Balkans than with the prospect of a return to the Austro-Russian condominium of the pre-1903 era, which would in turn have facilitated a return to the pre-1907 situation of open Anglo-Russian global rivalry, a scenario they felt even less well equipped to deal with in 1913 than they had been in the era of the Boer War.[39] In the summer of 1912, Nicolson even propagated the view that Russian expansion into the Balkan region was inevitable and should therefore not be opposed by Britain. 'The determination of Russia, now that she has got her finances in splendid order and reorganized her army,' he told the British ambassador in Vienna, 'is to reassert and re-establish her predominant position in the Balkans.'[40]

Détente interacted in complex ways with the mobile architecture of the alliance blocs. It could raise risk levels by muting the awareness of risk among key political actors. The Ambassadors' Conference in London, for which Grey took much of the credit, left him confident in his ability to solve crises and 'save peace', a confidence that would impede his ability to react in a timely fashion to the events of July 1914. Grey drew from the Anglo-German détente in the Balkans the lesson that Germany would continue restraining its Austrian ally, come what may. Jagow and Bethmann extracted the equally problematic insight that the eyes of London had at last been opened to the true character of Russian policy on the peninsula and that Britain would probably remain neutral if the Russians started a conflict in the region. Moreover, détente in one part of the European international system could also produce a hardening of commitments in another. Thus, for example, uncertainties about London – fuelled by Anglo-German collaboration in the Balkans – affected French relations with St Petersburg. 'The French government,' wrote the Belgian minister to Paris in April 1913, 'seeks to tighten more and more its alliance with Russia, for it is aware that the friendship of England is less and less solid and effective.'[41]

These reflections might seem to suggest that the pre-war European system had somehow locked itself into a position from which a war was the only way out. That would appear to be one possible deduction from the observation that even détente posed a danger to peace. But we should not forget how dynamic the system still was, or how open its future seemed to be. In the last months before the outbreak of war, it was gradually dawning on some of the most senior British policy-makers that the Convention with Russia over Persia might not survive its scheduled renewal in 1915.[42] Tyrrell's view in the spring of 1913 was that Britain should tolerate the misbehaviour of the Russians until the crisis in the Balkans subsided and then – in 1914 or 1915 perhaps? – get tough with them over Persia, Mongolia and China. A gap opened between Grey and Nicolson, who by 1914 was an increasingly isolated figure. Many senior Foreign Office colleagues viewed with deepening scepticism Nicolson's unconditional attachment to the Anglo-Russian Convention. Tyrrell and Grey – and other senior Foreign Office functionaries – were deeply annoyed by St Petersburg's failure to observe the terms of the agreement struck in 1907 and began to feel that an arrangement of some kind with Germany might serve as a useful corrective to

St Petersburg. By the spring of 1914, even Nicolson was getting the message: on 27 March 1914, he warned a colleague not to presume that the current constellation of powers would endure: 'I think it is extremely probable that before long we shall witness fresh developments and new groupings in the European political situation.'[43]

'NOW OR NEVER'

What did all of this mean for the Germans? In answering this question, it is helpful to emphasize the ambivalence of international developments in the last two years before the war. On the one hand, the post-Agadir period saw a waning of tension, especially between Germany and Britain, and signs that the continental alliance blocs might in time lose their functionality and cohesion. There was thus reason to believe that détente was not merely a temporary respite from mutual hostility, but a genuine potentiality of the international system. Viewed from this perspective, a general war was anything but inevitable.[44] On the other hand, the Agadir and Balkan crises produced a drastic stepping up of military preparedness and signs of a more aggressive Russian policy on the Balkan peninsula, backed by Paris. And the fear that the bonds of the Entente might be loosening produced in the short term a hardening of alliance commitments, a tendency reinforced by the ascendancy across Europe of relatively belligerent policy factions.

German policy reflected the incoherence and ambiguity of this larger picture. First, it is worth noting that the Germans were as impressed as everyone else by the spectacle of Russian economic growth and vitality. After his journey to Russia in the summer of 1912, Bethmann summarized his impressions for Jules Cambon in similar terms to Verneuil's account for Pichon nine months later:

> The Chancellor expressed a feeling of admiration and astonishment so profound that it affects his policy. The grandeur of the country, its extent, its agricultural wealth, as much as the vigour of the population, still bereft, he remarked, of any intellectualism. He compared the youth of Russia to that of America, and it seems to him that whereas [the youth] of Russia is saturated with futurity, America appears not to be adding any new element to the common patrimony of humanity.[45]

From the standpoint of the most influential German military command-ers, it seemed blindingly obvious that the geopolitical situation was shifting rapidly to Germany's disadvantage. Helmuth von Moltke, Schlieffen's successor (from January 1906) as chief of the General Staff adopted an unswervingly bleak and bellicose view of Germany's inter-national situation. His outlook can be reduced to two axiomatic assumptions. The first was that a war between the two alliance blocs was inevitable over the longer term. The second was that time was not on Germany's side. With each advancing year, Germany's prospective enemies, and Russia in particular with its swiftly expanding economy and virtually infinite manpower, would grow in military prowess until they enjoyed an unchallengeable superiority that would permit them to select the moment for a conflict to be fought and decided on their own terms.

There was a fundamental difference in kind between these two axi-oms. The first was an unverifiable psychological projection, born of Moltke's own paranoia and pessimism.[46] The second, by contrast, though it also incorporated a measure of paranoia, was at least justified

Helmuth von Moltke in 1914

by a comparative analysis of the relative military strengths of the European powers. Moltke's concern over the deepening imbalance between the two blocs and the steady deterioration in Germany's capacity to prevail in a future conflict steadily gained in plausibility after 1910, when the Russians initiated the first major cycle of rearmament in land weapons and forces.[47]

The next escalation in European war-readiness and armaments investment came in the wake of Agadir and the crisis triggered by the Balkan Wars. In November 1912, as the Russians stepped up their measures against Austria-Hungary and the French government cheered from the sidelines, the German government showed remarkable restraint – reservists were not called up, conscript classes were not retained, there was no trial mobilization.[48] But from mid-November, as the massive scale of the Russian military preparations became clear, the German command grew increasingly concerned. Especially alarming was the retention of the Russian senior conscript class, which sharply raised troop strengths along the German frontier in the Polish salient. And these concerns were nourished by intelligence from a range of sources and locations that the dominant view among the senior echelons of the Russian army was that conflict with Austria was inevitable and that 'the best time to strike was the present moment'.[49]

Unnerved by these auguries and by the troop movements on both sides of the Galician border and anxious to counter the impression that Germany was no longer interested in defending Austria-Hungary against regional threats, the German chancellor Theobald von Bethmann Hollweg delivered a ten-minute speech to the Reichstag on 2 December 1912. It was a redaction – in a more concise format and a more modest register – of Lloyd George's Mansion House speech of the previous year. The chancellor began by noting that Germany had to date 'used her influence in order to localise the war' and that 'hitherto it had in fact been localised' – an observation that brought cheers from the house. There followed a carefully worded warning:

> If – which I hope will not be the case – insoluble difficulties then appear, it will be the business of the Powers directly involved in the particular case to give effect to their claims. This applies to our allies. If in giving effect to their interests they, contrary to all expectation, are attacked from a third side, and so find their existence menaced, we, in loyalty to our duty as

allies, should have to take our stand firm and determined at their side. (Cheers from the Right and from the National Liberals.) In that case we should fight for the defence of our own position in Europe and for the protection of our own future and security. (Cheers on the Right.) I am convinced that in following such a policy we shall have the whole people behind us. (Cheers.)[50]

The Times, which published the text of the entire speech on the following day, found nothing 'new or sensational' in the chancellor's words. 'It has been perfectly clear,' the paper's Berlin correspondent wrote, 'that Germany is both desiring peace and ensuing [i.e. pursuing] it.'[51] Edward Grey saw the matter very differently. In a completely unexpected move, he summoned the German ambassador, Count Lichnowsky, to his office and informed him that in the event of a war between Germany and the Franco-Russian Alliance, Britain was likely to fight on the side of Germany's enemies. Lichnowsky's report of his conversation with Grey triggered panic in Berlin, or more precisely in the Kaiser, who, ever sensitive to signals from London, claimed to discern in Grey's warning a 'moral declaration of war'.[52] Deeply shaken, Wilhelm ordered Moltke, Tirpitz, Chief of the Admiralty Heeringen and Admiral Müller, Chief of the Naval Cabinet, to attend him at short notice for an emergency meeting in the Royal Palace at 11.00 a.m on Sunday 8 December. The meeting opened with belligerent bluster from the Kaiser: Austria must be firm in dealing with Serbia (whose troops were at this time still in Albania) and Germany must support her if Russia attacked. Should this occur, the Kaiser vociferated, Germany would throw the brunt of its army against France and use its submarines to torpedo British troop ships. Towards the end of the discussion that followed, he urged that the navy step up the pace of U-boat production, demanded that 'more should be done through the press to prepare the popularity of a war against Russia' and endorsed Staff Chief Hellmuth von Moltke's observation that 'war is unavoidable and the sooner the better'.[53]

Historians disagree about the significance of this 'war council', as it was ironically dubbed by Bethmann, who was not invited. Some have argued that the war council of December 1912 not only revealed the continuing centrality of the Kaiser to the decision-making process, but also set the scene for a comprehensive war-plan that involved placing the navy, the army, the German economy and German public opinion on a war footing in preparation for the unleashing of a premeditated conflict.[54] Others have seen the meeting as a reflex response to an international crisis, rejecting the notion that the German military and political leadership henceforth began the countdown to a pre-planned European war. Who is right? There is no doubting the belligerence of the military advice offered at the council, and it is clear that the Kaiser seemed willing for the moment to endorse the views of his most aggressive commanders. On the other hand, the meeting did not in fact trigger a countdown to preventive war. The only eyewitness report of the occasion that we possess, the diary of Admiral Müller, closes its comments on the council with the observation that its result amounted to 'almost 0'. No national propaganda campaign followed and no concerted effort was made to set the German economy on a wartime footing.[55] The key figure in the drama of 8 December was not Wilhelm, but Bethmann, who subsequently 'put the Kaiser in his place' and 'nullified' the decisions taken at the conference.[56] The war council of 8 December remained an episode: by the beginning of January, the sense of crisis in Berlin had dissipated and Wilhelm had regained his calm. Bethmann talked him out of plans for an expanded naval programme, the accelerated submarine building demanded by the Kaiser never took place, and when a new crisis broke out in the Balkans in April–May 1913 over the Serbo-Montenegrin occupation of the Albanian city of Scutari, it was apparent that Wilhelm still opposed any moves that would incur the risk of war.[57]

Far more significant than the meeting at the Neues Palais in December was the decision in the previous month to seek an unprecedented growth in German peacetime military strength. The roots of the army bill of 1913 lay in anxiety over Germany's deteriorating security position, compounded by alarm at Russia's handling of the Balkan crisis. In a detailed memorandum of December, Moltke made the case for an ambitious programme of expansion and improvement. Should a war break out, he argued, it appeared likely that Germany would face a conflict on two fronts against France and Russia, with little help from Austria and none from Italy. If, as appeared highly likely in the light of Grey's warning of 3 December, Britain too were to join the fray, the Germans would be able to field 192 fewer infantry battalions in the west than Britain, France and Belgium combined. And Russia was no longer a negligible quantity – its power was growing from year to year.[58] In presentations to secret sessions of the Reichstag Budget Commission during April, the generals painted a dark picture of German prospects; they saw little chance of a peaceful resolution of Germany's current encirclement and were downbeat about the German army's chances of success. The Russians would possess irreversible military superiority by 1916. The French already enjoyed superiority in strategic railways and mobilization and deployment times – whereas the Germans possessed thirteen through railway lines to the common border in 1913, France had sixteen, all of which were double-tracked, with junction lines to bypass loops, stations and intersections.[59]

After much haggling over details and finance, the new bill passed into law in July 1913. The peacetime army grew by 136,000 to 890,000 officers and men. Yet the new measures still failed to meet German security needs, because they triggered hikes in armaments expenditure in France and Russia that quickly offset German growth. During the first cycle of armaments expansion, it had been the Russians who had set the pace; now it was the Germans. The 1913 army law was crucial to the passage in France during August 1913 of the Three Year Law. And in Russia, the German army law (plus French goading) triggered the schedule of expansions and refurbishments known as the 'Great Programme'. In March 1913, massive sums were approved by the Tsar for artillery and other armaments in a vastly ambitious scheme that would by 1917 have increased Russian winter peacetime strength by 800,000 men, most of whom would (by contrast with the deployment plan of 1910) be concentrated in European Russia.[60] As a consequence, the peacetime strength of the Russian army in 1914 was double that of the German, at around one and a half million men and 300,000 more than the combined strengths of the German and Austro-Hungarian armies; by 1916–17, the Russian figure was expected to exceed 2 million.[61] And in 1914 these measures were complemented by the French-financed Russian strategic railways programme. Since 1905, Germany's answer to this predicament had been the Schlieffen Plan, which aimed to resolve the problem of a war on two fronts by first mounting a massive strike against France, accompanied by a holding operation in the east. Only when the situation on the western front had been resolved would Germany swing eastwards against Russia. But what if the balance of forces between the two alliance blocs shifted to the point where the Schlieffen Plan no longer made sense?

It has been pointed out that Germany was faster to implement its improvements than its two Entente opponents and that this furnished the German military leadership with a short-term strategic advantage in 1914.[62] And the economic foundations of Russia's military might remained fragile: between 1900 and 1913 Russian productive strength was actually decreasing in relation to Germany's.[63] But the outlook from Berlin's standpoint remained grim. In 1904, the combined strength of the Franco-Russian military had exceeded the Austro-German by 260,982. By 1914, the gap was estimated at around 1 million and it was widening fast. In a report dated 25 May 1914, the German military attaché in St Petersburg reported the latest enlargement of the recruit contingent (from 455,000 to 585,000) and calculated expected growth in peacetime strength over the next three to four years, concluding that 'The growth of the Russian army will thereby increase at a rate never before seen in the armed forces of any country.' Moltke viewed the Franco-Russian loan as 'one of the most sensitive strategic blows that France has dealt us since the war of 1870–71' and foresaw that it would bring about 'a decisive turning point to Germany's disadvantage'.[64] By 1916–17, German strategists believed, the striking power of Russia would be sufficient to nullify the calculations embodied in the Schlieffen Plan.[65]

Obsessed with the dangers looming from east and west and convinced that time was running out, Moltke became the eloquent exponent of a 'preventive war' that would enable the German Empire to resolve the coming conflict on terms advantageous to itself. He came to view each passing pre-war crisis as a failed opportunity to redress a deepening strategic imbalance that would soon place Germany at an irreversible disadvantage.[66] Preventive war thinking became widespread within the military command – a recent study has identified several dozen occasions on which senior commanders pressed for war 'sooner rather than later', even if this involved taking the initiative and accepting the opprobrium of the aggressor.[67] It was not just the Germans who saw the matter thus. Early in 1914, Poincaré remarked to the editor of *Le Matin* that the Germans feared the growth of Russia: 'They know that this great body gains each day in cohesion; they want to attack and destroy it before it has attained the plenitude of its power.'[68] In March 1914, when a summary of a dispatch outlining the improvements made to the Russian army since 1913 was sent to the British director of military operations, Major-General Henry Wilson, Wilson appended the following comment:

This is a most important despatch. It is easy to understand now why Germany is cautious about the future and why she may think that it is a case of 'now or never'.[69]

A vein of fatalism underlay the bellicism of the German military. When they spoke of war, the German military tended to speak less of victory than of the 'twin threats of defeat and annihilation'.[70] The danger inherent in such thinking, which allowed commanders to sanction even the most aggressive initiatives as essentially defensive, is clear enough. But to what extent did the preventive war arguments of the military shape German foreign policy? Even in a praetorian system like the Prusso-German one, much depended on the ability of the most senior commanders to persuade their civilian colleagues to adopt their strategic viewpoint. In this, they were not especially successful. Moltke pressed for war 'sooner rather than later' at the Neues Palais in December 1912, but although the Kaiser seemed briefly to endorse the staff chief's view, nothing came of it.

Paradoxically, the absence in Berlin of a collective decision-making organ like the Council of Ministers in St Petersburg made it more difficult for the militaries to build a political pressure group in support of their ideas, using military requisitions as a battering ram to smash through fiscal restraints. In Paris, the most powerful civilian and military officials worked closely together to achieve increased expenditure in support of a more offensively oriented strategy. In Germany, such deep institutional and constitutional barriers separated the military and civilian chains of command that this kind of synergy was far harder to achieve. There was no German equivalent of Krivoshein, and Chancellor Bethmann Hollweg was a more powerful and formidable figure than his Russian counterpart Vladimir Kokovtsov. After the Agadir crisis of 1911, Bethmann consistently pursued a policy focused on inconspicuous and pragmatic collaboration with Britain and Russia. 'Our most urgent task is a modus vivendi with England,' he declared in December 1911. 'We must keep France in check through a cautious policy towards Russia and England,' he wrote in March 1913. 'Naturally this does not please our chauvinists and is unpopular. But I see no alternative for Germany in the near future.'[71] Preventive war arguments thus never became the platform for policy in Germany before 1914 – they were rejected, like Conrad's even more vociferous demands in Vienna – by the civilian leadership. Neither in 1905 nor in 1908–9 or 1911 (when conditions were in fact much more favourable from the German standpoint than they would be in the summer of 1914) did the German government consider launching a preventive war. In the Agadir affair of 1911, it was the British, rather than the French or the Germans, who did most to militarize the crisis. And in the winter crisis of 1912–13, it was French rather than German policy that came close (though only intermittently) to embracing the notion of preventive war. Berlin was far more restrained in its advice to Vienna than Paris was in its communications with St Petersburg.

As for the Kaiser, though prone to outbursts of belligerent rhetoric, he panicked and counselled caution whenever a real conflict seemed likely, to the endless frustration of the generals. Wilhelm remained hopeful of a long-term accommodation with Britain. His remarks during 1913 suggest that he continued to regard an Anglo-German war as 'unthinkable'. He also remained confident that German military prowess would deter Russia from an armed intervention in a conflict between Austria and Serbia.[72] This complacency prompted the hawkish General Falkenhayn, soon to become minister of war, to observe in a letter of January 1913 that the deluded faith of the political leadership – including Wilhelm – in the possibility of a lasting peace left Moltke 'standing alone' in his 'struggle' with the Kaiser for a more aggressive foreign policy.[73] The Kaiser's refusal to embrace preventive war thinking became the *bête noire* of a growing 'military opposition'.[74] The primacy of the civilian over the military leadership remained intact.[75] Yet this does not mean that we should discount pro-pre-emption arguments as irrelevant to the actions of German or other policy-makers. On the contrary, preventive war logic exerted a stealthy but important pressure on the thinking of the key decision-makers during the crisis of summer 1914.

GERMANS ON THE BOSPHORUS

German policy-makers (other ones than those preoccupied with arming Germany for a future war on two fronts) also explored the possibilities of a future in which Germany would pursue its interests while avoiding the incalculable risks of war. An influential group of functionaries, including the state secretary of the Colonial Office Bernhard Dernburg,

Ambassador Paul Metternich in London and his colleague Richard von Kühlmann, later state secretary of the Foreign Office in Berlin, continued to press for a policy of détente and concessions vis-à-vis London. This line of thought found formal expression in the political tract *A German World Policy Without War!*, published anonymously in Berlin in 1913, but written by Richard Plehn, who had worked closely with Kühlmann in London.[76] And there were potential partners for such a policy in Whitehall, especially among members of the anti-Grey liberals, such as Colonial Secretary Lewis Harcourt.[77]

Despite the collapse of the Haldane mission, the quest for détente with Britain had yielded real fruits. A new round of negotiations over colonial questions opened in the summer of 1912; in April 1913, the two states signed an agreement on the African territories currently under the authority of the Portuguese Empire, whose financial collapse was expected imminently. The agreement was never ratified, because of differences between Berlin and London on when and how to publicize its contents, but it signalled a willingness in principle on both sides to demarcate spheres of interest and collaborate in excluding third parties from intervening.[78]

Given the very limited options available to Germany in the global imperial arena, and the relatively closed situation in the Europe of the alliance blocs, one region above all attracted the attention of statesmen interested in a 'world policy without war': the Ottoman Empire.[79] German policy had traditionally been rather restrained in this part of the world, where inter-imperial rivalries were especially fierce, but during the 1880s Berlin became more active. It was encouraged to do so by the government in Constantinople, which, alienated by the British occupation of Egypt (1882), actively courted partners in Berlin.[80] German banks, construction firms and railway companies began to move into the less developed areas of the Sultan's empire, acquiring concessions and spheres of interest. Work on a largely German-financed and -built Anatolian Railway began in 1888 to link Constantinople with Ankara and Konya; both lines were complete by 1896. Government support for these ventures, initially rather fitful, gradually became more pronounced and consistent. By 1911, it was possible for the German ambassador in Constantinople to speak of the Empire as a German 'political, military and economic sphere of interest'.[81] By investing in the Ottoman lands – especially in crucial infrastructural projects – the Germans hoped to stabilize the Ottoman Empire in the face of the threat posed to it by the other imperial powers, most importantly Russia. And should the collapse of the Ottoman Empire open the door to a territorial partition among the world empires, they wanted to be sure of a seat at the table where the spoils were divided.[82]

High hopes were invested in the Anatolian Railway. The Ottoman authorities in Constantinople intended to pacify and integrate the Anatolian 'wild east', still prey at this time to the depredations of Circassian bandits, and to civilize the most underdeveloped of the Ottoman lands. They viewed Anatolia through orientalist spectacles as a colony in need of improvement. New food crops were introduced in the areas opened up by the railway – including some, such as sugar beet and potatoes, that turned out to have been grown in the region for some time – and efforts were made to establish industrial plants, such as esparto grass, which could be processed to manufacture paper. Many of these projects made it no further than the experimental stage, either because the climate and soils were unsuitable, or because the locals refused to adopt the new techniques. For the inhabitants of rural Anatolia, some of whom brought bushels of grass to the stations to feed the horses that they had assumed would be pulling the trains, the appearance of steam locomotives was an unforgettable sensation.[83]

In Germany, too, the Anatolian venture had an inflaming effect on the colonial imagination. Some pan-Germans saw Anatolia (improbably enough) as a possible field for future German mass settlement; others were more interested in access to markets, trade routes and raw materials.[84] Railways (like hydroelectric dams in the 1930s–50s, or space travel in the 1960s) held a special place in the imperial imaginary at the turn of the twentieth century. In Britain and the Cape Colony plans were afoot to build a Cape to Cairo railway; at around the same time the French were planning a rival west–east African super-railway from Senegal to Djibouti. The history of the great global telegraph networks had already established the intimate connection between infrastructure and power, especially in those areas of the British Empire where telegraph stations were miniature outposts of imperial authority and discipline.

There was thus consternation in 1903 when it became known that a company owned by German banks had been entrusted by the Ottoman government with the construction of a gigantic railway line that would extend from the Ankara end of the Anatolian Railway via Adana and Aleppo across Mesopotamia to Baghdad and (ultimately) Basra on the Persian Gulf. The project, which in theory would one day make it possible to travel by train directly from Berlin to Baghdad, met with suspicion and obstruction from the other imperial powers. The British were concerned at the prospect of the Germans acquiring privileged access to the oil fields of Ottoman Iraq, whose importance was growing at a time when the British navy was planning the transition from coal- to oil-fired ships.[85] They feared that the Germans, freed through a land route to the east from the constraints imposed by British global naval dominance, might come to threaten Britain's pre-eminence in colonial trade. Although the route of the railway had been laid – at great inconvenience to the engineers and investors – as far as possible from Russian areas of interest, St Petersburg still feared that it would place the Germans in a position to pose a threat to Russian control of the Caucasus and northern Persia.

These projections of strategic anxiety appear far-fetched in retrospect, but they had a powerful hold on policy-makers at the time, who tended to assume that economic investment would inevitably be followed by geopolitical leverage. Kaiser Wilhelm II's intermittent pro-Ottoman and pro-Islamic political posturing did nothing to allay such suspicions. In 1898, during his second visit to the Middle East, Wilhelm had delivered an impromptu toast in the City Hall of Damascus that was cited in newspapers around the world: 'May His Majesty the Sultan and the 300 million Muslims living around the world who see in him their Caliph be assured that at all times the German Kaiser will be their friend.'[86] This effusion, the result of a euphoric mood brought on by the cheering of the Arab crowds, awakened fears of a Germany aligned with the forces of pan-Islamism and Arab nationalism that were already gaining ground in the British and Russian empires.[87]

In reality, German economic involvement was not disproportionate in international terms. There was intensive German investment in electrical utilities, agriculture, mining and municipal transportation; trade between Germany and the Ottoman Empire was on the increase. Yet the Germans still (in 1913) lagged behind Britain, France and Austria-Hungary in imports from, and behind Britain and Austria-Hungary in exports to, the Ottoman Empire. French investments still exceeded those of Germany by around 50 per cent. Nor could it be said that German capital behaved more aggressively than the European and British competition. In the race to secure strategic control of the prized oil concessions of Mesopotamia, for example, British banks and investors, backed by London, easily manoeuvred the Germans into positions of disadvantage with a combination of hard bargaining and ruthless financial diplomacy.[88] Even in the sphere of railway building, where more than half of all German investment was tied up (340 million gold francs), the French contribution was comparable in size (c. 320 million gold francs). While the French owned 62.9 per cent of the Ottoman Public Debt administered by an international agency on behalf of the Empire's creditors, Germany and Britain held roughly equal shares of most of the rest. And the most powerful financial institution in Constantinople, the Banque Impériale Ottomane, which in addition to controlling the lucrative tobacco monopoly and numerous other enterprises also possessed the exclusive right to issue bank notes in the Ottoman Empire, was a Franco-British enterprise, not a German one; it was also an instrument of French policy, in the sense that its credit and fiscal operations were steered from Paris.[89]

After long negotiations, a sequence of international accords did much to neutralize tension over the Baghdad Railway. A Franco-German agreement of 15 February 1914 marked out the boundaries between the spheres of interest of the key German and French investors (French capital was crucial to the financing of the project), and on 15 June, the Germans were able to overcome British objections by conceding, among many other things, British control of the crucial Basra–Persian Gulf section of the future railway – a concession that robbed the project of much of its supposed geostrategic value to the Germans. These and other episodes of collaboration, where political questions were laid aside in the interest of securing pragmatic arrangements in the economic sphere, gave reason to hope that the Ottoman Empire might indeed provide the theatre for a 'world policy without war' that would in time create the basis for a partnership of some kind with Britain.[90]

Much more serious than the wrangling over control of the Baghdad Railway was the crisis that broke in December 1913 over the arrival of a German military mission in Constantinople. After its disastrous campaigns in the Balkans, the Ottoman government looked desperately for foreign assistance in strengthening its armed forces through root-and-branch reform. Although the Ottoman military command did briefly consider inviting a French military mission, the Germans were the more obvious partners. German military advisers had been a fixture in Constantinople since the late 1880s and 90s, when 'Goltz Pasha' had run training courses for Turkish officer cadres.[91] But this mission was to be on a larger scale than earlier efforts. Its chief was to be assigned a command role (the refusal to cede such authority to the previous advisers was seen as a key reason for the failure of earlier efforts) and would be responsible for the entirety of Ottoman military education, including the training of the General Staff. He also possessed unlimited powers of military inspection and he would be accompanied by a phalanx of forty German officers on active service. Most importantly: as commanding general of the Ottoman 1st Army Corps, he was also to be responsible for the defence of the Straits and of Constantinople itself.[92] The man chosen to head up the mission was Lieutenant General Liman von Sanders, commander of the 22nd Division in Kassel.

Since neither the Kaiser nor Chancellor Bethmann Hollweg saw this mission as a fundamental departure from previous practice, and since the details were drawn up internally between the Ottoman and German military commands, it was not viewed as a matter for formal diplomatic negotiation with Russia. Instead, the Kaiser raised the question informally in May 1913 during a meeting with Nicholas II and George V on the occasion of the wedding of Princess Victoria Louise of Prussia and Prince Ernst August of Hanover. Neither sovereign raised any objections to the planned mission. No mention was made of it when Bethmann and Sazonov met for brief talks in November 1913, the chancellor assuming that Sazonov had been informed by the Tsar.[93] When news began to leak out about the details of Liman's assignment, however, there was a roar of protest from the Russian newspapers. Underlying the public outrage, which was encouraged by the Russian foreign ministry, was the apprehension that the mission would not only strengthen German influence in Constantinople, increasingly seen as a strategic choke-point of immense importance for Russia, but would renew the viability of the Ottoman Empire itself, whose collapse and partition were becoming an axiomatic element in Russian strategic thinking on the near and medium-term future.[94] The Russian military plenipotentiary in Berlin described Liman in a letter to the Tsar as a 'very energetic and self-aggrandising' character.[95] It did not help that the Kaiser, in a secret audience for the members of the mission, had urged its departing members to build him 'a strong army' that would 'obey my orders' and form a 'counterweight to the aggressive designs of Russia'. These words were passed back to St Petersburg by the Russian military attaché in Berlin, Bazarov.[96] Sazonov therefore saw in the German mission a matter of 'eminently political significance'.[97] There was consternation in St Petersburg – 'I have never seen them so excited,' Edward Grey confided to the German ambassador in London.[98]

Why did the Russians react so strongly to the Liman mission? We should recall that even during the crises of 1912–13, when Sazonov's policy had appeared to prioritize the Balkan peninsula over a bid for control of the Dardanelles, the Straits had remained at the centre of Russian strategic thinking. The importance of the Straits to Russian economic life had never been more obvious. In the years 1903–12, 37 per cent of Russian exports passed through the Dardanelles; the figure for wheat and rye exports, both vital to Russia's cash-hungry industrializing economy, was much higher, at around 75–80 per cent.[99] The urgency of this linkage was driven home by the two Balkan Wars. From the beginning of the conflict, Sazonov made numerous representations both to the belligerent states and to the allied great powers to the effect that a closure of the Straits to neutral commercial shipping would inflict 'enormous losses' on Russian exporters, and that measures must be avoided that might bring this about.[100] As it happened, the wars did cause two temporary closures of the Dardanelles, seriously disrupting Russian trade.

Disruptions were one thing, the permanent loss of influence in an area of crucial geopolitical interest was another, much more serious, concern. In the summer of 1911, Sukhomlinov had worried lest the Germans establish a foothold on the Bosphorus: 'Behind Turkey,' he warned, 'stands Germany.'[101] In November 1912, it was the Bulgarians who seemed close to seizing Constantinople. At that time, Sazonov had instructed Izvolsky to warn Poincaré that if the city were captured, the Russians would be obliged to deploy the entire Black Sea Fleet there immediately.[102] During the weeks that followed, Sazonov discussed with the General Staff and the Admiralty plans for a landing of Russian troops to protect Constantinople and project Russian interests. He rejected a British proposal to internationalize the Ottoman capital on the grounds that it was likely to dilute Russian influence in the region. New plans were drawn up to seize Constantinople and the entirety of the Straits by force.[103] In a paper prepared for Kokovtsov and the service chiefs on 12 November, Sazonov explained the advantages of a Russian seizure: it would secure one of the centres of world trade, the 'key to the Mediterranean Sea' and 'the basis for an unprecedented development of Russian power'. Russia, he argued, would be established 'in a global position that is the natural crown of her efforts and sacrifices over two centuries of our history'. In a revealing allusion to the importance of opinion, Sazonov concluded that an achievement of such grandeur would 'unite government and society' behind an issue of 'indisputable pan-national importance' and thereby 'bring healing to our internal life'.[104]

Russia had lost millions of roubles in trade during the recent disruption of the Straits, Sazonov pointed out to Nicholas II on 23 November 1912: 'Imagine what would happen if, instead of Turkey, the Straits were to go to a state which would be able to resist Russian demands'.[105] Anxieties on this score ensured that, throughout the summer and autumn of 1913 the Russian Black Sea naval command remained focused on the possibility of an imminent seizure of the Dardanelles. Russia, Captain A. V. Nemitz of the Naval General Staff declared, 'must be prepared to accomplish [the capture of the Straits] in the immediate future'.[106] Concerns about the growing strength of the Turkish fleet heightened the urgency of these proposals. The Turks had already ordered one dreadnought battleship, which was currently under construction in Britain, and two more were ordered in 1912–14, though none had arrived by the time war broke out. Nevertheless, the prospect of local Turkish superiority over Russian naval strength filled the navalists in St Petersburg with a foreboding that was in part no more than the inversion of their own imperial designs.[107]

The Russians – and Sazonov in particular, who was closely involved in all the relevant strategy discussions – were thus already highly sensitized to the question of control over the Straits when the Liman von Sanders mission arrived in Constantinople. What the foreign minister found particularly objectionable was the German command role. The Germans were at first reluctant to back down on this question, because the failure to assign real authority to previous generations of military advisers was seen (by both the Germans and the Ottomans) as the core reason for their failure to produce genuine reform. Experience suggested that the right to issue instructions was insufficient without the power to see that these were implemented. Sazonov was unimpressed and sought to step up pressure on Berlin. He proposed to London and Paris a joint note from the Entente powers objecting in the strongest terms to the mission and closing with the implicit threat that 'if Germany were to secure such a primacy in Constantinople, then the other powers would see themselves obliged to act in accordance with their own interests in Turkey'.[108]

This initiative was not a success, mainly because the Russians were alone in viewing the Liman von Sanders mission as a threat to their vital interests. Neither the French nor the British military attaché in Constantinople was especially alarmed at Liman's arrival. It made sense, they reported, for the Germans to insist on tighter controls after the failure of previous missions to achieve anything of lasting value. Grey pleaded that the urgency of the Irish Question and 'the difficult internal condition of the country' ruled out any direct British involvement in the issue.[109] In any case, the British were less concerned about German advances in Turkey than about the growing dominance of *French* capital. 'Turkey's independence is a vanishing quantity before the advances of the French financiers,' Sir Louis Mallet told Edward Grey in March 1914. In a furious speech to the House of Commons on 18 March, the Conservative MP Sir Mark Sykes, expert on Ottoman and Middle Eastern affairs, warned that the stranglehold of French finance in Ottoman Syria would ultimately 'pave the way to annexation'.[110]

Then there was the fact that there was already a British naval mission operating on the Bosphorus, the scope of which had been extended by the arrival in 1912 of Admiral Arthur Limpus, whose contract of employment stated that he was *'commandant de la flotte'*.[111] In addition to overseeing improvements to the training and supply of the Ottoman navy, Limpus coordinated the deployment of torpedo boats and the laying of mines in the Turkish Straits, one of the most important means by which access was denied to foreign warships.[112] Limpus understood his mission in a broad political sense – his correspondence with the Ottoman Admiralty covered not just questions of technical modernization, procurements and training, but also broader issues of strategic importance, such as the degree of naval strength required 'to make it hazardous for the Russians to move troops across the Black Sea'.[113] In other words, his presence in Constantinople served aims closely analogous to Liman's. Limpus viewed with sage equanimity the Anglo-German condominium over Ottoman sea- and land-based defence. 'England has the widest experience in naval matters and as regards shore establishments,' he told the Ottoman Admiralty in June 1912:

> Germany has the most powerful army and it is also believed to be the most efficient. I feel sure it has been most wise to get German advisers for everything connected with the army. I feel sure it will be most wise to obtain all advisers on naval matters from England.[114]

Sazonov therefore found it difficult to stir in his Entente partners the outrage felt in Russia at the arrival of the German mission. Grey rejected the threatening joint note proposed by Sazonov and suggested instead a much more innocuous *enquiry* to Constantinople as to the scope of the German mission. Notwithstanding Delcassé's vigorous nodding in St Petersburg,[115] the Quai d'Orsay was even less enthusiastic than the British Foreign Office, because it discerned in the language of Sazonov's menacing joint note the prospect of a comprehensive 'dissolution of Asiatic Turkey' with potentially disastrous consequences for French financial interests. Paris thus preferred to support Grey's more irenic proposal.[116] In other words: too many different forms of imperial ambition and paranoia were focused on the faltering Ottoman Empire to permit the Entente powers to rally together against one supposed threat.

Nevertheless: the Liman episode triggered a dangerous escalation of the mood among the key Russian policy-makers. Sazonov was furious at the lukewarmness of the British and French reactions to Russia's protests. In a telegram of 12 December 1913 to the Russian ambassador in London, he spoke bitterly of his declining trust in the effectiveness of British support, adding that the 'lack of solidarity between the powers of the Entente arouses our serious concern'.[117] In a report to the Tsar of 23 December, he adopted an openly militant position. He urged that 'joint military measures' should be prepared immediately and coordinated with France and Britain. The Entente powers should 'seize and occupy certain points in Asia Minor and declare that they would stay there until their aims were met'. Of course such a dramatic initiative risked triggering 'European complications', but it was more likely that a posture of 'firm resolve' would have the desired effect of forcing a German climbdown. Giving in, on the other hand, 'could have the most fatal consequences'. A summit conference should be convened to discuss the issues arising from the Liman affair.[118]

The conference, which opened on 13 January 1913, was chaired by Premier Vladimir Kokovtsov. Also present were Sazonov, Minister of War Sukhomlinov, Chief of Staff General Zhilinsky and Naval Minister Grigorovich. The meeting began with a discussion of the 'coercive measures' required to pressure Constantinople into withdrawing its request for the German military mission. The notion that economic sanctions could be used to apply pressure to the Ottoman government was dismissed – these would also hurt the very extensive French financial interests in the Ottoman Empire and strain the bonds of the Entente. An alternative was the armed seizure by Entente forces of key Ottoman strongpoints. The crucial precondition, Sazonov pointed out, was French support. Kokovtsov argued, as usual, against all this fighting talk, pointing out that war was simply too great a risk. Throughout the meeting he strove to impose a moderate and reasonable tone on the proceedings. Rather than acting in a spirit of pique with *ad hoc* reprisals, it was important, he suggested, to establish exactly the limits of what Russia would tolerate and what it would not. The Germans, Kokovtsov observed, were looking for a way of escaping 'from the situation created by the Russian demands' and had already expressed their readiness to make concessions. It was thus crucial to avoid 'categorical declarations of an ultimative character' that would force them to harden their own position.[119] But this time, the prime minister was challenged in chorus by Sukhomlinov, Sazonov, Grigorovich and Zhilinsky, who argued that the likelihood of a German armed intervention was minimal, and that, if the worst should come to the worst, war, though undesirable, was nonetheless acceptable. Minister of War Sukhomlinov and Chief of Staff Zhilinsky both categorically declared 'the full readiness of Russia for a one-to-one war with Germany, not to mention a one-to-one war with Austria'.[120]

These drastic scenarios became irrelevant, because the Germans quickly backed down and the crisis passed. Alarmed by the intensity of the Russian reaction and urged to conciliate by London and Paris, the Berlin government agreed to assign Liman to the Sultan's army: he remained inspector general, but his promotion to 'Field Marshal of the Ottoman Empire' meant that he could relinquish his command of the 1st Army Corps without loss of face.[121]

The Liman von Sanders affair never flared into a continental war, but it was, in retrospect, a revelatory moment. It showed, firstly, how belligerent the thinking of some of the Russian policy-makers had become. Sazonov in particular had moved from the vacillations of his early period in office towards a firmer and more Germanophobic stance – he had begun to construct a narrative of German-Russian relations that left no room for an understanding with Berlin: Russia had always been the docile, peace-loving neighbour and Germany the duplicitous predator, bullying and humiliating the Russians at every opportunity. Now the time had come to stand firm! The power of such narratives to shrink policy horizons should not be underestimated. And the repeated assurances from Paris had clearly left their mark: at the conference of 13 January Sazonov observed that, although it was unclear how the British would react to a war between Russia and Germany, it was certain that in the event of a war with Germany, the French would offer 'active assistance, even to the ultimate'. The French ambassador M. Delcassé, Sazonov reported, had recently assured him that 'France would go as far as Russia wished'. As for Britain, while there might be some hesitation in London at first, it was 'beyond doubt' that she would intervene as soon as the resulting conflict developed to the disadvantage of France and Russia.[122]

The Tsar too began to take a firmer view: in a conversation with Ambassador Buchanan at the beginning of April 1914, he observed that 'it was commonly supposed that there was nothing to keep Germany and Russia apart'. This, however, 'was not the case: there was the question of the Dardanelles', where the Tsar feared that the Germans were working to shut Russia into the Black Sea. Should Germany attempt such a thing, it was essential that the three powers of the Entente unite together more closely to make it clear to Berlin that 'all three would fight together against German aggression'.[123] For the Germans, on the other hand, the ferocity of the Russian reaction to the Liman mission coupled with bitterness over the German capitulation to Russian demands created the sense that an unbridgeable gulf now separated Berlin and St Petersburg. 'Russian–Prussian relations are dead for all time!' lamented the Kaiser. 'We have become enemies!'[124]

For the dovish Kokovtsov, the Liman von Sanders affair brought the final unravelling of his already enfeebled position. He had been in France negotiating the new railways loan when the crisis had broken. Sazonov asked him to go to Berlin to negotiate with the Germans. Kokovtsov's reports of those conversations reveal that he felt acutely the extent to which he had been sidelined. He had found it difficult, he commented in a thinly veiled complaint to Sazonov, to make his German interlocutors understand the 'peculiarities' of a Russian system that assigned such limited 'powers and prerogatives' to the chairman of the Council of Ministers.[125] Kokovtsov's chairmanship at the conference of 13 January was the last occasion on which he would play such a role. At the end of January 1914, he was dismissed by the Tsar both as chairman of the Council of Ministers and as minister of finance.

Kokovtsov's dismissal was a defeat not just for the man but for the policy and more generally for the cautious and conservative tendency in Russian politics that he represented. The new chairman of the Council of Ministers was Goremykin, who was widely viewed as a mere figurehead, 'an old man' as Sazonov later recalled, 'who had long ago lost not only his capacity for interesting himself in anything but his personal tranquillity and well-being, but also the power of being able to take into account the activities in progress around him'.[126] The real power-house on the new council was the exceptionally well-connected Krivoshein, who had been coordinating the campaign against Kokovtsov since 1913. Kokovtsov's replacement in finance, P. A. Bark, was a competent but undistinguished figure and a protégé of Krivoshein. Krivoshein was an enthusiastic supporter of the hard line pursued with increasing energy by Sukhomlinov and Sazonov. Without Kokovtsov as the exponent of caution, the balance of influence on the Council of Ministers shifted towards more militant solutions.

Finally, the Liman von Sanders crisis revealed how urgent the Russian preoccupation with the Straits had become.[127] At the same time, it raised troubling questions about how far the Entente partners still were from supporting a Russian bid for untrammelled access to the Straits. Sazonov's doubts on this score were reflected in the rather inconsequential conclusion to the conference of 13 January, in which it was agreed, on the one hand, that the Russians should launch, with Entente support, a sequence of increasingly coercive actions against Constantinople, and on the other, that if the Entente continued to *withhold* its support, the Russians should confine themselves to non-military measures of coercion. The Russians were right to be sceptical about Entente backing. Even after the crisis had passed, the British remained apprehensive at the prospect that Russia would 'raise the question [of the Turkish Straits] again in the not distant future'.[128]

Ivan Goremykin

It was difficult, in other words, to imagine a scenario in which the Russians would be able to secure the necessary international backing for a policy aimed directly and openly at securing control of the Straits. This was the problem Charykov had faced in November 1911, when he had explored the possibility of a bilateral deal with the Porte. At that time, Sazonov had opted to disavow his ambassador in Constantinople, because he believed a direct bid for the Straits was still premature. He had gravitated instead towards Hartwig, whose militant pan-Slavist policy was focused on the Balkan peninsula, and on Serbia in particular. The logic of that choice suggested that the failure or frustration of a Straits policy was likely to shift the emphasis back again to the Balkan salient. This was in some ways a default or residual option. But a forward policy in the Balkans did not by any means entail the abandonment of Russia's ultimate interest in the Straits. On the contrary, it represented a longer and more winding road to the same destination. Russian strategic thinking tended increasingly in 1912–14 to view the Balkans as the hinterland to the Straits, as the key to securing ultimate control of the Ottoman choke-point on the Bosphorus.[129] Underlying this conviction was the belief, increasingly central to Sazonov's thinking during the last years before the outbreak of war, that Russia's claim to the Straits would only ever be realized in the context of a general European war, a war that Russia would fight with the ultimate aim of securing control of the Bosphorus and the Dardanelles.[130]

These concerns were reflected in the protocols of the state Special Conference of 8 February 1914. Convened and chaired by Sazonov and marked by a distinctly post-Kokovtsovian disinhibition in tone and outlook, the conference reaffirmed the importance of Russian control of the Straits. And yet, as Sazonov acknowledged, it was hard to imagine how the Straits could be taken without triggering a 'general European war'. The discussion thus turned on how Russia should prioritize two quite different tasks: the seizure of the Dardanelles and the winning of a European war that would itself require the commitment of all available forces. Responding to Sazonov's remarks, Chief of Staff Zhilinsky noted that in the event of a European war, Russia would not be able to spare the troops required for a seizure of the Straits – these would be needed on Russia's western front. But – and this was the important conceptual step – if Russia prevailed in the war on the western front, the question of the Dardanelles would also solve itself, along with various other regional issues, as part of the larger conflict. Quartermaster-General Danilov agreed. He was against any military operation directed exclusively at securing the Straits:

> The war on the western front would demand the ultimate exertion of all forces of the state; we would not be able to dispense with even one Army Corps in order to keep it aside for other tasks. We must focus on securing success in the most important theatre of war. Victory in this theatre would entail advantageous decisions in all lesser questions.[131]

But this was not the only view taken at the conference. Captain Nemitz, head of the operations section of the Russian Admiralty, warned that the scenario envisaged by Sazonov, Zhilinsky and Danilov made sense only if the enemy threatening Constantinople happened to be the same as the one opposing Russia on the western front (i.e. Germany and/or Austria-Hungary). Then Russia could indeed focus exclusively on the primary conflict, in the assumption that the Straits would fall to her in due course. But in its striving for the Straits, Nemitz noted, Russia had other opponents than Germany and Austria. It was thus plausible, he observed in a veiled reference to Britain, that 'foreign fleets and armies' might occupy the Straits while Russia fought and bled on the German and Austrian fronts.[132] Nemitz had a point: the experience of recent years suggested that any Russian attempt to change unilaterally the regime in the Straits was likely to encounter the resistance of friends and foes alike.[133]

These reflections help in turn to explain why the Liman von Sanders crisis was such a crucial juncture in Russia's policy towards Britain.[134] Sazonov immediately began pressing for measures that would transform the Entente into a fully-fledged alliance, and he was the main protagonist behind the naval conversations with London that began on 7 June 1914. In his memoirs, Sazonov later recalled that the German military mission on the Bosphorus had 'forced' Russia to seek a 'concrete agreement' with Britain 'in consciousness of the shared danger' posed by Berlin – and this of course fits with our retrospective view, which is oriented towards the outbreak of war in 1914. But while there is no doubt that Sazonov dreamt of confronting and containing Germany with the 'greatest alliance known in human history',[135] it is also clear (though this was not a matter on which the foreign minister could afford to be forthcoming) that a naval agreement with England held the promise of *tethering* the world's greatest naval power and holding it back from unwelcome initiatives on the Straits. This inference is reinforced by the Russian protest formally submitted to London in May 1914 at the role British officers were playing in the development of the Turkish navy.[136] For Russia, as for Britain, this was still a world in which there was more than one potential enemy. Beneath the scaffolding of the alliances lurked older imperial rivalries.

THE BALKAN INCEPTION SCENARIO

In a letter of May 1913 to Hartwig whose contents were passed to Pašić, Sazonov sketched an overview of recent Balkan events and their significance for the kingdom. 'Serbia', he remarked, had completed only 'the first stage of its historical path':

> In order to reach its destination it must still undergo a terrible struggle, in which its entire existence is placed in question. [. . .] Serbia's promised land lies in the territory of today's Austria-Hungary and not in the direction in

which it currently strives, where the Bulgarians block its path. Under these circumstances it is in the vital interest of Serbia [. . .] to place itself through determined and patient work in a condition of readiness for the inescapable future struggle. Time is working for Serbia and for the downfall of her enemies, who already show clear signs of decomposition.[137]

What is interesting about this letter is not just the candour with which Sazonov deflected Serbian aggression away from Bulgaria in the direction of Austria-Hungary, but also his claim that in doing so he was merely acquiescing in the verdict of History, which had already decided that the days of the Habsburg polity were numbered. We often encounter such narratives of inevitable Austrian decline in the rhetoric of Entente statesmen, and it is worth noting how useful they were. They served to legitimate the armed struggle of the Serbs, who appeared in them as the heralds of a pre-ordained modernity destined to sweep away the obsolete structures of the dual monarchy. At the same time, they occluded the superabundant evidence that, whereas the Austro-Hungarian Empire was one of the centres of European cultural, administrative and industrial modernity, the Balkan states – and especially Serbia – were still locked in a spiral of economic backwardness and declining productivity. But the most important function of such master narratives was surely that they enabled decision-makers to hide, even from themselves, their responsibility for the outcomes of their actions. If the future was already mapped out, then politics no longer meant choosing among options, each of which implied a different future. The task was rather to align oneself with the impersonal, forward momentum of History.

By the spring of 1914, the Franco-Russian Alliance had constructed a geopolitical trigger along the Austro-Serbian frontier. They had tied the defence policy of three of the world's greatest powers to the uncertain fortunes of Europe's most violent and unstable region. For France, the commitment to the Serbian salient was a logical consequence of the commitment to the Franco-Russian Alliance, which was in itself the consequence of what French policy-makers saw as immovable policy constraints. The first of these was demographic. Even with the immense expansion made possible by the Three Year Law, the French army did not possess the numbers its commanders believed were necessary to counter the German threat alone. Success against the Germans would thus depend upon two things: the presence of a British expeditionary force on the Allied western front, and a rapid offensive through Belgium that would enable the French forces to circumvent the heavily fortified terrain of Alsace and Lorraine. Unfortunately, these two options were mutually exclusive, because breaching Belgian neutrality would mean forfeiting British support. Yet even forgoing the strategic advantages of an invasion of Belgium did not necessarily guarantee a British intervention in the first, decisive phase of the coming war, because the ambiguity of British policy had created a substantial margin of doubt.

France was thus obliged to seek a means of compensating in the east for its security deficits in the west. As the Belgian minister had put it in the spring of 1913, the less 'solid and effective' British friendship seemed, the more French strategists felt the need to 'tighten' the bonds of their alliance with Russia.[138] The French government focused from 1911 onwards on strengthening Russian offensive capacity and, in 1912–13 on ensuring that Russian deployment plans were directed against Germany rather than Austria, the ostensible opponent in the Balkans. Increasingly, intimate military relations were reinforced by the application of powerful financial incentives. This policy was purchased at a certain strategic cost, because betting so heavily on enabling Russia to seize the initiative against Germany inevitably involved a certain reduction in French autonomy. That French policy-makers were willing to accept the resulting constraints is demonstrated by their willingness to extend the terms of the Franco-Russian Alliance specifically in order to cover the Balkan inception scenario, a concession that in effect placed the initiative in Russian hands. The French were willing to accept this risk, because their primary concern was not that Russia would act precipitately, but rather that she would not act at all, would grow so preponderant as to lose interest in the security value of the alliance, or would focus her energies on defeating Austria rather than the 'principal adversary', Germany.

The Balkan inception scenario was attractive precisely because it seemed the most likely way of securing full Russian support for joint operations, not only because the Balkan region was an area of traditionally strong Russian interest, but because the conflict of the Serbs with Austria-Hungary was an issue that could be depended upon to stir Russian national feeling in a way that would leave the leaders with little option but to commit. Hence the importance of the vast French loans (at the time, among the largest in financial history), being tied to the programme of strategic railway construction that would throw the brunt of Russia's forces against Germany, thereby forcing Germany (so it was hoped) to divide its armies, reduce the weight of the assault on the west and provide France with the margin required to secure victory.

The Russian commitment to the Serbian salient was built of different stuff. The Russians had long pursued policies designed to secure a partnership of some kind with a league of Balkan states capable of forming a bulwark against Austria-Hungary. They revived this policy during the Italian war on Libya, brokering the creation of the Serbo-Bulgarian alliance that defined Russia as the arbitrating power on the peninsula. When the Second Balkan War broke out over the territorial spoils of the first, the Russians recognized that the League policy was now obsolete and chose, after some prevarication, to adopt Serbia as the principal client, to the detriment of Bulgaria, which quickly drifted into the financial and (later) political orbit of the central powers. The deepening commitment to Serbia tied Russia into a posture of direct confrontation with Austria-Hungary, as the events of December 1912–January 1913 had shown.

Yet the Russians were slow to embrace the strategic vision so insistently offered by the French General Staff. Sukhomlinov's Redeployment Plan of 1910 annoyed the French, because it had pulled the areas of concentration far back from Russia's western borders with Germany. Over the following years, the French worked hard and with success to overcome Russian resistance to a strategy focused on delivering the maximum strike power against the western frontier in the shortest possible time, by means of quadruple railway arteries designed to deliver massive forces against the enemy's heartland.

If Russian and French strategic thinking eventually fell to some extent into step, this was for several reasons. The promise of massive French loans offered a powerful incentive for collaboration. Since it was impossible to imagine that a Russian attack on Austria would not draw in Germany, it was increasingly clear that the breaking of Austrian power on the Balkan peninsula would be possible only if Russia were in a position to defeat Germany. Finally, and most importantly, the arrival of the Liman von Sanders mission in Constantinople prompted not just an escalation of Russian war-readiness and suspicion of German objectives, but also a clarification of how Balkan policy related to Russia's more fundamental interest in the Turkish Straits. As the Special Conference of 8 February made clear, Sazonov, Sukhomlinov and Zhilinsky had come to accept that the objective of securing access to or control of the Straits, though agreed to be of profound importance to Russia's economic and strategic future, would have to be subordinated to the task of prevailing in the European conflict against the central powers, not just or even primarily because of the fear that Germany might acquire a controlling interest in the Straits, but because the Entente powers were themselves as yet unready to support a direct Russian bid for this crucial strategic asset. Indeed, so diverse were the perspectives of the three Entente powers on the Straits that the Russian ministry of foreign affairs came to see a general war – which in effect meant a war begun in the Balkans – as the only context in which Russia could be sure of acting with the support of its western partners.[139]

We need to draw an important distinction: at no point did the French or the Russian strategists involved plan to launch a war of aggression against the central powers. We are dealing here with scenarios, not plans as such. But it is striking, nonetheless, how little thought the policy-makers gave to the effect that their actions were likely to have on Germany. French policy-makers were aware of the extent to which the balance of military threat had tilted against Germany – a French General Staff report of June 1914 noted with satisfaction that 'the military situation has altered to Germany's detriment', and British military assessments reported much the same. But since they viewed their own actions as entirely defensive and ascribed aggressive intentions solely to the enemy, the key policy-makers never took seriously the possibility that the measures they were themselves enacting might be narrowing the options available to Berlin. It was a striking example of what international relations theorists call the 'security dilemma', in which the steps taken by one state to enhance its security 'render the others more insecure and compel them to prepare for the worst'.[140]

Were the British aware of the risks posed by the Balkanization of Entente security policy? British policy-makers saw clearly enough that the drift in European geopolitics had created a mechanism that might, if triggered in the right way, transform a Balkan quarrel into a European war. And they viewed this possibility – as they viewed virtually every aspect of the European situation – with ambivalence. Even the most

Russophile British policy-makers were not uncritical of St Petersburg's Balkan policy: in March 1912, when he learned of the role of the Russians in brokering a Serbo-Bulgarian treaty, Arthur Nicolson deplored the latest Russian initiative, 'as it shows that the Russian government have no intention to work hand in hand with the Austrian government in Balkan affairs, and this, personally, I much regret'.[141] When he met with leading British statesmen in London and Balmoral in September 1912, Sazonov was struck by the 'exaggerated prudence' of British views on the Balkans and their suspicion of any Russian move that seemed calculated to apply pressure to the Ottoman government.[142] In November 1912, as the Serbian army pushed across Albania to the Adriatic coast, Viscount Bertie, the British ambassador in Paris, warned the French foreign minister that Britain would not go to war in order to secure an Adriatic seaport for Belgrade.[143]

Yet only a few days later, on 4 December, Edward Grey summoned the German ambassador Count Lichnowsky and issued a stark warning:

> If a European war were to arise through Austria's attacking Serbia, and Russia, compelled by public opinion, were to march into Galicia rather than again put up with a humiliation like that of 1909, thus forcing Germany to come to the aid of Austria, France would inevitably be drawn in *and no one could foretell what further developments might follow*.[144]

The pretext for this exchange, it should be recalled, was Chancellor Bethmann's ten-minute speech to the German parliament, in which he had warned that if, against all expectation, Austria were to be attacked by another great power (the reference was clearly to Russia, whose military measures along the Galician border had triggered the war scare), Germany would intervene to protect its ally. Lichnowsky read Grey's comment as a 'hint that cannot be misunderstood'; it meant that 'it was for England of vital necessity *to prevent [France] from being crushed by Germany*'.[145] Reading Lichnowsky's summary a few days later Wilhelm II panicked, seeing in it a 'moral declaration of war' against Germany. This was the warning that had triggered the Potsdam war council of 8 December 1912. And it is clear from the French documents that Grey subsequently – on the day of the warning itself – relayed the content of his conversation with Count Lichnowsky to Ambassador Paul Cambon, who in turn passed the details to Poincaré.[146]

What is remarkable about Grey's warning is how forcefully the causal linkages of the Balkan inception scenario were set out and how many assumptions were built into it. Grey aligned himself, firstly, with Sazonov's and Izvolsky's view of the 'humiliation' of 1909, seemingly forgetting that it was Britain's refusal to do business with Izvolsky over the Straits that had prompted the then Russian foreign minister to kick up the crisis by claiming that he had been duped by his Austrian colleague. The notion that Russia had suffered repeated humiliations at the hands of the central powers was dubious, to say the least – the truth was the contrary, namely that the Russians were lucky to have escaped so lightly from dangers of their own making.[147] Then there was the highly questionable notion that Russian decision-makers would have no choice but to attack Austria if a conflict between Austria and Serbia inflamed Russian domestic opinion. In fact it was not at all clear that Russian opinion demanded precipitate action over Serbia; some nationalist papers did, of course, but there were others, such as the conservative *Grazhdanin* of Prince Meshchersky, that denounced the 'impotent romanticism' of the Slavophiles and attacked the notion that Russia must inevitably take the side of Serbia in an Austro-Serbian conflict. In February 1913, at the height of the Balkan winter crisis, the former Russian prime minister Sergei Witte estimated that perhaps 10 per cent of the Russian population were in favour of war and 90 per cent against.[148] Equally remarkable was Grey's supposition that this intervention by Russia, though it would involve aggression against a state whose actions posed no direct threat to Russian security, must 'inevitably' bring in France – a point of view that essentially endorsed, or at least implicitly accepted, Poincaré's scaling up of the treaty commitment to cover the possibility of a Russian attack on another European great power. And this, Grey implied, would oblige Britain at some point to intervene on the side of France. Grey may have felt discomfort – he certainly expressed it intermittently – about the prospect of 'fighting for Serbia', but he had understood and legitimized the Balkan inception scenario and absorbed it into his thinking. And this scenario, it is important to remember, was not a neutral feature of the international system. It did not embody an impersonal necessity; rather, it was a fabric of partisan attitudes, commitments and threats. It revealed the extent to which Grey had forsaken a pure balance of power policy in favour of a policy oriented towards maximizing the security of the Entente.[149] In sketching the scenario for

Lichnowsky, Grey was not foretelling a preordained future, but himself articulating part of a set of understandings that made that future possible.

A crucial precondition for all these calculations was the refusal – whether explicit or implicit – to grant Austria-Hungary the right to defend its close-range interests in the manner of a European power. The French and British decision-makers were tantalizingly vague about the precise conditions under which an Austro-Serbian quarrel might arise. Poincaré made no effort to define criteria in his conversations with Izvolsky and the French minister of war and senior military command-ers pressed for aggressive action in the winter of 1912–13, although there had as yet been no Austrian assault on Serbia. Grey was a little more ambivalent and sought to differentiate: in a note to Bertie in Paris written on 4 December 1912, the same day as he had issued the warning to Lichnowsky, the British foreign minister suggested that British reac-tions to a Balkan conflict would depend upon 'how the war broke out':

> If Servia provoked Austria and gave her just cause of resentment, feeling would be different from what it would be if Austria was clearly aggressive.[150]

But what would constitute a 'just cause of resentment'? In an envir-onment as polarized as Europe in 1912–14, it was going to be difficult to agree what degree of provocation justified an armed response. And the reluctance to integrate Austro-Hungarian security imperatives into the calculation was further evidence of how indifferent the powers had become to the future integrity of the dual monarchy, either because they viewed it as the lapdog of Germany with no autonomous geopolitical identity, or because they suspected it of aggressive designs on the Balkan peninsula, or because they accepted the view that the monarchy had run out of time and must soon make way for younger and better successor states. One irony of this situation was that it made no difference whether the Habsburg foreign minister was a forceful character like Aehrenthal, or a more emollient figure like Berchtold: the former was suspected of aggression, the latter of subservience to Berlin.[151]

A supportive codicil to this death warrant for the Habsburg state was a rose-tinted view of Serbia as a nation of freedom-fighters to whom the future had already been vouchsafed. We can discern this ten-dency not just where we would most expect it, in Hartwig's enthusiastic reporting from Belgrade, but in the warmly supportive dispatches filed by Descos, the French minister stationed in the Serbian capital. The long-standing policy of French financial assistance continued. In January 1914, another large French loan (amounting to twice the entire Serbian state budget for 1912) arrived to cover Belgrade's immense military expenditures, and Pašić negotiated with St Petersburg a military aid package comprising 120,000 rifles, twenty-four howitzers, thirty-six cannon 'of the newest system' and appropriate munitions, claiming – falsely, as it happens – that Austria-Hungary was delivering similar goods to Bulgaria.[152]

Grey adopted a latently pro-Serbian policy in the negotiations at the London Conference of 1913, favouring Belgrade's claims over those of the new Albanian state, not because he supported the Great Serbian cause as such, but because he viewed the appeasement of Serbia as a key to the durability of the Entente.[153] The resulting borders left over half of the Albanian population outside the newly created Kingdom of Albania. Many of those who fell under Serb rule suffered persecution, deportation, mistreatment and massacres.[154] Yet the British acting minister Crackanthorpe, who had many good friends in the Serbian political elite, at first suppressed and then downplayed the news of atrocities in the newly conquered areas. When the evidence of misdeeds mounted up, there were intermittent internal expressions of disgust, but nothing strong enough to modify a policy oriented towards keeping the Russians on side.

Two further factors heightened the sensitivity of the Balkan trigger. The first was Austria's growing determination to check Serbian territorial ambitions. We have seen that as the situation on the Balkan peninsula deteriorated, the decision-makers in Vienna gravitated towards more hawkish solutions. The mood continued to fluctuate as crises came and went, but there was a cumulative effect: at each point, more of the key policy-makers aligned themselves with aggressive positions. And the jumpiness of the politicians was reinforced by financial and domestic morale factors. As the money ran out for further peacetime mobilizations and anxieties grew about their effects on minority nationality recruits, Austria-Hungary's repertoire of options narrowed, its political outlook became less elastic. Yet we should not forget that the last pre-war strategic overview of the region by an Austrian functionary, the gloomy Matscheko memorandum prepared for Berchtold in June 1914, made no mention of military action as a means of resolving the many problems Austria faced on the peninsula.

Finally, there was the deepening German dependency on a 'policy of strength'. The habit of seeking autonomy and security through the maximization of strength was a deeply established feature of German policy from Bismarck to Bülow to Bethmann Hollweg. That the pursuit of strength might antagonize Germany's neighbours and alienate potential alliance partners was a problem successive policy-makers failed to address. But as long as the policy continued to generate sufficient deterrent effect to exclude the possibility of a combined assault by the opposing camp, the threat of isolation, though serious, was not overwhelming. By 1912, the massive scaling up of Entente military preparedness undermined the longer-term feasibility of this approach.

Two questions preoccupied German strategists and policy-makers in the last years before the outbreak of war. The first, discussed above, was about how long Germany could be expected to remain in a position of sufficient relative strength to fight off its adversaries, should a war arise. The second preoccupation concerned Russian intentions. Was the Russia leadership actively preparing for a preventive war against Germany? The two questions were interlocked, because if one concluded that Russia really was *looking for a war* with Germany, then the arguments for avoiding one now by means of politically costly concessions appeared much weaker. If there was no question of avoiding war, but only of postponing it, then it made sense to accept the war offered by the antagonist now, rather than wait for a later reiteration of the same scenario under much less advantageous circumstances. These thoughts weighed heavily on the German decision-makers during the crisis that followed the assassinations at Sarajevo.

A CRISIS OF MASCULINITY?

If we survey the European chancelleries in the spring and early summer of 1914, it is impossible not to be struck by the unfortunate configuration of personalities. From Castelnau and Joffre to Zhilinsky, Conrad von Hötzendorf, Wilson and Moltke, the senior military men were all exponents of the strategic offensive who wielded a fluctuating but important influence on the political decision-makers. In 1913–14 first

Delcassé, then Paléologue, both hardliners, represented France in St Petersburg; Izvolsky, still determined to avenge the 'humiliation' of 1909, officiated in Paris. The French minister in Sofia, André Panafieu, observed in December 1912 that Izvolsky was the 'best ambassador in Paris', because he had 'personal interests against Germany and Austria', and his Russian colleagues noticed that whenever he came to speak of Austrian policy vis-à-vis Belgrade his voice took on 'a palpable tone of bitterness which had not left him since the times of the annexation'.[155] The excitable Austrophobe Miroslav Spalajković was now at the Serbian ministry in St Petersburg – his old enemy Count Forgách was helping to formulate policy in Vienna. One is reminded of a Harold Pinter play where the characters know each other very well and like each other very little.

This was a play with only male characters – how important was that? Masculinity is and was a broad category that encompassed many forms of behaviour; the manliness of these particular men was inflected by identities of class, ethnicity and profession. Yet it is striking how often the key protagonists appealed to pointedly masculine modes of comportment and how closely these were interwoven with their understanding of policy. 'I sincerely trust we shall keep our backs very stiff in this matter,' Arthur Nicolson wrote to his friend Charles Hardinge, recommending that London reject any appeals for rapprochement from Berlin.[156] It was essential, the German ambassador in Paris, Wilhelm von Schoen wrote in March 1912, that the Berlin government maintain a posture of 'completely cool calmness' in its relations with France and approach 'with cold blood' the tasks of national defence imposed by the international situation.[157] When Bertie spoke of the danger that the Germans would 'push us into the water and steal our clothes', he metaphorized the international system as a rural playground thronging with male adolescents. Sazonov praised the 'uprightness' of Poincaré's character and 'the unshakable firmness of his will';[158] Paul Cambon saw in him the 'stiffness' of the professional jurist, while the allure of the reserved and self-reliant 'outdoorsman' was central to Grey's identity as a public man. To have shrunk from supporting Austria-Hungary during the crisis of 1914, Bethmann commented in his memoirs, would have been an act of 'self-castration'.[159]

Such invocations of *fin-de-siècle* manliness are so ubiquitous in the correspondence and memoranda of these years that it is difficult to localize their impact. Yet they surely reflect a very particular moment in the history of European masculinity. Historians of gender have suggested that around the last decades of the nineteenth and the first of the twentieth century, a relatively expansive form of patriarchal identity centred on the satisfaction of appetites (food, sex, commodities) made way for something slimmer, harder and more abstinent. At the same time, competition from subordinate and marginalized masculinities – proletarian and non-white, for example – accentuated the expression of 'true masculinity' within the elites. Among specifically military leadership groups, stamina, toughness, duty and unstinting service gradually displaced an older emphasis on elevated social origin, now perceived as effeminate.[160] 'To be masculine [. . .] as masculine as possible [. . .] is the true distinction in [men's] eyes,' wrote the Viennese feminist and freethinker Rosa Mayreder in 1905. 'They are insensitive to the brutality of defeat or the sheer wrongness of an act if it only coincides with the traditional canon of masculinity.'[161]

Yet these increasingly hypertrophic forms of masculinity existed in tension with ideals of obedience, courtesy, cultural refinement and charity that were still viewed as markers of the 'gentleman'.[162] Perhaps we can ascribe the signs of role strain and exhaustion we observe in many of the key decision-makers – mood swings, obsessiveness, 'nerve strain', vacillation, psychosomatic illness and escapism, to name just a few – to an accentuation of gender roles that had begun to impose intolerable burdens on some men. Conrad von Hötzendorf combined the brittle persona of a belligerent martinet with a deep need for the support of women, in whose company the immobile mask of command fell away revealing an insatiable ego in dire need of comfort and psychological reinforcement. His mother Barbara lived with or near Conrad until she died in 1915. He filled the vacancy by finally marrying the now divorced Gina von Reininghaus and drafting her into the Austro-Hungarian headquarters in Teschen – much to the astonishment of his colleagues and of Viennese society.[163]

Another interesting case is the French envoy in Belgrade, Léon Descos. A Russian colleague who knew Descos well reported that the 'deep moral blow' of the two Balkan wars had damaged his 'nervous system'. 'He started to become more solitary [. . .] and from time to time he would repeat his favourite ditty on the inviolability of peace.'[164] During the Balkan wars, Berchtold complained constantly to his diary of nightmares, sleepless nights and headaches.[165] When the new French prime minister René Viviani, a man of fundamentally pacific temperament, travelled to St Petersburg for the summit talks of July 1914, he came close to suffering a complete nervous collapse. Hartwig, too, was under strain. Alexander Savinsky, the Russian minister in Sofia, believed that Hartwig had 'lost his balance' during the Balkan Wars; Hartwig, Savinsky observed, 'sees enemies everywhere that he has created himself'. By the early summer of 1914, Hartwig was constantly complaining about the poor state of his heart and longing for his summer break and cure in Bad Nauheim. He would not outlive the July Crisis.[166] The nervousness that many saw as the signature of this era manifested itself in these powerful men not just in anxiety, but also in an obsessive desire to triumph over the 'weakness' of one's own will, to be a 'person of courage', as Walther Rathenau put it in 1904, rather than a 'person of fear'.[167] However one situates the characters in this story within the broader contours of gender history, it seems clear that a code of behaviour founded in a preference for unyielding forcefulness over the suppleness, tactical flexibility and wiliness exemplified by an earlier generation of statesmen (Bismarck, Cavour, Salisbury) was likely to accentuate the potential for conflict.

HOW OPEN WAS THE FUTURE?

In his *System of Subjective Public Laws*, published in 1892, the Austrian public lawyer Georg Jellinek analysed what he called 'the normative power of the factual'. By this he meant the tendency among human beings to assign normative authority to actually existing states of affairs. Human beings do this, he argued, because their perceptions of states of affairs are shaped by the forces exerted by those states of affairs. Trapped in this hermeneutic circularity, humans tend to gravitate quickly from the observation of what exists to the presumption that an existing state of affairs is normal and thus must embody a certain ethical necessity. When upheavals or disruptions occur, they quickly adapt to the new circumstances, assigning to them the same normative quality they had perceived in the prior order of things.[168]

Something broadly analogous happens when we contemplate historical events, especially catastrophic ones like the First World War. Once they occur, they impose on us (or seem to do so) a sense of their necessity. This is a process that unfolds at many levels. We see it in the letters, speeches and memoirs of the key protagonists, who are quick to emphasize that there was no alternative to the path taken, that the war was 'inevitable' and thus beyond the power of anyone to prevent. These narratives of inevitability take many different forms – they may merely attribute responsibility to other states or actors, they may ascribe to the system itself a propensity to generate war, independently of the will of individual actors, or they may appeal to the impersonal forces of History or Fate.

The quest for the causes of the war, which for nearly a century has dominated the literature on this conflict, reinforces that tendency: causes trawled from the length and breadth of Europe's pre-war decades are piled like weights on the scale until it tilts from probability to inevitability. Contingency, choice and agency are squeezed out of the field of vision. This is partly a problem of perspective. When we look back from our remote vantage point in the early twenty-first century at the twists and turns of European international relations before 1914, we cannot help but view them through the lens of what followed. The events assemble themselves into something resembling Diderot's characterization of a well-composed picture: 'a whole contained under a single point of view'.[169] It would be perverse, of course, in attempting to correct for this problem, to fetishize contingency or inadvertancy. Among other things, this would merely replace the problem of over-determination with one of under-determination – of a war without causes. Important as it is to understand that this war might easily not have happened and why, this insight has to be balanced with an appreciation of how and why it did in fact happen.

A striking feature of the interactions between the European executives was the persistent uncertainty in all quarters about the intentions of friends and potential foes alike. The flux of power across factions and office-holders remained a problem, as did worries about the possible impact of popular opinion. Would Grey prevail against his opponents in cabinet and parliament? Would Poincaré stay in control of the French ministry? Military voices had recently been setting the tone in strategic debates in Vienna, but in the wake of the Redl Affair, Conrad's power appeared to be in decline, his dismissal was already on the cards. On the other hand, the hawks were in the ascendancy in St Petersburg. These domestically induced uncertainties were compounded by the difficulty of reading power relations within foreign political executives. British observers believed (wrongly, as we know in retrospect) that dovish conservatives like Kokovtsov (despite his recent dismissal) and Pyotr Durnovo had strengthened their influence over the Tsar and were about to make a comeback. There was anxious talk in Paris about the imminent victory of a pro-German faction led by the former premier Sergei Witte. Then there was the perennial nervousness about the susceptibility of key decision-makers to trends in public opinion. In a report filed from Berlin on the last day of February 1914, the Russian military plenipotentiary, Major-General Ilya Leonidovich Tatishchev, a friend of the German Kaiser, conceded that although he had noted high levels of hostility to Russia in the German press, he was unable to judge how this might influence Wilhelm II: 'I believe in general, however, that His Majesty's love of peace is unshakable. But perhaps it is getting weaker in his entourage.' Two weeks later, however, he sounded the all-clear, noting that the latest Russo-German press feud appeared to have left no impression whatsoever on the German sovereign.[170] Beneath all the paranoia and aggression was a fundamental uncertainty about how to read the mood and intentions of the other chancelleries, let alone how to anticipate their reactions to as yet unrealized eventualities.

The future was still open – just. For all the hardening of the fronts in both of Europe's armed camps, there were signs that the moment for a major confrontation might be passing. The Anglo-Russian alliance was under serious strain – it looked unlikely to survive the scheduled date for renewal in 1915. And there were even signs of a change of heart among the British policy-makers, who had recently been sampling the fruits of détente with Germany in the Balkans. It is far from obvious or certain that Poincaré could have sustained his security policy over the longer term. There were even tentative signs of an improvement in relations between Vienna and Belgrade, as agreements were sought and found on the exchange of political prisoners and the settlement of the Eastern Railway question. Above all, none of the European great powers was at this point contemplating launching a war of aggression against its neighbours. They feared such an initiative on each other's part, and as the military preparedness of the Entente soared, there was talk among the military in Vienna and Berlin of a pre-emptive strike to break the deadlock, but pre-emptive war had not become policy. Nor had Vienna resolved to invade Serbia unprovoked – an act that would have amounted to geopolitical suicide. The system still needed to be ignited from outside itself, by means of the trigger that the Russians and French had established on the Austro-Serbian frontier. Had Pašić's Serbian government pursued a policy aimed at domestic consolidation and nipped in the bud the irredentist movement that posed as great a threat to its own authority as it did to the peace of Europe, the boys might never have crossed the river Drina, a more clear-cut warning might have been given in good time to Vienna, the shots might never have been fired. The interlocking commitments that produced the catastrophic outcome of 1914 were not long-term features of the European system, but the consequence of numerous short-term adjustments that were themselves evidence of how swiftly relations among the powers were evolving.

And had the trigger not been pulled, the future that became history in 1914 would have made way for a different future, one in which, conceivably, the Triple Entente might not have survived the resolution of the Balkan crisis and the Anglo-German détente might have hardened into something more substantial. Paradoxically, the plausibility of the second future helped to heighten the probability of the first – it was precisely in order to avoid abandonment by Russia and to secure the fullest possible measure of support that France stepped up the pressure on St Petersburg. Had the fabric of the alliances seemed more dependable and enduring, the key decision-makers might have felt less under pressure to act as they did. Conversely the moments of détente that were so characteristic of the last years before the war had a paradoxical impact: by making a continental war *appear* to recede to the horizons of probability, they encouraged key decision-makers to underrate the risks attending their interventions. This is one reason why the danger of a conflict between the great alliance blocs appeared to be receding, just as the chain of events that would ultimately drag Europe into war got underway.

PART III

Crisis

7

Murder in Sarajevo

THE ASSASSINATION

On the morning of Sunday 28 June 1914, Archduke Franz Ferdinand, heir apparent to the Austro-Hungarian throne, and his wife Sophie Chotek von Chotkowa and Wognin arrived by train in the city of Sarajevo and boarded a motorcar for the ride down the Appel Quay to the City Hall. There were six vehicles in the motorcade. In the leading car were the mayor of Sarajevo, Fehim Effendi Čurčić, dressed in a fez and a dark suit, and the Sarajevo police commissioner, Dr Edmund Gerde. Sitting behind them in the second car, a splendid Graef und Stift sports coupé with the roof rolled back so the passengers could be seen by the crowds of well-wishers lining the streets, were the archduke and his wife. Opposite them on the folding seat sat General Oskar Potiorek, governor of Bosnia. Sitting in the passenger seat at the front beside the driver was Lieutenant-Colonel Count Franz von Harrach. Behind them followed three further cars carrying local policemen and members of the archduke's and the governor's suites.

A picturesque view unfolded before the couple as the motorcade swung on to the Appel Quay, a broad boulevard that runs along the embankment of the river Miljačka through the centre of Sarajevo. On either side of the river, which gushes from a gorge just above the town to the east, steep hills rise to a height of over 5,000 feet. The hillsides were dotted with villas and houses standing in orchards. Further up were the cemeteries with their glowing spots of white marble, crowned by dark firs and buffs of naked rock. The minarets of numerous mosques could be seen rising from among the trees and buildings along the river, a reminder of the city's Ottoman past. At the heart of the town just to

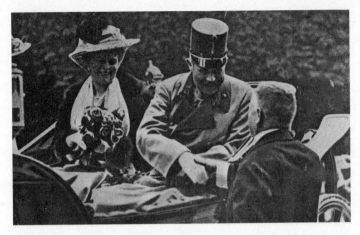

Franz Ferdinand and Sophie in Sarajevo, 28 June

the left of the Appel Quay was the bazaar, a labyrinth of lanes lined with shaded wooden booths backing on to warehouses of solid stone. Carpet traders, greengrocers, saddlers, coppersmiths, dealers in every craft, worked their trades here, each in their allotted quarter. A small house at the centre of the bazaar dispensed coffee free of charge to the poor at the expense of the *waqf*, an Ottoman charitable foundation. The previous day had been cool and rainy, but on the morning of 28 June the city was bathed in hot sunshine.

The Austrians had chosen an unlucky date for the visit. On this day, St Vitus's Day, in the year 1389, Ottoman forces had destroyed a Serb-led army on the Field of Blackbirds (Kosovo), putting an end to the era of Serb empire in the Balkans and creating the preconditions for the later integration of what remained of Serbia into the Ottoman Empire. The commemorations across the Serb lands were set to be especially intense in 1914, because this was the first St Vitus's Day since the 'liberation' of Kosovo during the Second Balkan War in the previous year. 'The holy flame of Kosovo, which has inspired generations [of Serbs] has now burst forth into a mighty fire,' the Black Hand journal *Pijemont* announced on 28 June 1914. 'Kosovo is free! Kosovo is avenged!'[1] For Serb ultra-nationalists, both in Serbia itself and across the Serbian irredentist network in Bosnia, the arrival of the heir apparent in Sarajevo on this of all days was a symbolic affront that demanded a response.

Seven terrorists organized in two cells gathered in the city during the days preceding the visit. On the morning of the archduke's arrival, they positioned themselves at intervals along the Quay. Strapped around their waists were bombs no bigger than cakes of soap with detonator caps and twelve-second chemical fuses. In their pockets were loaded revolvers. The surplus of weapons and manpower was essential to the success of the undertaking. If one man were searched and arrested or simply failed to act, another stood by to take his place. Each carried a paper packet of cyanide powder so that he could take his own life when the deed was done.

Official security precautions were conspicuous by their absence. Despite warnings that a terrorist outrage was likely, the archduke and his wife travelled in an open car along a crowded and entirely predictable route. The espalier of troops who usually lined the kerbs on such occasions was nowhere to be seen, so that the motorcade passed virtually unprotected in front of the dense crowds. Even the special security detail was missing – its chief had mistakenly climbed into one of the cars with three local Bosnian officers, leaving the rest of his men behind at the railway station.[2]

The archducal couple were strikingly unconcerned about their own safety. Franz Ferdinand had spent the last three days with his wife in the little resort town of Ilidze, where he and Sophie had seen nothing but friendly faces. There had even been time for an impromptu shopping visit to the Sarajevo bazaar, where they had walked unmolested in the narrow crowded streets. What they could not know was that Gavril Princip, the young Bosnian Serb who would shoot them dead just three days later, was also in the bazaar shadowing their movements. At a dinner in Ilidze on the last night before they took the train to Sarajevo, Sophie happened to meet the Bosnian Croat leader Dr Josip Sunarić, who had warned the local authorities against bringing the couple to Bosnia at a time of heightened national emotion for the local Serbs. 'Dear Dr Sunarić,' she told him, 'you are wrong after all [...]. Everywhere we have gone here, we have been treated with so much friendliness – and by every last Serb too – with so much cordiality and unsimulated warmth that we are very happy about it!'[3] Franz Ferdinand was in any case known for his impatience with security procedures and wanted this last part of his Bosnian journey to have a distinctly relaxed and civilian flavour. He had spent the past few days playing the role of inspector general at the army manoeuvres in the nearby Bosnian hills; now he wished to go among his future subjects as the heir to the Habsburg throne.

Most important of all: Sunday 28 June was Franz Ferdinand's and Sophie's wedding anniversary. Despite the many obstacles thrown in their path by Habsburg court etiquette, the archduke and his wife had since their marriage established an extremely contented family life. Marrying 'my Soph' was the most intelligent thing he had done in his life, Franz Ferdinand confided to a friend in 1904. She was his 'entire happiness' and their children were his 'whole delight and pride'. 'I sit with them and admire them the whole day because I love them so.'[4] There is no reason to believe that the warmth of this relationship – unusual in the context of dynastic marriages in this era – had in any way diminished by the time they came to visit Sarajevo. Sophie had insisted that she be allowed to remain at Franz Ferdinand's side during the anniversary day and there was doubtless a special pleasure in the fact that in this attractive and exotic outpost of the Austro-Hungarian Empire, they could officiate together in a way that was often impossible in Vienna.

The cars rolled past houses and shops decked with Habsburg black-and-yellow and Bosnian red-and-yellow banners, towards the Sarajevan Muhamed Mehmedbašić, who had taken up a position by the Ćumurija Bridge. As the cheers rose from around him he prepared to prime and throw his bomb. It was a tense moment, because once the percussion cap on the bomb was cracked – an action that itself generates a loud report – there was no going back, the bomb would have to be thrown. Mehmedbašić managed to free his bomb from its swaddling, but at the last moment he thought he sensed someone – a policeman perhaps – stepping up behind him and was paralysed by terror, just as he had been when he aborted the mission to kill Oskar Potiorek on the train in January 1914. The cars rolled on. The next assassin in line, and the first to go into action, was the Bosnian Serb Nedeljko Čabrinović, who had placed himself on the river side of the Quay. He freed his bomb and broke the detonator against a lamppost. Hearing the sharp bang of the percussion cap, the archduke's bodyguard, Count Harrach, assumed that a tyre had blown out, but the driver saw the bomb flying through the air towards the car and stepped on the accelerator. Whether the archduke himself saw the bomb and managed to bat it away with his hand, or whether it simply bounced off the folded fabric of the roof at the back of the passenger compartment, is not clear. At any rate, it missed, fell to the ground and exploded beneath the car behind, wounding several of the officers inside and gouging a hole in the road.

The archduke responded to this mishap with astonishing sang-froid. Looking back, he could see that the third vehicle had ground to a halt. The air was thick with dust and smoke and still ringing with the force of the explosion. A splinter had cut Sophie's cheek, but otherwise the couple were unharmed. The passengers in the third car were wounded but alive; some were attempting to dismount. The most seriously injured was General Potiorek's adjutant, Colonel Erik von Merizzi, who, though conscious, was bleeding heavily from a head wound. A number of bystanders had also been hurt.

As soon as Čabrinović had thrown his bomb, he ingested the cyanide powder he was carrying and threw himself over the parapet into the Miljačka. Neither of these actions had the intended result. The poison was of inferior quality, so that it seared the young man's throat and stomach lining, but did not kill him or even knock him out. And the river was too low in the summer heat to drown him or carry him away. Instead he merely fell twenty-six feet to the exposed sand at the side of the riverbed, where he was quickly captured by a shopkeeper, a barber armed with a handgun and two police officers.

Instead of leaving the danger zone immediately, the archduke saw to the treatment of the wounded and then ordered that the cavalcade should continue to the Town Hall in the centre of the city and then pass back along the Appel Quay, so that he and his wife could visit the wounded in hospital. 'Come on,' he said. 'That fellow is clearly insane; let us proceed with our programme.' The motorcade lurched back into motion, with the rearmost drivers picking their way around the smoking wreck of the fourth car. The remaining assassins, still waiting at their posts, were thus given every opportunity to complete their task. But they were young and inexperienced; three of them lost their nerve when the car and its passengers came within close range. Vaso Čubrilović, the youngest of the terrorists, froze like Mehmedbašić at the last moment – apparently because he was put off by the unexpected sight of the archduke's wife beside him in the imperial car. 'I did not pull out the revolver because I saw that the Duchess was there,' he later recalled; 'I felt sorry for her.'[5] Cvijetko Popović, too, was undone by fear. He remained at his station ready to throw his device, but was unable to do so because he 'lost [his] courage at the last moment when [he] caught sight of the archduke'.[6] When he heard the report of Čabrinović's bomb, Popović sprinted to the building of the Prosvjeta, a Serb cultural society, and hid his own bomb behind a box in the basement.

Gavrilo Princip was at first caught off guard. Hearing the explosion, he assumed that the plot had already succeeded. He ran towards Čabrinović's position, only to see him being borne away by his captors, bent over in agony as the poison burned his throat. 'I immediately saw that he had not succeeded and that he had not been able to poison himself. I intended to shoot him quickly with my revolver. At this moment the cars drove by.'[7] Princip abandoned the plan to kill his accomplice and turned his attention to the motorcade, but by the time he could see the archduke – unmistakable in his helmet adorned with brilliant green ostrich feathers – the car was moving too fast for him to get a clear shot. Princip stayed calm, an extraordinary feat under the circumstances. Realizing that the couple would soon be returning, he took up a new position on the right side of Franz Joseph Street, along the publicly advertised route by which the motorcade was to leave the city. Trifko Grabež had left his post to look for Princip, and had been caught up in the heaving of the crowd after the first explosion. When the motorcade passed him, he too failed to act, probably from fear, though he later claimed that the crowd had been so thick that he was unable to extract his bomb from under his clothes.

At first, it seemed the archduke was right to have insisted on continuing the programme. The motorcade reached its destination in front of the Sarajevo Town Hall without further incident. There followed a tragicomic interlude. It fell to the mayor, Fehim Effendi Čurčić, to deliver the usual speech of welcome to the august visitors. From his vantage point at the front of the motorcade, Čurčić knew that the day had already gone very wrong and that his innocuous text was now grossly inadequate to the situation, but he was far too nervous to improvise an alternative or even to modify his words so as to take account of what had just happened. In a state of high agitation and perspiring heavily, he stepped forward to deliver his speech, which included such gems as the following: 'All of the citizens of the capital city of Sarajevo find that their souls are filled with happiness, and they most enthusiastically greet Your Highness's most illustrious visit with the most cordial of welcomes . . .' Hardly had he got underway, but he was interrupted by a furious expectoration from the archduke, whose rage and shock, pent up since the attack, now burst forth. 'I come here as your guest and you people greet me with bombs!' In the horrified silence that followed, Sophie could be seen whispering into her husband's ear. Franz Ferdinand regained his calm: 'Very well. You may speak.'[8] Once the mayor had struggled through to the end of his address, there was another pause when it was discovered that the sheets bearing the text of Franz Ferdinand's own prepared reply were wet with the blood of the injured officer in the third car.[9] Franz Ferdinand gave a graceful address, in which he made tactful mention of the morning's events: 'I thank you cordially, Mr Mayor, for the resounding ovations with which the population has received me and my wife, the more so as I see in them an expression of pleasure over the failure of the assassination attempt.'[10] There were some closing remarks in Serbo-Croat, in which the archduke asked the mayor to convey his best regards to the people of the city.

After the speeches, it was time for the couple to separate. Sophie was scheduled to meet with a delegation of Muslim women in a room on the first floor of the City Hall. Men were barred from the chamber so that the women could remove their veils. The room was warm and close and the Duchess appeared sombre and preoccupied with thoughts of her children – seeing a little girl who had accompanied her mother to the gathering, she said: 'You see this girl is just about as tall as my Sophie.' At another point she declared that she and her husband were looking forward to rejoining their children – 'we have never left our children alone for so long.'[11] In the meanwhile, the archduke had dictated a telegram to the Emperor assuring him that both of them were well and was being shown the vestibule of the City Hall. The shock of the morning's events seemed to be catching up with him. He was speaking in a 'funny, thin voice', a local eyewitness later recalled. 'He was standing quite grotesquely, he was lifting his legs high as if he were doing the goosestep.

I suppose he was trying to show he was not afraid.'[12] There was some taunting of Potiorek, whose security arrangements had so manifestly failed.

How should the visit now proceed? The original plan had been to drive a short distance back down the Quay and then turn right just after the bazaar into Franz Joseph Street to the National Museum. The archduke asked Potiorek whether he thought a further attack was likely. According to his own testimony, Potiorek made the disheartening reply that he 'hoped not, but that even with every possible security measure, one could not prevent such an undertaking launched from close quarters'.[13] To be on the safe side, Potiorek proposed cancelling the rest of the programme and driving straight out of the city back to Ilidze, or alternatively to the governor's residential palace, the Konak, and from there to the Bistrik railway station on the left bank of the river. But the archduke wanted to visit Potiorek's wounded adjutant, now recovering in the garrison hospital on the western outskirts of the city. It was agreed that the tour of the museum should be cancelled, and that the motorcade should proceed straight back down the Appel Quay rather than up Franz Joseph Street, as any further prospective assassin would presumably be expecting. The original plan had foreseen that the couple would separate at this point, the archduke proceeding to the museum and his wife to the governor's palace. But Sophie took the initiative and announced to her husband in front of the entire retinue: 'I will go with you to the hospital.'[14] For good measure, Count Harrach decided to stand on the running-board on the leftward side of the car (towards the river), in case there should be a further attack.

The motorcade rolled back through the city in the gathering heat, westwards now, away from the City Hall. But no one had informed the drivers of the changed itinerary. As they passed the bazaar district, the lead vehicle swung to the right into Franz Joseph Street and the car carrying Franz Ferdinand and Sophie made to follow suit. Potiorek upbraided the driver: 'This is the wrong way! We are supposed to take the Appel Quay!' The engine was disengaged and the car (which had no reverse gear) pushed slowly back on to the main thoroughfare.

This was Gavrilo Princip's moment. He had positioned himself in front of a shop on the right side of Franz Joseph Street and he caught up with the car as it slowed almost to a stop. Unable to disentangle in time the bomb tied to his waist, he drew his revolver instead and fired twice from point-blank range, while Harrach, standing on the running board, looked on in horror from the left. Time – as we know from Princip's later testimony – seemed to slow as he left the shade of the shop awnings to take aim. The sight of the Duchess gave him momentary pause: 'as I saw that a lady was sitting next to him, I reflected for a moment whether to shoot or not. At the same time, I was filled with a peculiar feeling . . .'[15] Potiorek's recollection conveys a similar sense of unreality – the governor remembered sitting stock still in the car, gazing into the face of the killer as the shots were fired, but seeing no smoke or muzzle flash and hearing only muted shots, that seemed to come from far away.[16] At first it appeared the shooter had missed his mark, because Franz Ferdinand and his wife remained motionless and upright in their seats. In reality, they were both already dying. The first bullet had passed through the door of the car into the Duchess's abdomen, severing the stomach artery; the second had hit the archduke in the neck, tearing the jugular vein. As the car roared away across the river towards the Konak, Sophie teetered sideways until her face was between her husband's knees. Potiorek initially thought she had fainted with shock; only when he saw blood issuing from the archduke's mouth did he realize something more serious was afoot. Still straddling the running-board and leaning into the passenger compartment, Count Harrach managed to hold the archduke upright by clutching his collar. He heard Franz Ferdinand speaking in a soft voice words that would become famous throughout the monarchy: 'Sophie, Sophie, don't die, stay alive for our children!'[17] The plumed helmet, with the green ostrich feathers, slipped from his head. When Harrach asked him if he was in pain, the archduke repeated several times in a whisper 'It's nothing!' and then lost consciousness.

Behind the retreating vehicle, the crowd closed in around Gavrilo Princip. The revolver was knocked from his hands as he raised it to his temple to take his own life. So was the packet of cyanide he endeavoured without success to swallow. He was punched, kicked and beaten with walking sticks by the surrounding mob; he would have been lynched on the spot if police officers had not managed to drag him off into custody.

Sophie was already dead by the time they reached the Konak palace and the couple were rushed into two rooms on the first floor. Franz Ferdinand was comatose. His valet, Count Morsey, who had run all the way from the scene of the shooting to rejoin the archduke, tried to ease his breathing by cutting his uniform open at the front. Blood splashed up, staining the yellow cuffs of the valet's uniform. Kneeling beside the bed, Morsey asked Franz Ferdinand if he had a message for his children, but there was no reply; the archduke's lips were already stiffening. It was a matter of minutes before those present agreed that the heir apparent was dead. The time was just after 11 a.m. As the news fanned out from the palace, bells began to toll across Sarajevo.

FLASHBULB MOMENTS

The assassination first announced itself to Stefan Zweig as a disruption in the rhythm of existence. On the afternoon of 28 June he was holidaying in Baden, a little spa town near Vienna. Finding a quiet place away from the crowds in the Kurpark, he settled down with a book, an essay on Tolstoy and Dostoyevsky by the St Petersburg Symbolist Dmitrii Sergeyevich Merezhkovsky. He was soon deeply immersed in his reading,

> but the wind in the trees, the twittering of the birds and the music floating across from the park were at the same time part of my consciousness. I could clearly hear the melodies without being distracted, for the ear is so adaptable that a continuous noise, a roaring street, a rushing stream are quickly assimilated into one's awareness; only an unexpected pause in the rhythm makes us prick our ears. [. . .] Suddenly the music stopped in the middle of a bar. I didn't know what piece they had played. I just sensed that the music had suddenly stopped. Instinctively, I looked up from my book. The crowd, too, which was strolling through the trees in a single flowing mass, seemed to change; it, too, paused abruptly in its motion to and fro. Something must have happened.[18]

The Sarajevo murders, like the murder of President John F. Kennedy at Dallas in 1963, were an event whose hot light captured the people and places of a moment and burned them into memory. People recalled exactly where they were and whom they were with when the news reached them.[19] The Viennese freethinker and feminist Rosa Mayreder happened to be travelling in Germany with her husband Karl, a chronic depressive, when they saw the news of the murders posted up in the window of a Dresden department store across the street from their hotel bedroom.[20] Half a century after the event, Prince Alfons Clary-Aldringen remembered stalking roebuck in a Bohemian forest with his Kinski relatives. At dusk, as the hunters gathered on the road at the edge of the wood, the cook from the Kinski estate arrived on a bicycle bearing a message from the local postmaster.[21] For the parliamentarian Joseph Redlich, it was the telephone that brought the shocking news; the rest of his afternoon was spent in a hectic sequence of calls to friends, relatives and political associates. The dramatist Arthur Schnitzler, who had dreamt only four weeks before that the Jesuit order had commissioned him to murder the archduke, also learned of the murders by telephone.[22]

Joint Finance Minister Leon Biliński felt the shock of the news even before it had arrived. On the morning of 28 June, he was at home in Vienna reading the *Neue Freie Presse*. The horses were waiting in front of his house to take him to eleven o'clock mass. His eye happened to fall on an article outlining the arrangements for the archduke's visit to Bosnia.

Leon Biliński

To this day, I remember exactly the sensation of genuine physical pain that I felt while reading the details of this journey [into Sarajevo]. But not being aware of any rational cause for this pain, I had to persuade myself that I had no reason to be resentful of the Archduke on account of this festivity. A few moments later the telephone rang.[23]

The news seemed so horrific, the Russian ambassador in Vienna reported, that many at first refused to believe it. Only in the evening, when extra editions of the papers appeared and the first mourning flags were seen on public buildings, did the truth sink in. 'The residents of the capital gathered on the streets, discussing the terrible event deep into the night'.[24] Within twenty-four hours, the news was everywhere, even in the fictional Prague guest-house where Mr Švejk, Czech *idiot savant* and accredited trader in mongrel dogs, sat rubbing embrocation into his rheumatic knee. In the imagined world of Jaroslav Hašek's picaresque post-war masterpiece *The Good Soldier Švejk*, it is the news of the arch-duke's death – delivered by the charwoman Mrs Müller – that nudges the narrative into motion by eliciting from the hero a guileless political monologue (the first of many) that lands him in gaol on charges of sedition and then in a lunatic asylum on suspicion of imbecility.

'They bumped him off at Sarajevo, sir, with a revolver, you know. He drove there in a car with his Archduchess.'

'Well, there you have it, Mrs Müller, in a car. Yes, of course, a gentleman like him can afford it, but he never imagines that a drive like that might finish up badly. And at Sarajevo into the bargain! That's in Bosnia, Mrs Müller. I expect the Turks did it. You know, we never ought to have taken Bosnia and Herzegovina from them.'[25]

The news from Sarajevo would echo for years in the literary imagin-ation of the vanished Empire, from the ominous clamour of telephones in Karl Kraus's *Last Days of Mankind*, to Joseph Roth's Lieutenant Trotta von Sipolje, who received the ill tidings as 'the enactment of something he had often dreamed'.[26]

Assessing the contemporary impact of the archduke's assassination on his Austro-Hungarian contemporaries is difficult. The 'most out-standing feature' of Franz Ferdinand's public persona, one expert has written, 'was his pronounced unpopularity at all levels of public life'.[27]

Franz Ferdinand was no crowd-pleaser. He was uncharismatic, irritable, prone to sudden outbursts of anger. The pudgy, immobile features were unendearing to those who had never seen how his face could come to life, lit up by intensely blue eyes, in the company of his family or his closest friends. Contemporaries remarked on a constant craving for respect and affirmation. He was appalled by the slightest hint of insubordination. On the other hand, he hated grovellers, so he was difficult to please. He was, as his political ally and admirer Count Ottokar Czernin observed, 'a good hater' who never forgot an ill turn. So fearsome were his rages that ministers and senior officials 'rarely waited on him without beating hearts'.[28] He had few truly close friends. Distrust was the dominant emotion in his dealings with other people: 'I take everyone I meet for the first time to be a common scoundrel,' he once remarked, 'and only gradually allow myself to be persuaded to the contrary.'[29] His obsession with the hunt, which was extreme even by contemporary standards, occasioned much negative comment, especially in the valleys around his hunting lodge Schloss Blühnbach – in order to protect the local game reserves from any risk of disease, Franz Ferdinand sealed off the estate around the castle, to the fury of middle-class alpinists, who were denied access to the popular local trails, and of the local peasants, who could no longer pasture their goats in the mountains above their villages.[30] In a diary entry written on the day of the assassinations, the dramatist Arthur Schnitzler noted how quickly the 'first shock' of the murders had worn off, tempered by recollections of the archduke's 'appalling unpopularity'.[31]

There was thus no outpouring of collective grief when the news of the assassinations became known. This helps to explain why the assassinations have always been named for the place where they occurred, rather than for the victims. (By contrast, no one refers to the murder of John F. Kennedy as the 'Dallas Assassination'.[32]) Historians have sometimes inferred from the unpopularity of the archduke that his murder was not in itself an important trigger of events, but at best a pretext for decisions whose roots lay in a more remote past. But this conclusion is misleading. First there is the fact that, whether he was popular or not, the energy and reforming zeal of the heir to the throne were widely acknowledged. Franz Ferdinand, the Austrian minister in Constantinople told his Serbian colleague, was a man of 'rare dynamism and strong will' who was utterly dedicated to affairs of state and would have wielded great influence.[33] He was the man who had gathered around him all 'those who understood that only a complete change of course in the sphere of domestic policy' could safeguard the continued existence of the empire.[34] Moreover, it was not just the extinction of the person Franz Ferdinand that mattered, it was the blow to what he stood for: the future of the dynasty, of the empire and the 'Habsburg State Idea' that unified it.

Franz Ferdinand's reputation was in any case transfigured by the manner of his death, a process accomplished above all, and with incredible speed, by the print media. Within twenty-four hours of the assassination, most of the familiar Sarajevo narrative was in place, from Čabrinović's abortive bomb-throw and subsequent leap into the river Miljačka to the archduke's stoical refusal to call off the tour after the first bomb, his solicitude for the injured in the fourth car, his intemperate exchange with Mayor Čurčić, the fateful wrong turn at Franz Joseph Street, and even the last words of the dying archduke to his unconscious wife.[35] Newspaper coverage generated an overpowering sense of occasion. The thick stripes of mourning black on the front pages found an echo in the black flags and pennants that transformed the streets and buildings of the monarchy's cities – even the trams were decked out in black. Leader-writers dwelt on the energy and political foresight of the deceased archduke, the violent termination of a loving marriage, the grief of three orphaned children, the resigned dismay of an elderly emperor who had already suffered more than his fair share of bereavements.

For the first time, moreover, the private person and domestic life of the archduke were exposed to public view. One characteristic passage from the *Reichspost* of 30 June cited the archduke on the subject of his family: 'When I return to the circle of my family after a long and burdensome day of work, and see my wife at her sewing amongst my playing children, I leave all my cares behind the door and can scarcely absorb all the happiness that surrounds me.'[36] These authentic snippets reported by close associates of the dead man broke open the barrier that had separated the private individual from the rebarbative public persona, generating emotions that were no less real for the fact that they were media-induced. As Karl Kraus put it just two weeks after the murders, what had remained silent in Franz Ferdinand's life became eloquent in his death.[37]

Nevertheless, the meaning of the assassination was for most people essentially political rather than sentimental. Leader writers quickly built up a sense of the event's epochal significance. The *Neue Freie Presse*, journal of the educated Viennese bourgeoisie, spoke of a 'stroke of destiny' (the term '*Schicksalsschlag*' can be found all over the press in the days following the assassination).[38] When the 'horrific event [...] became known', the editors declared, 'it was as if a storm were sweeping through the monarchy, as if History had inscribed the hideous axiom of a new epoch with a blood-red pen'. The *Innsbrucker Nachrichten* wrote of 'a unique event in the history of Austria'. With the death of the archduke, the editors of the *Reichspost* observed, the monarchy had lost not merely its prospective sovereign, but a uniquely energetic and determined public figure, 'upon whom the peoples of the Habsburg Empire had hung all their hopes, all their future'.[39] These were Austrian voices, of course. The picture was rather different in Budapest, where many greeted with a sense of furtive relief the news that the nemesis of Magyardom had perished. But even here, the bourgeois press framed the event as a world-historical moment and fulminated against the suspected authors of the outrage.[40] Only the most introverted natures can have failed altogether to register the concentration and darkening of the public mood. The case of Franz Kafka in Prague, whose diary passed over the political events of that day in silence to dwell instead on a chronicle of purely private misfortunes – getting lost en route to an assignation, catching the wrong streetcar and missing a telephone call – was exceptional.[41]

THE INVESTIGATION BEGINS

The judicial inquiry into the assassination began as soon as Princip fired his shots. Within hours of the event, Gavril Princip, sick from the half-swallowed cyanide and covered in bruises and cuts from his near-lynching on Franz Joseph Street, faced Leo Pfeffer of Sarajevo, an Austrian judge. 'The young assassin,' Pfeffer later recalled, 'was undersized, emaciated, sallow, sharp-featured. It was difficult to imagine that so frail-looking an individual could have committed such a serious crime.' At first Princip seemed unable to speak, but when Pfeffer addressed him directly, he answered 'with perfect clarity in a voice that

The assassins in court

grew steadily stronger and more assured'.[42] Over the following days he made heroic efforts to prevent the Austrians from reconstructing the background to the crime. In his first interrogation on the afternoon of 28 June, he claimed that he had been acting entirely on his own and denied any link whatsoever with Čabrinović. 'When I heard the explosion [of the bomb thrown by Čabrinović],' Princip declared, 'I said to myself: here is someone who feels as I do.' On the following day, he added a further detail to bolster the authenticity of his account: he had been so taken aback by the noise of Čabrinović's explosion that he had forgotten to shoot at the archduke as he passed down the Appel Quay and was forced to find a new position from which to launch his attack. Čabrinović at first confirmed this view of the matter. On the afternoon of the assassination, he too claimed that he had acted without accomplices, using a bomb acquired from an 'anarchist' in Belgrade whose name he could not remember.

On the following morning, Monday 29 June, however, Čabrinović suddenly changed his story. He now admitted that he and Princip were accomplices who had planned the crime together in Belgrade. The weapons had come from 'former partisans' in the city, men who had fought in the Balkan Wars and kept their weapons after demobilization. Pressed to identify these 'partisans' Čabrinović named the railway orderly Ciganović, the lowest link in Apis's chain of command. When Princip was confronted with these details on Monday morning, he too admitted that the two were co-conspirators.

It is conceivable that the investigation might have come to a standstill at this point. The two young men had agreed on a plausible and self-contained story. Pfeffer was not an especially aggressive or searching interrogator. There was no physical intimidation of the prisoners, and no use of extra-judicial threats. Pfeffer seems to have been reluctant even to pressure each suspect with incriminating or contradictory details of the other's statements, because he saw independent and uncoerced testimony as the only sound means of getting at the truth. In reality there could be no question of independent testimony, since Čabrinović and Princip were able in their separate holding cells to communicate with each other using a system of coded knocks they had read about in a Russian novel.[43]

What pushed the investigation further was not the testimony of the bomber and the shooter, but the widening dragnet of routine police arrests, driven by the suspicion that there must be other accomplices.[44] Among those who fell into the hands of the police by this means was none other than Danilo Ilić. The police had no hard evidence against Ilić. They knew only that he was an associate of Princip and that he was affiliated with Serb nationalist circles. Ilić, on the other hand, had no idea how much the police knew and must have suspected that either Princip or Čabrinović or both of them had already incriminated him. When the police brought him before Judge Pfeffer on Wednesday 1 July, Ilić panicked and proposed a plea bargain. He would reveal everything he knew if the investigating judge would undertake to protect him from the death penalty. Pfeffer could make no binding promises, but he did advise Ilić that Austrian law viewed the provision of state evidence as a mitigating circumstance.

That was enough for Ilić. His statement blew open Princip's and Čabrinović's story and pushed the investigation into new territory. The bomber and the shooter had not been acting alone, Ilić stated. They were members of a seven-man team, three of whom had come from Belgrade. Ilić himself had recruited the other three. He named every

Arrest of a suspect

member of the group and offered intelligent guesses as to their current whereabouts. Electrified by these revelations, Pfeffer rushed from the interrogation room to the telephone. Orders went out to arrest all the persons named.

The first to be found was Trifko Grabež, the third member of the Belgrade cell. After Princip had fired his shots, Grabež had taken elaborate precautions to avoid arousing suspicion. He walked slowly from the scene to the house of an uncle in Sarajevo, where he hid his gun and his bomb. He then strolled across town to the house of another uncle, a deputy in the Bosnian Diet, where he ate lunch and spent the night. On the next morning, he took the train to Pale, his home town, from where he hoped to escape into Serbia. He was captured in a small town near the Serbian border. Within nine days of the assassinations, Čubrilović and Popović had also been arrested. Only Mehmedbašić remained at large. He had already crossed the border into Montenegro and was thus, for the moment, beyond the reach of the Austrian police. But even without Mehmedbašić in custody the Sarajevo police had plenty to go on. Ilić's confessions incriminated a crowd of further accomplices, including the schoolteacher, the smuggler and the various hapless peasants who had helped the boys along their way, either by putting them up for the night or by transporting or concealing their weapons.

Reconstructing the links with Serbia was more difficult. The weapons themselves were of Serbian make; the revolvers were manufactured under Serbian licence and the recovered bombs hailed from the Serbian state armoury at Kragujevac. On 29 June, Čabrinović named Ciganović as the man who had supplied the team with their guns and bombs in Belgrade. But Ciganović was a lowly figure in the network and in any case a Bosnian exile. Implicating him did not in itself point in the direction of official Serbian complicity. If Ciganović was, as the Italian historian Albertini concluded, working as Nikola Pašić's agent and informant within the Black Hand,[45] this role was informal and would have eluded even the most thorough investigation. The situation was different for Major Voja Tankosić, a Serbian national who was prominent in the partisan movement, and a personal aide to Apis, the chief of Serbian Military Intelligence. His name was volunteered by Ilić, who stated that Tankosić had not only provided the assassins with weapons, but had also trained them in marksmanship in Belgrade and issued the instruction that they should kill themselves rather than be taken alive. The Belgrade boys initially denied any knowledge of Tankosić; only after they were confronted one by one with Ilić (one of the very few occasions in which prisoner confrontations were used to elicit confessions) did Princip, Čabrinović and Grabež concede that Tankosić had been involved in the preparation of the plot.

By this time, however, over two weeks had elapsed and the Austrians were getting no nearer to Apis, the real author of the conspiracy. Looking over the witness statements, it is hard not to agree with the historian Joachim Remak that Princip, Grabež and Čabrinović pursued a strategy of deliberate obfuscation that led 'by way of splendid confusion from initial denial to reluctant – and incomplete – admission'.[46] All three took pains to limit the damage done by Ilić's revelations and to prevent as far as possible the inculpation of official circles in Belgrade. None made any mention of the Black Hand; instead they hinted at links between Ciganović and the Narodna Odbrana, a red herring that would lead the

Austrian investigators far from the true trail. And Judge Pfeffer's rather languorous mode of proceeding gave the imprisoned assassins plenty of time to harmonize their stories, thereby ensuring that a fuller picture was slow to emerge.

The ponderous progress of the police investigation did not, of course, prevent the Austrian leadership from intuiting a link to Belgrade, or from forming a view of the broader background to the plot. Telegrams fired off by Governor Potiorek of Bosnia within hours of the assassinations already hinted at Serbian complicity. The 'bomb-thrower' Čabrinović, he reported, belonged to a Serbian socialist group 'that usually takes its orders from Belgrade'. The 'Serbian-Orthodox' school student Princip had been studying for some time in the Serbian capital, and police searches had revealed 'an entire library of nationalist-revolutionary publications of Belgrade origin' in the house of Princip's older brother in Hadzici.[47] From the Austrian embassy in Belgrade came a coded telegram reporting that Čabrinović had been employed at a publishing house in Belgrade until a few weeks before the assassination. In a longer report, dispatched on 29 June, the Austrian minister observed that the boys had received their 'political education' in Belgrade and linked the murders to the culture of Serbian national memory. Of particular significance was the celebrated medieval suicide-assassin Miloš Obilić, who 'passes for a hero wherever Serbs live'.

> I would not yet be so bold as to accuse the Belgrade [government] directly
> of the murder, but they are surely indirectly guilty, and the ring-leaders are
> to be found not just among the uneducated masses, but in the Propaganda
> Department of the [Serbian] Foreign Ministry, among those Serbian univer-
> sity professors and newspaper editors who for years have sown hatred and
> now have reaped murder.[48]

Governor Potiorek was even less restrained. In a coded telegram to the minister of war, he noted that the killers had admitted receiving their arms in Belgrade. But even without a confession, the governor was 'fully convinced' that the true causes of the outrage were to be sought in Serbia. It was not his business to judge which measures should be taken, but his personal view was that only 'firm action in the domain of foreign policy would restore peace and normality to Bosnia-Herzegovina'.[49] The shock of the event still resonates in these early reports: 'we have still not recovered from the crushing impact of yesterday's catastrophe', wrote the Austrian minister in Belgrade, 'so that I find it difficult to assess the bloody drama in Sarajevo with the necessary composure, objectivity and calm . . .'[50] Vengeful rage, hostile underlying assumptions about Serbian objectives and a growing body of circumstantial evidence shaped official Austrian perceptions of the crime from the first hour, in a process that was only obliquely linked to the discoveries generated by the legal investigation itself.

SERBIAN RESPONSES

Especially close attention was paid in Austria to Serbian reactions to the crime. The Belgrade government made an effort to observe the expected courtesies, but from the outset Austrian observers discerned a gaping discrepancy between the show of official condolence and the jubilation felt and expressed by most Serbs. The Austrian minister in Belgrade reported on the day after the event that a celebration scheduled for the evening of 28 June in memory of the assassin Miloš Obilić had been cancelled. But he also passed on reports from informers that there had been private expressions of satisfaction throughout the city.[51] From the fields of Kosovo, where massive celebrations of St Vitus's Day had been planned, the Austrian consul reported that the news from Sarajevo was greeted by the 'fanaticised mass' with expressions of elation 'that I can only describe as bestial'.[52] A preliminary announcement that the Serbian court would observe six weeks of state mourning was subsequently corrected: there would be only eight days of official mourning. But even this modest acknowledgement belied the reality that the streets and coffee-houses were full of Serb patriots rejoicing at the blow to the Habsburgs.[53]

Austrian doubts were further reinforced by the continuing vituperations of the Serbian nationalist press. On 29 June, the mass distribution in Belgrade of pamphlets decrying the alleged 'extermination' of the Serbs in Bosnia-Herzegovina by 'hired masses', while the Habsburg authorities sat back 'with folded hands', annoyed the staff of the Austrian embassy, as did a leader article in the nationalist organ *Politika* on the following day blaming the Austrians themselves for the murders and denouncing the Vienna government for manipulating the situation to propagate the 'lie' of Serbian complicity. Other pieces praised the assassins as 'good, honourable youths'.[54] Articles of this stripe (and there were many of them) were regularly translated and excerpted in the Austro-Hungarian press, where they helped to stir popular resentment. Particularly dangerous – because they contained an element of truth – were articles claiming that the Belgrade government had formally warned Vienna in advance of the plot against the archduke. A piece published under the title 'An Unheeded Warning' in the Belgrade newspaper *Stampa* stated that Jovan Jovanović, the Serbian minister in Vienna, had passed details of the plot to Count Berchtold, who had been 'very grateful' for the minister's confidence and had alerted both the Emperor and the heir to the throne.[55] There was a morsel of truth in this claim, which cut in two directions because it implied Austrian negligence on the one hand and Serbian government foreknowledge on the other.

There was, of course, little that Serbian leaders could have done to avoid these recriminations. The Belgrade government could not forbid merrymakers to celebrate the murders in the coffee-houses, nor could they control the behaviour of the crowds at Kosovo Field. The press was a grey area. From Vienna, Jovanović recognized the threat posed by the more intemperate Belgrade papers and repeatedly urged Pašić to take action against the worst offenders in order to avoid the exploitation of extremist statements by the Viennese press.[56] The Austrians too communicated their displeasure, and warnings to rein in the press were heard from the Serbian foreign legations.[57] But the Pašić government was formally correct in insisting that it lacked the constitutional instruments to control the organs of the free Serbian press. And Pašić did in fact instruct the head of the Serbian press bureau to urge caution upon Belgrade's journalists.[58] It is also notable that stories about an official warning to Vienna by the Belgrade government quickly evaporated after Pašić's official denial on 7 July.[59] Whether Pašić could have used emergency powers to moderate the tone of the newspapers is another question – at any rate he chose not to, possibly because he judged tough measures against the nationalist press to be politically inopportune so soon after the bitter conflict of May 1914 between the Radical cabinet and the praetorian elements in the Serbian army. New elections were scheduled, moreover, for 14 August; in the heated atmosphere of an election campaign, Pašić could hardly afford to offend nationalist opinion.

There were other, more avoidable lapses. On 29 June, Miroslav

Spalajković, the Serbian minister in St Petersburg, issued statements to the Russian press justifying Bosnian agitation against Vienna and denouncing the Austrian measures against Serbian subjects suspected of involvement with irredentist groups. For years, Spalajković told the *Vecherneye Vremya*, the political leadership in Vienna had been manufacturing anti-Austrian organizations, including 'the so-called "Black Hand", which is an invention'. There were no revolutionary organizations whatsoever in Serbia, he insisted. In an interview granted on the following day to *Novoye Vremya*, the Serbian diplomat denied that the murderers had received their weapons from Belgrade, blamed the Jesuits for stirring up a feud between Croats and Serbs in Bosnia and warned that the arrest of prominent Serbs in Bosnia might even provoke a military assault by Serbia against the monarchy.[60] Spalajković had a long history of rancorous relations with his Austrian diplomatic counterparts and a reputation for excitability. Even the Russian foreign minister Sazonov, a friend of the Serbian envoy, described him as 'unbalanced'.[61] But these public utterances, which were conveyed immediately to the decision-makers in Vienna, helped to poison the atmosphere in the early days after the assassinations.

Pašić, too, muddied the waters with ill-judged displays of bravado. In a speech held in New Serbia on 29 June, attended by several cabinet ministers, twenty-two members of the Skupština, numerous local functionaries and a delegation of Serbs from various regions of the Austro-Hungarian monarchy, Pašić warned that if the Austrians should attempt to exploit the 'regrettable event' politically against Serbia, the Serbs 'would not hesitate to defend themselves and to fulfil their duty'.[62] This was an extraordinary gesture at a time when the feeling generated by the event was still so fresh. In a circular sent to all the Serbian legations on 1 July, Pašić took a similar line, juxtaposing the honest and strenuous efforts of the Belgrade government with the nefarious manipulations of the Viennese press. Serbia and its representatives must resist any attempt by Vienna to 'seduce European opinion'. In a later communication on the same theme, Pašić accused the Viennese editors of deliberately misrepresenting the tone of Serbian press coverage and rejected the notion that the Belgrade government should act to curb what were in effect justified reactions to Austrian provocations.[63] In short, there were moments when Pašić seemed closer to leading the Serbian papers into the fray than tempering the tone of their coverage.

Pašić's contacts with Austrian ministers and diplomats had never been easy; they were especially awkward during the first days after the assassinations. On 3 July, for example, during an official requiem in Belgrade in memory of the archduke, Pašić assured the Austrian minister that Belgrade would treat this matter 'as if it concerned one of their own rulers'. The words were doubtless well meant, but in a country with such a vibrant and recent history of regicide they were bound to strike his Austrian interlocutor as tasteless, if not macabre.[64]

More important than Pašić's tone was the question of whether he or his government could be depended upon to collaborate with the Austrians in investigating the roots of the conspiracy to kill the heir apparent and his wife. Here, too, there was ample reason for doubt. On 30 June, the Austrian minister in Belgrade, Ritter von Storck, met with the secretary-general of the Serbian foreign ministry, Slavko Gruić, and enquired as to what the Serbian police had been doing to follow up the threads of the conspiracy which, it was well known, led into Serbian territory. Gruić retorted with striking (and possibly disingenuous) naivety that the police had done nothing whatsoever – did the Austrian government wish to request such an investigation? At this point Storck lost his temper and declared that he regarded it as an elementary duty on the part of the Belgrade police to investigate the matter to the best of their ability, whether Vienna requested it or not.[65]

Yet, despite official assurances, the Serbian authorities never conducted an investigation proportionate to the gravity of the crime and the crisis to which it had given rise. At Gruić's prompting, Interior Minister Protić did, to be sure, order Vasil Lazarević, chief of police in the Serbian capital, to look into the assassins' links with the city. A week later, Lazarević closed his 'investigation' with a cheerful announcement to the effect that the assassination in Sarajevo had no connection whatsoever with the Serbian capital. No one by the name of 'Ciganović', the chief of police added, 'existed or had ever existed' in Belgrade.[66] When Storck solicited the assistance of the Serbian police and foreign ministry in locating a group of students suspected of planning a further assassination, he was provided with such a muddle of obfuscation and contradictory information that he concluded that the Serbian foreign ministry was incapable of operating as a trustworthy partner, despite the assurances of Nikola Pašić. There was no pre-emptive crackdown against the Black Hand; Apis remained in office; and Pašić's tentative investigation of the border regiments involved in smuggling operations fell far short of what was needed.

Instead of meeting the Austrians halfway, Pašić (and the Serbian authorities more generally) fell back on customary postures and attitudes: the Serbs themselves were the victims in this affair, both in Bosnia-Herzegovina and now after Sarajevo; the Austrians had it coming to them anyway; the Serbs had the right to defend themselves, both with words and, if necessary, with armed force, and so forth. As Pašić saw it, this was all in keeping with his view that the assassination had nothing whatsoever to do with 'official Serbia'.[67] Seen from this perspective, any independent measure against persons or groups implicated in the assassination would have implied an acceptance of Belgrade's responsibility for the crime. A posture of cool aloofness, by contrast, would send out the message that Belgrade regarded this issue as a purely domestic Habsburg crisis that unscrupulous Vienna politicians were endeavouring to exploit against Serbia. In keeping with this view, Serbian official communications depicted Austrian recriminations as an utterly unprovoked assault on Serbia's reputation, the appropriate response to which was haughty official silence.[68] All of this made sense when viewed through the lens of Belgrade politics, but it was bound to infuriate the Austrians, who saw in it nothing but insolence, deceitfulness and evasion, not to mention further confirmation of the Serbian state's co-responsibility for the disaster. Above all, the glib denials from Belgrade suggested that the Serbian government was not, and would not perform the role of, a partner or neighbour in resolving the urgent issues raised by the assassinations. There was nothing surprising in this for Vienna, which had come to expect evasion and duplicity in its dealings with Belgrade, but it was important nonetheless, because it made it very difficult to imagine how relations could be normalized after the outrage without some measure of external coercion.

WHAT IS TO BE DONE?

The impact of the murders on the Austro-Hungarian decision-making elite was immediate and profound. Within a few days of the assassinations of 28 June, a consensus formed among the key Austrian decision-makers that only military action would solve the problem of the monarchy's relations with Serbia. Something must be done to answer the provocation. More numerous and united than ever before, the hawks pressed in on Foreign Minister Leopold von Berchtold with demands for swift action. 'Last year I took the liberty of writing to you to say that we would have to learn how to tolerate Serbian impertinences without resorting to war,' Ritter von Storck told Berchtold on 30 June. 'Now,' he wrote, 'the matter has acquired an entirely different aspect'.

> In answering the question of peace or war, we must no longer be led by the thought that we cannot gain anything through a war with Serbia, but rather we must seize the first opportunity for a pulverising blow against the kingdom without giving any consideration to such scruples.[69]

Prince Gottfried von Hohenlohe-Schillingsfürst, a senior diplomat who had already been appointed to succeed the long-serving Szögyényi as Austrian minister in Berlin, confronted Berchtold on the morning after the murders. If serious measures were not taken now, Hohenlohe threatened, with an insolence verging on insubordination, he would refuse to take up his Berlin posting.[70] That evening, after an afternoon in which Berchtold must have endured many similar conversations, Conrad arrived. Freed by the assassinations at Sarajevo of the most formidable restraint on his political influence, the chief of the General Staff launched into his familiar refrain. Now was the time to take action: mobilization should be ordered without any further negotiations with Belgrade. 'If you have a poisonous adder at your heel, you stamp on its head, you don't wait for the deadly bite.' The staff chief's advice could be summarized, Berchtold later recalled, in three words: 'War! War! War!'[71] Much the same was heard from Minister of War Krobatin, freshly returned from a tour of inspection in South Tyrol, who met with Berchtold and Conrad on the morning of Tuesday 30 June. The army was ready for action, Krobatin declared; war was the only way out of the monarchy's current predicament.[72]

Leon Biliński, the joint finance minister, joined the chorus. As one of the three joint ministers who constituted what passed for an imperial government in Austria-Hungary, he would play an important role in formulating policy during the crisis. Biliński was no Serbophobe. As the minister responsible for the administration of Bosnia, he had been known for the supple and approachable manner of his dealings with the national minorities in the province. He taught himself how to read and understand Serbo-Croat and spoke Russian rather than German with his South Slav colleagues; it was easier for them to follow and drew attention to their shared Slav heritage. Meetings were conducted in a markedly informal and friendly fashion, and debates were lubricated with large helpings of strong black coffee and a plentiful supply of good cigarettes.[73] Until the events at Sarajevo, Biliński had continued to work on building a constructive long-term relationship with the national minorities in Bosnia-Herzegovina. Even after the assassinations, he opposed the efforts of the martinet *Landeschef* Potiorek to impose repressive measures in Bosnia.[74]

On the question of external relations with Serbia, Biliński had veered between conciliatory and bellicose views during the recent Balkan turbulence. He was warlike during the stand-off over northern Albania in May 1913, and again during the Albanian crisis of October, though he warned on this occasion that since neither the Emperor nor the heir apparent would agree to an all-out war, Vienna should probably stop short of ordering a mobilization.[75] On the other hand, he cultivated excellent relations with Jovanović, the Serbian minister in Vienna, and used these effectively to help bring the dispute over Serbian–Albanian border rectifications to a harmonious resolution. During the second Balkan War, he opposed the policy of backing Bulgaria against Belgrade, pressing instead for a rapprochement with victorious, expanding Serbia. He consistently and vehemently opposed Conrad's idea of deliberately engineering a war against the neighbouring state, on the grounds that this would stigmatize Austria-Hungary as the aggressor and isolate it among the great powers.[76]

The assassinations put an abrupt end to this equivocation. From the afternoon of 28 June, Biliński was an unstinting advocate of direct action against Serbia. He had never been especially close to Franz Ferdinand, but found it hard to shake off a sense that he had failed in his duty of care to the victims of the assassination. In retrospect, it is clear that he was entirely blameless. He had not been informed by Potiorek of the plan to bring the archduke and his wife into the city – hence the attack of nausea he suffered when he read the details of the projected visit in the newspaper. Nor had he been consulted on the security arrangements. Yet the minister spent his first post-Sarajevo meetings with the Emperor and with Berchtold pedantically defending himself – with documentary evidence – against the imagined accusation that he had been negligent in discharging his duties.[77]

One of the fiercest hawks was Biliński's subordinate, Potiorek. Unlike Biliński, the governor had ample reason to accuse himself of negligence. It was Potiorek who had pressed to have the manoeuvres conducted in Bosnia in the first place. He had been responsible for the risible security arrangements on the day of the visit. And it was he who had mishandled the archduke's departure from the city after the reception at the Town Hall. But if he experienced pangs of self-reproach, Potiorek masked them with a posture of impetuous bellicosity.[78] In reports dispatched from Sarajevo to the General Staff and the ministry of war, Potiorek pressed for a rapid military strike against Belgrade. Time was running out for the monarchy. Bosnia would soon be rendered ungovernable by the operations of the Serb irredentist networks, to the extent that it would become impossible to deploy large troop units there. Only by cracking down on Serbian national organizations in the province and eliminating the root of the problem in Belgrade would the monarchy resolve its Balkan security problem. Potiorek was not a decision-maker of the inner circle, but his reports were important nonetheless. Franz Ferdinand had always argued that the fragility of the Austro-Hungarian Empire categorically ruled out any consideration of war with an external foe. Potiorek turned this argument on its head, asserting that war would resolve, not exacerbate, the Empire's domestic problems. This rather contrived appeal to what historians would later term the 'primacy of domestic politics' helped Conrad and Krobatin to overturn the objections of some of their civilian colleagues.

The upper tiers of the foreign ministry were quick to embrace a militant policy. As early as 30 June, the German minister in Vienna, Baron Tschirschky, reported that his contacts – most of them foreign ministry people – were expressing the wish for a 'thorough settling of accounts with Serbia'.[79] The motivations for embracing a militant policy varied to some extent from one individual to the next: Baron Alexander von Musulin, the self-proclaimed Foreign Office 'Serbia expert' who would later draft the ultimatum to Belgrade and took part in several important early meetings at the Foreign Office, was a Croat deeply hostile to greater-Serbian nationalism who saw in the post-Sarajevo crisis the last opportunity to halt the advance of pan-Serbianism with the support of the empire's Croats.[80] Frigyes ('Fritz') Szapáry, the Austrian minister in St Petersburg, who happened to be in Vienna during the first fortnight after the assassination because of his wife's illness, was mainly concerned with the deepening grip of the Russians on the Balkan peninsula. Count Forgách, head of the foreign ministry's Political Section from October 1913, had not forgotten his miserable years in Belgrade or his rancorous dealings with Spalajković. A militant group-think seized hold of the ministry. Underlying the preference for a policy of confrontation was the familiar topos of the active foreign policy – seen as the polar opposite of the passivity and muddling-through that had supposedly dogged Austrian policy. Aehrenthal had argued his case in these terms during the Bosnian annexation crisis of 1908–9, contrasting his own proactive approach with the 'fatalism' of his predecessors. Forgács, Count Alexander ('Alek') Hoyos (Berchtold's *chef de cabinet*), Szapáry, the department chief Count Albert Nemes and Baron Musulin were all enthusiastic disciples of Aehrenthal. During the Balkan crises of 1912 and 1913, these men had repeatedly pressed Berchtold not to give way either to Russian intimidation or to Serbia's 'growing impertinence' and privately lamented what they saw as his excessively conciliatory approach.[81]

Sarajevo did not just stir the hawks to war. It also destroyed the best hope for peace. Had Franz Ferdinand survived his visit to Bosnia in 1914, he would have continued to warn against the risks of a military adventure, as he had done so often before. On his return from the summer manoeuvres, he would have removed Conrad from his post. This time there would have been no coming back for the bellicose staff chief. 'The world has no idea that the archduke was always against war,' a senior Austrian diplomat told the politician Joseph Redlich in the last week of July. 'Through his death he has helped *us* find the energy that *he* would never have found as long as he lived!'[82]

No one was under more pressure during the first few days after the assassinations than the Austro-Hungarian joint foreign minister Leopold von Berchtold. He was personally deeply affected by the news from Sarajevo. He and Franz Ferdinand were close in age and had known each other since childhood. For all the differences between the hot-tempered, confident, opinionated archduke and the refined, sensitive and effeminate count, the two men had respected each other deeply.

Berchtold had ample opportunity to acquaint himself with the vivacious, impulsive individual behind the cantankerous public persona of the heir apparent. And there was a broader familial dimension to the relationship: Berchtold's wife Nandine had been the intimate childhood friend of Sophie Chotek and the two had remained close ever since. Berchtold was speechless when he received the news during a charitable event near his castle at Buchlau and rushed by train to Vienna, where he was immediately swept up in a frenzy of meetings. 'The shadow of a dead man, of a great dead man, lay upon these discussions,' Berchtold later recalled. 'I found them unbearably painful. Always I seemed to see before me the image of him who had been blamelessly slain, [. . .] the large shining eyes blue as water beneath the dark resolute brow . . .'[83]

Did Berchtold have to be pushed into accepting the case for war against Serbia? Certainly the hawks who besieged him with advice on the morrow of the assassination presumed that the foreign minister would need to be bullied into adopting a policy of confrontation. Although Berchtold had on occasion taken up firm positions (over Albania, for example), he was still widely viewed as a man of prudence and conciliation, and thus a soft touch on foreign affairs. Berchtold, one senior Habsburg ambassador claimed in May 1914, was a 'dilettante', whose 'inconsequentiality and lack of will' had deprived the monarchy's foreign policy of any clear sense of direction.[84] In order to goad the minister into action after Sarajevo, the most hawkish colleagues coupled their advice on the current crisis with biting critiques of Austro-Hungarian policy since the death of Aehrenthal in 1912. Conrad, as ever, was the most forthright. It was thanks to Berchtold's hesitancy and caution during the Balkan Wars, Conrad told the minister on 30 June, that Austria-Hungary now found itself in this mess.

In fact, however, it seems that Berchtold himself made an early, and probably independent, commitment to a policy of direct action. The man of manoeuvre and restraint became overnight an unshakably strong leader.[85] He had an opportunity to set out his view of the crisis at his first post-Sarajevo audience with the Emperor in Schönbrunn Palace at one o'clock on the afternoon of 30 June. This encounter was of crucial importance; in his unpublished memoirs, Berchtold later recalled it in detail. It is worth noting that he found the Emperor deeply grieved by the murders at Sarajevo, notwithstanding his difficult relationship with the archduke and his morganatic wife. Breaking with protocol, the

83-year-old monarch took the minister's hand in his own and asked him to sit down. His eyes became wet as they discussed the recent events.[86] Berchtold declared – and the Emperor agreed – that the monarchy's 'policy of patience' had exhausted its plausibility. If Austro-Hungary were to show weakness in such an extreme case as this, Berchtold warned, 'the neighbours to the south and the east would become even more confident of our impotence and pursue their work of destruction with ever more determination'. The empire now found itself in a 'position of constraint'. The Emperor, Berchtold recalled, seemed extremely well informed on the current situation and fully accepted the need for action. But he also insisted that Berchtold agree any further steps with Count István Tisza, the prime minister of Hungary, who was at that time staying in Vienna.[87]

Here was the germ of a potentially serious problem: Tisza fiercely objected to any policy designed to engineer an immediate conflict. Tisza, prime minister during the years 1903–5 and again from 1913, was the dominant figure in Hungarian politics. This exceptionally energetic and ambitious man, a fervent admirer of Bismarck, had built up his power though a combination of electoral corruption, the ruthless police intimidation of political opponents, and modernizing economic and infrastructural reforms designed to appeal to the Magyar-speaking middle classes and assimilationist elements in the other national elites. Tisza embodied the Compromise system created in 1867. He was a nationalist, but he believed deeply in the union with Austria, which he saw as indispensable to the future security of Hungary. He was utterly determined to uphold the hegemony of the Magyar elite and thus firmly opposed to any broadening of the restrictive franchise that kept the non-Magyars out of politics.

For Tisza, the assassination of the heir apparent was a cause not of grief but of raw relief. The reforms envisaged by Franz Ferdinand would have placed at risk the entire power structure in which Tisza had made his career. The archduke's close links with parts of the Romanian intelligentsia were especially distasteful. His assassination therefore represented an unhoped-for deliverance, and the Hungarian prime minister shared neither the rage nor the sense of urgency that animated so many of his Austrian colleagues. At a meeting with Berchtold on the afternoon of 30 June and again in a letter to the Emperor on the following day, Tisza warned against allowing the assassination to become the 'pretext' for a war with Serbia. The chief reason for restraint lay in the currently disadvantageous constellation among the Balkan states. The key problem was Romania, which was well on the way by the summer of 1914 to aligning itself with St Petersburg and the powers of the Entente. In view of the immense size of the Romanian minority in Transylvania and the indefensibility of the long Romanian frontier, Bucharest's realignment posed a serious security threat. It was folly, Tisza argued, to risk a war with Serbia while the question of Romania's allegiance and comportment in a possible conflict remained unresolved. Tisza envisaged two options: either the Romanians must be persuaded – with Berlin's help – to re-enter the orbit of the Triple Alliance; or they must be restrained through the establishment of closer Austro-Hungarian and German ties with Bulgaria, Romania's enemy in the Second Balkan War.

> For all the grandiose delusions of the Romanians, the driving force in the psyche of this people is the fear of Bulgaria. Once they see that they cannot prevent us from contracting an alliance with Bulgaria, they will perhaps seek to be admitted to the [Triple] Alliance in order by this means to be protected from Bulgarian aggression.[88]

This was the familiar Balkan calculus, refracted through the prism of a specifically Hungarian view of the Empire's security predicament. Romania loomed large on the policy horizons of the Magyar elite, and this preoccupation was amplified in Tisza's case by the fact that he was the descendant of a Transylvanian gentry family. Tisza and his closest advisers regarded good relations with St Petersburg as the key to Hungarian security, and the idea of rebuilding the old entente with Russia was fashionable at this time within the Magyar leadership. The Hungarian prime minister's objection to war was not, it should be noted, absolute. Tisza had supported a military intervention against Serbia during the second Albanian crisis in October 1913 and he was happy to consider the possibility of a war with Serbia at some later date, should an appropriate provocation arise under more auspicious circumstances. But he was firmly opposed to the policy of direct action favoured by most of the Austrian decision-makers.[89]

However powerful the emotions circulating within the Austrian political elite during the days after the assassinations, it quickly became clear that an immediate military response was out of the question. First there was the problem of persuading Tisza to support the view emerging in Vienna; it was politically and constitutionally impossible simply to overrule this powerful player in the dualist system. Then there was the question of actually proving Serbia's involvement. In a meeting with Berchtold on the afternoon of 30 June, Tisza argued that the Serbian government should be given time to 'demonstrate its good will'. Berchtold was sceptical on this point, but he did accept that any military action should be delayed until further confirmation of Serbian culpability.[90] It would take some days before a fuller picture emerged of the links with Belgrade. A further sensitive issue was the lead-time required for a military action. Conrad repeatedly urged his civilian colleagues to 'strike immediately' (i.e. without waiting for the outcome of the investigation), yet he informed Berchtold on the morning of 30 June that the General Staff would need sixteen days to mobilize the armed forces for a strike against Serbia – this subsequently proved to be a gross underestimate.[91] A substantial delay was thus inevitable, even if the leadership should agree on a precise plan of action.

Finally, and most importantly, there was the question of Germany. Would Berlin support a policy of confrontation with Belgrade? German backing for Austro-Hungarian Balkan policy had been patchy of late. It was only eight weeks since Ambassador Fritz Szapáry, writing from St Petersburg, had complained of Germany's systematic 'sacrifice' of Austria-Hungary's Balkan interests. During the first days of the crisis, mixed messages emanated from Berlin. On 1 July, the well-known German journalist Viktor Naumann called on Berchtold's *chef de cabinet*, Count Alek Hoyos, to say that he believed the German leadership would look kindly on an Austro-Hungarian strike against Serbia and were ready to accept the risk of a war with Russia, should St Petersburg decide to force the issue. Naumann had no official standing, but since he was known to be in close touch with Wilhelm von Stumm, head of the political department at the Berlin Foreign Office, his words carried a certain weight.[92] At the same time, however, the German ambassador, Baron Tschirschky, was urging the Austrians to observe caution. Whenever the Austrians spoke to him of the need for harsh measures, Tschirschky wrote on 30 June, 'I availed myself of such openings to issue a warning, calmly but very emphatically and seriously, against hasty measures.'[93] And in a conversation with the Austrian ambassador in Berlin, the under-secretary of state of the Berlin Foreign Office, Arthur

Zimmermann, expressed his sympathy for Vienna's plight, but warned against confronting Belgrade with 'humiliating demands'.[94]

The views of the German Emperor were further reason for concern. In the autumn and winter of 1913 Wilhelm II had repeatedly advised the Austrians to win over Belgrade with cash gifts and exchange programmes. As recently as June 1914, during his last meeting with Franz Ferdinand, the Kaiser had refused to commit himself. Asked whether Austria-Hungary 'could continue to count unconditionally on Germany in the future', Wilhelm had 'dodged the question and failed to provide us with an answer'.[95] In a report submitted to Emperor Franz Joseph on 1 July, Tisza warned that the German Emperor harboured a 'pro-Serbian bias' and would need some persuading before he would be willing to support Vienna's Balkan policy.[96] The Austro-Hungarian leaders at first hoped that the two emperors might be able to exchange views face-to-face when Wilhelm II came to Vienna to attend the archduke's funeral, but that visit was cancelled following rumours of a further Serbian assassination plot against the German Kaiser. Some other means would have to be found of synchronizing policy with Berlin.

Here, at least, was a step on which Berchtold, Tisza and the other Austrian decision-makers could agree: Germany must be properly consulted before any further action was taken. Berchtold oversaw the preparation of a diplomatic mission to Berlin. Two documents were to be forwarded to the German ally. The first was a personal letter from Franz Joseph to Kaiser Wilhelm II, signed in the Emperor's own hand but in fact drafted by Berchtold's staff chief Alek Hoyos; the second was a hastily revised version of the pre-Sarajevo Matscheko memorandum, to which was appended a brief post-assassination postscript.

These two documents make extremely strange reading today. The revised Matscheko memorandum offered the same sprawling overview of the deteriorating Balkan alignment as the original, but with a stronger emphasis on the ruinous consequences of Romanian infidelity – a point directed both at Berlin's friendly relations with Bucharest and at Tisza's preoccupation with Transylvania. The aggressiveness of the Franco-Russian alliance was brought more clearly to the fore, and this was framed as a threat not only to Austria-Hungary, but also to Germany. At the end of the document was a postscript introduced by the words: 'the aforegoing Memorandum had just been completed when the terrible events of Sarajevo took place'. It spoke of the 'danger and intensity' of a 'greater-Serbian agitation that will stop short of nothing' and noted that the efforts of the monarchy to secure good relations with Serbia through a policy of goodwill and compromise now appeared completely pointless. No direct reference was made to war, but the postscript referred to the 'irreconcilability' of the Austro-Serbian antagonism in the light of recent events. The document closed with an ungainly metaphor: the Austro-Hungarian eagle 'must now tear with resolute hand the threads that its enemies are weaving into a net over its head'.[97]

The personal note from Franz Joseph to Kaiser Wilhelm II was more straightforward. It, too, dwelt at some length on Romania and the machinations of the Russians, but it closed with a clear intimation of impending action against Serbia. The assassination, it pointed out, was not the act of an individual but a 'well-organised conspiracy [. . .] whose threads extend to Belgrade'. Only when Serbia was 'neutralised as a power factor in the Balkans' would Austria-Hungary be safe.

> You too will be convinced after the recent terrible events in Bosnia that there can be no further question of bridging by conciliation the difference that separates Serbia from us, and that the policy pursued by all European monarchs of preserving the peace will be at risk for as long as this hotbed of criminal agitation in Belgrade remains unpunished.[98]

What strikes the present-day reader about these communications is their panicky lack of focus, the preference for swollen metaphors over clear formulations, the employment of histrionic devices to achieve an emotional effect, the juxtaposition of different perspectives in the absence of a unifying meta-narrative. There is no explicit request for German assistance; there are no policy proposals, no lists of options, just a grim, unfocused panorama of threat and foreboding. Nor was it clear how the passages diagnosing the Balkan situation in general terms – which hint at the need for a diplomatic solution – related to the passages on Serbia, which leave the reader in no doubt that the authors have war in mind.

Berchtold had initially intended to send the imperial letter and the revised Matscheko memorandum to Berlin by regular government courier. Late on Saturday 4 July, however, he telegraphed Ambassador Szögyéni in Berlin to inform him that his *chef de cabinet*, Count Hoyos, would be bringing the documents to Berlin by hand. Szögyéni was to arrange interviews with the Kaiser and Chancellor Theobald von

Bethmann Hollweg. Though young – he was only thirty-six – Hoyos was one of the most energetic and ambitious of the hawkish younger cohort of foreign ministry officials. He was also well connected in Berlin. In 1908, on his recall from a posting in the German capital, Ambassador Szögyényi had commented approvingly on the relations of unusual 'intimacy and trust' Hoyos had built with the leading German political circles.[99] During a posting in China, Hoyos had also met and got to know Arthur Zimmermann, currently standing in for his boss, Secretary of State Gottlieb von Jagow, who was on his honeymoon when the crisis broke. Hoyos regarded the relationship with Germany as the cornerstone of Austro-Hungarian security and the prerequisite for an active policy in the Balkans – this, in his view, was the lesson of the 1908–09 annexation crisis, in which he had himself played a peripheral role. Most importantly, Hoyos was a hardliner who favoured a military solution from the outset; during the struggle to secure Tisza's agreement, the young staff chief provided his beleaguered boss with much-needed moral support.[100]

By selecting Hoyos for the mission to Berlin, Berchtold ensured that an unequivocally bellicose construction would be placed upon the two policy documents from Vienna. There would be no doubt in the minds of the Germans that the Austrians meant business. While ostensibly complying with the advice of Tisza, who had refused to agree any further steps until the Germans were consulted, Berchtold used the mission in effect to shut the Hungarian leader out of the decision-making process and to ensure that Habsburg policy evolved in conformity with his own preference for a swift and decisive response to the outrage at Sarajevo.[101] This was a matter of some importance because, as the German ambassador pointedly reminded Berchtold on 3 July, grandiose talk, for which the Austrians had an undeniable talent, did not in itself constitute a plan of action.[102]

Mobilization schedules, political dissension, the progress of the Sarajevo police enquiry, the need to secure German support – these were excellent reasons for delaying a military action against Serbia. Not even Conrad was able to offer a credible alternative to his civilian colleagues. And yet, throughout the July Crisis the Austrians would be haunted by the suspicion that it might actually have been better simply to strike at Belgrade without full mobilization and without a declaration of war, in what would universally have been seen as a reflex response to a grave provocation. Why didn't Austria-Hungary simply attack Serbia straight away and be done with it, asked Prime Minister Ion Brătianu of Romania on 24 July, as the crisis entered its critical phase. 'Then [you] would have had the sympathies of Europe on your side.'[103] How differently the crisis might then have evolved is a matter on which we can only speculate, but one thing is clear: by the time Alek Hoyos boarded the night train for Berlin, the window of opportunity for that virtual scenario had already closed.

8

The Widening Circle

REACTIONS ABROAD

On the afternoon of Sunday 28 June, the Kaiser was off the north-sea coast of Germany, preparing to race his yacht *Meteor* in the Kiel regatta. The motor launch *Hulda* came alongside blowing its horn, and Admiral Müller, chief of the Emperor's naval cabinet, shouted the news of the assassinations across the water. After a brief meeting on board the yacht, it was decided that Wilhelm must return to Berlin immediately 'to take things in hand and preserve the peace of Europe'.[1] At around the same time, a telegram was passed to President Raymond Poincaré at the Longchamp racecourse in Paris, where he was attending the Grand Prix together with other members of the diplomatic corps. Count Szécsen, the Austro-Hungarian ambassador, withdrew immediately. The president and most of the other foreign representatives remained to enjoy the afternoon's racing.

These vignettes, insignificant in themselves, hint at a divergence of responses and perspectives that would bedevil the July Crisis of 1914. In Germany, according to the British ambassador to Berlin, the news of the assassinations caused general consternation. The Emperor had only just returned from a visit to the archduke at Konopischte (today Konopiště), his residence in Bohemia, and the 'intimacy' between the two men was 'a matter of common knowledge as well as of great satisfaction to Germans'. Then there was the sympathy felt in Germany for the elderly Emperor.[2] For Germans, as for Austrians, the impact of the event manifested itself in countless personal impressions, like that of the historian Friedrich Meinecke, who felt everything turning black before his eyes as he read the headlines posted on the offices of a newspaper.[3]

In Romania, too, the regret at the news was deep and widely felt, despite the recent political alienation between Bucharest and Vienna. The Romanian press was unanimous in praising the dead man as a 'protector of minorities and supporter of national aims' within his empire.[4] The Russian envoy in Bucharest reported that Romanians on both sides of the Carpathian mountains had seen in Franz Ferdinand the driving force behind the recent efforts to broker a compromise between the Magyar administration and the Romanians of Transylvania; there were many 'statesmen and politicians', he noted, who had hoped that the accession of the archduke would open the doors to a restoration of good relations with Vienna. The Serbian envoy in Bucharest also noted ruefully that Romanian reactions to the murders were 'much less friendly to Serbia than we might have expected'.[5]

Elsewhere, the picture was different. The crassest contrast was with Serbia itself, where the British ambassador reported 'a sensation of stupefaction rather than one of regret' among the populace.[6] In neighbouring Montenegro, the Austrian legation secretary Lothar Egger Ritter von Möllwald reported that while there were expressions of sympathy for the deaths at Sarajevo, the Austrians were blamed for bringing the disaster upon themselves.[7] In the little town of Metalka, just across the Austrian border with Montenegro, festive flags were still flying on 2 July; enquiries by the Austrians revealed that the flags had gone up only on 30 June – they were not there to mark Kosovo Day, but to taunt the Austrian border troops stationed nearby.[8] From St Petersburg, the headstrong Serbian minister Spalajković reported on 9 July that the news of Franz Ferdinand's assassination had been greeted 'with pleasure'.[9]

In Italy, Austria's ally and rival, the death of the archduke and his consort prompted mixed feelings. The archduke had been almost as hostile to the Italians in Austria-Hungary as he was to the Magyars. Amid all the official expressions of regret it was obvious, wrote the British ambassador in Rome, Rennell Rodd, 'that people in general have regarded the elimination of the late archduke as almost providential'. The Austrian ambassador's reports and those of the Serbian minister confirmed this impression.[10] According to a report from the Russian ambassador, the Sunday afternoon crowds in an overfilled Rome cinema had greeted the news with cheers and calls for the orchestra to play the national anthem – '*Marcia reale! Marcia reale!*'. When the orchestra complied, there was wild applause. 'The crime is horrific,' Foreign

Minister San Giuliano remarked to the Ambassador Sverbeyev, 'but world peace will be no worse off.' In a conversation with the Serbian minister in Rome, one Italian journalist summarized his feelings in the words: 'Grazie Serbia!'[11]

In Paris, the news from Sarajevo was pushed off the front pages by a scandal of momentous proportions. On 16 March 1914, Madame Caillaux, wife of the former prime minister Joseph Caillaux, had walked into the office of Gaston Calmette, editor of *Figaro*, and fired six bullets into him. The reason for the murder was the campaign the newspaper had waged against her husband, in the course of which Calmette had published love letters she had written to Joseph Caillaux while he was still married to his first wife. The trial was due to open on 20 July and the public interest in this story, which combined sexual scandal and a *crime passionel* by a woman highly visible in French public life, was naturally intense. As late as 29 July, the reputable *Le Temps* devoted twice as many column inches to Madame Caillaux's acquittal (on the grounds that the provocation to her honour justifed the crime) as it did to the crisis brewing in Central Europe.[12] Inasmuch as the Parisian press did respond to the news from Sarajevo, the predominant attitude was that Vienna had no right to accuse the Serbian government of complicity in the murders – on the contrary, French papers blamed the Viennese press for stirring up anti-Serbian emotion.[13]

From London, by contrast, the Serbian minister reported with dismay that the British press appeared to be 'following the propaganda of the Austrians' and blaming Serbia for the assassination: 'They are saying these were the actions of a Serbian revolutionary and that he had ties with Belgrade; this is not good for Serbia.'[14] A leader in *The Times* of 16 July declared that the Austrians had every right to insist on vigorous investigation of all the ramifications of the plot and to demand that Serbia henceforth suppress irredentist agitation against the monarchy.[15]

As these variations suggest, attitudes to the murders were refracted through the geopolitics of the relations between states. Romania is an interesting case. Public opinion had in general been well disposed towards the dead archduke, who was known for his pro-Romanian outlook. But King Carol, the man at the centre of Romania's recent realignment towards the Entente powers, adopted a pro-Belgrade view; he was confident that the Serbian government would carry out a full and rigorous investigation of the crime and that Austria therefore had no right to impose demands on Belgrade.[16]

A much more ominous development was the accumulation of a fabric of assumptions that minimized the significance of the event and thereby delegitimized it as a potential *casus belli*. First there was the claim, widely echoed in the diplomatic traffic of the Entente powers and their Italian sleeping partner, that the dead archduke had been at the head of an Austro-Hungarian war party – a view that was at variance with the truth. The emphasis on the victim's unpopularity served to cast doubt on the authenticity of Austria's sense of outrage at the crimes, while supporting the claim that the plot reflected the local unpopularity of the Habsburg dynasty among the South Slavs of the monarchy and therefore had nothing whatsoever to do with Serbia. Then there was the highly adventurous assumption – asserted as if it were the fruit of long and deep research – that official Serbia was completely uninvolved in the attacks at Sarajevo. According to a dispatch of 13 July 1914 from the Serbian minister in Berlin, the Russian ministry of foreign affairs had informed the Russian ambassador in Berlin that there was 'no Serbian involvement in the assassination at Sarajevo' – this at a time when the Austrian investigation, for all its lassitude, had already produced clear evidence to the contrary. From St Petersburg, Miroslav Spalajković approvingly reported that, despite the dossier of evidence forwarded by the Austrian Korrespondenz-Bureau to the Russian press, the papers in St Petersburg were following the Russian government line and treating the Sarajevo incident as a 'purely internal Austrian affair'.[17]

If we follow this theme through the Russian dispatches, we can see how these viewpoints fused into an argument that denied Vienna the right to counter-measures and turned the murders into a manufactured pretext for an action whose real motivations must be sought elsewhere. Franz Ferdinand had in recent years been little more than a stooge of the Kaiser, Ambassador Shebeko reported from Vienna. Inasmuch as there was any genuine anti-Serbian feeling in Vienna after the assassinations, this was the work of 'German elements' (Shebeko made no mention of the important role played by Croats in the anti-Serbian demonstrations that followed the assassinations, though in a later dispatch he added mysteriously that 'Bulgarian elements' were also involved). The German ambassador Heinrich von Tschirschky in particular, Shebeko reported on 1 July, was doing his best to 'exploit the sad event' by stirring up public opinion against Serbia and Russia (in fact Tschirschky was at this time doing exactly the opposite: he was urging caution on all and sundry, much to the chagrin of the Emperor in Berlin; only later did he change tack).[18]

From Belgrade, Hartwig reported to St Petersburg that all the claims of the Austro-Hungarian authorities were false: there was no *schadenfreude* in Serbia, on the contrary, the entire Serbian nation was moved to sympathy by the appalling murders at Sarajevo; the Belgrade-based networks that had supposedly helped the terrorists in their plot against the archduke did not exist; Čabrinović had not obtained his bombs or his weapons from the Kragujevac armoury and so on. The allegation that the Austrians were manufacturing evidence was important, not just because it recalled the scandal of the Friedjung trials, still unforgotten in Serbia (see chapter 2), or because it was false (though it certainly was), but because it implied that Vienna was deliberately manipulating the shootings at Sarajevo into the pretext for an assault on Belgrade motivated by predatory expansionism.[19] And behind all these machinations, supposedly, were the Germans, who, as the Russian envoy in Sofia remarked, might well see in the current events the chance to launch a preemptive attack on their eastern neighbour and thereby halt the growing military preponderance of the Franco-Russian Alliance.[20] A chain of arguments was born – weeks before the war had even broken out! – that would enjoy a long afterlife in the historical literature.

From all this it naturally followed, in the eyes of the Russian policymakers, that Austria had no right to take measures of any kind against Serbia. Axiomatic to the Russian position was the contention that a sovereign state could not be made responsible for the actions of private persons on foreign soil, especially as those in question were 'immature anarchists' – the Russian sources scarcely ever refer to the Serbian or South Slav nationalist orientation of the assassins.[21] It would be wrong and mistaken to hold an entire race responsible for the misdeeds of individuals committed on foreign soil.[22] It was 'unfair', Ambassador Shebeko told a British colleague in Vienna on 5 July, for the Austrians even to accuse Serbia of having 'indirectly favoured by her antipathy the plot to which the Archduke fell victim'.[23] A conversation of 8 July between Sazonov and the Austrian chargé d'affaires in St Petersburg, Ottokar von Czernin, reveals how short was the tether Russian policy was prepared to allow Vienna after Sarajevo. Czernin had mentioned the 'possibility' that the Austro-Hungarian government might 'demand the support of the Serbian government in an investigation within Serbia of the latest assassination'. Sazonov's response was to warn the Austrian diplomat that this step would 'make a very bad impression in Russia'. The Austrians should drop this idea, 'lest they set their foot upon a dangerous path'.[24] In a conversation of 18 June with Austrian ambassador Fritz Szapáry, who had meanwhile returned to St Petersburg after a period of leave spent nursing his dying wife in Vienna, Sazonov asserted the same view in even more trenchant terms, announcing that 'no proof that the Serbian government had tolerated such machinations would ever be produced'.[25]

This framing of events was important, because it was part of the process by which Russia decided how to respond in the event of Austrian measures against Serbia. The blood-deed at Sarajevo, whose morally abhorrent character could be accepted as a given, was to be surgically separated from its Serbian context in order to expose Austria's putative intention to 'exploit the crime for the purpose of delivering a mortal blow against Belgrade'.[26] This was, of course, a very Russian view of events, pervaded with historic sympathy for the heroic struggle of the Serbian 'little brothers'. But since it was the Russians who would determine whether and when the Austro-Serbian quarrel justified their own intervention, it was their view of the question that counted most. And there was little reason to expect that the other Entente powers would insist on a more rigorous form of arbitration. The French government had already granted St Petersburg *carte blanche* in the matter of an Austro-Serbian conflict. Without having looked into the matter himself, Poincaré adamantly denied any link between Belgrade and the assassinations. In an interesting conversation on 4 July 1914 with the Austrian ambassador in Paris, the French president compared the murders at Sarajevo with the assassination of the French president Sadi Carnot by an Italian anarchist in 1894. It was a gesture that seemed to express fellow feeling, but was in fact intended to frame the Sarajevo outrage as the act of an aberrant individual for which no political agency, and certainly no sovereign state, could be held liable. The Austrian replied by reminding the president – in vain – that the assassination of Carnot had borne 'no relation to any anti-French agitation in Italy, whereas one must now admit that in Serbia they have been agitating against the Monarchy for years using every permitted and illicit means'.[27]

Count Benckendorff

Edward Grey had at least expressed a theoretical interest in establishing whether Austria or Serbia was the provocateur, on the grounds that British public opinion would not support a war by the Triple Entente on behalf of a Serbian aggressor. But he had been very vague about how one might go about adjudicating such a quarrel, and his comments in the early days after the assassinations did not suggest that he intended to hold the Russians to very stringent criteria. On 8 July, Count Benckendorff, the Russian ambassador in London, remarked to Edward Grey that he 'did not see on what a démarche against Servia could be founded'. The foreign secretary's reply was characteristically tentative:

I said that I did not know what was contemplated. I could only suppose that some discovery made during the trial of those implicated in the murder of the Archduke – for instance, that the bombs had been obtained in Belgrade – might, in the eyes of the Austrian Government, be foundation for a charge of negligence against the Servian Government. But this was only imagination and guess on my part.

Count Benckendorff said that he hoped that Germany would restrain

Austria. He could not think that Germany would wish a quarrel to be precipitated.[28]

Grey made (or recorded) no reply to this last point, which was of considerable importance, because it placed the onus upon Germany to restrain its ally and glibly accepted the inevitability of a 'quarrel' – meaning in this context a war among the great powers – in the event that it should fail to do so. The same argument was conveyed more explicitly in a telegram from Vienna that reached Grey on the following day. It described a conversation between the British ambassador to Vienna and his Russian colleague, in which the Russian announced that he could not believe that Austria would be foolish enough to allow itself to be 'rushed into war',

> for an isolated combat with Servia would be impossible and Russia would
> be compelled to take up arms in defence of Servia. Of this there could be
> no question. A Servian war meant a general European war.[29]

Within ten days, the Russians had established a seamless counter-narrative of the event at Sarajevo. There were contradictions in the picture, to be sure. As one Austrian diplomat pointed out, it made no sense for the Russians to say, on the one hand, that the South Slavs of Bosnia-Herzegovina were united in their loathing of Habsburg tyranny and on the other to complain at the attacks on Serbian property there by crowds of angry Croats. And the Russian assertion that Serbia wished nothing more than to live in peace and harmony with her neighbour sat uncomfortably with Sazonov's earlier assurances to Pašić (via Hartwig) that Serbia would soon inherit the South Slav lands of the crumbling Habsburg Empire. Spalajković's widely reported claim to the press in St Petersburg that the Belgrade government had warned Vienna of the assassination plot in advance raised awkward questions – disregarded by the Russians – about Serbian foreknowledge. Above all, the entire history of Russia's sponsorship of Serbian expansionism and of Balkan instability in general was elided from view. Conspicuously missing from the picture was, finally, any acknowledgement of Russia's own links with the Serbian undergound networks. After the war, Colonel Artamonov, the Russian military attaché in Belgrade, candidly admitted his close pre-war relationship with Apis. He even admitted that he had supplied the head of the Black Hand with funds in support of their espionage operations in Bosnia, though he denied any fore-knowledge of the plot to kill the archduke.[30]

In any case it was already clear that neither London nor Paris intended to challenge the Russian version of events. An unpopular, war-mongering martinet had been cut down by citizens of his own country driven to frenzy by years of humiliation and ill-treatment. And now the corrupt, collapsing and yet supposedly rapacious regime he had repre-sented intended to blame his unregretted death on a blameless and peaceful Slav neighbour. Framing the event at Sarajevo in this way was not in itself tantamount to formulating a decision for action. But it removed some of the obstacles to a Russian military intervention in the event of an Austro-Serbian conflict. The Balkan inception scenario had become an imminent possibility.

COUNT HOYOS GOES TO BERLIN

Even before Alek Hoyos arrived by night train in Berlin on the morning of Sunday 5 July, the view had gained ground there that Austria-Hungary would be justified in mounting a démarche of some kind against Belgrade. A key figure in the change of mood was the Kaiser. When Wilhelm read Tschirschky's dispatch of 30 June reporting that he had been urging calm on the Austrians, Wilhelm appended angry marginal comments:

> Who authorised him to do so? This is utterly stupid! It is none of his busi-ness, since it is entirely Austria's affair [to determine] what she intends to do. Later on, if things went wrong, it would be said: Germany was not willing! Will Tschirschky be so kind as to stop this nonsense! It was high time a clean sweep was made of the Serbs.[31]

Someone must have passed this to Tschirschky, because by 3 July, he was assuring Berchtold of Berlin's support for an Austrian action, pro-vided the objectives were clearly defined and the diplomatic situation favourable.[32] Hoyos was thus assured of a sympathetic hearing when he arrived in the German capital. His first task was to brief Szögyényi, the Austrian ambassador in Berlin, on the two documents he had brought with him, the revised Matscheko memorandum and the personal letter from the Austrian to the German Emperor. Szögyényi then left with copies of both documents for Potsdam, where he lunched with the Kaiser, while Hoyos met with Arthur Zimmermann, under-secretary of the Berlin Foreign Office.

Wilhelm II received the ambassador at the Neues Palais, a vast baroque structure at the western end of the palace park at Potsdam. According to Szögyényi's report, Wilhelm read quickly through both documents and then remarked that he had 'expected a serious action on our part against Serbia' but that he must also consider that such a course might well bring about 'a serious European complication'. He would therefore be unable to give a 'definitive answer before conferring with the Reich Chancellor'. The Emperor then retired for lunch. Szögyényi wrote:

After the meal, when I once again stressed the seriousness of the situation in the most emphatic way, His Majesty empowered me to convey to our Supreme Sovereign [Franz Joseph] that we can count, in this case too, upon the full support of Germany. As he had said, he must hear the opinion of the Reich Chancellor, but he did not doubt in the slightest that Herr von Bethmann Hollweg would completely agree with his view. This was particularly true as regards the action on our part against Serbia. According to his [Kaiser Wilhelm's] view, however, this action should not be delayed. Russia's attitude would be hostile in any event, but he had been prepared for this for years, and if it should come to a war between Austria-Hungary and Russia, we should be confident that Germany would stand by our side with the customary loyalty of allies. Russia, incidentally, as things stood today, was not by any means prepared for war and would certainly think long and hard over whether to issue the call to arms. [...] But if we had truly recognised the necessity of a military action against Serbia, then he (the Kaiser) would regret it if we failed to exploit the present moment, which is so advantageous to us.[33]

While the ambassador and the Emperor talked at Potsdam, Hoyos met with Under Secretary Zimmermann at the Foreign Office in Berlin for an informal talk – the secretary of state, Gottlieb von Jagow, was still away on his honeymoon and thus unavailable for an interview. Hoyos and Zimmermann agreed in principle that Germany would support an Austrian action against Serbia. Zimmermann read the two documents through, noted that he was not in a position to offer an official view and then remarked – according to Hoyos's later recollection – that if the Austrians took action against Serbia, there was 'a 90% likelihood of a European war', before assuring the ambassador nonetheless of German support for Austria's plan.[34] The under-secretary's earlier mood of apprehension, expressed in his call of 4 July for circumspection in Vienna, had clearly dissipated.

At five o'clock that evening, a small group met at the Neues Palais to discuss the morning's events and to coordinate views. Present were the Kaiser, his adjutant General Plessen, the chief of his military cabinet, General Lyncker, and War Minister General Falkenhayn. Under-Secretary Zimmermann and the imperial chancellor, who had in the meanwhile returned from his estate, also attended. Plessen recorded the details in his diary. The Kaiser read out the letter from Franz Joseph, from which everyone concluded that the Austrians were 'getting ready for a war on Serbia' and wanted 'first to be sure of Germany'. 'The opinion prevailed among us that the sooner the Austrians make their move against Serbia the better, and that the Russians – though friends of Serbia – will not join in after all.'[35]

On the following day, 6 July, Bethmann Hollweg received Count Hoyos and Ambassador Szögyényi with Zimmermann in attendance to offer the Austrians a formal reply to their representations (Kaiser Wilhelm had in the meanwhile left Berlin for his annual yacht tour of Scandinavia). Bethmann dwelt first at some length on the general security situation in the Balkans. Bulgaria should be integrated more closely into the Triple Alliance, Bucharest should be asked to scale down its support for Romanian irridentism in Transylvania, and so on. Only then did he turn to the proposed military action:

> In the matter of our relationship with Serbia, [Szögyényi reported] he said that it was the view of the German government that we must judge what ought to be done to sort out this relationship; whatever our decision turned out to be, we could be confident that Germany as our ally and a friend of the Monarchy would stand behind us. In the further course of the conversation, I gathered that both the Chancellor and his Imperial master view an immediate intervention by us against Serbia as the best and most radical solution of our problems in the Balkans. From an international standpoint he views the present moment as more favourable than a later one.[36]

Notwithstanding the oddities of this short address – among other things, only nine of the fifty-four lines of the printed text of Szögyényi's summary were actually about the proposed measures against Serbia and there was no mention of a possible Russian response – we have here a clear decision, and one of momentous importance. For once, the German government was speaking with one voice. The Kaiser and the chancellor (who was also the foreign minister) were in agreement, as was the under-secretary of the Foreign Office, standing in for Jagow, the secretary of state for foreign affairs. The minister of war had been informed and had advised the Emperor that the German army was ready for all eventualities. The result was the assurance of German support that has become known as the 'blank cheque'.

Inasmuch as this otherwise slightly misleading metaphor connotes a promise of support for the alliance partner, it is a fair description of German intentions. The Kaiser and the chancellor believed that the Austrians were justified in taking action against Serbia and deserved to be able to do so without the fear of Russian intimidation. Much more problematic is the claim that the Germans over-interpreted the Austrian messages, made commitments that surpassed Austrian intentions, and thereby pressured them into war.[37] While it is true that Franz Joseph's note did not refer directly to 'war' against Serbia, it left the reader in absolutely no doubt that Vienna was contemplating the most radical possible action. How else should one understand his insistence that 'a conciliation of the conflict' between the two states was no longer possible and that the problem would be resolved only when Serbia had been 'eliminated as a power-factor in the Balkans'? In any case Count Hoyos had left no margin of doubt about Vienna's thinking. He asserted personal control over the Austrian representations during his 'mission' in Berlin; he later revealed to the historian Luigi Albertini that it was he, not the veteran ambassador, who had composed Szögyényi's dispatch summarizing Bethmann's assurances.[38]

How did the German leadership assess the risk that an Austrian attack on Serbia would bring about a Russian intervention, force Germany to assist its ally, trigger the Franco-Russian alliance and thereby bring about a continental war? Some historians have argued that Wilhelm, Bethmann and their military advisers saw the crisis brewing over Sarajevo as an opportunity to seek conflict with the other great powers on terms favourable to Germany. Over preceding years, elements of the German military had repeatedly made a case for preventive war, on the grounds that since the balance of military striking power was tilting fast away from the Triple Alliance, time was running out for Germany. A war fought now might still be winnable; in five years' time the armaments gap would have widened to the point where the odds in favour of the Entente powers were unbeatable.

Exactly how much weight did such arguments carry in the deliberations of the German leadership? In answering this question, we should note first that the key decision-makers did not believe a Russian intervention to be likely and did not wish to provoke one. On 2 July Salza Lichtenau, the Saxon envoy in Berlin, reported that although certain senior military figures were arguing that it would be desirable to 'let war come about now', while Russia remained unprepared, he felt it unlikely that the Kaiser would accept this view. A report filed on the following day by the Saxon military plenipotentiary noted that, by contrast with those who looked with favour on the prospect of a war sooner rather than later, 'the Kaiser is said to have pronounced in favour of maintaining peace'. Those present at the meeting with Wilhelm II in Potsdam on the afternoon of 5 July all took the view that the Russians, though friends of Serbia, 'would not join in after all'. Thus, when at that meeting War Minister Falkenhayn asked the Kaiser whether he wished that 'any kind of preparations should be made' for the eventuality of a great power conflict, Wilhelm replied in the negative. The reluctance of the Germans to make military preparations, which remained a feature of the German handling of the crisis into late July, may in part have reflected the army's confidence in the existing state of readiness, but it also reflected the German leadership's wish to confine the conflict to the Balkans, even if this policy risked jeopardizing their readiness, should confinement fail.[39]

The Kaiser in particular remained confident that the conflict could be localized. On the morning of 6 July, before his departure from Berlin, he told the acting secretary of state for the navy, Admiral von Capelle, that 'he did not believe there would be any further military complications', since 'the Tsar would not in this case place himself on the side of the regicides. Besides, Russia and France were not prepared for war.' He briefed other senior military figures along the same lines. This was not just whistling in the dark: the Kaiser had long been of the opinion that although Russian military preparedness was on the increase, it would be some time before the Russians would be willing to risk a strike.

Late in October 1913, in the aftermath of the Albanian crisis, he had told Ambassador Szögyényi that 'for the moment Russia gave him no cause for anxiety; for the next six years one need fear nothing from that quarter'.[40]

This line of reasoning was not an alternative to the preventive war argument; on the contrary, it was partly interwoven with it. The argument in favour of launching a preventive war consisted of two distinct and separable elements. The first was the observation that Germany's chances of military success in a European war were diminishing fast; the second was the inference that Germany should address this problem by itself seeking a war before it was too late. It was the first part that entered into the thinking of the key civilian decision-makers, not the second. After all, the evidence that suggested diminishing chances of success also implied that the risk of a Russian intervention was minimal. If the Russians' chances of success in a war with Germany really were going to be much better in three years' time than they were be in 1914, why would St Petersburg risk launching a continental conflict now, when it was only half-prepared?

Thinking along these lines opened up two possible scenarios. The first, which appeared much the more probable to Bethmann and his colleagues, was that the Russians would abstain from intervening and leave the Austrians to sort out their dispute with Serbia, perhaps responding diplomatically in concert with one or more other powers at a later point. The second scenario, deemed less probable, was that the Russians would deny the legitimacy of Austria's case, overlook the incompleteness of their own rearmament programme, and intervene nonetheless. It was on this secondary level of conditionality that the logic of preventive war fell into place: for if there was going to be a war *anyway*, it would be better to have one now.

Underlying these calculations was the strong and, as we can see in retrospect, erroneous assumption that the Russians were unlikely to intervene. The reasons for this gross misreading of the level of risk are not hard to find. Russia's acceptance of the Austrian ultimatum in October 1913 spoke for that outcome. Then there was the deeply held belief already alluded to that time was on Russia's side. The assassinations were seen in Berlin as an assault on the monarchical principle launched from within a political culture with a strong propensity to regicide (a view that can also be found in some British press coverage). Strong as

Russia's pan-Slav sympathies might be, it was difficult to imagine the Tsar siding 'with the regicides', as the Kaiser repeatedly observed. To all this, we must add the perennial problem of reading the intentions of the Russian executive. The Germans were unaware of the extent to which an Austro-Serbian quarrel had already been built into Franco-Russian strategic thinking. They failed to understand how indifferent the two western powers would be to the question of who had provoked the quarrel.

Moreover, the Germans had not yet grasped the significance of Kokovtsov's removal from office as chairman of the Council of Ministers and found it difficult to read the balance of power within the new Council. In this they were not alone – British diplomats too struggled to read the new constellation and came to the entirely misleading conclusion that the influence of anti-war conservatives such as Kokovtsov and Durnovo was once again in the ascendant, and in Paris there was concern that a 'pro-German' faction led by Sergei Witte might be about to secure control over policy.[41] The opacity of the system made it difficult – now, as on so many previous ocasions – to assess risk. At the same time, the recent German experience of hand-in-hand collaboration with London on Balkan matters suggested that England might well – despite the latest naval talks – understand Berlin's standpoint and press St Petersburg to observe restraint. This was one of the dangers of détente: that it encouraged decision-makers to underrate the dangers attendant upon their actions.

One could thus speak, as some historians have, of a policy of calculated risk.[42] But this characterization excludes from view a further important link in the chain of German thinking. This was the supposition that a Russian intervention – being a policy indefensible in ethico-legal or in security terms – would in reality be evidence of something else more ominous, namely St Petersburg's desire to *seek* a war with the central powers, to exploit the opportunity offered by the Austrian démarche in order to commence a campaign that would break the power of the Triple Alliance. Seen from this perspective, the Austro-Serbian crisis looked less like an opportunity to seek war and more like a means of establishing the true nature of Russia's intentions. And if Russia were found to want war (which was plausible in German eyes, given the immense scope of its rearmament, the intense collaboration with France, the outrage over the Liman mission and the recent naval talks with Britain), then – here again the diminishing chances/preventive war argument fell into place as part of a second-tier conditionality – it would be better to accept the war offered by the Russians now than dodge it by backing down. If one did the latter, then Germany faced the prospect of losing its one remaining ally and of coming under steadily intensifying pressure from the Entente states, whose ability to enforce their preferences would increase as the balance of military power tilted irreversibly away from Germany and whatever remained of Austria-Hungary.[43]

This was not, then, strictly speaking, a strategy centred on risk, but one that aimed to establish the true level of threat posed by Russia. To put it a different way, if the Russians *chose* to mobilize against Germany and thereby trigger a continental war, this would not express the risk generated by Germany's actions, but the strength of Russia's determination to rebalance the European system through war. Viewed from this admittedly rather circumscribed perspective, the Germans were not taking risks, but testing for threats. This was the logic underlying Bethmann's frequent references to the threat posed by Russia during the last months before the outbreak of war.

In order to understand this preoccupation, we need briefly to recall how prominent this issue was in the public world shared by policy-makers and newspaper editors in the spring and summer of 1914. On 2 January 1914, the Paris newspaper *Le Matin* began to publish a sensational series of five long articles under the title 'La plus grande Russie'. Composed by the paper's editor-in-chief Stéphane Lauzanne, who had just come back from a journey to Moscow and St Petersburg, the series impressed readers in Berlin not only by the sneering belligerence of its tone, but also by the apparent accuracy and texture of the information contained in it. Most alarming of all was a map bearing the caption 'Russia's dispositions for war' and depicting the entire terrain between the Baltic and the Black Sea as a densely packed archipelago of troop concentrations linked with each other by a lattice of railways. The commentary attached to the map reported that these were 'the exact dispositions of the Russian army corps as of 31 December 1913' and urged readers to note 'the extraordinary concentration of forces on the Russo-Prussian frontier'. These articles expressed a somewhat fantastical and exaggerated view of Russian military strength and may in fact have been aimed at undermining the opposition to the new Russian loan, but for German readers who were aware of the massive loans recently agreed between France and Russia, they made alarming reading. Their effect was amplified by the suspicion that the information in them derived from a government source – *Le Matin* was notoriously close to Poincaré and it was known that Lauzanne had met with Sazonov and senior Russian military commanders during his trip to Russia.[44] There were many other similarly hair-raising ventures into inspired journalism: in a New Year's editorial published at around the same time, the military journal *Razvechik*, widely viewed as an organ of the imperial General Staff, offered a bloodcurdling view of the coming war with Germany:

> Not just the troops, but the entire Russian people must get used to the fact that we are arming ourselves for the war of extermination against the Germans and that the German empires [*sic*] must be destroyed, even if it costs us hundreds of thousands of lives.[45]

Semi-official panic-mongering of this kind continued into the summer. Particularly unsettling was a piece of 13 June in the daily *Birzheviia Vedomosti* (Stock Exchange News) whose headline read: 'We Are Ready. France Must Be Ready Too'. It was widely reprinted in the French and German press. What especially alarmed policy-makers in Berlin was the (accurate) advice from Ambassador Pourtalès in St Petersburg that it was inspired by none other than the minister of war Vladimir Sukhomlinov. The article sketched an impressive portrait of the immense military machine that would fall upon Germany in the event of war – the Russian army, it boasted, would soon count 2.32 million men (Germany and Austria, by contrast, would have only 1.8 million between them). Thanks to a swiftly expanding strategic railway network, moreover, mobilization times were plummeting.[46]

Sukhomlinov's primary purpose was in all probability not to terrify the Germans, but to persuade the French government of the size of Russia's military commitment to the alliance and to remind his French counterparts that they too must carry their weight. All the same, its effect on German readers was predictably disconcerting. One of these was the Kaiser, who splattered his translation with the usual spontaneous jottings, including the following: 'Ha! At last the Russians have placed their cards on the table! Anyone in Germany who still doesn't believe that Russo-Gaul is working towards an imminent war with us

[. . .] belongs in the Dalldorf asylum!'[47] Another reader was Chancellor Bethmann Hollweg. In a letter of 16 June to Ambassador Lichnowsky in London, the chancellor observed that the war-lust of the Russia 'militarist party' had never been 'so ruthlessly revealed'. Until now, he went on, it was only the 'extremists', pan-Germans and militarists, who had suspected Russia of preparing a war of aggression against Germany. But now, 'even calmer politicians', among whom Bethmann presumably counted himself, were 'beginning to incline towards this view'.[48] Among these was Foreign Secretary Gottlieb von Jagow, who took the view that although Russia was not *yet* ready for war, it would soon 'overwhelm' Germany with its vast armies, Baltic Fleet and strategic railway network.[49] General Staff reports of 27 November 1913 and 7 July 1914 provided updated analyses of the Russian strategic railway programme, accompanied by a map on which the new arterial lines – most with numerous parallel rails, reaching deep into the Russian interior and converging on the German and Austrian frontiers – were marked in stripes of brightly coloured ink.[50]

These apprehensions were reinforced by the Anglo-Russian naval talks of June 1914, which suggested that the strategizing of the Entente powers had entered a new and dangerous phase. In May 1914, in response to pressure from the French foreign ministry, the British cabinet sanctioned joint naval staff talks with the Russians. Despite the strict secrecy in which they were held, the Germans were in fact well informed of the details of the Anglo-Russian discussions through an agent in the Russian embassy in London, the second secretary, Benno von Siebert, a Baltic German in Russian service. Through this source Berlin learned, among other things, that London and St Petersburg had discussed the possibility that in the event of war, the British fleet would support the landing of a Russian Expeditionary Corps in Pomerania. The news caused alarm in Berlin. In 1913–14, Russian naval spending exceeded Germany's for the first time. There was concern about a more aggressive Russian foreign policy and a steady tightening of the Entente that would soon deprive German policy of any freedom of movement. The discrepancies between Edward Grey's evasive replies to enquiries by Count Lichnowsky and the details filed by Siebert conveyed the alarming impression that the British had something to hide, producing a crisis in trust between Berlin and London, a matter of some import to Bethmann Hollweg, whose policy had always been founded on the presumption that Britain, though partially integrated into the Entente, would never support a war of aggression against Germany by the Entente states.[51]

The diaries of the diplomat and philosopher Kurt Riezler, Bethmann's closest adviser and confidant, convey the tenor of the chancellor's thinking at the time the decision was made to back Vienna. After the meeting with Szögyényi and Hoyos on 6 July, the two men had travelled back out to the chancellor's estate at Hohenfinow. Riezler recalled his conversation of that evening with Bethmann:

> On the verandah under the night sky long talk on the situation. The secret information [from the German informant at the Russian embassy in London] he divulges to me conveys a shattering picture. He sees the Russian-English negotiations on a naval convention, a landing in Pomerania, as very serious, the last link in the chain. [. . .] Russia's military power growing swiftly; strategic reinforcement of the Polish salient will make the situation untenable. Austria steadily weaker and less mobile [. . .]

Intertwined with these concerns about Russia were doubts about the reliability and longevity of the alliance with Austria:

> The Chancellor speaks of weighty decisions. The murder of Franz Ferdinand. Official Serbia involved. Austria wants to pull itself together. Letter from Franz Joseph with enquiry regarding the readiness of the alliance to act.
>
> It's our old dilemma with every Austrian action in the Balkans. If we encourage them, they will say we pushed them into it. If we counsel against it, they will say we left them in the lurch. Then they will approach the western powers, whose arms are open, and we lose our last reasonable ally.[52]

During a conversation with Riezler on the following day, Bethmann remarked that Austria was incapable of 'entering a war as our ally on behalf of a German cause'.[53] By contrast, a war 'from the east', born of a Balkan conflict and driven in the first instance by Austro-Hungarian interests, would ensure that Vienna's interests were fully engaged: 'If war comes from the east, so that we enter the field for Austria-Hungary and not Austria-Hungary for us, we have some prospect of success.'[54] This argument mirrored exactly one of the core arguments of the French policy-makers, namely that a war of Balkan origin was most likely to engage Russia fully in support of the common enterprise against Germany. Neither the French nor the German policy-makers trusted their respective allies to commit fully to a struggle in which their own country's interests were principally at stake.

THE ROAD TO THE AUSTRIAN
ULTIMATUM

A decision of sorts had been made: the Austrians, or at least the group around Berchtold, intended to seek a military resolution of their conflict with Serbia. But on all other issues, the composite policy-mind in Vienna had as yet failed to deliver coherent positions. There was still no agreement at the time Hoyos left for Berlin, for example, on what policy should be pursued vis-à-vis Serbia after an Austrian victory. When Zimmermann enquired after Austria's post-war objectives, Hoyos responded with a bizarre improvisation: Serbia, he declared, would be partitioned between Austria, Bulgaria and Romania. Hoyos had no authority to propose such a course to Zimmermann, nor had a policy of partition been agreed by his Austrian colleagues. Hoyos later recalled that he had invented the partition policy because he feared that the Germans would lose faith in the Austrians if they felt 'that we could not formulate our Serbian policy precisely and had unclear objectives'; it was irrelevant what aims were identified, what mattered was that an appearance of determination and firmness be conveyed to the ally.[55] Tisza was furious when he learned of Hoyos's indiscretion; the Hungarians, even more than the political elite in Vienna, regarded the prospect of yet more angry South Slav Habsburg subjects with unalloyed horror. Vienna subsequently made it clear that no annexation of Serbian territory was intended. But Hoyos's extraordinary gaffe conveys something of the disjointed way in which Austrian policy evolved during the crisis.

Timing was another problem. The Germans had insisted that if there was to be an action against Serbia, it must happen fast, while popular outrage at the murders was still fresh. But promptness was not a prominent feature of the Austrian political culture. It soon became clear that it would be some time before any military action could begin. There were two main reasons for this sluggishness. The first was political. At a meeting of the Joint Ministerial Council, held in Vienna on 7 July, the day after Hoyos's return from Berlin, it became clear that there was still disagreement among the principal decision makers about how to proceed. Berchtold opened the proceedings by reminding his colleagues that Bosnia and Herzegovina would be stabilized only if the external threat posed by Belgrade were dealt with. If no action were taken, the monarchy's ability to deal with the Russian-sponsored irredentist movements in its South Slav and Romanian areas would steadily deteriorate. This was an argument calculated to appeal to the Hungarian premier Count Tisza, for whom the stability of Transylvania was a central concern. Tisza was not convinced. In his reply to Berchtold, he conceded that the attitude of the Serbian press and the results of the police investigation in Sarajevo strengthened the case for a military strike. But first, the diplomatic options must be exhausted. Belgrade must be presented with an ultimatum, whose stipulations must be 'firm, but not unfulfillable'. Sufficient forces must be made available to secure Transylvania against an opportunist attack by Romania. Then Vienna must look to consolidate its position among the Balkan powers: Vienna should seek closer relations with Bulgaria and the Ottoman Empire, in the hope of creating a Balkan counterweight to Serbia and 'forcing Romania to return to the Triple Alliance'.[56]

There was nothing here to surprise anyone around the table – this was the familiar Budapest view, in which Transylvania occupied centre stage. But Tisza faced a solid bloc of colleagues determined to confront Serbia with demands they expected Belgrade to reject. A purely diplomatic success, War Minister Krobatin warned, would have no value at all, since it would be read in Belgrade, Bucharest, St Petersburg and the South Slav areas of the monarchy as a sign of Vienna's weakness and irresolution. Time was running out for Austria-Hungary – with each passing year, the monarchy's security position on the Balkan peninsula became increasingly fragile. The conclusions stated in the minutes, which were kept by none other than Count Hoyos, reflected a curious and not entirely coherent blend of the salient positions. Everyone concurred, firstly, on the need for a swift resolution of the quarrel with Serbia, 'either by military or by peaceful means'. Secondly, the ministers agreed to accept Count Tisza's suggestion that mobilization against Serbia should occur only after Belgrade had been confronted with an ultimatum. Lastly, it was noted that everyone in the room, with the exception of the Hungarian premier, was of the opinion that a purely diplomatic success, even if it entailed a 'sensational humiliation' of Serbia, would be worthless and that the ultimatum must therefore be framed in terms harsh enough to ensure a rejection, 'so that the way is open to a radical solution by means of military intervention'.[57]

After lunch, Conrad and Karl Kailer, representing the naval chief of staff, joined the meeting and the ministers reviewed the military plans. Questioned by Minister of War Krobatin, Conrad explained that while the war plan against Serbia (named 'Plan B', for 'Balkan') would involve deploying large numbers of troops to the southern periphery, an intervention in the conflict by Russia would oblige the Austrians to shift the focus of operations from the south to the north-east. It might take some time to ascertain whether and when this shift would be necessary, but Conrad hoped that he would know by the fifth day after mobilization whether he needed to take Russia into account. This delay might even mean ceding a part of northern Galicia in the first instance to the Russians. It remained unclear how exactly the logistically complex business of changing gear from one war plan to another would be accomplished, and the ministers did not ask.[58]

This discussion marked a watershed. The chance of a peaceful outcome was slim once the meeting was over.[59] Yet there was still no sign of precipitate action. The option of an immediate surprise attack without a declaration of war was rejected. Tisza, whose agreement was constitutionally necessary for a resolution of such importance, continued to insist that Serbia should first be humiliated diplomatically. Only after a further week did he yield to the majority view, mainly because he became convinced that failure to address the Serbian question would have an unsettling effect on Hungarian Transylvania. But there was a more intractable obstacle to swift action. In rural areas of the Habsburg lands, military service in summertime created serious disruption by keeping young men away from their homes and fields at the time when most crops were harvested. In order to alleviate the problem, the Austrian General Staff had devised a system of harvest leaves that allowed men on active service to return to their family farms to help with the crops and then rejoin their units in time for the summer manoeuvres. On 6 July, the day before the meeting, Conrad had ascertained that troops serving in units at Agram (Zagreb), Graz, Pressburg (Bratislava), Craców, Temesvar (Timisoara), Innsbruck and Budapest were currently on harvest leave and would not be returning to service until 25 July.

So Conrad had little choice: he could issue an order to cancel new leaves (and he did), but he could not recall the many thousands of men already on summer leave without seriously disrupting the harvest, disaffecting peasant subjects in many national minority areas, overcrowding the railway system and awakening suspicion across Europe that Austria was planning an imminent military strike. It is odd, to say the least, that Conrad, who was the architect of these leave arrangements, did not foresee this problem when he proposed to Berchtold, on the evening of the day after the murders, that Austria mount an immediate attack on Serbia in the manner of the Japanese assault on the Russian fleet at Port Arthur in 1904, which had been launched without a prior declaration of war.[60]

In the meanwhile, a measure of unanimity was achieved in Vienna over the course of action to be followed. At a further summit meeting in the city on 14 July, it was agreed that a draft of the ultimatum would be checked and approved by the Council of Ministers on Sunday 19 July. But the ultimatum itself would be presented to the Belgrade government only on Thursday 23 July. This was in order to avoid its coinciding with a state visit by President Raymond Poincaré and his new prime minister, René Viviani, to St Petersburg, scheduled for 20–23 July. Berchtold and Tisza were in agreement that 'the sending of an ultimatum during this meeting in St Petersburg would be viewed as an affront and that personal discussion between the ambitious President of the Republic and His Majesty the Emperor of Russia [. . .] would heighten the likelihood of a military intervention by Russia and France'.[61]

From this moment onwards, secrecy was of the greatest possible importance, both for strategic and diplomatic reasons. It was essential, Conrad informed Berchtold on 10 July, to avoid any action that might give the Serbs prior notice of Austrian intentions and thereby give them time to steal a march on the Austrian army.[62] Recent Austrian appraisals of Serbian military strength suggested that the Serbian army would not be a trivial opponent. (How right they were became clear in the winter of 1914, when the Serbian army succeeded in throwing the Austrians back out of the kingdom.) Secrecy was also essential because it presented Vienna's only hope of conveying its demands to Belgrade before the Entente powers had the opportunity for joint deliberations on how to respond – hence the importance of avoiding the days when Poincaré and Viviani would be in St Petersburg. Berchtold therefore ordered that the press be firmly instructed to avoid the subject of Serbia. This step was apparently effective: there was a remarkable evacuation of Serbian subject matter from the daily papers during the middle weeks of the crisis – a state of affairs that helped to produce a deceptive public sense of calm, just as the crisis was in fact about to enter its most dangerous phase. In its official relations with Russia, Vienna went out of its way to avoid even the slightest friction; Szapáry, the Austrian ambassador in St Petersburg, was particularly assiduous in his efforts to tranquillize the Russian foreign ministry with assurances that all would be well.[63]

Unfortunately, this policy of stealth was compromised by a leak originating, oddly enough, in Berlin. On 11 July, the German secretary of state Gottlieb von Jagow, informed the German ambassador in Rome of Austria's intentions. Flotow passed this information to the Italian foreign minister, San Giuliano, and the Italian Foreign Office promptly conveyed the information by coded telegram to the Italian legations in St Petersburg, Bucharest and Vienna. The Austrians, who had broken the Italian code and were closely watching diplomatic traffic between Vienna and Rome, learned almost immediately that the Italians had acquired knowledge of Austrian plans from a German source and had passed it to two unfriendly capitals, with the intention that the Russians and the Romanians should be encouraged to prevent the Austrian démarche by adopting a 'threatening demeanour' in Vienna and Berlin.[64] The Austrians also had good reason to suppose that the Russians, whose code-breaking was unequalled anywhere in Europe, had themselves intercepted the Italian telegrams and found out about the forthcoming ultimatum. In fact the Russians had no need of these Italian intercepts, since they also learned of the planned ultimatum via other German *and* Austrian leaks. On 16 July, in conversation with the retired Austrian diplomat Count Lützow, the Russian ambassador in Vienna learned that the Austrians were drawing up a note worded 'in very harsh terms' and containing, as the ambassador put it, 'demands unacceptable to any independent state'. Lützow's source, astonishingly enough, was a long and candid conversation in Vienna with Berchtold and Forgách. Shebeko's report on this sensational discovery went straight via the Russian foreign ministry to Tsar Nicholas II. The Tsar appended a remarkable comment: 'In my view, no country can present demands to another, unless it has decided to wage war'.[65] Nothing could express more clearly the Russian denial of Austria's right to insist on any kind of satisfaction from Belgrade.

These breaches of Austrian secrecy had two important effects. The first was simply that by around 20 July, the Russians and their great power partners were pretty fully apprised of what the Austrians had in store. The Serbian authorities too, were informed, as we know from a report of 17 July by Crackanthorpe, the British minister in Belgrade.[66] In both St Petersburg and in Belgrade, this prior knowledge facilitated the formulation and coordination – *in advance of the presentation of the ultimatum to Belgrade* – of a firmly rejectionist position, eloquently expressed in Pašić's circular of 19 July to the Serbian legations abroad: 'we cannot accept those demands which no other country that respects its own independence and dignity would accept'.[67] What this meant, among other things, was that there had been ample opportunity for views on a possible ultimatum to mature by the time the French head of state and his prime minister arrived in St Petersburg on 20 July. The notion – promulgated by Sazonov and later put about in the literature – that the news of the ultimatum came as a terrible shock to the Russians and the French on 23 July, when the note was presented to the Serbian foreign ministry, is nonsense.

The second effect related to Vienna's handling of the German partner. Berchtold blamed the Germans for compromising his strategy of stealth and responded to the leaks by shutting down communications with Berlin, with the result that the Germans were no better informed of the precise contents of the forthcoming Austrian ultimatum than their Entente opponents. It is one of the strangest features of Austria's handling of the crisis that a copy of the ultimatum was forwarded to the leadership in Berlin only on the evening of 22 July.[68] Yet German protestations of ignorance naturally rang false with the diplomats of the Entente, who viewed them as evidence that the Germans and the Austrians were together in secret planning a long-prepared joint enterprise that must be met with a coordinated and firm response – an assumption that did not augur well for peace as the crisis entered its final phase.

It is worth touching once again on the oddities of the Austro-Hungarian decision-making process. Berchtold, disparaged by many of the hawks in the administration as a soft touch incapable of forming clear resolutions, took control of the policy debate after 28 June in a rather impressive way. But he could do this only through an arduous and time-consuming process of consensus-building. The puzzling dissonances in the documents that track the emergence of the Austrian decision for war reflect the need to incorporate – without necessarily reconciling – opposed viewpoints.

Perhaps the most striking defect of Austrian decision-making was the narrowness of the individual and collective fields of vision. The Austrians resembled hedgehogs scurrying across a highway with their eyes averted from the rushing traffic.[69] The momentous possibility of a Russian general mobilization and the general European war that would inevitably follow was certainly glimpsed by the Austrian decision-makers, who discussed it on several occasions. But it was never integrated into the process by which options were weighed up and assessed. No sustained attention was given to the question of whether Austria-Hungary was in any position to wage a war with one or more other European great powers.[70] There are several possible reasons for this. One was the extraordinary confidence of the Austro-Hungarian administration in the strength of German arms, which, it was believed, sufficed in the first instance to deter and, failing that, to defeat Russia.[71] The second was that the hive-like structure of the Austro-Hungarian political elite was simply not conducive to the formulation of decisions through the careful sifting and balancing of contradictory information. The contributors to the debate tended to indulge in strong statements of opinion, often sharpened by mutual recriminations, rather than attempting to view the problems facing Vienna in the round. The solipsism of Austrian decision-making also reflected a profound sense of geopolitical isolation. The notion that Austro-Hungarian statesmen had a 'responsibility to Europe' was nonsense, one political insider noted, 'because there is no Europe. Public opinion in Russia and France [. . .] will always maintain that we are the guilty ones, even if the Serbs, in the midst of peace, invade us by the thousands one night, armed with bombs'.[72] But the most important reason for the perplexing narrowness of the Austrian policy debate is surely that the Austrians were so convinced of the rectitude of their case and of their proposed remedy against Serbia that they could conceive of no alternative to it – even Tisza, after all, had accepted by 7 July that Belgrade was implicated in the crimes at Sarajevo and was willing in principle to countenance a military response, provided the timing and diplomatic context were right. Inaction would merely confirm the widely held conviction that this was an empire on its last legs. On the other hand, the moral effect of a bold action would be transformative: 'Austria-Hungary [. . .] would again believe in itself. It would mean: "I have the will, therefore I am."'[73]

In short, the Austrians were in the process of making what decision theorists have called an 'opting decision', one in which the stakes are unimaginably high, the impact transformative and irrevocable, levels of emotion elevated, and the consequences of not acting potentially lasting. Decisions of this kind may acquire an existential dimension, in that they promise to re-invent the decision-making entity, to fashion it into something it was not before. At the core of such decisions is something rooted in identity that is not easily susceptible to rationalization.[74] This is not to suggest that Austrian decision-making was 'irrational'. The present crisis was assessed in the light of past developments, and various factors and risks were brought to bear on the discussion. Nor is it easy to see how the Austrians could made a less drastic solution work, given the reluctance of the Serbian authorities to meet Austrian expectations, the absence of any international legal bodies capable of arbitrating in such cases, and the impossibility in the current international climate of enforcing the future compliance of Belgrade. Yet at the core of the Austrian response – to an extent that does not apply to any of the other actors in 1914 – was a temperamental, intuitive leap, a 'naked act of decision'[75] founded in a shared understanding of what the Austro-Hungarian Empire was and must be if it were to remain a great power.

THE STRANGE DEATH OF NIKOLAI HARTWIG

It was during the tranquillization phase of Austrian policy that the Russian minister in Belgrade suddenly died. Hartwig had been suffering from angina pectoris for some time. He was obese, and prone to increasingly fierce headaches, the result not just of stress, but probably also of hypertension. It was his practice each summer to take the cure at Bad Nauheim, whence he would return with his spirits restored and his weight reduced. When his subordinate Basil Strandmann, on hearing the news of the assassinations, broke off his own vacation in Venice and returned to Belgrade, he found Hartwig in poor physical condition and longing to take his cure. The minister informed Strandmann that 'as no important events could be expected before Autumn', he had put in an application to take his vacation on 13 July.

On 10 July, three days before he was due to leave, Hartwig learned that the Austrian minister Baron Giesl had just returned to Belgrade. He telephoned the Austrian legation and arranged a visit in order to clarify various misunderstandings. It was widely reported in Belgrade that on 3 July, the day of the archduke's requiem service, the Russian legation had been the only one in the Serbian capital not to fly its flag at half-mast. Both the Italian and the British mission chiefs in Belgrade had noticed the omission.[76] On the evening following the assassinations, moreover, it was said that Hartwig had hosted a reception in his legation, from which cheering and laughter could be heard in the nearby streets. The Russian minister was probably also anxious lest reports of other indiscretions had reached the ears of his Austrian colleague.[77] In fact, the interview went quite amicably. Giesl cordially accepted Hartwig's explanations and excuses and the two men settled down for a long talk in Giesl's office.

Having spoken at some length of his poor health and his vacation plans, Hartwig came to the chief concern of his visit, a defence of Serbia's innocence of the murders and of its intentions for the future. But he had scarcely got through the first sentence when, at about 9.20 p.m., he lost consciousness and slowly slid, his cigarette still burning between his fingers, from the divan on to the carpet. Hartwig's carriage was sent at haste to collect his daughter Ludmilla and a local Serbian doctor appeared, followed by Hartwig's physician, but despite the application of water, Eau de Cologne, ether and ice, it proved impossible to bring him back to consciousness. Baroness Giesl's expressions of sympathy for Hartwig's daughter were brushed off with the comment that 'Austrian words' were of no interest to her. Ludmilla von Hartwig, who had been spending the evening with Crown Prince Alexandar of Serbia, made a point of inspecting the room in which her father had died, digging around in some large Japanese vases, sniffing at the bottle of Eau de Cologne that had been used to try to rouse him and curtly enquiring whether her father had been given anything to eat or drink. Giesl replied that the minister had merely smoked a few Russian cigarettes that he had brought with him. The daughter asked for the butts and took them away in her purse. Neither the evidence of Hartwig's illness, of which he had made no secret, nor the assurances of the Austrian minister prevented assassination theories from circulating across the capital.[78] One newspaper referred to Giesl and his wife as 'modern Borgias' who poisoned unwelcome guests, and a few days later Giesl himself overheard a conversation between two clients in his barber's shop:

> Austria sends us strange ambassadors. First we had an imbecile [Forgách] and now we have an assassin. Giesl has brought an electric chair from Vienna that causes the immediate death of anyone who sits down on it and leaves not the slightest trace.[79]

Fortunately, neither of the two interlocutors recognized Giesl in the next chair. At the request of Hartwig's family and the Belgrade government, Sazonov gave permission for Hartwig to be buried in Serbia, a highly unusual procedure for a Russian diplomat who had died in foreign service.[80] The expressions of public grief and the unprecedented pomp that accompanied his state funeral in Belgrade bore witness to the extraordinary place he occupied in Serbian public awareness. However one assesses Hartwig's contribution to Balkan politics, it would be churlish to deny that the Russian minister had already achieved his primary objectives when he collapsed on Giesl's divan. In the words of the French envoy Descos, Hartwig died at the very moment when his 'indomitable will' had triumphed by 'imposing on Serbism his absolute authority, and on Europe the Serbian question in the violent form dear to his heart'.[81]

9

The French in St Petersburg

COUNT DE ROBIEN CHANGES TRAINS

On 6 July 1914, the 26-year-old French diplomat Louis de Robien left
Paris for St Petersburg, where he had been appointed attaché at the
French embassy. The date of his departure had been pulled forward so
that he would arrive in good time to help with the preparations for the
state visit by President Poincaré, which was scheduled for 20 July. To
gain time, de Robien did not take the Nord Express, which did not leave
every day, but boarded an ordinary sleeping car in the fast train to
Cologne. There was time to look briefly at the Rhine and the great
Gothic cathedral before the connecting train crossed the industrial
region of the Ruhr, 'always so impressive and not without a certain
beauty'. From there the train made its way eastwards, traversing Germany at its widest point, until it reached Wirballen (today the Lithuanian
town of Kybartai) on the eastern border of East Prussia. Here, much to
his annoyance, de Robien had to leave his comfortable German sleeping
car and change trains because of the difference between the Russian and
European gauges. His first encounter with the locals on the far side of
the border made a lasting impression: as soon as the train had stopped,
the carriages were invaded by a 'horde of bearded persons' wearing
boots and white aprons who took charge of his baggage with such haste
that he was unable to follow them. De Robien and his fellow passengers
were channelled towards a barricade before which stood 'soldiers with
great sabres'. Here their passports were verified, a procedure that astonished de Robien, because 'in that era of liberty, one travelled everywhere
in Europe except for Russia without carrying a passport'. After present-
ing his travel documents, de Robien waited in a vast room in whose

corners were icons, lit by stands of burning candles, a 'strange accoutre-
ment', he felt, for what was effectively a waiting room. At last the
formalities were complete and the train passed through a countryside
'of terrible sadness' studded with villages over which loomed the onion
domes of churches. He tried to speak with some officers, who appeared
to be engineers, but they spoke only a few words of German. 'We felt,'
he recalled, 'as if we were in China.'[1]

His arrival in St Petersburg, where he would spend the war years and
live through the cataclysm of two revolutions, did nothing to dispel the
sense of strangeness. On the contrary, it merely 'completed our disappointment'. The Russian capital was full of 'horrible little carriages, long,
poorly maintained roads, and bearded, exotic-looking coachmen'. He
initially booked in at the Hotel France, where the rooms were large but
the furniture so ugly and the ambience so comfortless and 'different from
what we were used to in Europe' that he decided to cancel his reserva-
tion and move instead to the Hotel d'Europe on the 'famous Nevsky
Prospekt'. But even the Hotel d'Europe was not especially European and
the shops along the great riverside avenue were disappointing – the best
of them, the Parisian nobleman wrote, were reminiscent of a French
provincial town.[2]

Getting about was difficult, because scarcely any passers-by could
understand him, which was a shock, since his colleagues in Paris had
assured him that the French language would be familiar to everybody.
The food and drink of the city brought little comfort to the fastidious
count: Russian cuisine, he reported, was awful, especially the fish soups,
which were 'detestable'; only borshch struck him as 'a recipe worth
keeping on the menu'. As for 'their vodka', drunk at one draught, it was
'unworthy of a civilized palate educated to the slow enjoyment of our
cognacs, our armagnacs, our marcs and our kirsch'.[3]

Having found his bearings in the city, de Robien made his way to his
new place of work. There was some consolation in the fact that the
French embassy, housed in a fine palace that had belonged to the Dolgo-
ruki family, was situated at one of the most beautiful points along the
banks of the Neva. De Robien was especially impressed by the footmen
in their blue livery and short breeches. On the ground floor looking out
over the river could be found the ambassador's office, decorated with
tapestries and paintings by Van der Meulen. Next door was a smaller
room where the telephone was kept – it was here that the embassy staff

gathered each afternoon for the ritual taking of tea. Next to this room was the office of the counsellor M. Doulcet, whose walls were decorated with portraits of all the ambassadors of France to the court of Russia. At the back, behind an office crowded with secretaries and archival files, was a door opening on to the embassy strongroom, where secret documents and the transmissions code were stored. The pride of the embassy was the reception room on the first floor, a fine boudoir with walls of green and gold damask hung with paintings by Guardi belonging to the ambassador, and gilt armchairs that were supposed to have furnished the rooms of Marie Antoinette.[4]

De Robien already knew Ambassador Maurice Paléologue, a larger-than-life figure who had been in post since January and would dominate the life of the embassy until his departure three years later. Photographs from 1914 show a dapper man of medium height with a shaven head and 'very brilliant eyes deeply lodged within their sockets'. Paléologue was a 'romancer, rather than a diplomat', de Robien recalled. He viewed all events from their dramatic and literary angle. 'Whenever he recounted an event or sought to retrace a conversation, he recreated them almost entirely in his imagination, endowing them with more vividness than truth.' Paléologue was extremely proud of his name, which he claimed (speciously) to have inherited from the emperors of ancient Byzantium. He compensated for his 'exotic' ancestry (his father was a Greek political refugee and his mother a Belgian musician) with a passionate and demonstrative patriotism and a desire to project himself as the embodiment of French refinement and cultural superiority.

Once installed in St Petersburg, Paléologue, who had never held such a senior post before, soon filled out the dimensions of his new office. De Robien observed the ways in which the ambassador would make his importance felt to the representatives of 'lesser' countries: when the secretary announced the arrival of the Belgian envoy Buisseret or his Dutch colleague Sweerts, it was Paléologue's habit to go out by the back door for a walk, in order to greet them in the anteroom an hour later with arms opened, saying 'My dear fellow, I've had so much on today . . .' He displayed a taste for extravagance and ostentation that was exceptional, even in the world of the senior ambassadors. Much was made in St Petersburg society of the fact that embassy dinners were prepared by the chef Paléologue had brought with him from Paris. De Robien put all this down to Paléologue's 'oriental' ancestry, adding archly that, as with many parvenus, Paléologue's love of magnificence had something affected and unnatural about it.[5]

Paléologue had a horror of the kind of detailed dispatches that were the bread and butter of workaday diplomacy, preferring to shape his impressions into lively scenes invigorated by dialogues in which catchy phrases replaced the long and often ambiguous verbal circumlocutions that were the day-to-day traffic of diplomats working in Russia. De Robien recalled one particular day on which the ambassador was scheduled to be received in audience by the Tsar for a conversation on an important military matter. Paléologue wished the dispatch to be sent as soon as he returned to the embassy, so that it would reach Paris at the time when it would 'have the greatest effect'. In order to achieve this he composed the account of his meeting before he had even left the embassy to see the Russian sovereign. De Robien and his colleagues got busy encoding the detailed narative of a conversation that had never taken place. Amid all the faux-reportage, the count remembered one highly characteristic Paléologian phrase: 'At this point, the interview reached a crucial turning point and the Emperor offered me a cigarette.'[6]

De Robien's comments on the ambassador, though hostile, were probably fair. Paléologue was one of the most iridescent personalities to hold ambassadorial office in the French service. For many years he had languished in the Parisian Centrale, condemned to tedious copying tasks. Later he was placed in charge of keeping the secret files, especially those relating to the Franco-Russian Alliance and liaison between foreign ministry and army intelligence services, work that he relished. His long years as the custodian of the ministry's accumulated understanding of the alliance and of the military threats facing it – he had access, for example, to French intelligence on Germany's two-pronged mobilization plan – imbued him with a view of French foreign relations that was tightly focused on the German threat and the paramount importance of allied cohesion.[7] His historical writings convey a romantic conception of the great man as one who gives himself to moments of world-historical decision:

> In certain cases [Paléologue wrote in his biography of Count Cavour], the wise man leaves much to chance; reason prompts him to follow blindly after impulses or instincts beyond reason, that seem to be heaven-sent. No man can say when these should be dared or when deserted; nor book, nor

rules, nor experience can teach him; a certain sense and a certain daring alone can inform him.[8]

Paléologue's pronounced and unwavering Germanophobia was coupled with a taste for catastrophic scenarios that many colleagues recognized as dangerous. During his stint in Sofia (1907–12), one of the few foreign posts he held before accepting the mission to St Petersburg, a colleague there reported that Paléologue's dispatches and conversation alike were full of wild talk of 'horizons, of clouds and menacing storms'. Indeed it is hard to find any contemporary comment on the future ambassador that unequivocally praises him. There were simply too many bad reports, one senior foreign office functionary observed in May 1914, for there to be any question of 'confidence' in the new ambassador.[9] Izvolsky characterized him as a 'phrase-maker, a fantasist and very smooth'. Even his British colleagues in Sofia described Paléologue in 1912 as 'excitable', 'inclined to spread sensational and alarmist rumours' and a 'trafficker in tall tales'.[10]

Paléologue's appointment to the St Petersburg embassy, the most strategically sensitive and important posting in French diplomacy, might thus seem rather remarkable. He owed his rise through the service more to the prevalent political alignment than to the usual array of professional qualifications. Delcassé discovered Paléologue and energetically promoted him, mainly because they shared the same views on the German threat to France – in Paléologue, Delcassé found a subordinate who could echo and reinforce his own ideas. Paléologue's star waned after Delcassé's fall in 1905 and he wound up making do with various minor posts. It was Poincaré who rescued him; the two men had been intimate since the days when they were both pupils at the Lycée Louis le Grand in Paris. Paléologue's 'great gift', de Robien unkindly remarked, consisted in having been one of Poincaré's and Millerand's classmates at high school – 'it was to their friendship that he owed his astonishing career'.[11] As prime minister, Poincaré recalled Paléologue from Sofia in 1912 and appointed him political director at the Quai. This dramatic promotion – an amazing leap in seniority for such a quirky and controversial man – shocked many of the veteran ambassadors. The French ambassador to Madrid commented to Bertie that Paléologue was 'not of the right stuff for the directorship', while the French ambassador to Japan described him as a 'lamentable choice'.[12] These were strong words, even by the standards of the diplomatic service, where the upwardly mobile often attract envious sniping. 'We must hope,' Eyre Crowe noted in London, 'that the atmosphere of Paris will have a sedative effect on M. Paléologue, but this is not usually the effect of Paris'.[13]

Poincaré was aware of Paléologue's reputation and did what he could to curb his excesses, but the two friends entered into a close working relationship based on a profound agreement on all key questions. Poincaré came to depend on Paléologue's judgement.[14] Indeed, it was Paléologue who encouraged Poincaré to commit France more firmly in the Balkans. Paléologue did not believe that a reconciliation between Austrian and Russian interests in the region would be possible and his obsession with the nefarious designs of Berlin and Vienna made him blind to the machinations of Russian policy. He saw in the two Balkan Wars an opportunity for Russia to consolidate its position on the peninsula.[15] The close link with Poincaré was one reason why Sazonov, although he knew of Paléologue's idiosyncrasies, welcomed the new ambassador's appointment to St Petersburg.[16] Here was a man who could be trusted to take up in January 1914 where Delcassé had left off. In a conversation with a Russian diplomat who happened to be passing through Paris, Paléologue declared on the eve of his departure that he was taking the St Petersburg post so that he could put an end to the policy of concessions that had hitherto prevailed, and that 'he would fight for a future hardline policy without compromise or vacillation'. 'Enough of all this, we should show Germany our strength!'[17] These were the convictions, attitudes and relationships that would guide the new ambassador during the summer crisis of 1914.

M. POINCARÉ SAILS TO RUSSIA

At 11.30 p.m. on Wednesday 15 July, the presidential train left the Gare du Nord in Paris for Dunkirk. On board were Raymond Poincaré, the new prime minister René Viviani and Paléologue's successor as political director at the Quai d'Orsay, Pierre de Margerie. Early the following morning, the three men joined the battleship *France* for the journey through the Baltic to Kronstadt and St Petersburg. Viviani was new in post – the former socialist had been prime minister for only four weeks and had no experience or knowledge whatsoever of external affairs. His

Raymond Poincaré

René Viviani

principal utility to Poincaré consisted in the fact that he had recently converted to the cause of the Three Year Law, commanded a sizeable following in the chamber and was prepared to support Poincaré's views on defence. As the state visit to Russia unfolded, it would quickly become apparent that he was politically out of his depth. Pierre de Margerie, by contrast, was an experienced career diplomat who had been brought to Paris by Poincaré in the spring of 1912, at the age of fifty-one, to occupy the post of associate director at the Quai d'Orsay. Poincaré had created this watchdog post in the hope that de Margerie would keep an eye on Paléologue and check any major indiscretions. As it happened, this proved unnecessary. Paléologue performed to Poincaré's satisfaction, and when his reward came in the form of the posting to St Petersburg, de Margerie succeeded to the political directorship. In this role he proved himself efficient and – most importantly of all in the president's eyes – politically loyal.[18] Neither Viviani nor de Margerie was capable of mounting an effective challenge to the president's control over policy.

Poincaré had much to think about as he boarded the *France* at Dunkirk at 5.00 a.m. on 16 July. First there was Charles Humbert's sensational indictment of the French military administration. In a speech before the Senate of 13 July to mark the submission of his report on the special budgetary vote for army matériel, Humbert, senator for the Meuse (a department on the border with Belgium), had delivered a swingeing attack on the French military administration. French forts, he claimed, were of poor quality, fortress guns lacked ammunition and the wireless installations for fort-to-fort communications were faulty. Whenever the German wireless installation at Metz was transmitting, Humbert claimed, the station at Verdun went on the blink. French artillery was quantatively inferior to the German, especially in heavy guns. One detail above all caught the attention of the French public, and particularly of the nation's mothers: the army was woefully short of boots; if war broke out, Humbert declared, French soldiers would have to take to the field with only one pair of boots, plus a single thirty-year-old reserve boot in their knapsacks. The speech triggered a political sensation. In his reply, Minister of War Adolphe Messimy did not deny the substance of the charges, but insisted that rapid progress was being made on all fronts.[19] The deficiencies in artillery provision would be made good by 1917.

This was all the more annoying for the fact that the man at the fore-front of the resulting parliamentary agitation was Poincaré's old enemy Georges Clemenceau, who was claiming that the incompetence revealed in the report justified withholding parliamentary support for the new military budget. It had only just been possible to resolve the issue and pass the new military budget in time to avoid a postponement of the president's departure. On the day they left for Dunkirk, Viviani seemed nervous and preoccupied by the thought of intrigues and conspiracies, despite Poincaré's efforts to calm him.[20]

As if this were not enough, Madame Caillaux's trial was due to open on 20 July and there was reason to fear that exposures and revela-tions in court might trigger a chain of scandals that would shake the government. The scope of the threat became apparent when rumours circulated that the murdered newspaper editor Calmette had also had in his possession deciphered German telegrams revealing the extent of Caillaux's negotiations with Germany during the Agadir crisis in 1911. In these communications – according to the telegrams, at least – Caillaux had spoken of the desirability of a rapprochement with Berlin. Caillaux also claimed to possess affidavits proving that Poincaré had orchestrated the campaign against him. On 11 July, three days before the president's departure for Russia, Caillaux threatened to make these known to the public if Poincaré did not press for the acquittal of his wife.[21] The occult machines of Parisian political intrigue were still turning at full throttle.

Despite these concerns, Poincaré embarked on his journey across the Baltic Sea in a surprisingly calm and resolved mood. It must have been a huge relief to escape Paris at a time when the Caillaux trial had thrown the newspapers into a frenzy. He spent much of the first three days of the crossing on the deck of the *France* briefing Viviani, whose ignorance of foreign policy he found 'shocking', for the mission in St Petersburg.[22] His summary of these tutorials, which gives us a clear sense of Poin-caré's own thinking as he left Paris, included 'details on the alliance', an overview of 'the various subjects raised in St Petersburg in 1912', 'the military conventions of France and Russia', Russia's approach to Eng-land regarding a naval convention and 'relations with Germany'. 'I have never had difficulties with Germany,' Poincaré declared, 'because I have always treated her with great firmness.'[23] The 'subjects raised in St Petersburg in 1912' included the reinforcement of strategic railways, the importance of massive offensive strikes from the Polish salient and the need to focus on Germany as the principal adversary. And the reference to England is an indication that Poincaré was thinking in terms not just of the alliance with Russia, but of the embryonic Triple Entente. Here in a nutshell was Poincaré's security credo: the alliance is our bedrock; it is the indispensable key to our military defence; it can only be maintained by intransigence in the face of demands from the opposing bloc. These were the axioms that would frame his interpretation of the crisis unfolding in the Balkans.

To judge from the diary entries, Poincaré found the days at sea profoundly relaxing. While Viviani fretted over the news of Parisian scandal and intrigue arriving in fragments via the radio-telegraph from Paris, Poincaré enjoyed the warm air on deck and the play of the sunshine on a blue sea brushed by 'imperceptible waves'. There was just one small hitch: while approaching the harbour at Kronstadt, the *France*, steaming along at 15 knots in the early morning darkness of 20 July, managed to ram a Russian tugboat towing a frigate towards its berth. The incident woke Poincaré in his cabin. How vexing that a French warship sailing in neutral waters under the command of an admiral of the fleet should have struck and damaged a tugboat of the allied nation. It was, he noted irritably in the diary, 'a gesture lacking in dexterity and elegance'.

The president's good cheer was restored by the brilliant scene that greeted the *France* as it sailed into Kronstadt harbour. From all directions, naval vessels and festively decorated packet and pleasure boats motored out to welcome the visitors and the imperial launch pulled alongside to transfer Poincaré to the Tsar's yacht *Alexandria*. 'I leave the *France*,' Poincaré noted, 'with the emotion that always overcomes me when, to the noise of cannonfire, I leave one of our warships.'[24] Across the water, standing beside the Tsar on the bridge of the *Alexandria*, where he had an excellent view of the entire scene, Maurice Paléologue was already mentally composing a paragraph for his memoirs:

> It was a magnificent spectacle. In a quivering, silvery light, the *France* slowly surged forward over the turquoise and emerald waves, leaving a long white furrow behind her. Then she stopped majestically. The mighty warship which has brought the head of the French state is well worthy of her name. She was indeed France coming to Russia. I felt my heart beating.[25]

THE POKER GAME

The minutes of the summit meetings that took place over the next three days have not survived. In the 1930s, the editors of the *Documents Diplomatiques Français* searched for them in vain.[26] And the Russian records of the meetings, less surprisingly perhaps, given the disruptions to archival continuity during the years of war and civil war, have also been lost. Nevertheless, it is possible by reading the accounts in Poincaré's diaries alongside the memoirs of Paléologue and the notes kept by other diplomats present during those fateful days, to get a fairly clear sense of what transpired.

The meetings were centrally concerned with the crisis unfolding in Central Europe. It is important to emphasize this, because it has often been suggested that as this was a long-planned state visit rather than an exercise in crisis summitry, the matters discussed must have followed a pre-planned agenda in which the Serbian question occupied a subordinate place. In fact, quite the opposite is the case. Even before Poincaré had left the *France*, the Tsar was already telling the ambassador how much he was looking forward to his meeting with the president of the Republic: 'We shall have weighty matters to discuss. I am sure we shall agree on all points ... But there is one question which is very much in my mind – our understanding with England. We *must* get her to come into our alliance.'[27]

As soon as the formalities were done with, the Tsar and his guest made their way to the stern of the *Alexandria*, and entered into conversation. 'Or perhaps I should say a discussion,' wrote Paléologue, 'for it was obvious that they were talking business, firing questions at each other and arguing.' It seemed to the ambassador that Poincaré was dominating the conversation; soon he was doing 'all the talking, while the Tsar simply nodded acquiescence, but [the Tsar's] whole appearance showed his sincere approval'.[28] According to Poincaré's diary, the conversation in the yacht touched first on the alliance, of which the Tsar spoke 'with great firmness'. The Tsar asked him about the Humbert scandal, which he said had made a very bad impression in Russia, and he urged Poincaré to do whatever was necessary to prevent the Three Year Law from falling. Poincaré in turn assured him that the new French chamber had shown its true will by voting to retain the law and that

Viviani too was a firm supporter. Then the Tsar raised the matter of the relations between Sergei Witte and Joseph Caillaux, who were said to be the exponents of a new foreign policy based on rapprochement between Russia, France, Germany and Britain. But the two men agreed that this was an unfeasible project that posed no threat to the current geopolitical alignment.[29]

In short, even as they made their way to shore, Poincaré and the Tsar established that they were both thinking along the same lines. The key point was alliance solidarity, and that meant not just diplomatic support, but the readiness for military action. On the second day (21 July), the Tsar came to see Poincaré in his apartments at the Peterhof and the two men spent an hour tête-à-tête. This time, the conversation focused first on the tension between Russia and Britain in Persia. Poincaré adopted a conciliating tone, insisting that these were minor vexations that ought not to compromise good Anglo-Russian relations. Both men agreed that the source of the problem did not lie in London or St Petersburg, but with unspecified 'local interests' of no broader relevance. And the Tsar noted with some relief that Edward Grey had not allowed Berlin's discovery of the naval talks to scupper the search for a convention. Some other issues were touched on – Albania, Graeco-Turkish tension over the Aegean islands and Italian policy – but the Tsar's 'most vivid preoccupation', Poincaré noted, related to Austria and to her plans in the aftermath of the events at Sarajevo. At this point in the discussion, Poincaré reported, the Tsar made a highly revealing comment: 'He repeats to me that under the present circumstances, the complete alliance between our two governments appears to him more necessary than ever.' Nicholas left soon afterwards.[30]

Here again, the central theme was the unshakeable solidarity of the Franco-Russian Alliance in the face of possible provocations from Austria. But what did this mean in practice? Did it mean that the alliance would respond to an Austrian démarche against Serbia with a war that must, by necessity, be continental in scope? Poincaré offered a coded answer to this question on that afternoon (21 July), when, together with Viviani and Paléologue, he received the various ambassadors. The second in line was the Austro-Hungarian ambassador Fritz Szapáry, newly returned from Vienna, where he had been at the bedside of his dying wife. After a few words of sympathy on the assassination, Poincaré asked whether there had been any news of Serbia. 'The judicial enquiry is proceeding,' Szapáry answered. Paléologue's account of Poincaré's reply accords closely with that given in Szapary's dispatch:

Of course I am anxious about the results of this enquiry *Monsieur l'Ambassadeur*. I can remember two previous enquiries which did not improve your relations with Serbia . . . Don't you remember? The Friedjung affair and the Prochaska affair?[31]

This was an extraordinary response for a head of state visiting a foreign capital to make to the representative of a third state. Quite apart from the taunting tone, it was in effect denying in advance the credibility of any findings the Austrians might produce in their enquiry into the background of the assassinations. It amounted to declaring that France did not and would not accept that the Serbian government bore any responsibility whatsoever for the murders in Sarajevo and that any demands made upon Belgrade would be illegitimate. The Friedjung and Prochaska affairs were pretexts for an a priori rejection of the Austrian grievance. In case this was not clear enough, Poincaré went on:

I remark to the ambassador with great firmness that Serbia has friends in Europe who would be astonished by an action of this kind.[32]

Paléologue remembered an even sharper formulation:

Serbia has some very warm friends in the Russian people. And Russia has an ally, France. There are plenty of complications to be feared![33]

Szapáry, too, reported the president as saying that an Austrian action would produce 'a situation dangerous for peace'. Whatever Sazonov's exact words, the effect was shocking, and not just for Szapáry, but even for the Russians standing nearby, some of whom, de Robien reported, were 'known for their antipathy towards Austria'.[34] At the close of his dispatch, Szapáry noted – and it is hard to fault his judgement – that the 'tactless, almost threatening demeanour' of the French president, a 'foreign statesman who was a guest in this country', stood in conspicuous contrast with the 'reserved and cautious attitude of Mr Sazonov'. The whole scene suggested that the arrival of Poincaré in St Petersburg would have 'anything but a calming effect'.[35]

In commenting on the contrast between Sazonov and Poincaré, Szapáry identified a raw nerve in the Franco-Russian relationship. During an embassy dinner that evening – a splendid affair in honour of the president – Poincaré sat next to Sazonov. In stifling heat – the room was poorly ventilated – they discussed the Austro-Serbian situation. To his dismay, Poincaré found Sazonov preoccupied and little disposed to firmness. 'The timing is bad for us,' Sazonov said, 'our peasants are still very busy with their work in the fields.'[36] In the meanwhile, in the *petit salon* next door, where the less important guests were being entertained, a different mood prevailed. Here, a colonel from Poincaré's entourage was heard proposing a toast 'to the next war and to certain victory'.[37] Poincaré was unsettled by Sazonov's irresolution. 'We must,' he told Paléologue, 'warn Sazonov of the evil designs of Austria, encourage him to remain firm and promise him our support.'[38] Later that night, after a reception by the municipal assembly, Poincaré found himself sitting at the back of the imperial yacht with Viviani and Izvolsky, who had travelled back from Paris to take part in the meetings. Izvolsky seemed preoccupied – perhaps he had been talking with Sazonov. Viviani appeared 'sad and surly'. As the yacht sailed along towards the Peterhof in virtual silence, Poincaré looked up into the night sky and asked himself, 'What does Austria have in store for us?'[39]

The next day, 22 July, was particularly difficult. Viviani appeared to be having a breakdown. It came to a head in the afternoon, when the French prime minister, who happened to be seated at lunch to the left of the Tsar, seemed to find it impossible to answer any of the questions addressed to him. By mid-afternoon, his behaviour had become more outlandish. While Nicholas and Poincaré sat listening to a military band, Viviani was seen standing alone near the imperial tent muttering, grumbling, swearing loudly and generally drawing attention to himself. Paléologue's efforts to calm him were of no avail. Poincaré's diary registered the situation with a lapidary comment: 'Viviani is getting sadder and sadder and everyone is starting to notice it. The dinner is excellent.'[40] Eventually it was announced that Viviani was suffering from a 'liver crisis' and would have to retire early.

Why the prime minister was feeling so poorly is impossible to establish with certainty. His collapse may well, as some historians have suggested, have been precipitated by his anxieties about developments in Paris – a telegram had arrived on Wednesday reporting that Caillaux had threatened to expose various sensitive transcripts in court.[41] But it is more likely that Viviani – a deeply pacific man – was alarmed by the steadily intensifying mood of belligerence at the various Franco-Russian gatherings. This is certainly what de Robien thought. It was clear to the French attaché that Viviani was 'overwrought by all these expressions of the military spirit'. On 22 July, de Robien noted, the talk was of nothing but war – 'one felt that the atmosphere had changed since the night before'. He laughed when the marines who crewed the *France* told him that they were worried about the prospect of coming under attack on the home crossing, but their nervousness was an ominous sign. The highpoint was Thursday 23 July – Poincaré's last day in Russia – when the heads of state witnessed a military review involving 70,000 men against a backdrop of military music consisting mainly of the *Sambre et Meuse* and the *Marche Lorraine*, which the Russians appeared to consider 'the personal hymn of Poincaré'. Particularly striking was the fact that the troops were not wearing their elaborate ceremonial uniforms, but the khaki battledress they had worn for training – de Robien interpreted this as yet another symptom of a general eagerness for war.[42]

Poincaré and Paléologue witnessed one of the most curious expressions of alliance solidarity on the evening of 22 July, when Grand Duke Nikolai Nikolaevich, commander of the Imperial Guard, gave a dinner for the guests at Krasnoye Selo, a recreational suburb of St Petersburg with many handsome villas, including the summer residences of the Tsars. The scene was picturesque: three long tables were set in half-open tents around a freshly watered garden bursting with fragrant blooms. When the French ambassador arrived, he was greeted by Grand Duke Nikolai's wife, Anastasia, and her sister Militza, who was married to Nikolai's brother, Pyotr Nikolaevich. The two sisters were daughters of the remarkably energetic and ambitious King Nikola of Montenegro. 'Do you realise,' they said (both talking at once), 'that we are passing through historic days!

> At the review to-morrow the bands will play nothing but the *Marche Lorraine* and *Sambre et Meuse*. I've had a telegram (in pre-arranged code) from my father to-day. He tells me we shall have war before the end of the month . . . What a hero my father is! . . . He's worthy of the Iliad! Just look at this little box I always take about with me. It's got some Lorraine soil in it, real Lorraine soil I picked up over the frontier when I was in France with my husband two years ago. Look there, at the table of honour: it's covered with thistles. I didn't want to have any other flowers there. They're Lorraine thistles, don't you see! I gathered several plants on the

annexed territory, brought them here and had the seeds sown in my garden . . . Militza, go on talking to the ambassador. Tell him all to-day means to us while I go and receive the Tsar . . .[43]

Militza was not speaking figuratively. A letter of November 1912 from the French military attaché in St Petersburg, General Laguiche, confirms that in the summer of that year, while her husband was attending the French manoeuvres near Nancy, the grand duchess had sent someone over the border into German-controlled Lorraine with instructions to collect a thistle and some soil. She brought the thistle back to Russia, cared for it until it germinated, then planted the seeds in the Lorraine earth, watered it carefully until new thistles grew, then mixed the Lorraine soil with Russian soil to symbolize the Franco-Russian Alliance and passed it to her gardener for propagation with the warning that if the thistles died, he would lose his job. It was from this garden that she harvested the samples she showed to Poincaré in July 1914.[44] These extravagant gestures had real political import; Anastasia's husband Grand Duke Nikolai, a pan-Slavist and the first cousin once removed of the Tsar, was among those most active in pressing Nicholas II to intervene militarily on Serbia's behalf, should Austria press Belgrade with 'unacceptable' demands.

The Montenegrin rhapsody continued during dinner, as Anastasia regaled her neighbours with prophecies: 'There's going to be a war . . . There'll be nothing left of Austria . . . You're going to get back Alsace and Lorraine . . . Our armies will meet in Berlin . . . Germany will be destroyed . . .'[45] and so on. Poincaré, too, saw the princesses in action. He was sitting next to Sazonov during an entràcte in the ballet when Anastasia and Militza approached and began upbraiding the foreign minister for insufficient ardour in Serbia's support. Once again, the limpness of the foreign minister's manner gave pause for thought, but Poincaré noted with satisfaction that 'the Tsar, for his part, without being quite as ecstatic as the two grand duchesses, seems to me more determined than Sazonov to defend Serbia diplomatically'.[46]

These dissonances did not prevent the alliance partners from agreeing on a common course of action. At 6 p.m. on 23 July, the evening of the departure of the French, Viviani, who seemed somewhat recovered from his 'attack of liver', agreed with Sazonov the instructions to be sent to the Russian and French ambassadors in Vienna. The ambassadors were to mount a friendly joint démarche recommending moderation to Austria and expressing the hope that she would do nothing that could compromise the honour or the independence of Serbia. These words were of course carefully chosen to interdict in advance the note that both parties already knew the Austrians were about to present. George Buchanan agreed to suggest that his own government send an analogous message.[47]

That evening, during the pre-departure dinner held on the deck of the *France*, there was a highly emblematic dispute between Viviani and Paléologue over the wording of a communiqué to be drawn up for the press. Paléologue's draft ended by alluding to Serbia with the words:

The two governments have discovered that their views and intentions for the maintenance of the European balance of power, especially in the Balkan Peninsula, are absolutely identical.

Viviani was unhappy with this formulation – 'I think it involves us a little too much in Russia's Balkan policy', he said. Another more anodyne draft was drawn up:

The visit which the president of the Republic has just paid to H.M. the Emperor of Russia has given the two friendly and allied governments an opportunity of discovering that they are in entire agreement in their views on the various problems which concern for peace and the balance of power in Europe has laid before the powers, especially in the Balkans.[48]

This was a fine exercise in the art of euphemism. Yet despite its prudent tone, the revised communiqué was easily decoded and exploited by the liberal and pan-Slav Russian papers, which began pushing openly for military intervention in support of Belgrade.[49]

Poincaré was not especially happy with how the dinner had gone. The heavy afternoon rain had virtually torn down the marquee on the aft deck where the guests were supposed to be sitting and the ship's cook did not cover himself in glory – the soup course was late and 'no one praised the dishes', Poincaré later noted. But the president could afford to be satisfied with the overall impact of the visit. He had come to preach the gospel of firmness and his words had fallen on ready ears. Firmness in this context meant an intransigent opposition to any Austrian measure against Serbia. At no point do the sources suggest that Poincaré or his Russian interlocutors gave any thought whatsoever to what measures Austria-Hungary might legitimately be entitled to take in the aftermath of the assassinations. There was no need for improvisations or new policy statements – Poincaré was simply holding fast to the course he had plotted since the summer of 1912. This may help explain why, in contrast to many of those around him, he remained so conspicuously calm throughout the visit. This was the Balkan inception scenario envisaged in so many Franco-Russian conversations. Provided the Russians, too, stayed firm, everything would unfold as the policy had foreseen. Poincaré called this a policy for peace, because he imagined that Germany and Austria might well back down in the face of such unflinching solidarity. But if all else failed, there were worse things than a war at the side of mighty Russia and, one hoped, the military, naval, commercial and industrial power of Great Britain.

De Robien, who observed all this from close quarters, was not impressed. Poincaré, he felt, had deliberately overridden the authority of Viviani, who as premier and minister of foreign affairs was the responsible office-holder, pressing assurances and promises upon Nicholas II. Just before they separated, Poincaré reminded the Tsar: 'This time we must hold firm.'

> At almost exactly the same moment [de Robien recalled], the Austrian ultimatum was presented to Belgrade. Our opponents, too, had decided to 'hold firm'. On both sides they imagined that 'bluffing' would suffice to achieve success. None of the players thought that it would be necessary to go all the way. The tragic poker game had begun.[50]

It was in the nature of great men, Paléologue would later write, to play such fateful games. The 'man of action' he observed in his study of Cavour, becomes 'a gambler, for each grave action implies not only an anticipation of the future, but a claim to be able to decide events, to lead and control them'.[51]

10

The Ultimatum

AUSTRIA DEMANDS

While Poincaré and Viviani were steaming towards the harbour at Kronstadt, the Austrians put the final touches to the ultimatum to be presented in Belgrade. Travelling in unmarked vehicles to avoid notice, the members of the Joint Ministerial Council made their way to Berchtold's private apartments on Sunday 19 July for a meeting to resolve the 'forthcoming diplomatic action against Serbia'. There was an informal discussion about the note to be sent to Belgrade and the text was definitively settled. It was agreed that the ultimatum would be presented at 5 p.m. on 23 July (subsequently postponed to 6 p.m. to ensure that it would arrive after Poincaré's departure). Berchtold declared quixotically that he believed it unlikely 'that word of our step would be publicly known before [Poincaré] left St Petersburg', but since he was aware that news of Vienna's plans had already reached Rome, speed was of the essence. The Serbian government would be given forty-eight hours to respond; if it was not accepted in full by the Serbs, the ultimatum would expire early in the evening of Saturday 25 July.

What would happen next? The rest of the discussion touched on various aspects of the post-ultimatum scenario. Conrad assured Tisza that sufficient forces would be made available to secure Transylvania against possible Romanian attack. Tisza insisted that Austria-Hungary must declare at the outset that it had 'no plans of aggrandizement against Serbia' and did not intend to annex any of the kingdom's territory. The Hungarian premier was strongly opposed, as at the previous meeting, to any measure that would bring more angry South Slavs into the monarchy; he also feared that the prospect of Austrian annexations would make it impossible for the Russians to back down. This demand triggered some hefty discussion. Berchtold in particular maintained that the territorial reduction of Serbia might, in the aftermath of a conflict, prove to be an indispensable means of neutralizing the threat it posed to Austro-Hungarian security. Tisza stood his ground and the meeting agreed on a compromise: Vienna would formally announce in due course that the dual monarchy was not waging a war of conquest and had no designs on Serbian territory. However, it would leave open the possibility that other states, notably Bulgaria, might secure areas of territory currently controlled by the Serbs.[1]

Neither this nor the other Austrian summit meetings produced anything even remotely resembling what we would today call an exit strategy. Serbia was not a rogue state in an otherwise quiet neighbourhood: adjacent Albania remained extremely unstable; there was always the possibility that Bulgaria, once engorged with lands from Serbian-controlled Macedonia, would return to its earlier Russophile policy; and how would one balance Bulgarian annexations in Macedonia against the need to mollify Romania with territorial compensations?[2] Would the Austrophobe Karadjordjević dynasty remain in place, and if not, who or what would replace it? And there were practical questions of a lesser order: who would take care of the Austrian legations in Belgrade and Cetinje if Austria-Hungary were obliged to break off relations – the Germans perhaps?[3] All of this remained unclear. And once again, as at the meeting of 7 July, the possibility of Russian intervention received only the most perfunctory attention. Conrad's comments on the military situation focused exclusively on Austria's Plan B, a purely Balkan military scenario, rather than on Plan R, which provided for the possibility of a Russian attack on Austrian Galicia. Yet none of the ministers present thought to press Conrad on the question of how he would respond if the Russians did in fact intervene, or to ask him how easy it would be to transition from one deployment scenario to the other.[4] The eyes of the Austrian political elite were still riveted on the quarrel with Belgrade, to the exclusion of broader concerns. Even when news reached Vienna of Poincaré's extraordinary warning to Szapáry that Serbia had 'friends' – a message revealing that France and Russia had harmonized their views on how they would respond to an Austrian démarche – Berchtold did not consider a change of course.[5]

The note and the ultimatum were drafted by Baron Musulin von

Gomirje, a relatively junior figure, counsellor from 1910 in the sections for church policy and East Asia. Musulin was tasked with drafting the ultimatum because he had a reputation as an excellent stylist. He was, as Lewis Namier later put it, 'one of those average, personally honest, well-meaning men whom a dark fate had chosen for pawns in the game that was to result in the greatest disaster of European history'.[6] Musulin filed away at his text like a jeweller with a precious stone.[7] The covering note to the ultimatum opened by recalling that Serbia had promised in the aftermath of the Bosnian annexation crisis to get along 'on a footing of good neighbourliness' with Austria-Hungary. Despite this undertaking, the letter went on, the Serbian government had continued to tolerate the existence on its territory of a 'subversive movement' which had sponsored 'acts of terrorism, by a series of outrages and by murders' – a somewhat histrionic reference to the dozen or so abortive South Slav terrorist plots that had preceded the assassinations at Sarajevo. Far from attempting to suppress such activity, the letter claimed, the Serbian government had 'tolerated the criminal machinations of various societies and associations' and 'tolerated all the manifestations of a nature to inculcate in the Serbian population hatred for the monarchy and its institutions'.[8] The preliminary investigation into the plot to slay the archduke had revealed that it was planned and supplied in Belgrade, and that the passage of the killers into Bosnia had been expedited by officials of the Serbian frontier service. The time was therefore over for the atttitude of 'forbearance' that the monarchy had hitherto shown in its relations with Serbia. The last part of the letter stipulated that the Belgrade government must post a public notice across the kingdom (the text was provided) repudiating pan-Serbian irredentism.

Perhaps the most interesting feature of this text, which provided the raw material for the letter that would be circulated to the other powers when Austria declared war on Belgrade five days later, is that it does not assert direct complicity on the part of the Serbian state in the murders at Sarajevo. Instead, it makes the more modest claim that the Serbian authorities had 'tolerated' the organizations and activities that gave rise to the assassinations. This careful wording was in part simply a reflection of what the Austrians knew and did not know. The ministry of foreign affairs in Vienna had sent Section Counsellor Dr Friedrich von Wiesner to Sarajevo to collate and analyse all the available evidence on the background to the plot. On 13 July, after a scrupulous investigation,

Wiesner dispatched a report concluding that there was as yet no evidence to prove the responsibility or complicity of the Belgrade government.[9] This report would later be cited by those who claimed that Austria, being determined to wage war, had merely used Sarajevo as a pretext. But the situation at the time was more complex. As Wiesner later explained to the American historian Bernadotte Everly Schmitt, his telegram had been 'widely misunderstood'.

> Personally [Wiesner recalled], he was at the time quite convinced by the evidence secured at the investigation of the moral culpability of the Serbian government for the Sarajevo crime, but as the evidence was not of the kind which a court of law would accept, he had been unwilling to have it used in the formal case against Serbia. He had, he said, made this clear on his return to Vienna.[10]

Since the Austrians were determined to make their case as legally tight as possible, there could be no question of alleging direct culpability on the part of the Serbian state in the murders at Sarajevo. There was enough, in the evidence relating to the preparation and training of the boys and of their passage across the Serbian border, only to confirm the involvement of various subordinate state agencies. In chasing the nebulous structures of the Narodna Odbrana, moreover, the Austrians had missed the much more important Black Hand, whose networks reached deep into the Serbian state. They had not been able to trace the trail to Apis, nor had they been able to nail down the question of Serbian government foreknowledge of the conspiracy, perhaps because Biliński, embarrassed by his own failure to report to Berchtold his brief conversation with the Serbian ambassador, subsequently kept a lid on the entire episode. Had they possessed fuller knowledge, the Austrians would doubtless have felt even more justified in the measures they planned to undertake. For the moment, the opprobrium of the Friedjung trial, which was already being brandished by the Russians and the French as an argument against accepting Vienna's claims, obliged the drafters of the ultimatum to trim their language to what could be proven beyond doubt on the basis of the information that had already emerged from the investigation in Sarajevo.

There followed the ten demands of the ultimatum proper. The first three points focused on the suppression of irredentist organs and of the anti-Austrian propaganda they generated. Points 4, 6 and 8 addressed the need to take action against persons implicated in the Sarajevo outrage, including compromised military personnel and frontier officials and 'accessories to the plot of 28 June who are on Serbian territory'. Point 7 was more specific: it demanded the arrest 'without delay' of Major Voja Tankosić and Milan Ciganović. Tankosić was, unbeknown to the Austrians, a Black Hand operative close to Apis; it was he who had recruited the three youths who formed the core of the assassination team. Ciganović was known to the Austrians only as 'a Serbian state employee implicated by the findings of the preliminary investigation at Sarajevo', but he was also, according to the later testimony of Ljuba Jovanović, a member of the Black Hand who doubled as an agent working secretly for Pašić.[11] Point 9 requested that Belgrade furnish Vienna with explanations regarding the 'unjustifiable utterances of high Serbian officials, both in Serbia and abroad, who notwithstanding their official position have not hesitated since the outrage of 28 June to express themselves in interviews in terms of hostility towards the Austro-Hungarian monarchy'. This point referred among other things to the interviews given by Spalajković in St Petersburg; it also reminds us of how deeply Austrian attitudes were affected by Serbian responses to the outrage. Point 10 simply requested official notification 'without delay' of the measures undertaken to meet the preceding points.

The most controversial points were 5 and 6. Point 5 demanded that the Belgrade government 'accept the collaboration in Serbia of organs of the Imperial and Royal Government [of Austria-Hungary] in the suppression of the subversive movement directed against the territorial integrity of the monarchy' and point 6 stated that 'organs delegated' by Austria-Hungary would 'take part in the investigations' relating to accessories in the crime. As usual in Vienna, this text was composed by many hands, but it was Berchtold who had insisted on incorporating a reference to Austrian involvement.[12] The reason is obvious enough: Vienna did not trust the Serbian authorities to press home the investigation without some form of Austrian supervision and verification. And it must be said that nothing the Serbian government did between 28 June and the presentation of the ultimatum gave them any reason to think otherwise.

This was the demand irreconcilable with Serbian sovereignty that had already been identified in Paris, St Petersburg and Belgrade as the prospective trigger for a broader confrontation. One can legitimately ask, of course, whether a state can be made responsible for the actions of private citizens planned on its territory. But framing the issue in terms of Serbia's inviolable sovereignty skewed the picture somewhat. First, there was the question of reciprocity. The Serbian state – or at least the statesmen who directed it – accepted responsibility for the eventual 'reunion' of all Serbs, including those living within the Austro-Hungarian dual monarchy. This implied at best a limited acknowledgement of the empire's sovereign rights within the unredeemed lands of 'Serbdom'. Then there was the fact that the Serbian state under Pašić could exercise only very limited control over the irredentist networks. The interpenetration of the conspiratorial networks with the Serbian state, and the transnational affiliations of ethnic irredentism made a nonsense of any attempt to understand the friction between Serbia and Austria-Hungary in terms of an interaction between sovereign territorial states. And of course the transnational organs and legal framework that today arbitrate in such conflicts and monitor their resolution were not in existence.

When Edward Grey saw the full text of the Austrian ultimatum, he described it famously as 'the most formidable document he had ever seen addressed by one State to another that was independent'; in a letter to his wife, Winston Churchill described the note as 'the most insolent document of its kind ever devised'.[13] We do not know what comparators Grey and Churchill had in mind and the specificity of the historical situation created by the Sarajevo crimes makes comparative judgements difficult. But it would certainly be misleading to think of the Austrian note as an anomalous regression into a barbaric and bygone era before the rise of sovereign states. The Austrian note was a great deal milder, for example, than the ultimatum presented by NATO to Serbia-Yugoslavia in the form of the Rambouillet Agreement drawn up in February and March 1999 to force the Serbs into complying with NATO policy in Kosovo. Its provisions included the following:

> NATO personnel shall enjoy, together with their vehicles, vessels, aircraft and equipment free and unrestricted passage and unimpeded access through the Former Republic of Yugoslavia, including associated airspace and territorial waters. This shall include, but not be limited to, the right of bivouac, manoeuvre, billet and utilization of any areas or facilities as required for support, training, and operations.[14]

Henry Kissinger was doubtless right when he described Rambouillet as 'a provocation, an excuse to start bombing', whose terms were unacceptable even to the most moderate Serbian.[15] The demands of the Austrian note pale by comparison.

Vienna's ultimatum was, to be sure, drawn up on the assumption that the Serbs would probably not accept it. This was not a last-ditch attempt to save the peace between the two neighbours, but an uncompromising statement of the Austrian position. On the other hand, it was not, unlike Rambouillet, a demand for the complete prostration of the Serbian state; its terms were tightly focused on the threat posed by Serbian irredentism to Austrian security, and even points 5 and 6 reflected concerns about the reliability of Serbian compliance that the drafters had reason to believe were valid. Let us remember that as late as 16 July, when the British minister Dayrell Crackanthorpe put it to Slavko Gruić, secretary-general of the ministry of foreign affairs in Belgrade, that it might be a good idea to launch an independent Serbian investigation of the crimes, Gruić had insisted on the 'impossibility of adopting any definite measures before learning the findings of the Sarajevo investigation'. Once the report was published, Gruić continued, the Serbian government would comply with 'whatever request for further investigation the circumstances might call for and which would be compatible with international usage'. Should the worst come to the worst, Gruić added ominously, 'Serbia would not stand alone. Russia would not remain quiet were Serbia wantonly attacked.'[16] These obfuscating formulations suggested that the chances of compliance without coercion to the demands of a hostile neighbour were slim indeed. It was precisely the issues of enforcement and compliance that the Serbian government had addressed in its circular to the powers justifying the attack of the Balkan states on the Ottoman Empire in 1912. The repeated failure of the Ottomans to address the need for reforms in Macedonia, they argued, meant that their refusal to accept any form of 'foreign participation' in such reforms and their promises 'to apply serious reforms by themselves' were greeted 'throughout the world' with 'a deeply rooted distrust'.[17] Whether anyone in Belgrade noticed the parallel in July 1914 is doubtful.

SERBIA RESPONDS

On the morning of 23 July, the Austrian minister Baron Giesl telephoned the ministry of foreign affairs in Belgrade to inform them that Vienna would be delivering an 'important communication' for the Serbian prime minister that evening. Pašić was away from Belgrade, campaigning for the elections; the finance minister Lazar Paču had been appointed to replace him in his absence. On receiving the advance warning of the note, Paču managed to reach Pašić by telephone in Niš. Despite the pleas of the minister, Pašić refused to return to the capital. 'Receive [Giesl] in my place' was his instruction. When Giesl appeared in person at the ministry at 6 p.m. (the deadline having been postponed by an hour), he was received by Paču and Gruić, who had been asked to attend the meeting because the finance minister did not speak French.

Giesl handed to Paču the ultimatum, a two-page annexe and a covering note addressed to Paču as acting prime minister and informed him that the time limit for a reply was exactly forty-eight hours. When that deadline expired, if there were an unsatisfactory reply or none at all, Giesl would break off diplomatic relations and return to Vienna with the entire legation staff. Without opening the dossier, Paču answered that as the elections were in full swing and many ministers were away

Nikola Pašić in 1919

from Belgrade, it might be physically impossible to assemble the responsible office-holders in time to deliver a decision. Giesl replied that 'in the age of railways and telegraphs and in a country of this size the return of the ministers could only be a matter of a few hours'. In any case, he added, 'this was an internal matter for the Serbian government, on which he [Giesl] need take no view'.[18] Giesl's telegram dispatch to Vienna closes with the words: 'there was no further discussion', but in post-war conversations with the Italian historian Luigi Albertini, the former Austrian minister recalled that Paču hesitated, saying he was unable to accept the note. Giesl responded that in that case he would place it on the table and 'Paču could do what he liked with it'.[19]

As soon as Giesl left, Paču gathered the Serbian ministers still present in the capital and they went through the text together. Paču in particular was shocked because he had been expecting, despite all the evidence to the contrary, that the Germans would ultimately hold Vienna back from any step that 'might also drag her [Germany] into war'. For a time the men studied the note in 'deathly silence, because no one ventured to be the first to express his thoughts'. The first to speak was the minister of education Ljuba Jovanović, who paced the room back and forth several times and then declared: 'We have no other choice but to fight it out.'[20]

A curious interlude followed. In view of the extreme importance of the note, it was clear to all present that Pašić must return immediately to Belgrade. Pašić had spent the morning campaigning in Niš in southern Serbia for the elections of 14 August. After giving a speech, the prime minister seemed suddenly to lose interest in the campaign. 'It would be a good thing if we were to take a little rest,' he told Sajinović, the political director of the foreign ministry, who was travelling with him. 'What do you think of going off to Salonika [i.e. Thessaloniki, annexed to Greece by the Treaty of Bucharest in 1913] where we could stay two or three days incognito?' While Pašić and the political director waited for the prime minister's special coach to be coupled on to the train to Thessaloniki, Pašić was informed by a station attendant that there was an urgent telephone call from Belgrade. It was Lazar Paču, begging him to return to the capital. Pašić had no intention of hurrying back. 'I told Laza that when I get back to Belgrade, we shall give the answer. Laza told me from what he had heard that it was to be no ordinary note. But I stood firmly by my reply.' Sure enough, he and Sajinović went to take their seats in the train to Thessaloniki. Only when the train reached Lescovac, nearly fifty kilometres south of Niš, was the prime minister persuaded to return by a telegram from Prince-Regent Alexandar.[21]

This was bizarre but not uncharacteristic behaviour. We may recall that in the summer of 1903, when the details of the planned assassination of King Alexandar and Queen Draga were passed to him in advance by the regicides, Pašić had reacted by taking his family by train to the Adriatic coast, then under Austrian rule, where he could wait out the consequences. What exactly he had in mind on the afternoon on 23 July is impossible to establish. He may simply, as Albertini suggested, have hoped to avoid the weighty responsibility of accepting the note. Interestingly enough, Berchtold had learned through unspecified secret channels that Pašić intended to resign immediately on receiving it.[22] He may just have panicked, or perhaps he felt the need to clear his head and think over his options. The exigencies of a national election, coupled with the greatest external crisis in the history of the modern Serbian state had doubtless placed him under considerable strain. Whatever it was, the moment passed and the prime minister and the political director arrived in Belgrade at 5 a.m. on 24 July.

It took a little time for a Serbian response to the ultimatum to crystallize. On the evening of 23 July, while Pašić was travelling back to the capital, Paču dispatched a circular note to the Serbian legations stating that the demands set out in the Austrian note were 'such as no Serbian government could accept them in their entirety'. Paču reaffirmed this view when he paid a visit to Chargé d'Affaires Strandmann, who, following the death of Hartwig, was acting chief of the Russian mission. After Paču had left, Prince Alexandar appeared to discuss the crisis with Strandmann. He too insisted that acceptance of the ultimatum was 'an absolute impossibility for a state which has the slightest regard for its dignity', and added that he placed his trust in the magnanimity of the Tsar of Russia 'whose powerful word alone could save Serbia'. Early on the next morning, it was Pašić's turn to see Strandmann. The prime minister took the view that Serbia should neither accept nor reject the Austrian note and must immediately seek a postponement of the deadline. An appeal would be made to the powers to protect the independence of Serbia. 'But,' Pašić added, 'if war is unavoidable, we shall fight.'[23]

All of this might seem to suggest that the Serbian political leadership came almost immediately to the unanimous view that Serbia must resist and – if necessary – go to war. But these utterances were all reported by Strandmann. It is likely that the desire to elicit Russian support encouraged the ministers on hand in Belgrade to insist on the impossibility of acceptance. Other testimony suggests that, among themselves, the decision-makers were deeply alarmed at the prospect of an Austrian attack and saw no alternative to acceptance.[24] The memory of October 1913, when Sazonov had advised Belgrade to back down in the face of an Austrian ultimatum over Albania, was still fresh enough to nourish doubts about whether the Russians would support Serbia in the current crisis. Ascertaining the attitude of France was difficult, because the key French leaders were on their way back from Russia and the French envoy Descos, who for some time had been showing signs of strain, had collapsed and been recalled to Paris; his replacement had not yet arrived.

No decision was reached at the first cabinet meeting convened by Paču on the evening of 23 July and the situation remained unresolved after Pašić's return on the following morning. Pašić merely determined that no decision should be taken until the Russians had made their view known. In addition to the conversations with Strandmann, which were of course reported immediately to St Petersburg, there were two official requests for clarification. Pašić cabled Spalajković, asking him to ascertain the views of the Russian government. On the same day, Prince Regent Alexander sent a telegram to the Tsar stating that Serbia 'could not defend itself' and that the Belgrade government was prepared to accept any points of the ultimatum 'whose acceptance shall be advised by Your Majesty [i.e. the Russian Tsar]'.[25] The Italian historian Luciano Magrini concluded from his interviews with key Serbian decision-makers and other witnesses to the events of those days that the Belgrade government had in effect decided to accept the ultimatum and avoid war. 'It was thought that in the condition she was known to be in, Serbia could not be expected to do otherwise than yield to so terrible a threat.'[26] It was evidently in a mood of resignation that Pašić composed his telegram of 25 July to the Serbian missions declaring that Belgrade intended to send a reply that would be 'conciliatory on all points' and offer Vienna 'full satisfaction'.[27] This was unmistakably a major step back from Paču's much firmer circular of two days before. A telegram from Crackanthorpe to Grey, dispatched just after midday on 25 July, confirms that at this point the Serbs were even willing to accept the notorious points 5 and 6 calling for a mixed commission of enquiry, 'provided that the appointment of such commission can be proved to be in accordance with international usage'.[28]

It may have been reassurance from the Russians that stiffened the backs of the Serbs. At around 8.30 a.m. on 23 July, a telegram dispatched on the evening of the previous day arrived from Spalajković, reporting his conversation with Poincaré during the state visit. The French president had asked the Serbian envoy if there was news from Belgrade; when Spalajković replied that the situation was very bad, Poincaré had said: 'We will help you to improve it.'[29] This was gratifying, but not especially substantial. At around midnight on 24 July, a telegram reached Belgrade announcing that 'a bold decision' was imminent.[30]

The most important of Spalajković's dispatches were two telegrams sent on the night of 24–25 July, detailing a conversation with Sazonov some time before 7 p.m. on 24 July in which the Russian foreign minister had conveyed to the Serbian envoy the results of a meeting of the Council of Ministers held at three o'clock that afternoon. In the first telegram, Spalajković reported that the Russian foreign minister had 'condemned the Austro-Hungarian ultimatum with disgust', declaring that no state could accept such demands without 'committing suicide'. Sazonov had assured Spalajković that Serbia could 'count unofficially on Russian support'. But he did not specify which form this help would take, because these were matters 'for the Tsar to decide and consult on with France'. In the meanwhile, Serbia should avoid any unnecessary provocations. If the country were attacked and unable to defend itself, it should in the first instance withdraw its armed forces south-eastwards into the interior.[31] The aim was not to accept an Austrian occupation, but rather to keep Serbia's armies in readiness for a subsequent deployment. The second telegram of that night, dispatched at 1.40 a.m. on 25 July, reported that the Russian Ministerial Council had decided to take 'energetic measures, even mobilization', and were about to publish an 'official communiqué in which Russia takes Serbia under its protection'.[32]

At 8 p.m. on 25 July, Spalajković fired off a further dispatch reporting that he had spoken with the Serbian military attaché, who had just returned from the Tsar's residence at Tsarskoe Selo. The attaché had been talking with the chief of the Russian General Staff and told Spalajković that the Military Council had shown the 'greatest readiness for war' and was resolved to 'go to any length in protecting Serbia'. The Tsar in particular had surprised everybody with his determination.

Moreover, it had been ordered that at exactly 6 p.m., the deadline for the Serbian reply, all the final-year cadets in Russia were to be raised to officer rank, a clear signal of imminent full mobilization. 'In all circles without exception, the greatest resolve and jubilation reigns on account of the stance adopted by the tsar and his government'.[33] Other dispatches reported on the military measures that were already being taken, the mood of 'pride and [readiness for] any sacrifice' that pervaded the ruling circles and the public sphere and the excitement that greeted the news from London that the British fleet had been ordered to a state of readiness.[34]

It was probably the news from Russia that dispelled the mood of fatalism in Belgrade and dissuaded the ministers from attempting to avoid war by acquiescing in the demands of the ultimatum.[35] Spalajković's telegram of 24 July conveying Sazonov's vague assurance of support arrived in Belgrade in two parts, the first at 4.17 a.m. and the second at 10 a.m. on 25 July. The telegram hinting at Russian mobilization arrived at 11.30 a.m. on the same day, in good time to reach the Serbian ministers before they had drafted their reply to the Austrian note.[36]

Notwithstanding this firming of the mood, the Serbian ministers invested immense effort in polishing their reply to Vienna in order to create the appearance of offering the maximum possible compliance without compromising Serbian sovereignty. Pašić, Ljuba Jovanović and most of the ministers then present in Belgrade, including those of the interior, economics and justice, Stojan Protić, Velizar Janković and Marko Djuričić, all had a hand in the numerous redactions of the text. Slavko Gruić, secretary-general of the Serbian foreign ministry, later described to Luigi Albertini the hectic activity that preceded the presentation of the reply. During the afternoon of Saturday 25 July there were numerous drafts as the ministers took turns in adding and scratching out various passages; even the final version was so covered in alterations, insertions and crossings-out that it was virtually illegible.

At last after 4 pm the text seemed finally settled and an attempt was made to type it out. But the typist was inexperienced and very nervous and the typewriter refused to work, with the result that the reply had to be written out by hand in hectographic ink, copies being jellied off. [. . .] The last half-hour was one of feverish work. The reply was corrected by pen here and there. One whole phrase placed in parenthesis was crossed out in ink and made illegible. At 5.45 Gruić handed the text to Pašić in an envelope.[37]

Pašić had hoped that Gruić or some other subordinate figure would convey the reply to Baron Giesl, but when no one volunteered, he said: 'Very well, I will take it myself,' descended the stairs and walked to the meeting with Giesl, while the ministers and officials all rushed to make the train to Niš, to which the Serbian government was relocating in preparation for the coming conflict.

The Serbian reply may have looked messy, but it was a masterpiece of diplomatic equivocation. Baron Musulin, who had composed the first draft of the Austrian ultimatum, described it as 'the most brilliant specimen of diplomatic skill' that he had ever encountered.[38] The reply opened with a confident flourish. The Serbian government, it was asserted, had demonstrated on many occasions during the Balkan Wars its moderate and peaceful attitude. Indeed, it was 'thanks to Serbia and to the sacrifice that she has made in the exclusive interest of European peace that that peace [had] been preserved'. The drafters of the reply were therefore confident that their response would remove any misunderstanding between the two countries. Since the government could not be held responsible for the actions of private individuals, and exercised no direct controls over the press or the 'peaceable work of societies', it had been surprised and pained by the accusations emanating from Vienna.[39]

In their replies to the individual points, the drafters offered a subtle cocktail of acceptances, conditional acceptances, evasions and rejections. They agreed officially to condemn all propaganda aimed at the dissolution of the Austro-Hungarian Empire or the annexation of its territories (though they used a modal form of the verb that avoided the implication that there had ever actually been any such propaganda). On the question of the suppression of irredentist organizations, the reply stated that the Serbian government possessed 'no proof that the Narodna Odbrana or other similar societies' had as yet committed 'any criminal act' – nevertheless, they agreed to dissolve the Narodna Odbrana and any other society 'that may be directing its efforts against Austria-Hungary'. Point 3 stated that the government would happily remove from Serbian public education any anti-Austrian propaganda, 'whenever the Imperial and Royal Government furnish them with facts and proofs of this propaganda'. Point 4 agreed to the removal from the military of suspect persons, but again, only once the Austro-Hungarian authorities had communicated to them 'the names and acts of these officers and functionaries'. On the question of the creation of mixed Austro-Serbian commissions of enquiry (point 5) the reply stated that the Serbian government 'did not clearly grasp the meaning or scope of the demand', but that they undertook to accept such collaboration, inasmuch as it could be shown to agree with 'the principle of inter-national law, with criminal procedure and with good neighbourly relations'. Point 6 (on the participation of Austrian officials in the pros-ecution of implicated persons) was rejected outright on the grounds that this would be contrary to the Serbian constitution – this was the issue touching on Serbia's sovereignty, on which Sazonov had urged Belgrade to stand firm. As for point 7, calling for the arrest of Tankosić and Ciganović, the Serbian government stated that it had already arrested Tankosić 'on the very evening of the delivery of the note'; it had 'not yet been possible to arrest Ciganović'. Again, the Austrian government were asked to provide the 'presumptive evidence of guilt, as well as the proofs of guilt, if there are any [. . .] for the purposes of the later enquiry'. This was a somewhat devious response: as soon as the name of Ciganović had cropped up in connection with the Sarajevo enquiry, the prefecture of police in Belgrade had hustled him out of the capital on a special commission, all the while officially denying that any person by the name of Milan Ciganović existed in the city.[40] The reply accepted without condition points 8 and 10 regarding the prosecution of frontier officials found guilty of illegal activity and the duty to report to the Austro-Hungarian government on the measures undertaken. But point 9, under which the Austrians had demanded an explanation of hostile public comments by Serbian officials during the days following the assassina-tions, elicited a more equivocal response: the Serbian government would 'gladly give' such explanations, once the Austrian government had 'communicated to them the passages in question in these remarks and as soon as they have shown that the remarks were actually made by said officials'.[41]

It is hard to dissent from Musulin's breathless admiration for this finely wrought text. The claim often made in general narratives that this reply represented an almost complete capitulation to the Austrian demands is profoundly misleading. This was a document fashioned for

Serbia's friends, not for its enemy. It offered the Austrians amazingly little.[42] Above all, it placed the onus on Vienna to drive ahead the process of opening up the investigation into the Serbian background of the conspiracy, without, on the other hand, conceding the kind of collaboration that would have enabled an effective pursuit of the relevant leads. In this sense it represented a continuation of the policy the Serbian authorities had followed since 28 June: flatly to deny any form of involvement and to abstain from any initiative that might be taken to indicate the acknowledgement of such involvement. Many of the replies on specific points opened up the prospect of long, querulous and in all likelihood ultimately pointless negotiations with the Austrians over what exactly constituted 'facts and proofs' of irredentist propaganda or conspiratorial activity by officers and officials. The appeal to 'international law', though effective as propaganda, was pure obfuscation, since there existed no international jurisprudence for cases of this kind and no international organs with the authority to resolve them in a legal and binding way. Yet the text was perfectly pitched to convey the tone of voice of reasonable statesmen in a condition of sincere puzzlement, struggling to make sense of outrageous and unacceptable demands. This was the measured voice of the political, constitutional Serbia disavowing any ties with its expansionist pan-Serbian twin in a manner deeply rooted in the history of Serbian external relations. It naturally sufficed to persuade Serbia's friends that in the face of such a full capitulation, Vienna had no possible ground for taking action.

In reality, then, this was a highly perfumed rejection on most points. And one can reasonably ask whether any other course was open to Pašić, now that, by refusing to take the initiative in shutting down the irredentist networks, he had allowed the crisis to reach this point. Various reasons have already been considered for the prime minister's peculiar passivity after 28 June – his continuing vulnerability after the recent struggles with the military party and the Black Hand network, the deeply ingrained habits of reticence and secretiveness that he had acquired over thirty years at the dangerous summit of Serbian politics, and the fundamental ideological sympathy of Pašić and his colleagues for the irredentist cause. To these one could add a further consideration. Pašić must have had good reason to fear any thoroughgoing investigation of the crime, because this might well have unearthed linkages leading into the heart of the Serbian political elite. Any light shed on the machinations of Apis would have damaged Belgrade's cause, to put it mildly. But far more worrying was the possibility that the pursuit and investigation of the double agent Ciganović, whom the Austrians had identified as a suspect, might have revealed the foreknowledge of Pašić and his fellow ministers, foreknowledge that Pašić had vehemently denied in his interview with *Az Est* (The Evening) on 7 July. In a sense, perhaps, the Austrians really were demanding the impossible, namely that the official Serbia of the political map shut down the expansionist ethnic Serbia of irredentism. The problem was that the two were inter-dependent and inseparable, they were two sides of the same entity. In the ministry of war in Belgrade, an official location if there ever was one, there hung, in front of the main reception hall, the image of a Serbian landscape, before which stood an armed allegorical female figure on whose shield were listed the 'provinces still to be liberated': Bosnia, Herzegovina, Voivodina, Dalmatia, and so on.[43]

Even before he took delivery of the reply, Giesl knew that the accept-ance would not be unconditional. An order for Serbian general mobilization had been in effect since three o'clock that afternoon, the city garrison had departed with great noise and haste to occupy the heights around the city, the National Bank and the state archives were evacuating Belgrade, making for the interior of the country, and the dip-lomatic corps was already preparing to follow the government to its interim location at Kragujevac, en route to Niš.[44] There was also a con-fidential warning from one of the ministers involved in drafting the reply.[45] Five minutes before the deadline, at 5.55 p.m. on Saturday 25 July, Pašić appeared at the Austrian legation and handed over the note, saying in broken German (he did not speak French): 'Part of your demands we have accepted [. . .] for the rest we place our hopes on your loyalty and chivalry as an Austrian general,' and left. Giesl cast a super-cilious eye over the text, saw it was wanting, and signed a pre-prepared letter informing the prime minister that he would be leaving Belgrade that evening with his staff. The protection of Austro-Hungarian citizens and property was formally entrusted to the German legation, the codes were taken from the strongroom and burned, and the luggage – already packed – was carried out to the cars waiting at the door. By 6.30 p.m., Giesl, his wife and the legation staff were on the train out of Belgrade. They crossed the Austrian border ten minutes later.

Did this mean war? In a curious telegram of 24 July to Mensdorff in

London, Berchtold instructed the ambassador to inform Edward Grey that the Austrian note was not a formal ultimatum, but a 'time-limited démarche' whose expiry without a satisfactory result would bring about the cessation of diplomatic relations and the commencement of necessary military preparations. Yet war was still not inevitable: if Serbia subsequently decided to back down, 'under the pressure of our military preparations', Berchtold continued, she would be asked to pay an indemnity in respect of Austria's costs.[46] On the following day, as Berchtold was travelling westwards to Bad Ischl to meet with Emperor Franz Joseph, a telegram from First Section Chief Count Macchio in Vienna reached him at Lambach. Macchio reported that the Russian chargé d'affaires in Vienna, Kudashchev, had made an official request for an extension of the deadline. In his reply, Berchtold stated that an extension was impossible, but he added that even after expiry of the deadline, Serbia could still avoid war by complying with Austria's demands.[47] Perhaps these words reflected, as Albertini believed, a momentary failure of nerve;[48] perhaps, on the other hand, they were merely a play for time – we have seen how anxious the Austrians were not to get behindhand with their military preparations, once these became necessary.

In retrospect, it is clear that there was no mileage in these last-minute manoeuvres. On 26 and 27 July, exultant dispatches arrived from Spalajković, bringing news that the Russians were mobilizing an army of 1,700,000 men and planned 'immediately to commence an energetic offensive against Austria-Hungary as soon as it attacks Serbia'. The Tsar was convinced, Spalajković reported on 26 July, that the Serbs would 'fight like lions' and might even destroy the Austrians single-handedly from their redoubt in the interior of the country. The stance of Germany was as yet unclear, but even if the Germans did not enter the fray, the Tsar believed there was a good chance of bringing about 'a partition of Austria-Hungary'; failing that, the Russians would 'execute the French military plans so that victory against Germany is also certain'.[49]

So excited was Spalajković, the former political chief of the Serbian minstry of foreign affairs, that he turned to proposing policy: 'In my opinion, this presents to us a splendid opportunity to use this event wisely and achieve the full unification of the Serbs. It is desirable, therefore, that Austria-Hungary should attack us. In that case, onwards in the name of God!' These effusions from St Petersburg contributed to a further hardening of the mood. Last-minute concessions to Austrian demands were now inconceivable. Pašić had long believed that the union of the Serbs would not be achieved in peacetime, that it would be forged only in the heat of a great war and with the help of a great power. This was not and had never been a plan as such – it was an imagined future whose hour now seemed imminent. Nearly two weeks would pass before any serious fighting took place, but the road to war was already in sight. For Serbia, there would be no looking back.

A 'LOCAL WAR' BEGINS

On the morning of 28 July 1914, Emperor Franz Joseph signed his declaration of war on Serbia with an ostrich-feather quill at the desk in his study in the imperial villa at Bad Ischl. In front of him was a bust in brilliant white marble of his dead wife. At his right elbow was a state-of-the-art electric cigar lighter, an unwieldy bronze structure on a plinth of dark wood, whose plaited cord led to a wall-socket behind the desk. The text followed the manifesto format the Austrians had used for declaring war on Prussia in 1866:

> To my peoples! It was my fervent wish to consecrate the years which, by the grace of God, still remain to me, to the works of peace and to protect my peoples from the heavy sacrifices and burdens of war. Providence, in its wisdom, has otherwise decreed. The intrigues of a malevolent opponent compel me, in the defence of the honour of my Monarchy, for the protection of its dignity and its position as a power, for the security of its possessions, to grasp the sword after long years of peace.[50]

By this time, Belgrade was already a depopulated city. All men of serving age had been called up and many families had left to take refuge with relatives in the interior of the country. Most of the foreign nationals had gone. At two o'clock in the afternoon of 28 July, the rumour of imminent war spread like a bush fire through the city. Extra editions of all newspapers sold as soon as the vendors could carry them on to the street.[51] Before the day was out, two Serbian Danube steamers carrying ammunition and mines had been seized by Austrian pioneers and watchmen. Shortly after one o'clock on the following morning, Serbian troops blew up the bridge over the river Save between Semlin and Belgrade.

Austrian gunboats opened fire and after a brief engagement the Serbian troops withdrew.

The news that war had finally been declared filled Sigmund Freud, now fifty-eight years of age, with elation: 'For the first time in thirty years, I feel myself to be an Austrian, and feel like giving this not very hopeful empire another chance. All my libido is dedicated to Austria-Hungary.'[52]

11

Warning Shots

FIRMNESS PREVAILS

After four hectic days of receptions, military reviews, speeches, dinners and toasts, Maurice Paléologue needed some rest. Having seen Poincaré off on the *France* on the evening of 23 July, he told his servant to let him sleep in on the following morning. But it was not to be: at seven o'clock came an urgent telephone call announcing the Austrian ultimatum. As the ambassador lay in bed still half-asleep, the news entered his mind like a waking dream:

> The occurrence seemed to me unreal and yet definite, imaginary but authentic. I seemed to be continuing my conversation of yesterday with the Tsar, putting my theories and conjectures. At the same time I had a sensation, a potent, positive and compelling sensation, that I was in the presence of a *fait accompli*.[1]

Paléologue cancelled his lunchtime date and agreed instead to a meeting at the French embassy with Foreign Minister Sazonov and the British ambassador Sir George Buchanan.[2] According to his own memoirs, Paléologue reminded his two guests of the toasts exchanged between the president and the Tsar on the previous night and repeated that the three Entente powers must adopt a policy of 'firmness'. Sazonov was taken aback: 'But suppose that policy is bound to lead to war?' Firmness would lead to war, Paléologue replied, only if the 'Germanic powers' had *already* 'made up their minds to resort to force to secure their hegemony over the East' (here the French ambassador mirrored exactly the argument Bethmann had made to Riezler during the second week of July).

Whether Sazonov was really as passive as Paléologue's account suggests may be doubted: in the despatch George Buchanan filed on the same conversation, it was Sazonov who raised the stakes, declaring that 'Russia would at any rate have to mobilise'.[3] Whoever said what, the three men clearly took a drastic view of the situation created by Austria's presentation of the note to Belgrade. Sazonov and Paléologue joined forces in urging Buchanan to dissuade his government from a policy of neutrality that would be 'tantamount to suicide'. Buchanan agreed and undertook to make 'strong representations' to Grey in favour of a policy of 'resistance to German arrogance'.[4] Count de Robien, who spoke with the ambassador that afternoon, was aghast. 'At this noxious lunch,' he recalled, 'they all goaded each other on. Paléologue was apparently particularly vehement, boasting of his conversations with Poincaré . . .'[5]

In fact, Sazonov needed no persuading from Paléologue or anyone else. Even before his lunch at the French embassy, he had dressed down the Austrian ambassador in terms that left no doubt about how he read the situation and how he intended to respond to it. After Fritz Szapáry, following the customary practice in such cases, had read aloud the text of the Austrian note, Sazonov barked several times over: 'I know what it is. You want to make war on Serbia! The German newspapers have been egging you on. You are setting fire to Europe. It's a great responsibility you are taking on, you will see what effect this has in London and Paris and maybe elsewhere too.' Szapáry proposed to send him a dossier of evidence supporting Vienna's claims, but Sazonov waved the offer aside, saying he was not interested: 'You want war and you've burned your bridges.' When Szapáry replied that Austria had a right to defend its vital interests and was 'the most peace-loving power in the world', Sazonov responded with a sarcastic retort: 'One can see how peaceful you are, now that you are setting fire to Europe.'[6] Szapáry left the meeting in an excited state and rushed straight to the Austrian embassy to encode and dispatch his report.

No sooner had the Austrian ambassador left than Sazonov summoned the chief of the Russian General Staff, General Yanushkevich, to the ministry of foreign affairs. The government, he declared, would soon be issuing an official press announcement to the effect that Russia did not intend to 'remain inactive' if the 'dignity and integrity of the Serb people, brothers in blood, were under threat' (a corresponding note was released to the press on the following day). Then he discussed with Yanushkevich plans for a 'partial mobilisation against Austria-Hungary alone'.[7] During the days that followed the presentation of the note, the Russian foreign minister stuck to his policy of firmness, striking postures and making decisions that escalated the crisis.

At 3 p.m. that afternoon, there was a two-hour meeting of the Council of Ministers. Sazonov, fresh from his lunch with Paléologue and Buchanan, was the first to speak. He began by sketching out what he saw as the broader background to the current crisis. Germany, he declared had long been engaged in 'systematic preparations' aimed not just at increasing its power in Central Europe but at securing its objectives 'in all international questions, without taking into consideration the opinion and influence of the powers not included in the Triple Alliance'. Over the last decade, Russia had met these challenges with unfailing moderation and forbearance, but these concessions had merely 'encouraged' the Germans to use 'aggressive methods'. The time had come to take a stand. The Austrian ultimatum had been drawn up 'with German connivance'; its acceptance by Belgrade would transform Serbia into a de facto protectorate of the central powers. Were Russia to abandon its 'historic mission' to secure the independence of the Slav peoples, she would be 'considered a decadent state', would forfeit 'all her authority' and her 'prestige in the Balkans' and 'would henceforth have to take second place among the powers'. A firm stand, he warned, would bring the risk of war with Austria and Germany, a prospect all the more dangerous for the fact that it was as yet still uncertain what position Great Britain would take.[8]

The next to speak was the minister of agriculture, A. V. Krivoshein, one of the ministers who had opposed and intrigued against Vladimir Kokovtsov. He enjoyed the special favour of the Tsar and was closely associated with the nationalist lobby in the Duma. As minister of agriculture, he was also closely affiliated with the *zemstvos*, noble-dominated elected organs of local government that spanned most of the Russian Empire. He had been linked for years to the *Novoye Vremya*, known for its nationalist campaigns on Balkan questions and the Turkish Straits.[9] He had supported Sukhomlinov's policy of partial mobilization against Austria in November 1912 on the grounds that it was 'high time Russia stopped cringeing before the Germans'.[10] He also appears to have been on quite close terms with the garrulous Militza of Montenegro, who viewed him as an ally in Montenegro's struggle to redeem South Slav-dom.[11] After Kokovtsov's departure, Krivoshein was the most powerful man on the Council of Ministers. His views on foreign policy were hawkish and increasingly Germanophobic.

In his words to the Council of Ministers on 24 July, Krivoshein invoked a complex array of arguments for and against a military response, but ultimately opted for a firm reaction to the Austrian démarche. Russia, he noted, was without question in an incomparably better political, financial and military position than after the catastrophe of 1904–1905. But the rearmament programme was not yet complete and it was doubtful whether Russia's armed forces would ever be able to compete with those of Germany and Austria-Hungary in terms of 'modern technical efficiency'. On the other hand, 'general conditions' had improved in recent years (perhaps he was referring to the strengthening of the Franco-Russian Alliance), and it would be difficult for the imperial government to explain to the public and the Duma why it was 'reluctant to act boldly'. Then came the nub of the argument. In the past, Russia's 'exaggeratedly prudent attitudes' had failed to 'placate' the Central European powers. To be sure, the risks to Russia in the event of hostilities were great, the Russo-Japanese War had made that clear. But while Russia desired peace, further 'conciliation' was not the way to achieve it. 'War could break out in spite of our efforts at conciliation.' The best policy under the present circumstances was therefore 'a firmer and more energetic attitude towards the unreasonable claims of the Central Powers'.[12]

Krivoshein's statement made a profound impression on the meeting and none of the speakers who followed said anything to modify his conclusions. War Minister Sukhomlinov and Naval Minister Grigorovich admitted that the rearmament programme was still unfinished, but both 'stated nevertheless that hesitation was no longer appropriate' and saw 'no objection to a display of greater firmness'. Peter Bark, speaking for the finance ministry, expressed some concerns about the capacity of Russia to sustain the financial and economic strains of a continental war, but even he acknowledged that further concessions were in themselves no guarantee of peace, and 'since the honour, dignity and authority of Russia were at stake', he saw no reason to dissent from the opinion of the majority. Summing up that opinion, premier Goremykin concluded that 'it was the Imperial Government's duty to decide immediately in favour of Serbia'. Firmness was more likely to secure peace than conciliation and, failing that, 'Russia should be ready to make the sacrifices required of her'.[13] Finally, the meeting agreed the following five resolutions: (i) Austria would be requested to extend the time-limit of the ultimatum; (ii) Serbia would be advised not to offer battle on the frontier, but to withdraw its armed forces to the centre of the country; (iii) the Tsar would be requested to approve 'in principle' the mobilization of the military districts of Kiev, Odessa, Kazan and Moscow; (iv) the minister of war would be instructed to accelerate the stockpiling of military equipment and (v) Russian funds currently invested in Germany and Austria were to be withdrawn.[14]

'IT'S WAR THIS TIME'

On the next day (25 July), there was a further, more solemn meeting of the Council of Ministers, presided over by the Tsar and attended both by Chief of Staff Yanushkevich and by Grand Duke Nikolai, commander of the St Petersburg District and the husband of Anastasia of Montenegro, who had spoken so forthrightly with President Poincaré during the state visit. This meeting confirmed the Council's decisions of the previous day and agreed on further, more elaborate military measures. Most importantly of all, the Council decided to authorize a complex batch of regulations known as the 'Period Preparatory to War'. These measures, which involved numerous dispositions intended to prepare for mobilization, were not to be confined to the districts bordering on Austria, but would apply right across European Russia.[15]

It would be difficult to overstate the historical importance of the meetings of 24 and 25 July. In one sense, they represented a kind of last-minute renaissance of the Council of Ministers, whose influence over foreign policy had been in decline since the death of Stolypin. It was rather unusual for foreign policy to be debated in this way by the Council.[16] In focusing the minds of his colleagues on Germany as the alleged instigator of the current crisis, Sazonov revealed the extent to which he had internalized the logic of the Franco-Russian Alliance, according to which Germany, not Austria, was the 'principal adversary'. That this was an Austrian rather than a German crisis made no difference, since Austria was deemed to be the stalking horse for a malevolent German policy whose ultimate objectives – beyond the acquisition of 'hegemony in the Near East' remained unclear. As for the problem of Russia's relative unreadiness for war (by comparison with its prospective condition in three years), the ministers addressed this issue by referring in vague terms to a war which would come 'anyway', even if Russia chose to 'conciliate' the Germans by not attacking their Austrian allies. This line of argument superficially resembled the train of thought that preoccupied Bethmann during the first weeks of July: that one could view the Sarajevo crisis as a means of testing Russia's intentions – if the Russians opted, despite everything, for a European war, that would mean they had wanted war anyway. But there was a crucial difference: in Bethmann's case, this argument was deployed to justify *accepting* a war, should Russia choose to start one; at no point (until after Russian general mobilization) was this argument used to justify *pre-emptive* military measures by Germany. In St Petersburg, by contrast, the measures being considered were proactive in nature, did not arise from a direct theat to Russia, and were highly likely (if not certain) to further escalate the crisis.

The practical military measures adopted at the two meetings are especially baffling. First, there was the fact that the partial mobilization agreed by Sazonov and Yanushkevich and subsequently adopted in principle at the meeting of 24 July, was a grossly impractical and potentially dangerous procedure. Even a partial mobilization, if it posed a direct threat to Austria-Hungary, would inevitably, by the logic of the Austro-German alliance, call forth counter-measures by Berlin, just as a German partial mobilization against Russia would inevitably have triggered counter-measures by France, whether or not Germany chose to mobilize on its western front. And should these counter-measures occur, the frontier areas in which mobilization had *not* occurred would be doubly exposed, as would be the right flank of the southern army group that had mobilized against Austria. The room for manoeuvre created by the partial nature of the mobilization was thus largely illusory. Even more worrying was the fact that Russian plans simply did not provide for a partial mobilization. There existed no separate schedule for a mobilization against Austria alone. The current planning regime, known as Mobilization Schedule no. 19, was a 'seamless whole, an all-or-nothing proposition' that made no distinction between the two adversaries.[17] Variations in population density across the different districts meant that most of the army corps drew on reservists from other mobilization zones. Moreover, some army corps in the areas adjoining Austria were earmarked, in the event of full mobilization, for deployment into parts of the Polish salient adjoining Germany. As if all this were not bad enough, a mobilization restricted to some sectors would wreak havoc on the immensely complex arrangements for rail transit into and across the concentration zones. Improvising an Austria-only mobilization would therefore not only be risky in its own right, it would jeopardize Russia's ability to make the transition to a full mobilization, should this subsequently become necessary.[18]

In view of these difficulties, it is astonishing that the partial mobilization policy was ever given serious consideration. Why did Sazonov press for it? One can understand the superficial appeal of a measure that seemed to offer something short of the full mobilization that must by necessity trigger a continental war. Sazonov doubtless remembered the winter crisis of 1912–13, when the army had improvised a stop-gap mobilization plan against Austria-Hungary. And as a civilian in an environment where military expertise was jealously guarded and civil–military communications were poor, Sazonov, whose ignorance of military matters was notorious, may have known no better. He clearly received extremely poor advice from the chief of the General Staff, Yanushkevich, a man of very modest abilities who was still somewhat out of his depth after only five months in office. Yanushkevich, a courtier rather than a soldier, had seen no service in the field and his promotion, which was said to have excited general surprise, was probably due more to the Tsar's affection for him than to his professional qualifications.[19] Yet even after Yanushkevich's subordinates and Yanushkevich himself had pointed up the absurdity of the partial mobilization plan, Sazonov refused to discard it. Perhaps he felt he needed to be able to offer the Tsar an alternative to full mobilization; perhaps he hoped that partial mobilization would suffice to persuade the Austrians and the Germans to back down. Perhaps, on the other hand, he hoped with the offer of partial mobilization to coax the Tsar into a situation from which he would be forced to progress to the real thing. At the very least, these uncertainties suggest a certain disjointedness at the apex of the Russian executive, an impression reinforced by the fact that the Tsar was allowed to add the Baltic Fleet to Sazonov's partial mobilization plan, although this made a nonsense of the foreign minister's intention to avoid antagonizing Germany.[20]

In any case, for the moment, the policy of partial mobilization remained a red herring – at least until 28 July, when the government chose actually to announce it. In the meanwhile, the Council of Ministers had resolved an even more important decision, namely the activation of the 'Regulation on the Period Preparatory to War of 2 March 1913'. This pre-mobilization law provided for heightened security and readiness at magazines and supply depots, the accelerated completion of railway repairs, readiness checks in all departments, the deployment of covering troops to positions on threatened fronts and the recall of reservists to training camps. And there were other measures: troops in training at locations remote from their bases were to be recalled immediately; around 3,000 officer cadets were to be promoted to officer rank to bring the officer corps up to wartime strength; harbours were to be mined, horses and wagons assembled, and the state of war was to be declared in all fortresses in the Warsaw, Vilnius and St Petersburg districts, so that the military authorities would possess the fullness of powers required to ensure speedy general mobilization when the order came. And these measures were put in force not only in the Austrian border zones, but across the entirety of European Russia.[21]

Needless to say, these measures were fraught with risk. How would the Germans and the Austrians be able to tell the difference between Russia's far-reaching pre-mobilization measures and the opening phase of a mobilization proper? The text of the Regulation of 2 March conveys an impression of the scale of the measures underway. According to its stipulations, reserves were to be recalled to frontier divisions and 'instructed as to the uniforms and probable dispositions of the enemy.

> Horses are to be reshod. No more furloughs are to be granted and officers and men on furlough or detailed elsewhere are to return at once to their troop divisions. Espionage suspects are to be arrested. Measures to prevent the export of horses, cattle and grain are to be worked out. Money and valuable securities are to be removed from banks near the frontier to the interior. Naval vessels are to return to their harbours and receive provisions and full war equipment.[22]

Yanushkevich raised the likelihood of misunderstandings by expressly advising the commanders in each district not to feel bound by the letter of the Regulation of 2 March and to overstep the prescribed measures if they judged it appropriate.

And sure enough, many obervers mistook the pre-mobilization for a partial mobilization. The Belgian military attaché in St Petersburg reported on 26 July that the Tsar had ordered the mobilization of 'ten army corps in military circumscriptions of Kiev and Odessa', adding that the news had been 'received with the greatest enthusiasm in military circles' and pointing out in a dispatch of the following day that the press had been informed that any public discussion of the 'mobilization of the army' was strictly forbidden.[23] German and Austrian consuls, diplomats and attachés began firing off alarmed reports. From Copenhagen, the Austrian minister Count Széchényi reported on 26 July that the Danish foreign minister Eric Scavenius had received news from St Petersburg suggesting that Russia had already begun to mobilize – though in view of these precipitate offensive measures, Széchényi thought it unlikely that France or England would feel obliged to intervene.[24] On the following day, the Austrian Consul Hein in Kiev reported the recall of officers to garrisons and long lines of artillery units marching westwards out of the Kiev encampment, their destination unknown. Later on the same day (27 July), he reported sixteen trains loaded with artillery and Cossacks leaving Kiev and twenty-six military trains carrying artillery and sappers en route from Odessa, all bound for the Austrian border. The vast Kiev military camp was now empty – the troops had either moved to their winter quarters or were assembling at the station for embarkation.[25] From Szczakowa in the Polish salient came a coded dispatch reporting that manoeuvres taking place in the area had been broken off and all troops concentrated in the city; a 'large contingent' of artillery had been loaded into wagons at the city's Vienna station. During the previous night, seven trains full of sappers had passed out of the station.[26] From Moscow came reports that the Imperial Russian Airforce, second only to the French in size, had pushed westwards, while a cavalry regiment had arrived in the city from far-off Ekaterinoslav (today: Dniepropetrovsk) nearly 600 miles to the south.[27] From the Austrian authorities in Galicia, there were reports of 'decidedly large' masses of troops, including artillery and Cossacks, moving into positions just across the border.[28] From Batum on the east coast of the Black Sea came news of regiments of infantry, Cossacks and dragoons on their way to Warsaw.[29] Consular dispatches sent from across Russia to the German embassy in St Petersburg reported the mining of rivers, the seizure of rolling stock, an entire Russian artillery division seen marching westwards out of Kiev, the interdiction of German encrypted telegraphy through the Moscow telegraph office, troops on their way back from manoeuvres, infantry and cavalry units approaching Lublin and Kovel, the assembly of masses of horses at their points of concentration, large convoys of military vehicles on the move and other signs of a mass army preparing to make war.[30] As early as the evening of 25 July, when Maurice Paléologue went to the Warsaw station in St Petersburg to say goodbye to Izvolsky, who was travelling back to Paris 'in hot haste', the two men were struck by the commotion around them:

> There was great bustle on the platforms. The trains were packed with officers and men. This looked like mobilization. We rapidly exchanged impressions and came to the same conclusion: 'It's war this time.'[31]

RUSSIAN REASONS

In taking these steps, Sazonov and his colleagues escalated the crisis and greatly increased the likelihood of a general European war. For one thing, Russian pre-mobilization altered the political chemistry in Serbia, making it unthinkable that the Belgrade government, which had originally given serious consideration to accepting the ultimatum, would back down in the face of Austrian pressure. It also heightened the domestic pressure on the Russian administration, for the sight of uniformed men and the news that Russia would not 'remain indifferent' to the fate of Serbia stirred euphoria in the nationalist press. It sounded alarm bells in Austria-Hungary. Most importantly of all, these measures drastically raised the pressure on Germany, which had so far abstained from military preparations and was still counting on the localization of the Austro-Serbian conflict.

Why did Sazonov do it? He was not a candid man and never produced a reliable account of his actions or motivations during these days, but the most plausible and obvious answer lies in his very first reaction to the news of the ultimatum: 'C'est la guerre européenne!' Sazonov believed from the outset that an Austrian military action against Serbia must trigger a Russian counter-attack. His response to the ultimatum was entirely consistent with his earlier commitments. Sazonov had never acknowledged that Austria-Hungary had a right to counter-measures in the face of Serbian irredentism. On the contrary, he had endorsed the politics of Balkan irredentism and had explicitly aligned himself with the view that Serbia was the rightful successor to the lands of unredeemed South Slavdom within the dual monarchy, an obsolete multi-ethnic structure whose days, in his view, were in any case numbered. It does not seem to have occurred to him that the days of the autocratic, multi-ethnic Russian Empire, whose minority relations were in worse condition than Austria-Hungary's, might also be numbered.

Sazonov had denied from the start Austria's right to take action *of any kind* against Belgrade after the assassinations. He had repeatedly indicated in a range of contexts that he would respond militarily to any action against the client state. Already on 18 July, shortly after it became known that an Austrian note of some sort was in preparation, Sazonov had told Sir George Buchanan that 'anything resembling an Austrian ultimatum in Belgrade could not leave Russia indifferent, and she might be forced to take some precautionary military measures'.[32] Sazonov must have been aware of the immense risks involved, for he had joined Kokovtsov in opposing such a partial mobilization against Austria in November 1912 at the height of the Balkan crisis, on the grounds – as Kokovtsov put it – that 'whatever we chose to call the projected measures, a mobilisation remained a mobilisation, to be countered by our adversaries with actual war'.[33]

The situation in 1914 was different, of course. The risks were greater and, with Kokovtsov out of the way, the mood was less inhibited. But there was another important difference: even in November 1912, Sazonov had added a rider to his support for a stand-down, saying that 'even if we were ready for war [. . .] we had no right to undertake such steps without first coming to an understanding with our allies'.[34] About this understanding – at least with France – there could no longer be any doubt in the summer of 1914. It was not just that Poincaré and Paléologue had pressed so hard for Russian firmness on the Serbian question, it was that a crisis of this kind conformed exactly to the Balkan inception scenario that the alliance, over many discussions and summit meetings, had come to define in recent years as the optimal *casus belli*. In a fascinating dispatch filed on 30 July, the Russian military attaché in Paris, Count Ignatiev, who had numerous contacts among the most senior French military commanders, reported that he saw in all around him 'unconcealed joy at the prospect of having the chance to use, as the French see it, beneficial strategic circumstances'.[35] The Belgian minister in Paris registered the same upbeat mood: 'The French general staff is favourable to war,' he wrote on 30 July. 'The general staff desires war, because in its view the moment is favourable and the time has come to make an end of it.'[36]

It is simply not the case, as has sometimes been claimed, that Paléologue misrepresented French intentions and made undertakings to St Petersburg for which he had no authorization from Paris. Nor is it true that he misinformed Paris about Russian mobilization in order to allow the crisis to mature to the point where Paris would be unable to restrain her ally. On the contrary, he alerted the French foreign ministry throughout to the measures adopted by the Russian government. A telegram composed at 6.30 on the evening of 24 July endorsed the principle of alliance solidarity in the interests of 'preserving peace by the use of force'; a further telegram of eleven o'clock that night referred to the measures that Russia 'would without doubt be obliged to take if Serbia were to be threatened in her independence or her territorial integrity'. And a further telegram composed at 4.45 p.m. on the following day and marked 'urgent' and 'secret' reported that the Council of Ministers had that day agreed 'in principle' the mobilization 'of the 13 army corps that are destined to operate against Austria'. There followed the crucial sentence:

> The mobilisation will be made public and effective only when the Austro-Hungarian government attempts to constrain Serbia by force of arms. However, secret preparations [*preparatifs clandestins*] will begin from today.[37]

Viviani would later explode with indignation at the news that things had been allowed to go so far so quickly and would demand from Paléologue a full account of his doings during the crucial days of the crisis, accusing him of having withheld vital information on Russian measures (this is where the myth of Paléologue's unauthorized manipulations began). But athough Viviani was out of the loop (as Poincaré no doubt intended him to be), Poincaré and Paris were not. In case the notes from Paléologue did not suffice, there were parallel dispatches streaming in from the French military attaché General Laguiche, who reported on 26 July, for example, that 'secret military dispositions' were already underway in Warsaw, Vilna and St Petersburg, all districts abutting the German frontier.[38] Yet there was no call for restraint from the Quai d'Orsay. Nor did Poincaré, though he later falsified key details of his own involvement in the crisis, ever disavow Paléologue or the policy he had so enthusiastically represented in St Petersburg.

To be sure, there were moments when Sazonov's belief in a peaceful outcome seemed to revive. We have seen that the Austrians paused after receiving the ultimatum on 25 July, in the hope that the actuality of Austrian military preparations might prompt last-minute concessions from Belgrade. Sazonov mistakenly read this as a sign that Vienna might be looking for a climbdown and began to talk of a negotiated settlement. 'Until the very last moment,' he told the French ambassador on 26 July, 'I will show myself ready to negotiate.' What he meant by this became clear when he summoned Szapáry for a 'frank and loyal explanation' of his views. Working through the Austrian note point by point, Sazonov insisted on the 'unacceptable, absurd and insulting' character of every clause and closed with an offer: 'Take back your ultimatum, modify its form and I guarantee you we will have a result.'[39] This 'negotiation' was hardly the basis for fruitful further discussions. In any case, the brief Austrian lull after the submission of the ultimatum was grounded not in Austrian doubts about the rectitude of their own course, but in the hope that Belgrade might back down at the last minute. The news of the Russian pre-mobilization naturally rendered these hopes groundless. No one was more excited by the spectacle of Cossacks boarding trains than Miroslav Spalajković, who saw in them the portents of a final struggle for Serbian unity and freedom. With the Tsar urging the Serbs to fight 'like lions', it was unlikely that Belgrade would entertain second thoughts about the terms of the ultimatum. And, in the meantime, Sazonov had explicitly advised Belgrade *not* to accept a British offer of mediation.

Even as they allowed the crisis to escalate, the Russians had to observe a certain caution. The French were committed to support Russia in a Balkan intervention, regardless of the precise circumstances in which that intervention was deemed to be necessary. But it was still important to placate French and British public opinion and to keep the Germans quiescent for as long as possible. Since November 1912, it had been an established assumption of Russian mobilization practice that the concentration of troops and matériel should be completed, if possible, 'without beginning hostilities, in order not to deprive the enemy irrevocably of the hope that war can still be avoided'. During this period of latent mobilization, 'clever diplomatic negotiations' would be used to 'lull to sleep as much as possible the enemy's fears'.[40] When mobilization is ordered in Russia, Paléologue reported to Paris on 25 July after a conversation with Sazonov, it will take place against Austria only and will avoid taking the offensive, 'in order to leave Germany with a pretext for *not invoking straight away* the *casus foederis*'.[41] It was also essential, for the sake of Russian, French and British public opinion, that *Austria*, not Russia, be seen as the aggressor. 'We must let Austria place herself entirely in the wrong,' Sazonov told Paléologue on 24 July.[42] This thought, that the opponent must be allowed to appear the aggressor, would crop up in all the key decision-centres on both sides during the last days of the crisis.

Was all this done on Serbia's behalf alone? Was Russia really willing to risk war in order to protect the integrity of its distant client? We have seen that Serbia's importance in Russian eyes grew during the last years before the war, partly because of the deepening alienation from Sofia and partly because Serbia was a better instrument than Bulgaria for applying pressure to the Austro-Hungarian monarchy. Sympathy with the Serbian cause was strong in Russian pan-Slavist and nationalist circles – this was an issue with which the government could build useful bridges to its middle-class public. On the other hand, St Petersburg had been willing to leave Belgrade to its own devices in October 1913, when the Austrians had issued an ultimatum demanding their withdrawal from northern Albania. And unlike Russia's neighbour Bulgaria, which possessed a piece of Black Sea coast, Serbia could hardly be seen as geopolitically crucial to Russian security.

The robustness of the Russian response fully makes sense only if we read it against the background of the Russian leadership's deepening anxiety about the future of the Turkish Straits. The Russians (or, more precisely, the Russian naval command) had been wishfully planning Bosphorus-seizing expeditions since the 1890s.[43] And we have seen how the Bulgarian march on Constantinople, the disruption of grain exports during the Balkan Wars and the Liman von Sanders crisis pushed this issue to the head of the agenda in 1912–1914.[44] By the summer of 1914, further factors were conspiring to heighten Russian apprehensions about the Turkish Straits. Most importantly, a regional arms and naval race had broken out between the Ottoman Empire and Greece, driven by a dispute over the future of the northern Aegean islands. In order to retain their edge over the Greeks, the Ottoman naval authorities had ordered two dreadnought-class battleships from the British firms Armstrong and Vickers, the first of which was due to arrive in late July 1914.[45]

This local power struggle was extremely alarming to the Russians. First, there was the danger, in the event of hostilities, of a further closure of the Straits to Russian commercial shipping, with all the costs and economic disruption that entailed. Then there was the possibility that some lesser state (Greece or Bulgaria) might suddenly grab a piece of Ottoman territory that the Russians themselves had their eyes on. A further worry was that a Graeco-Turkish war might bring the British navy on to the scene, just when the Russians were pressing London to scale down the British naval mission. But most important by a long margin was the prospect of a Turkish dreadnought presence in the Black Sea, where the Russians possessed no battleships of this class. The arrival of the new Turkish dreadnoughts, the Russian naval minister warned in January 1914, would create a naval power with 'crushing, nearly six-fold superiority' over the Russian Black Sea Fleet.[46] 'It is clear what calamitous results the loss of our superior position on the Black Sea would have for us,' Sazonov told the Russian ambassador in London in May 1914. 'And therefore we cannot stand idly by and watch the continued and also very rapid expansion of the Ottoman naval forces.'[47] At the end of July 1914, Sazonov was still entreating the British to retain the dreadnoughts destined for Constantinople.[48]

Exactly how much weight these concerns carried in Russian thinking during the July Crisis is difficult to ascertain.[49] Since the official documents tended to focus on the Austro-Serbian epicentre of the crisis, there was a tendency to rationalize Russian decisions exclusively in terms of solidarity with the Slavic 'little brothers' and the need to maintain Russian prestige on the Balkan peninsula. Sazonov had learned his lesson and knew that an open bid for control of the Straits was unlikely to play well with his allies. The picture is complicated somewhat, however, by the fact that the Bosphorus was a specifically naval obsession, not shared by the army General Staff.

On the other hand, the Straits issue doubtless carried considerable weight for Krivoshein, whose responsibility for agricultural exports made him especially aware of the vulnerability of Russian commercial shipping. Recent instability in the Balkans had tended to fuse the Balkan theatre with the Straits question, so that the pensinsula came increasingly to be seen as the crucial strategic hinterland to the Straits.[50] Russian control of the Balkans would place St Petersburg in a far better position to prevent unwanted intrusions on the Bosphorus. Designs on the Straits were thus an important reinforcing factor in the decision to stand firm over the threat to Serbia.

Whatever the precise order of geopolitical priorities, the Russians were already on the road to war. At this point, the horizons of possibility began to narrow. It becomes in retrospect harder (though not impossible) to imagine alternatives to the war that actually did break out in the first days of August 1914. This is doubtless what General Dobrorolsky, head of the Russian army's mobilization department, meant when he remarked in 1921 that after the St Petersburg meetings of 24 and 25 July 'the war was already a decided thing, and all the flood of telegrams between the governments of Russia and Germany were nothing but the staging for an historical drama'.[51] And yet throughout the crucial days of the fourth week of July, the Russians and their French partners continued to speak of a policy of peace. The policy of 'firmness', as expounded by Poincaré, Sazonov, Paléologue, Izvolsky, Krivoshein and their colleagues was a policy that aimed, in the words of the Tsar, 'to safeguard peace by the demonstration of force'.

It is tempting to dismiss this language as a smokescreen of euphemisms intended to disguise the aggressiveness of Russian and French policy and perhaps also to avoid putting off the policy-makers in London. But we find the same formulations in internal correspondance and private utterances. There is an interesting contrast here with the analogous German documents, which speak more directly of war as an external threat, a necessity and an instrument of policy. Yet a closer look at what Russian and French statesmen were actually doing when they spoke of the need to safeguard peace suggests that the difference was discursive, rather than substantial. Why this difference should have existed is not immediately clear, but we should be wary of seeing in it the symptom of Germanic militarism or war-lust. It may well reflect the deep impact of Clausewitz on German political language. The war of 1914–18 was the absolute negation of everything that Clausewitz had stood and argued for, but his subtle writings on conflict had depicted war as an eminently political tool, whose deployment – as a measure of last resort – should always serve political ends. By contrast, the language of the Russian and French decision-makers reflected the assumption that war and peace were stark existential alternatives. However, neither Clausewitz's sage injunctions on the primacy of politics nor heartfelt invocations of peace as the highest human good did anything to inhibit the decision-makers who took Europe into war in July 1914.

12

Last Days

A STRANGE LIGHT FALLS UPON THE MAP OF EUROPE

Throughout most of the July Crisis of 1914, the eyes of the decision-makers in London were riveted on the nine counties of Ulster in the north of Ireland. On 21 May 1914, a bill introducing Irish Home Rule was passed by the Commons at the third reading but rejected by the House of Lords. Dependent on Irish nationalist votes, Asquith's Liberal government resolved to use the provisions of the Parliament Act, which allows a government in such circumstances to circumvent the Lords and pass a bill by means of the Royal Assent. The prospect of a partial devolution of government functions to Catholic Ireland stirred deep and bitter controversy. The thorniest question concerned which counties, if any, of confessionally mixed Ulster should be exempted from Home Rule and thus allowed to remain in the Union. Despairing of a solution that would meet their demands, both sides – Catholic Irish nationalists and Protestant Unionists – began preparing for an armed power struggle. In the spring, Ireland was on the brink of a fully-fledged civil war. This was the seed-bed of the Troubles that would continue to bedevil northern Irish politics into the early twenty-first century.[1]

The tensions generated by the Ulster Question reached deep into the political life of the United Kingdom, because they touched on the past, present and future identity of the British polity. The Conservative Party (officially known as the Conservative and Unionist Party) was passionately opposed to Home Rule. Unionist feeling also ran high in the officer corps of the British army, many of whose recruits hailed from Protestant Anglo-Irish families with a strong stake in the Union. Indeed, it appeared

H. H. Asquith

doubtful whether the army would remain loyal if it were called upon to enforce Home Rule. In the Curragh Incident of 20 March 1914, fifty-seven British officers based at the Curragh Camp in County Kildare proposed to resign their commissions rather than enforce the introduction of Home Rule against unionist resistance.[2]

Among those within the army leadership who supported unionist insubordination was Director of Military Operations Henry Wilson, who had played such an important role in expanding the scope of the British contingency plans for a continental intervention. Wilson made less and less effort to mask his contempt for 'Squiff' (as he called Asquith) and his 'filthy cabinet'. He did not shrink from using the Home Rule question to blackmail the prime minister into meeting unionist demands. In a memorandum presented to the Army Council to be put before the cabinet on 29 June 1914, Wilson and his colleagues argued that the army would need to deploy the entire British Expeditionary Force to Ireland if it were to impose Home Rule and restore order there.[3] In other words: if the British government wished to impose

Home Rule, it would have to renounce any military intervention in Europe for the foreseeable future; conversely, a continental military intervention would mean forgoing the introduction of Home Rule. This meant in turn that officers of unionist sympathies – which were extremely widespread in an officer corps dominated by Protestant Anglo-Irish families – were inclined to see in a British continental intervention one possible means of postponing or preventing altogether the introduction of Home Rule. Nowhere else in Europe, with the possible exception of Austria-Hungary, did domestic conditions exert such direct pressure on the political outlook of the most senior military commanders.

Ulster was still consuming the attention of the British government when the news from Sarajevo broke. The prime minister did not keep a diary, but his intimate correspondence with his young friend and soulmate Venetia Stanley, an elegant and intelligent socialite, is diary-like in its candid and detailed accounts of Asquith's daily preoccupations. The letters suggest that the violent death of the 'Austrian royalties' on 28 June scarcely impinged on the prime minister's political awareness, which was wholly focused on 'the queer things that are going on about Ulster'.[4] Asquith made no further mention of the international situation until 24 July, when he reported ruefully that yet another round of haggling over Ulster had collapsed, stymied by the complex confessional geography of Tyrone and Fermanagh. Only at the end of a long discussion of Northern Irish matters did the prime minister mention, almost as an afterthought, that Austria had just sent 'a bullying and humiliating Ultimatum to Servia, who cannot possibly accept it'.

> We are within measurable, or imaginable distance of a real Armageddon, which would dwarf the Ulster and Nationalist Volunteers to their true proportion. Happily there seems to be no reason why we should be anything more than spectators.[5]

This letter opened with the startling announcement that 'the light has failed', but Asquith was referring to Venetia's departure from London that morning for her family's country home on Anglesey, not to the impending extinction of European civilization.

For Edward Grey, these were days heavy with personal preoccupations: his sight was deteriorating – he was finding it increasingly difficult to follow the ball during games of squash and could no longer pick out his favourite star at night. He was planning to spend more time in the country and there was talk of a visit to a renowned German oculist. By contrast with Asquith, however, Grey immediately perceived the seriousness of the crisis brewing in south-eastern Europe.

In his conversations during July with the London ambassadors of the powers, Grey plotted, as so often before, a meandering path that steered clear of straightforward commitments. On 8 July, he warned Paul Cambon that if the Austrian Emperor were forced by Austrian public opinion to undertake a démarche against Serbia, France and Britain would have to do everything in their power to calm St Petersburg; Cambon 'warmly agreed'.[6] On the same day, Grey reminded the Russian ambassador that Berlin was nervous about the recent Anglo-Russian naval conversations and that it was crucial Russia not give Germany any reason to suspect that a coup was being prepared against her.[7] On 9 July, he assured the German ambassador, Count Lichnowsky, that there existed no secret and binding understandings between Britain and France or Russia. But he also added that Britain's relations with its Entente partners had lost nothing of their 'warmth' and that Lichnowsky should be aware that certain 'conversations' had taken place since 1906 between the various military and naval authorities, albeit without any 'aggressive intent'.[8]

The foreign secretary's talks with the Austrian ambassador were polite, but reserved and noncommittal. When Count Mensdorff complained to Grey on 17 July of the excesses of the Belgrade press, Grey enquired – rather oddly – whether there was not perhaps *one* Serbian paper that had behaved decently. Mensdorff conceded that this might be the case, but went on to say that the dual monarchy could no longer tolerate political subversion at this level of intensity. 'Sir Edward Grey conceded this,' Mensdorff reported, 'but did not enter into any further discussion of the subject.'[9] After receiving the text of the Austrian note to Belgrade, Grey invited Mensdorff to come to see him again on 24 July – it was on that occasion that he described the note as the most 'formidable' document of its type that he had ever seen. But even on that occasion, the foreign secretary conceded that Austria's claims concerning the complicity of certain Serbian state agencies and even some of the demands listed in the note were 'justified'.[10] On the same day, after securing approval from the cabinet, he proposed that a concert of the four powers less directly involved in the quarrel – Britain, France,

Italy and Germany – should intervene in the event of a flare-up between Russia and Austria.[11]

None of this gave any indication that Grey intended to enter the conflict. He had often remarked that public opinion (by which he essentially meant published opinion) would be the ultimate determinant of British action, but there was little support for intervention in that sphere. Almost all the major papers viewed the prospect of British participation in a European war with distaste. The *Manchester Guardian* declared that Britain was in no danger of being dragged into the Austro-Serbian conflict by 'treaties of alliance' and famously announced that Manchester cared for Belgrade as little as Belgrade cared for Manchester. On 29 July, the *Daily News* expressed disgust at the notion that British lives might be sacrificed 'for the sake of Russian hegemony of the Slav world'.[12] On 1 August, its liberal editor, Alfred George Gardiner, published a piece entitled 'Why we must not fight', of which the two central arguments were that there were no fundamental conflicts of interest between Britain and Germany, and that crushing Germany would in effect establish a Russian dictatorship over 'Europe and Asia'. These were liberal titles, but even the Tory papers were unenthusiastic. The *Yorkshire Post*, for example, was doubtful that an Austro-German victory over the Franco-Russian Alliance would leave England any worse off than a Franco-Russian victory and could 'see no reason why Britain should be drawn in'. The *Cambridge Daily News* agreed on 28 July that Britain's interest in the looming conflict was negligible and the *Oxford Chronicle* announced on 31 July that the government's duty was to localize the quarrel and keep well out of it.[13] Only *The Times* argued consistently for British intervention: although there was moderately sympathetic coverage of the Austrian position by Wickham Steed on 17 July, the paper anticipated a continental conflict from 22 July and spoke out on 27, 29 and 31 July in favour of British involvement. Particularly vehement were the rantings of the journalist, self-publicist and fraudster Horatio Bottomley, whose editorial for his own *John Bull* in the first week of July opened with the words: 'We have always looked at Serbia as a hotbed of cold-blooded conspiracy and subterfuge' and demanded 'Servia must be wiped out' before going on, inconsequentially, to recommend that the British government 'avail itself of the crisis' to 'annihilate' the German fleet.[14] The Serbian minister in London, Bošković, was so appalled by the coverage in *John Bull* that he presented a formal protest to the British foreign office and sought legal advice on suing the paper for its 'lies' about Serbia.[15]

At least until the beginning of August, then, it cannot be said that public opinion was pressuring the British government to intervene. Nor did it seem likely that the cabinet would seize the initiative. The majority of the ministers was still staunchly non-interventionist. It was the same constellation that had produced the cabinet revolt against Grey's policy in November 1911. This was the fundamental problem Grey had always had to confront: that his foreign policy was distrusted by a large part of his own party. He had been able to count for some time on the support of the Conservatives in parliament, but in the summer of 1914, with anti-Home-Rule feeling running high, this support base, too, looked fragile. In the face of these pressures, he fell back on his customary practice of confining discussions of the international situation to his three liberal imperialist associates Asquith, Haldane and Churchill.

Not until the cabinet meeting of 24 July, after long and and difficult discussions on the minutiae of local government boundaries in Ulster, did he raise the issue of British policy on the current crisis, proposing that a concert of the four powers less closely connected with the Austro-Serbian quarrel be established to mediate between the two antagonists. It was the first time the cabinet had discussed foreign policy for more than a month. In a slightly purple but oddly effective passage, Churchill later evoked the cabinet's dawning awareness of the import of Grey's words: 'The parishes of Fermanagh and Tyrone faded back into the mists and squalls of Ireland and a strange light began by perceptible gradations to fall upon the map of Europe.'[16] The cabinet approved Grey's proposal for a four-power intervention and then broke up for the weekend.

As the fourth week of July reached its end, Grey began to press harder for a clarification of the circumstances under which the government might be prepared to intervene. On Monday 27 July, he enquired whether the cabinet would support intervention if France were to be attacked by Germany. Grey's old opponents, Morley, Simon, Burns, Beauchamp and Harcourt, all threatened to resign immediately if such a decision were taken. At a late-night meeting on 29–30 July, after a long discussion failed to produce a resolution, Grey pressed for a promise of support for France. Only four cabinet colleagues (including Asquith, Haldane and Churchill) backed the proposal; the rest were opposed.

Even the question of Belgium seemed unlikely to trigger an intervention. It was widely assumed, on the basis both of military intelligence secured by the French General Staff and of military inference, that the Germans would approach France through Belgium, breaching the 1839 international treaty guaranteeing its neutrality. But the cabinet took the view that, while Britain was indeed a signatory to the treaty, the obligation to uphold it fell on all the signatories collectively, not on any one of them individually. Should the matter actually arise, they concluded, the British response would be 'one of policy rather than obligation'.[17] Indeed, it is striking with what sang-froid senior British military and political leaders contemplated a German breach of Belgian neutrality. On the basis of Anglo-French staff conversations in 1911, Henry Wilson had come to the conclusion that the Germans would choose to cross the Ardennes through southern Belgium, confining their troops to the area south of the rivers Sambre and Meuse; these findings were presented to the 114th meeting of the Committee of Imperial Defence.[18] The same scenario was discussed by the cabinet on 29 July, when Lloyd George showed, using a map, why it was likely that the Germans would cross 'only [...] the furthest southern corner' of Belgium. Far from greeting this prospect with outrage, the ministers accepted it as strategically necessary (from Germany's standpoint) and thus virtually inevitable. British strategic concerns were focused primarily on Antwerp and the mouth of the river Schelde, which had always been regarded as one of the keys to British security. 'I don't see,' Churchill commented, 'why we should come in if they go only a little way into Belgium.'[19] Lloyd George later claimed that he would have refused to go to war if the German invasion of Belgium had been confined to the route through the Ardennes.[20] British policy-makers assumed in any case that the Belgians themselves would not make their last stand in the south, but would, after offering token resistance to demonstrate that they had not permitted the violation, fall back on their lines of fortification further to the north.[21] There would thus be nothing automatic about the relationship between a German invasion of Belgium and British intervention in the conflict.

It would be a mistake, however, to infer from these indications of reluctance that Grey himself or his closest associates had abandoned their long-standing commitment to the Entente. On the contrary, Grey viewed the crisis unfolding in Europe almost entirely through the lens of the Entente. The prospect that parliament might not honour the moral obligation to France that he had worked so hard to create and protect caused him profound anxiety. He shared the personal distaste of his colleagues for the adventurist politics of Belgrade and was aware of the massacres and harassment in the newly conquered areas. He certainly possessed enough information to understand the kind of threat that Serbia posed to the Austro-Hungarian monarchy. He expressed disgust at the notion that any great power should be 'dragged into a war by Servia'.[22] Yet he showed no interest in the kind of intervention that might have provided Austria with other options than the ultimatum. The four-power mediation proposed at the cabinet meeting of 24 July was a non-starter.[23] Of the four powers involved (Britain, Germany, Italy and France) only one was likely to defend the interests of Austria-Hungary. Moreover, Austria-Hungary and the international system lacked the means to ensure compliance with whatever stipulations might have been agreed. Finally, the great power most directly involved in sponsoring Serbian irredentism would not have been involved in, or bound by, the decisions of the concert. Grey's confidence in his ability to patch together some form of mediation doubtless derived in part from the good fame he had earned by chairing the Ambassadors' Conference of 1913 in London. But arguments over Albanian border strips and a peace–war mediation among the great powers were very different things.

In his reactions to the crisis, Grey subordinated his understanding of the Austro-Serbian quarrel to the larger imperatives of the Entente, which meant, in effect, tacitly supporting Russian policy. Grey did speak at intervals of the importance of 'calming' Russia, and he did ask St Petersburg to avoid unnecessarily provocative measures, but he showed remarkably little knowledge of, or interest in, what was actually happening in Russia during the crucial days following the presentation of the Austrian note. This ignorance was not entirely his fault, for the Russians deliberately concealed the extent of their 'clandestine preparations' from Sir George Buchanan, telling him on 26 July that the 'protective measures' in Moscow and St Petersburg had been put into effect merely to deal with a wave of strikes currently disrupting Russian industry. Buchanan was not entirely convinced: in a brief dispatch to Grey on 26 July, he noted that, since the strikes were 'practically over', the measures he had observed must 'doubtless' be connected with 'intending mobilization'.[24] But Grey was not interested; there was no attempt on Buchanan's part to follow up on these indications, and no instruction from London to do so. And this approach was characteristic of the Foreign Ministry's handling of communications with Russia. On 26 July, the day Buchanan filed his report, Nicolson met with Count Lichnowsky, who appeared with an urgent telegram from his government reporting that Russia seemed to be calling in 'classes of reserves', which in effect signalled mobilization. Nicolson replied that London 'had no information as to a general mobilization or indeed of any mobilization immediately'. But then he added:

> It would, however, be difficult and delicate for us to ask Petersburg not to mobilise at all when Austria was contemplating such a measure; we should not be listened to. The main thing was to prevent, if possible, *active* military operations.[25]

This was an odd reading of the situation, to say the least, for it implied an equivalence between Austrian and Russian mobilization, overlooking the fact that whereas Austrian measures were focused exclusively on Serbia, Russian ones were directed against Austria (and Germany, inasmuch as the Regulation of 2 March 1913 applied to nearly all the western Russian military districts and had in any case been extended to cover the mobilization of the Baltic Fleet). Grey's comments also revealed a blank (or perhaps partially wilful) ignorance of the meaning of mobilization measures in an era when the speed of concentration and attack was seen as a crucial determinant of military success. Finally, had Grey been interested in adopting an impartial approach to the admittedly tangled problem of mediation and localization, he might have wished to examine closely the strengths and weaknesses of the Austrian case against Serbia, and to prevent Russian counter-measures that were certain to trigger a broader conflict. But he did nothing of the kind. At his meeting with Benckendorff on 8 July and at various points thereafter, Grey had, after all, acquiesced in the Russian view that a 'Servian war inevitably meant a European war'.[26]

Grey knew in general terms what had transpired during the French visit to St Petersburg. In a dispatch of 24 July (following Poincaré's departure) Ambassador Buchanan reported that the meetings in the

Russian capital had revealed a 'perfect community of views' between Russia and France on 'the general peace and the balance of power in Europe' and that the two states had made 'a solemn affirmation of [the] obligations imposed by [their] alliance'; Sazonov had asked Buchanan to convey to Grey his hope that the British government would 'proclaim [its] solidarity with France and Russia'.[27] Commenting on this dispatch, Eyre Crowe used more trenchant formulations than Grey would have chosen, but captured the inner logic of the position that the foreign secretary would adopt:

> Whatever we may think of the merits of the Austrian charges against Servia, France and Russia consider that these are the pretexts, and that the bigger cause of Triple Alliance versus Triple Entente is definitely engaged. I think it would be impolitic, not to say dangerous, for England to attempt to controvert this opinion, or to endeavour to obscure the plain issue, by any representation at St. Petersburg and Paris. [. . .] Our interests are tied up with those of France and Russia in this struggle, which is not for the possession of Servia, but one between Germany aiming at a political dictatorship in Europe and the Powers who desire to retain individual freedom.[28]

Grey assured Lichnowsky that Britain had no legal obligations to its Entente partners. But he also warned the German ambassador on 29 July (without specific authorization from the cabinet beforehand) that if Germany and France were drawn into the war, Britain might find it necessary to take precipitous action.[29] When Bethmann Hollweg contacted London on 30 July to suggest that Germany would abstain from annexations of French territory if Britain agreed to remain neutral, Grey cabled Goschen (the British ambassador in Berlin) to inform him that the proposal 'cannot for a moment be entertained'.[30]

Grey's actions and omissions revealed how deeply Entente thinking structured his view of the unfolding crisis. This was, in effect, a new iteration of the Balkan inception scenario that had become the animating logic of the Franco-Russian Alliance, and that Grey had internalized in his warning to the German ambassador in early December 1912 (see chapter 5). There would be a quarrel in the Balkans – it didn't really matter who started it – Russia would pile in, pulling in Germany, France would 'inevitably' intervene on the side of her ally; in that situation, Britain could not stand aside and watch France be crushed by Germany.

This is precisely the script – notwithstanding momentary doubts and prevarications – that Grey followed in 1914. He did not inspect or weigh up the Austrian case against Serbia, indeed he showed no interest in it whatsoever, not because he believed the Serbian government was innocent of the charges against it,[31] but because he acquiesced in the Franco-Russian view that the Austrian threat to Serbia constituted a 'pretext' as Eyre Crowe put it, for activating the alliance.

A central feature of that scenario was that Britain accepted – or at least did not challenge – the legitimacy of a Russian strike against Austria to resolve an Austro-Serbian quarrel, and the inevitability of French support for the Russian initiative. The precise circumstances of the Austro-Serbian dispute and questions of culpability were matters of subordinate interest; what mattered was the situation that unfolded once the Russians (and the French) were involved. And defining the problem in this way naturally placed the onus on Germany, whose intervention in Austria's defence must necessarily trigger French mobilization and a continental war.

POINCARÉ RETURNS TO PARIS

As Grey was proposing his four-power mediation idea at the end of the cabinet meeting of 24 July, Poincaré and Viviani were crossing the Gulf of Finland on board the *France*, escorted by Russian torpedo boats. When they arrived in Sweden on the following day, Poincaré exploited the access to secure telegraphic links to ensure that control over the formulation of policy remained with himself and (nominally) Viviani. He instructed the premier to issue a statement to the French press announcing that Viviani was in communication with all relevant parties and had resumed direction of external affairs. 'It is important,' Poincaré noted, 'that they not get the impression in France that Bienvenu-Martin [the inexperienced acting foreign minister in Paris] has been left to his own devices.'[32] Over the past twenty-four hours, bits and pieces of information on the evolving Austro-Serbian crisis had made it through to the wireless station on board the *France*. As a fuller picture emerged, Poincaré stuck to the position he had outlined in St Petersburg: the Austrian démarche was illegitimate, Vienna's demands were 'obviously unacceptable to Serbia', indeed they constituted a 'violation of human rights'. The responsibility for saving peace no longer lay with Russia, whose military preparations were entirely in accordance with the positions affirmed and agreed during the French state visit, but with the Germans, who must restrain their Austrian ally. If the Germans failed to do this, Poincaré noted in his diary on 25 July, 'they would place themselves in a very wrongful position in taking upon themselves the responsibilities for the violent acts of Austria'.[33]

The most revealing glimpse of how proactively Poincaré viewed his own part in events is furnished by his reaction to the news, which reached him in Stockholm, that Sazonov had urged the Serbs not to offer resistance to the Austrians at the border, but to withdraw their forces to the interior of the country, to protest to the international community that she had been invaded and to appeal to the powers for judgement. Sazonov's aims in proffering this advice were to win international sympathy for the Serbian cause, but at the same time to draw the Austrians as deeply as possible into their Plan B deployments and thereby weaken the dispositions available to meet a Russian attack on Galicia. Poincaré misread this news as an indication that Sazonov had lost his nerve and was counselling an 'abdication' of Russia's responsibilities to the Balkan state. 'We assuredly cannot show ourselves *braver* [i.e. more committed to Belgrade] *than the Russians*,' he wrote. 'Serbia has every chance of being humiliated.'[34] It was, or rather it looked like, a return to those days of winter 1912–13 when French policy-makers had pressed the Russians to adopt a firmer position against Austria in the Balkans. At that time, the Russian military attaché in Paris had reacted with puzzlement to the bellicose talk of the French military. Now the situation was different. The policy had been agreed, and Poincaré's fears that Sazonov was about to wobble again were unfounded.

It may seem odd that Poincaré did not, in view of the escalating crisis in Central Europe, simply cancel his scheduled visit to Sweden on the home leg. The stopover in Stockholm has sometimes been cited as evidence of the French leader's essential passivity in relation to the crisis. Why, if Poincaré intended to play a proactive role in events, would he and Viviani have indulged in maritime tourism on the way home to Paris?[35] The answer to the question is that the visit to Sweden was not tourism at all, but a crucial part of the alliance strategy reaffirmed in St Petersburg. Poincaré and the Tsar had discussed the need to secure

Swedish neutrality (in preparation, one must infer, for an impending European war). Swedish-Russian relations had been troubled in recent times by aggressive Russian espionage activity and fears in Stockholm of an imminent Russian attack, either across their shared border or across the Baltic.[36] On their last day together in St Petersburg, Nicholas II had asked Poincaré personally to convey to King Gustav V of Sweden his (the Tsar's) peaceful intentions towards Sweden. Poincaré was to inform the king that the Tsar harboured no aggressive intentions against his Baltic neighbour and that while he had until now been unaware of any espionage activity, he would put a stop to it forthwith.[37] Above all, it was crucial that Sweden be prevented from falling into the arms of the Germans, with the severe strategic complications this might entail. On 25 July, during an afternoon spent with Gustav V, Poincaré successfully performed this errand and was able to report that the king heartily reciprocated the Tsar's desire that Sweden should remain neutral.[38]

It was, of course, awkward to be stuck wining and dining in Sweden while the European crisis deepened, especially as the strain was beginning to tell once more on poor Viviani. But French public opinion was still calm – attention remained focused on the Caillaux trial, which

Nicholas II and Poincaré

ended only on 28 July with the surprise acquittal of Madame Caillaux. Under these circumstances, as Poincaré knew well, an early return was more likely to alarm than to reassure French and European opinion. Moreover, it would 'give rise to the impression that France may involve herself in the conflict'.[39] But once it became known, on 27 July, that the Kaiser had returned early to Berlin from his Baltic journey on the imperial yacht, Poincaré, who was now being bombarded with telegrams from ministers urging him to return to Paris, lost no time in cancelling the remaining state visits to Denmark and Norway, which were in any case much less pressing from the strategic point of view, and instructing the crew of the *France* to return directly to Dunkirk.[40]

Hardly had they changed their course, but the *France* and her escort, the dreadnought-class battleship *Jean Bart*, were met by a German battle cruiser crossing the Bay of Mecklenburg out of Kiel, followed by a German torpedo boat that turned tail and left the scene. The German battle cruiser offered the usual salute, firing blanks from all guns singly on the beam, and the *Jean Bart* responded in kind – the *France* remained silent, as was the custom for any ship carrying a head of state. Minutes later, the telegraph station on the *France* intercepted an encrypted radio transmission sent from the battle cruiser immediately after the salute – presumably to alert Berlin to the fact that the French president was now on his way back to Paris.[41]

Poincaré and Viviani found themselves adopting increasingly divergent views of the international situation. Poincaré noticed that the prime minister seemed 'more and more troubled and worried' and was preoccupied by 'the most contradictory ideas'.[42] When a telegram arrived on 27 July reporting Edward Grey's affirmation that England would not remain inactive should a war break out in the Balkans, Poincaré 'made an example of this firmness to Viviani' in order to buck him up. The president spent much of that day, as he had on the journey to St Petersburg, explaining to Viviani 'that weakness is [. . .] always the mother of complications' and that the only sensible course was to manifest 'an enduring firmness'. But Viviani remained 'nervous, agitated [and] kept uttering disturbing words or phrases that denote a bleak vision of foreign policy matters'. Pierre de Margerie (head of the political department of the Quai d'Orsay), too, was unsettled by Viviani's 'singular state of mind'. To Poincaré's consternation, the prime minister seemed unable to speak coherently of anything but party congresses and the political alliances around the socialist leader Jean Jaurès.[43]

Poincaré, too, was feeling the strain. Particularly vexing was a sequence of confused and almost unintelligible radiogrammes on 27 July reporting various statements by Sir Edward Grey. Having warned the Austrian ambassador that Britain would not stand aside in a war of Balkan origin, Grey was now warning the French ambassador, Paul Cambon, that British public opinion would not support British involvement in a war over the Serbian question. But whereas Viviani feared a headlong rush towards war, what Poincaré feared above all was a failure to confront and oppose an Austria démarche against Serbia.

> . . . if Austria wants to push her victory further [by 'victory', Poincaré meant Belgrade's supposed acceptance of the Austrian demands], if she declares war or if she enters Belgrade, will Europe let her do it? Is it only between Austria and Russia that [Europe] will intervene to put a stop to [a further escalation]? That would mean taking Austria's part and giving it open season vis-à-vis Serbia. I set out all these objections to Viviani . . .[44]

On 28 July, as they entered the North Sea and approached the French coast, Poincaré had the telegraph officer radio ahead to cancel the reception at Dunkirk – the president's train should be made ready so that the party could travel directly from the harbour to Paris. The air over the North Sea was colder and greyer, the sea was choppy, and there were frequent drenching showers. The latest radiogrammes reported that the British supported a 'collective démarche' by the powers to defuse the crisis, encouraging news for the president, because it meant that the Russians would be expected to stand down only if the Austrians did. And lastly there was very cheering news from Paris: in reply to the German ambassador von Schoen, who had insisted that the Austro-Serbian quarrel was a matter for the two countries to resolve between themselves, the acting foreign minister Bienvenu-Martin had declared that France would do nothing to restrain Russia unless Germany restrained Austria-Hungary. Delighted with this unexpectedly firm riposte, Poincaré instructed de Margerie to have Viviani telegraph to Paris his – i.e. Viviani's – approval of the acting minister's reply. It was a neat illustration of the chain of command driving French foreign policy in the last days of July 1914.[45]

By the time of his arrival in France, Poincaré had made up his mind – though there were still no signs of military counter-measures from Germany – that a European war could no longer be avoided.[46] He found the ministers in a calm and resolute mood and was relieved to see that their attitude was more energetic than that of the faint-hearted Viviani. Poincaré had already telegraphed Bienvenu-Martin, instructing him to liaise with his colleagues in the ministries of war, the navy, the interior and finance to ensure that all the 'necessary precautions' were in place in case of a heightening of tension; he was pleased to find that great progress had been made in all relevant sectors. Abel Ferry, the under-secretary of state for foreign affairs, and René Renoult, minister of public works, who had travelled to Dunkirk to meet the presidential party, informed Poincaré that soldiers on leave had been recalled, troops in training camps had returned to their garrisons, the prefects had been placed on alert, civil servants had been instructed to remain at their posts and key supplies had been purchased by Paris; 'in short, the steps had been taken which, in the event of need, would permit an immediate mobilization'.[47] When Renoult asked him in the train from Dunkirk to the capital whether a political settlement among the great powers was still possible, Poincaré replied: 'No, there can be no settlement. There can be no arrangement.'[48] Most telling of all is the description in Poincaré's diary of the crowds that gathered to greet him on the way to Paris; it suggests the state of mind of a political leader already at war:

> Immediately we note that the morale of the population is excellent, especially of the labourers and dockers. A very dense multitude had poured onto the wharves and quays and greeted us with repeated cries of Vive la France! Vive Poincaré! I master my emotion and exchange a few words with the mayor, senators and deputies. They all tell me, and the Prefect confirms, that we can count on the unity and on the determination of the country.[49]

The Russian government had already implemented far-reaching pre-mobilization measures. Paris was well informed of these, both by Paléologue, in the brief note of 25 July and, in more detail on the following day, by the French military attaché in St Petersburg, General Pierre de Laguiche.[50] Then came the news, brought by Ambassador Izvolsky on the morning of 29 July, that a Russian partial mobilization against Austria-Hungary was planned for the same day. It is difficult to retrace Poincaré's reponse to this news, because he later (while preparing his memoirs) removed the latter half of the entry for 29 July from the manuscript of his diary, a page that appears to have been concerned with the Russian measures.[51] And there are no extant minutes of the discussion at the Council of Ministers convened that day. But according to an account confided to Joseph Caillaux that evening by a minister who had been present (Minister of the Interior Louis Malvy), the Council of Ministers expressly approved the Russian measures.[52] Neither on 26–27 nor on 29 July did Paris see fit to urge restraint on the alliance partner.

All of this was in accordance with the Balkan inception scenario and with French strategic thinking, which laid great weight upon the speed and effectiveness of Russian mobilization. But this priority had to be balanced with the need to secure British intervention. At the end of July, the British government remained undecided on the question of whether, when and in what way it would take part in the impending European war. One thing was clear: if France were seen to be entering a war of aggression at the side of its ally, this would thoroughly undermine its moral claim to British support. Yet French security in the face of a German westward attack required that Paris insist on the swiftest possible military response by St Petersburg. This was the familiar paradox: the war that needed to be fought defensively in the west had to begin aggressively in the east. These conflicting imperatives placed immense pressure on the decision-makers in Paris. And the pressure became especially acute on the night of 29 July, when the Germans warned St Petersburg that they would consider mobilizing their own forces unless Russia halted its own mobilization.

Late in the night of 29–30 July, a telegram from Sazonov arrived at the Russian embassy in Paris informing Izvolsky of the German warning. Since Russia could not back down, Sazonov wrote, it was the Russian government's intention to 'accelerate our defence measures and to assume the likely inevitability of a war'. Izvolsky was instructed to thank the French government, on Sazonov's behalf, for its generous assurance 'that we can count absolutely on the support of France as an ally'.[53] Since the Russians had already advised France of the earlier decision to launch a *partial* mobilization (against Austria only), it can be inferred that Sazonov's 'acceleration' referred to an imminent Russian *general* mobilization, a measure that would indeed make a continental war virtually inevitable.[54] Unsurprisingly, this message triggered a flurry of activity in Paris. Izvolsky sent his legation secretary in the dead of night to the Quai d'Orsay and went himself to Viviani to present him with Sazonov's telegram. Shortly thereafter, at four o'clock on the morning of 30 July, Viviani met with War Minister Adolphe Messimy and Poincaré in the Elysée Palace to discuss the news. The result was a carefully worded French reply, dispatched on the morning of that day:

> France is resolved to fulfil all the obligations of the alliance. But, in the interest of general peace and given that discussions are still underway among the less interested powers, I believe that it would be desirable that, in the measures of precaution and defence to which Russia believes it must proceed, it does not make immediately any disposition that might offer Germany a pretext for a total or partial mobilization of its forces.[55]

This reply is sometimes cited as evidence that the French government, alarmed by the Russian measures, were willing for the sake of peace to jeopardize the security arrangements of the Franco-Russian Alliance.[56] Certaintly this was how it seemed to Viviani: during a meeting that evening with the former foreign minister Gabriel Hanotaux, he complained that the Russians 'are confronting us with faits accomplis and are hardly consulting us at all'.[57] But the purpose of the note was more complex. It was intended to persuade the British that France was endeavouring to restrain its ally – with this purpose in mind, a copy of the message was dispatched immediately to Paul Cambon in London. The link with the Anglo-French Entente is made explicit in Poincaré's diary, which records that the message to St Petersburg was formulated 'on account of the ambiguous attitude of England'.[58] At the same time, however, de Margerie and Messimy were instructed by Poincaré – apparently without Viviani's knowledge – to clarify to Izvolsky the true nature of the French government's intentions. Izvolsky's report of conversations with the diplomat and the minister substantially muted the impact of the earlier telegram urging restraint:

> Margerie, with whom I have just spoken, told me that the French government *has no wish to intervene in our military preparations*, but believes it to be extremely desirable, in the interests of the continuation of negotiations for the preservation of peace, that these preparations should avoid as far as possible an overt and provocative character. Developing the same

thought, the minister of war also said to Count Ignatiev [the Russian military attaché in Paris] that we could make a declaration to the effect that we are willing, for the sake of the higher interests of peace, temporarily to slow our mobilization measures, *which need not prevent us on the other hand from continuing our military preparations and indeed pursuing them more energetically, as long as we refrain from mass transports of troops.*[59]

These two telegrams, both dispatched on 30 July, capture the complex triangulations of a French policy that had to mediate between the hard imperatives of the Franco-Russian Alliance and the fuzzy logic of the Anglo-French Entente. Appealing to the 'higher interests of peace' in essence meant offering the opponent an opportunity to back down – an eventuality that looked increasingly unlikely. In the meanwhile, Russia's preparations for war continued, in the form of an almost-mobilization that stopped short of the concentration of masses of troops at the western frontier. As he jotted down notes in the Council of Ministers on the morning of 30 July, the under-secretary of state at the Quai d'Orsay, Abel Ferry, summarized French policy thus: '*Do not stop Russian mobilization. Mobilize, but do not concentrate.*'[60] In Poincaré's diary, the passage from that day reporting the dispatch of the telegram urging restraint on St Petersburg is followed by the sentence: 'At the same time, we take the necessary measures to establish our covering troops in the East.'[61]

RUSSIA MOBILIZES

On the evening of 29 July, the chief of the Russian General Staff passed the *Ukaz* for general mobilization to General Sergei Dobrorolsky. As director of mobilization, it was Dobrorolsky's task to collect the ministerial signatures without which the order could not come into effect. The general later recalled his visits to the ministries of war, the navy and the interior. The mood was sombre. Sukhomlinov, once so outspoken in his belligerence, had grown very quiet in recent days. Perhaps, Dobrorolsky reflected, he now regretted the incendiary article he had planted some months before in the *Birzheviia Vedomosti* declaring that Russia was 'ready for war'.[62] The minister of the navy, Admiral Grigorovich, was shocked to see the *Ukaz*: 'What, war with Germany? Our fleet is in no state to hold its own against the German fleet.' He called Sukhom-linov on the telephone for confirmation and then signed 'with a heavy heart'. In the office of the reactionary ultra-monarchist minister of the interior, Nikolai Maklakov, Dobrorolsky found 'an atmosphere of prayers': large icons standing on a narrow table glowed in the light of a church lamp. 'In Russia,' the minister said, 'war will never be popular with the profound masses of the people. Revolutionary ideas are more to their taste than a victory over Germany. But one does not escape one's destiny . . .' Crossing himself, Maklakov, too, signed the order.[63]

At around 9 p.m., with all the necessary signatures collated, Dobro-rolsky made his way to St Petersburg's Central Telegraph Office, where the director-in-chief of posts and telegrams had been warned in advance to make himself available for a transmission 'of the greatest import-ance'. With scrupulous care, the text was typed up in multiple copies so that it could be sent simultaneously from the machines in the main hall that linked St Petersburg to the principal centres of the Russian Empire. From these it would be retransmitted to all towns in all districts. Fol-lowing the protocol for the dispatch of mobilization orders, the telegraph office had shut down all other traffic. At 9.30 p.m., just before transmis-sion, the phone rang: it was Yanushkevich, chief of the General Staff, ordering Dobrorolsky not to transmit the text, but to stand by for fur-ther instructions. A few minutes later a messenger, in the form of Staff Captain Tugan-Baranowsky, arrived in a state of agitation. The Tsar had changed his mind. Instead of the mobilization order, an order for *partial* mobilization was to be promulgated, along the lines resolved 'in principle' at the meetings of 24 and 25 July. The new order was duly drawn up and transmitted at around midnight on 29–30 July, trigger-ing mobilization measures in the Kiev, Odessa, Moscow and Kazan districts.[64]

This sudden reversal produced almost comical levels of confusion at the French embassy. General Laguiche, the military attaché, was advised of the impending mobilization just after 10 p.m., but told by the Rus-sians not to inform Ambassador Paléologue, lest the latter's indiscretion compromise the secrecy of the decision. But Paléologue learned of it an hour later from a different source (i.e. an indiscreet Russian) and imme-diately sent his first secretary, Chambrun, to the Russian foreign ministry to alert Paris by urgent telegram to the fact that a secret general mobili-zation was underway (the ministerial telegram link was chosen because it was feared that the French ciphers might not be secure; at the same time, Paléologue dispatched a telegram to the Quai d'Orsay in French cipher bearing the text: 'Please collect from the Russian Embassy, as a matter of extreme urgency, my telegram no. 304'). On reaching the ministry, Chambrun bumped into Laguiche, who had just learned that the Tsar had rescinded the mobilization order. Laguiche ordered Chambrun to delete the section of his telegram referring to the decision 'secretly to begin mobilization'. The telegram dispatched to the Russian embassy in Paris now merely announced the Russian mobilization against Austria, so that Viviani and his colleagues remained unaware of how close St Petersburg had come to a general mobilization. On the following morning, Paléologue was incandescent at the efforts of the military attaché and his own first secretary to obstruct his communications with Paris.

In any case, the partial mobilization announced on 29 July was not a sustainable arrangement. Partial mobilization posed insuperable difficulties to the Russian staff planners, because it threatened to disrupt the arrangements for a subsequent full mobilization. Unless the order were rescinded or replaced by an order for general mobilization within twenty-four hours, irreparable damage would be done to Russian preparedness for a westward attack. Early on the morning of 30 July Sazonov and Krivoshein conferred by telephone – both were 'greatly disturbed at the stoppage of the general mobilization'.[65] Sazonov proposed that Krivoshein request an audience of the Tsar in order to persuade him of the urgency of general mobilization. At 11 a.m., Sazonov and Yanushkevich met in the latter's office, and the staff chief set out once again the reasons for proceeding at once to general mobilization. Standing in the office of the chief of staff, Sazonov had a telephone call put through to the Peterhof palace. After some pained minutes of waiting, Sazonov heard the voice, unrecognizable at first, of a man 'little accustomed to speaking on the telephone, who desired to know with whom he was speaking'.[66] The Tsar agreed to receive Sazonov at three o'clock that afternoon (he refused to receive Krivoshein at the same time, because he hated it when ministers joined forces to form a lobby).

At the Peterhof, Sazonov was admitted immediately to the Emperor's study, where he found the sovereign 'tired and preoccupied'. At the Tsar's request, the audience took place in the presence of General Tatishchev, who was about to return to his posting as Russian military attaché to the German Emperor. Sazonov spoke for fifty minutes, setting out the technical difficulties, reminding Nicholas that the Germans had rejected 'all our conciliatory offers, which went far beyond the spirit of concession one would expect of a Great Power whose forces are intact' and concluding that 'no hope remained of saving peace'. The Tsar ended the meeting with a final decision: 'You are right, there is nothing else left than to prepare ourselves for an attack. Transmit to the chief of the general staff my orders of mobilization.'[67]

At last, with profound relief, Yanushkevich received the call he had been waiting for. 'Issue your orders, General,' Sazonov told him, 'and then – disappear for the rest of the day.' But Sazonov's fear that there would be another countermanding order proved groundless. Once again, it fell to General Dobrorolsky to make his way to the central telegraph office and transmit the telegram ordering a general mobilization. This time, everyone knew what was at stake. When Dobrorolsky entered the main hall of the telegraph office at around six p.m., 'solemn silence reigned among the telegraphers, men and women'. Each was seated before his or her machine, waiting for the copy of the telegram. There was no messenger from the Tsar. Several minutes after 6 p.m., though the human operators remained silent, the machines began clicking and tapping, filling the hall with dense, purposeful rustling.[68]

The Russian general mobilization was one of the most momentous decisions of the July Crisis. This was the first of the general mobilizations. It came at a moment when the German government had not yet even declared the State of Impending War, the German counterpart to the Russian Period Preparatory to War which had been in force since 26 July. Austria-Hungary, for its part, was still locked into a partial mobilization focused on defeating Serbia. There would later be some discomfort among French and Russian politicians about this sequence of events. In the Orange Book produced after the outbreak of war by the Russian government to justify its actions during the crisis, the editors backdated by three days the Austrian order of general mobilization so as to make the Russian measure appear a mere reaction to developments elsewhere. A telegram dated 29 July from Ambassador Shebeko in Vienna stating that an order of general mobilization was 'anticipated' for the following day, was backdated to 28 July and reworded to say 'The Order for General Mobilization has been signed' – in fact, the order for Austrian general mobilization would not be issued until 31 July, to go into effect on the following day. The French Yellow Book played even more adventurously with the documentary record, by inserting a fictional communiqué from Paléologue dated 31 July stating that the Russian order had been issued 'as a result of the general mobilization of Austria' and of the 'measures for mobilization taken secretly, but continuously, by Germany for the past six days . . .' In reality, the Germans had remained, in military terms, an island of relative calm throughout the crisis.[69]

Why did the Russians take this step? For Sazonov, the decisive factor was undoubtedly the Austrian declaration of war on Serbia on 28 July, to which he responded almost immediately with a telegram to the embassies in London, Paris, Vienna, Berlin and Rome to the effect that Russia would announce on the following day the (partial) mobilization of the military districts adjoining Austria.[70] (This is the telegram that was discussed by the French Council of Ministers on 29 July.) At this point, it was still important to Sazonov that the Germans be assured of the 'absence on the part of Russia of any aggressive intentions regarding Germany' – opting for partial, as opposed to general, mobilization was part of that policy.[71] Why, then, did he so rapidly shift from partial to general mobilization? Four reasons spring to mind. We have already considered the first, namely the technical impossibility of combining partial mobilization (for which no proper plan existed) with the option of a general mobilization thereafter.

A further factor was Sazonov's conviction – entertained from the beginning of the crisis, but increasingly indignant and dominant – that Austria's intransigence was in fact Germany's policy. This was an idea deeply rooted in Russian Balkan policy, which had for some time ceased to take Austria-Hungary seriously as an autonomous factor in European affairs – witness Sazonov's injunction to Bethmann at Baltic Port in the summer of 1912 not to encourage Austrian adventures. And it was reinforced by reports suggesting (correctly) that Germany was continuing to support the Austrian position, rather than pressuring its ally to back down. In his memoirs, Sazonov recalled receiving on 28 July, the day of the Austrian declaration of war on Serbia, a telegram from Ambassador Benckendorff in London reporting that a conversation with Count Lichnowsky (the German ambassador there) had 'confirmed his conviction' that Germany was 'supporting the obstinacy of

Austria'. This was an idea of great importance, because it allowed the Russians to establish Berlin as the moral fulcrum of the crisis and the agent upon which all hope of peace rested. As Benckendorff pithily put it: 'The key to the situation is clearly to be found in Berlin.'[72]

Sazonov himself articulated this view in a brief telegram dispatched to the Paris and London embassies on 28 July, in which he declared that he inferred from a conversation with the German ambassador to St Petersburg, Count Pourtalès, that 'Germany favours the unappeasable attitude of Austria'.[73] The Russian foreign minister's position hardened considerably on the following day, when Pourtalès called in on him during the afternoon to read out a message from the German chancellor in which it was stated that if Russia continued with her military preparations, Germany too would find herself compelled to mobilize. To this, Sazonov, who viewed the chancellor's warning as an ultimatum, curtly replied: 'Now I am in no doubt as to the true cause of Austrian intransigence,' prompting Pourtalès to rise from his chair and exclaim: 'I protest with all my force, *M. le Ministre*, against this wounding assertion.'[74] The meeting ended on a cold note. The point, as the Russian saw it, was that if Germany, despite its outward quiescence, was in fact the driving force behind Austrian policy, then partial mobilization made no sense, given the solidity of the Austro-German bloc – why not recognize the true nature of the threat and mobilize all-out against both powers? Finally, Sazonov's support for general mobilization was reinforced by the assurance given by Maurice Paléologue on 28 July, 'on the instructions of his government', that the Russians could count 'in case of necessity' on 'the complete readiness of France to fulfil her obligations as an ally'.[75] The Russians may even have felt confident at this early hour of British help. 'Today they are firmly persuaded in St Petersburg, indeed they have even been assured of it,' wrote the Belgian military attaché Bernard de l'Escaille on 30 July, 'that England will support France. This support carries enormous weight and has made no small contribution to giving the advantage to the war party.'[76] Which 'assurance' (if any) de l'Escaille was referring to and when exactly it became known is unclear, but he was almost certainly right that Russian leaders remained confident of British intervention, at least in the longer term.

Yet no sooner had the decision for general mobilization been reached and then accepted by the Tsar, but it was rescinded in favour of the officially agreed but unfeasible option of a partial mobilization against

Austria. The reason for this lay fundamentally in the Tsar's fear and abhorrence of war, now that he faced the task of making it a reality. Virtually all of those who knew the Tsar and left behind written observations of the sovereign's personality agree that he combined two characteristics that were in tension with each other. One was a very understandable dread at the prospect of war and the disruption it would cause to his country; the other was a susceptibility to the elevated tone of nationalist politicians and rhetoric, a preference for men and measures that stirred patriotic emotion. What tilted the Tsar towards caution on 29 July was the arrival at 9.20 p.m., just as the order for general mobilization was about to be dispatched from the central telegraph office, of a telegram from Kaiser Wilhelm II, in which the Tsar's German cousin pleaded that his government was still hoping to promote a 'direct understanding' between Vienna and St Petersburg and closed with the words:

> Of course, military measures on the part of Russia which could be looked upon by Austria as threatening would precipitate a calamity we both wish to avoid, and jeopardise my position as mediator which I readily accepted on your appeal to my friendship and my help.[77]

Saying 'I will not be responsible for a monstrous slaughter', the Tsar insisted that the order be cancelled. Yanushkevich reached for the phone to stay Dobrorolsky's hand, and the messenger was sent running to the telegraph office to explain that an order for partial mobilization was to be promulgated instead.

It is worth pausing for a moment to ponder on the fact that the impact of a telegram from the Emperor's third cousin in Berlin was sufficient to stay an order of general mobilization for nearly twenty-four hours. After the revolution of February 1917, the Russian revolutionary publicist and scourge of Tsarism Vladimir Burtsev was placed in charge of the Tsar's private papers, in which he discovered a cache of personal telegrams exchanged between the German and Russian emperors. Signing as 'Willy' and 'Nicky', the two men communicated with each other in English, adopting an informal, at times even intimate tone. The discovery of these documents was a sensation. In September 1917, the journalist Hermann Bernstein, who was reporting on the revolutionary events, published them in the *New York Herald* and they were reissued in book form (with a foreword by Theodore Roosevelt) four months later.[78]

The 'Willy–Nicky telegrams', as they came to be known, have exerted an enduring fascination, partly because, reading them, one seems to be eavesdropping on a private conversation between two emperors from a now vanished Europe, and partly because they convey the sense of a world in which the destinies of nations still rested in the hands of extremely powerful individuals. In fact, both impressions are misleading, at least as far as the famous telegrams of 1914 are concerned. Those exchanged during the July Crisis were neither secret – since their existence was widely known and discussed[79] – nor private. They were in effect diplomatic cables couched in the form of personal correspondence. At both ends of the conversation, the content was carefully vetted by foreign office personnel. They were an example of that curious monarch-to-monarch signalling that remained a feature of the European system until the outbreak of war, though in this case the monarchs were the transmitters, rather than the generators, of the signals exchanged. Their existence reflects the monarchical structure of the European executives, not the power of the monarchs to shape policy. The telegram of 29 July was exceptional: it arrived at a very special moment, when, for once, everything hung on the decision of the Tsar, not because he was the dominant player in the policy-making process, but because his permission (and signature) was required for an order of general mobilization. And this was a matter not of political influence as such, but of the residual military absolutism of the autocratic system. At a moment when the Tsar found it agonizingly difficult to give his assent – understandably, given the stakes involved – the telegram from 'Willy' was enough to tip the balance away from general mobilization. But the effect lasted for less than a day, because both monarchs were merely articulating the fundamentally opposed positions of their respective executives. On the morning of 30 July, when the Tsar received a telegram from Wilhelm II reiterating the warning issued by Ambassador Pourtalès on the previous day, Nicholas II abandoned any hope that a deal between the cousins could save peace and returned to the option of general mobilization.[80]

One last thought on the Russian decision to mobilize: when Sazonov saw the Tsar on the afternoon of 30 July, he found him preoccupied with the threat posed to Russia by Austrian mobilization. 'They [the Germans] don't want to acknowledge that Austria mobilized before we did. Now they demand that our mobilization be stopped, without mentioning that of the Austrians. [. . .] At present, if I accepted Germany's demands, we would be disarmed against Austria.'[81] Yet we know that the Austrian preparations were at this point still entirely focused on the task of securing victory over Serbia, regardless of the growing threat of a Russian response. The Tsar's anxiety was not the expression of an individual paranoia; rather, it reflected a broader tendency in Russian military threat analysis. Russian military intelligence consistently overrated Austrian military capability and, more importantly, presumed a very formidable capacity for pre-emption by stealth, an assumption fortified by the Balkan crisis of 1912–13, when the Austrians had managed to raise troop strengths in Galicia without at first attracting the Russians' notice.[82] These tendencies were reinforced, paradoxically, by the very detailed knowledge the Russians possessed (thanks to the now-deceased Colonel Redl and other well-placed sources) of Austrian deployment plans. This was not a new problem: already in 1910, Sukhomlinov, newly appointed as minister of war, boasted that he had seen specific Austrian army and naval deployment plans for the 'conquest of Macedonia'. Such evidence, he claimed, revealed the immense scale of the threat posed to Russian interests by Austro-Hungarian expansionism on the Balkan peninsula and made a nonsense of all diplomatic assurances. That these – in fact antiquated and obsolete – documents might have been contingency plans rather than expressions of Austrian policy appears not to have occurred to Sukhomlinov, who presumably intended to use them as arguments for a hike in military funding.[83] A tendency towards paranoid over-reading of captured planning documents continued to dog Russian security policy until 1914. Precisely because they were so well acquainted with Austrian mobilization schedules, the Russians tended, on the one hand, to read individual measures as part of a coherent whole and, on the other, to view any departure from the expected sequence as potentially threatening.

In 1913, for example, the Russians had learned from their intelligence sources that the Austrians had earmarked as many as seven army corps for the eventuality of a war with Serbia. But in July 1914, reports (of dubious accuracy) from Ambassador Shebeko and the Russian military attaché Vineken suggested that the number of corps currently in preparation might be as high as eight or nine. Russian intelligence read this discrepancy as an indication that Conrad might be shifting from his Serbian-focused Plan B to the Russian-centred Plan R, in other words embarking on a 'covert shift to full or near-full Austrian mobilization'.[84] In retrospect, we know that Austrian estimates of Serbian effectiveness had indeed been rising, pushing up the deployments they believed would be needed to subdue the country's armed forces. And the course of the first year of the war was to show that even these revised Austrian estimates were not large enough to secure a decisive victory against the Serbs, who really did 'fight like lions', as the Tsar had predicted. It was a classic example of the misreadings that can arise when a dose of high-level, textured intelligence tempts the receiver to shoehorn incoming data into a pattern that is denuded of context and may be outdated. In an environment saturated by paranoia, sober assessments of actual threat levels were virtually impossible. But what matters most about these interpetations of Austrian measures is that they were taken seriously by the Tsar, who was an avid reader of the General Staff's daily intelligence surveys. And this in turn explains the otherwise puzzling tendency of the Russians to view their own general mobilization as equivalent to, and justifed by, Austrian measures. Like nearly everyone else in this crisis, the Russians could claim to be standing with their backs against the wall.

THE LEAP INTO THE DARK

Throughout the middle weeks of July 1914, the German decision-makers stuck like barnacles to their policy of localization. During the early days it was still quite easy to imagine a very swift resolution of the crisis. Wilhelm II told Emperor Franz Joseph on 6 July that 'the situation would be cleared up within a week because of Serbia's backing down . . .', though it was possible, as he remarked to War Minister Erich von Falkenhayn, that the 'period of tension' might last a little longer, perhaps as long as 'three weeks'.[85] But even in the third week of July, when the hope of a swift resolution no longer seemed realistic, the political leadership remained committed to localization. On 17 July, the chargé d'affaires at the Saxon legation in Berlin learned that 'a localisation of the conflict is expected, since England is absolutely pacific and France as well as Russia likewise do not feel inclined towards war'.[86] In a circular of 21 July to the German ambassadors in Rome, London and St Petersburg, Bethmann declared: 'We urgently desire a localisation of

Theobald von Bethmann Hollweg

the conflict; an intervention by any another power will, in view of the divergent alliance commitments, lead to incalculable consequences.'[87]

One condition for successful localization was that the Germans themselves must avoid any action likely to trigger an escalation. It was partly with this end in mind, and partly to secure the autonomy and freedom from distraction he needed to manage the crisis, that Bethmann encouraged the Kaiser to leave Berlin for his scheduled cruise of the Baltic. For the same reason, the senior military commanders were encouraged to go or remain on holiday. Chief of the General Staff Helmut von Moltke, Imperial Naval Office chief Admiral von Tirpitz and the chief of the Admiralty Staff Hugo von Pohl were already on holiday, Quarter-Master General Count Waldersee left Berlin for a few weeks' rest on his father-in-law's estate in Mecklenburg, as did War Minister Erich von Falkenhayn, who set off for a brief inspection tour, to be followed by his annual holiday.

It would be a mistake to make too much of these departures. The individuals involved were aware of the gravity of the crisis and confident in the existing state of readiness of the German military; they also understood that a further escalation was unlikely until the Austrians took some kind of action vis-à-vis Belgrade.[88] On the other hand, it is going too far to speak of an elaborate German feint to distract the attention of the world from preparations for a continental war that had already been resolved upon and planned in advance. The internal memoranda and correspondence of these days suggest that both the political leadership and the military and naval commands were confident that the strategy of localization would work. There were no summit discussions among the senior German commanders, and Helmut von Moltke did not return from taking the waters in Carlsbad, Bohemia until 25 July. On the 13th, he wrote to the German military attaché in Vienna that Austria would be well advised to 'beat the Serbs and then make peace quickly, demanding an Austro-Serbian alliance as the sole condition, as Prussia did with Austria in 1866' – at this point he apparently still believed it possible that Austria would launch and complete its strike on Serbia without triggering a Russian intervention.[89]

Particularly noteworthy is the lack of activity on the part of the military intelligence networks. Major Walter Nicolai, head of Department IIIb of the General Staff, responsible for espionage and counter-intelligence, was away on a family holiday in the Harz mountains and was not recalled. The intelligence posts on the eastern frontier were issued with no special instructions after the meetings at Potsdam and appear to have taken no special precautions. Only on 16 July did it occur to someone in the operations department that it might be 'desirable to watch developments in Russia more closely than this is done in times of complete political calm', but even this circular made it clear that there was no call for 'special measures of any kind'.[90] In several of the districts adjoining Russian territory, the local intelligence officers were allowed to remain on leave, like Moltke, until 25 July.[91]

In order not to compromise the localization plan, Bethmann and the German Foreign Office repeatedly urged the Austrians to get their skates on and produce their tensely awaited *fait accompli*. But the decision-makers in Vienna were unable or unwilling to comply. The cumbersome machinery of the Habsburg state did not lend itself to swift and decisive measures. Already by 11 July, Bethmann was starting to fret at the agonizing slowness of Austrian preparations. In a diary entry composed on Bethmann's estate, Kurt Riezler summed up the problem: 'Apparently [the Austrians] need a horribly long time to mobilise. 16 days, says [Conrad von] Hoetzendorff. This is very dangerous. A quick *fait accompli* and then friendly to the Entente – that way the shock can be withstood.'[92] As late as 17 July, Secretary Stolberg at the German embassy in Vienna notified Bethmann that 'negotiations' were still taking place between Berchtold and Tisza.[93] It was in order to meet the need for speed and minimize the likelihood of international complications that Berchtold set the deadline for the reply to the Austrian note to only forty-eight hours. For the very same reason, Jagow pressed the Austrians to bring forward the projected date of their declaration of war on Serbia from 29 to 28 July.

If the sluggishness of the Austrian response removed one of the preconditions for the success of the policy of localization, why did the Germans stick so doggedly to it? One reason was that they continued to believe that deeper structural factors – such as the incompleteness of the Russian armaments programme – militated against an armed intervention. The French government was harder to read, all the more so as the president, the prime minister and the head of the political department of the Quai d'Orsay were all in Russia or at sea for the third and fourth week of July. But German confidence in the likely inaction of the Entente was reinforced by the Humbert report on French military readiness.

The Germans greeted Humbert's sensational revelations on the supposed inadequacy of French military preparations with scepticism, recognizing in the intemperate language of Humbert's report an essentially political attack on War Minister Adolphe Messimy and his staff. German military experts were quick to point out that the smaller French field guns were in fact superior in quality to their German counterparts. Since the French army had abandoned its earlier defensive approach in favour of an offensive strategy, the relative decline of the border fortifications was a red herring.[94] In a secret memorandum following up the Humbert revelations, however, Moltke concluded that French military preparations on the eastern frontier were indeed deficient, especially in the areas of heavy artillery, mortars and bomb-proof ammunition storage.[95] At the very least, the Humbert report suggested that the French government, and in particular the French military command, would be in no mood to press the Franco-Russian Alliance into a war over Serbia; the Russians, too, would surely be discouraged.[96]

A further reason for the commitment to localization was the

paucity – as the Germans saw it – of alternative options. Abandoning the Habsburg ally was out of the question, and not just for reputational and power-political reasons, but also because the German decision-makers really did accept the justice of the Austrian case against Serbia. If the balance of military striking-power was shifting to Germany's disadvantage, the situation would be incalculably worse, were Germany to be denuded of its only great power ally – German planners had already written off Italy as too unreliable to be counted as a substantial asset.[97] Italian ambivalence also undermined the plausibility of the proposal, favoured by Grey, that a concert of the four less involved powers work together to resolve the dispute – if Italy, as seemed very likely, given its anti-Austrian Balkan policy – sided with the two Entente powers, Britain and France, what chance would there be of securing a fair outcome for Austria-Hungary? The Germans were willing to pass British suggestions to Vienna, but Bethmann's view was that Germany should support a multilateral intervention only between Russia and Austria, not between Austria and Serbia.[98]

Underlying the localization strategy – and preventing the emergence of alternatives – was still the belief, so important to Bethmann, that if the Russians decided, despite everything, to intervene on behalf of their client, the resulting war would arise as something beyond Germany's control, as a destiny visited on the central powers by an aggressive Russia and its Entente partners. We find this train of thought in a letter of 12 July from Foreign Secretary Gottlieb von Jagow to Ambassador Lichnowsky in London:

> We need to see to localising the conflict between Austria and Serbia. Whether this is possible will depend in the first place on Russia and in the second place on the influence of the other members of the entente. [. . .] I have no wish for a preventive war, but if the fight offers itself, we dare not flinch.[99]

Here again is the tendency we can discern in the reasoning of so many of the actors in this crisis, to perceive oneself as operating under irresistible external constraints while placing the responsibility for deciding between peace and war firmly on the shoulders of the opponent.

Through their support for Austria-Hungary and through their blithe confidence in the feasibility of localization, the German leaders made their own contribution to the unfolding of the crisis. And yet nothing in how they reacted to the events of summer 1914 suggests that they viewed the crisis as the welcome opportunity to set in train a long-laid plan to unleash a preventive war on Germany's neighbours. On the contrary, Zimmermann, Jagow and Bethmann were remarkably slow to grasp the scale of the disaster unfolding around them. On 13 July, Zimmermann was still confident that there would be no 'great European conflict'. As late as the 26th, it was still the view of the senior Foreign Office staff that both France and England would stay out of any Balkan conflict. Far from being masters of the situation, the German policymakers appeared to be struggling to stay abreast of developments. During the decisive days of the crisis, Jagow struck senior colleagues as 'nervous, irresolute, fearful' and 'inadequate to the responsibilities of his office', while Bethmann reminded Tirpitz of 'a drowning man'.[100]

During these hot July weeks, the Kaiser was taking his Scandinavian cruise. Extended journeys by ship, mostly in the Baltic, had long been a fixture in Wilhelm II's summer calendar. They allowed him to escape from the tension, complexity and the sense of impotence that dogged him in Berlin. On board the royal yacht *Hohenzollern*, surrounded by agreeable sycophants who could always be press-ganged into imperial amusements, the Kaiser could be master of all he surveyed and give free rein to the impetuous currents of his personality. After a few pleasant days at the Kiel regatta, accompanied by much jovial fraternizing with officers of the Royal Navy, Wilhelm sailed on to the Norwegian coastal town of Balholm, where he remained anchored until 25 July. It was from here, on 14 July, that he sent a first personal reply to Franz Joseph's message requesting German help. The letter reiterated the earlier assurance of support and denounced the 'crazed fanatics' whose 'pan-Slavist agitation' threatened the dual monarchy, but interestingly enough, it made no reference to the waging of war. Wilhelm stated that although he must 'refrain from taking a view on the question of current relations between Vienna and Belgrade', he saw it as a 'moral duty of all civilized states' to counter anti-monarchist 'propaganda of the deed' with 'all the available instruments of power'. But the rest of the letter referred exclusively to *diplomatic* initiatives in the Balkan region to prevent the emergence of an anti-Austrian 'Balkan League under Russian patronage'. It closed with best wishes for the Emperor's swift recovery from his bereavement.[101]

The Kaiser's comments on the state papers that reached him on the yacht reveal that, like many of the leading political and military figures in Berlin, he was impatient to hear of a decision from Vienna.[102] His chief concern appears to have been that allowing too much time to elapse would squander the benefits of international indignation at the Sarajevo murders, or that the Austrians might lose their nerve altogether. He was pleased to hear, on around 15 July, that 'an energetic decision' was imminent. His only regret was that there would be a further delay before Austrian demands were delivered to Belgrade.[103]

On 19 July, however, Wilhelm was shocked into a state of 'high anxiety' by a telegram to the *Hohenzollern* from the secretary of state for foreign affairs, Jagow. The telegram contained nothing essentially new, but its warning that an ultimatum was now planned for 23 July and that measures were to be taken to make sure that the Kaiser could be reached 'in case unforeseen circumstances should make important decisions [mobilization] necessary' brought home to Wilhelm the potential scope of the crisis that now loomed.[104] He immediately issued an order that the High Seas Fleet should cancel a planned visit to Scandinavia and instead remain together in a state of readiness for immediate departure. His anxiety was understandable, given that the British navy happened at this time to be in the midst of a trial mobilization and was thus at a high level of battle-readiness. But Bethmann and Jagow rightly took the view that this would merely arouse suspicion and exacerbate the crisis by discouraging a British demobilization; on 22 July, they overruled Wilhelm and ordered that the sojourn in Norway proceed as planned. At this point, diplomatic priorities still outweighed strategic considerations.[105]

Despite the rising tension, Wilhelm remained confident that a more general crisis could be avoided. Presented with a copy of the text of the ultimatum to Belgrade, he commented: 'Well, what do you know, that *is* a firm note after all' – Wilhelm had evidently shared the view widely held within his entourage that the Austrians would ultimately shrink from confronting Serbia. When Admiral Müller suggested that the ultimatum meant that war was imminent, the Kaiser energetically contradicted him. The Serbs, he insisted, would never risk a war against Austria. Müller interpreted this – correctly, as it turned out – as a sign that the Kaiser was psychologically completely unprepared for military complications and would cave in as soon as he realized that war was a real possibility.[106]

Wilhelm returned to Potsdam on the afternoon of 27 July. It was very early on the morning of the following day that he first read the text of the Serbian reply to the ultimatum served by Vienna five days before. His response was unexpected, to say the least. He inscribed on his copy of the Serbian reply the words: 'An excellent result for a forty-eight hour [deadline]. This is more than we could have expected! But this does away with any need for war.' He was astonished to hear that the Austrians had already issued an order for partial mobilization: '*I* would never have ordered a mobilization on that basis.'[107] At ten o'clock that morning, the Kaiser dashed off a letter to Jagow in which he declared that since Serbia had tendered a 'capitulation of the most humiliating kind', 'any reason for war has now been eliminated'. Instead of invading the country outright, he went on, they should consider temporarily occupying the evacuated city of Belgrade as a means of ensuring Serbian compliance. More importantly, Wilhelm ordered Jagow to inform the Austrians that this was his wish, that 'every cause for war [had] vanished', and that Wilhelm himself was prepared to 'mediate for peace with Austria'. 'This I will do in my own way and as sparingly of Austria's national feeling and of the honour of her arms as possible.'[108] He also let Moltke know in writing that if Serbia abided by her undertakings to Austria-Hungary, the grounds for war would no longer exist. During that day, according to the minister of war, he made 'confused speeches which give the clear impression that he no longer wants war and is determined to [avoid it], even if it means leaving Austria-Hungary in the lurch'.[109]

Historians have seen this sudden bout of circumspection as evidence of a failure of nerve. On 6 July, when the Kaiser had met Gustav Krupp in Kiel, he had repeatedly assured the industrialist: 'This time, I shall not chicken out' – Krupp was struck by the pathos of these feeble attempts to prove his mettle.[110] As Luigi Albertini aptly put it: 'Wilhelm was full of bluster when danger was a long way off but piped down when he saw a real threat of war approaching.'[111] There is something in this: the Emperor's readiness to commit himself to the defence of Austrian interests had always been inversely proportional to his assessment of the risk of conflict. And on 28 July, the risks appeared very grave indeed. The latest telegrams from Lichnowsky in London reported Sir Edward Grey as saying that Serbia had given satisfaction to a degree 'he would never have believed possible' and warning that a major conflagration was in prospect if Austria did not moderate its position.[112] Hypersensitive as he was to the British viewpoint, Wilhelm must have taken these warnings seriously – indeed they may even account for his interpretation of the Serbian reply, which was so at odds with the view of the chancellor and the Foreign Office. In some respects, however, Wilhelm's note of 28 July was less out of line with his previous interventions than the idea of a failure of nerve might imply; his comments during the crisis suggest that, unlike those figures in Vienna and Berlin who saw the ultimatum as a mere pretext for military action, he regarded it as an authentic diplomatic instrument with a role to play in resolving the crisis and that he remained wedded to the notion of a political resolution of the Balkan problem.

A fissure had opened within the German decision-making structure. The view of the sovereign was at odds with that of the most senior political decision-makers. But the fissure was soon closed. The most remarkable thing about the letter to Jagow of 28 July is that it was not acted upon. Had Kaiser Wilhelm II enjoyed the plenitude of power that is sometimes attributed to him, this intervention might have changed the course of the crisis and possibly of world history. But he was out of touch with developments in Vienna, where the leadership was now impatient to press ahead with the strike on Serbia. And, more importantly, having been away at sea for the better part of three weeks, he was out of touch with developments in Berlin. His instructions to Jagow had no influence on Berlin's representations to Vienna. Bethmann did not inform the Austrians of Wilhelm's views in time to prevent them from issuing their declaration of war on 28 July. And the chancellor's urgent telegram to Tschirschky, dispatched only a quarter of an hour after the Kaiser's letter to Jagow, incorporated some of Wilhelm's proposals, but omitted the crucial insistence that there could now be no reason for war. Instead, Bethmann stuck to the earlier line, since abandoned by Wilhelm, that the Germans must 'avoid very carefully giving rise to the impression that we wish to hold the Austrians back'.[113]

Why Bethmann did this is difficult to establish. The view that he had already harnessed his diplomacy to a policy of preventive war cannot be supported from the documents. It is more probable that he was simply already committed to an alternative strategy that focused on working alongside Vienna to persuade Russia not to overreact to Austrian measures. On the evening of 28 July, Bethmann persuaded the Kaiser to send a telegram to Nicholas II assuring him that the German government was doing its level best to bring about a satisfactory understanding between Vienna and St Petersburg; only twenty-four hours before, Wilhelm had rejected such a move as premature.[114] The result was the note mentioned earlier to Nicky, begging him not to compromise Willy's role as intermediary. Bethmann was thinking in terms of localizing the conflict, not of preventing it, and he was determined to protect that policy against interventions from above.

From 25 July onwards, there was growing evidence of military movement in Russia. The intelligence officer in Königsberg reported that an 'unusually long' batch of encrypted transmissions had been intercepted between the Eiffel Tower and the Russian wireless station at Bobruysk.[115] On the morning of Sunday 26 July, Lieutenant-General Chelius, the German military plenipotentiary to the court of Nicholas II, reported that the authorities appeared to have inaugurated 'all preparations for mobilization against Austria'.[116] In order to acquire a fuller picture of what was happening across the border, Major Nicolai of Department IIIb returned to Berlin, cut short his holiday leave and issued orders that the 'tension travellers' (*Spannungreisende*) were to be mobilized. These were volunteers from a range of backgrounds whose task was, at the first sign of international tension, to enter Russia and France under the guise of vacationers or commercial travellers and record covert observations in order to establish, as Major Nicolai put it in their brief, 'whether war preparations are taking place in France and Russia'.[117] Some of them made repeated short trips across the border and reported their observations in person, like the indefatigable Herr Henoumont, who managed to visit Warsaw twice in the space of three days and was trapped for a time in Russian Poland when the borders closed. Others travelled further afield and sent lightly coded cables through the public telegraph service. There was as yet no sense of hurry – the intelligence officers handling the travellers were informed on 25 July that the period of tension might be quite protracted. If, on the other hand, the tension waned, those travellers whose leave had been cancelled would be able to go back on vacation.[118]

The tension travellers and other agents operating out of the intelligence stations on the eastern frontier soon began to generate a picture of Russian military preparations. From the station at Königsberg came reports of empty freight trains moving eastwards, troop movements around Kovno and alerts to frontier guard units. At 10 p.m. on 26 July, tension traveller Ventski reported from Vilna, using the commercial telegram service, that war preparations were already well underway in the city. Throughout the 27th and 28th, a steady flow of details from tension travellers and other agents reached the newly created 'intelligence assessment board' at the General Staff. On the afternoon of 28 July, the board produced an appraisal summarizing the latest information to hand:

> Russia apparently partial mobilization. Extent not yet discernible with certainty. Military districts Odessa and Kiev fairly certain. Moscow still uncertain. Isolated reports regarding mobilization of the Warsaw military district not yet verified. In other districts, notably Vilna, mobilization not yet ordered. Nevertheless, it is certain that Russia taking some military measures also on the German border which must be regarded as preparation for a war. Probably proclamation of her 'Period preparatory to War', proclaimed for the whole empire. Frontier guard everywhere equipped for combat and ready to march.[119]

This dramatic worsening of the situation, further reinforced by the news of partial mobilization on 29 July, injected an element of panic into German diplomacy: worried by messages from London and by the steady stream of data on Russian military preparations, Bethmann suddenly changed his tack. Having undermined Wilhelm's efforts to restrain Vienna on 28 July, he now attempted to do so himself in a series of urgently worded telegrams to Ambassador Tschirschky the next day.[120] But his efforts were rendered futile in their turn by the speed of Russian preparations, which threatened to force the Germans into countermeasures before mediation could begin to take effect.

After the news of Russia's mobilization on 30 July, it was merely a matter of time before Berlin responded with military measures of its own. Two days earlier, the minister of war Erich von Falkenhayn had succeeded, after a struggle with Bethmann, in getting troops in training areas ordered back to their bases. The early preparatory measures ordered at this time – buying wheat in the western attack zone, setting special guards on railways and ordering troops to garrisons – could still be kept secret, and could thus, in theory, proceed in parallel with diplomatic efforts to contain the conflict. But the same did not apply to the

State of Imminent Danger of War (SIDW), the last stage of prepared-ness before mobilization. The question whether and when Germany should adopt this measure, which had been in force in Russia since 26 July, was one of the central bones of contention within the Berlin lead-ership during the last days of peace.

At a meeting on 29 July, the day of Russia's partial mobilization, there was still disagreement among the military chiefs: Falkenhayn, the minister of war, was in favour of declaring the SIDW, while the chief of the General Staff Helmuth von Moltke and Chancellor Bethmann Hol-lweg were for merely extending guard duties on important transport structures. The Kaiser appears to have oscillated between the two options. In Berlin, as in St Petersburg, the deepening concentration of the political leadership on momentous and controversial *sovereign* deci-sions enabled the head of state to re-emerge as a central participant in the policy-making process. The telegram Wilhelm had received that morning from the Tsar threatening 'extreme [Russian] measures that would lead to war' disposed him at first to support the minister of war. But under pressure from Bethmann, he changed his mind, and it was decided that the SIDW would not be declared. Falkenhayn regretted this outcome, but noted in his diary that he could understand the moti-vations for it, 'because anyone who believes in, or at least wishes for, the maintenance of peace can hardly support the declaration of the "threat of war"'.[121]

On 31 July, after further wavering over military measures, news arrived from Ambassador Pourtalès in Moscow that the Russians had ordered total mobilization from midnight on the previous evening. The Kaiser now ordered by telephone that the SIDW be declared, and the order was issued to the armed forces by Falkenhayn at 1.00 p.m. on 31 July. The responsibility for mobilizing first now lay squarely with the Russians, a matter of some importance to the Berlin leadership, who were concerned, in the light of pacifist demonstrations in some of the German cities, that there should be no doubt about the defensive char-acter of Germany's entry into war. Of particular concern was the leadership of the Social Democrats (SPD), who had secured more than a third of all German votes in the last Reichstag elections. Bethmann had met on 28 July with the right-wing SPD leader Albert Südekum, who had promised that the SPD would not oppose a government obliged to defend itself against Russian attack (anti-Russian feeling was as strong within the SPD as it was in the British liberal movement). On 30 July, the chancellor was able to reassure his colleagues that they need not fear, in the event of war, subversion from within by the organized working class.[122]

In view of developments in Russia, Wilhelm could hardly continue to block declaration of the SIDW, but it is interesting to note that, according to the testimony of the Bavarian military plenipotentiary von Weininger, this decision had to be 'wrung out of him' by Falkenhayn. By afternoon, the sovereign had regained his sang-froid, mainly because he had persuaded himself that he was now acting under external constraint, a matter of great import to nearly all the actors in the July Crisis. During a meeting at which War Minister Falkenhayn was present, Wilhelm gave a spirited exposé of the current situation, in which the entire responsibility for the impending conflict was laid at Russia's door. 'His demeanour and language,' Falkenhayn noted in his diary, 'were worthy of a German Emperor, worthy of a Prussian king' – these were striking words from a soldier at the forefront of those hawks who had excoriated the monarch for his love of peace and his fear of war.[123] When the Russian government refused to rescind its mobilization order, Germany declared war on Russia on 1 August 1914.

'THERE MUST BE SOME MISUNDERSTANDING'

During the last days of July, the German Kaiser's attention remained focused on Britain. This was partly because, like many Germans, he saw Britain as the power at the fulcrum of the continental system, upon which depended the avoidance of a general war. Wilhelm shared in a broader tendency both to overestimate Britain's weight in continental diplomacy and to underestimate the degree to which its key policymakers (Grey in particular) had already committed themselves to a specific course. But there was surely also a psychological dimension: England was the place where Wilhelm had desperately sought – but only sometimes achieved – applause, recognition and affection. It represented much that he admired – a navy equipped with the best guns and equipment that modern science could build, wealth, sophistication, worldliness and (at least in the circles he encountered on his visits) a kind of aristocratic, poised comportment that he admired but found impossible to emulate. It was the home of his dead grandmother, of whom Wilhelm later remarked that, had she lived on, she would never have allowed Nicky and George to gang up on him like this. It was the kingdom of his envied and detested uncle, Edward VII, who had succeeded (where Wilhelm had failed) in improving the international standing of his country. And of course it was the birthplace of his mother, now dead for thirteen years, with whom he had had such a troubled and unresolved relationship. A tangle of emotions and associations was always in play when Wilhelm attempted to interpret British policy.

The Kaiser was hugely encouraged by a message from his brother Prince Henry of Prussia on 28 July, suggesting that George V intended to keep Britain out of the war. Early on the morning of the 26th, Henry, who had been yachting at Cowes, rushed to Buckingham Palace to take his leave from the British king before returning to Germany. A conversation had taken place between the two men, in which Henry claimed that George V had said: 'We shall try all we can to keep out of this and shall remain neutral.'[124] These words were cabled to the Kaiser as soon as the prince reached Kiel harbour on 28 July. William viewed this statement as tantamount to an official assurance of British neutrality. When Tirpitz challenged him on his reading, Wilhelm replied, with a characteristic blend of pomposity and naivety, 'I have the word of a king, and that is enough for me.'[125] Whether the British king had in fact uttered these words is unclear. His diary is predictably uninformative on the subject – it states simply: 'Henry of Prussia came to see me early; he returns at once to Germany.' But another account of the meeting, probably composed by the monarch at the request of Edward Grey, provides more detail. According to this source, when Henry of Prussia asked George V what England would do in the event of a European war, the British monarch replied:

> I don't know what we shall do, we have no quarrel with anyone, and I hope we shall remain neutral. But if Germany declared war on Russia, & France joins Russia, then I am afraid we shall be dragged into it. But you can be sure that I and my Government will do all we can to prevent a European war![126]

There was, then, a stiff measure of wishful thinking in Henry's report of the exchange, though we cannot absolutely rule out the possibility that

George V adjusted his own account of the meeting to the expectations of the foreign secretary, in which case the truth may lie somewhere between the two. In any case, Henry's telegram was enough to replenish the Kaiser's confidence that Britain would stay out, and his optimism seemed to be borne out by the reluctance of the British government, and specifically of Grey, to make known their intentions.

Wilhelm was thus shocked to learn, on the morning of 30 July, of a conversation between Grey and the German ambassador, Prince Lichnowsky, in which the former had warned that whereas Britain would stand aside if the conflict remained confined to Austria, Serbia and Russia (a bizarre notion), it would intervene on the side of the Entente if Germany and France were to become involved. The ambassador's dispatch provoked a rush of enraged jottings from the German monarch: the English were 'scoundrels' and 'mean shopkeepers' who wanted to force Germany to leave Austria 'in the lurch' and who dared to threaten Germany with dire consequences while refusing to pull their continental allies back from the fray.[127] When news arrived of the

Count Lichnowsky

Russian general mobilization on the following day, Wilhelm's thinking turned once again to Britain. Seen in combination with Grey's warnings, the Russian mobilization 'proved' to Wilhelm that England now planned to exploit the 'pretext' provided by the widening conflict in order to 'play the card of all the European nations in England's favour against us!'[128]

Then, shortly after 5 p.m. on the afternoon of Saturday 1 August, came sensational news. Just a few minutes after Berlin had issued the order for a general mobilization, a telegram arrived from Lichnowsky in London describing a meeting that morning with the British foreign secretary. It seemed that Grey was offering not just to stay out of the war if Germany refrained from attacking France, but to vouch for French neutrality as well. The text of the cable was as follows:

> Sir Edward Grey has just sent word to me by Sir W. Tyrrell that he hopes that he will be able this afternoon, as a result of a council of ministers that is just taking place [Lichnowsky dispatched the telegram at 11.14 a.m.] to make a statement to me which may prove helpful in preventing the great catastrophe. To judge by a remark of Sir W. Tyrrell's this seems to mean that in the event of our not attacking France, England, too, would remain neutral and would guarantee France's passivity. I shall learn the details this afternoon. Sir Edward Grey had just called me upon the telephone and asked whether I thought I could give an assurance that in the event of France remaining neutral in a war between Russia and Germany we should not attack the French. I assured him that I could take the responsibility for such a guarantee and he will use this assurance at today's Cabinet meeting. Supplementary: Sir W. Tyrrell urgently begged me to use my influence to prevent our troops from violating the French frontier. Everything depended upon that. He said that in one case where German troops had already crossed the frontier, the French troops had withdrawn.[129]

Stunned by this unexpected offer, the decision-makers in Berlin got busy drafting a warmly positive reply to the note. But the draft was incomplete when a further telegram arrived from London at around 8 p.m.: 'As follow-up to [my previous telegram], Sir W. Tyrrell has just been to see me and told me that Sir Edward Grey wants this afternoon to make proposals for England's neutrality, even in the event of our being at war with France as well as with Russia. I shall be seeing Sir Edward Grey at 3.30 and shall report at once.'[130]

The messages from London set the scene for a violent dispute between the Emperor and the chief of the General Staff. The German mobilization was already underway, which meant that the vast machinery of the Schlieffen Plan was in motion. After seeing Lichnowsky's first telegram, Wilhelm took the view that although the mobilization *order* could not for the moment be revoked, he would be willing to halt any move against France in return for a promise of Anglo-French neutrality. Supported by Bethmann, Tirpitz and Jagow, he ordered that there were to be no further troop movements until the arrival of a further message from London clarifying the nature of the British offer. But whereas Wilhelm and Bethmann wished to seize the opportunity to avoid war in the west, Moltke took the view that, once set in motion, the general mobilization could not be halted. 'This gave rise to an extremely lively and dramatic dispute,' one oberver recalled. 'Moltke, very excited, with trembling lips, insisted on his position. The Kaiser and the Chancellor and all the others pleaded with him in vain.'[131] It would be suicidal, Moltke argued, to leave Germany's back exposed to a mobilizing France; in any case the first patrols had already entered Luxembourg and the 16th Division from Trier was following close behind. Wilhelm was unimpressed. He had the order put through to Trier that the 16th Division be halted before the borders of Luxembourg. When Moltke implored the Kaiser not to hinder the occupation of Luxembourg on the grounds that this would jeopardize German control of its railway route, Wilhelm retorted: 'Use other routes!' The argument reached a deadlock. In the process, Moltke had become almost hysterical. In a private aside to Minister of War Erich von Falkenhayn, the chief of the General Staff confided, close to tears, 'that he was a totally broken man, because this decision by the Kaiser demonstrated to him that the Kaiser still hoped for peace'.[132]

Even after the arrival of the later telegram, Moltke continued to argue that the mobilization plan could not at this late stage be altered to exclude France, but Wilhelm refused to listen: 'Your illustrious uncle would not have given me such an answer. If I order it, it must be possible.'[133] Wilhelm ordered that champagne be brought in, while Moltke stomped off in a huff, telling his wife that he was perfectly prepared to fight with the enemy, but not with 'a Kaiser like this one'. The stress of this encounter was such, Moltke's wife believed, that it caused the chief of the General Staff to suffer a mild stroke.[134]

As the champagne corks flew from their bottles, Bethmann and Jagow were still drafting their reply to the first cable from London. Germany would accept the proposal, they wrote, 'if England could guarantee with its entire armed strength the unconditional neutrality of France in a German-Russian conflict'. The mobilization would continue, but no German troops would cross the French border until 7 a.m. on 3 August, pending a finalization of the agreement. The Kaiser reinforced the message in a telegram of his own to King George V, in which he warmly accepted the offer of 'French neutrality under guarantee of Great Britain', and expressed the hope that France would not become 'nervous'. 'The troops on my frontier are in the act of being stopped by telegraph and telephone from crossing into France.'[135] Jagow, too, sent a telegram asking Lichnowsky to thank Grey for his initiative.[136]

Shortly afterwards, a new dispatch arrived from Lichnowsky. The eagerly awaited 3.30 p.m. appointment with Grey had in the meanwhile taken place but, to the German ambassador's surprise, Grey had not offered a proposal for British or French neutrality, nor did it seem that he had raised the matter with his colleagues in cabinet. Instead, he merely hinted at the possibility that the German and French armies might 'in the event of a Russian war, remain facing each other without either side attacking', and then focused on those German actions that might trigger a British intervention. In particular, Grey warned, 'it would be very difficult to restrain English feeling on any violation of Belgian neutrality by either [France or Germany].' Lichnowsky responded with a question that turned the tables on the foreign secretary: would Grey be prepared to give him an assurance of Britain's neutrality if Germany agreed not to violate Belgian territory? Oddly enough, this overture caught Grey off-guard – he was obliged to state that he could not give any such assurance, since England must keep its hands free. In other words, Grey appeared to be backing away from his earlier proposal. At the same time he revealed – perhaps inadvertently – that he had made his proposal without consulting the French beforehand. In his account of this somewhat inconclusive conversation, Lichnowsky reported simply that the British did not appear prepared to make any engagement that would limit their freedom of action, but that Grey had agreed to enquire into the possibility of a Franco-German armed stand-off.[137] In Berlin, this dispatch, which arrived early in the evening, gave rise to general confusion and no reply was sent.

In the meanwhile, however, the Kaiser's telegram to King George V warmly accepting his government's proposal of French neutrality had reached its destination, causing consternation in London. No one, it seems, had been initiated into the twists and turns of Grey's operations that day and the foreign secretary was summoned urgently to Buckingham Palace to provide an explanation and draft a reply. At around 9 p.m., he pencilled the text that became George V's answer to Kaiser Wilhelm's telegram:

> There must be some misunderstanding as to a suggestion that passed in friendly conversation between Prince Lichnowsky and Sir Edward Grey this afternoon when they were discussing how actual fighting between German and French armies might be avoided while there is still chance of some agreement between Austria and Russia. Sir Edward Grey will arrange to see Prince Lichnowsky early tomorrow to ascertain whether there is a misunderstanding on his part.[138]

Any remaining ambiguity was dispelled by a further telegram from Prince Lichnowsky, who had received Jagow's 'acceptance' of the British 'proposal' at around the same time as King George had received the exuberant telegram from his cousin. With deadpan clarity, Lichnowsky wrote: 'Since there is no British proposal at all, your telegram inoperative. Therefore have taken no further steps.'[139]

By this time it was past 11 p.m. in Berlin. Relief was in sight for Moltke, who was at General Staff headquarters, weeping tears of despair over the Kaiser's order halting the 16th Division. Shortly before midnight, Moltke was ordered back to the palace to hear news of the latest dispatch. On his arrival, Wilhelm showed the staff chief a further telegram he had received outlining the (corrected) British position and said: 'Now you can do what you want.'[140]

What was Grey up to? His communications with Lichnowsky, Cambon and various British colleagues during 1 August are so difficult to unravel that the effort to make sense of them has produced a sub-debate within the war-origins literature. On 29 July, Grey had warned Lichnowsky that Britain might be obliged to take swift action if Germany and France were drawn into the war – this was the warning that elicited the Kaiser's angry jottings about 'scoundrels' and 'mean shopkeepers'.[141] Yet on 31 July he had also warned his ambassador in Paris, Bertie, that the British public could not be expected to support British intervention in a quarrel that was so remote from the country's own interests.[142] Perhaps Grey really did hold up the prospect of British neutrality to Lichnowsky – that would mean that there was in fact no misunderstanding by Lichnowsky of his fundamental intentions.[143] By this reading, the 'misunderstanding' becomes Grey's way of wriggling out of the mess he had got himself into. Or perhaps he was trying to accommodate his uncertainty about whether the British cabinet would back his policy of support for France. If they did not, then the proposal of neutrality would at least offer Britain a lever by which to secure various German assurances (a promise to abstain from a pre-emptive attack on France, for example).[144] Or maybe Grey was not interested in neutrality at all, but briefly came under pressure from his liberal imperialist ally, Lord Chancellor Haldane, to find a way of preventing or delaying the commencement of hostilities between France and Germany so that there would be time better to prepare and train the British Expeditionary Force. Anxiety about the increasing fragility of the international financial markets in the last week of July may also have given him pause.[145]

Whichever view we take – and the disagreement among historians is itself telling – it is clear that Grey's ambiguities were on the verge of becoming open contradictions. To propose British neutrality, even in the face of a continental war involving France, would have amounted to a crass reversal of the positions the foreign secretary had earlier adopted – so much so, indeed, that it is hard to believe that this was truly his intention. On the other hand, the proposal that France and Germany should maintain an armed stand-off is unambiguously instantiated in the documents. In a telegram dispatched to Bertie at 5.25 p.m. on 1 August, Grey himself reported that he had put it to the German ambassador that 'after mobilisation on the western frontier French and German armies should remain, neither crossing the border so long as the other did not do so. I cannot say whether this would be consistent with French obligations under her alliance.'[146] But even this suggestion was bizarre, since it was based on the supposition that France might be willing to abandon the Russian alliance Poincaré and his colleagues had worked so hard in recent years to reinforce. It suggests at best a very weak grip on the realities of the wider political and military situation. In any case, Grey was soon called to order by Bertie, who vented his frustration with the foreign secretary's speculations in a remarkably impertinent reply:

> I cannot imagine that in the event of Russia being at war with Austria and being attacked by Germany it would be consistent with French obligations towards Russia to remain quiescent. If France undertook to remain so, the Germans would first attack Russians and, if they defeated them, would then turn round on the French. Am I to enquire precisely what are the obligations of the French under Franco-Russian alliance?[147]

As we know, nothing came of this curious policy option; Grey himself discarded it even before Bertie's acidic note reached the foreign secretary's desk. One thing we do know for sure: during these days, Grey was operating under extreme pressure. He was getting very little sleep. He had no way of knowing whether or when the cabinet would support his pro-intervention policy, and he was being pressed in different directions by various colleagues, including the anti-interventionists of his own government (who still controlled a majority in cabinet) and the pro-interventionists of the Conservative opposition.

One additional source of pressure that may help to explain the prevarications of 1 August was the Russian mobilization order of 30 July. Late in the night of the 31st the German embassy informed London that in response to the Russian order, Berlin had declared the State of Imminent Danger of War, and announced that if Russia did not immediately rescind its order of general mobilization, Germany would be obliged to mobilize its own forces, which in turn would 'mean war'.[148] This news sounded alarm bells in London. At 1.30 in the morning, Prime Minister Herbert Asquith and Grey's private secretary Sir William Tyrrell rushed to Buckingham Palace in a taxi to have the king woken so that he could send a telegram appealing to the Tsar to halt the Russian mobilization. Asquith later described the scene:

> The poor king was hauled from his bed and one of my strangest experiences (& as you know I have had a good lot) was sitting with him – he in a brown dressing gown over his night shirt & with copious signs of having been wakened from his 'beauty sleep' – while I read the message & the proposed answer. All he did was suggest that it should be made more personal and direct – by the insertion of the words 'My dear Nicky' – and the addition at the end of the signature 'Georgie'![149]

The diplomatic activity intensified from dawn that morning.

We might consider the impact of the news from St Petersburg in the light of what we know of the ambivalence of Foreign Office thinking on Russia during the last months before the July Crisis broke. As we have seen, Grey and Tyrrell had been rethinking the relationship with Russia for some time. In the light of continuing Russian pressure on Persia and other peripheral imperial territories, there had been talk of abandoning the Anglo-Russian Convention in favour of a more open-ended policy that would not necessarily exclude a rapprochement of some kind with Germany. This never became Foreign Office policy, but the news that Russian mobilization had just triggered German counter-measures at least temporarily foregrounded the Russian aspect of the growing crisis. British policy-makers had no particular interest in or sympathy for Serbia. This was a war from the east, sparked by concerns remote from the official mind of Whitehall. Did this prompt in Grey misgivings about the Balkan inception scenario?

On the morning of 29 July, Grey reminded Cambon (much to the latter's horror) that France was allowing herself to be 'drawn into a quarrel which [is] not hers, but in which, owing to her alliance, her honour and interest obliged her to engage'; Britain, by contrast, was 'free of engagements and would have to decide what British interests required the government to do'. 'Our idea,' Grey added, 'had always been to avoid being drawn into war over a Balkan question.'[150] Two days later, following the news of the declaration of SIDW in Berlin, he retraced the same argument, insisting, contrary to Cambon's claims, that there was no comparison between the current crisis and Agadir in 1911, when Britain had come to the support of France, because 'in this case France is being drawn into a quarrel which is not hers'.[151] When Cambon expressed great disappointment at this reply, and asked whether Britain would be ready to help France if Germany made an attack on her, Grey made his case even more pointedly: 'The latest news was that Russia had ordered a complete mobilisation of her fleet and army. This, it seemed to me, would precipitate a crisis, and would make it appear that German mobilisation was being forced by Russia.'[152] Only in the light of this perspective on events could it seem to make sense to propose a stand-off between Germany and France, while Russia, abandoned by her ally, faced Germany and Austria alone in the east. 'If France could not take advantage of this [offer]' Grey told Cambon on the afternoon of 1 August, 'it was because she was bound by an alliance to which we were not parties, and *of which we did not know the terms*.'[153] When he wrote these words, Grey was doing more than merely cooling the temperature by withholding his support or buying time for military preparations; he was struggling with the automatism of a specific understanding of the Triple Entente – an understanding he had himself at various moments shared and articulated. It clearly unnerved him, at least at this juncture, that a remote quarrel in south-eastern Europe could be accepted as the trigger for a continental war, even though none of the three Entente powers was under direct attack or threat of attack. Grey ultimately remained true to the Ententiste line he had pursued since 1912, but these moments of circumspection remind us of a complicating feature of the July Crisis, namely that the bitter choices between opposed options divided not only parties and cabinets, but also the minds of key decision-makers.

THE TRIBULATIONS OF PAUL CAMBON

These were the worst days of Paul Cambon's life. From the moment when he learned of the Austrian note to Belgrade, he was convinced that a European war was imminent. Although he had sometimes been critical of Poincaré's encouragement of Russia's Balkan commitments, he now took the view that the Franco-Russian Alliance must hold firm in the face of the Austrian threat to Serbia. Indeed he left London on the afternoon of 25 July in order to brief the inexperienced acting foreign minister Bienvenu-Martin; it was probably as a consequence of Cambon's prompting that the acting minister issued the firm response to the German ambassador that so delighted Poincaré when he learned of it at sea on 28 July.[154]

For Cambon, just as for Wilhelm, everything depended upon Britain. 'If the British government puts its foot on the whole thing today, peace might be saved,' he told the journalist André Géraud on 24 July.[155] At a meeting with Grey early on 28 July, he pressed the same argument: 'if once it were assumed that Britain would certainly stand aside from a European war, the chance of preserving peace would be very much imperilled'.[156] Here again was that reflex deflection of responsibility that placed the onus of deciding between peace and war on another's shoulders. It was, by this reading, Britain that now carried the responsibility for preserving peace by adding its immense naval and commercial might to the balance against Berlin and thereby deterring it from supporting its ally. For years Cambon had been telling his political masters that they could rely absolutely on British support.

He was in an unenviable situation. This was not, after all, strictly speaking a defensive war, but one in which France had been called upon to support Russia's intervention in a Balkan conflict – an obligation about which he himself had earlier expressed concern. The French government did its utmost to offset this disadvantage by scrupulously avoiding any aggressive measures against Germany: on the morning of 30 July, the Council of Ministers in Paris agreed that French covering troops would take positions along a line from the Vosges mountains to Luxembourg, but without getting closer than ten kilometres from the frontier. The idea was to avoid any possibility of border skirmishes with German patrols and to persuade London of the pacific nature of French policy. It was felt that the moral effect and propaganda value of the exclusion zone outweighed the military risks. London was immediately notified through Cambon of the new policy.[157] But the fact remained that Britain was not, as Grey repeatedly pointed out, a party to the alliance which supposedly obliged France to intervene, nor had it been officially apprised of the terms of that alliance. Neither Russia nor France had been attacked or placed under direct threat of attack. It was all very well for Cambon to plead with Grey that France was 'obliged to aid Russia in the event of her being attacked', but for the moment there was no indication that either Austria or Germany intended to attack Russia.[158] Nor did it seem very likely that a British declaration of intention to intervene would deter the central powers from a policy they had embarked upon without consulting Britain.

Underlying this predicament was a divergence of perspectives rooted deep in the history of the Anglo-French Entente. Cambon had always wishfully presumed that Britain, like France, viewed the Entente as an instrument for balancing and containing Germany. He failed to see that for British policy-makers, the Entente served more complex objectives. It was, among other things, a means of deflecting the threat posed to the dispersed territories of the British Empire by the power best placed to do them harm, namely Russia. One likely reason for Cambon's misprision was that he came to depend too much on the assurances and advice of the permanent under-secretary Sir Arthur Nicolson, who was passionately attached to the Russian and the French connection and intent on seeing both hardened into a fully-fledged alliance. But Nicolson, though influential, was not the arbiter of policy in London, and his views were increasingly out of sync with the group around Grey who were becoming increasingly distrustful of Russia and increasingly open to a more pro-German (or at least less anti-German) course.[159] This is a classic example of how difficult even the best informed contemporaries found it to read the intentions of allies and enemies.

Divergences in geopolitical perspective were reinforced by the profound antipathy of the British political establishment to any form of binding commitment, an antipathy compounded by deep hostility towards Russia, especially among leading liberal radicals. The Entente Cordiale thus came to represent two rather different things to the two partners.[160] Throughout the lifetime of the alliance, the Foreign Office 'sought to minimise the extent of the Entente, while the Quai d'Orsay took pains to make the very most of it'.[161] And all these dissonances were amplified by the two individuals who personifed the Entente in London – Edward Grey and Paul Cambon, the former wary, evasive and totally ignorant of France and of Europe, the latter hypertrophically French and utterly invested in the Entente, which was and remained the crowning achievement not just of his political career but of his life as a patriot.

Grey, too, was operating under narrow constraints. He failed to secure cabinet support for intervention on 27 July. He failed again two days later, when his request for a formal promise of assistance to France was supported by only four of his colleagues (Asquith, Haldane, Churchill and Crewe). This was the meeting at which the cabinet rejected the view that Britain's status as a signatory to the 1839 Belgian neutrality treaty obliged it to oppose a German breach with military force. The obligation to uphold the treaty did not fall on Britain specifically, the radicals argued, but on all of the signatory powers. Should the matter arise, the cabinet resolved, the decision would be 'one of policy rather than legal obligation'.[162] Both the French and Russians were insisting that only a clear declaration of British solidarity with the Anglo-French alliance would persuade Germany and Austria to 'draw in their horns'.[163] And Grey was under pressure from his own closest colleagues – Nicolson and Eyre Crowe were both pushing him hard towards a declaration of solidarity with the Entente states. In a memorandum of 31 July, Crowe provided Grey with ammunition to use against his opponents in cabinet. There might be no obligation to France, he wrote, but Britain's 'moral' obligation to its 'friend' across the Channel was surely undeniable:

> The argument that there is no written bond binding us to France is strictly correct. There is no contractual obligation. But the Entente has been made, strengthened, put to the test and celebrated in a manner justifying the belief that a moral bond was being forged. The whole policy of the Entente can have no meaning if it does not signify that in a just quarrel England would stand by her friends. This honourable expectation has been raised. We cannot repudiate it without exposing our good name to grave criticism.[164]

Nicolson, by contrast, focused on Belgium and the British obligation to defend its neutrality. But the conditions under which the Grey group had made policy in the past no longer prevailed. The epicentre of the decision-making process had shifted from the Foreign Office to the cabinet, leaving Grey's penumbra of Ententiste advisers out in the cold.

After a morning cabinet meeting on 1 August, Grey explained to a distraught Cambon that the cabinet was quite simply opposed to any intervention. Cambon protested that he would not transmit this message to Paris; he would simply state that no decision had been reached. But there *was* a decision, Grey retorted. Cabinet had decided that British interests were not deeply enough implicated to justify the sending of an expeditionary force to the continent. Desperate, the French ambassador shifted the ground of the argument: he reminded Grey that under the terms of the naval convention of 1912, France had denuded its northern ports of naval defences, in effect entrusting the security of its coastline to the Royal Navy. Even in the absence of a formal alliance, he pleaded, 'does not Britain have a moral obligation to help us, to at least give us the help of your fleet, since it is on your advice that we have sent ours away?' It is rather extraordinary that Grey needed to be told this by Cambon, but the argument struck home. The foreign secretary acknowledged that a German attack on the French coastline and/or a

German violation of Belgian neutrality might alter the complexion of British public opinion. Most importantly of all, he undertook to raise the question of the French coasts in cabinet on the following day. Cambon left this meeting as white as a sheet and close to tears. Staggering into the ambassadors' room next to Grey's office, he was guided to a chair by Nicolson, muttering, 'They are going to drop us. They are going to drop us.'[165]

BRITAIN INTERVENES

In fact, the position was less dire than Cambon supposed. In the crisis situation of the first days of August 1914, emotions were running high. The fear of abandonment for Cambon and the fear, for Grey, of being drawn out of his depth before there had been time to secure support for his policy produced a heightening and polarization of utterance that may lead us to misread the underlying realities of the situation. The balance of initiative was already shifting by imperceptible degrees in favour of a British continental intervention. On 29 July, the cabinet had agreed to Churchill's request as First Lord for a precautionary mobilization of the fleet. And on that evening, Asquith managed to convey to Churchill by means of a 'hard stare' and a 'sort of grunt' his tacit consent to a deployment of the fleet to war stations. On 1 August, without securing the agreement of cabinet (but with the prime minister's implicit approval) Churchill mobilized his fleet.

At the same time, the Conservative opposition started to lobby in earnest for intervention. The Tory press had already begun to come out in favour of a British intervention. While the *Manchester Guardian*, the *Daily News* and the *Standard*, all Liberal organs, stuck to a policy of neutrality, *The Times* led the Tory papers in demanding a strong stand against Austria and Germany and participation in the imminent continental war. And behind the scenes, the director of military operations, Henry Wilson, a staunch supporter of intervention who was often seen during these days darting between the French embassy and the Foreign Office, alerted the Conservative leadership that Britain was in danger of abandoning France.

On 1 August, shortly after Cambon's interview with Grey, the Conservative MP George Lloyd paid a call on the French ambassador.

Cambon was still incensed: what, he asked, had become of the Anglo-French naval arrangements or the General Staff consultations, both of which presupposed an interlocked security policy? And what of the many assurances of British support over recent years? 'All our plans have been arranged in common,' the ambassador exclaimed. 'Our General Staffs have consulted. You have seen all our schemes and preparations.'[166] Overcoming his consternation, Cambon handled his interlocutor skilfully. The Foreign Office, he said, had in effect placed the blame for its own inaction on the Conservative opposition, by suggesting that the Tories could not be relied upon to support any initiative that might lead to war. Lloyd vigorously denied this and left the meeting determined to mobilize a Conservative pro-intervention lobby. A meeting took place late that night at the home of Austen Chamberlain and by ten o'clock the next morning (2 August), a troupe of prominent Conservatives, including Lansdowne and Bonar Law, the Conservative leaders in the two Houses of Parliament, had been won over to the cause of positive action. A letter was sent to Asquith stating that the opposition would support intervention and warning that a decision for British neutrality would not only damage the country's reputation, but undermine its security.[167]

It was in the cabinet, however, that the crucial battle would be fought. Here, opinion was still firmly on the side of non-intervention. The majority were suspicious of the Entente with France and deeply hostile to the Convention with Russia.[168] 'Everybody longs to stand aside,' Asquith told Venetia Stanley on 31 July.[169] At least three quarters of its members, Churchill later recalled, were determined not be drawn into a 'European quarrel' unless Britain itself were attacked, 'which seemed unlikely'.[170] And the anti-interventionists could claim, with some justice, to have the support of the banking and commercial interests in London – on 31 July, a delegation of City financiers visited Asquith to warn him against allowing Britain to be drawn into a European conflict.

The cabinet meeting on the morning of 1 August brought a polarization and clarification of views. Morley and Simon led the anti-interventionist group, calling for a declaration, 'now and at once' that '*in no circumstances*' would the British government take a hand. Churchill, by contrast, was 'very bellicose' and demanded 'immediate mobilization'. Grey appeared likely to resign if the cabinet committed itself to neutrality. Haldane was 'diffuse' and 'nebulous'.[171] The cabinet decided against the immediate deployment of the British Expeditionary Force to the continent – a decision that was not opposed by Grey or the other liberal imperialists (this was the decision that plunged Paul Cambon into despair). So sure was John Morley of non-intervention that he flaunted the victory of the 'peace party' before Churchill, saying: 'We have beaten you after all'.[172]

And yet, by the close of the following day – Sunday 2 August – the British government had taken the crucial steps towards intervention. At the first cabinet meeting of that day, from eleven in the morning until two in the afternoon, Grey was authorized to inform the French ambassador that if the German fleet crossed the North Sea or entered the Channel in order either to disrupt French shipping or to attack the French coast, the British fleet would extend full protection. Walter Runciman, president of the Board of Agriculture and Fisheries, later described this as 'the Cabinet which decided that war with Germany was inevitable'.[173] At a later meeting, held between 6.30 and 8 p.m., it was agreed that a 'substantial violation' of Belgian neutrality would 'compel us to take action'.[174] It was understood that this latter undertaking would inevitably entail intervention, since the Germans had made it clear to the British government that they intended to advance on France through Belgium. Recognizing that the writing was on the wall for the proponents of non-intervention, Burns announced his retirement after the first meeting; at the end of the second, Viscount John Morley, too, gave notice of his imminent retirement. The 'peace party' was in disarray.

How was such a dramatic reversal possible? In answering this question, it is worth noting, first, the skill with which the interventionist group set the terms of the debate. The cabinet minister Herbert Samuel helped to frame the discussion by drawing up in advance of the two meetings two formulae identifying, firstly, a German bombardment of the French coast and, secondly, a 'substantial violation' of Belgian neutrality as potential triggers for a British armed response. Part of the appeal of these two proposals lay in the fact that they were designed to ensure that it was 'an action of Germany's and not of ours' which would 'cause the failure'.[175] Grey stated at the morning meeting of 2 August with great emotion that Britain had a moral obligation to support France in the coming conflict, adding that 'We have led France to rely upon us and unless we support her in her agony, I cannot continue at the Foreign Office . . .'.[176] And while the pro-interventionists gathered around Grey and the prime minister, the 'peace party' failed to rally cross-party or extra-parliamentary support and proved unable to generate a leader capable of challenging the imperialists and their Conservative allies.

How important were the arguments put forward by the liberal imperialists? Since Britain's declaration of war on Germany on 4 August did indeed follow upon the German invasion of Belgium and since the Entente swiftly hardened into a fully-fledged alliance, whose history would later be rewritten as a story of abiding Anglo-French friendship, it has generally been assumed that Belgium and France were the issues that drew cabinet, parliament and the British people into war. This view is not wrong: it is impossible to deny their importance both in legitimating the policy adopted and in cementing the *union sacrée* between the cabinet, parliament and popular opinion that was such a striking feature of early wartime Britain.[177] In a brilliantly judged speech to the House of Commons on 3 August, Grey integrated the Anglo-French Entente into the emerging pro-war consensus. British undertakings to France, he said, had always stopped short of 'an engagement to cooperate in war'. But the very fact of naval cooperation between the two countries implied a moral obligation:

> The French fleet is now in the Mediterranean, and the Northern and Western coasts of France are absolutely undefended. The French fleet being concentrated in the Mediterranean, the situation is very different from what it used to be, because the friendship which had grown up between the two countries has given them a sense of security that there was nothing to be feared from us. The French coasts are absolutely undefended. The French fleet is in the Mediterranean, and has for some years been concentrated there because of the feeling of confidence and friendship which has existed between the two countries.[178]

And to this moral calculation Grey appended an argument from interest by suggesting that were France to withdraw its fleet from the eastern Mediterranean, Italy might seize the opportunity to depart from her own neutrality and Britain might at some later date be forced to enter the fray in order to defend Mediterranean trade routes that were 'vital to this country'. This was, by all accounts, the most successful speech of Grey's political career – no one who reads it today can fail to be impressed by the way in which he, in the beguilingly hesitant, gentlemanly style that was his trademark, established the moral credentials of the imperialist position. One of the most telling tributes came from the formerly anti-interventionist Liberal Christopher Addison: '[Grey's speech] satisfied, I think, all the House, with perhaps three or four exceptions, that we were compelled to participate.'[179] And once the decision was made, the nation fell in line behind it with astonishing speed, creating a British *union sacrée* that extended all the way from the unionists of all stripes to the Labour Party and even the Irish nationalists.[180] Cambon's trust in the British foreign secretary was thus vindicated. There had been a few painful moments, to be sure, but the French ambassador was right in the longer run, and the run was only a few days long, after all.

Nevertheless, the fact that neither Belgium nor France had carried much weight with the cabinet in the last days of July suggests that we need to nuance the argument and distinguish between the reasons for decisions and the arguments chosen to advertise and justify them. Other factors must have catalysed the transition from neutrality to intervention, especially for those waverers among the ministers whose support was necessary for the passage of a cabinet resolution. Within this more circumscribed setting, party-political anxieties about how the Liberal government would survive the resignation of Grey and Asquith were surely crucial. Given the support of the Conservative opposition for intervention (which was in turn powered in part by attitudes to the Irish Question, the assumption being that intervention would necessitate the indefinite postponement of Home Rule), the collapse of the Liberal cabinet would simply have resulted in the slightly belated adoption of Grey's policy. For those who remained unmoved by Belgian neutrality and the Anglo-French naval arrangement, this was a powerful argument against allowing the intervention debate to break the government.[181]

Underlying these calculations were deeper concerns about the threat posed to British security by the looming conflict. Since around 1900, the need to ward off Russian menaces had been a central theme in British policy-making. In 1902, Britain had used the Anglo-Japanese alliance to balance against Russia in the Far East. The Anglo-French Entente of 1904 had further weakened Russia, at least as an opponent of Britain, and the Convention of 1907 with Russia provided – in theory at least – a means of managing tensions along an imperial periphery that Britain could no longer afford effectively to garrison. The Russian threat had not disappeared by 1914; in fact it was resurfacing during the last year before the outbreak of war. At that time, the extremely high-handed and provocative behaviour of the Russians in Persia and Central Asia encouraged some policy-makers in London to believe that the Anglo-Russian Convention might be on its last legs, and others to press yet harder for an alliance with St Petersburg. As Buchanan put it in a letter to Nicolson in April 1914: 'Russia is rapidly becoming so power-ful that we must retain her friendship at almost any cost. If she acquires the conviction that we are unreliable and useless as a friend, she may one day strike a bargain with Germany and resume her liberty of action on Turkey and Persia.[182] Or in Nicolson's more explicit formulation of 1912:

> ... it would be far more disadvantageous to have an unfriendly France and Russia than an unfriendly Germany. [Germany can] give us plenty of annoyance, but it cannot really threaten any of our more important inter-ests, while Russia especially could cause us extreme embarrassment and, indeed, danger in the Mid-East and on our Indian frontier, and it would be most unfortunate, were we to revert to the state of things which existed before 1904 and 1907.[183]

Yet it was to contain Germany, not Russia, that Britain went to war in 1914. There has been controversy among historians about the respective impact of what appear to be two quite distinct security paradigms – while the older studies (and some newer ones) stress the centrality of the continental balance of power to British thinking and policy, recent revisionist accounts have globalized the field of vision, arguing that Britain's vulnerability as a world power obliged it to focus on Russia as the more fundamental threat. It is true that continentalist arguments acquired more weight in British thinking after the crises of 1905 and 1911.[184] But it is misleading to overstate the tension between the two viewpoints, which were often blended in the arguments offered by decision-makers. An example is the minute appended by Eyre Crowe on 25 July to a telegram from Ambassador Buchanan in St Petersburg. Crowe's view was and always had been that of a balance-of-power con-tinentalist focused on the containment of Germany. Yet he also made an explicit appeal to Britain's imperial security:

Should the war come, and England stand aside, one of two things must happen. (a) Either Germany and Austria win, crush France, and humiliate Russia. What will be the position of a friendless England? (b) Or France and Russia win. What would then be their attitude towards England? What about India and the Mediterranean?[185]

In short, the key British decision-makers were not forced to choose between continentalist and imperial options in 1914. Whether one identified Russia or Germany as the chief threat, the outcome was the same, since British intervention on the side of the Entente offered a means *both* of appeasing and tethering Russia *and* of opposing and containing Germany. In the conditions of 1914, the logics of global and continental security converged in the British decision to support the Entente powers against Germany and Austria.

BELGIUM

French policy combined an offensive posture in the Russian theatre with a defensive one in their own. In Germany's case, the poles were reversed. The need to fight on two fronts obliged German planners to seek a decisive victory first on one front and then on the other. The westward strike was given priority, because it was here that the Germans expected to encounter the most determined and effective resistance. On the eastern front, in the meanwhile, a mere holding force was left to meet the Russian advance. The balance between the eastern and the western contingents changed in the last years before the war as Moltke struggled to address the threat posed by Russian military expansion and infrastructural improvements, but the underlying logic of the plan remained the same: Germany would strike first and hardest in the west and destroy its western opponent before turning to face its enemy in the east. Since 1905 it had been assumed by German planners that military success in the west would be possible only if Germany struck at France through neutral Luxembourg and Belgium. The assault would pass along two corridors on either side of the Ardennes Forest, one leading through Luxembourg, the other squeezing around the tongue of Dutch territory known as the Maastricht salient to cross southern Belgium. A broad, five-armed, concentric attack into northern France would bypass the *places fortes* around Verdun, Nancy, Epinal and Belfort, enabling the German armies to threaten Paris from the north-east and thereby to achieve a swift resolution of the conflict in the west.

Moltke and his subordinates in the General Staff viewed this deployment plan as the pure expression of an incontrovertible military necessity. No alternative plans were devised that might have provided the civilian leadership with options to play with. The only alternative deployment scenario, the Eastern Campaign Plan, which envisaged a mobilization against Russia alone, was shelved in 1913. The military leaders were remarkably unconcerned about the political impact that the violation of Belgian neutrality might have on Germany's diplomatic freedom of manoeuvre during the crucial crisis phase between peace and war. Historians have rightly criticized the rigidity of German military planning, seeing in it the fruits of a political system in which the army pursued its own dreams of 'absolute destruction', free of civilian control or oversight.[186] But there was also careful reasoning behind the narrowing of options: the increasingly interdependent defence arrangements within the Franco-Russian Alliance made a war on one front virtually inconceivable – hence the abandonment of the Eastern Campaign Plan. And the German military (by contrast with their French counterparts and with German *civilian* leaders) did not attach great importance to the question of British intervention, which was seen by most German planners as militarily irrelevant – another failure of strategic and political imagination.

As the moment approached for German mobilization on 1 August, the policy-makers in Berlin made two further epic blunders. The execution of the western deployment plan required the swift and immediate invasion of Belgium. Delaying the violation was out of the question, Moltke argued, because the completion of Belgian defence measures in and around fortified Liège would block the German advance and cost huge casualties. This insistence on immediate action was politically problematic. Had Germany waited until its forces were actually concentrated and ready for attack before crossing the Belgian border, the Belgian and French armies would have acquired more time to consolidate their defensive arrangement. On the other hand, it would have been much harder (though probably not impossible) for Grey and his colleagues to make a case for intervention. Grey's opponents could have pointed out that Russia and (by extension) France, not Germany, were forcing the pace; the British interventionists would have been deprived of one of their most effective arguments. Recognizing this, Admiral Tirpitz, a navalist who understood the importance of the British role, later posed the angry question: 'Why did we not wait?'[187]

The presentation of an ultimatum to the Belgian government on 2 August was another disastrous mistake. Given the decision to breach Belgian neutrality and the pressing need for speed, it might well have been better (from Germany's point of view) simply to break into and across Belgian territory, making one's excuses as one went and dealing with the matter afterwards as a *fait accompli* by means of an indemnity. This is exactly what the British government had been expecting the Germans to do. And the ministers in Asquith's cabinet – including Churchill – had repeatedly expressed the view that Britain would not necessarily regard a German *transit* through Belgium as a *casus belli*, so long as the Germans stayed south of the Sambre–Meuse line and thus kept clear of the strategically sensitive region around Antwerp and the Schelde estuary.

The German civilian leaders, on the other hand, could see no alternative to an ultimatum, for this seemed the only possible way to strike a deal of some kind with Brussels and thereby keep Britain out of the war. The ultimatum, drawn up by Moltke on 26 July and subsequently revised by the Foreign Office in Berlin, was formulated to appeal to a reasoned Belgian appraisal of the national interest in the light of the huge imbalance in the forces engaged. The text opened by stating that the Germans believed a French attack through Belgian territory to be imminent and that the German government would view it as a matter of the 'deepest regret if Belgium regarded as an act of hostility against herself the fact that the measures of Germany's opponents force Germany, for her own protection, to enter Belgian territory'. Then followed a series of points: Germany would (point 1) guarantee all Belgian territory and possessions, (point 2) evacuate Belgian territory as soon as hostilities were completed, and (point 3) cover all Belgian costs and damages with a cash indemnity. Should Belgium oppose the German troops, however (point 4), 'Germany would, to her regret, be compelled to consider Belgium as an enemy'. But if this outcome were avoided, the 'friendly ties that bind the two neighbouring states' would 'grow stronger and more enduring'.[188]

Two telling last-minute changes were made to the note. The deadline offered for the Belgian reply was reduced from twenty-four to twelve hours at the request of Moltke, who was keen to get moving as quickly as possible. Second, a clause suggesting that the Belgians could, if they maintained a 'friendly attitude', expect territorial compensation 'at the cost of France' was deleted from the text because it had suddenly occurred to the Foreign Office that it might well enrage Britain even more than the intended violation of Belgian territory. That Bethmann had at first failed to see this does not cast a flattering light on his political judgement at the height of the crisis.[189]

From the moment when the German minister Below Saleske delivered the note to Davignon, the Belgian minister of foreign affairs, everything started to go horribly wrong for the Germans. Had Moltke simply barged through the south of Belgium, it might have been possible to frame the breach in terms of military expediency. But the note forced the Belgian government to articulate a principled view in advance of the anticipated action. The task of doing that fell to the Belgian king and to the head of the Belgian government Count Charles de Broqueville. De Broqueville brought a French translation of the text with him when he went to see the king at the palace at 8 p.m. There could be no doubt about how these two would respond. The Belgian king was famed for his uprightness and resolve and de Broqueville was a genteel, old-fashioned Belgian patriot. They viewed the note as an affront to Belgian honour – how could they have done otherwise? One hour later, at 9 p.m., the German ultimatum was discussed by the Council of Ministers and then by a Crown Council at which the portfolio ministers were joined by a number of distinguished statesmen with titular ministerial titles. There was no debate – it was clear from the outset that Belgium would resist. During the hours of darkness the ministry of foreign affairs composed a reply of profoundly impressive dignity and clarity, culminating in a high-minded rejection of the German offer: 'The Belgian government, were they to accept the proposal submitted to them, would sacrifice the honour of the nation and betray at the same time their duties towards Europe.'[190]

On the morning of 3 August, the texts of the ultimatum and of the Belgian reply were shown to the French minister in Brussels, M. Klobukowski, who immediately passed the news to the Havas agency. A media storm swept through Belgium and the Entente countries, stirring outrage everywhere. In Belgium, there was an explosion of patriotic emotion. Across Brussels and other major towns, the streets filled with national flags; all the parties, from the anticlerical liberals and socialists across to the clerical Catholics, pledged their determination to defend their homeland and their national honour against the invader.[191] At the Chamber of Deputies, where the king spoke on 5 August of the need for national unity in defence of the fatherland and asked the assembled deputies, 'Are you determined at any cost to maintain the sacred heritage of our ancestors?', there was delirious cheering from all sides.[192] The German ultimatum thus turned out to be a 'terrible psychological blunder'.[193] It resonated in wartime propaganda, overshadowing the complexities of the war's causation and endowing the Entente war effort with an unshakeable sense of moral superiority.

Many Germans were shocked by the Belgian decision to resist à l'outrance. 'Oh, the poor fools,' one diplomat at the German legation in Brussels exclaimed. 'Oh, the poor fools! Why don't they get out of the way of the steamroller. We don't want to hurt them, but if they stand in our way they will be ground into the dirt. Oh, the poor fools!'.[194] It was perhaps because they recognized this that the Germans renewed their appeal to Belgian reason only six days later, on 8 August. The fortress of Liège, so important to Moltke, had in the meanwhile been taken after a determined defence, at considerable cost in life. In a note passed to Brand Whitlock, the American minister in Brussels, the Berlin government expressed its regret at the 'bloody encounters before Liège', and added:

> Now that the Belgian army has upheld the honour of its arms by its heroic resistance to a very superior force, the German Government beg the King of the Belgians and the Belgian Government to spare Belgium the further horrors of war. [. . .] Germany once more gives her solemn assurance that it is not her intention to appropriate Belgium to herself and that such an intention is far from her thoughts. Germany is still ready to evacuate Belgium as soon as the state of war will allow her to do so.[195]

This offer, too, was rejected.

BOOTS

With the sequence of general mobilizations, ultimatums and declarations of war, the story this book set out to tell comes to an end. During his last meeting with Sazonov in St Petersburg on Saturday 1 August,

Ambassador Pourtalès muttered 'incomprehensible words', burst into tears, stammered 'So this is the result of my mission!' and ran from the room.[196] When Count Lichnowsky called on Asquith on the 2nd, he found the prime minister 'quite broken', with tears 'coursing down his cheeks'.[197] In Brussels, the departing counsellors of the German legation sat on the edge of their chairs in a shuttered room among their packed boxes and files, mopping their brows and chain-smoking to master their agitation.[198]

The time of diplomacy was drawing to a close, the time of the soldiers and sailors had begun. When the Bavarian military plenipotentiary to Berlin visited the German ministry of war after the order for mobilization had gone out, he found 'everywhere beaming faces, shaking of hands in the corridors; one congratulates oneself for having taken the hurdle'.[199] In Paris on 30 July Colonel Ignatiev reported the 'unconcealed joy' of his French colleages 'at having the chance to use, as the French think, beneficial strategic circumstances'.[200] The First Sea Lord Winston Churchill was cheered by the thought of the impending struggle. 'Everything tends towards catastrophe, & collapse,' he wrote to his wife on 28 July. 'I am interested, geared-up and happy.'[201] In St Petersburg, a jovial Alexander Krivoshein assured a delegation of Duma deputies that Germany would soon be crushed and that the war was a 'boon' for Russia: 'Depend upon us, gentlemen, everything will be superb.'[202]

Mansell Merry, vicar of St Michael's, Oxford, had travelled to St Petersburg in mid-July in order to officiate over the summer months as chaplain at the city's English Church. When the order to mobilize was announced, he tried to make his escape by steamer to Stockholm. But his ship, the *Døbeln*, was confined to harbour – the lighthouses had been extinguished along the whole length of the Finnish Bight and the forts at Kronstadt had been ordered to fire at once on any boat that attempted to pass the minefield. On 31 July, an ugly, grey, blustery day in St Petersburg, Merry found himself confined on board with all the other would-be travellers, watching throngs of soldiers and naval reservists tramp along the Nicolaevskaya Quay. A few marched to the 'lilting strains' of a brass band, but most 'trudged along, bundle on back or in hand, in sullen silence, the womenfolk, many of them weeping as if their hearts would break, breathlessly struggling to keep pace with their husbands, sons or lovers on either side, as company after company [swung] past'.[203]

In the small hours of the night of 1–2 August, the Boulevard du Palais in central Paris was filled with the same sound of marching men making their way in long columns northwards to the Gares de l'Est and du Nord. There was no music, singing or cheering, just the scraping of boots, the clip-clopping of hundreds of horses, the growl of motor lorries and the crunching of iron wheels on cobbles as artillery pieces rolled under the unlit windows of apartments, many of whose occupants must have lain awake or sleepily watched the sombre spectacle from their windows.[204]

Public reactions to the news of war gave the lie to the claim, so often voiced by statesmen, that the hands of the decision-makers were forced by popular opinion. There was, to be sure, no resistance against the call to arms. Almost everywhere men went more or less willingly to their assembly points.[205] Underlying this readiness to serve was not enthusiasm for war as such, but a defensive patriotism, for the aetiology of this conflict was so complex and strange that it allowed soldiers and civilians in all the belligerent states to be confident that theirs was a war of defence, that their countries had been attacked or provoked by a determined enemy, that their respective governments had made every effort to preserve the peace.[206] As the great alliance blocs prepared for war, the intricate chain of events that had sparked the conflagration was swiftly lost from view. 'Nobody seems to remember,' an American diplomat in Brussels noted in his diary on 2 August, 'that a few days ago Serbia was playing a star rôle in this affair. She seems to have faded away behind the scenes.'[207]

There were isolated expressions of chauvinist enthusiasm for the coming fight, but these were the exception. The myth that European men leapt at the opportunity to defeat a hated enemy has been comprehensively dispelled.[208] In most places and for most people, the news of mobilization came as a profound shock, a 'peal of thunder out of a cloudless sky'. And the further one moved away from the urban centres, the less sense the news of mobilization seemed to make to the people who were going to fight, die or be maimed or bereaved in the coming war. In the villages of the Russian countryside a 'stunned silence' reigned, broken only by the sound of 'men, women and children weeping'.[209]

In Vatilieu, a small commune in the Rhône-Alpes region of south-eastern France, the ringing of the tocsin brought workers and peasants into the village square. Some, who had run straight from the fields, were still carrying their pitchforks.

> 'What can it mean? What is going to happen to us?' asked the women. Wives, children, husbands, all were overcome by emotion. The wives clung to the arms of their husbands. The children, seeing their mothers weeping, started to cry too. All around us was alarm and consternation. What a disturbing scene.[210]

An English traveller recalled the reaction in an Altai (Semipalatinsk) Cossack settlement when the 'blue flag' borne aloft by a rider and the noise of bugles playing the alarm brought news of mobilization. The Tsar had spoken, and the Cossacks, with their unique military calling and tradition, 'burned to fight the enemy'. But who *was* that enemy? Nobody knew. The mobilization telegram provided no details. Rumours abounded. At first everyone imagined that the war must be with China – 'Russia had pushed too far into Mongolia and China had declared war.' Then another rumour did the rounds: 'It is with England, with England.' This view prevailed for some time.

> Only after four days did something like the truth come to us, and then nobody believed it.[211]

Conclusion

'I shall never be able to understand how it happened,' the novelist Rebecca West remarked to her husband as they stood on the balcony of Sarajevo Town Hall in 1936. It was not, she reflected, that there were too few facts available, but that there were too many.[1] That the crisis of 1914 was complex has been one of the central contentions of this book. Some of that intricacy derived from behaviours that are still part of our political scene. The last section of the book was written at the height of the Eurozone financial crisis of 2011–12 – a present-day event of baffling complexity. It was notable that the actors in the Eurozone crisis, like those of 1914, were aware that there was a possible outcome that would be generally catastrophic (the failure of the euro). All the key protagonists hoped that this would not happen, but in addition to this shared interest, they also had special – and conflicting – interests of their own. Given the inter-relationships across the system, the consequences of any one action depended on the responsive actions of others, which were hard to calculate in advance, because of the opacity of decision-making processes. And all the while, political actors in the Eurozone crisis exploited the *possibility* of the general catastrophe as leverage in securing their own specific advantages.

In this sense, the men of 1914 are our contemporaries. But the differences are as significant as the commonalities. At least the government ministers charged with solving the Eurozone crisis agreed in general terms on what the problem *was* – in 1914, by contrast, a profound sundering of ethical and political perspectives eroded consensus and sapped trust. The powerful supranational institutions that today provide a framework for defining tasks, mediating conflicts and identifying remedies were conspicuously absent in 1914. Moreover, the complexity of the 1914 crisis arose not from the diffusion of powers and

Gavrilo Princip's footsteps, Sarajevo (a photo from 1955)

responsibilities across a single politico-financial framework, but from rapid-fire interactions among heavily armed autonomous power-centres confronting different and swiftly changing threats and operating under conditions of high risk and low trust and transparency.

Crucial to the complexity of the events of 1914 were rapid changes in the international system: the sudden emergence of an Albanian territorial state, the Turco-Russian naval arms race in the Black Sea, or the reorientation of Russian policy away from Sofia to Belgrade, to name just a few. These were not long-term historical transitions, but short-range realignments. Their consequences were amplified by the fluidity of the power relations within the European executives: Grey's struggle to contain the threat posed by the liberal radicals, the fragile ascendancy of Poincaré and his alliance policy, or the campaign waged by Sukhomlinov against Kokovtsov. After Vladimir Kokovtsov's fall from office in January 1914, according to the unpublished memoir of a political insider, Tsar Nicholas II offered his post in the first instance to the deeply conservative Pyotr N. Durnovo, a forceful and determined man who was adamantly opposed to Balkan entanglements of any kind. But Durnovo turned the post down and it passed instead to Goremykin, whose weakness allowed Krivoshein and the military command to wield disproportionate influence in the councils of July 1914.[2] It would be a mistake to hang too much on this detail, but it draws our attention to the place of short-range, contingent realignments in shaping the conditions under which the crisis of 1914 unfolded.

This in turn made the system as a whole more opaque and unpredictable, feeding a pervasive mood of mutual distrust, even within the respective alliances, a development that was dangerous for peace. Levels of trust between the Russian and British leaderships were relatively low by 1914 and they were getting lower, but this did not diminish the readiness of the British Foreign Office to accept a European war on terms set by Russia; on the contrary, it reinforced the case for intervention. The same can be said for the Franco-Russian Alliance: doubts about its future had the effect on both sides of heightening, rather than muting the readiness to risk conflict. Fluctuations in power relations within each government – coupled with swiftly changing objective conditions – in turn produced the policy oscillations and ambiguous messaging that were such a crucial feature of the pre-war crises. Indeed it is not clear that the term 'policy' is always appropriate in the pre-1914 context, given the looseness and ambiguity of many of the commitments involved. Whether Russia or Germany had a Balkan policy in the years 1912–14 is questionable – what we see instead is a multiplicity of initiatives, scenarios and attitudes whose overall trend is sometimes hard to discern. Within the respective state executives, the changeability of power relations also meant that those entrusted with formulating policy did so under considerable domestic pressure, not so much from the press or public opinion or industrial or financial lobbies, as from adversaries within their own elites and governments. And this, too, heightened the sense of urgency besetting decision-makers in the summer of 1914.

We need to distinguish between the objective factors acting on the decision-makers and the stories they told themselves and each other about what they thought they were doing and why they were doing it. All the key actors in our story filtered the world through narratives that were built from pieces of experience glued together with fears, projections and interests masquerading as maxims. In Austria, the story of a nation of youthful bandits and regicides endlessly provoking and goading a patient elderly neighbour got in the way of a cool-headed assessment of how to manage relations with Belgrade. In Serbia, fantasies of victimhood and oppression by a rapacious, all-powerful Habsburg Empire did the same in reverse. In Germany, a dark vision of future invasions and partitions bedevilled decision-making in the summer of 1914. And the Russian saga of repeated humiliations at the hands of the central powers had a similar impact, at once distorting the past and clarifying the present. Most important of all was the widely trafficked narrative of Austria-Hungary's historically necessary decline, which, having gradually replaced an older set of assumptions about Austria's role as a fulcrum of stability in Central and Eastern Europe, disinhibited Vienna's enemies, undermining the notion that Austria-Hungary, like every other great power, possessed interests that it had the right robustly to defend.

That the Balkan setting was central to the outbreak of war may seem self-evident, given the location of the assassinations that started the crisis. But two points in particular deserve emphasis. The first is that the Balkan Wars recalibrated the relationships among the greater and lesser powers in dangerous ways. In the eyes of both the Austrian and the Russian leaderships, the struggle to control events on the Balkan peninsula took on a new and more threatening aspect, especially during the winter crisis of 1912–13. One consequence was the Balkanization of the

Franco-Russian Alliance. France and Russia, at different paces and for different reasons, constructed a geopolitical trigger along the Austro-Serbian frontier. The Balkan inception scenario was not a policy or a plan or plot that steadily matured over time, nor was there any necessary or linear relationship between the positions adopted in 1912 and 1913 and the outbreak of war in the following year. It was not that the Balkan inception scenario – which was in effect a Serbian inception scenario – drove Europe forwards towards the war that actually happened in 1914, but rather the other way round, that it supplied the conceptual framework within which the crisis was interpreted, once it had broken out. Russia and France thereby tied the fortunes of two of the world's greatest powers in highly asymmetrical fashion to the uncertain destiny of a turbulent and intermittently violent state.

For Austria-Hungary, whose regional security arrangements were ruined by the Balkan Wars, the Sarajevo murders were not a pretext for a pre-existing policy of invasion and warfare. They were a transformative event, charged with real and symbolic menace. It is easy from the perspective of the twenty-first century to say that Vienna should have resolved the issues arising from the assassinations through calm bilateral negotiations with Belgrade, but in the setting of 1914 this was not a credible option. Nor, for that matter, was Sir Edward Grey's half-hearted proposal of 'four-power mediation', which was founded upon a partisan indifference to the power-political realities of Austria-Hungary's situation. It was not just that the Serbian authorities were partly unwilling and partly unable to suppress the irredentist activity that had given rise to the assassinations in the first place; it was also that Serbia's friends did not concede to Vienna the right to incorporate in its demands on Belgrade a means of monitoring and enforcing compliance. They rejected such demands on the ground that they were irreconcilable with Serbian sovereignty. There are parallels here with the debate that took place within the UN Security Council in October 2011 over a proposal – favoured by the NATO states – that sanctions should be imposed on the Assad regime in Syria to prevent further massacres of that country's dissident citizens. Against this proposal the Russian representative argued that the idea reflected an inappropriately 'confrontational approach' that was typical of the western powers, while the Chinese representative argued that sanctions were inappropriate because they were irreconcilable with Syrian 'sovereignty'.

Where does this leave the question of culpability? By asserting that Germany and her allies were morally responsible for the outbreak of war, Article 231 of the Versailles Peace Treaty ensured that questions of culpability would remain at or near the centre of the debate over the war's origins. The blame game has never lost its appeal. The most influential articulation of this tradition is the 'Fischer thesis' – shorthand for a bundle of arguments elaborated in the 1960s by Fritz Fischer, Imanuel Geiss and a score of younger German colleagues, who identified Germany as the power chiefly culpable in the outbreak of war. According to this view (leaving aside the many variations within the Fischer school), the Germans did not stumble or slither into war. They *chose* it – worse, they planned it in advance, in the hope of breaking out of their European isolation and launching a bid for world power. Recent studies of the resulting Fischer controversy have highlighted the links between this debate and the fraught process by which German intellectuals came to terms with the contaminating moral legacy of the Nazi era, and Fischer's arguments have been subjected to criticism on many points.[3] Nonetheless, a diluted version of the Fischer thesis still dominates in studies of Germany's road to war.

Do we really need to make the case against a single guilty state, or to rank the states according to their respective share in responsibility for the outbreak of war? In one classical study from the origins literature, Paul Kennedy remarked that it is 'flaccid' to dodge the search for a culprit by blaming all or none of the belligerent states.[4] A stiffer approach, Kennedy implies, ought not to shrink from pointing the finger. The problem with a blame-centred account is not that one may end up blaming the wrong party. It is rather that accounts structured around blame come with built-in assumptions. They tend, firstly, to presume that in conflictual interactions one protagonist must ultimately be right and the other wrong. Were the Serbs wrong to seek to unify Serbdom? Were the Austrians wrong to insist on the independence of Albania? Was one of these enterprises more wrong than the other? The question is meaningless. A further drawback of prosecutorial narratives is that they narrow the field of vision by focusing on the political temperament and initiatives of one particular state rather than on multilateral processes of interaction. Then there is the problem that the quest for blame predisposes the investigator to construe the actions of decision-makers as planned and driven by a coherent intention. You have to show that someone willed war as well as caused it. In its extreme form, this mode of procedure produces conspiratorial narratives in which a coterie of powerful individuals, like velvet-jacketed Bond villains, controls events from behind the scene in accordance with a malevolent plan. There is no denying the moral satisfaction delivered by such narratives, and it is not, of course, logically impossible that war came about in this manner in the summer of 1914, but the view expounded in this book is that such arguments are not supported by the evidence.

The outbreak of war in 1914 is not an Agatha Christie drama at the end of which we will discover the culprit standing over a corpse in the conservatory with a smoking pistol. There is no smoking gun in this story; or, rather, there is one in the hands of every major character. Viewed in this light, the outbreak of war was a tragedy, not a crime.[5] Acknowledging this does not mean that we should minimize the belligerence and imperialist paranoia of the Austrian and German policy-makers that rightly absorbed the attention of Fritz Fischer and his historiographical allies. But the Germans were not the only imperial-ists and not the only ones to succumb to paranoia. The crisis that brought war in 1914 was the fruit of a shared political culture. But it was also multipolar and genuinely interactive – that is what makes it the most complex event of modern times and that is why the debate over the origins of the First World War continues, one century after Gavrilo Princip fired those two fatal shots on Franz Joseph Street.

One thing is clear: none of the prizes for which the politicians of 1914 contended was worth the cataclysm that followed. Did the pro-tagonists understand how high the stakes were? It used to be thought that Europeans subscribed to the deluded belief that the next continen-tal conflict would be a short, sharp cabinet war of the eighteenth-century type; the men would be 'home before Christmas', as the saying went. More recently, the prevalence of this 'short-war illusion' has been called into question.[6] The German Schlieffen Plan was predicated on a mas-sive, lightning-fast strike into France, but even within Schlieffen's own staff there were voices warning that the next war would bring not quick victories but rather a 'tedious and bloody crawling forward step-by-step'.[7] Helmuth von Moltke hoped that a European war, if it broke out, would be resolved swiftly, but he also conceded that it might drag on for years, wreaking immeasurable ruin. British Prime Minister Herbert Asquith wrote of the approach of 'Armageddon' in the fourth week of

July 1914. French and Russian generals spoke of a 'war of extermination' and the 'extinction of civilisation'.

They knew it, but did they really feel it? This is perhaps one of the differences between the years before 1914 and the years after 1945. In the 1950s and 60s, decision-makers and the general public alike grasped in a visceral way the meaning of nuclear war – images of the mushroom clouds over Hiroshima and Nagasaki entered the nightmares of ordinary citizens. As a consequence, the greatest arms race in human history never culminated in nuclear war between the superpowers. It was different before 1914. In the minds of many statesmen, the hope for a short war and the fear of a long one seem, as it were, to have cancelled each other out, holding at bay a fuller appreciation of the risks. In March 1913, a journalist writing for the *Figaro* reported on a series of lectures recently given in Paris by the leading lights of French military medicine. Among the speakers was Professor Jacques-Ambroise Monprofit, who had just returned from a special mission to the military hospitals of Greece and Serbia, where he had helped to establish better standards of military surgery. Monprofit observed that 'the wounds caused by the French cannon [sold to Balkan states before the outbreak of the First Balkan War] were not merely the most numerous, but also horrifically grave, with crushed bones, lacerated tissues, and shattered chests and skulls'. So terrible was the resulting suffering that one prominent expert in military surgery, Professor Antoine Depage, proposed an international embargo on the future use of such arms in battle. 'We understand the generosity of his motivation,' the journalist commented, 'but if we must expect to be outnumbered one day on the field of battle, then it is as well that our enemies know that we have such weapons to defend ourselves with, weapons that are to be feared . . .' The article closed with the declaration that France should congratulate herself both on the horrific force of her arms and on possessing 'a medical organisation that we may confidently describe as marvellous'.[8] We can find such glib reflections wherever we look in pre-war Europe. In this sense, the protagonists of 1914 were sleepwalkers, watchful but unseeing, haunted by dreams, yet blind to the reality of the horror they were about to bring into the world.

Notes

ABBREVIATIONS

AMAE – Archive Ministère des Affaires Ètrangères, Paris

AN – Archives Nationales, Paris

AS – Arkhiv Srbije, Belgrade

AVPRI – Arkhiv Vneshnei Politiki Rossiiskoi Imperii (Archive of Foreign Policy of the Russian Empire), Moscow

BD – G. P. Gooch and H. Temperley (eds.), *British Documents on the Origins of the War: 1898–1914* (11 vols, London, 1926–38)

BNF – Bibliothèque Nationale de France, Paris

DD – Karl Kautsky, Count Max Montgelas and Walter Schücking (eds.), *Deutsche Dokumente zum Kriegsausbruch* (4 vols., Berlin, 1919)

DDF – Commission de publication de documents relatifs aux origines de la guerre de 1914 (ed.), *Documents diplomatiques français relatifs aux origines de la guerre de 1914* (41 vols., Paris, 1929–59)

DSP – Vladimir Dedijer and Života Anić (eds.), *Dokumenti o Spoljnoj Politici Kraljevine Srbije* (7 vols., Belgrade, 1980)

GARF – Gosudarstvennyi Arkhiv Rossiiskoi Federatsii (State Archive of the Russian Federation), Moscow

GP – Johannes Lepsius, Albrecht Mendelssohn-Bartholdy and Friedrich Wilhelm Thimme (eds.), *Grosse Politik der europäischen Kabinette, 1871–1914* (40 vols., Berlin 1922–7)

HHStA – Haus- Hof- und Staatsarchiv, Vienna

HSA – Hauptstaatsarchiv, Stuttgart

IBZI – Kommission beim Zentralexekutivkomitee der Sowjetregierung under dem Vorsitz von M. N. Pokrowski (ed.,) *Die internationalen Beziehungen im Zeitalter des Imperialismus. Dokumente aus den Archiven der zarischen und der provisorischen Regierung*, trans. Otto Hoetzsch (9 vols., Berlin, 1931–9)

KA – *Krasnyi Arkhiv*

MAEB AD – Ministère des Affaires Étrangères Belgique – Archives Diplomatiques, Brussels

MFA – Ministry of Foreign Affairs

MID-PO – Ministerstvo Inostrannikh Del – Politicko Odelenje (Serbian Ministry of Foreign Affairs, Political Department)

NA – Nationaal Archief, The Hague

NMM – National Maritime Museum, Greenwich

ÖUAP – Ludwig Bittner and Hans Uebersberger (eds.), *Österreichs-Ungarns Aussenpolitik von der bosnischen Krise bis zum Kriegsausbruch 1914*

PA-AA – Das Politische Archiv des Auswärtigen Amtes, Berlin

PA-AP – Papiers d'Agents – Archives Privées

RGIA – Rossiiskii Gosudarstvennyi Istoricheskii Arkhiv (Russian State Historical Archive), St Petersburg

RGVIA – Rossiiskii Gosudarstvennyi Voenno-istoricheskii Arkhiv (Russian State Military History Archive), Moscow

TNA – The National Archives, Kew

INTRODUCTION

1. Cited in David Fromkin, *Europe's Last Summer. Who Started the Great War in 1914?* (New York, 2004), p. 6.

2. The German Foreign Office sponsored the activities of the Arbeitsauschuss Deutscher Verbände dedicated to coordinating the campaign against war guilt and unofficially supported a Zentralstelle zur Erforschung der Kriegsursachen staffed by scholars; see Ulrich Heinemann, *Die verdrängte Niederlage: politische Öffentlichkeit und Kriegsschuldfrage in der Weimarer Republik* (Göttingen, 1983), esp. pp. 95–117; Sacha Zala, *Geschichte unter der Schere politischer Zensur. Amtliche Aktensammlung im internationalen Vergleich* (Munich, 2001), esp. pp. 57–77; Imanuel Geiss, 'Die manipulierte Kriegsschuldfrage. Deutsche Reichspolitik in der Julikrise 1914 und deutsche Kriegsziele im Spiegel des Schuldreferats des Auswärtigen Amtes, 1919–1931', *Militäreschichtliche Mitteilungen*, 34 (1983), pp. 31–60.

3. Barthou to Martin, letter of 3 May 1934, cited in Keith Hamilton, 'The Historical Diplomacy of the Third Republic', in Keith M. Wilson (ed.), *Forging the Collective Memory. Government and International Historians through Two World Wars* (Providence, Oxford, 1996), pp. 29–62, here p. 45; on French criticism of the German edition, see for example, E. Bourgeois, 'Les archives d'État et l'enquête sur les origines de la guerre mondiale. À propos de la publication allemande: Die grosse Politik d. europ. Kabinette et de sa traduction française', *Revue historique*, 155 (May–August 1927), pp. 39–56. Bourgeois accused the German editors of structuring the edition in a way that concealed tactical omissions in the documentary record; for a reply from the German editor, see Friedrich Thimme, 'Französische Kritiken

zur deutschen Aktenpublikation', *Europäische Gespräche*, 8/9 (1927), pp. 461–79.

4. Ulfried Burz, 'Austria and the Great War. Official Publications in the 1920s and 1930s', in Wilson, *Forging the Collective Memory*, pp. 178–91, here p. 186.

5. J.-B. Duroselle, *La grande guerre des Français, 1914–1918: L'incompréhensible* (Paris, 1994), pp. 23–33; J. F. V. Keiger, *Raymond Poincaré* (Cambridge, 1997), pp. 194–5.

6. Keith M. Wilson, 'The Imbalance in British Documents on the Origins of the War, 1898–1914. Gooch, Temperley and the India Office', in id. (ed.), *Forging the Collective Memory*, pp. 230–64, here p. 231; see also in the same volume Wilson's 'Introduction. Governments, Historians and "Historical Engineering"', pp. 1–28, esp. pp. 12–13.

7. Bernhard Schwertfeger, *Der Weltkrieg der Dokumente. Zehn Jahre Kriegsschuldforschung und ihr Ergebnis* (Berlin, 1929). On this problem more generally, see Zala, *Geschichte unter der Schere*, esp. pp. 31–6, 47–91, 327–38.

8. Theobald von Bethmann Hollweg, *Betrachtungen zum Weltkriege* (2 vols., Berlin, 1919), esp. vol. 1, pp. 113–84; Sergei Dmitrievich Sazonov, *Les Années fatales* (Paris, 1927); Raymond Poincaré, *Au service de la France – neuf années de souvenirs* (10 vols., Paris, 1926–33), esp. vol. 4, *L'Union sacrée*, pp. 163–431. For a more detailed but not necessarily more revelatory discussion of the crisis by the former president, see the statements recorded in René Gerin, *Les responsabilités de la guerre: quatorze questions, par René Gerin . . . quatorze réponses, par Raymond Poincaré* (Paris, 1930).

9. Edward Viscount Grey of Fallodon, *Twenty-Five Years, 1892–1916* (London, 1925).

10. Bernadotte Everly Schmitt, *Interviewing the Authors of the War* (Chicago, 1930).

11. Ibid., p. 11.

12. Luigi Albertini, *The Origins of the War of 1914*, trans. Isabella M. Massey (3 vols., Oxford, 1953), vol. 2, p. 40; Magrini was working at the behest of the Italian historian Luigi Albertini.

13. Derek Spring, 'The Unfinished Collection. Russian Documents on the Origins of the First World War', in Wilson (ed.), *Forging the Collective Memory*, pp. 63–86.

14. John W. Langdon, *July 1914: The Long Debate, 1918–1990* (Oxford, 1991), p. 51.

15. It would be pointless to offer a sample from the literature here. For useful discussions of the debate and its history, see John A. Moses, *The Politics of Illusion: The Fischer Controversy in German Historiography* (London, 1975); Annika Mombauer. *The Origins of the First World War:*

Controversies and Consensus (London, 2002); W. Jäger, *Historische Forsc-hung und politische Kultur in Deutschland. Die Debatte um den Ausbruch des Ersten Weltkriegs 1914–1980* (Göttingen, 1984); Langdon, *The Long Debate*; id., 'Emerging from Fischer's Shadow: Recent Examinations of the Crisis of July 1914', *The History Teacher*, vol. 20, no. 1 (Nov 1986), pp. 63–86; James Joll, 'The 1914 Debate Continues: Fritz Fischer and His Critics', *Past & Present*, 34/1 (1966), pp. 100–113 and the reply in P. H. S. Hatton, 'Britain and Germany in 1914: The July Crisis and War Aims', *Past & Present*, 36/1 (1967), pp. 138–43; Konrad H. Jarausch, 'Revising German History. Bethmann Hollweg Revisited', *Central European History*, 21/3 (1988), pp. 224–43; Samuel R. Williamson and Ernest R. May, 'An Identity of Opinion. Historians and July 1914', *Journal of Modern History*, 79/2 (June 2007), pp. 335–87; Jay Winter and Antoine Prost, *The Great War in History. Debates and Controversies, 1914 to the Present* (Cambridge, 2005).

16. On 'ornamentalism', see David Cannadine, *Ornamentalism. How the British Saw Their Empire* (London, 2002); for a superb example of the distancing 'world-that-was' approach to the pre-1914 world, see Barbara Tuchman, *Proud Tower. A Portrait of the World before the War, 1890–1914* (London, 1966) and ead., *August 1914* (London, 1962).

17. Richard F. Hamilton and Holger Herwig, *Decisions for War 1914–1917* (Cambridge, 2004), p. 46.

18. Svetoslav Budinov, *Balkanskite Voini (1912–1913). Istoricheski predstavi v sistemata na nauchno-obrezovatelnata komunikatsia* (Sofia, 2005), p. 55.

19. See esp. Holger Afflerbach, 'The Topos of Improbable War in Europe before 1914', in id. and David Stevenson (eds.), *An Improbable War? The Outbreak of World War I and European Political Culture before 1914* (Oxford, 2007), pp. 161–82 and the editors' introduction to the same volume, pp. 1–17.

CHAPTER I

1. Sir George Bonham to Marquess of Lansdowne, telegram (copy), Belgrade, 12 June 1903, TNA, FO 105/157, fo. 43.

2. Conflicting accounts of the regicide circulated in Belgrade during the weeks following the assassinations, as various individuals sought to conceal the most incriminating details or to minimize or magnify their own roles in the plot. For detailed and well-informed early press reports on the events of 10–11 June, see *Neue Freie Presse*, 12 June, pp. 1–3, and 13 June 1903, pp. 1–2; the British envoy reports are particularly informative about the steady accumulation of facts amid the rumours; these can be consulted in TNA, FO 105/157, 'Servia. Coup d'Etat. Extirpation of the Obrenovitch dynasty

& Election of King Peter Karageorgević. Suspension of diplomatic relations with Servia June 1903'; also Wayne S. Vucinich, *Serbia Between East and West. The Events of 1903–1906* (Stanford, 1954), pp. 55–9; for authoritative accounts in the secondary literature, see Slobodan Jovanović, *Vlada Aleksandra Obrenovica* (3 vols., Belgrade, 1934–6), vol. 3, pp. 359–62; Dragisa Vasić, *Devetsto treća (majski prevrat) prilozi za istoriju Srbije od 8. jula 1900. do 17. januara 1907* (Belgrade, 1925), pp. 75–112; Rebecca West, *Black Lamb and Grey Falcon. A Journey through Yugoslavia* (London, 1955), pp. 11–12, 560–64.

3. David MacKenzie, *Apis: The Congenial Conspirator. The Life of Colonel Dragutin T. Dimitrejević* (Boulder, 1989), p. 26; Alex N. Dragnich, *Serbia, Nikola Pašić and Yugoslavia* (New Brunswick, 1974), p. 44.

4. MacKenzie, *Apis*, p. 29.

5. See, for example, the passages from the diary of Vukasin Petrović describing a conversation with Alexandar Obrenović transcribed in Vladan Georgevitch, *Das Ende der Obrenovitch. Beiträge zur Geschichte Serbiens 1897–1900* (Leipzig, 1905), pp. 559–88.

6. Vucinich, *Serbia between East and West*, p. 9.

7. Ibid., p. 10.

8. Branislav Vranesević, 'Die Aussenpolitischen Beziehungen zwischen Serbien und der Habsburgermonarchie', in Adam Wandruszka and Peter Urbanitsch (eds.), *Die Habsburgermonarchie 1848–1918* (10 vols., Vienna, 1973–2006), vol. 6/2, pp. 319–86, here pp. 36–7.

9. See *The Times*, 7 April, p. 3, issue 37048, col. B; 23 April, issue 37062, col. A.

10. Vucinich, *Serbia between East and West*, p. 21; Gale Stokes, 'The Social Role of the Serbian Army before World War I: A Synthesis', in Stephen Fischer-Galati and Béla K. Király (eds.), *War and Society in Central Europe, 1740–1920* (Boulder, 1987), pp. 105–17.

11. On 'coterie charisma', see Roger Eatwell, 'The Concept and Theory of Charismatic Leadership', *Totalitarian Movements and Political Religions*, 7/2 (2006), pp. 141–56, here pp. 144, 153, 154; id., 'Hacia un nuevo modelo de liderazgo carismático de derecha', in Miguel Ángel Simon Gomez (ed.), *La extrema derecha en Europa desde 1945 a nuestros días* (Madrid, 2007), pp. 19–38.

12. Both comments cited in MacKenzie, *Apis*, p. 50.

13. Vucinich, *Serbia between East and West*, p. 47.

14. MacKenzie, *Apis*, p. 35; Vucinich, *Serbia between East and West*, p. 51; Vladimir Dedijer, *The Road to Sarajevo* (London, 1967), p. 85.

15. *The Times*, 27 April, p. 6, issue 37065, col. B.

16. Jovanović, *Vlada Aleksandra Obrenovica*, vol. 3, p. 359.

17. Sir G. Bonham to Marquess of Lansdowne, deciphered telegram, Belgrade, 7.45 p.m. 11 June 1903, TNA, FO 105/157, fo. 11.

18. Bonham to Marquess of Lansdowne, telegram (copy), Belgrade, 12 June 1903, TNA, FO 105/157, fo. 43.

19. Sir F. Plunkett to Marquess of Lansdowne, Vienna, 12 June 1903, ibid., fo. 44.

20. See Petar's proclamation of 25 June (OS) in Djurdje Jelenić, *Nova Srbija i Jugoslavija. Istorija nacionalnog oslobodjenja i ujedinjenja Srba, Hrvata i Slovenaca, od Kočine krajine do vidovdanskog ustava (1788–1921)* (Belgrade, 1923), p. 225.

21. For accounts that depict the coup of 1903 as the threshold to a Serbian golden age, see M. Popović, *Borba za parlamentarni režim u Srbiji* (Belgrade, 1938), esp. pp. 85–108, 110–11; Z. Mitrović, *Srpske politicke stranke* (Belgrade, 1939), esp. pp. 95–114; Alex N. Dragnich, *The Development of Parliamentary Government in Serbia* (Boulder, 1978), pp. 95–8; id., *Serbia, Nikola Pašić and Yugoslavia*.

22. Comments by M. Kalievć, reported in Bonham to Marquess of Lansdowne, 21 June 1903, TNA, FO 105/157, fos. 309–11, here fo. 310; see also Vucinich, *Serbia between East and West*, pp. 70–71.

23. Wilfred Thesiger to Marquess of Lansdowne, Belgrade, 15 November 1905, TNA, FO 105/158, fos. 247–52, here fo. 250. (Thesiger was the father of the famous explorer and writer.)

24. Thesiger to Marquess of Lansdowne, Belgrade, 5 December 1905, ibid., fos. 253–5, here fos. 254–5; Dragnich, *Serbia, Nikola Pašić and Yugoslavia*, pp. 73–4.

25. MacKenzie, *Apis*, p. 56.

26. Count Mérey von Kapos-Mére to Aehrenthal, 27 November 1903, cited in F. R. Bridge, *From Sadowa to Sarajevo. The Foreign Policy of Austria-Hungary, 1866–1914* (London, 1972), p. 263; Mérey's assessment is corroborated in Kosztowits (Netherlands consul in Belgrade) to Melvil van Lijnden, Belgrade, 4 September 1903, NA, 2.05.36, doc. 10, Rapporten aan en briefwisseling met het Ministerie van Buitenlandse Zaken.

27. David MacKenzie, 'Officer Conspirators and Nationalism in Serbia, 1901–1914', in S. Fischer-Galati and B. K. Kiraly (eds.), *Essays on War and Society in East Central Europe, 1720–1920* (Boulder, 1987), pp. 117–50, here p. 125; D. Djordjević, 'The Role of the Military in the Balkans in the Nineteenth Century', in R. Melville and H.-J. Schroeder (eds.), *Der Berliner Kongress von 1878* (Wiesbaden, 1982), pp. 317–47, esp. pp. 343–5.

28. D. T. Bataković, 'Nikola Pašić, les radicaux et la "Main Noire"', *Balcanica*, 37 (2006), pp. 143–69, here p. 154; for a narrative account of the 'Niš counter-conspiracy', see Vasić, *Devetsto treća*, pp. 131–84.

29. For an astute analysis of Pašić's personality, see Djordje Stanković, *Nikola Pašić. Prilozi za biografiju* (Belgrade, 2006), pt 2, ch. 8, p. 322.

30. Slobodan Jovanović, 'Nicholas Pašić: After Ten Years', *Slavonic and East European Review*, 15 (1937), pp. 368–76, here p. 369.

31. On Pašić's Russophilia, which was pragmatic rather than ideological, see Čedomir Popov, 'Nova Osvetljenja Rusko-Srpskih odnosa' (review of Latinka Petrović and Andrej Šemjakin (eds.), *Nikola Pašić. Pisma članci i govori* (Belgrade, 1995)), in *Zbornik Matice Srpske za Slavistiku*, 48–9 (1995), pp. 278–83, here p. 278; Vasa Kazimirović, *Nikola Pašić i njegovo doba 1845–1926* (Belgrade, 1990), pp. 54–5, 63. For an account that stresses the ideological dimension of Pašić's Russophilia, see Andrej Šemjakin, *Ideologia Nikole Pašića. Formiranje i evolucija (1868–1891)* (Moscow, 1998); on the mission to St Petersburg, see MacKenzie, *Apis*, p. 27.

32. Nikac Djukanov, *Bajade: anegdote o Nikoli Pašiću* (Belgrade, 1996), p. 35.

33. Stanković, *Nikola Pašić*, pp. 315–16.

34. Bataković, 'Nikola Pašić', pp. 150–51; Dragnich, *Serbia, Nikola Pašić and Yugoslavia*, pp. 3, 6, 7, 27–8; MacKenzie, *Apis*, pp. 26–8.

35. Bataković, 'Nikola Pašić', p. 151; Dragnich, *Serbia, Nikola Pašić and Yugoslavia*, p. 76; MacKenzie, *Apis*, p. 57; Constantin Dumba, *Memoirs of a Diplomat*, trans. Ian F. D. Morrow (London, 1933), pp. 141–3.

36. Vucinich, *Serbia between East and West*, p. 102.

37. For the text of *Načertanije*, see Dragoslav Stranjaković, 'Kako postalo Garašaninovo "Načertanije"', in *Spomenik Srpske Kraljevske Akademije*, VCI (1939), pp. 64–115, here p. 75, cited in Wolf Dietrich Behschnitt, *Nationalismus bei Serben und Kroaten 1830–1914* (Munich, 1980), p. 55.

38. Cited in Behschnitt, *Nationalismus*, p. 57; see also Horst Haselsteiner, 'Nationale Expansionsvorstellungen bei Serben und Kroaten im 19. Jahrhundert', *Österreichische Osthefte*, 39 (1997), pp. 245–54, here pp. 247–8.

39. For the text of *Srbi svi i svuda*, see Vuk Stefanović Karadžić, *Kovčežic za istoriju, jezik, običaje Srba sva tri zakona* [A Treasury of History, Language and Folkways of the Serbs of All Three Confessions] (Vienna, 1849), pp. 1– 27, here pp. 1, 7, 19, 22; on the puzzling refusal of Croats to adopt the name 'Serb', pp. 2–3; Haselsteiner, 'Nationale Expansionsvorstellungen', pp. 246–7.

40. Karadžić, *Kovčežic*, pp. 2–3; Haselsteiner, 'Nationale Expansionsvorstellungen', p. 248.

41. Stranjaković, 'Kako postalo Garašaninovo "Načertanije"', p. 84, cited in Behschnitt, *Nationalismus*, p. 56; Haselsteiner, 'Nationale Expansionsvorstellungen', p. 249.

42. David MacKenzie, 'Serbia as Piedmont and the Yugoslav Idea, 1804–1914', *East European Quarterly*, 28 (1994), pp. 153–82, here p. 160.

43. Leopold von Ranke, *The History of Servia and the Servian Revolution*, trans. Mrs Alexander Kerr (London, 1853), p. 52.

44. Tim Judah, *The Serbs. History, Myth and the Destruction of Yugoslavia* (2nd edn, New Haven, 2000), pp. 29–47.

45. Arthur J. Evans, *Through Bosnia and the Herzegovina on Foot during the Insurrection, August and September, 1875* (London, 1877), p. 139.

46. Barbara Jelavich, 'Serbia in 1897: A Report of Sir Charles Eliot', *Journal of Central European Affairs*, 18 (1958), pp. 183–9, here p. 185.

47. Dedijer, *Road to Sarajevo*, pp. 250–60.

48. The exact population numbers for 'Old Serbia' (comprising Kosovo, Metohija, Sandzak and Bujanovac) are unknown; see Behschnitt, *Nationalismus*, p. 39.

49. See Justin McCarthy, *Death and Exile. The Ethnic Cleansing of Ottoman Muslims, 1821–1922* (Princeton, 1996), pp. 161–4 and passim.

50. For an excellent overview (with map) see Andrew Rossos, *Macedonia and the Macedonians. A History* (Stanford, 2008), p. 4.

51. John Shea, 'Macedonia in History: Myths and Constants', *Österreichische Osthefte*, 40 (1998), pp. 147–68; Loring M. Danforth, 'Competing Claims to Macedonian Identity: The Macedonian Question and the Breakup of Yugoslavia', *Anthropology Today*, 9/4 (1993), pp. 3–10; Rossos, *Macedonia*, p. 5.

52. Jelavich, 'Serbia in 1897', p. 187.

53. Carnegie Foundation Endowment for International Peace, *Enquête dans les Balkans: rapport présenté aux directeurs de la Dotation par les membres de la commission d'enquête* (Paris, 1914), pp. 448, 449.

54. Cited in Djordje Stanković, *Nikola Pašić, saveznivi i stvaranje Jugoslavije* (Zajecar, 1995), p. 29; on Pašić's belief in the essential unity of Serbs, Croats and Slovenes, see also id., *Nikola Pašić. Prilozi za biografiju*, esp. the first chapter.

55. Cited in David MacKenzie, *Ilja Garašanin: Balkan Bismarck* (Boulder, 1985), p. 99.

56. Vucinich, *Serbia between East and West*, p. 122.

57. Kosztowits to Melvil de Lijnden, Belgrade, 25 August 1903, NA, 2.05.36, doc. 10, Rapporten aan en briefwisseling met het Ministerie van Buitenlandse Zaken.

58. MacKenzie, 'Officer Conspirators', pp. 128–9; Vucinich, *Serbia between East and West*, pp. 158–9.

59. Haselsteiner, 'Nationale Expansionsvorstellungen', p. 249.

60. Cited in Vucinich, *Serbia between East and West*, pp. 172, 174.

61. Bridge, *From Sadowa to Sarajevo*, pp. 122–3.

62. Kazimirović, *Nikola Pašić*, p. 607.

63. On the trade and armaments questions, see Jovan Jovanović, *Borba za Narodno Ujedinjenje, 1903–1908* (Belgrade, [1938]), pp. 108–16.

64. Kosztowits to W. M. de Weede, Belgrade, 24 May 1905, NA, 2.05.36, doc. 10, Rapporten aan en briefwisseling met het Ministerie van Buitenlandse Zaken.

65. M. B. Hayne, *The French Foreign Office and the Origins of the First World War 1898–1914* (Oxford, 1993), pp. 52, 150.

66. Herbert Feis, *Europe, the World's Banker 1870–1914. An Account of European Foreign Investment and the Connection of World Finance with Diplomacy before the War* (New Haven, 1930), p. 264.

67. Čedomir Antić, 'Crisis and Armament. Economic Relations between Great Britain and Serbia 1910–1912', *Balcanica*, 36 (2006), pp. 151–61.

68. J. B. Whitehead, 'General Report on the Kingdom of Servia for the Year 1906', in David Stevenson (ed.), *British Documents on Foreign Affairs. Reports and Papers from the Foreign Office Confidential Print, Part 1, From the Mid-Nineteenth Century to the First World War*, Series F, *Europe, 1848–1914*, vol. 16, *Montenegro, Romania, Servia 1885–1914*, doc. 43, pp. 205–20, here p. 210.

69. Michael Palairet, *The Balkan Economies c. 1800–1914. Evolution without Development* (Cambridge, 1997), p. 28.

70. Ibid., pp. 86–7.

71. Holm Sundhaussen, *Historische Statistik Serbiens. Mit europäischen Vergleichsdaten, 1834–1914* (Munich, 1989), pp. 26–8.

72. Palairet, *Balkan Economies*, p. 23.

73. Ibid., pp. 112, 113, 168; John R. Lampe, 'Varieties of Unsuccessful Industrialisation. The Balkan States Before 1914', *Journal of Economic History*, 35 (1975), pp. 56–85, here p. 59.

74. Palairet, *Balkan Economies*, p. 331.

75. Martin Mayer, 'Grundschulen in Serbien während des 19. Jahrhunderts. Elementarbildung in einer "Nachzüglergesellschaft"', in Norbert Reiter and Holm Sundhaussen (eds.), *Allgemeinbildung als Modernisierungsfaktor. Zur Geschichte der Elementarbildung in Südosteuropa von der Aufklärung bis zum Zweiten Weltkrieg* (Berlin, 1994), pp. 77–102, here pp. 87, 88, 91, 92.

76. Andrei Simić, *The Peasant Urbanites. A Study of Rural-Urban Mobility in Serbia* (New York, 1973), pp. 28–59, 148–51.

77. See Mira Crouch's reflections on interwar Belgrade in 'Jews, Other Jews and "Others": Some Marginal Considerations Concerning the Limits of Tolerance', in John Milfull (ed.), *Why Germany? National Socialist Anti-Semitism and the European Context* (Providence, 1993), pp. 121–38, here p. 125.

78. Whitehead, 'General Report . . . 1908', pp. 312–34, here p. 314.

79. Cited in Violeta Manojlović, 'Defense of National Interest and Sovereignty: Serbian Government Policy in the Bosnian Crisis, 1906–1909', MA thesis, Simon Fraser University, 1997, p. 58.

80. Cited in ibid., pp. 68–9.

81. Ibid., p. 3.

82. Paul Miliukov, *Political Memoirs 1905–1917*, trans. Carl Goldberg (Ann Arbor, 1967), p. 182.

83. Whitehead, 'General Report . . . 1908', pp. 314–15.

84. Jovan Cvijić, *The Annexation of Bosnia and Herzegovina and the Serb Problem* (London, 1909), p. 14; on his influence on Pašić, see Vladimir Stojancević, 'Pašićevi pogledi na resavanje pitanja Stare Srbije i Makedonije do 1912. godine', in Vasilije Krestic, *Nikola Pašić. Zivot i delo. Zbornik*

radova za Naucnog Skupa u Srpskoj Akademiji Nauka i Utmetnosti (Belgrade, 1997), pp. 284–301, here p. 285.

85. Prince Lazarovich-Hrebelianovich, *The Servian People. Their Past Glory and Destiny* (New York, 1910), p. 142.

86. Behschnitt, *Nationalismus*, p. 108.

87. MacKenzie, 'Officer Conspirators', pp. 130–31; id., *Apis*, p. 63.

88. Cited in Milorad Radusinović, 'Antanta i aneksiona kriza', *Istorija 20. Veka*, 9 (1991), pp. 7–22, here p. 9.

89. Aleksandar Pavlović, *Liudi i dogadaji, ideje i ideali* (Belgrade, 2002), pp. 30–38. Pavlović was a social-democrat politician and a member of Belgrade's intellectual elite – this edition of his diary, whose existence had been unknown to the public, was published by his daughters in 2002.

90. Cited in Manojlović, 'Defense of National Interest and Sovereignty', p. 78.

91. Radusinović, 'Antanta i aneksiona kriza', p. 18

92. Cited in Milan St. Protić, *Radikali u Srbjii: Ideje i Pokret* (Belgrade, 1990), p. 246.

93. Manojlović, 'Defense of National Interest and Sovereignty', p. 109.

94. Milovije Buha, *'Mlada Bosna' – Sarajevski atentat. Zavod za udžbenike i nastavna sredstva* (Sarajevo, 2006), p. 171.

95. Behschnitt, *Nationalismus*, p. 117.

96. For details on the foundation of Ujedinjenje ili smrt!, see MacKenzie, 'Serbia as Piedmont', pp. 153–82; id., *Apis*, pp. 64–8; Dragoslav Ljubibratic, *Mlada Bosna i Sarajevski atentat* (Sarajevo, 1964), pp. 35–7; Behschnitt, *Nationalismus*, pp. 115–17.

97. Buha, *'Mlada Bosna'*, p. 170.

98. *Pijemont*, 12 November 1911, cited in Bataković, 'Nikola Pašić', pp. 143–69, here p. 158; the link with proto-fascism is also made in Vladimir Dedijer and Branko Pavičević, 'Dokazi za jednu tezu', *Novi Misao* (Belgrade), June 1953.

99. Cited in Joachim Remak, *Sarajevo. The Story of a Political Murder* (London, 1959), p. 46; on Jovanović's authorship and involvement, see David MacKenzie, 'Ljuba Jovanović-Čupa and the Search for Yugoslav Unity', *International History Review*, 1/1 (1979), pp. 36–54.

100. Dedijer, *Road to Sarajevo*, p. 379.

101. Remak, *Sarajevo*, p. 49.

102. Cited in MacKenzie, *Apis*, p. 71.

103. Vojislav Vučković, *Unutrašnje krize Srbije i Prvi Svetski Rat* (Belgrade, 1966), p. 179.

104. Bataković, 'Nikola Pašić', p. 160.

105. MacKenzie, *Apis*, p. 73.

106. Ugron to Aehrenthal, Belgrade, 12 November 1911, HHStA Vienna, PA Serbien XIX 62, no. 94a.

107. Buha, *'Mlada Bosna'*, pp. 143, 175.

108. See, for example, *Politika*, Belgrade, 18 August 1910, which hails Žerajić as a 'noble scion of [his] race' whose name 'is spoken today among the people as something sacred'. The article appeared to mark the birthday of King Petar Karadjordjević; it is cited in the Austrian 'Red Book', but sourced here online at *http://209.85.135.104/search?q=cache:0YxuZRIgw9YJ:www .geocities.com/veldes1/varesanin.html+%22bogdan+zerajic%22=en&ct=cl nk&cd=4&gl=uk&ie=UTF-8.*

109. Remak, *Sarajevo*, pp. 36–7.

110. Dedijer, *Road to Sarajevo*, p. 236; Jean-Jacques Becker, 'L'ombre du nationalisme serbe', *Vingtième Siècle*, 69 (2001), pp. 7–29, here p. 13.

111. Paget to Grey, Belgrade, 6 June 1913, TNA, FO 371/1748.

112. Crackanthorpe to Grey, Belgrade, 7 September 1913, ibid., fos. 74–6.

113. Carnegie Foundation, *Enquête dans les Balkans*, p. 144; Katrin Boeckh, *Von den Balkankriegen zum Ersten Weltkrieg. Kleinstaatenpolitik und ethnische Selbstbestimmung auf dem Balkan* (Munich, 1996), pp. 125–6.

114. Boeckh, *Von den Balkankriegen*, p. 164.

115. Peckham to Crackanthorpe, Üsküb, 23 October 1913; Crackanthorpe to Grey, Belgrade, 17 November, TNA, FO 371/1748, fos. 147–8, 158.

116. Greig to Crackanthorpe, Monastir, 25 November 1913, ibid., fo. 309.

117. Greig to Crackanthorpe, Monastir, 30 November 1913, ibid., fos. 341–50, here fo. 341.

118. Greig to Crackanthorpe, Monastir, 16 December 1913, ibid., fo. 364.

119. Greig to Crackanthorpe, Monastir, 24 December 1913, TNA, FO 371/2098, fos. 11–15, here fos. 13–14.

120. Marginal note by 'RGV' (Robert Gilbert Vansittart) on Foreign Office Circular, 9 December 1913, TNA, FO 371/1748, fo. 327.

121. See Pašić's comments, dated 3 April 1914, appended to Djordjević to Foreign Ministry Belgrade, Constantinople, 1 April 1914, in *DSP* (7 vols., Belgrade, 1980), vol. 7/1, doc. 444, p. 586.

122. Assistance was refused on the grounds that the Russian member of the team, Paul Miliukov, was an 'enemy of Serbia' because he had spoken before the Duma in support of autonomy for Macedonia; see Boeckh, *Von den Balkankriegen*, p. 172.

123. Remak, *Sarajevo*, p. 57.

124. Buha, 'Mlada Bosna', pp. 173–4.

125. On the radicalizing effect of the wars on the Serbian army: Descos to Doumergue, Belgrade, 7 May 1914, *DDF*, 3rd series, vol. 10, doc. 207, pp. 333–5.

126. Whether Apis intended to carry out such a coup is unclear and still disputed, see MacKenzie, *Apis*, pp. 119–20; on the links between the Black Hand and the parliamentary opposition, see Vučković, *Unutrašnje krize*, p. 187.

127. Dedijer, *Road to Sarajevo*, p. 389.

128. Apis claimed during his trial at Salonika in 1917 that he had entrusted the agent Rade Malobabić with organizing all the details of the assassination.

Whether the whole of Ujedinjenje ili smrt! was involved, or just a coterie of officers and agents around Apis is controversial, see David MacKenzie, *The 'Black Hand' on Trial: Salonika, 1917* (Boulder, 1995), pp. 45, 261–2; Fritz Würthle, *Die Sarajewoer Gerichtsakten* (Vienna, 1975), Miloš Bogičević, *Le Procès de Salonique, Juin 1917* (Paris, 1927), pp. 36, 63; MacKenzie, *Apis*, pp. 258–9.

129. Bogičević, *Procès de Salonique*, pp. 78–80, 127.

130. Luigi Albertini, *The Origins of the War of 1914*, trans. Isabella M. Massey (3 vols., Oxford, 1953), vol. 2, p. 73; MacKenzie, *Apis*, p. 128.

131. Session of 12 October 1914, transcribed in Albert Mousset, *Un drame historique: l'attentat de Sarajevo* (Paris, 1930), p. 131.

132. Albertini, *Origins*, vol. 2, pp. 86–8.

133. Köhler, *Prozess*, p. 44.

134. Remak, *Sarajevo*, p. 63.

135. Köhler, *Prozess*, p. 4.

136. Ibid., p. 23.

137. On the vexed question of Bosnia's economic condition relative to Serbia, see Evelyn Kolm, *Die Ambitionen Österreich-Ungarns im Zeitalter des Hochimperialismus* (Frankfurt am Main, 2001), pp. 235–40; Robert J. Donia, *Islam under the Double Eagle. The Muslims of Bosnia and Herzegovina, 1878–1914* (New York, 1981), p. 8; Peter F. Sugar, *The Industrialization of Bosnia-Herzegovina, 1878–1918* (Seattle, 1963); Palairet, *Balkan Economies*, pp. 171, 231, 369; Robert A. Kann, 'Trends towards Colonialism in the Habsburg Empire, 1878–1918: The Case of Bosnia-Hercegovina 1878–1918', in D. K. Rowney and G. E. Orchard (eds.), *Russian and Slavic History* (Columbus, 1977), pp. 164–80; Kurt Wessely, 'Die wirtschaftliche Entwicklung von Bosnien-Herzegowina', in Wandruszka and Urbanitsch (eds.), *Die Habsburgermonarchie*, vol. 1, pp. 528–66.

138. *The Mountain Wreath* is not strictly speaking about Miloš Obilić, but his name, which occurs twenty times in the course of the text, is repeatedly invoked as the symbol of all that is best in the Serbian tradition of courageous and sacrificial struggle. For a full text in English with a useful critical apparatus, see *http://www.rastko.rs/knjizevnost/njegos/njegos-mountain_wreath.html*.

139. Testimony of Gavril Princip in Professor Pharos (pseud.), *Der Prozess gegen die Attentäter von Sarajewo* (Berlin, 1918), p. 40.

140. Köhler, *Prozess*, p. 41.

141. Ibid., pp. 30, 53.

142. Ibid., p. 5.

143. Ibid., p. 6.

144. Ibid., p. 6.

145. Ibid., p. 9.

146. Ibid., p. 24.

147. Ibid., pp. 137, 147.
148. Ibid., pp. 145–6, 139.
149. On Čubrilović's fights with his teachers, see Zdravko Antonić, 'Svedočenje Vase Čubrilovića o sarajevskom atentatu i svom tamnovanju 1914–1918', *Zbornik Matice srpske za istoriju*, 46 (1992), pp. 163–80, here pp. 165, 167.
150. Ljuba Jovanović, 'Nach dem Veitstage des Jahres 1914', *Die Kriegsschuldfrage. Berliner Monatshefte für Internationale Aufklärung*, 3/1 (1925), pp. 68–82, here pp. 68–9; on the significance of this document, see Albertini, *Origins*, vol. 2, p. 90; but this version of events is not universally accepted: see, for example, Buha, '*Mlada Bosna*', p. 343, who argues (from the lack of any direct proof) that Pašić knew of the boys' crossing, but was ignorant of the nature of their mission; see also Bataković, 'Nikola Pašić', p. 162; Stanković, *Nikola Pašić*, esp. p. 262.
151. The evidence for Pašić's knowledge before the fact is discussed in Albertini, *Origins*, vol. 2, pp. 90–97 – Albertini focuses on the testimony from L. Jovanović, reinforced by the supposition that Ciganović was Pašić's agent; Albertini's collaborator Luciano Magrini added two further testimonies from Pašić associates, recorded during the war, see id., *Il dramma di Seraievo. Origini i responsabilità della guerra europea* (Milan, 1929), pp. 106–8, 114–16. The information available at the time is judiciously appraised in Sidney Bradshaw Fay, *The Origins of the First World War* (2 vols., New York, 1929), vol. 2, pp. 140–46; Hans Uebersberger, *Österreich zwischen Russland und Serbien. Zur südslawischen Frage und der Entstehung des Ersten Weltkrieges* (Cologne, Graz, 1958), pp. 264–5 supplements this evidence with a scribbled note in Pašić's hand referring to 'schoolboys', 'bombs' and 'revolvers' found among the papers of the Serbian Foreign Ministry. Vladimir Dedijer's extremely detailed account of the background to the plot, *Road to Sarajevo*, concedes that Pašić probably knew in advance of the plot, but proposes that he did so only because he was able to intuit its existence from the incomplete information he had to hand. The more recent accounts, including Friedrich Würthle's very detailed *Die Spur führt nach Belgrad* (Vienna, 1975), offer a range of interpretations, but add no new evidence to this corpus.
152. The evidence for Ciganović's role as informant is indirect but strong, see Bogičević, *Procès de Salonique*, pp. 32, 131–2; Fay, *Origins*, vol. 2, pp. 146–8; and Albertini, *Origins*, vol. 2, p. 98. Pašić's nephew was also a member of Ujedinjenje ili smrt!
153. See Chief of Podrinje District to Protić, Sabac, 4 June 1914; Protić to Pašić (with a summary of reports from the border), Belgrade, 15 June 1914; Chief of Podrinje District to Commander 5th Border Guards at Loznice, Sabac, 16 June 1914; Commander of Drina Divisional Area, Valevo, to Minister of War, 17 June 1914, *DSP* vol. 7, docs. 155, 206, 210, 212, pp. 290, 337–9, 344–5, 347.

154. Minister of the Interior to Chief of Podrinje District in Sabac, 10 June 1914, ibid., reply from Protić appended to doc. 155, p. 290.
155. Chief of Podrinje District to Protić, Sabac, 'Top Secret', 14 June 1914, ibid., doc. 198, p. 331.
156. Captain 4th Border Guards to Commander 5th Border Area, 19 June 1914; Commander 5th Border Area to Chief of General Staff, same date, ibid., both appended to doc. 209, p. 343; see also Dedijer, *Road to Sarajevo*, pp. 390–91; Buha, *'Mlada Bosna'*, p. 178.
157. The full Serbian text of Apis's court deposition can be found in Milan Z. Živanović, *Solunski process hiljadu devetsto sedamnaeste. Prilog zaproucavanje politicke istorije Srbije od 1903. do 1918. god.* (Belgrade, 1955), pp. 556–8; see also MacKenzie, *'Black Hand' on Trial*, p. 46.
158. Royal General Staff Reporting Department (Apis) to General Staff Operational Department, 21 June 1914, in *DSP*, vol. 7/2, doc. 230, pp. 364–5.
159. Pašić to Stepanović, Belgrade, 24 June 1914, in ibid., doc. 254, pp. 391–2.
160. Albertini, *Origins*, vol. 2, p. 99; Stanković, *Nikola Pašić, saveznivi i stvaranje Jugoslavije*, p. 40.
161. See 'Die Warnungen des serbischen Gesandten', *Neue Freie Presse*, 3 July 1914, p. 4.
162. 'Note de M. Abel Ferry', 1 July 1914, *DDF*, series 3, vol. 10, doc. 466, pp. 670–71.
163. Testimony of Lešanin, reported in Magrini, *Il dramma di Seraievo*, p. 115.
164. Letter of Jovanović to *Neues Wiener Tageblatt*, 177, 28 June 1924, cited in Albertini, *Origins*, vol. 2, p. 105; Bogičević, *Procès de Salonique*, pp. 121–5; Magrini, *Il dramma di Seraievo*, pp. 115–16; Fay, *Origins*, vol. 2, pp. 152–66.
165. Remak, *Sarajevo*, p. 75.
166. Ibid., p. 74; Albertini, *Origins*, vol. 2, p. 102.
167. Vučković, *Unutrašnje krize*, p. 192.
168. Stanković, *Nikola Pašić. Prilozi za biografiju*, p. 264.
169. Radusinović, 'Antanta i aneksiona kriza', p. 18.
170. Stanković, *Nikola Pašić, saveznivi i stvaranje Jugoslavije*, pp. 30–32; Dragnich, *Serbia, Nikola Pašić and Yugoslavia*, p. 106.
171. Stanković, *Nikola Pašić, saveznivi i stvaranje Jugoslavije*, p. 36.
172. Ibid., p. 41.
173. On Pašić's understanding of Russian Balkan policy, see A. Šemjakin, 'Rusofilstvo Nikole Pasica', p. 28.
174. Cited in Behschnitt, *Nationalismus*, p. 128.
175. Reports from the Serbian military attaché in St Petersburg are summarized in Protić to Pašić, Belgrade, 12 June 1914; there were further excited reports of Russian military preparedness in the Serbian embassy in Belgrade (Spalajković) to Minister of Foreign Affairs, St Petersburg, 13 June 1914, *DSP*, vol. 7, docs. 185, 189, pp. 317, 322.
176. Bogičević, *Procès de Salonique*, p. iii.

CHAPTER 2

1. Norman Stone, 'Constitutional Crises in Hungary, 1903–1906', *Slavonic and East European Review*, 45 (1967), pp. 163–82; Peter F. Sugar, 'An Underrated Event: The Hungarian Constitutional Crisis of 1905–6', *East European Quarterly* (Boulder), 15/3 (1981) pp. 281–306.

2. A. Murad, *Franz Joseph and His Empire* (New York, 1978), p. 176; Andrew C. Janos, 'The Decline of Oligarchy: Bureaucratic and Mass Politics in the Age of Dualism (1867–1918)', in Andrew C. Janos and William B. Slottman (eds.), *Revolution in Perspective: Essays on the Hungarian Soviet Republic of 1919* (Berkeley, 1971), pp. 1–60, here pp. 23–4.

3. Cited in Alan Sked, *The Decline and Fall of the Habsburg Empire 1815–1918* (New York, 1991), p. 190.

4. Samuel R. Williamson, *Austria-Hungary and the Origins of the First World War* (Houndmills, 1991), p. 24; figures for 1880 in Sked, *Decline and Fall*, pp. 278–9.

5. Sked, *Decline and Fall*, pp. 210–11; Janos, 'The Decline of Oligarchy', pp. 50–53.

6. Brigitte Hamann, *Hitlers Wien. Lehrjahre eines Diktators* (Munich, 1996), pp. 170–74.

7. Steven Beller, *Francis Joseph* (London, 1996), p. 173; Arthur J. May, *The Hapsburg Monarchy, 1867–1914* (Cambridge, MA, 1951), p. 440; C. A. Macartney, *The House of Austria. The Later Phase, 1790–1918* (Edinburgh, 1978), p. 240; R. A. Kann, *A History of the Habsburg Empire, 1526–1918* (Berkeley, 1977), pp. 452–61; Robin Okey, *The Habsburg Monarchy, c. 1765–1918. From Enlightenment to Eclipse* (London, 2001), pp. 356–60.

8. For an interesting reflection on this problem, see Arthur J. May, 'R. W. Seton-Watson and British Anti-Hapsburg Sentiment', *American Slavic and East European Review*, vol. 20, no. 1 (Feb 1961), pp. 40–54.

9. For an excellent brief analysis, see Lothar Höbelt, 'Parliamentary Politics in a Multinational Setting: Late Imperial Austria', CAS Working Papers in Austrian Studies Series, Working Paper 92–6; his arguments are set out in more detail in id., 'Parteien und Fraktionen im Cisleithanischen Reichsrat', in Adam Wandruszka and Peter Urbanitsch (eds.), *Die Habsburgermonarchie 1848–1918* (10 vols., Vienna, 1973–2006), vol. 7/1, pp. 895–1006.

10. László Katus, 'The Common Market of the Austro-Hungarian Monarchy', in András Gerö (ed.), *The Austro-Hungarian Monarchy Revisited*, trans. Thomas J. and Helen D. DeKornfeld (New York, 2009), pp. 21–49, here p. 41.

11. István Deák, 'The Fall of Austria-Hungary: Peace, Stability, and Legitimacy', in Geir Lundestad (ed.), *The Fall of Great Powers* (Oxford, 1994), pp. 81–102, here pp. 86–7.

12. György Köver, 'The Economic Achievements of the Austro-Hungarian

Monarchy. Scales and Speed', in Gerö (ed.), *Austro-Hungarian Monarchy*, pp. 51–83, here p. 79; Nachum T. Gross, 'The Industrial Revolution in the Habsburg Monarchy 1750–1914', in Carlo C. Cipolla (ed.), *The Emergence of Industrial Societies* (6 vols., New York, 1976), vol. 4/1, pp. 228–78; David F. Good, ' "Stagnation" and "Take-Off" in Austria, 1873–1913', *Economic History Review*, 27/1 (1974), pp. 72–88 argues that while there was no Austrian 'take-off', strictly speaking, growth in the Austrian part of the monarchy remained robust throughout the pre-war period; John Komlos, 'Economic Growth and Industrialisation in Hungary 1830–1913', *Journal of European Economic History*, 1 (1981), pp. 5–46; id., *The Habsburg Monarchy as a Customs Union. Economic Development in Austria-Hungary in the Nineteenth Century* (Princeton, 1983), esp. pp. 214–20; for an account that stresses the vitality of Austrian (as opposed to Hungarian), per capita GDP growth, see Max Stephan Schulze, 'Patterns of Growth and Stagnation in the Late Nineteenth-Century Habsburg Economy', *European Review of Economic History*, 4 (2000), pp. 311–40.

13. Henry Wickham Steed, *The Hapsburg Monarchy* (London, 1919), p. 77.

14. John Leslie, 'The Antecedents of Austria-Hungary's War Aims. Policies and Policy-makers in Vienna and Budapest before and during 1914', in Elisabeth Springer and Leopold Kammerhold (eds.), *Archiv und Forschung. Das Haus-, Hof- und Staatsarchiv in seiner Bedeutung für die Geschichte Österreichs und Europas* (Vienna, 1993), pp. 307–94, here p. 354.

15. Kann, *History*, p. 448; May, *Hapsburg Monarchy*, pp. 442–3; Sked, *Decline and Fall*, p. 264; Sazonov to Nicholas II, 20 January 1914, GARF, Fond 543, op. 1, del. 675.

16. Okey, *Habsburg Monarchy*, pp. 303, 305.

17. Wolfgang Pav, 'Die dalmatinischen Abgeordneten im österreichischen Reichsrat nach der Wahlrechtsreform von 1907', MA thesis, University of Vienna, 2007, p. 144, viewed on line at *http://othes.univie.ac.at/342/1/11 -29-2007_0202290.pdf*.

18. On this tendency, see John Deak, 'The Incomplete State in an Age of Total War. Or: The Habsburg Monarchy and the First World War as a Historiographical Problem', unpublished typescript, University of Notre Dame, 2011; John Deak presented a version of this paper at the Cambridge Modern European History Seminar in 2011; I am extremely grateful to him for letting me see a pre-publication version of the full text.

19. Maureen Healy, *Vienna and the Fall of the Habsburg Empire. Total War and Everyday Life in World War I* (Cambridge, 2004), p. 24; John W. Boyer, 'Some Reflections on the Problem of Austria, Germany and Mitteleuropa', *Central European History*, 22 (1989), pp. 301–15, here p. 311.

20. On the growth of the state in these years, see Deak, 'The Incomplete State in an Age of Total War'.

21. Gary B. Cohen, 'Neither Absolutism nor Anarchy: New Narratives on

Society and Government in Late Imperial Austria', *Austrian History Yearbook*, 29/1, (1998), pp. 37–61, here p. 44.

22. Robert Musil, *Der Mann ohne Eigenschaften* (Hamburg, 1978), pp. 32–3.

23. Barbara Jelavich, *History of the Balkans* (2 vols., Cambridge, 1983), vol. 2, p. 68.

24. F. Palacky to the Frankfurt Parliament's 'Committee of Fifty', 11 April 1848, in Hans Kohn, *Pan-Slavism. Its History and Ideology* (Notre Dame, 1953), pp. 65–9.

25. Cited in May, *Hapsburg Monarchy*, p. 199.

26. Lawrence Cole, 'Military Veterans and Popular Patriotism in Imperial Austria, 1870–1914', in id. and Daniel Unowsky (eds.), *The Limits of Loyalty. Imperial Symbolism, Popular Allegiances and State Patriotism in the Late Habsburg Monarchy* (New York, Oxford, 2007), pp. 36–61, here p. 55.

27. On Franz Joseph as an 'unpersonality' and a 'demon of mediocrity', see Karl Kraus, *The Last Days of Mankind. A Tragedy in Five Parts*, trans. Alexander Gode and Sue Ellen Wright, ed. F. Ungar (New York, 1974), Act IV, Scene 29, p. 154; see also Hugh LeCaine Agnew, 'The Flyspecks on Palivec's Portrait. Franz Joseph, the Symbols of Monarchy and Czech Popular Loyalty', in Cole and Unowsky (eds.), *Limits of Loyalty*, pp. 86–112, here p. 107.

28. Lothar Höbelt, *Franz Joseph I. Der Kaiser und sein Reich. Eine politische Geschichte* (Vienna, 2009); on the Emperor's role in the making of laws and constitutions: Lászlo Péter, 'Die Verfassungsentwicklung in Ungarn', in Wandruszka and Urbanitsch (eds.), *Die Habsburgermonarchie*, vol. 7/1, pp. 239–540, esp. pp. 403–14.

29. Beller, *Francis Joseph*, p. 173.

30. Joseph Maria Baernreither, *Fragmente eines politischen Tagebuches. Die südslawische Frage und Österreich-Ungarn vor dem Weltkrieg*, ed. Joseph Redlich (Berlin, 1928), p. 210.

31. On loyalty to the Emperor, see Stephen Fischer-Galati, 'Nationalism and Kaisertreue', *Slavic Review*, 22 (1963), pp. 31–6; Robert A. Kann, 'The Dynasty and the Imperial Idea', *Austrian History Yearbook*, 3/1 (1967), pp. 11–31; Lawrence Cole and Daniel Unowsky, 'Introduction. Imperial Loyalty and Popular Allegiances in the Late Habsburg Monarchy', in id. (eds.), *Limits of Loyalty*, pp. 1–10; in the same volume, see also the following chapters: Christiane Wolf, 'Representing Constitutional Monarchy in Late Nineteenth-Century and Early Twentieth-Century Britain, Germany and Austria', pp. 199–222, esp. p. 214; Alice Freifeld, 'Empress Elisabeth as Hungarian Queen: The Uses of Celebrity Monarchy', pp. 138–61.

32. Joseph Roth, *The Radetzky March*, trans. Michael Hofmann (London, 2003), p. 75.

33. F. R. Bridge, *From Sadowa to Sarajevo. The Foreign Policy of Austria-Hungary, 1866–1914* (London, 1972), p. 71.

34. Noel Malcolm, *Bosnia. A Short History* (London, 1994), p. 140.

35. Michael Palairet, *The Balkan Economies c. 1800–1914. Evolution without Development* (Cambridge, 1997), pp. 171, 369; Peter F. Sugar, *The Industrialization of Bosnia-Herzegovina, 1878–1918* (Seattle, 1963); a less enthusiastic appraisal emphasizing the instrumental, self-interested character of Austrian investment is Kurt Wessely, 'Die wirtschaftliche Entwicklung von Bosnien-Herzegovina', in Wandruszka and Urbanitsch (eds.), *Die Habsburgermonarchie*, vol. 1, pp. 528–66.

36. Robert J. Donia, *Islam under the Double Eagle. The Muslims of Bosnia and Herzegovina 1878–1914* (New York, 1981), p. 8; Robert A. Kann, 'Trends towards Colonialism in the Habsburg Empire, 1878–1914: The Case of Bosnia-Hercegovina 1878–1918', in D. K. Rowney and G. E. Orchard (eds.), *Russian and Slavic History* (Columbus, 1977), pp. 164–80.

37. Martin Mayer, 'Grundschulen in Serbien während des 19. Jahrhunderts. Elementarbildung in einer "Nachzüglergesellschaft"', in Norbert Reiter and Holm Sundhaussen (eds.), *Allgemeinbildung als Modernisierungsfaktor. Zur Geschichte, der Elementarbildung in Südosteuropa von der Aufklärung bis zum Zweiten Weltkrieg* (Berlin, 1994), p. 93.

38. Malcolm, *Bosnia*, p. 144.

39. Vladimir Dedijer, *The Road to Sarajevo* (London, 1967), p. 278.

40. Comment recorded by former Austrian trade minister Joseph Maria Baernreither, *Der Verfall des Habsburgerreiches und die Deutschen. Fragmente eines politischen Tagebuches 1897–1917*, ed. Oskar Mitis (Vienna, 1939), pp. 141–2.

41. William Eleroy Curtis, *The Turk and His Lost Provinces: Greece, Bulgaria, Servia, Bosnia* (Chicago and London, 1903), p. 275; President Roosevelt may well have been reading Curtis, who also makes the link to the Philippines.

42. Edvard Beneš, *Le Problème Autrichien et la Question Tchèque* (Paris, 1908), p. 307, cited in Joachim Remak, 'The Ausgleich and After – How Doomed the Habsburg Empire?' in Ludovik Holotik and Anton Vantuch (eds.), *Der Österreich-Ungarische Ausgleich 1867* (Bratislava, 1971), pp. 971–88, here p. 985.

43. Wickham Steed, letter to the editor, *TLS*, 24 September 1954; id., *The Hapsburg Monarchy*, p. xiii.

44. Tomáš G. Masaryk, *The Making of a State. Memories and Observations, 1914–1918* (London, 1927 [orig. Czech and German editions appeared in 1925]), p. 8. For a discussion of Steed's view and of this passage, see Deak, 'The Incomplete State in an Age of Total War'.

45. Oszkár Jászi, *The Dissolution of the Habsburg Monarchy* (Chicago, 1929), pp. 23, 451.

46. Oszkár Jászi, 'Danubia: Old and New', *Proceedings of the American Philosophical Society*, 93/1 (1949), pp. 1–31, here p. 2.

47. Mihály Babits, *Keresztükasul életemen* (Budapest, 1939), cited in Mihály Szegedy-Maszák, 'The Re-evaluated Past. The Memory of the Dual Monarchy in Hungarian Literature', in Gerö (ed.), *Austro-Hungarian Monarchy*, pp. 192–216, here p. 196.

48. For a useful compilation of country-by-country studies, see Marian Kent (ed.), *The Great Powers and the End of the Ottoman Empire* (London, 1984).

49. Williamson, *Austria-Hungary*, pp. 59–61; Bridge, *From Sadowa to Sarajevo*, pp. 211–309.

50. The text of the Three Emperors' League treaty (1881 version) and separate protocol may be consulted in Bridge, *From Sadowa to Sarajevo*, pp. 399–402.

51. Cited in ibid., p. 141. But see also Ernst R. Rutkowski, 'Gustav Graf Kálnoky. Eine biographische Skizze', *Mitteilungen des Österreichischen Staatsarchivs*, 14 (1961), pp. 330–43.

52. Kálnoky memorandum to Taaffe, September 1885, cited in Bridge, *From Sadowa to Sarajevo*, p. 149.

53. Edmund Glaise von Horstenau, *Franz Josephs Weggefährte: das Leben des Generalstabschefs, Grafen Beck nach seinen Aufzeichnungen und hinterlassenen Dokumenten* (Zurich, Vienna, 1930), p. 391.

54. Bridge, *From Sadowa to Sarajevo*, p. 263.

55. Kosztowits to Tets van Goudriaan, Belgrade, 22 Janury 1906, NA, 2.05.36, doc. 10, Rapporten aan en briefwisseling met het Ministerie van Buitenlandse Zaken.

56. For an illuminating discussion of these agreements, based on the memoirs and diaries of the Bulgarian diplomat Christophor Khesapchiev, see Kiril Valtchev Merjanski, 'The Secret Serbian-Bulgarian Treaty of Alliance of 1904 and the Russian Policy in the Balkans before the Bosnian Crisis', MA thesis, Wright State University, 2007, pp. 30–31, 38–9, 41–2, 44, 50–51, 53–78. See also Constantin Dumba, *Memoirs of a Diplomat*, trans. Ian F. D. Morrow (London, 1933), pp. 137–9; Miloš Bogičević, *Die auswärtige Politik Serbiens 1903–1914* (3 vols., Berlin, 1931), vol. 3, p. 29.

57. For a classic discussion of this problem, see Solomon Wank, 'Foreign Policy and the Nationality Problem in Austria-Hungary, 1867–1914', *Austrian History Yearbook*, 3 (1967), pp. 37–56.

58. Pomiankowski to Beck, Belgrade, 17 February 1906, cited in Günther Kronenbitter, *'Krieg im Frieden'. Die Führung der k.u.k. Armee und die Grossmachtpolitik Österreich-Ungarns 1906–1914* (Munich, 2003), p. 327.

59. 'Konzept der Instruktion für Forgách anlässlich seines Amtsantrittes in Belgrad', Vienna, 6 July 1907, in Solomon Wank (ed.), *Aus dem Nachlass Aehrenthal. Briefe und Dokumente zur österreichisch-ungarischen Innen- und Aussenpolitik 1885–1912* (2 vols., Graz, 1994), vol. 2, doc. 377, pp. 517–20, here p. 518.

60. Solomon Wank, 'Aehrenthal's Programme for the Constitutional Trans-formation of the Habsburg Monarchy: Three Secret Memoires', *Slavonic and East European Review*, 42 (1963), pp. 513–36, here p. 515.

61. On the background to the annexation, see Bernadotte E. Schmitt, *The Annexation of Bosnia 1908–1909* (Cambridge, 1937), pp. 1–18.

62. Okey, *Habsburg Monarchy*, p. 363.

63. Holger Afflerbach, *Der Dreibund. Europäische Grossmacht- und Allianz-politik vor dem Ersten Weltkrieg* (Vienna, 2002), p. 629.

64. N. Shebeko, *Souvenirs. Essai historique sur les origines de la guerre de 1914* (Paris, 1936), p. 83.

65. Harold Nicolson, *Die Verschwörung der Diplomaten. Aus Sir Arthur Nicol-sons Leben 1849–1928* (Frankfurt am Main, 1930), pp. 301–2; Williamson, *Austria-Hungary*, pp. 68–9; Schmitt, *The Annexation of Bosnia*, pp. 49–60; a contemporary account confirming this view: Baron M. de Taube, *La politique russe d'avant-guerre et la fin de l'empire des Tsars* (Paris, 1928), pp. 186–7.

66. Theodor von Sosnosky, *Die Balkanpolitik Österreich-Ungarns seit 1866* (Berlin, 1913), pp. 170–72; Schmitt, *Annexation of Bosnia*, pp. 43–4; Affler-bach, *Dreibund*, pp. 750–54, 788–814; R. J. B. Bosworth, *Italy, the Least of the Great Powers: Italian Foreign Policy before the First World War* (Cam-bridge, 1979), pp. 87–8, 223–4, 245.

67. W. M. Carlgren, *Iswolsky und Aehrenthal vor der bosnischen Annexion-skrise. Russische und österreichisch-ungarische Balkanpolitik 1906–1908* (Uppsala, 1955), pp. 86–7.

68. David Stevenson, *Armaments and the Coming of War. Europe 1904–1915* (Oxford, 1996), pp. 162–3.

69. Paul Miliukov, *Political Memoirs 1905–1917*, trans. Carl Goldberg (Ann Arbor, 1967), p. 242; V. N. Strandmann, *Balkanske Uspomene*, trans. from the Russian into Serbian by Jovan Kachaki (Belgrade, 2009), p. 238.

70. G. Schödl, *Kroatische Nationalpolitik und 'Jugoslavenstvo'. Studien zur nationalen Integration und regionaler Politik in Kroatien-Dalmatien am Beginn des 20. Jahrhunderts* (Munich, 1990), p. 289.

71. Tomáš G. Masaryk, *Der Agramer Hochverratsprozess und die Annexion von Bosnien und Herzegowina* (Vienna, 1909), a pamphlet containing most of the key speeches by Masaryk on the Agram trial scandal; see also von Sosnosky, *Die Balkanpolitik*, pp. 221–4; Baernreither, *Fragmente. Die süds-lawische Frage*, pp. 133–45.

72. Forgách to Aehrenthal, Belgrade, 9 November 1910, ÖUAP, vol. 3, doc. 2296, p. 40; Forgách to Aehrenthal, Belgrade, 13 November 1910, ibid., doc. 2309, p. 49; Forgách to Aehrenthal, Belgrade, 15 November 1910, ibid., doc. 2316, pp. 56–8; Forgách to Aehrenthal, Belgrade, 22 November 1910, ibid., doc. 2323, pp. 64–6.

73. Forgách to Aehrenthal, Belgrade, 26 November 1910, ibid., doc. 2329, pp. 72–4.

74. Forgách to Macchio, Belgrade, 17 January 1911, ibid., doc. 2413, p. 146.
75. Forgách to Aehrenthal, Belgrade, 12 December 1910, ibid., doc. 2369, pp. 109–10.
76. Forgách to Aehrenthal, Belgrade, 1 April 1911, ibid., doc. 2490, p. 219.
77. See Miroslav Spalajković, *La Bosnie et l'Herzégovine. Étude d'histoire diplomatique et de droit international* (Paris, 1897), esp. pp. 256–79, 280–316.
78. Notes on a conversation with Descos by Jean Doulcet, St Petersburg, 8 December 1913, AMAE Papiers Jean Doulcet, vol. 23, Saint Petersbourg IV, Notes personnelles, 1912–1917.
79. Leslie, 'Antecedents', p. 341; on the hostility between Forgách and Spalajković, see also Friedrich Würthle, *Die Spur führt nach Belgrad* (Vienna, 1975), pp. 186–92.
80. Tschirschky to Bethmann Hollweg, Vienna, 13 February 1910, PA-AA, R 10984.
81. Notes on a conversation with André Panafieu, St Petersburg, 11 December 1912, AMAE Papiers Jean Doulcet, vol. 23.
82. Strandmann, *Balkanske Uspomene*, p. 249.
83. Malenković to Pašić, Budapest, 12 July 1914, AS, MID – PO, 416, fo. 162.
84. Andrew Lamb, 'Léhar's *Die Lustige Witwe* – Theatrical Fantasy or Political Reality?', article in programme of *The Merry Widow*, Royal Opera, London, 1997; revised and accessible online at *http://www.josef-weinberger.com/mw/politics.html*.
85. Egon Erwin Kisch, *Mein Leben für die Zeitung 1906–1913. Journalistische Texte 1* (Berlin and Weimar, 1983), pp. 140–42.
86. Polivanov to Neratov, St Petersburg, 14 August 1911, *IBZI*, series 3, vol. 1, part 1, doc. 318, pp. 383–4.
87. Kronenbitter, *Grossmachtpolitik Österreich-Ungarns*, p. 321; Christopher Seton Watson, *Italy from Liberalism to Fascism, 1870–1925* (London, 1967), pp. 333–8.
88. Seton Watson, *Italy*, p. 344.
89. The text of Racconigi (in French and Russian) is in Narodnii komissariat po inostrannym delam (ed.), *Materialy po istorii franko-russkikh otnoshenii za 1910–1914 g.g. Sbornik sekretnykh diplomaticheskikh dokumentov byvshego Imperatorskogo rossiiskogo ministerstva inostrannykh del* (Moscow, 1922), p. 298; on the subsequent agreement between Austria-Hungary and Italy see Guido Donnino, *L'Accordo Italo-Russo di Racconigi* (Milan, 1983), pp. 273–9.
90. Čedomir Antić, 'Crisis and Armament. Economic Relations between Great Britain and Serbia 1910–1912', *Balcanica*, 36 (2006), pp. 158–9.
91. Aehrenthal to Szögyényi, Erlass nach Berlin, 29 December 1911, ÖUAP, vol. 3, doc. 3175, p. 733; Radoslav Vesnić, *Dr Milenko Vesnić, Gransenjer Srbske Diplomatije* (Belgrade, 2008), pp. 275, 280.

92. Von Haymerle to MFA Vienna, Belgrade, 9 October 1910, *ÖUAP*, vol. 3, doc. 2266, pp. 13–14.

93. Ugron to Aehrenthal, Belgrade, 12 November 1911, *ÖUAP*, vol. 3, doc. 2911, p. 539; Ugron to Aehrenthal, Belgrade, 14 November 1911, ibid., doc. 2921, pp. 545–6; Gellinek to Chief of General Staff, Belgrade, 15 November 1911, ibid., doc. 2929, pp. 549–50.

94. Gellinek to Chief of General Staff, Belgrade, 22 November 1911, ibid., doc. 2966, p. 574; see also Ugron to Aehrenthal, Belgrade, 29 January 1912, transcribed in Barbara Jelavich, 'What the Habsburg Government Knew about the Black Hand', *Austrian History Yearbook*, 22 (1991), pp. 131–50, here p. 141.

95. Gellinek to Chief of General Staff, Belgrade, 15 November 1911, *ÖUAP*, vol. 3, doc. 2928, p. 549; Gellinek to Chief of General Staff, Belgrade, 15 November 1911, ibid., doc. 2929, pp. 549–50.

96. Gellinek to Chief of General Staff, Belgrade, 3 December 1911, ibid., doc. 3041, p. 627; Gellinek to Chief of General Staff, Belgrade, 2 February 1912, ibid., doc. 3264, pp. 806–7.

97. Ugron to MFA Vienna, Belgrade, 6 February 1912, ibid., doc. 3270, pp. 812–14.

98. Jelavich, 'What the Habsburg Government Knew', p. 138.

99. Gellinek to Chief of General Staff, Belgrade, 18 January 1914, transcribed in Jelavich, 'What the Habsburg Government Knew', pp. 142–4, here p. 143.

100. Gellinek to Chief of General Staff, Belgrade, 10 May 1914, transcribed in ibid., pp. 145–7, here p. 145.

101. Gellinek to Chief of General Staff, Belgrade, 21 May 1914, transcribed in ibid., pp. 147–9, here pp. 147–8.

102. Gellinek to Chief of General Staff, Belgrade, 21 June 1914, transcribed in ibid., pp. 149–50, here p. 150.

103. Hugo Hantsch, *Leopold Graf Berchtold. Grandseigneur und Staatsmann* (2 vols., Graz, 1963), vol. 2, p. 489.

104. Leon Biliński, *Wspomnienia i dokumenty* (2 vols., Warsaw, 1924), vol. 1, pp. 260–62; for a subtle analysis of this encounter, see also an unpublished manuscript chapter by Samuel R. Williamson, entitled 'Serbia and Austria-Hungary: The Final Rehearsal, October 1913', pp. 13–15. I am extremely grateful to Professor Williamson for letting me see this chapter, which helped me to understand the evolution of Austro-Serbian relations after the Second Balkan War.

105. On Berchtold's 'politesse exquise, mais peu sincère, léger, peu sûr de lui-même, et à cause de cela réservé et peu communicatif', see Shebeko, *Souvenirs*, p. 167.

106. Jelavich, 'What the Habsburg Government Knew', pp. 131–50.

107. Kronenbitter, *Grossmachtpolitik Österreich-Ungarns*, p. 386.

108. Gellinek, Resumé on the Serbian army after its campaign against Bulgaria in the summer of 1913, cited in ibid., pp. 434–5; on Austrian assessments of Serbian military strength, see also Rudolf Jerábek, *Potiorek. General im Schatten von Sarajevo* (Graz, 1991), p. 106.

109. For a brilliant analysis of decision-making structures in Austria-Hungary, see Leslie, 'Antecedents', passim.

110. Gina Countess Conrad von Hötzendorf, *Mein Leben mit Conrad von Hötzendorf* (Leipzig, 1935), p. 12.

111. Lawrence Sondhaus, *Franz Conrad von Hötzendorf: Architect of the Apocalypse* (Boston, 2000), p. 111.

112. Holger Herwig, *The First World War. Germany and Austria-Hungary, 1914–1918* (London, 1997), p. 10.

113. Hans Jürgen Pantenius, *Der Angriffsgedanke gegen Italien bei Conrad von Hötzendorf. Ein Beitrag zur Koalitionskriegsführung im Ersten Weltkrieg* (2 vols., Cologne, 1984), vol. 1, pp. 350–57: Herwig, *The First World War*, pp. 9–10.

114. Roberto Segre, *Vienna e Belgrado 1876–1914* (Milan, [1935]), p. 43.

115. Countess Conrad von Hötzendorf, *Mein Leben mit Conrad*, p. 44.

116. Conrad, Memorandum of 31 December 1907, cited in Kronenbitter, *Grossmachtpolitik Österreich-Ungarns*, p. 330.

117. Countess Conrad von Hötzendorf, *Mein Leben mit Conrad*, p. 101.

118. Herwig, *First World War*, pp. 19–21.

119. On Conrad's view of armed conflict, see Kronenbitter, *Grossmachtpolitik Österreich-Ungarns*, pp. 135–7, 139, 140; István Deák, *Beyond Nationalism. A Social and Political History of the Habsburg Officer Corps* (New York, 1990), p. 73; Pantenius, *Angriffsgedanke*, pp. 231, 233–6.

120. Aehrenthal, memorandum of 22 October 1911, cited in Kronenbitter, *Grossmachtpolitik Österreich-Ungarns*, pp. 363–5.

121. Conrad von Hötzendorf, *Aus meiner Dienstzeit, 1906–1918* (5 vols., Vienna, 1921–5), vol. 2, p. 282.

122. Deák, *Beyond Nationalism*, p. 73.

123. Bridge, *From Sadowa to Sarajevo*, p. 336; Sondhaus, *Architect of the Apocalypse*, p. 106.

124. Rudolf Sieghart, *Die letzten Jahrzehnte einer Grossmacht* (Berlin, 1932), p. 52; Georg Franz, *Erzherzog Franz Ferdinand und die Pläne zur Reform der Habsburger Monarchie* (Brünn, 1943), p. 23.

125. Lawrence Sondhaus, *The Naval Policy of Austria-Hungary 1867–1918. Navalism, Industrial Development and the Politics of Dualism* (West Lafayette, 1994), p. 176; it was the Austrian prime minister, Koerber, who used the phrase 'shadow government', see Franz, *Erzherzog Franz Ferdinand*, p. 25.

126. Cited in Kronenbitter, *Grossmachtpolitik Österreich-Ungarns*, p. 66.

127. Lavender Cassels, *The Archduke and the Assassin* (London, 1984), p. 23; Franz, *Erzherzog Franz Ferdinand*, p. 18.

128. Keith Hitchins, *The Nationality Problem in Austria-Hungary. The Reports of Alexander Vaida to Archduke Franz Ferdinand's Chancellery* (Leiden, 1974), pp. x, 8–14, 176–9 and passim.

129. Stephan Verosta, *Theorie und Realität von Bündnissen. Heinrich Lammasch, Karl Renner und der Zweibund, 1897–1914* (Vienna, 1971), pp. 244, 258–9, 266.

130. Kronenbitter, *Grossmachtpolitik Österreich-Ungarns*, pp. 74, 163; Sondhaus, *Architect of the Apocalypse*, p. 118.

131. Sondhaus, *Architect of the Apocalypse*, pp. 104–5.

132. Franz Ferdinand to Aehrenthal, 6 August 1908, cited in Leopold von Chlumecky, *Erzherzog Franz Ferdinands Wirken und Wollen* (Berlin, 1929), p. 98.

133. Franz Ferdinand to Aehrenthal, 20 October 1908, cited in Kronenbitter, *Grossmachtpolitik Österreich-Ungarns*, pp. 338–9.

134. Franz Ferdinand to Major Alexander Brosch von Aarenau, 20 October 1908, cited in Chlumecky, *Erzherzog Franz Ferdinands Wirken und Wollen*, p. 99; Rudolf Kiszling, *Erzherzog Franz Ferdinand von Österreich-Este. Leben, Pläne und Wirken am Schicksalsweg der Donaumonarchie* (Graz, 1953), pp. 127–130; Sondhaus, *Architect of the Apocalypse*, p. 102.

135. On his motives for accepting the post, see Berchtold, diary entry 2 February 1908, cited in Hantsch, *Berchtold*, vol. 1, p. 88.

136. Ibid., p. 86.

137. Berchtold to Aehrenthal, St Petersburg, 19 November 1908, cited in ibid., pp. 132–4.

138. Ibid., pp. 206; for Berchtold's views on the philistinism of St Petersburg high society, see p. 233.

139. Leslie, 'Antecedents', p. 377.

140. Franz Ferdinand to Berchtold, Vienna, 16 January 1913, cited in Bridge, *From Sadowa to Sarajevo*, p. 342.

141. Cited in Hantsch, *Berchtold*, vol. 1, p. 265.

142. Report of Consul-General Jehlitschka in Üsküb, 24 October 1913, copied as annexe to Griesinger to German Foreign Office, Belgrade, 30 October, PA-AA, R14 276, cited in Katrin Boeckh, *Von den Balkankriegen zum Ersten Weltkrieg. Kleinstaatenpolitik und ethnische Selbstbestimmung auf dem Balkan* (Munich, 1996), p. 168.

143. Jovanović to Pašić, Vienna, 6 May 1914, AS, MID – PO, 415, fo. 674.

144. Storck to Berchtold, Belgrade, 28 October 1913, cited in Katrin Boeckh, *Von den Balkankriegen zum Ersten Weltkrieg. Kleinstaatenpolitik und ethnische Selbstbestimmung auf dem Balkan* (Munich, 1996), pp. 171–2.

145. Giesl to MFA Vienna, Belgrade, 30 May 1914, in *ÖUAP*, vol. 8, doc. 9774, pp. 96–7.

146. Gellinek to MFA Vienna, ibid., doc. 9883, pp. 158–9.

147. For an English text of the Matscheko memorandum, see Bridge, *From Sadowa to Sarajevo*, pp. 443–8, here p. 443.

148. On the need for external help, see De Veer and Thomson (Dutch mission to Albania) to Netherlands Ministry of War, NA, 2.05.03, doc. 652 Algemeine Correspondentie over Albanië, Ministerie van Buitenlandse Zaken.

149. All quotations from the Matscheko memorandum are from the transcription in Bridge, *From Sadowa to Sarajevo*. On the paranoia expressed by the memorandum and the 'shrillness' of its tone, see Williamson, *Austria-Hungary*, pp. 165–70; on its irenic general outlook: Bridge, *From Sadowa to Sarajevo*, pp. 334–5; for a different view suggesting that the objectives set out in the memorandum (namely the cooption of Romania) could not have been achieved without triggering a crisis, see Paul Schroeder, 'Romania and the Great Powers before 1914', *Revue Roumaine d'Histoire*, 14/1 (1975), pp. 39–53.

150. See Kronenbitter, *Grossmachtpolitik Österreich-Ungarns*, pp. 236–7; on Hötzendorf junior's involvement, see Bruce W. Menning, 'Russian Military Intelligence, July 1914. What St Petersburg Perceived and Why It Mattered', unpublished typescript. I am extremely grateful to Professor Menning for sharing this paper with me in advance of its publication by the *Journal of Modern History*, and for discussing with me his thoughts on the place of intelligence in Russian decision-making. For Svechin's memoirs, discussed by Menning, see Mikhail Svechin, *Zapiski starogo generala o bylom* (Nice, 1964), esp. p. 99.

151. Williamson, *Austria-Hungary*, p. 146.

152. Cited in Sondhaus, *Architect of the Apocalypse*, p. 122.

153. Von Hötzendorf, *Aus meiner Dienstzeit*, vol. 3, p. 169; Karl Bardolff, *Soldat im alten Österreich* (Jena, 1938), p. 177; Kiszling, *Erzherzog Franz Ferdinand*, p. 196.

154. Cited in Kronenbitter, *Grossmachtpolitik Österreich-Ungarns*, p. 71.

155. Strandmann, *Balkanske Uspomene*, pp. 245–50; for complaints by the Serbian negotiators about interventions by Pašić, see Mikhail Ilić to Pašić, Vienna, 9 March 1914; same to same, Vienna, 10 March 1914, and esp. same to same, 11 March 1914, where Ilić asks Pašić to desist from disrupting the negotiations with 'novelties', AS, MID – PO, 415, fos. 9–12, 14–24, 25–7; on the readiness of both parties to come to an agreement, see Hartwig to Sazonov, Belgrade, 4 March 1914, *IBZI*, series 3, vol. 1, doc. 379, p. 375.

CHAPTER 3

1. For the text of the treaty, see The Avalon Project. Documents in Law, History and Diplomacy, Yale Law School, consulted at *http://avalon.law.yale.edu/19th_century/frrumil.asp*.

2. Claude Digeon, *La Crise allemande dans la pensée française 1870–1914* (Paris, 1959), pp. 535–42.

3. Klaus Hildebrand, *Das vergangene Reich. Deutsche Aussenpolitik von Bismarck bis Hitler 1871–1945* (Stuttgart, 1995), p. 18.

4. For an acute analysis of this problem, see Paul W. Schroeder, 'The Lost Intermediaries: The Impact of 1870 on the European System', *International History Review*, 6/1 (1984), pp. 1–27.

5. J. B. Eustis, 'The Franco-Russian Alliance', *The North American Review*, 165 (1897), pp. 111–18, here p. 117.

6. Ulrich Lappenküper, *Die Mission Radowitz. Untersuchungen zur Russlandpolitik Otto von Bismarcks (1871–1875)* (Göttingen, 1990), p. 226.

7. The quotation is from the famous Bad Kissingen Memorandum of 15 June 1877, which was composed with an eye to the Balkans, but captures many of the central themes of the chancellor's policy; the text is in *GP*, vol. 2, pp. 153–4.

8. Otto von Bismarck, speech to the Reichstag of 5 December 1876, in Horst Kohl (ed.), *Politische Reden Bismarcks. Historisch-kritische Gesamtausgabe* (14 vols., Stuttgart, 1892–1905), vol. 6, p. 461.

9. Hildebrand, *Das vergangene Reich*, pp. 50–51; see also Hermann Oncken, *Das Deutsche Reich und die Vorgeschichte des Weltkrieges* (2 vols., Leipzig, 1933), vol. 1, p. 215.

10. For a good summary of the Bulgarian crisis, see J. M. Roberts, *Europe, 1880–1945* (3rd edn, Harlow, 2001), pp. 75–8.

11. Herbert von Bismarck to his brother Wilhelm, 11 November 1887, in Walter Bussmann (ed.), *Staatssekretär Graf Herbert von Bismarck: aus seiner politischen Privatkorrespondenz* (Göttingen, 1964), pp. 457–8.

12. On the Bismarck *fronde*, see J. A. Nicholls, *Germany After Bismarck* (Cambridge, MA, 1958), pp. 101–3, 132–4; Katherine Lerman, *Bismarck. Profiles in Power* (Harlow, 2004), pp. 244–8; Konrad Canis, *Bismarcks Aussenpolitik 1870 bis 1890: Aufstieg und Gefährdung* (Paderborn, 2004), pp. 381–3; Ernst Engelberg, *Bismarck. Das Reich in der Mitte Europas* (Munich, 1993), pp. 309–13; Otto Pflanze, *Bismarck and the Development of Germany* (3 vols., Princeton, 1990), vol. 3, *The Period of Fortification 1880–1898*, pp. 313–16.

13. William L. Langer, 'The Franco-Russian Alliance (1890–1894)', *The Slavonic Review*, 3/9 (1925), pp. 554–75, here pp. 554–5.

14. On the impact in St Petersburg of non-renewal, see Peter Jakobs, *Das Werden des französsch-russischen Zweibundes, 1890–1894* (Wiesbaden, 1968), pp. 56–8; George F. Kennan, *The Decline of Bismarck's European Order. Franco-Prussian Relations, 1875–1890* (Princeton, 1979), p. 398.

15. *Morning Post*, 1 July 1891 and *Standard*, 4 July 1891, both cited in Patricia A. Weitsman, *Dangerous Alliances, Proponents of Peace, Weapons of War* (Stanford, 2004), p. 109.

16. Antoine Laboulaye to Alexandre Ribot, 22 June 1890, cited in ibid., p. 105.

17. Giers to Mohrenheim, 19–21 August 1891, cited in ibid., pp. 105–6.

18. George F. Kennan, *The Fateful Alliance. France, Russia and the Coming of the First World War* (Manchester, 1984), pp. 153–4.

19. Francis R. Bridge and Roger Bullen, *The Great Powers and the European States System 1815–1914* (Harlow, 1980), p. 259; on the anti-British orientation of the new alliance (in Russian eyes), see also Jakobs, *Das Werden des französisch-russischen Zweibundes*, pp. 73–8.

20. Kennan, *Fateful Alliance*, passim.

21. Weitsman, *Dangerous Alliances*, p. 117.

22. On the alliance and popular culture, see I. S. Rybachenok, *Rossiia i Frantsiia: soiuz interesov i soiuz serdets, 1891–1897: russko-frantsuzskyi soiuz v diplomaticheskikh dokumentakh, fotografiakh, risunkakh, karikaturakh, stikhakh, tostakh i meniu* (Moscow, 2004).

23. Thomas M. Iiams, *Dreyfus, Diplomatists and the Dual Alliance: Gabriel Hanotaux at the Quai d'Orsay, 1894–1898* (Geneva, 1962), pp. 27–8.

24. Conversation between Lamzdorf and Lobanov-Rostovsky recorded on 9 October 1895, in V. N. Lamzdorf, *Dnevnik: 1894–1896*, ed. V. I. Bovykin and I. A. Diakonova (Moscow, 1991), pp. 264–6; D. C. B. Lieven, *Nicholas II. Emperor of All the Russias* (London, 1993), p. 93.

25. On Hanotaux's view of colonies as crucial to the restoration of lost prestige, see Peter Grupp, *Theorie des Kolonialimperialismus und Methoden der imperialistischen Aussenpolitik bei Gabriel Hanotaux* (Bern and Frankfurt, 1962), esp. pp. 78–84, 122–7, 142–5; see also Alf Heggoy, *The African Policies of Gabriel Hanotaux, 1894–1898* (Athens, GA, 1972), esp. pp. 10–11; Christopher Andrew and A. S. Kanya-Forstner, 'Gabriel Hanotaux, the Colonial Party and the Fashoda Strategy', in E. F. Penrose (ed.), *European Imperialism and the Partition of Africa* (London, 1975), pp. 55–104.

26. Cited in Christopher Andrew, *Théophile Delcassé and the Making of the Entente Cordiale. A Reappraisal of French Foreign Policy 1898–1905* (London, 1968), p. 19; M. B. Hayne, *The French Foreign Office and the Origins of the First World War, 1898–1914* (Oxford, 1993), p. 95.

27. G. N. Sanderson, *England, Europe and the Upper Nile, 1882–1889* (Edinburgh, 1965), pp. 140–61.

28. Hayne, *French Foreign Office*, p. 97.

29. Andrew, *Delcassé*, p. 168.

30. Ibid., p. 171.

31. Jules Clarétie, 'Vingt-huit ans à la Comédie-Française – Journal', entry of 8 March 1900, *Revue des deux mondes* (November 1949/6), pp. 122–40, here p. 129.

32. Ibid., p. 129; Andrew, *Delcassé*, pp. 307–8; Hayne, *French Foreign Office*, p. 113.

33. Andrew, *Delcassé*, p. 172; on the French reaction to signs of Anglo-German rapprochement in the late 1890s, see also P. J. V. Rolo, *Entente Cordiale*.

The Origins and Negotiation of the Anglo-French Agreements of 8 April 1904 (London, 1969), p. 73.

34. Rolo, *Entente Cordiale*, p. 106.

35. Maurice Paléologue, *Un grand tournant de la politique mondiale (1904–1906)* (Paris, 1914), p. 196.

36. Hayne, *French Foreign Office*, p. 55.

37. Disraeli speech to House of Commons, accessed online at Hansard 1803–2005, *http://hansard.millbanksystems.com/commons/1871/feb/09/address-to-her-majesty-on-her-most*.

38. Leader article, *The Times*, 15 February 1871, p. 9, col. C.

39. 'The Eastern Question: The Russian Repudiation of the Treaty of 1856, A New Sebastopol Wanted ...' *New York Times*, 1 January 1871, p. 1.

40. Disraeli speech to House of Commons, accessed online at Hansard 1803–2005, *http://hansard.millbanksystems.com/commons/1871/feb/09/address-to-her-majesty-on-her-most*.

41. Keith Neilson, *Britain and the Last Tsar. British Policy and Russia 1894–1917* (Oxford, 1995), p. xiii.

42. For the definitive analysis of the China Question, see Thomas Otte, *The China Question. Great Power Rivalry and British Isolation, 1894–1905* (Oxford, 2007).

43. Payson J. Treat, 'The Cause of the Sino-Japanese War, 1894', *The Pacific Historical Review*, 8 (1939), pp. 149–57; Stewart Lone, *Japan's First Modern War. Army and Society in the Conflict with China, 1894–95* (London, 1994), p. 24.

44. Keith Neilson, 'Britain, Russia and the Sino-Japanese War', in Keith Neilson, John Berryman and Ian Nish, *The Sino-Japanese War of 1894–5 in its International Dimension* (London, [1994]), pp. 1–22.

45. Rolo, *Entente Cordiale*, pp. 64, 108.

46. D. Gillard, *The Struggle for Asia, 1828–1914. A Study in British and Russian Imperialism* (London, 1977), pp. 153–66.

47. Godley (permanent under-secretary, India Office) to Curzon, 10 November 1899, cited in Neilson, *Britain and the Last Tsar*, p. 122.

48. Intelligence Department, War Office, 'Military Needs of the Empire in a War with France and Russia', 12 August 1901, cited in ibid., p. 123.

49. Cited in ibid., pp. 16–17.

50. Cited in Otte, *China Question*, p. 71.

51. Cited from a letter from the British military attaché in Peking to Kimberley in ibid., p. 71.

52. On British reactions to French encroachments from Indo-China and the link to the policy of entente, see J. D. Hargreaves, 'Entente Manquée: Anglo-French Relations, 1895–1896', in *Historical Journal*, 11 (1953–5), pp. 65–92; Otte, *China Question*, p. 330.

53. Neilson, *Britain and the Last Tsar*, p. xiv; Rolo, *Entente Cordiale*, p. 273;

on Delcassé, Keith M. Wilson, *The Policy of the Entente. Essays on the Determinants of British Foreign Policy, 1904–1914* (Cambridge, 1985), p. 71.

54. Cited in Wilson, *Policy of the Entente*, p. 71.

55. Cited in Neilson, *Britain and the Last Tsar*, p. 22.

56. Ibid., pp. 124–5.

57. On the 'feverish haste' of Russian military preparations near the Indian frontier, see the secret report by the British military attaché H. D. Napier, St Petersburg, 9 November 1904, enclosed with Charles Hardinge to Lansdowne, 10 November 1904, Hardinge Papers, Cambridge University Library, vol. 46.

58. 'Demands for Reinforcements by the Government of India', 20 February 1905, cited in Neilson, *Britain and the Last Tsar*, p. 131.

59. Stanley Wolpert, *Morley and India, 1906–1910* (Berkeley, 1967), p. 80.

60. Neilson, *Britain and the Last Tsar*, pp. 134–5; Wilson, *Policy of the Entente*, p. 7.

61. Grey to Spring Rice, London, 22 December 1905, cited in Neilson, *Britain and the Last Tsar*, p. 12.

62. Otto, *China Question*, pp. 71, 90, 333.

63. On the German bid for Angra Pequeña, see Hildebrand, *Das vergangene Reich*, pp. 87–8; also Canis, *Bismarcks Aussenpolitik*, pp. 209–17.

64. On the 'four months of haughty silence' with which the Salisbury government greeted President Cleveland's note of 20 July 1895 protesting British aggressions in Venezuela, and the 'condescending' reply of the British government to subsequent US communications, see Bradford Perkins, *The Great Rapprochement: England and the United States 1895–1914* (London, 1969), pp. 13–16; also H. C. Allen, *Great Britain and the United States: A History of Anglo-American Relations (1783–1952)* (London, 1954), pp. 532–41.

65. Bismarck comment on letter from Count Hatzfeldt to Bismarck, 24 May 1884, *GP*, vol. 4, p. 58.

66. Bülow to Eulenburg, 2 March 1890, cited in Peter Winzen, *Bülow's Weltmachtkonzept. Untersuchungen zur Frühphase seiner Aussenpolitik 1897–1901* (Boppard am Rhein, 1977), p. 50.

67. Konrad Canis, *Von Bismarck zur Weltpolitik. Deutsche Aussenpolitik, 1890 bis 1902* (Berlin, 1997), pp. 93–4.

68. Ibid., p. 124.

69. Rolo, *Entente Cordiale*, p. 116.

70. Gordon Martel, *Imperial Diplomacy: Rosebery and the Failure of Foreign Policy* (London, 1986), p. 187.

71. On German objections to the treaty, see Jacques Willequet, *Le Congo Belge et la Weltpolitik (1894–1914)* (Brussels, 1962), pp. 14–21; Canis, *Von Bismarck zur Weltpolitik*, pp. 134–5; cf. A. J. P. Taylor, 'Prelude to Fashoda:

The Question of the Upper Nile, 1894–5', *English Historical Review*, 65 (1950), pp. 52–80.

72. Canis, *Von Bismarck zur Weltpolitik*, pp. 142–3.

73. Full text of the Kruger telegram is in *GP*, vol. 11, doc. 2610, pp. 31–2.

74. On the course and consequences of the Transvaal crisis, see Harald Rosenbach, *Das deutsche Reich, Grossbritannien und der Transvaal (1896–1902). Anfänge deutsch-britischer Entfremdung* (Göttingen, 1993).

75. Friedrich Kiessling, *Gegen den grossen Krieg? Entspannung in den internationalen Beziehungen 1911–1914* (Munich, 2002), p. 137.

76. P. Winzen, 'Zur Genesis von Weltmachtkonzept und Weltpolitik', in J. C. G. Röhl (ed.), *Der Ort Kaiser Wilhelms in der deutschen Geschichte* (Munich, 1991), pp. 189–222; here pp. 192–3.

77. Jan Rüger, *The Great Naval Game. Britain and Germany in the Age of Empire* (Cambridge, 2007).

78. Gregor Schöllgen, *Imperialismus und Gleichgewicht. Deutschland, England und die orientalische Frage, 1871–1914* (Munich, 1984), p. 76; Christopher Clark, *Kaiser Wilhelm II. A Life in Power* (London, 2008), p. 184.

79. Jonathan Steinberg, *Yesterday's Deterrent; Tirpitz and the Birth of the German Battle Fleet* (London, [1965]), pp. 71, 101–2, 109; Ivo Nikolai Lambi, *The Navy and German Power Politics, 1862–1914* (Boston, 1984), pp. 68–86.

80. Steinberg, *Yesterday's Deterrent*, p. 201; also pp. 125–48.

81. Cited in Rosenbach, *Transvaal*, p. 70.

82. The text of this memorandum is given in Steinberg, *Yesterday's Deterrent*, pp. 209–21. See also Volker R. Berghahn and Wilhelm Deist (eds.), *Rüstung im Zeichen der wilhelminischen Weltpolitik* (Düsseldorf, 1988), esp. docs. II/11, II/12 and VII/1.

83. See James Ainsworth, 'Naval Strategic Thought in Britain and Germany 1890–1914', PhD thesis, University of Cambridge, 2011; on the persistence of the British fear of French naval power around 1900 and the relatively low priority assigned to the 'German threat', see Andreas Rose, *Zwischen Empire und Kontinent. Britische Aussenpolitik vor dem Ersten Weltkrieg* (Munich, 2011), pp. 209–11.

84. Even Lord Selborne, often cited as crown witness for the thesis that the fear of German naval power transformed British strategy, was as concerned about the Russian and French fleets as he was about the German, see Dominik Geppert and Andreas Rose, 'Machtpolitik und Flottenbau vor 1914. Zur Neuinterpretation britischer Aussenpolitik im Zeitalter des Hochimperialismus', *Historische Zeitschrift*, 293 (2011), pp. 401–37, here p. 409; Rose, *Zwischen Empire und Kontinent*, pp. 223–6.

85. The literature on Anglo-German naval rivalry has for some time been in a state of flux. The older view espoused in Arthur J. Marder, *From the Dreadnought to Scapa Flow. The Royal Navy in the Fischer Era, 1904–1919*

(5 vols., Oxford, 1961–70), that the German threat dominated and transformed British naval thinking has been questioned by numerous more recent studies; see, for example: Jon T. Sumida, 'Sir John Fischer and the Dreadnought. The Sources of Naval Mythology', *The Journal of Military History*, 59 (1995), pp. 619–38; Charles H. Fairbanks Jr, 'The Origins of the Dreadnought Revolution. A Historiographical Essay', *International History Review*, 13 (1991), pp. 246–72; Nicholas A. Lambert, 'Admiral Sir John Fischer and the Concept of Flotilla Defence, 1904–1909', *The Journal of Military History*, 59 (1995), pp. 639–60. The most important revisionist study in this tradition is now Rose, *Zwischen Empire und Kontinent*.

86. Cited in Niall Ferguson, *Pity of War* (London, 1998), p. 71.

87. Hardinge, Wilson and Grey cited in Wilson, *Policy of the Entente*, p. 106.

88. Rose, *Zwischen Empire und Kontinent*, pp. 202–17 and 404–24; on Tirpitz's 'renunciation' of the arms race, see Hew Strachan, *The First World War* (Oxford, 2001), p. 33.

89. Hans Delbrück in *Preussische Jahrbücher*, 87 (1897), p. 402, cited in Canis, *Von Bismarck zur Weltpolitik*, p. 225.

90. Bernhard von Bülow, speech to the Reichstag on 6 December 1897, in Johannes Penzler (ed.), *Fürst Bülows nebst urkundlichen Beiträgen zu seiner Politik. Mit Erlaubnis des Reichskanzlers gesammelt und herausgegeben* (2 vols., Berlin, 1907), vol. 1, *1897–1903*, p. 6.

91. Canis, *Von Bismarck zur Weltpolitik*, pp. 255–6.

92. Waldersee, diary entry 13 July 1900, in Heinrich Otto Meisner, *Denkwürdigkeiten des General-Feldmarschalls Alfred Grafen von Waldersee* (3 vols., Stuttgart, 1922–3), vol. 2, p. 449.

93. George C. Herring, *From Colony to Superpower: US Foreign Relations since 1776* (New York, 2009), p. 307; Ferguson, *Pity of War*, pp. 54–5.

94. Cited in Paul Kennedy, *The Rise of the Anglo-German Antagonism, 1860–1914* (London, 1980), pp. 365, 236.

95. On *Weltpolitik* as a 'social imperialist' instrument devised for domestic ends, see above all Hans-Ulrich Wehler's classic, *Das deutsche Kaiserreich 1871–1918* (Göttingen, 1973), p. 178; id., *Deutsche Gesellschaftsgeschichte* (5 vols., Munich, 1987–2008), vol. 3, p. 1139; a similar view is presented in Wolfgang M. Mommsen, *Grossmachtstellung und Weltpolitik. Die Aussenpolitik des Deutschen Reiches, 1870 bis 1914* (Frankfurt am Main, 1993), pp. 139–40; on the navy as an instrument of domestic 'crisis management', see Volker Berghahn, *Der Tirpitz-Plan. Genesis und Verfall einer innenpolitischen Krisenstrategie unter Wilhelm II.* (Düsseldorf, 1971), pp. 11–20, 592–604 and passim.

96. Wilhelm II to Bülow, Syracuse, 19 April 1904, in *GP*, vol. 20/1, doc. 6378, pp. 22–3.

97. Wilhelm II to Tsar Nicholas II, 11 February 1904, in W. Goetz (ed.), *Briefe Kaiser Wilhelms II. an den Zaren, 1894–1914* (Berlin, 1920), pp. 337–8.

98. Wilhelm II to Nicholas II, 6 June, 19 August 1904, in ibid., pp. 340–41.

99. Delcassé to Barrère, 28 February 1900, cited in Andrew, *Delcassé*, p. 151.

100. Abel Combarieu, *Sept ans à l'Élysée avec le président Émile Loubet: de l'affaire Dreyfus à la conférence d'Algésiras, 1899–1906* (Paris, 1932), pp. 183–4.

101. Cited in Andrew, *Delcassé*, p. 271; Samuel R. Williamson, *The Politics of Grand Strategy. Britain and France Prepare for War, 1904–1914* (Cambridge, MA, 1969), p. 14; cf. J. C. G. Röhl, *Wilhelm II. Der Weg in den Abgrund, 1900–1941* (Munich, 2008), p. 372.

102. Metternich (German ambassador in London) to German Foreign Office, London, 4 June 1904, *GP*, vol. 20/1, doc. 6384, pp. 29–30.

103. Hildebrand, *Das vergangene Reich*, pp. 222–3; Williamson, *Grand Strategy*, pp. 31–2.

104. 'The German Emperor at Tangier', *The Times*, 1 April 1905, p. 5, col. A.

105. 'The Morocco Question', *The Times*, 8 January 1906, p. 9, col. A.

106. Katherine Lerman, *The Chancellor as Courtier: Bernhard von Bülow and the Governance of Germany, 1900–1909* (Cambridge, 1990), pp. 147–8; on the 'uselessness' of the Triple Alliance, see Prince Max von Lichnowsky, *My Mission to London, 1912–1914* (London, 1929), p. 3.

107. Kennedy, *Anglo-German Antagonism*, p. 280.

108. Hardinge to Nicolson, London, 26 March 1909, cited in Zara S. Steiner, *The Foreign Office and Foreign Policy, 1898–1914* (Cambridge, 1969), p. 95.

109. Marina Soroka, *Britain, Russia and the Road to the First World War. The Fateful Embassy of Count Aleksandr Benckendorff (1903–16)* (London, 2011), p. 146; Rogers Platt Churchill, *The Anglo-Russian Convention of 1907* (Cedar Rapids, 1939), p. 340; David MacLaren McDonald, *United Government and Foreign Policy in Russia, 1900–1914* (Cambridge, MA, 1992), p. 110.

110. For an account that does justice to the pressures operating on European diplomacy from the periphery, see Thomas Otte, *China Question*, id., *The Foreign Office Mind. The Making of British Foreign Policy, 1865–1914* (Cambridge, 2011); Nils Petersson, *Imperialismus und Modernisierung. Siam, China und die europäischen Mächte, 1895–1914* (Munich, 2000); for a powerful critique on theoretical and empirical grounds of the 'consensus view' that the German powers themselves 'caused' their own isolation through egregious international behaviour, see Paul W. Schroeder, 'Embedded Counterfactuals and World War I as an Unavoidable War', consultable online at *http://ir.emu.edu.tr/staff/ekaymak/courses/IR515/Articles/Schroeder%20on%20counterfactuals.pdf*; pp. 28–9 and passim.

111. Fiona K. Tomaszewski, *A Great Russia. Russia and the Triple Entente* (Westport, 2002), p. 68.

112. Lansdowne to Bertie, London, 22 April 1905, *BD*, vol. 3, doc. 90, pp. 72–3.

113. Aide-Mémoire of the British embassy in Paris, Paris, 24 April 1905, *DDF*, series 2, vol. 6, doc. 347, pp. 414–15; on Delcassé's ignorance of supposed German designs on a west Moroccan port, see note 5 to same.

114. Conversation between Delcassé and Paléologue of 26 April, recounted in Maurice Paléologue, *The Turning Point. Three Critical Years 1904–1906*, trans. F. Appleby Holt (London, 1935), p. 233.

115. Andrew, *Delcassé*, pp. 283–5; on Fisher's 'anti-Germanism': Strachan, *First World War*, p. 18.

116. Steiner, *Foreign Office*, pp. 100, 102.

117. See, for example, the minutes appended by Grey, Crowe and Edward VII to various letters from Cartwright to Grey, Munich, 12 January 1907, 23 April 1907, 7 August 1907, 8 January 1908, *BD*, vol. 6, docs. 2, 16, 23 and the minutes to Cartwright's dispatch from Munich of 8 January 1908, pp. 11, 32, 42, 108. Sidney B. Fay discusses London's reactions to Cartwright's dispatches in his review of this volume of Gooch and Temperley's *British Documents* in *American Historical Review*, 36 (1930), pp. 151–5.

118. G. S. Spicer, minutes to Bertie to Grey, Paris, 12 September 1907, *BD*, vol. 6, doc. 35, pp. 55–8, here p. 56.

119. Edward Grey, *Twenty-Five Years, 1892–1916* (2 vols., London, 1925), vol. 1, p. 33.

120. Eyre Crowe, Memorandum on the Present State of British Relations with France and Germany, 1 January 1907, *BD*, vol. 3, appendix to doc. 445, pp. 397–420, here p. 406.

121. Grey, *Twenty-Five Years*, vol. 2, p. 29; J. A. S. Grenville, *Lord Salisbury and Foreign Policy. The Close of the Nineteenth Century* (London, 1970), p. 213.

122. Minute by Hardinge, dated 10 November 1909, to Goschen to Grey, Berlin, 4 November 1909, *BD*, vol. 6, doc. 204, pp. 304–12, here p. 311; for a suggestive and trenchantly revisionist discussion of this and other utterances, see Keith M. Wilson, *The Policy of the Entente. Essays on the Determinants of British Foreign Policy, 1904–1914* (Cambridge, 1985), p. 100.

123. Eyre Crowe, Memorandum on the Present State of British Relations with France and Germany, 1 January 1907, *BD*, vol. 3, appendix to doc. 445, pp. 397–420, here p. 406. On the consolidation of the 'anti-German phalanx' at the apex of the Foreign Office, see Jürgen Angelow, *Der Weg in die Urkatastrophe. Der Zerfall des alten Europas 1900–1914* (Berlin, 2010), pp. 51–2.

124. These figures are drawn from Hans-Ulrich Wehler, *Deutsche Gesellschaftsgeschichte* (5 vols., Munich, 2008), vol. 3, *Von der 'deutschen Doppelrevolution' bis zum Beginn des Ersten Weltkrieges, 1849–1914*, pp. 610–12.

125. Clive Trebilcock, *The Industrialisation of the Continental Powers 1780–1914* (London, 1981), p. 22.

126. Keith Neilson, 'Quot homines, tot sententiae: Bertie, Hardinge, Nicolson and British Policy, 1906–1916', unpublished manuscript; I am extremely grateful to Professor Neilson for letting me see a copy of this text prior to publication.

127. Hardinge to Bertie, private letter, 14 February 1904, Bertie Papers, TNA, FO 800/176; Hardinge to Bertie, private letter, 11 May 1904, Bertie Papers, ibid., FO 800/183, both cited in Neilson, 'Quot homines, tot sententiae'.

128. Keith Neilson, '"My Beloved Russians": Sir Arthur Nicolson and Russia, 1906–1916', International History Review, 9/4 (1987), pp. 521–54, here pp. 524–5.

129. 'The Invention of Germany' is the title of the sixth chapter of Wilson, Policy of the Entente, pp. 100–120.

130. On British concerns about defensive capability after the Boer War, see Aaron L. Friedberg, The Weary Titan. Britain and the Experience of Relative Decline, 1895–1905 (Princeton, 1988), pp. 232–4 and passim; David Reynolds, Britannia Overruled. British Policy and World Power in the Twentieth Century (2nd edn, Harlow, 2000), pp. 63–7.

131. On this feature of US foreign policy, see John A. Thompson, 'The Exaggeration of American Vulnerability: The Anatomy of a Tradition', Diplomatic History, 16/1 (1992), pp. 23–43.

132. For examples of this kind of fantasizing, see A. Dekhnewallah (pseud.), The Great Russian Invasion of India. A Sequel to the Afghanistan Campaign of 1879–9 (London, 1879); William Le Queux, The Great War in England in 1897 (London, 1894) (foresees a Franco-Russian invasion of Britain that is thwarted by the gallant intervention of Imperial Germany); for an excellent overview, see I. F. Clarke, Voices Prophesying War, 1763–1984 (London, 1970).

133. Diary entry 29 November 1906, in Paléologue, The Turning Point, p. 328.

134. David M. McDonald, United Government and Foreign Policy in Russia 1900–1914 (Cambridge, MA, 1992), pp. 103–11.

135. E. W. Edwards, 'The Franco-German Agreement on Morocco, 1909', English Historical Review, 78 (1963), pp. 483–513, here p. 413; on the hostile British and Russian response, see Paul Cambon to Jules Cambon, 9 December 1911, in Paul Cambon, Correspondance 1870–1924 (3 vols., Paris, 1940–46), vol. 2, pp. 354–5; Jean-Claude Allain, Agadir, 1911. Une Crise impérialiste en Europe pour la conquête du Maroc (Paris, 1976), pp. 232–46.

136. Hildebrand, Das vergangene Reich, pp. 256–7; Uwe Liszkowski, Zwischen Liberalismus und Imperialismus. Die zaristische Aussenpolitik vor dem Ersten Weltkrieg im Urteil Miljukovs und der Kadettenpartei, 1905–1914 (Stuttgart, 1974), pp. 70, 156; on détentist tendencies in general during this period, see Kiessling, Gegen den grossen Krieg?, passim.

CHAPTER 4

1. Johannes Paulmann, *Pomp und Politik: Monarchenbegegnungen in Europa zwischen Ancien Régime und Erstem Weltkrieg* (Paderborn, 2000), pp. 338–40.
2. On the Kaiser's capacity to shape the language with which ordinary Germans grasped foreign relations, see Michael A. Obst, *'Einer nur ist Herr im Reiche'. Wilhelm II als politischer Redner* (Paderborn, 2010), pp. 406–7.
3. Christopher Hibbert, *Edward VII. A Portrait* (London, 1976), p. 282.
4. Virginia Cowles, *Edward VII and His Circle* (London, [1956]), p. 110.
5. Zara S. Steiner, *The Foreign Office and Foreign Policy, 1898–1914* (Cambridge, 1969), pp. 69–71.
6. Robert and Isabelle Tombs, *That Sweet Enemy. The French and British from the Sun King to the Present* (London, 2006), p. 438; Hibbert, *Edward VII*, pp. 259 (quotation), 258; Roderick McLean, *Royalty and Diplomacy in Europe, 1890–1914* (Cambridge, 2001), pp. 147–8.
7. Cited in Hibbert, *Edward VII*, pp. 261–2.
8. Harold Nicolson, *King George the Fifth* (London, 1952), p. 175.
9. Kenneth Rose, *George V* (London, 1983), p. 166.
10. Nicolson, *King George the Fifth*, p. 175.
11. Cited in Miranda Carter, *The Three Emperors. Three Cousins, Three Empires and the Road to World War One* (London, 2009), p. 82.
12. D. C. B. Lieven, *Nicholas II. Emperor of All the Russias* (London, 1993), p. 117.
13. Cited in David M. McDonald, *United Government and Foreign Policy in Russia 1900–1914* (Cambridge, MA, 1992), p. 31.
14. Cited in Lieven, *Nicholas II*, p. 97.
15. McDonald, *United Government*, pp. 38–57.
16. Lieven, *Nicholas II*, p. 100.
17. McDonald, *United Government*, p. 106.
18. Ibid., pp. 168–98.
19. J. C. G. Röhl, *Germany Without Bismarck. The Crisis of Government in the Second Reich, 1890–1900* (London, 1967); id., 'The "kingship mechanism" in the Kaiserreich', in Röhl, *The Kaiser and His Court. Wilhelm II and the Government of Germany*, trans. T. F. Cole (Cambridge, 1994), pp. 107–30; Hans-Ulrich Wehler, *Das deutsche Kaiserreich, 1871–1918* (Göttingen, 1973), pp. 60–69; id., *Deutsche Gesellschaftsgeschichte* (5 vols. Munich, 1995), vol. 3, pp. 1016–20.
20. L. Cecil, 'Der diplomatische Dienst im kaiserlichen Deutschland', in K. Schwabe (ed.), *Das diplomatische Korps, 1871–1945* (Boppard am Rhein, 1985), pp. 15–39, here p. 39.
21. Cited in J. C. G. Röhl, 'Kaiser Wilhelm II: A Suitable Case for Treatment?',

in id., *The Kaiser and His Court. Wilhelm II and the Government of Germany* (Cambridge, 1994), pp. 2–27, here p. 12.

22. J. C. G. Röhl, 'The Splendour and Impotence of the German Diplomatic Service', in id., *The Kaiser and His Court*, pp. 150–61, here p. 159; F.-C. Stahl, 'Preussische Armee und Reichsheer, 1871–1914', in O. Hauser, *Zur Problematik Preussen und das Reich* (Cologne and Vienna, 1984), pp. 181–245, here p. 202; Johannes Paulmann, '"Dearest Nicky ..." Monarchical Relations between Prussia, the German Empire and Russia during the Nineteenth Century', in R. Bartlet and K. Schönwalder (eds.), *The German Lands and Eastern Europe. Essays on the History of Their Social, Cultural and Political Relations* (London, 1999), pp. 157–81.

23. The most authoritative critical account is J. C. G. Röhl, *Wilhelm II. Der Weg in den Abgrund 1900–1941* (Munich, 2008), p. 26.

24. O'Brien to Elihu Root, Berlin, 7 April 1906, cited in Alfred Vagts, *Deutschland und die vereinigten Staaten in der Weltpolitik* (2 vols., New York, 1935), p. 1878, cited in Röhl, *Der Weg in den Abgrund*, p. 488.

25. Ragnhild Fiebig-von Hase, 'Die Rolle Kaiser Wilhelms II. in den deutsch-amerikanischen Beziehungen, 1890–1914', in John C. G. Röhl (ed.), *Wilhelm II.* (Munich, 1991), pp. 223–57, here p. 251; id., *Der Weg in den Abgrund*, p. 653.

26. Röhl, *Der Weg in den Abgrund*, pp. 253, 125, 109, 269.

27. See Holstein to Eulenburg, Berlin, 20 October 1891, in Röhl (ed.), *Philipp Eulenburgs Politische Korrespondenz* (3 vols., Boppard am Rhein, 1976–83), vol. 1, p. 716.

28. Röhl, *Der Weg in den Abgrund*, pp. 82, 90.

29. Harald Rosenbach, *Das deutsche Reich, Grossbritannien und der Transvaal (1896–1902). Anfänge deutsch-britischer Entfremdung* (Göttingen, 1993), pp. 58–61; for similar confusion in the Kaiser's Far Eastern policy, see Gordon Craig, *Germany 1866–1945* (Oxford, 1981), p. 244.

30. Röhl, *Der Weg in den Abgrund*, p. 375; Holger Afflerbach, *Falkenhayn: Politisches Denken und Handeln im Kaiserreich* (Munich, 1994), pp. 58–9.

31. This episode is discussed in Röhl, *Der Weg in den Abgrund*, p. 348.

32. K. Hildebrand, *Das vergangene Reich. Deutsche Aussenpolitik von Bismarck bis Hitler 1871–1945* (Stuttgart, 1995), pp. 155–6; Rainer Lahme, *Deutsche Aussenpolitik 1890–1894. Von der Gleichgewichtspolitik Bismarcks zur Allianzstrategie Caprivis* (Göttingen, 1994), p. 18; N. Rich, M. H. Fisher and W. Frauendienst (eds.), *Die geheimen Papiere Friedrich von Holsteins* (4 vols., Göttingen, Berlin, Frankfurt, 1957), vol. 1, p. 130.

33. Wilhelm to Bülow, 11 August 1905, in *GP*, vol. 19/2, pp. 496–8; see also Katherine Lerman, *The Chancellor as Courtier Bernhard von Bülow and the Governance of Germany, 1900–1909* (Cambridge, 1990), pp. 129–30; Christopher Clark, *Kaiser Wilhelm II. A Life in Power* (London, 2008), pp. 99–100.

34. Röhl, *Der Weg in den Abgrund*, p. 543.

35. Ibid., pp. 366, 473; Holstein, undated note, Rich, Fischer and Frauendienst (eds.), *Geheime Papiere*, vol. 4, p. 366.

36. Jules Cambon to Maurice Paléologue, Berlin, 10 May 1912, AMAE PA-AP, 43 Jules Cambon 56, fo. 204.

37. Jean-Paul Bled, *Franz Joseph*, trans. Theresa Bridgeman (London, 1994), pp. 200–203.

38. R. J. B. Bosworth, *Italy, the Least of the Great Powers: Italian Foreign Policy before the First World War* (Cambridge, 1979), pp. 14–17.

39. Fortunato Minniti, 'Gli Stati Maggiori e la politica estera italiana', in R. J. B. Bosworth and Sergio Romano (eds.), *La Politica estera italiana (1860–1985)* (Bologna, 1991), pp. 91–120, here p. 120; Bosworth, *Italy, the Least of the Great Powers*, p. 219.

40. Lieven, *Nicholas II*, p. 105.

41. His children, for example, played with the children of the friendly ambassadors, see Helene Izvolsky, 'The Fateful Years: 1906–1911', *Russian Review*, 28/2 (1969), pp. 191–206.

42. David MacLaren McDonald, *United Government and Foreign Policy in Russia, 1900–1914* (Cambridge, MA, 1992), pp. 84–5, 94–6.

43. Memorandum by Edward Grey, 15 March 1907; Grey to Nicolson, London, 19 March 1907, TNA FO 418/38, fos. 79, 90–91.

44. Paul Miliukov, *Political Memoirs 1905–1917*, trans. Carl Goldberg (Ann Arbor, 1967), p. 184.

45. McDonald, *United Government*, pp. 153, 157–8; Andrew Rossos, *Russia and the Balkans. Inter-Balkan Rivalries and Russian Foreign Policy 1908–1914* (Toronto, 1981), p. 11; Ronald Bobroff, *Roads to Glory. Late Imperial Russia and the Turkish Straits* (London, 2006), pp. 13–15.

46. On the background to the Potsdam Agreement, see I. I. Astaf'ev, *Russko-germanskie diplomaticheskie otnosheniia, 1905–1911 g.g.* ([Moscow], 1972).

47. On Hartwig, see Rossos, *Russia and the Balkans*, pp. 50–51; on Charykov's diplomacy in 1911, see Bobroff, *Roads to Glory*, pp. 23–6.

48. McDonald, *United Government*, p. 166.

49. Cited in Lieven, *Nicholas II*, p. 82.

50. Rossos, *Russia and the Balkans*, p. 9; Uwe Liszkowski, *Zwischen Liberalismus und Imperialismus. Die zaristische Aussenpolitik vor dem Ersten Weltkrieg im Urteil Miljukovs und der Kadettenpartei 1905–1914* (Stuttgart, 1974), pp. 173–4.

51. On this aspect of Russian policy, see Dietrich Geyer, *Russian Imperialism. The Interaction of Domestic and Foreign Policy 1860–1914*, trans. Bruce Little (Leamington Spa, 1987), pp. 293–317 and passim.

52. M. B. Hayne, *The French Foreign Office and the Origins of the First World War, 1898–1914* (Oxford, 1993), p. 34.

53. Ibid., p. 81.

54. 'Un Diplomate' (pseud.), *Paul Cambon, ambassadeur de France* (Paris, 1937), p. 234.

55. Hayne, *French Foreign Office*, pp. 84, 103.

56. Ibid., p. 85.

57. Ibid., pp. 174, 200.

58. On the Moroccan Accord of 8 February 1909, see Paul Cambon to Henri Cambon, 7 February 1909, in Cambon, *Correspondance*, vol. 2, pp. 272–3.

59. Hayne, *French Foreign Office*, pp. 199, 207

60. Herbette, 'Relations avec la France de 1902 à 1908. Notes de Maurice Herbette', AMAE NS Allemagne 26, esp. fos. 3 verso, 25, 27, 34, 36, 37, 58, 87, 91, 113, 150, 160, 175, 182, 200, 212, 219, 249, 343; for a discussion of this document, see Hayne, *French Foreign Office*, p. 209.

61. Cited in Jean-Claude Allain, *Agadir. Une Crise impérialiste en Europe pour la conquête du Maroc* (Paris, 1976), p. 284; see also Hayne, *French Foreign Office*, p. 212; on French handling of the relationship with Germany in Morocco, see also E. Oncken, *Panthersprung nach Agadir. Die deutsche Politik während der zweiten Marokkokrise 1911* (Düsseldorf, 1981), pp. 98–109.

62. E.W. Edwards, 'The Franco-German Agreement on Morocco, 1909', *English Historical Review*, 78 (1963), pp. 483–513.

63. For a subtle analysis of the transition to 'adventurist diplomacy' in Paris in 1910–11, see Allain, *Agadir*, pp. 279–97.

64. Hildebrand, *Das vergangene Reich*, p. 161.

65. Wolfgang J. Mommsen, *Grossmachtstellung und Weltpolitik. Die Aussenpolitik des Deutschen Reiches, 1870 bis 1914* (Frankfurt am Main, 1993), p. 125.

66. Geoff Eley, 'The View from the Throne: The Personal Rule of Kaiser Wilhelm II', *Historical Journal*, 28/2 (1985), pp. 469–85.

67. Holstein to Eulenburg, Berlin, 3 February 1897; see also Eulenburg to Holstein, Vienna, 7 February 1897, in Rich, Fisher and Frauendienst (eds.), *Die geheimen Papiere*, docs. 599 and 601, vol. 4, pp. 8, 12; see also Hohenlohe to Eulenburg, Berlin, 4 February 1897, in C. z. Hohenlohe-Schillingsfürst, *Denkwürdigkeiten der Reichskanzlerzeit*, ed. K. A. v. Müller (Stuttgart, Berlin, 1931), p. 297.

68. Lerman, *Chancellor as Courtier*, p. 110.

69. Wilhelm to Bülow, 11 August 1905, in *GP*, vol. 19/2, pp. 496–8; see also Lerman, *Chancellor as Courtier*, pp. 129–30.

70. Peter Winzen, *Reichskanzler Bernhard Fürst von Bülow: Weltmachtstratege ohne Fortune, Wegbereiter der grossen Katastrophe* (Göttingen, 2003), pp. 134–46.

71. Lerman, *Chancellor as Courtier*, p. 258.

72. Konrad H. Jarausch, *The Enigmatic Chancellor. Bethmann Hollweg and the Hubris of Imperial Germany* (New Haven, 1973), pp. 72, 110.

73. Sir Edward and Lady Grey, *Cottage Book. The Undiscovered Country Diary of an Edwardian Statesman*, ed. Michael Waterhouse (London, 2001), p. 63; on Grey's avowed dislike of political life, see also p. 21.

74. Spring-Rice to Ferguson (Lord Nova), 16 July 1898, in Stephen Gwynn (ed.), *The Letters and Friendships of Sir Cecil Spring-Rice* (London, 1929) pp. 252–3.

75. Arthur Ponsonby, cited in Steiner, *British Foreign Office*, p. 84.

76. Ibid., p. 92.

77. Ibid., p. 91.

78. Dominik Geppert, *Pressekriege. Öffentlichkeit und Diplomatie in den deutsch-britischen Beziehungen (1896–1912)* (Munich, 2007), pp. 412–18.

79. On elite relations with Germany, see Thomas Weber, 'Our Friend "The Enemy"'. *Elite Education in Britain and Germany before World War I* (Stanford, 2008).

80. Speech given by Grey at the Eighty Club, reported in *The Times*, 1 June 1905, p. 12, col. B.

81. Jean-Claude Allain, *Joseph Caillaux* (2 vols., Paris, 1978), vol. 1, esp. pp. 327–3; W. Henry Cooke, 'Joseph Caillaux. Statesman of the Third Republic', *Pacific Historical Review*, 13/3 (1944), pp. 292–7.

82. Allain, *Joseph Caillaux*, vol. 1, p. 388.

83. John Keiger, *France and the Origins of the First World War* (London, 1983), pp. 35, 42.

84. Allain, *Agadir*, p. 402.

85. Ralf Forsbach, *Alfred von Kiderlen-Wächter (1852–1912). Ein Diplomatenleben im Kaiserreich* (2 vols., Göttingen, 1997), vol. 2, pp. 500–501.

86. Oscar Freiherr von der Lancken-Wakenitz to Langwerth von Simmern, Paris, 21 August 1911, *GP*, vol. 29, doc. 10717.

87. On Kiderlen's failure to keep Bethmann Hollweg informed of developments, see the diary entry by Kurt Riezler, 30 July 1911, in Karl Dietrich Erdmann (ed.), *Kurt Riezler. Tagebücher, Aufsätze, Dokumente* (Göttingen, 1972), pp. 178–9.

88. Report Schoen to Foreign Office Berlin, Paris, 7 May 1911, *GP*, vol. 29, doc. 10554, fo. 113.

89. David Stevenson, *Armaments and the Coming of War: Europe 1904–1914* (Cambridge, 1996), pp. 182–3; Oncken, *Panthersprung*, pp. 136–44; on the *Panther*'s mission as a manifestation of Kiderlen's 'prudence' and desire to avoid 'warlike complications', see esp. Allain, *Agadir*, p. 333.

90. G. P. Gooch, 'Kiderlen-Wächter', *Cambridge Historical Journal*, 5/2 (1936), pp. 178–92, here p. 187.

91. Forsbach, *Kiderlen-Wächter*, pp. 469, 471, 474, 476, 477.

92. These comments are recorded in 'Indications données à M. Stéphen Pichon

à M. de Margerie, 18 October 1918', in AMAE, NS Allemagne 51, fo. 202, cited in Stefan Schmidt, *Frankreichs Aussenpolitik in der Julikrise 1914. Ein Beitrag zur Geschichte des Ausbruchs des Ersten Weltrieges* (Munich, 2009), p. 228.

93. Grey to Bertie, 19 and 20 July 1911, Bertie to Grey, 21 July 1911, *BD*, vol. 7, docs. 397, 405, 408, pp. 376, 382, 385; see also Samuel R. Williamson, *The Politics of Grand Strategy. Britain and France Prepare for War, 1904–1914* (Cambridge, MA, 1969), pp. 146–7.

94. Keith M. Wilson, 'The Agadir Crisis, the Mansion House Speech and the Double-edgedness of Agreements', *Historical Journal*, 15/3 (1972), p. 517.

95. Bertie to Grey, Paris, 17 July 1911, *BD*, vol. 7, doc. 391, pp. 370–71.

96. Grey to Goschen, London, 21 July 1911, ibid., doc. 411, p. 390.

97. 'Mr Lloyd George on British Prestige', *The Times*, 22 July 1911, p. 7, col. A.

98. Stevenson, *Armaments*, p. 186.

99. Timothy Boyle, 'New Light on Lloyd George's Mansion House Speech', *Historical Journal*, 23/2 (1980), pp. 431–3; on the anti-German orientation of the speech, see Richard A. Cosgrove, 'A Note on Lloyd George's Speech at the Mansion House, 21 July 1911', *Historical Journal*, 12/4 (1969), pp. 698–701; on the liberal imperialist planning behind the speech, see Wilson, 'The Agadir Crisis', pp. 513–32; also id., *The Policy of the Entente. Essays on the Determinants of British Foreign Policy, 1904–1914* (Cambridge, 1985), p. 27; Williamson, *Grand Strategy*, pp. 153–5.

100. Cited in Wilson, 'Agadir Crisis', pp. 513–14.

101. Wilson, *Policy of the Entente*, p. 27.

102. Steiner, *British Foreign Office*, p. 125.

103. On the place of the 'war option' in Grey's policy, see Jost Dülffer, Martin Kröger and Rolf-Harald Wippich, *Vermiedene Kriege. Deeskalation von Konflikten der Grossmächte zwischen Krimkrieg und Ersten Weltkrieg 1856–1914* (Munich, 1997), p. 639.

104. Bethmann to Metternich, 22 November 1911, *GP*, vol. 29, doc. 10657, pp. 261–6 (on the British government's 'order to prepare for war'); Bethmann to Metternich, 22 November 1911, *GP*, vol. 31, doc. 11321, pp. 31–3 (p. 32 on the 'readiness to strike'). On Britain's role in escalating the crisis: Hew Strachan, *The First World War* (Oxford, 2001), p. 26.

105. Aehrenthal, audience with Emperor Franz Joseph, Mendel, 3 August 1911, *ÖUAP*, vol. 3, doc. 2579, pp. 292–4, here p. 294.

106. Conversation between Kiderlen and Osten-Sacken, reported in Osten-Sacken to Neratov, Berlin, 20 August 1911, *IBZI*, series 3, vol. 1, part 1, doc. 238, p. 344.

107. Friedrich Kiessling, *Gegen den grossen Krieg? Entspannung in den internationalen Beziehungen, 1911–1914* (Munich, 2002), p. 59.

108. Wilson, *Policy of the Entente*, pp. 31–6.

109. Ibid., p. 29.

110. Williamson, *Grand Strategy*, p. 46; Christopher Andrew, *Théophile Delcassé and the Making of the Entente Cordiale. A Reappraisal of French Foreign Policy (1898–1905)* (London, 1968), pp. 283–4; on Haldane's involvement in these developments, see Edward M. Spiers, *Haldane. An Army Reformer* (Edinburgh, 1980), p. 78.

111. Williamson, *Grand Strategy*, esp. chap. 7.

112. Wilson, *Policy of the Entente*, p. 123.

113. Schmidt, *Frankreichs Aussenpolitik*, pp. 156–171, 196.

114. Baron Guillaume to Davignon, 14 April 1913, MAEB AD, France 11, Correspondance politique – légations.

115. Edward House, *The Intimate Papers of Edward House* (2 vols., London, 1926), vol. 1, *Behind the Political Curtain, 1912–1915*, pp. 254–5.

116. I owe this tidbit to Professor Laurence W. Martin, author of *Peace Without Victory. Woodrow Wilson and the British Liberals* (Port Washington, 1973).

117. Peter Gatrell, *Government, Industry and Rearmament in Russia, 1900–1914. The Last Argument of Tsarism* (Cambridge, 1994), pp. 128–9; William C. Fuller, *Strategy and Power in Russia, 1600–1914* (New York, 1992), p. 411; Stevenson, *Armaments*, p. 156.

118. Gatrell, *Government*, pp. 147–8.

119. V. A. Sukhomlinov, *Erinnerungen* (Berlin, 1924), pp. 271–7; V. N. Kokovtsov, *Out of My Past: The Memoirs of Count Kokovtsov, Russian Minister of Finance, 1904–1914, Chairman of the Council of Ministers, 1911–1914*, ed. H. H. Fischer, trans. Laura Matveev (Stanford, 1935), pp. 229, 313–5.

120. Stevenson, *Armaments*, p. 178.

121. Peter-Christian Witt, *Die Finanzpolitik des Deutschen Reiches von 1903 bis 1913. Eine Studie zur Innenpolitik des wilhelminischen Deutschland* (Lübeck, 1970), pp. 318–20, 323.

122. Stig Förster, *Der doppelte Militarismus. Die deutsche Heeresrüstungspolitik zwischen Status-Quo-Sicherung und Aggression, 1890–1913* (Stuttgart and Wiesbaden, 1985), pp. 112–16, 224.

123. See Terence Zuber, *Inventing the Schlieffen Plan* (Oxford, 2002), passim.

124. On the structural constraints on Reich military expenditure, see Niall Ferguson, 'Public Finance and National Security. The Domestic Origins of the First World War Revisited', *Past & Present*, 142 (1994), pp. 141–68.

125. Karl von Einem to Bernhard von Bülow, 18 June 1906, cited in Herrmann, *The Arming of Europe*, p. 67.

126. Annika Mombauer, *Helmuth von Moltke and the Origins of the First World War* (Cambridge, 2001), p. 88.

127. David G. Herrmann, *The Arming of Europe and the Making of the First World War* (Princeton, 1996), pp. 64–5.

128. Conrad cited in ibid., p. 98; Stevenson, *Armaments*, p. 6; Norman Stone, 'Army and Society in the Habsburg Monarchy 1900–1914', *Past & Present*,

33 (April 1966), pp. 95–111; István Deák, 'The Fall of Austria-Hungary: Peace, Stability, and Legitimacy' in Geir Lundestad (ed.), *The Fall of Great Powers* (Oxford, 1994), p. 89.

129. On the struggle for funds, see Joseph Joffre, *Mémoires du Maréchal Joffre (1910–1917)* (Paris, 1932), pp. 41–59, citation p. 58; Gerd Krumeich, *Armaments and Politics in France on the Eve of the First World War. The Introduction of the Three-Year Conscription 1913–1914*, trans. Stephen Conn (Leamington Spa, 1984); Stevenson, *Armaments*, p. 218; on realignments in opinion, see Paul B. Miller, *From Revolutionaries to Citizens. Antimilitarism in France, 1870–1914* (Durham and London, 2002), pp. 173–200.

130. Krumeich, *Armaments and Politics*, p. 47.

131. Förster, *Der doppelte Militarismus*, pp. 216–220, 272; Herrmann, *The Arming of Europe*, p. 190; Witt, *Die Finanzpolitik*, pp. 356–7.

132. William C. Fuller, *Civil-Military Conflict in Imperial Russia 1881–1914* (Princeton, 1985), p. 225; quotation: H. H. Fisher (ed.), *Out of My Past. The Memoirs of Count Kokovtsov Russian Minister of Finance, 1904–1911, Chairman of the Council of Ministers, 1911–1914*, trans. Laura Matveev (Stanford, 1935), p. 340.

133. Joseph Caillaux, *Mes Mémoires* (3 vols., Paris, 1942–7), vol. 2, *Mes audaces – Agadir . . . 1909–12*, pp. 211–15; Krumeich, *Armaments and Politics*, p. 24.

134. Lieven, *Nicholas II*, p. 175; the reference to 'civilian attitudes' is Durnovo's, see D. C. B. Lieven, *Russia's Rulers Under the Old Regime* (New Haven, 1989), p. 218.

135. Bruce W. Menning, *Bayonets Before Bullets. The Imperial Russian Army, 1861–1914* (Bloomington, 1992), pp. 221–37.

136. Fuller, *Strategy and Power*, pp. 424–33.

137. Fisher (ed.), *Memoirs of Count Kokovtsov*, p. 348.

138. David M. McDonald, 'A Lever without a Fulcrum: Domestic Factors and Russian Foreign Policy, 1904–1914', in Hugh Ragsdale (ed.), *Imperial Russian Foreign Policy* (Cambridge, 1993), pp. 268–314, here p. 302; on support for Sukhomlinov in the Council, see Fisher (ed.), *Memoirs of Count Kokovtsov*, p. 349.

139. See, for example, Peter Rassow, 'Schlieffen und Holstein', *Historische Zeitschrift*, 173 (1952), pp. 297–313.

140. Widenmann to Tirpitz, London, 28 October and 30 October 1911, *GP*, vol. 31, docs. 11313, 11314, pp. 11–15, 16–17.

141. For an illuminating analysis of the Widenmann reports, to which my discussion is indebted, see Kiessling, *Gegen den grossen Krieg?*, pp. 73–4.

142. Bethmann Hollweg to Metternich, Berlin, 31 October 1911; Metternich to Bethmann Hollweg, London, 1 November 1911, *GP*, vol. 31, docs. 11315, 11316, pp. 17–18, 18–24.

143. Kiessling, *Gegen den grossen Krieg?*, p. 74.

144. 'Der Kaiser machte eine, der Kanzler eine andere Politik, der Generalstab seine Antworthen für sich'. Alfred von Waldersee to Jagow (State Secretary for Foreign Affairs), 6 May 1919, cited in Dieter Hoffmann, *Der Sprung ins Dunkle: Oder wie der 1. Weltkrieg entfesselt wurde* (Leipzig, 2010), p. 137.

145. D. Ralston, *The Army of the Republic* (Cambridge, MA, 1967), pp. 338–40 observes that Moltke, unlike Joffre, had to contend with an emperor who took his duties as 'supreme warlord' seriously; critical of this view: Douglas Porch, *The March to the Marne. The French Army, 1871–1914* (Cambridge, 1981), pp. 171–2.

146. Wilson diary entries 9 August 1911 and 16 November 1911, Imperial War Museum London; third quotation: Hew Strachan, *The Politics of the British Army* (Oxford, 1997), p. 114; on Wilson's political and constitutional views see ibid., pp. 114–15, 125–6.

147. Samuel Williamson and Russell Van Wyk, *Soldiers, Statesmen and the Coming of the Great War. A Brief Documentary History* (Boston, 2003), p. 218.

148. Raymond Poincaré, 'Entretien avec Kokowtsoff – Chemins de fer stratégiques', St Petersburg, August 1912, AMAE, NS Russie 41, fo. 280.

149. Porch, *March to the Marne*, p. 175; on the binding effect of the Russian alliance on French security arrangements, see also comments of 17 June 1914 by Maurice Herbette reported in Georges Louis, *Les Carnets de Georges Louis* (2 vols., Paris, 1926), vol. 2, p. 114.

150. Krumeich, *Armaments and Politics*, p. 214.

151. Mombauer, *Moltke*, p. 45.

152. Fuller, *Civil-Military Conflict*, p. 225.

153. Marc Trachtenberg, 'The Coming of the First World War: A Reassessment', in id., *History and Strategy* (Princeton, 1991).

154. Pourtalès to Bethmann Hollweg, St Petersburg, 1 February 1913, reporting a conversation with Sazonov, PA-AA, R 10896.

155. Ibid., 11 March 1914, PA-AA, R 10898.

156. Miliukov, *Political Memoirs*, p. 235.

157. Modris Eksteins, 'Sir Edward Grey and Imperial Germany in 1914', *Journal of Contemporary History*, 6/3 (1971), pp. 121–31.

158. Bernhard von Bülow, speech to the Reichstag, 29 March 1909, cited in Bernhard Rosenberger, *Zeitungen als Kriegstreiber? Die Rolle der Presse im Vorfeld des Ersten Weltkrieges* (Cologne, 1998), p. 33.

159. On these developments and their impact on German politics, see Joachim Radkau, *Das Zeitalter der Nervosität. Deutschland zwischen Bismarck und Hitler* (Munich, 1998); Mommsen, *Bürgerstolz und Weltmachtstreben*, p. 187; Hans-Ulrich Wehler, *Deutsche Gesellschaftsgeschichte* (5 vols., Munich, 1987–2008), vol. 3, p. 905; J. Sperber, *The Kaiser's Voters. Electors and Elections in Imperial Germany* (Cambridge, 1997); J. N. Retallack, *Notables of the Right. The Conservative Party and Political Mobilization in Germany* (Winchester, 1988; G. Eley, *The Reshaping of the German Right*.

Radical Nationalism and Political Change after Bismarck (New Haven, 1980); T. Nipperdey, *Die Organisation der deutschen Parteien vor 1918* (Düsseldorf, 1961); D. Blackbourn, 'The Politics of Demagogy in Imperial Germany', in id., *Populists and Patricians. Essays in Modern German History* (London, 1987), pp. 217–45, here pp. 222ff.

160. Bosworth, *Italy*, p. 44.

161. On Corradini and his influence, in a pan-European context, see Monique de Taeye-Henen, *Le Nationalisme d'Enrico Corradini et les origines du fascisme dans la revue florentine Il Regno, 1903–1906* (Paris, 1973); and the useful introduction to Enrico Corradini, *Scritti e discorsi*, ed. Lucia Strappini (Turin, 1980), pp. vii–lix.

162. William Mulligan, *The Origins of the First World War* (Cambridge, 2010), p. 139.

163. McDonald, *United Government*, p. 182; Louise McReynolds, *The News Under Russia's Old Regime. The Development of a Mass-Circulation Press* (Princeton, 1991), pp. 223–52.

164. See Bosworth, *Italy*, p. 17; Clark, *Kaiser Wilhelm II*, pp. 218–55; Geppert, *Pressekriege*, passim.

165. Lieven, *Nicholas II*, p. 96.

166. Buisseret (Belgian minister in St Petersburg) to Davignon (Belgian Minister of Foreign Affairs), 17 January 1914, MAEB AD, Empire Russe 34, 1914.

167. Hardinge to Nicolson, 28 October 1908, cited in Keith Neilson, '"My Beloved Russians": Sir Arthur Nicolson and Russia, 1906–1916', *International History Review*, 9/4 (1987), pp. 538–9.

168. Judith A. Head, 'Public Opinions and Middle-Eastern Railways. The Russo-German Railway Negotations of 1910–11', *International History Review*, 6/1 (1984), pp. 28–47, here pp. 46–7.

169. Theodore Roosevelt, *America and the World War* (London, 1915), p. 36.

170. Hibbert, *Edward VII*, pp. 256–7; Tombs and Tombs, *That Sweet Enemy*, pp. 438–40.

171. Kosztowits to Tets van Goudriaan, 7 March 1906, NA, 2.05.36, doc. 10, Rapporten aan en briefwisseling met het Ministerie van Buitenlandse Zaken.

172. Stevenson, *Armaments*, p. 193; Allain, *Agadir*, pp. 379–82.

173. Descos (French minister in Belgrade) to Doumergue (French foreign minister), 23 March 1914, 22 April 1914, 9 June 1914 in *DDF*, 3rd series (1911–14), vol. 10, docs. 17, 145, 347, pp. 26–7, 252–5, 513–15.

174. Fuller, *Civil-Military Conflict*, p. 210.

175. Kohlhaas, memorandum to Pourtalès, Moscow, 3 December 1912, PA-AA, R 10895.

176. Guillaume to Davignon, Paris, 5 May 1913, MAEB AD, France 11, 1914.

177. Keith Robbins, 'Public Opinion, the Press and Pressure Groups', in F. H. Hinsley (ed.), *British Foreign Policy under Sir Edward Grey* (Cambridge, 1977), pp. 70–88, here p. 72; Geppert, *Pressekriege*, pp. 59–69.

178. Denis Mack Smith, *Italy and Its Monarchy* (New Haven, 1989), p. 191.

179. D. W. Spring, 'Russia and the Coming of War', in R. J. W. Evans and H. Pogge von Strandmann (eds.), *The Coming of the First World War* (Oxford, 1988), pp. 57–86, here pp. 59–60.

180. Report from an unnamed German journalist on the *Lokal-Anzeiger* of St Petersburg, forwarded in Pourtalès to Bethmann, St Petersburg, 17 March 1911, PA-AA, R 10544.

181. Hayne, *French Foreign Office*, pp. 43–4.

182. McDonald, *United Government*, pp. 133, 134, 191.

183. Hayne, *French Foreign Office*, p. 47.

184. Krumeich, *Armaments and Politics*, pp. 46–7.

185. Fuller, *Strategy and Power in Russia*, pp. 419–20.

186. Buisseret to Davignon, St Petersburg, 17 January 1914, 27 March 1914, 9 June 1914, MAEB AD, Empire Russe 34, 1914.

187. Leopold Kammerhofer, *Diplomatie und Pressepolitik 1848–1918*, in Adam Wandruszka and Peter Urbanitsch (eds.), *Die Habsburgermonarchie 1848–1918* (10 vols., Vienna, 1973–2006), vol. 6/1, *Die Habsburger Monarchie im System der internationalen Beziehungen*, pp. 459–95, here pp. 489–90; Joseph Goričar and Lyman Beecher Stowe, *The Inside Story of Austro-German Intrigue or How the World War Was Brought About* (New York, 1920).

188. Hayne, *French Foreign Office*, p. 45.

189. On subsidies to journalists in St Petersburg: Pourtalès to Bethmann Hollweg, St Petersburg, 2 December 1911, PA-AA, R 10544; on British subsidies: Mulligan, *Origins of the First World War*, p. 169.

190. Georges Louis to Political and Commercial Department, MFA, St Petersburg, 24 February 1912, AMAE NS Russie 41.

191. Genther Kronenbitter, *'Krieg im Frieden'. Die Führung der k.u.k. Armee und die Grossmachtpolitik Österreich-Ungarns 1906–1914* (Munich, 2003), p. 450.

192. 'English money': Count Mirbach-Sorquitten to Bethmann Hollweg, 3 July 1914, PA-AA, R 10544; Constantinople: Sean McMeekin, *The Berlin–Baghdad Express. The Ottoman Empire and Germany's Bid for World Power 1898–1918* (London, 2010), p. 69.

193. Jules Cambon to Maurice Paléologue, Berlin, 10 May 1912, AMAE PA-AP, 43 Cambon Jules, 56, fo. 204.

194. Jules Cambon to Raymond Poincaré, Berlin, 26 October 1912, AMAE PA-AP, 43 Cambon Jules 56, fos. 51–2.

195. Moltke to Bethmann, 2 December 1912 PA-AA Berlin, R789.

196. Krumeich, *Armaments and Politics*, p. 48; Schmidt, *Frankreichs Aussenpolitik*, pp. 216–18, 227.

197. Cited in H. Temperley and L. Penson, *Foundations of British Foreign Policy from Pitt to Salisbury* (Cambridge, 1938), pp. 519–20.

198. Justin de Selves to Georges Louis, 21 August 1911, *DDF*, 2nd series, vol. 14, doc. 200, pp. 255–6; Louis to de Selves, 1 September 1911, ibid., doc. 234, pp. 305–7.

199. Tschirschky to Bethmann Hollweg, reporting a conversation with Jovanović, 18 November 1912; Pourtalès to Bethmann Hollweg, reporting a conversation with Sazonov, St Petersburg, 10 December 1912, PA-AA, R 10895.

200. Pourtalès to Bethmann Hollweg, St Petersburg, 17 November 1912, ibid.; on this practice in Russian diplomacy, see also Geyer, *Russian Imperialism*, p. 315.

201. Ronald Bobroff, 'Behind the Balkan Wars. Russian Policy towards Bulgaria and the Turkish Straits, 1912–13', *Russian Review*, 59/1 (2000), pp. 76–95, here p. 79.

202. Pourtalès to Bülow, St Petersburg, 11 December 1908, *GP*, vol. 26/1, doc. 9187, pp. 387–8; Wilhelm II to Franz Joseph, Berlin, 26 January 1909, *GP*, vol. 26/2, doc. 9193, pp. 401–2; Nicholas II to Wilhelm II, St Petersburg, 25 January 1909, *GP*, vol. 26/2, doc. 9194, pp. 402–4.

203. Grey to Asquith, 13 September 1911, cited in Kiessling, *Gegen den grossen Krieg?*, p. 40; Pourtalès to Bethmann Hollweg, St Petersburg, 12 February 1910, PA-AA, R 10894.

204. Stevenson, *Armaments*, p. 160.

205. Radolin to Bethmann Hollweg, Paris, 10 February 1910, PA-AA, R 10894.

206. Guillaume to Davignon, 5 January 1914, MAEB AD, France 12, 1914.

207. Geppert, *Pressekriege*, pp. 123, 230.

208. Lieven, *Nicholas II*, p. 192.

209. Geppert, *Pressekriege*, p. 358.

210. Tatishchev to Nicholas II, 27 February 1913, GARF, Fond 601, op. 1, del 746 (2).

211. Rosenberger, *Zeitungen*, passim; Geppert, *Pressekriege*, p. 27.

212. Friedrich von Bernhardi, *Germany and the Next War*, trans. Allen H. Powles (London, 1912), esp. chap. 1.

213. Kiessling, *Gegen den grossen Krieg?*, pp. 70, 99.

214. James Joll, *1914: The Unspoken Assumptions. An Inaugural Lecture Delivered 25 April 1968* (London, 1968).

215. On 'defensive patriotism' as the default position of all the European public spheres, see Mulligan, *Origins*, p. 159.

216. R. B. Brett, 2nd Viscount Esher, 'To-day and to-morrow', in id., *To-day and To-morrow and Other Essays* (London, 1910), p. 13; id., *Modern War and Peace* (Cambridge, 1912), p. 19.

217. Cited in John Gooch, 'Attitudes to War in Late Victorian and Edwardian England' in id., *The Prospect of War: Studies in British Defence Policy, 1847–1942* (London, 1981), pp. 35–51.

218. On 'sacrificial ideology', see Alexander Watson and Patrick Porter, 'Bereaved and Aggrieved: Combat Motivation and the Ideology of Sacrifice in the First

World War', *Historical Research*, 83 (2010), pp. 146–64; on positive depictions of conflict, see Glenn R. Wilkinson, '"The Blessings of War": The Depiction of Military Force in Edwardian Newspapers', *Journal of Contemporary History*, 33 (1998), pp. 97–115.

219. Cited in C. E. Playne, *The Pre-War Mind in Britain: A Historical Review* (London, 1928), p. 148.

220. For an excellent account of these issues, see Zara Steiner, 'Views of War: Britain Before the Great War – and After', *International Relations*, 17 (2003), pp. 7–33.

221. Fuller, *Civil-Military Conflict*, p. 197, id., *Strategy and Power*, p. 395.

222. Krümeich, *Armaments and Politics*, pp. 101–2; Herrmann, *The Arming of Europe*, p. 194.

223. Stevenson, *Armaments*, p. 150; Herrmann, *The Arming of Europe*, pp. 113–14.

224. Playne, *The Pre-War Mind*, pp. 147–8.

225. Brendan Simms, *The Impact of Napoleon. Prussian High Politics, Foreign Policy and the Crisis of the Executive, 1797–1806* (Cambridge, 1997).

226. Andrew Preston, *The War Council: McGeorge Bundy, the NSC, and Vietnam* (Cambridge, MA, 2006).

227. Philip E. Mosely, 'Russian Policy in 1911–12', *Journal of Modern History*, 12 (1940), pp. 69–86, here p. 86.

CHAPTER 5

1. G. F. Abbott, *The Holy War in Tripoli* (London, 1912), pp. 192–5.

2. Lt-Col Gustavo Ramaciotti, *Tripoli. A Narrative of the Principal Engagements of the Italian-Turkish War* (London, 1912), p. 117.

3. Ernest N. Bennett, *With the Turks in Tripoli. Being Some Experiences of the Turco-Italian War of 1911* (London, 1912), pp. 24–5.

4. Ibid., p. 77.

5. George Young, *Nationalism and War in the Near East* (Oxford, 1915).

6. 'M. Miroslaw Spalaïkovitch', interview with Spalajković in *La Revue Diplomatique*, 31 July 1924, cutting filed in AS, Personal fonds Miroslav Spalajković, Fiche 101, fo. 95.

7. William C. Askew, *Europe and Italy's Acquisition of Libya 1911–1912* (Durham, NC, 1942), p. 19; on the incorporation of a Libyan guarantee into the second renewal of the Triple Alliance in 1887, see Holger Afflerbach, *Der Dreibund. Europäische Grossmacht- und Allianzpolitik vor dem Ersten Weltkrieg* (Vienna, 2002), p. 691.

8. R. J. B. Bosworth, *Italy, the Least of the Great Powers. Italian Foreign Policy before the First World War* (Cambridge, 1979), pp. 137–8.

9. Enrico Serra, 'La burocrazia della politica estera italiana', in R. J. B. Bosworth and Sergio Romano (eds.), *La Politica estera italiana (1860–1985)*, (Bologna, 1991), pp. 69–90, here p. 80.

10. Miles Ignotus (pseud.), 'Italian Nationalism and the War with Turkey', *Fortnightly Review*, 90 (December 1911), pp. 1084–96, here pp. 1088–91; Askew, *Europe and Italy's Acquisition of Libya*, pp. 25, 27; Francesco Malgeri, *Guerra Libica (1911–1912)* (Rome, 1970), pp. 37–96.

11. On socialist jingoism at the time of the invasion, see Bennett, *With the Turks*, p. 7.

12. Bosworth, *Italy*, p. 151.

13. Pietro di Scalea to San Giuliano, 13 August 1911, cited in ibid., p. 158.

14. Thus Grey summarized his conversation with the ambassador in a subsequent letter to Sir Rennell Rodd, see Grey to Rodd, 28 July 1911, TNA FO 371/1250, fo. 311.

15. Bosworth, *Italy*, pp. 152–3.

16. Grey to Nicolson, London, 19 September 1911, *BD*, vol. 9/1, doc. 231, p. 274.

17. Bosworth, *Italy*, p. 159; Afflerbach, *Dreibund*, p. 693.

18. Cited in Bosworth, *Italy*, p. 160.

19. The ambassador was the former secretary of state for foreign affairs Marschall von Bieberstein, who strongly opposed the Italian campaign. On the tensions in German policy, see W. David Wrigley, 'Germany and the Turco-Italian War, 1911–1912', *International Journal of Middle Eastern Studies*, 11/3 (1980), pp. 313–38, esp. pp. 315, 319–20; also Malgeri, *Guerra Libica*, p. 138; Afflerbach, *Dreibund*, pp. 693–4.

20. Malgeri, *Guerra Libica*, p. 119.

21. Memorandum San Giuliano to Giolitti, Fiuggi, 28 July 1911, in Claudio Pavone, *Dalle carte di Giovanni Giolitti: quarant'anni di politica italiana* (3 vols., Milan, 1962), vol. 3, *Dai prodromi della grande guerra al fascismo, 1910–1928*, doc. 49, pp. 52–6.

22. Timothy W. Childs, *Italo-Turkish Diplomacy and the War Over Libya* (Leiden, 1990), pp. 44–5.

23. Report San Giuliano to Giolitti, 28 July 1911, in Pavone, *Dalle carte*, pp. 52–6.

24. Childs, *Italo-Turkish Diplomacy*, pp. 46–7.

25. Chevalier Tullio Irace, *With the Italians in Tripoli. The Authentic History of the Turco-Italian War* (London, 1912), pp. 11–12.

26. For a good account of the fighting around Tripoli in October and November 1911, despite a strong pro-Italian bias, see W. K. McLure, *Italy in North Africa. An Account of the Tripoli Enterprise* (London, 1913), pp. 60–109; on international reports of Italian atrocities and Arab resistance more generally, see Malgeri, *Guerra Libica*, pp. 195 and 165–94.

27. Texts of the treaties and the Imperial *Ferman* conceding autonomy in Childs, *Italo-Turkish Diplomacy*, pp. 243–53.

28. Sergio Romano, *La Quarta Sponda: La Guerra di Libia, 1911–1912* (Milan, 1977), p. 14.

29. Malgeri, *Guerra Libica*, pp. 303, 306–8, 309.

30. Ibid., pp. 327–9.

31. Paul Cambon to Poincaré, 25 January 1912, *DDF*, 3rd series, vol. 1, doc. 516, pp. 535–8, here p. 536.

32. On the failure of the 'concert system' in the last years before the war, see Richard Langhorne, *The Collapse of the Concert of Europe. International Politics, 1890–1914* (New York, 1981), esp. pp. 97–107; Günther Kronenbitter, 'Diplomatisches Scheitern: Die Julikrise 1914 und die Konzertdiplomatie der europäischen Grossmächte', in Bernhard Chiari and Gerhard P. Gross (eds.), *Am Rande Europas? Balkan – Raum und Bevölkerung als Wirkungsfelder militärischer Gewalt* (Munich, 2009), pp. 55–66. F. R. Bridge, 'Österreich(-Urgarn) unter der Grossmächten', in Wandruszka and Urbanitsch (eds.), *Die Habsburgermonarchie*, vol. 6/1, pp. 196–373, here pp. 329–32.

33. Rainer Lahme, *Deutsche Aussenpolitik 1890–1894. Von der Gleichgewichtspolitik Bismarcks zur Allianzstrategie Caprivis* (Göttingen, 1990), pp. 316–337, 494.

34. Cited in William L. Langer, *The Franco-Russian Alliance, 1890–1894* (Cambridge, 1929), p. 83.

35. Treadway, *Falcon and Eagle*, pp. 88–9.

36. Andrew Rossos, *Russia and the Balkans. Inter-Balkan Rivalries and Russian Foreign Policy, 1908–1914* (Toronto, 1981), p. 36.

37. Richard C. Hall, *The Balkan Wars, 1912–1913. Prelude to the First World War* (London, 2000), p. 11.

38. Cited in Robert Elsie (ed.), *Kosovo. In the Heart of the Balkan Powder Keg* (Boulder, 1997), p. 333.

39. Figures calculated from Hall, *Balkan Wars*, p. 24.

40. Richard C. Hall, *Bulgaria's Road to the First World War* (Boulder, 1997), pp. 78–9.

41. Alex N. Dragnich, *Serbia, Nikola Pašić and Yugoslavia* (New Brunswick, 1974), p. 101

42. Rapaport (Netherlands Consul-General) to Vredenburch (Netherlands minister in Bucharest, formally responsible for Serbia), Belgrade, 23 March 1913, NA, 2.05.36, 9 Consulaat-Generaal Belgrado en Gezantschap Zuid-Slavië.

43. Rossos, *Russia and the Balkans*, p. 161; Ivan T. Teodorov, *Balkanskite voini (1912–1913). Istorischeski, diplomaticheski i strategicheski ocherk* (Sofia, 2007), p. 182.

44. Teodorov, *Balkanskite voini*, pp. 259, 261.

45. Kiril Valtchev Merjansky, 'The Secret Serbian-Bulgarian Treaty of Alliance of 1904 and the Russian Policy in the Balkans before the Bosnian Crisis', MA thesis, Wright State University, 2007, pp. 19, 27, 52, 79.

46. Rossos, *Russia and the Balkans*, p. 175.

47. Rapaport to Vredenburch, Belgrade, 27 May 1913, NA, 2.05.36, doc. 9, Consulaat-Generaal Belgrado en Gezantschap Zuid-Slavië, 1891–1940.

48. Philip E. Mosely, 'Russian Policy in 1911–12', *Journal of Modern History*, 12 (1940), pp. 73–4; Rossos, *Russia and the Balkans*, pp. 12, 15.

49. Ronald Bobroff, *Roads to Glory. Late Imperial Russia and the Turkish Straits* (London, 2006), pp. 23–4.

50. See David Schimmelpenninck van der Oye, 'Russian Foreign Policy: 1815–1917', in D. C. B. Lieven (ed.), *Cambridge History of Russia* (3 vols., Cambridge, 2006), vol. 2, *Imperial Russia, 1689–1917*, pp. 554–74, here p. 573.

51. Cited in Rossos, *Russia and the Balkans*, p. 27.

52. V. N. Strandmann, *Balkanske Uspomene*, trans. from the Russian into Serbian by Jovan Kachaki (Belgrade, 2009) pp. 238–9.

53. Hartwig to Neratov, Belgrade, 6 October 1911 in *IBZI*, series 3, vol. 1, part 2, doc. 545.

54. Mosely, 'Russian Policy', p. 74; for an account of these developments, see Edward C. Thaden, 'Charykov and Russian Foreign Policy at Constantinople in 1911', *Journal of Central European Affairs*, 16 (1956–7), pp. 25–43; also Alan Bodger, 'Russia and the End of the Ottoman Empire', in Marian Kent (ed.), *The Great Powers and the End of the Ottoman Empire* (London, 1984), pp. 76–110; Bobroff, *Roads to Glory*, pp. 24–5.

55. Buchanan to Nicolson, St Petersburg, 21 March 1912, *BD*, vol. 9/1, doc. 563, pp. 561–2; Edward C. Thaden, *Russia and the Balkan Alliance of 1912* (University Park, TX, 1965), pp. 56–7 and 'Charykov and Russian Foreign Policy at Constantinople', in id. and Marianna Forster Thaden, *Interpreting History. Collective Essays on Russia's Relations with Europe* (Boulder, 1990), pp. 99–119.

56. Bobroff, *Roads to Glory*, pp. 26–7.

57. Ibid., pp. 30–31.

58. Sazonov to Izvolsky, St Petersburg, 2 October 1912, AVPRI, Fond 151 (PA), op. 482, d. 130, l. 5.

59. Sazonov, conversation with Nekliudov, Davos, October 1911, cited in Thaden, *Russia*, p. 78.

60. For Sazonov's belief that the Austrians would have occupied the Sanjak if the Russians had not 'bound' Vienna with a status quo agreement, see Sazonov, Confidential letter to the Russian ambassadors in Paris, London, Berlin, Vienna, Rome, Constantinople, Sofia, Belgrade, Cetinje, Athens, Bucharest and St Petersburg, 18 October 1912, AVPRI, Fond 151 (PA), op. 482, d. 130, ll. 79–81.

61. Katrin Boeckh, *Von den Balkankriegen zum Ersten Weltkrieg. Kleinstaatenpolitik und ethnische Selbstbestimmung aufden Balkan* (Munich, 1996), pp. 26–7; David Stevenson, *Armaments and the Coming of War. Europe 1904–1915* (Oxford, 1996), pp. 232–3.

62. Rossos, *Russia and the Balkans*, p. 45.

63. On the secret articles and the subsequent military convention of 12 May 1912, see Boeckh, *Von den Balkankriegen*, pp. 25–7; Thaden, *Russia*, pp. 56, 101, 103; Bobroff, *Roads of Glory*, pp. 43–4.

64. Sazonov to Benckendorff, 24 October 1912, transcribed in 'Pervaya Balkanskaya voina (okonchanie)', *KA*, 16 (1926), pp. 3–24, doc. 36, p. 9; see also Benno Siebert (ed.), *Benckendorffs diplomatischer Schriftwechsel* (3 vols., Berlin, 1928), vol. 2, doc. 698, pp. 462–3; David M. McDonald, *United Government and Foreign Policy in Russia 1900–1914* (Cambridge, MA, 1992), p. 180.

65. McDonald, *United Government*, Cambridge, MA, 1992 p. 181.

66. Radoslav Vesnić, *Dr Milenko Vesnić, Gransenjer Srbske Diplomatije* (Belgrade, 2008), p. 296.

67. Stevenson, *Armaments*, p. 234; Ernst Christian Helmreich, *The Diplomacy of the Balkan Wars, 1912–1913* (Cambridge, MA, 1938), p. 153; Thaden, *Russia*, p. 113.

68. Helmreich, *Balkan Wars*, pp. 156–7.

69. Conversation with Sazonov reported in Buchanan to Grey, 18 September 1912, *BD*, vol. 9/1, doc. 722, pp. 693–5, here p. 694.

70. Sazonov to Nekliudov, St Petersburg, 18 October 1912, AVPRI Fond 151 (PA), op. 482, d. 130, ll. 69–70.

71. Rossos, *Russia and the Balkans*, pp. 87–8.

72. *Novoye Vremya*, cited in Buchanan to Grey, 30 October 1912, *BD*, 9/2, doc. 78, pp. 63–6.

73. Sazonov to Izvolsky, Benckendorff, Sverbeev etc., 31 October 1912, *KA*, vol. 16, doc. 45, cited in Bobroff, *Roads to Glory*, p. 48.

74. Buchanan to Grey, 30 October 1912, *BD*, vol. 9/2, doc. 78, pp. 63–6; Sazonov to Krupensky (Russian ambassador in Rome), St Petersburg, 8 November 1912; Sazonov to Hartwig, St Petersburg, 11 November 1912, both in AVPRI, Fond 151 (PA), op. 482, d. 130, ll. 110, ll. 121–121 verso.

75. Sazonov to Hartwig, 'secret telegram', St Petersburg, 11 November 1912, AVPRI, Fond 151 (PA), op. 482, d. 130, ll. 121–2; 'Note de l'ambassade de Russie', 12 November 1912, *DDF*, 3rd series, vol. 4, doc. 431, pp. 443–4; Rossos, *Russia and the Balkans*, p. 97.

76. Pourtalès to Bethmann Hollweg, St Petersburg, 17 November 1912, PA-AA, R 10895.

77. Sazonov to Izvolsky, St Petersburg, 14 November 1912, in Friedrich Stieve (ed.), *Der diplomatische Schriftwechsel Iswolskis, 1911–1914* (Berlin, 4 vols., 1925), vol. 2, *Der Tripoliskrieg und der Erste Balkankrieg*, doc. 566, p. 345.

78. Report by Buchanan dated 28 November 1912, cited in L. C. F. Turner, *Origins of the First World War* (London, 1973), p. 34; see also supporting comment from Pourtalès in Pourtalès to Bethmann Hollweg, St Petersburg, 17 November 1912, PA-AA, R 10895.

79. Buchanan to Nicolson, St Petersburg, 9 January 1913, *BD*, vol. 9, doc. 481, p. 383.

80. Cited in Rossos, *Russia and the Balkans*, p. 109; on Russia's inability more generally to 'set and follow its own agenda', see Hew Strachan, *The First World War* (Oxford, 2001), p. 20.

81. Stevenson, *Armaments*, p. 234; Helmreich, *Russia and the Balkans*, pp. 157–62.

82. Sazonov to Kokovtsov, 'highly confidential', St Petersburg, 23 October 1912, AVPRI, Fond 151 (PA), op. 482, d. 130, ll. 46–46 verso.

83. Ibid., ll. 47–47 verso.

84. V. I. Bovykin, *Iz istorii vozniknoveniya pervoi mirovoi voiny: Otnosheniya Rossii i Frantsii v 1912–1914 gg* (Moscow, 1961), pp. 136–7.

85. Bruce W. Menning, 'Russian Military Intelligence, July 1914. What St Petersburg Perceived and Why It Mattered', unpublished typescript.

86. Laguiche to Ministry of War, St Petersburg, 16 December 1912, cited in Stevenson, *Armaments*, p. 237.

87. McDonald, *United Government*, p. 185.

88. Stevenson, *Armaments*, p. 260.

89. Bovykin, *Iz istorii vozniknoveniya*, pp. 152–3.

90. On the response in Vienna to this overture, see Tschirschky to MFA Vienna, 28 December 1912; Zimmermann to Tschirschky, Berlin, 3 January 1913; Tschirschky to Bethmann Hollweg, Vienna, 2 January 1913, *GP*, vol. 34/1, docs. 12580, 12605, 12607, pp. 91, 117–9, 120–21.

91. On Russian military measures, see Grey to Buchanan, 2 January 1913; Buchanan to Grey, 30 December 1912, *BD*, vol. 9/2, docs. 438, 419; on 'mobilization', see Louis to Poincaré, 25 and 27 December 1912, *DDF*, 3rd series, vol. 5, docs. 122, 131, pp. 142–3, 153.

92. On the situation in Austria, see Stevenson, *Armaments*, p. 262; on Russia: Pourtalès to Bethmann Hollweg, St Petersburg, 20 February 1913, PA-AA, R 10896.

93. On the crisis and the subsequent climbdown, see Lucius to Foreign Ministry, 23 December 1912, *GP*, 43/1, doc. 12570; Buchanan to Grey, 30 December 1912, Grey to Buchanan, 2 January 1913, *BD*, 9 (2), docs. 419, 438; Louis to Poincaré, 25 and 27 December 1912, *DDF*, 3rd series, vol. 5, docs. 122, 131.

94. On the impact of the winter crisis on Austro-Russian Balkan relations, see Samuel R. Williamson, 'Military Dimensions of Habsburg-Romanov Relations During the Era of the Balkan Wars', in Béla K. Király and Dimitrije Djordjević (eds.), *East Central European Society and the Balkan Wars* (Boulder, 1987), pp. 317–37.

95. Buisseret to Davignon, St Petersburg, 7 January 1913, MAEB AD, Russie 3, 1906–1913.

96. V. I. Gurko, *Cherty i Siluety Proshlogo. Pravitel'stvo i Obshchestvennost' v*

Tsarstvovanie Nikolaya II v Izobrazhenii Sovremennika (Moscow, 2000), p. 241.

97. A. Yu Ariev (ed.), *Sud'ba Veka. Krivosheiny* (St Petersburg, 2002), p. 91.

98. S. E. Kryzhanovskii, *Vospominaniia* (Berlin, 1938), p. 20.

99. In 1910, Krivoshein even wrote to Stolypin asking for raised troop strengths along the Amur river valley on the eastern march of Russian settlement. Krivoshein to Stolypin, St Petersburg, 30 April 1910, RGIA, F. 1276, op. 6, d. 690, L 129–130 ob.

100. Ariev (ed.), *Sud'ba Veka*, p. 189.

101. H. H. Fisher (ed.), *Out of My Past. The Memoirs of Count Kokovtsov Russian Minister of Finance, 1904–1914, Chairman of the Council of Ministers, 1911–1914*, trans. Laura Matveev (Stanford, 1935), p. 349.

102. I. V. Bestuzhev, *Bor'ba v Rossii po Voprosam Vneshnei Politiki Nakanune Pervoi Mirovoi Voiny* (Moscow, 1965) pp. 74, 162; Krivoshein also clashed with Kokovtsov over subsidized credits for farmers, a measure Kokovtsov opposed in the name of fiscal rigour; on the political tensions generated on both sides by Russo-German trade relations, see Horst Linke, *Das Zarische Russland und der Erste Weltkrieg. Diplomatie und Kriegsziele 1914–1917* (Munich, 1982), pp. 23–4.

103. Ariev (ed.), *Sud'ba Veka*, p. 189.

104. McDonald, *United Government*, p. 185.

105. Paul Miliukov, *Political Memoirs 1905–1917*, trans. Carl Goldberg (Ann Arbor, 1967), p. 177.

106. Sir George Buchanan, *My Mission to Russia and Other Diplomatic Memories* (2 vols., London, 1923), vol. 1, p. 71.

107. Rossos, *Russia and the Balkans*, p. 19.

108. Cited in ibid., p. 28.

109. Ibid., p. 29.

110. Sazonov's advice to Sofia: Sazonov to Nekliudov, St Petersburg, 31 October 1912; suspicions of France: Sazonov to Izvolsky, St Petersburg, 8 November 1912, both cited in Bovykin, *Iz istorii vozniknoveniya*, pp. 138, 142.

111. Thus Sazonov's account of the Tsar's view, cited in Teodorov, *Balkanskite voini*, p. 192.

112. Sazonov to Bobchev, 12 June 1913, cited in ibid., p. 233.

113. Rossos, *Russia and the Balkans*, p. 192; Teodorov, *Balkanskite voini*, pp. 42, 212.

114. Carnegie Endowment for International Peace (ed.), *Report of the International Commission to Enquire into the Causes and Conduct of the Balkan Wars* (Washington, 1914), p. 264.

115. Hall, *Balkan Wars*, p. 135.

116. Wolfgang-Uwe Friedrich, *Bulgarien und die Mächte 1913–1915* (Stuttgart, 1985), pp. 21–26.

117. Panafieu to Pichon, Sofia, 20 January 1914, *DDF*, 3rd series, vol. 9, doc. 118, pp. 139–41.

118. Savinsky to Sazonov, Sofia, 1 February 1914, *IBZI*, 3rd series, vol. 1, 157, pp. 144–8, esp. p. 147.

119. Friedrich, *Bulgarien und die Mächte*, p. 27.

120. Department note, conditions for a Bulgarian loan, Paris, 16 February 1914, *DDF*, 3rd series, vol. 9, doc. 306, pp. 389–90.

121. Malenic to Pašić, Berlin, 30 June 1914, AS, MID – PO, 415, fos. 613–20.

122. Alexander Savinsky, *Reflections from a Russian Diplomat* (London, 1927), pp. 215–23; Dard (French minister in Sofia) to Doumergue (French foreign minister), Sofia, 18 May 1914, *DDF*, 3rd series, vol. 10, doc. 246, pp. 379–82.

123. Friedrich, *Bulgarien und die Mächte*, pp. 33–5; Doumergue to Izvolsky, Paris, 30 May 1914, *DDF*, 3rd series, vol. 10, doc. 305, p. 455.

124. Matthew A. Yokell, 'Sold to the Highest Bidder. An Investigation of Diplomacy Regarding Bulgaria's Entry into World War I (MA thesis, University of Richmond, 2010), pp. 33–5, viewed online at: *https://dspace.lasrworks .org/bitstream/handle/10349/911/10HIS-YokellMatthew.pdf?sequence=1*; Dard to Doumergue, Sofia, 29 May 1914, *DDF*, 3rd series, vol. 10, doc. 302, p. 452.

125. Savinsky, *Reflections*, pp. 223–4.

126. Samuel R. Williamson, 'Vienna and July 1914: The Origins of the Great War Once More', in id. and Peter Pastor (eds.), *Essays on World War I: Origins and Prisoners of War* (New York, 1983), pp. 9–36, esp. p. 19.

127. Czernin to Berchtold, Bucharest-Sinaia, 22 June 1914, *ÖUAP*, vol. 8, doc. 9902, pp. 173–6, here p. 174.

128. The conversation between Sazonov and Bratianu is reported in Sazonov, 'Audience text for Nicholas II', 18 June 1914, in *IBZI*, series 1, vol. 3, doc. 339, p. 296 (emphasis added); French Foreign Ministry, Department of Political and Commercial Affairs (Europe), 'Note pour le Président du Conseil', Paris, 11 July 1914, AMAE NS, Russie 46 (Politique étrangère. Autriche-Hongrie-Russie), fos. 312–4, here fo. 314.

129. Buisseret to Davignon, St Petersburg, 25 November 1913, MAEB AD, Russie 3 1906–1914.

130. Hartwig to Sazonov, Belgrade, 24 February 1914, *IBZI*, series 3, vol. 1, 314, pp. 311–13.

131. Spalajković to Pašić, St Petersburg, 8–21 January 1914, AS, MID – PO, 416, fos. 420–21.

132. Spalajković to Pašić, St Petersburg, 14–27 March 1914, ibid., fo. 451.

133. Spalajković to Pašić, St Petersburg, 24 April–7 May 1914, ibid., fo. 475.

134. Descos (French minister in Belgrade) to Doumergue (French minister of foreign affairs), Belgrade, 6 April 1914, *DDF*, 3rd series (1911–1914), vol. 10, doc. 80, pp. 124–6.

135. Milos Bogičević, *Die auswärtige Politik Serbiens 1903–1914* (3 vols., Berlin, 1931), vol. I, p. 280; Friedrich Würthle, *Die Spur führt nach Belgrad* (Vienna, 1975), p. 28.

136. Hartwig to Sazonov, Belgrade, 14 January 1914, *IBZI*, series 3, vol. I, doc. 7, pp. 5–6.

137. 'Austrian Sympathies', *The Times*, 18 October 1912, p. 5 col. B.

138. Boeckh, *Balkankriegen*, pp. 26–7.

139. F. R. Bridge, *From Sadowa to Sarajevo. The Foreign Policy of Austria-Hungary, 1866–1914* (London, 1972), p. 346; see also 'Servia and the Sea', *The Times*, 9 November 1912, p. 7, col. A.

140. [Wickham Steed], 'The Problem of Albania', *The Times*, 18 November 1912, p. 5 col. A. The Russian pan-Slav and nationalist press took a similar line.

141. Samuel R. Williamson, *Austria-Hungary and the Origins of the First World War* (Houndmills, 1991), pp. 127–8; Bridge, *From Sadowa to Sarajevo*, p. 347; a fine detailed study of the Prochaska Affair is Robert A. Kann, *Die Prochaska-Affäre vom Herbst 1912. Zwischen kaltem und heissem Krieg* (Vienna, 1977).

142. Cited in Treadway, *Falcon and Eagle*, p. 125.

143. Friedrich Kiessling, *Gegen den grossen Krieg? Entspannung in den internationalen Beziehungen* (Munich, 2002), p. 186.

144. Cited in Treadway, *Falcon and Eagle*, p. 137.

145. Rapaport to Vredenburch, Belgrade, 23 April 1913, NA, 2.05.36, 9, Consulaat-Generaal Belgrado en Gezantschap Zuid-Slavië 1891–1940.

146. Giers (Russian envoy to Montenegro) to Nicholas II, Cetinje [beginning of January] 1913 and 21 January 1913, GARF, Fond 601, op. 1, del. 785.

147. Buisseret to Davignon, St Petersburg, 11 April 1913, MAEB AD, Russia 3.

148. Buchanan to Nicolson, 1 May 1913, cited in Treadway, *Falcon and Eagle*, p. 148.

149. For the text of this resolution, see Robert Elsie, 'Texts and Documents of Albanian History', viewed online at *http://www.albanianhistory.net/texts20_1/AH1913_2.html*.

150. This narrative follows the sequence plotted in Samuel R. Williamson's unpublished manuscript chapter, 'Serbia and Austria-Hungary: The Final Rehearsal, October 1913'.

151. Statement by the Serbian minister in Vienna, Jovanović, to *Neue Freie Presse*, reported in 'The Albanian Outbreak', *The Times*, 27 September, 1913, p. 5, col. A; 'Return of M. Pashitch to Belgrade; *The Times*, 1 October, p. 6, col. E.

152. Williamson, 'Serbia and Austria-Hungary', pp. 14–15.

153. 'M. Pashitch in Vienna', *The Times*, 4 October 1913, p. 5, col. C; Williamson, 'Serbia and Austria-Hungary', p. 19.

154. Williamson, 'Serbia and Austria-Hungary', p. 21.

155. 'Servian Aggression in Albania', *The Times*, 16 October 1913, p. 7, col. C.

156. Cited in Williamson, *Austria-Hungary*, p. 153.

157. Report on Sazonov's comment in O'Beirne (British chargé d'affaires in St Petersburg) to Grey, St Petersburg, 28 October 1913, in *BD*, vol. 10 (i), doc. 56, p. 49.

158. Paul Schroeder, 'Stealing Horses to Great Applause. Austria-Hungary's Decision in 1914 in Systemic Perspective', in Holger Afflerbach and David Stevenson (eds.), *An Improbable War*, pp. 17–42, esp. pp. 38–40.

159. Major von Fabeck to General Staff, Berlin, 11 February 1913, attached: draft of a letter from Moltke to Conrad, Berlin, 10 February 1913, PA-AA, R 10896.

160. Wilhelm II, marginal comment on a telegram from the Wolffsches Telegraphenbureau to Wilhelm II, Berlin, 4 November, 1912, in *GP*, vol. 33, pp. 276–7 (doc. 12321); Varnbüler to Weizsäcker, Berlin, 18 November 1812, HSA Stuttgart E50/03 206.

161. Wilhelm II, marginal comment on Kiderlen-Wächter to Wilhelm II, Berlin, 3 November 1912, in *GP*, vol. 33, pp. 274–6 (doc. 12320).

162. Wilhelm II to German Foreign Office, Letzlingen, 9 November 1912, in ibid., vol. 33, p. 302 (doc. 12348).

163. E. C. Helmreich, 'An Unpublished Report on Austro-German Military Conversations of November 1912', *Journal of Modern History*, 5 (1933), pp. 197–207, here p. 206. Thus Archduke Franz Ferdinand reported the content of the conversation; the Austrian ambassador Szögyényi reported a more aggressive posture, namely that the Kaiser had expressed a readiness to accept the risk of a war with all three Entente powers.

164. Stevenson, *Armaments*, pp. 250, 259; Helmreich, 'Unpublished Report', pp. 202–3.

165. Wilhelm II to Franz Ferdinand (draft), 24 February 1913, PA-AA, R 10896.

166. Szögyényi to MFA Vienna, Berlin, 28 October 1913, *ÖUAP*, vol. 7, doc. 8934, p. 512.

167. Velics to Berchtold, Munich, 16 December 1913, ibid., doc. 9096, p. 658.

168. Szapáry to Foreign Ministry, St Petersburg, 25 April 1914, ibid., doc. 9656, pp. 25–7.

169. Lawrence Sondhaus, *Architect of the Apocalypse* (Boston, 2000), p. 120.

170. Williamson, 'Serbia and Austria-Hungary', p. 23; Hugo Hantsch, *Leopold Graf Berchtold. Grandseigneur and Staatsmann* (2 vols. Graz, 1963), vol. 2, pp. 499–500.

171. Treadway, *Falcon and Eagle*, pp. 143–4, 145.

172. Ibid., pp. 150–56.

173. Stevenson, *Armaments*, p. 271; see also Williamson, *Austria-Hungary*, pp. 155–6.

174. Williamson, *Austria-Hungary*, pp. 157–8.

175. Norman Stone, 'Army and Society in the Habsburg Monarchy 1900–1914', *Past & Present*, 33 (April 1966), pp. 95–111; on infantry numbers, see

Holger Herwig, *The First World War. Germany and Austria-Hungary, 1914–1918* (London, 1997), p. 12.

176. Kronenbitter, *Grossmachtpolitik Österreich-Ungarns*, pp. 146, 147, 149, 154.

177. See the text of the convention in the appendix of George F. Kennan, *The Fateful Alliance. France, Russia and the Coming of the First World War* (Manchester, 1984), p. 271.

178. Ibid., pp. 250–52.

179. Hanotaux to Montebello (French ambassador to St Petersburg), Paris, 10 April 1897, *DDF*, series 1, vol. 13, doc. 193, pp. 340–46.

180. Stevenson, *Armaments*, p. 125.

181. For a discussion of these issues, to which my own account is substantially indebted, see Stefan Schmidt, *Frankreichs Aussenpolitik in der Julikrise 1914. Ein Beitrag zur Geschichte des Ausbruchs des Ersten Weltkrieges* (Munich, 2009), pp. 246–50; see also Murielle Avice-Hanoun, 'L'Alliance franco-russe (1892–1914)', in Ilja Mieck and Pierre Guillen (eds.), *Deutschland – Frankreich – Russland. Begegnungen und Konfrontationen. La France et l'Allemagne face à la Russie* (Munich, 2000), pp. 109–24, here pp. 113–14.

182. Friedrich Stieve, *Iswolski und der Weltkrieg. Auf Grund der neuen Dokumenten-Veröffentlichung des Deutschen Auswärtigen Amtes* (Berlin, 1924), p. 45.

183. On this issue, see D. C. B. Lieven, *Russia and the Origins of the First World War* (London, 1983), p. 48; Luigi Albertini, *The Origins of the War of 1914*, trans. Isabella M. Massey (3 vols., Oxford, 1953), vol. 1, pp. 372–3; Thaden, *Russia*, pp. 115–18; for Poincaré's apologetic account of these conversations which he denies had any political significance, see id., *Au service de la France – neuf années de souvenirs* (10 vols., Paris, 1926–33), vol. 2, p. 202.

184. Poincaré to Izvolski, Paris, 16 November 1912, *DDF*, 3rd series, vol. 4, doc. 468, pp. 480–81.

185. Gerd Krumeich, *Armaments and Politics in France on the Eve of the First World War. The Introduction of the Three-Year Conscription 1913–1914*, trans. Stephen Conn (Leamington Spa, 1984), p. 28.

186. Paul Cambon to Jules Cambon, Paris, 5 November 1912, AMAE PA-AP, 43, fos. 251–7, here fo. 252.

187. Jules Cambon to Paul Cambon, Berlin, 14 December 1912, ibid., 100, fos. 178–180.

188. Douglas Porch, *The March to the Marne. The French Army, 1871–1914* (Cambridge, 1981), pp. 169–70.

189. Ibid.

190. Izvolsky to Sazonov, Paris, 28 March 1912, *IBZI*, series 3, vol. 2, part 2, doc. 699.

191. Risto Ropponen, *Die Kraft Russlands. Wie beurteilte die politische und militärische Führung der europäischen Grossmächte in der Zeit von 1905 bis 1914 die Kraft Russlands?* (Helsinki, 1968), p. 235.

192. Krumeich, *Armaments and Politics*, p. 28; Mosely, 'Russian Policy', p. 84; Sergei Dmitrievic Sazonov, *Les Années fatales* (Paris, 1927), p. 57.

193. Raymond Poincaré, 'Entretien avec M. Sazonoff', August 1912, AMAE, AE NS, Russie 41, fos. 270–72, 282–3. For Sazonov's account of the same meeting, which notes the French minister's displeasure but observes that he soon found good reasons for appreciating the 'great political importance' of the Serbo-Bulgarian treaty, see Sazonov, *Les Années fatales*, p. 60.

194. Notes on various conversations, St Petersburg, 12 August 1913, AMAE, Papiers Jean Doulcet, vol. 23, Saint Petersbourg IV, Notes personnelles, 1912–1917, fo. 312.

195. Ropponen, *Die Kraft Russlands*, p. 236.

196. Izvolsky to Sazonov, Paris, 12 September 1912, in Stieve, *Schriftwechsel Iswolskis*, vol. 2, doc. 429, pp. 249–52, here p. 251.

197. Izvolsky to Sazonov, Paris, 24 October 1912, cited in Bovykin, *Iz istorii vozniknoveniya*, p. 137.

198. Poincaré to Izvolsky, 4 November 1912, in Narodnogo komissariata po inostrannym delam (ed.), *Materialy po istorii franko-russkikh otnoshenii za 1910–1914 gg: sbornik sekretnykh diplomaticheskikh dokumentov byvshego Imperatorskogo rossiiskogo ministerstva inostrannykh del* (Moscow, 1922), p. 297; see also Bovykin, *Iz istorii vozniknoveniya*, p. 142.

199. Izvolsky to Sazonov (letter), Paris, 7 November 1912, in ibid., pp. 295–7; Stieve, *Schrifwechsel Iswolskis*, vol. 2, doc. 554, pp. 335–7, here p. 336 (emphasis added).

200. Rossos, *Russia and the Balkans*, p. 100.

201. Izvolsky to Sazonov, 17 November 1912, in Narodnogo komissariata po inostrannym delam (ed.), *Materialy po istorii franko-russkikh otnoshenii za 1910–1914 g.g: sbornik sekretnykh diplomaticheskikh dokumentov byvshego Imperatorskogo rossiikogo ministerstva inostrannykh del* (Moscow, 1922), pp. 299–300, doc. 169; on Poincaré's assurances, see Stieve, *Iswolski und der Weltkrieg*, pp. 99, 121; id. (ed.), *Schriftwechsel Iswolskis*, vol. 2, doc. 567, p. 346; see also Bovykin, *Iz istorii vozniknoveniya*, p. 146.

202. Izvolsky to Sazonov, 20 November 1912 and Izvolsky to Sazonov, 20 November, *IBZI*, series 3, vol. 4, part 1, docs. 298 and 300.

203. Poincaré, *Au service de la France*, vol. 2, pp. 199–206, where the author accused Izvolsky of fashioning his conversations with the ambassador into 'a picturesque and somewhat over-coloured tale'.

204. Schmidt, *Frankreichs Aussenpolitik*, p. 256.

205. Alexandre Ribot, Note of 31 October 1912, AN, 563 AP 5, cited in ibid., p. 257.

206. 'Note de l'État-Major de l'Armée', 2 September 1912 and Paul to Jules

Cambon, Dieppe, 3 September 1912, *DDF*, 3rd series, vol. 3, dos. 359, 366, pp. 439–40, 449–51.

207. Paul Cambon to Jules Cambon, Paris, 5 November 1912, AMAE, PA-AP, 43, Cambon, Jules, Lettres de Paul à Jules 1882–1922, 101, fos. 251–7, here fos. 252–3.

208. Ignatiev to Zhilinsky (chief of the Russian General Staff), Paris, 19 December 1912, cited in Bovykin, *Iz istorii vozniknoveniya*, p. 149.

209. Ibid., p. 149.

210. On Millerand as minister of war in January 1912–January 1913, see Marjorie M. Farrar, 'Politics Versus Patriotism: Alexandre Millerand as French Minister of War', *French Historical Studies*, 11/4 (1980), 577–609; on the minister's earlier career as a moderate socialist, see Leslie Derfler, *Alexandre Millerand. The Socialist Years* (The Hague, 1977); for a balanced overview of the transition, see Marjorie M. Farrar, *Principled Pragmatist: The Political Career of Alexandre Millerand* (New York, 1991); there are interesting reflections on the tensions in Millerand's career in Antoine Prost, Marie-Louise Goorgen, Noelle Gérome and Danielle Tartakowsky, ' Four French Historians Review English Research on the History of French Labour and Socialism', *The Historical Journal*, 37/3 (1994), pp. 709–15, esp. p. 714.

211. Ignatiev to Zhilinsky, Paris, 4 December 1912, cited in Bovykin, *Iz istorii vozniknoveniya*, p. 150.

212. Lucius to Bethmann Hollweg, St Petersburg, 8 January 1913, reporting a conversation with Sazonov, PA-AA, R 10896.

213. Raymond M. B. Poincaré, 'Notes journalières', 29 January 1914, BNF (NAF 16026), Poincaré MSS; Hayne, *The French Foreign Office and the Origins of the First World War, 1898–1914* (Oxford, 1993), p. 239.

214. G. Wright, *The Reshaping of French Democracy. The Story of the Founding of the Fourth Republic* (New York, 1948), p. 10.

215. John Keiger, *France and the Origins of the First World War* (London, 1983), p. 117.

216. For his relations with Foreign Minister Jonnart, see Paléologue's diary entries 22 January and 13 February 1913, in M. Paléologue, *Au Quai d'Orsay à la veille de la tourmente. Journal 1913–1914* (Paris, 1947), pp. 15, 42.

217. Cited in Keiger, *France and the Origins*, p. 120.

218. William C. Fuller, *Strategy and Power in Russia, 1600–1914* (New York, 1992), pp. 440, 444.

219. Stevenson, *Armaments*, p. 161.

220. Fuller, *Strategy and Power*, p. 439.

221. '8ème Conférence. Procès-verbal de l'entretien du 13 Juillet 1912 entre les Chefs d'État-Major des armées française et russe', AMAE, AE NS, Russie 41, fos. 131–7, here fos. 134–5.

222. État-Major de l'Armée, 3ème bureau, 'Note sur l'action militaire de la Russie en Europe', ibid., fos. 255–63.

223. Stevenson, *Armaments*, p. 162.

224. Raymond Poincaré, 'Entretien avec l'Empéreur – Chemins de fer stratégiques'; 'Entretien avec M. Sazonoff – Mobilisation', St Petersburg, August 1912, AMAE, AE NS Russie 41, fos. 278–9, 288.

225. Raymond Poincaré, 'Entretien avec Kokowtsoff – Chemins de fer stratégiques', St Petersburg, August 1912, ibid., fo. 280.

226. Bovykin, *Iz istorii vozniknoveniya*, p. 147.

227. S. R. Williamson, 'Joffre Reshapes French Strategy, 1911–1913', in Paul Kennedy (ed.), *The War Plans of the Great Powers, 1880–1914* (London, 1979), pp. 133–54, here pp. 134–6.

228. On the German version of the same conundrum, see Jonathan Steinberg, 'A German Plan for the Invasion of Holland and Belgium, 1897', in Kennedy (ed.), *War Plans*, pp. 155–70, here p. 162. Steinberg refers here to German strategic thinking, but the same problem confronted the decision-makers in Paris.

229. Hayne, *French Foreign Policy*, p. 266.

230. D. N. Collins, 'The Franco-Russian Alliance and Russian Railways, 1891–1914', *The Historical Journal*, 16/4 (1973), pp. 777–88, here p. 779.

231. Buisseret to Davignon, St Petersburg, 25 February 1913, MAEB AD, Russia 3, 1906–13.

232. François Roth, 'Raymond Poincaré et Théophile Delcassé: Histoire d'une relation politique', in Conseil général de l'Ariège (ed.), *Delcassé et l'Europe à la veille de la Grande Guerre* (Foix, 2001), pp. 231–46, here p. 236.

233. Bovykin, *Iz istorii vozniknoveniya*, p. 151.

234. Delcassé to Pichon, St Petersburg, 24 March 1913, *DDF*, 3rd series, vol. 6, doc. 59, pp. 81–2; on the same question raised with Sazonov, see Delcassé to Jonnart, St Petersburg, 21 March 1913, ibid., doc. 44, p. 66.

235. Report of a conversation with Delcassé of 18 June 1914 by General Laguiche, military attaché in St Petersburg, in Georges Louis, *Les Carnets de Georges Louis* (2 vols., Paris, 1926) vol. 2, p. 126.

236. B. V. Ananich, *Rossiya I mezhdunarodyi kapital 1897–1914. Ocherki istorii finansovykh otnoshenii* (Leningrad, 1970), pp. 270–71.

237. On the Three Year Law and Poincaré's role in getting it passed, see J. F. V. Keiger, *Raymond Poincaré* (Cambridge, 1997), pp. 152–3, 162–3; Krumeich, *Armaments and Politics*, pp. 112–13.

238. Keiger, *France and the Origins*, p. 144.

239. Guillaume to Davignon, Paris, 17 April 1913, 12 June 1913, MAEB AD, France 11, Correspondance politique – légations.

240. Guillaume to Davignon, Paris, 16 January 1914, ibid.

241. Guillaume to Davignon, Paris, 28 May 1914, ibid.

242. Keiger, *France and the Origins*, pp. 136–7.

243. Diary entry Thursday 18 April 1913 in Maurice Paléologue, *Journal,*
1913–1914, p. 103.

244. Keiger, *France and the Origins,* p. 136; on these events, see also the diary entries
16 April to 5 May 1913, in Paléologue, *Journal, 1913–1914,* pp. 100–124.

245. Krumeich, *Armaments and Politics,* passim.

246. Guillaume to Davignon, Paris, 9 June 1914, MAEB AD, France 12, Correspondance politique – légations.

247. On the growing opposition to the Three Year Law, see Guillaume to Davignon, Paris, 16 January 1914, ibid.

248. On the collapse of the Ribot government on the day of its first appearance
in parliament, see Guillaume to Davignon, Paris, 13 June 1914, ibid.

249. Report by Captain Parchement on 'stage' in Vilna District in October 1912,
cited in Pertti Luntinen, *French Information on the Russian War Plans,*
1880–1914 (Helsinki, 1984), p. 175.

250. Verleuil to [Pichon], Brolles, 7 July 1913, AMAE NS, Russie 42, fos. 58–60,
here fo. 59.

251. Cited in Schmidt, *Frankreichs Aussenpolitik,* pp. 271–3.

252. Charles Rivet, 'Lettre de Russie: L'Effort militaire russe', in *Le Temps,* 13
November 1913, cutting in Buisseret to Davignon, St Petersburg, 15 November 1913, MAEB AD, Russie 3 1906–1914.

253. Ibid., p. 275.

254. Laguiche to Dupont, 14 February 1914, cited in ibid., p. 279.

255. Paul Kennedy, 'The First World War and the International Power System', in
Steven E. Miller (ed.), *Military Strategy and the Origins of the First World
War* (Princeton, 1985), pp. 7–40, here p. 28.

CHAPTER 6

1. Cited in Zara S. Steiner, *The Foreign Office and Foreign Policy, 1898–1914*
(Cambridge, 1969), p. 153.

2. On the Baltic Port meetings of 4–6 July 1912, see H. H. Fisher (ed.), *Out of
My Past. The Memoirs of Count Kokovtsov, Russian Minister of Finance,
1904–1911, Chairman of the Council of Ministers, 1911–1914,* trans.
Laura Matveev (Stanford, 1935), p. 322.

3. Notes by Bethmann Hollweg on conversation with Sazonov, 6 July 1912,
GP, vol. 31, doc. 11542, pp. 439–44.

4. Fisher (ed.), *Memoirs of Count Kokovtsov,* p. 320.

5. Notes by Pourtalès, 29 June 1912, *GP,* vol. 31, doc. 11537, pp. 433–6.

6. Sergei Dmitrievich Sazonov, *Les Années fatales* (Paris, 1927), pp. 48–9.

7. Fisher (ed.), *Memoirs of Count Kokovtsov,* pp. 320–21.

8. Bethmann to Foreign Office, Baltic Port, on board the *Hohenzollern,* 6 July
1912, *GP,* vol. 31, doc. 11540, pp. 437–8.

9. On détente as a potential of the international system before 1914, see Friedrich Kiessling, *Gegen den grossen Krieg? Entspannung in den internationalen Beziehungen, 1911–1914* (Munich, 2002), pp. 77–148.

10. Bethmann to Foreign Office, Baltic Port, on board the *Hohenzollern*, 6 July 1912, *GP*, vol. 31, doc. 11540, pp. 437–8.

11. Klaus Hildebrand, *Das vergangene Reich. Deutsche Aussenpolitik von Bismarck bis Hitler, 1871–1945* (Stuttgart, 1995), pp. 269–76.

12. Cf. Volker Berghahn, *Germany and the Approach of War in 1914* (Basingstoke, 1993), pp. 120–22 and Imanuel Geiss, 'The German Version of Imperialism: Weltpolitik', in G. Schöllgen, *Escape into War? The Foreign Policy of Imperial Germany* (Oxford, New York, Munich, 1990), pp. 105–20; here p. 118.

13. Thus Bethmann's 'Sketch of a Conceivable Formula' for the Anglo-German negotiations, cited in R. Langhorne, 'Great Britain and Germany, 1911–1914', in Francis Harry Hinsley (ed.), *British Foreign Policy under Sir Edward Grey* (Cambridge, 1977), pp. 288–314, here pp. 293–4.

14. Niall Ferguson, *Pity of War* (London, 1998), p. 72; Langhorne, 'Great Britain and Germany', pp. 294–5.

15. R. Langhorne, 'The Naval Question in Anglo-German Relations, 1912–1914, *Historical Journal*, 14 (1971), pp. 359–70, here p. 369; cf. Fritz Fischer, *War of Illusions. German Policies from 1911 to 1914*, trans. Marian Jackson (London, 1975), pp. 123–31.

16. R. J. Crampton, *Hollow Détente. Anglo-German Relations in the Balkans, 1911–1914* (London, 1980), pp. 56–8, 72–3; Kiessling, *Gegen den grossen Krieg?*, p. 103.

17. On the mission's objectives and Haldane's 'disavowal' by the British government, see B. D. E. Kraft, *Lord Haldane's Zending naar Berlijn in 1912. De duitsch-engelsche onderhandelingen over de vlootquaestie* (Utrecht, 1931), pp. 209–11, 214–17, 220–21; draft note to the German government, March 1912, cited in Gregor Schöllgen, *Imperialismus und Gleichgewicht. Deutschland, England und die orientalische Frage, 1871–1914* (Munich, 1984), p. 330.

18. Kraft, *Zending naar Berlijn*, p. 246.

19. Samuel R. Williamson, *The Politics of Grand Strategy. Britain and France Prepare for War, 1904–1914* (Cambridge, MA, 1969), p. 258.

20. Nicolson to Bertie, 8 February 1912, TNA FO 800 / 171, cited in Steiner, *Foreign Office*, p. 127.

21. Bertie to Nicolson, Paris, 11 February 1912, cited in Thomas Otte, *The Foreign Office Mind. The Making of British Foreign Policy, 1865–1914* (Cambridge, 2011), p. 364; on Nicolson's involvement in and commitment to the Anglo-Russian Convention, see Keith Neilson, '"My Beloved Russians": Sir Arthur Nicolson and Russia, 1906–1916', *International History Review*, 9/4 (1987).

22. Jonathan Steinberg, 'Diplomatie als Wille und Vorstellung: Die Berliner Mission Lord Haldanes im Februar 1912' in Herbert Schottelius and Wilhelm Deist (eds.), *Marine und Marinepolitik im kaiserlichen Deutschland, 1871–1914* (Düsseldorf, 1972), pp. 263–82, here p. 264; on the mission and its failure, see also Michael Epkenhans, *Die wilhelminische Flottenrüstung. Weltmachtstreben, industrieller Fortschritt, soziale Integration* (Munich, 1991), pp. 113–37; David Stevenson, *Armaments and the Coming of War: Europe 1904–1914* (Cambridge, 1996), pp. 205–7.

23. Goschen to Nicolson, Berlin, 20 April 1912, TNA FO 800/355, fos. 20–22.

24. 'Foreign Affairs. The Morocco Crisis. Sir E. Grey's Speech', *The Times*, 28 November 1911, p. 13, col. B.

25. Kühlmann to Bethmann, London, 14 October 1912, *GP*, vol. 33, doc. 12284, p. 228; see also the discussion in Jost Dülffer, Martin Kröger and Rolf-Harald Wippich, *Vermiedene Kriege. Deeskalation von Konflikten der Grossmächte zwischen Krimkrieg and Ersten Weltkring 1856–1914* (Munich,1997), p. 650.

26. Crampton, *Hollow Détente*.

27. Kiessling, *Gegen den grossen Krieg?*, pp. 89, 122; Paul W. Schroeder, 'Embedded Counterfactuals and World War I as an Unavoidable War', pp. 28–9.

28. Ronald Bobroff, *Roads to Glory. Late Imperial Russia and the Turkish Straits* (London, 2006); on French concerns about George V: Guillaume to Davignon, Paris, 11 April 1913, MAEB AD, France 11, Correspondance politique – légations.

29. Ira Klein, 'The Anglo-Russian Convention and the Problem of Central Asia, 1907–1914', *Journal of British Studies*, 11 (1971), pp. 126–47, here p. 128.

30. Ibid., p. 141.

31. Grey to Buchanan, London, 11 February 1914, Grey to Buchanan, London, 18 March 1914, TNA, Grey Papers, FO 800/74, cited in Thomas McCall, 'The Influence of British Military Attachés on Foreign Polich Towards Russia, 1904–1917', M.Phil thesis, University of Cambridge, 2011, p. 53.

32. Prince Max von Lichnowsky, *My Mission to London, 1912–1914* (London, 1918), p. 29.

33. Steiner, *Foreign Office*, pp. 121–40, 49; Otte, *Foreign Office Mind*, p. 380.

34. McCall, 'British Military Attachés', pp. 33–75.

35. Hamilton to Haldane, 1 September 1909, cited in ibid., p. 60.

36. Notes by H. A. Gwynne, editor of the *Morning Post*, on a confidential interview at the FO, probably with Sir William Tyrrell, cited and analysed in Keith M. Wilson, 'The British Démarche of 3 and 4 December 1912: H. A. Gwynne's Note on Britain, Russia and the First Balkan War', *Slavonic and East European Review*, 60/4 (1984), pp. 552–9, here p. 556.

37. Nicolson to Goschen, London, 15 April 1912, *BD*, vol. 6, doc. 575, p. 747.

38. Nicolson to Goschen, London, 25 May 1914, TNA, FO fos. 162–14, here fo. 163. 800/374.

39. Kiessling, *Gegen den grossen Krieg?*, pp. 82–3, Bovykin, *Iz istorii vozniknoveniya*, p. 180.

40. Cited in Steiner, *British Foreign Office*, p. 134; on Nicolson's views more generally, see pp. 128, 129, 131, 133, 134, 136–7; Otte, *Foreign Office Mind*, p. 384.

41. Guillaume to Davignon, Paris, 14 April 1914, MAEB AD, France 11, Correspondance politique – légations.

42. Otte, *Foreign Office Mind*, pp. 358–9, 387–8.

43. Nicolson to Bunsen, London, 30 March 1914, TNA, FO 800/373, fos. 80–83, here fo. 83.

44. These aspects of the international system are explored in Kiessling, *Gegen den grossen Krieg?*, and Holger Afflerbach and David Stevenson (eds.), *An Improbable War? The Outbreak of World War I and European Political Culture before 1914* (Oxford, 2007), both passim.

45. Jules Cambon to Poincaré, Berlin, 28 July 1912, AMAE, PA-AP, 43, Cambon Jules 56, fo. 45.

46. Annika Mombauer, *Helmuth von Moltke and the Origins of the First World War* (Cambridge, 2001), pp. 145, 211, 281.

47. Stevenson, *Armaments*, pp. 159–63.

48. Ibid., p. 247.

49. For German readings of attitudes among senior Russian commanders, see e.g. Pourtalès to Bethmann Hollweg, St Petersburg, 20 November 1912; Griesinger (German minister in Belgrade) to Bethmann Hollweg, 5 February 1913; the quotation is from Romberg (German minister in Bern) to Bethmann Hollweg, Bern, 1 February 1913, reporting a conversation between the Russian military attaché in the city and a member of the Austro-Hungarian legation, all in PA-AA, R 10895.

50. *The Times*, 3 December 1912, p. 6, col. B.

51. Ibid.

52. Cited in Lamar Cecil, *Wilhelm* II (2 vols., Chapel Hill, 1989 and 1996), vol. 2, *Emperor and Exile, 1900–1941*, p. 186; on Bethmann's speech and its significance, see Dülffer, Kröger and Wippich, *Vermiedene Kriege*, pp. 652–4.

53. For a full reconstruction of the meeting and a discussion of its significance, see J. C. G. Röhl, 'Dress Rehearsal in December: Military Decision-making in Germany on the Eve of the First World War', in id., *The Kaiser and His Court. Wilhelm II and the Government of Germany* (Cambridge, 1994), pp. 162–89, here pp. 162–3.

54. Röhl, 'Dress Rehearsal', passim; also id., 'Admiral von Müller and the Approach of War, 1911–1914, *Historical Journal*, 12 (1969), pp. 651–73. Röhl's reading of the 'war council' of December 1912 as the moment at which the countdown was started for a war planned in advance by Germany

is a minority view. At a conference in London in October 2011 ('The Fischer Controversy 50 Years On', 13–15 October 2011, German Historical Institute London), Röhl radicalized the argument, suggesting that the War Council was the moment at which the Germans decided not to wage war immediately, but to 'postpone' it until the summer of 1914, an argument expounded earlier by Fischer, *War of Illusions*, pp. 164, 169. The postponement thesis is also central to the argument presented in the third volume of Röhl's biography of the Kaiser, see J. C. G. Röhl, *Wilhelm II. Der Weg in den Abgrund, 1900–1941* (Munich, 2008).

55. Röhl, 'Dress Rehearsal'; Stevenson, *Armaments*, pp. 288–9; F. Fischer, 'The Foreign Policy of Imperial Germany and the Outbreak of the First World War', in Schöllgen, *Escape into War?*, pp. 19–40; here p. 22; M. S. Coetzee, *The German Army League* (New York, 1990), pp. 36–7; Wolfgang J. Mommsen, 'Domestic Factors in German Foreign Policy before 1914', *Central European History*, 6 (1973), pp. 3–43, here pp. 12–14.

56. E. Hölzle, *Die Selbstentmachtung Europas. Das Experiment des Friedens vor und im Ersten Weltkrieg* (Göttingen, 1975), pp. 180–83; Hildebrand, *Das vergangene Reich*, p. 289.

57. Jagow to Lichnowsky, Berlin, 26 April 1913; Jagow to Flotow, Berlin, 28 April 1913, *GP*, 34/2, pp. 737–8, 752; on submarine building and other naval measures, see Holger H. Herwig, *'Luxury' Fleet. The Imperial German Navy, 1888–1918* (London, 1980), pp. 87–9; Gary E. Weir, 'Tirpitz, Technology and Building U-boats 1897–1916', *International History Review*, 6 (1984), pp. 174–90; Hew Strachan, *The First World War* (Oxford, 2001), pp. 53–5.

58. Moltke to Bethmann and Heeringen, 21 December 1912, cited in Stevenson, *Armaments*, pp. 291–2.

59. David Stevenson, 'War by Timetable? The Railway Race Before 1914', *Past & Present*, 162 (1999), pp. 163–94, here p. 175.

60. Peter Gattrell, *Government, Industry and Rearmament in Russia, 1900–1914. The Last Argument of Tsarism* (Cambridge, 1994), pp. 133–4.

61. Fritz Fischer, *Griff nach der Weltmacht. Die Kriegszielpolitik des kaiserlichen Deutschland 1914–18* (Düsseldorf, 1961), p. 48.

62. See Stevenson, *Armaments*, pp. 298, 314; I. V. Bestuzhev, 'Russian Foreign Policy, February–June 1914', *Journal of Contemporary History*, 1/3 (1966), pp. 93–112, here p. 96.

63. Paul Kennedy, 'The First World War and the International Power System', in Steven E. Miller (ed.), *Military Strategy and the Origins of the First World War* (Princeton, 1985), p. 29.

64. Militär-Bericht Nr. 28, St Petersburg, 8–21 May 1914 (copy for the Reich Admiralty), BA-MA Freiburg, RM5/1439. I am grateful to Oliver Griffin for sending me a photocopy of this document. Moltke's views (of 15 December 1913 and 11 July 1914) are cited in Stevenson, 'War by Timetable?', p. 186.

65. Matthew Seligmann and Roderick McLean, *Germany from Reich to Republic* (London, 2000), pp. 142–4.

66. Ferguson, 'Public Finance and National Security. The Domestic Origins of the First World War Revisited', *Past & Present*, 142 (1994); on Moltke's calls for preventive war in 1908–9, see Fischer, *Griff nach der Weltmacht*, pp. 49–50; id., *War of Illusions*, p. 88; Norman Stone, 'Moltke-Conrad: Relations Between the German and Austro-Hungarian General Staffs', *Historical Journal*, 9 (1966), pp. 201–28; Isabel V. Hull, 'Kaiser Wilhelm II and the "Liebenberg Circle"', in J. C. G. Röhl and N. Sombart (eds.), *Kaiser Wilhelm II. New Interpretations* (Cambridge, 1982), pp. 193–220, esp. 212; Holger H. Herwig, 'Germany', in Richard F. Hamilton and Holger H. Herwig (eds.), *The Origins of World War I* (Cambridge, 2003), pp. 150–87, esp. p. 166.

67. Dieter Hoffmann, *Der Sprung ins Dunkle oder wie der 1. Weltkrieg entfesselt wurde* (Leipzig, 2010) see esp. the table on pp. 325–330.

68. Cited in Stefan Schmidt, *Frankreichs Aussenpolitik in der Julikrise 1914. Ein Beitrag zur Geschichte des Ausbruchs des Ersten Weltkrieges* (Munich, 2009), p. 276.

69. Henry Wilson, marginal comment on a staff summary of the latest dispatch from Colonel Knox in St Petersburg, 23 March 1914, TNA, WO 106/1039.

70. Kevin Kramer, 'A World of Enemies: New Perspectives on German Military Culture and the Origins of the First World War', *Central European History*, 39 (2006), pp. 270–98, here p. 272; on the relationship between the fear of war and the readiness for it, see also Kiessling, *Gegen den grossen Krieg?*, p. 57.

71. Bethmann Hollweg to Eisendecher, 26 December 1911 and 23 March 1913, both cited in Konrad H. Jarausch, 'The Illusion of Limited War: Chancellor Bethmann Hollweg's Calculated Risk, July 1914', *Central European History*, 2/1(1969), pp. 48–76.

72. Cecil, *Wilhelm II*, vol. 2, p. 195.

73. Falkenhayn to Hanneken, 29 January 1913, cited in Holger Afflerbach, *Falkenhayn: Politisches Denken und Handeln im Kaiserreich* (Munich, 1994), p. 102 (Falkenhayn would become minister of war on 7 June 1913).

74. Ibid., p. 76.

75. On the primacy of civilian leaders in 1914 Europe, see Marc Trachtenberg, 'The Coming of the First World War: A Reassessment', in id., *History and Strategy* (Princeton, 1991), pp. 47–99.

76. Anon., *Deutsche Weltpolitik und kein Krieg!* (Berlin, 1913).

77. Hildebrand, *Das vergangene Reich*, p. 278.

78. Strachan, *First World War*, p. 33.

79. On German policy options, see Hildebrand, *Das vergangene Reich,* pp. 277–82.

80. Mehmet Yerçil, 'A History of the Anatolian Railway, 1871–1914', PhD thesis, Cambridge, 2010.

81. Marschall von Biberstein to Bethmann, Constantinople, 4 December 1911, *GP*, vol. 30, doc. 10987.

82. Carl Mühlmann, *Deutschland und die Türkei 1913–1914. Die Berufung der deutschen Militärmission nach der Türkei 1913, das deutsch-türkische Bündnis 1914 und der Eintritt der Türkei in den Weltkrieg* (Berlin, 1929), p. 5.

83. Yerçil, 'Anatolian Railway', p. 91.

84. Ibid., pp. 95–120.

85. Helmut Mejcher, 'Oil and British Policy Towards Mesopotamia', *Middle Eastern Studies*, 8/3 (1972), pp. 377–91, esp. pp. 377–8.

86. Cited in J. C. G. Röhl, *Wilhelm II. The Kaiser's Personal Monarchy, 1888–1900*, trans. Sheila de Bellaigue (Cambridge, 2004), p. 953.

87. On German interest in pan-Islamism as an instrument of foreign policy, see Sean McMeekin, *The Berlin–Baghdad Express. The Ottoman Empire and Germany's Bid for World Power, 1898–1918* (London, 2010), pp. 7–53.

88. Fischer, *Griff nach der Weltmacht*, p. 54.

89. Herbert Feis, *Europe, The World's Banker 1870–1914* (New York, 1939), p. 53; Ulrich Trumpener, *Germany and the Ottoman Empire 1914–1918* (Princeton, 1968), pp. 3–11; Harry N. Howard, *The Partition of Turkey, 1913–1923* (Norman, 1931), pp. 49–50.

90. Hildebrand, *Das vergangene Reich*, pp. 281–2.

91. On 'Goltz Pascha' and other German military advisers in Constantinople before Liman, see Bernd F. Schulte, *Vor dem Kriegsausbruch 1914. Deutschland, die Türkei und der Balkan* (Düsseldorf, 1980), pp. 17–38.

92. Mühlmann, *Deutschland und die Türkei*, pp. 10–11; Hildebrand, *Das vergangene Reich*, p. 297.

93. Theobald von Bethmann Hollweg, *Betrachtungen zum Weltkriege* (2 vols., Berlin, 1919), vol. 1, pp. 88–9.

94. On the officially inspired press campaign in *Novoye Vremya*, see David MacLaren McDonald, *United Government and Foreign Policy in Russia, 1900–1914* (Cambridge, MA, 1992), p. 191; on the determination of the Ottoman authorities to use the German mission to improve their armed forces and thereby guard against further annexations, see Sverbeyev (Russian ambassador to Berlin) to Sazonov, 16 January 1914, *IBZI*, series 3, vol. 1, doc. 21, pp. 22–3.

95. Tatishchev to Nicholas II, Berlin, 6 November 1913, GARF, Fond 601, op. 1, del 746 (2).

96. Cited from Bazarov's report of 16 December 1913, in Fischer, *War of Illusions*, p. 334. How Bazarov learned of the content of this speech is unclear.

97. Pourtalès to German Foreign Office, 28 November and 5 December 1913, *GP*, vol. 38, docs. 15457, 15466; Mühlmann, *Deutschland und die Türkei*, p. 12.

98. Cited in Lichnowsky, *My Mission to London*, p. 14.

99. Bovykin, *Iz istorii vozniknoveniya*, pp. 125–6; Fischer, *War of Illusions*, pp. 147–8.

100. Sazonov to Demidov (Russian minister in Athens), St Petersburg, 16 October 1912, with copies to Constantinople, Paris and London; Sazonov to Girs, St Petersburg, 18 October 1912; Sazonov to Russian ambassadors in Paris, London, Berlin, Vienna and Rome, 5 October 1912, all in AVPRI, Fond 151 (PA), op. 482, d. 130, ll. 14, 20, 22.

101. Sukhomlinov to Neratov, 11 August 1911, *IBZI* series 3, vol. 1, doc. 310, pp. 375–8, here p. 376.

102. Sazonov to Izvolsky, 4 November 1912 (copies to London and Constantinople); Sazonov to Girs (ambassador in Constantinople), 'secret telegram', St Petersburg, 2 November 1912, both in AVPRI, Fond 151 (PA), op. 482, d. 130, ll. 96, 87.

103. Bobroff, *Roads to Glory*, pp. 52–3.

104. Sazonov to Kokovtsov and service chiefs, 12 November 1912, cited in ibid., p. 55.

105. Sazonov to Nicholas II, 23 November 1912, cited in Bovykin, *Iz istorii vozniknoveniya*, p. 126.

106. Ia. Zakher, 'Konstantinopol i prolivy', *KA*, 6 (1924), pp. 48–76, here p. 55, and 7 (1924), pp. 32–54.

107. Bobroff, *Roads to Glory*, pp. 76–95.

108. Sazonov to Russian chargé d'affaires, London, 7 December 1913, in B. von Siebert (ed.), *Graf Benckendorffs diplomatischer Schriftwechsel* (Berlin, 1928), vol. 3, doc. no. 982, pp. 208–9.

109. D. C. B. Lieven, *Russia and the Origins of the First World War* (London, 1983), p. 47; Etter (Russian chargé d'affaires, London) to Sazonov, London, 14 January 1914, *IBZI*, series 3, vol. 1, doc. 3, pp. 2–3.

110. Louis Mallet to Edward Grey, London, 23 March 1914, TNA FO 800/80; Great Britain, House of Commons Debates, 1914, vol., 59 cols. 2169–70, both cited in William I. Shorrock, 'The Origin of the French Mandate in Syria and Lebanon: The Railroad Question, 1901–1914', *International Journal of Middle East Studies*, 1/2 (1970), pp. 133–53, here p. 153; see also Stuart Cohen, 'Mesopotamia in British Strategy, 1903–1914', *International Journal of Middle East Studies*, 9/2 (1978), pp. 171–81, esp. pp. 174–7.

111. Note of understanding between HE Khourshid Pasha, minister of the navy, in the name of the Ottoman government and Admiral Limpus, 25 May 1912, Limpus Papers. Caird Library, NMM, LIM/12; on Limpus's appointment, see also Paul G. Halpern, *The Mediterranean Naval Situation, 1908–1914* (Cambridge, MA, 1971), p. 321.

112. See 'Instructions for Hallifax Bey', 11 May 1914, ibid., LIM/9.

113. Limpus to Ottoman Admiralty, 5 June 1912, ibid., LIM 8/1 (letter-book), fos. 63–7.

114. Limpus to Ottoman Admiralty, 5 June 1912, ibid., LIM 8/1 (letter-book), fos. 68–9.

115. Delcassé to Ministry of Foreign Affairs, 29 January 1914, AMAE NS, Russie 42, fos. 223–4; see also Izvolsky to Sazonov, Paris, 15 January 1914, *IBZI*, series 3, vol. 1, doc. 12, pp. 12–14, reporting French opposition to a Russian financial boycott of the Ottoman Empire.

116. lzvolski to Sazonov, Paris, 18 December 1913; Izvolski to Sazonov, Paris, 18 December 1913, in Stieve (ed.), *Der diplomatische Schriftwechsel Izwolskis*, vol. 3, docs. 1179, 1181, pp. 425–5, 428–31; Dülffer, Kröger and Wipplich. *Vermiedene Kriege*, pp. 663–4.

117. Sazonov to Benckendorff, St Petersburg, 11 December 1913, in Benno Siebert (ed.), *Benckendorffs diplomatischer Schriftwechsel* (3 vols., Berlin, 1928), vol. 3, doc. 991, p. 217.

118. On this report, see McDonald, *United Government*, p. 193; on the 'focusing' effect of the Liman affair, see Strachan, *First World War*, p. 61.

119. M. Pokrowski, *Drei Konferenzen. Zur Vorgeschichte des Krieges*, trans. Anon ([Berlin], 1920), pp. 34, 38.

120. Ibid., p. 42.

121. Hildebrand, *Das vergangene Reich*, p. 298.

122. Pokrowski, *Drei Konferenzen*, pp. 39, 41; on Sazonov's role in these discussions, see Horst Linke, *Das Zarische Russland and der Erste Weltkrieg. Diplomatie and Kriegsziele 1914–1917* (Munich, 1982), p.22.

123. Buchanan to Grey, 3 April 1914, cited in Lieven, *Russia and the Origins*, p. 197.

124. Concluding marginal comment to Pourtalès to Bethmann, St Petersburg, 25 February 1914, *GP*, vol. 39, doc. 15841, p. 545; see also the discussion in Dülffer, Kröger and Wippich, *Vermiedene Kriege*, p. 670.

125. Cited in McDonald, *United Government*, p. 193.

126. Sergei Dmitrievich Sazonov, *Fateful Years, 1909–96: The Reminiscences of Serge Sazonov*, trans. N. A. Duddington (London, 1928), p. 80.

127. Liszkowski, *Zwischen Liberalismus und Imperialismus. Die Zaristische Aussenpolitik vor dem Ersten Weltkrieg im Urteil Miljukovs und der Kadettenpartei, 1905–1914* (Stuttgart, 1974), pp. 224–5.

128. Mallet to Grey (no. 400), 2 June 1914, and minutes by Russell and Crowe, 9 and 14 June 1914, cited in Thomas Otte, *Foreign Office Mind*, pp. 378–9.

129. Lieven, *Russia and the Origins*, pp. 42–6; see also Bovykin, *Iz istorii vozniknoveniya*, p. 129.

130. Bobroff, *Roads to Glory*, p. 151; id., 'Behind the Balkan Wars', p. 78.

131. 'Journal der Sonderkonferenz, 8. Februar 1914', in Pokrowski, *Drei Konferenzen*, pp. 47, 52.

132. Ibid., pp. 52–3.

133. Bovykin, *Iz istorii vozniknoveniya*, p. 128.

134. Stephen Schröder, *Die englisch-russische Marinekonvention* (Göttingen, 2006), pp. 97–101; Linke, *Das Zarische Russland*, pp. 28–30.

135. Cited in Schröder, *Die englisch-russische Marinekonvention*, p. 128.

136. William A. Renzi, 'Great Britain, Russia and the Straits, 1914–1915', *Journal of Modern History*, 42/1 (1970), pp. 1–20, here pp. 2–3; Mustafa Aksakal, *The Ottoman Road to War in 1914. The Ottoman Empire and the First World War* (Cambridge, 2008), p. 46.

137. Sazonov to Hartwig, cited in Friedrich Stieve, *Iswolski and der Weltkrieg, auf Gund der neuen Dokumenten-Veröffentlichung des Deutschen Auswärtigen Amtes* (Berlin, 1924), p. 178.

138. Guillaume to Davignon, Paris, 14 April 1914, MAEB AD, France 11, Correspondance politique – légations.

139. On the centrality of this idea to Sazonov's thinking, see Bobroff, *Roads to Glory*, pp. 151–6.

140. John H. Herz, 'Idealist Internationalism and the Security Dilemma', *World Politics*, 2/2 (1950), pp. 157–180, here p. 157; on the relevance of this problem to the crisis of 1914, see Jack L. Snyder, 'Perceptions of the Security Dilemma in 1914', in Robert Jervis, Richard Ned Lebow and Janice Gross Stein, *Psychology and Deterrence* (Baltimore, 1989), pp. 153–79; Klaus Hildebrand, 'Julikrise 1914: Das europäische Sicherheitsdilemma. Betrachtungen über den Ausbruch des Ersten Weltkrieges', *Geschichte in Wissenschaft und Unterricht*, 36 (1985), pp. 469–502; Gian Enrico Rusconi, *Rischio 1914. Come si decide una guerra* (Bologna, 1987), pp. 171–87.

141. Nicolson to Cartwright, London, 18 March 1912, TNA, FO, 800/354, fos. 253–4.

142. Sazonov, *Les Années fatales*, p. 63.

143. Bertie to Grey, Paris, 26 November 1912, in *BD*, vol. 9/2, doc. 280, p. 206.

144. Prince Max von Lichnowksy, *Heading for the Abyss* (New York, 1928), pp. 167–8, italics as in original.

145. Ibid., pp. 167–8, italics as in original.

146. Cambon to Poincaré, London, 4 December 1912, *DDF*, 3rd series, vol. 4, doc. 622, pp. 642–3; see also Wilson, 'The British Démarche', p. 555.

147. Schroeder, 'Embedded Conterfactuals', p. 37.

148. Report of a conversation with Witte by a special agent of the Hamburg-Amerika Line, forwarded in Müller to Bethmann Hollweg, Hamburg, 21 February 1913, PA-AA, R 10137, Allgemeine Angelegenheiten Russlands, 1 January 1907–31 December 1915; for another report arguing that war was popular only with a small part of the Russian elite, see Kohlhaas (German consul-general in Moscow), memorandum, Moscow, 3 December 1912, PA-AA, R 10895.

149. On this tendency in British policy, see Christopher John Bartlett, *British Foreign Policy in the Twentieth Century* (London, 1989), p. 20; Paul W. Schroeder, 'Alliances, 1815–1914: Weapons of Power and Tools of Management', in Klaus Knorr (ed.), *Historical Dimension of National Security Problems* (Lawrence, KS, 1976), pp. 227–62, here p. 248; Christel Gade,

Gleichgewichtspolitik oder Bündnispflege? Maximen britischer Aussenpolitik (1909–1914) (Göttingen, 1997), p. 22; on France's abandonment of a 'balance of power' policy, see Bovykin, *Iz istorii vozniknoveniya*, p. 133.

150. Grey to Bertie, London, 4 December 1912, *BD*, vol. 9/2, doc. 328, p. 244; Grey said much the same to Ambassador Buchanan in St Petersburg, see Grey to Buchanan, 17 February 1913, ibid., doc. 626, p. 506.

151. On British suspicion of Austrian designs, the assumption that Vienna was a satellite of Berlin and the dysfunctionality of the Austro-Hungarian system, see Kiessling, *Gegen den grossen Krieg?*, pp. 127–9; Strachan, *First World War*, p. 81.

152. Katrin Boeckh, *Von den Balkankriegen zum Ersten Weltkrieg. Kleinstaatenpolitik und ethnische Selbstbestimmung auf dem Balkan* (Munich, 1996), pp. 121, 131; V. N. Strandmann, *Balkanske Uspomene*, trans. from the Russian into Serbian by Jovan Kachaki (Belgrade, 2009), p. 244; Pašić to Sazonov, 2 February 1914, *IBZI*, series 3, vol. 1, doc. 161, pp. 149–50. On these deliveries, which took some time to work their way through the Russian system: Sukhomlinov to Sazonov, 30 March 1914; Sazonov to Hartwig, St Petersburg, 9 April 1914; Sazonov to Hartwig, St Petersburg, 14 April 1914; Hartwig to Sazonov, 28 April 1914 – all in *IBZI*, series 1, vol. 1, doc. 161, pp. 149–50; ibid., series 1, vol. 2, docs. 124, 186, 218, 316, pp. 124, 198, 227–8 and 309.

153. Miranda Vickers, *The Albanians. A Modern History* (London and New York, 1999), p. 70.

154. Mark Mazower, *The Balkans* (London, 2000), pp. 105–6.

155. Notes on conversation with André Panafieu by Jean Doulcet, secretary at the French embassy in St Petersburg, St Petersburg, 11 December [1912], AMAE, Papiers Jean Doulcet, vol. 23, Notes personnelles, 1912–1917; Strandmann, *Balkanske Uspomene*, p. 239.

156. Nicolson to Hardinge, London, 1 February 1912, cited in Richard Langhorne, 'Anglo-German Negotiations Concerning the Future of the Portuguese Colonies, 1911–1914', *Historical Journal*, 16/2 (1973), pp. 361–87, here p. 371.

157. Schoen to Bethmann Hollweg, Paris, 22 March 1912, *GP*, vol. 31, doc. 11520, pp. 396–401, here pp. 400–401.

158. Sazonov, *Les Années fatales*, p. 61.

159. Bethmann, *Betrachtungen zum Weltkrieg*, vol. 2, p. 133.

160. On the 'hardening' of officer masculinity before 1914, see Markus Funck, 'Ready for War? Conceptions of Military Manliness in the Prusso-German Officer Corps before the First World War', in Karen Hagemann and Stephanie Schüler-Springorum (eds.), *Home/Front. The Military, War and Gender in Twentieth-Century Germany* (New York, 2002), pp. 43–68.

161. Rosa Mayreder, 'Von der Männlichkeit', in Mayreder, *Zur Kritik der Weiblichkeit*, Essays ed. Hana Schnedl (Munich, 1981), pp. 80–97, here p. 92.

162. Christopher E. Forth, *The Dreyfus Affair and the Crisis in French Masculinity* (Baltimore, 2004); see also the essays in Hagemann and Schüler-Springorum (eds.), *Home/Front*, esp. Karen Hagemann, 'Home/Front. The Military, Violence and Gender Relations in the Age of the World Wars', pp. 1–42; on elite masculinities in Anglo-German comparison, see Sonja Levsen, 'Constructing Elite Identities. University Students, Military Masculinity and the Consequences of the Great War in Britain and Germany', *Past & Present*, 198/1 (2008), pp. 147–83; on tensions within hegemonic models of masculinity, Mark Connellan, 'From Manliness to Masculinities', *Sporting Traditions*, 17/2 (2001), pp. 46–63.

163. Samuel R. Williamson, 'Vienna and July: The Origins of the Great War Once More', in id. and Peter Pastor (eds.), *Essays on World War I: Origins and Prisoners of War* (New York, 1983), pp. 9–36, esp. pp. 13–14.

164. Strandmann, *Balkanske Uspomene*, p. 241.

165. Hugo Hantsch, *Leopold Graf Berchtold. Grandseigneur und Staatsmann* (2 vols., Graz, 1963), vol. 2, pp. 374, 455, 475 n. 14, 500, 520.

166. Strandmann, *Balkanske Uspomene*, p. 244.

167. Joachim Radkau, *Das Zeitalter der Nervosität. Deutschland zwischen Bismarck und Hitler* (Munich, 1998), pp. 396–7.

168. Georg Jellinek, *System der subjektiven Öffentlichen Rechte* (Freiburg. 1892), pp. 8–17, 21–8; on Jellinek's 'normative Kraft des Faktischen', see Oliver Lepsius, *Besitz und Sachherrschaft im öffentlichen Recht* (Tübingen, 2002), pp. 176–9.

169. Denis Diderot, 'Composition in Painting', *Encyclopédie*, vol. 3 (1753), in Beatrix Tollemache, *Diderot's Thoughts on Art and Style* (New York, 1893–1971), pp. 25–34.

170. Tatishchev to Nicholas II, Berlin, 28 February 1914 and 13 March 1914, GARF, Fond 601, op. 1, del 746 (2).

CHAPTER 7

1. *Pijemont*, 28 June 1914, cited in Wolf Dietrich Behschnitt, *Nationalismus bei Serben und Kroaten, 1830–1914* (Munich, 1980), p. 132.

2. Leon Biliński, *Wspomnienia i dokumenty* (2 vols., Warsaw, 1924–5), vol. 1, p. 282.

3. Cited in Vladimir Dedijer, *The Road to Sarajevo* (London, 1967), p. 10.

4. Cited in Joachim Remak, *Sarajevo. The Story of a Political Murder* (London, 1959), p. 25.

5. Deposition by Veljko Čubrilović, in J. Kohler (ed.), *Der Prozess gegen die Attentäter von Sarajevo. Nach dem amtlichen Stenogramm der Gerichtsverhandlung aktenmässig dargestellt* (Berlin, 1918), p. 72.

6. Deposition by Cvijetko Popović, in ibid., p. 77.

7. Deposition by Gavril Princip, in ibid., p. 30.

8. Igelstroem (Russian consul-general in Sarajevo) to Shebeko, Sarajevo, 7 July 1914, *IBZI*, series 3, vol. 4, doc. 120, p. 123.

9. Rebecca West, *Black Lamb and Grey Falcon. A Journey through Yugoslavia* (London, 1955), p. 332.

10. Cited in Remak, *Sarajevo*, p. 131.

11. Cited in ibid., p. 134.

12. The recollections are those of the Yugoslav head of the Sarajevo tourist bureau, as recorded by Rebecca West when she visited the city in 1936–7, see West, *Black Lamb and Grey Falcon*, pp. 333, 350.

13. Deposition by Oskar Potiorek, in Kohler (ed.), *Der Prozess*, pp. 156–7.

14. Cited in Dedijer, *Road to Sarajevo*, p. 15; Rudolf Jeřábek, *Potiorek. General im Schatten von Sarajevo* (Graz, 1991), pp. 82–6.

15. Kohler (ed.), *Der Prozess*, p. 30.

16. Deposition by Oskar von Potiorek, in ibid., p. 157.

17. Deposition by Franz von Harrach, in ibid., p. 159.

18. Stefan Zweig, *Die Welt von gestern. Erinnerungen eines Europäers* (2nd edn, Hamburg, 1982), p. 251.

19. R. J. W. Evans, 'The Habsburg Monarchy and the Coming of War', in id. and H. Pogge von Strandmann (eds.), *The Coming of the First World War* (Oxford, 1988), pp. 33–57.

20. Diary entry 17 September 1914 in Rosa Mayreder, *Tagebücher 1873–1936*, ed. Harriet Anderson (Frankfurt am Main, 1988), p. 145.

21. Prince [Alfons] Clary[-Aldringen], *A European Past*, trans. Ewald Osers (London, 1978), p. 153.

22. Diary entry 1 June 1914 in Arthur Schnitzler, *Tagebücher 1913–1916*, ed. P. M. Braunwarth, R. Miklin, S. Pertlik, W. Ruprechter and R. Urbach (Vienna, 1983), p. 117.

23. Biliński, *Wspomnienia i dokumenty*, vol. 1, p. 276.

24. Shebeko to Sazonov, 1 July 1914, *IBZI*, series 3, vol. 4, doc. 46, p. 52.

25. Jaroslav Hašek, *The Good Soldier Švejk*, trans. Cecil Parrott (London, 1974; repr. 2000), p. 4.

26. Joseph Roth, *The Radetzky March*, trans. Michael Hofmann (London, 2003), p. 327.

27. Robert A. Kann, 'Gross-Österreich', in id., *Erzherzog Franz Ferdinand Studien* (Munich, 1976), pp. 26–46, here p. 31.

28. Count Ottokar Czernin, *In the World War* (London, 1919), p. 36.

29. Rudolf Kiszling, *Erzherzog Franz Ferdinand von Österreich-Este. Leben, Pläne und Wirken am Schicksalsweg der Donaumonarchie* (Graz, 1953), pp. 49–50.

30. Robert Hoffmann, *Erzherzog Franz Ferdinand und der Fortschritt. Altstadterhaltung und bürgerliche Modernisierungswille in Salzburg* (Vienna, 1994), pp. 94–5.

31. Diary entries 28 June and 24 September 1914, in Schnitzler, *Tagebücher*, pp. 123, 138.

32. See Bernd Sösemann, 'Die Bereitschaft zum Krieg. Sarajevo 1914', in Alexander Demandt (ed.), *Das Attentat in der Geschichte* (Cologne, 1996), pp. 295–320.

33. Djordjević to Pašić, Constantinople, 30 June 1914, AS, MID – PO, 411, fos. 744–8, here fos. 744–5.

34. Shebeko to Sazonov, 1 July 1914, *IBZI*, series 3, vol. 4, doc. 47, p. 53.

35. See, for example, 'Die Ermordung des Thronfolgerpaares', in *Prager Tagblatt*, 29 June 1914, 2nd Extra-Ausgabe, p. 1; 'Ermordung des Thronfolgerpaares', in *Innsbrucker Nachrichten*, 29 June 1914, p. 2; 'Die erste Nachricht', 'Das erste Attentat', 'Das tödliche Attentat', in *Pester Lloyd*, 29 June 1914, p. 2; 'Die letzten Worte des Erzherzogs', in *Vorarlberger Volksblatt*, 1 July 1914, p. 2.

36. 'Franz Ferdinand über Seine Ehe', in *Die Reichspost*, 30 June 1914, afternoon edition, p. 4.

37. Karl Kraus, 'Franz Ferdinand und die Talente', *Die Fackel*, 10 July 1914, pp. 1–4.

38. See, for example, 'Nichtamtlicher Teil', in *Wiener Zeitung*, 29 June 1914, p. 2.

39. 'Ermordung des Thronfolgerpaares', in *Innsbrucker Nachrichten*, 29 June 1914, p. 1; 'Die Ermordung des Thronfolgers und seiner Gemahlin', in *Die Reichspost*, 29 June 1914, p. 1; on the archduke as carrier of the Habsburg future, see also, 'Erzherzog Franz Ferdinand. Das Standrecht in Sarajevo', in *Neue Freie Presse*, 30 June 1914, p. 1.

40. Józef Galántai, *Hungary in the First World War* (Budapest, 1989), pp. 26–7.

41. Franz Kafka, *Tagebücher*, ed. Hans-Gerhard Koch, Michael Müller and Malcolm Pasley (Frankfurt am Main, 1990), p. 543.

42. Cited in Remak, *Sarajevo*, p. 183.

43. Ibid., p. 186.

44. Potiorek to Biliński, Sarajevo, 29 June 1914, *ÖUAP*, vol. 8, doc. 9947, pp. 213–14, here p. 214.

45. Luigi Albertini, *The Origins of the War of 1914*, trans. Isabella M. Massey (3 vols. Oxford, 1953), vol. 2, pp. 55, 97–8.

46. Remak, *Sarajevo*, pp. 194–6, 198.

47. Potiorek to Biliński, Sarajevo, 28 June 1914; Potiorek to Biliński, Sarajevo, 28 June 1914; Potiorek to Biliński, Sarajevo, 29 June 1914, *ÖUAP*, vol. 8, docs. 9939, 9940, and 9947, pp. 208, 209, 213–14; on Potiorek's need to assuage his possibly unconscious feelings of guilt in connection with the murders by ordering the arrest of all supposedly suspect Serbs in Bosnia, see Jeřábek, *Potiorek*, p. 88.

48. Wilhelm Ritter von Storck to MFA Vienna, Belgrade, 29 June 1914; Wilhelm Ritter von Storck to MFA Vienna, Belgrade, 29 June 1914, *ÖUAP*, vol. 8, docs. 9941, 9943, pp. 209–10, 210–12.

49. Potiorek to Krobatin, Sarajevo, 29 June 1914, ibid., doc. 9948, p. 214; on Potiorek's insistence on Belgrade's complicity in the crime, see also Roberto Segre, *Vienna e Belgrado 1876–1914* (Milan, [1935]), p. 48.

50. Wilhelm Ritter von Storck to MFA Vienna, Belgrade, 29 June 1914, ÖUAP, vol. 8, doc. 9943, pp. 210–12.

51. Storck to MFA Vienna, Belgrade, 29 June 1914, ibid., doc. 9943, pp. 210–12.

52. Heinrich Jehlitschka to MFA Vienna, telegram, Üsküb, 1 July 1914, ibid., doc. 9972, pp. 237–40, here p. 239.

53. Storck to MFA Vienna, Belgrade, 30 June 1914, ibid., doc. 9951, pp. 218–19. Similar reports were sent from other parts of Serbia: see, for example, Report of the consulate manager Josef Umlauf in Mitrovica, 5 July 1914, ibid., doc. 10064, pp. 311–12.

54. Attachments to Storck to MFA Vienna, Belgrade, 1 July 1914, ibid., doc. 9964, pp. 232–4; pamphlet published by Straza on 30 June, HHStA, PA I, Liasse Krieg, 810, fo. 78.

55. In fact the 'warning' was couched in vague generalities, no details of the plot were provided and Jovanović spoke to Biliński, not to Berchtold; transcript from *Stampa*, 30 June 1914, ibid., fo. 24.

56. Jovanović (Serbian minister in Vienna) to Pašić, Vienna, 1 July 1914; see also same to same, Vienna, 6 July 1914, AS, MID – PO, 411, fos. 659, 775.

57. Djordjević (Serbian minister in Constantinople) to Pašić, Constantinople, 29 June 1914. Djordjević reported that the Romanian minister in Constantinople had warned that the Serbian press should be careful 'not to celebrate this act, but to condemn [it]'; Djordjević disagreed and urged Pašić to aim for a tone of 'dignified reserve'; Vesnić to Pašić, Paris, 1 July 1914, ibid., 411, fos. 662, 710.

58. Mark Cornwall, 'Serbia', in Keith M. Wilson (ed.), *Decisions for War 1914* (London, 1995), pp. 55–96, here p. 62.

59. On Pašić's denial, see Albertini, *Origins*, vol. 2, p. 99; Djordje Stanković, *Nikola Pašić, saveznivi i stvaranje Jugoslavije* (Zajecar, 1995), p. 40.

60. See report Czernin (Austro-Hungarian minister in St Petersburg) to MFA Vienna, St Petersburg, 3 July 1914, ÖUAP, vol. 8, doc. 10017, pp. 282–3; full transcript of the article in *Vecherneye Vremya*, 29 June 1914, ibid., doc. 10017, pp. 283–4.

61. Szapáry to MFA Vienna, St Petersburg, 21 July 1914, ibid., doc. 10461, pp. 567–8.

62. Consul-General Heinrich Jehlitschka to MFA Vienna, telegram, Üsküb, 1 July 1914, ibid., doc. 9972, pp. 237–40, here p. 239.

63. Pašić to all Serbian legations, Belgrade, 1 July 1914; Pašić to all Serbian legations, Belgrade, 14 July 1914, in DSP, vol. 7/1, docs. 299, 415.

64. Storck to MFA Vienna, Belgrade, 3 July 1914; Storck to MFA Vienna, Belgrade, 3 July 1914, ÖUAP, vol. 8, docs. 10000, 10004, pp. 274, 276.

65. Storck to MFA Vienna, Belgrade, 30 June 1914, ibid., doc. 9950, p. 218.

66. *Neue Freie Presse*, 7 July 1914 (no. 17911), p. 4, col. 1.

67. Cornwall, 'Serbia', passim.

68. On the policy of haughty silence, see, for example, Hartwig to Sazonov, 9 July 1914, *IBZI*, series 3, vol. 4, doc. 148, p. 147.

69. Storck to MFA Vienna, Belgrade, 30 June 1914, *ÖUAP*, vol. 8, doc. 9951, pp. 218–19.

70. Hugo Hantsch, *Leopold Graf Berchtold. Grandseigneur und Staatsmann*, (2 vols., Graz, 1963), vol. 2, p. 557.

71. Cited in ibid., p. 558.

72. Ibid., p. 559.

73. Biliński, *Wspomnienia i dokumenty*, vol. 1, p. 238.

74. See for example, Biliński to Potiorek, Vienna, 30 June and 3 July 1914, *ÖUAP*, vol. 8, docs. 9962, 10029, pp. 227–31, 289–91.

75. See the account of the meeting of 13 October 1913 in Conrad von Hötzendorf, *Aus meiner Dienstzeit, 1906–1918* (5 vols., Vienna, 1921–5), vol. 3, pp. 464–6.

76. John Leslie, 'The Antecedents of Austria-Hungary's War Aims. Policies and Policy-makers in Vienna and Budapest before and during 1914', in Elisabeth Springer and Leopold Kammerhold (eds.), *Archiv und Forschung. Das Haus- Hof und Staatsarchiv in seiner Bedeutung für die Geschichte Österreichs und Europas* (Vienna, 1993) pp. 366–7.

77. Biliński, *Wspomnienia i dokumenty*, vol. 1, p. 277.

78. N. Shebeko, *Souvenirs. Essai historique sur les origins de la guerre de 1914* (Paris, 1936), p. 185.

79. Tschirschky to Bethmann Hollweg, Vienna, 30 June, in *DD*, vol. 1, doc. 7, pp. 10–11.

80. On Musulin's motivations, see the memoir composed by Count Alexander Hoyos and transcribed in Fritz Fellner, 'Die Mission "Hoyos"', in id., *Vom Dreibund zum Völkerbund. Studien zur Geschichte der internationalen Beziehungen 1882–1919*, ed. H. Maschl and B. Mazohl-Wallnig (Vienna, 1994), pp. 112–41, here p. 135.

81. Leslie, *Antecedents*, p. 378 (quotation: Szapáry to Berchtold, 19 November 1912).

82. Joseph Redlich, diary entry 24 July 1914, in Fritz Fellner (ed)., *Schicksalsjahre Österreichs, 1908–1919: Das politische Tagebuch Josef Redlichs*, (2 vols., Graz, 1953–4), vol. 1, p. 239.

83. Berchtold, 'Die ersten Tage nach dem Attentat vom 28. Juni', cited in Hantsch, *Berchtold*, vol. 2, p. 552.

84. Ambassador Mérey (Rome) to his father, 5 May 1914, cited in Fellner, 'Die Mission "Hoyos"', p. 119.

85. See R. A. Kann, *Kaiser Franz Joseph und der Ausbruch des Krieges* (Vienna,

1971), p. 11, citing a newspaper interview with Biliński; William Jannen, 'The Austro-Hungarian Decision for War in July 1914', in Samuel R. Williamson and Peter Pastor (eds.), *Essays on World War I: Origins and Prisoners of War* (New York, 1983), pp. 55–81, esp. p. 72.

86. This comment was supposedly reported to Margutti by the Emperor's aide-de-camp, General Count Paar, see [Albert Alexander] Baron von Margutti, *The Emperor Francis Joseph and His Times* (London, [1921]), pp. 138–9.

87. Berchtold's memoirs, cited in Hantsch, *Berchtold*, vol. 2, pp. 559–60.

88. Tisza, memorandum to Emperor Franz Joseph, Budapest, 1 July 1914, ÖUAP, vol. 8, doc. 9978, pp. 248–9.

89. Günther Kronenbitter, *Krieg in Frieden'. Die Führung der k.u.k. Armee und die Grossmachtpolitik Österreich-Ungarns 1906–1914* (Munich, 2003), pp. 465–6; Segre, *Vienna e Belgrado*, p. 49; Sidney Bradshaw Fay, *The Origins of the First World War* (2 vols., New York), vol. 2, pp. 224–36.

90. Berchtold's memoirs, cited in Hantsch, *Berchtold*, vol. 2, pp. 560, 561.

91. Conrad, *Aus meiner Dienstzeit*, vol. 4, p. 34; Samuel R. Williamson, *Austria-Hungary and the Origins of the First World War* (Houndmills, 1991), pp. 199–200.

92. Notes by Hoyos on conversation with Naumann, 1 July 1914, ÖUAP, vol. 8, doc. 9966, pp. 235–6; also Albertini, *Origins*, vol. 2, pp. 129–30; Dieter Hoffmann, *Der Sprung ins Dunkle: Oder wie der 1. Weltkrieg entfesselt wurde* (Leipzig, 2010), pp. 181–2; Fritz Fischer, *War of Illusions. German Policies from 1911 to 1914*, trans. Marian Jackson (London, 1975), p. 473.

93. Cited Albertini, *Origins*, vol. 2, p. 138.

94. Szögyényi to Berchtold, Berlin, 4 July 1914, ÖUAP, vol. 8, doc. 10039, p. 295.

95. Ibid., p. 36; cf. Fischer, *War of Illusions*, p. 418.

96. Tisza, memorandum to Emperor Franz Joseph, Budapest, 1 July 1914, ÖUAP, vol. 8, doc. 9978, pp. 248–9.

97. Ibid., appendix to doc. 9984, pp. 253–61.

98. Franz Joseph to Kaiser Wilhelm II, 2 July 1914, ibid., doc. 9984, pp. 250–52.

99. Report by Szögyényi on Hoyos (1908) cited in Verena Moritz, '"Wir sind also fähig, zu wollen!" Alexander Hoyos und die Entfesselung des Ersten Weltkrieges', in Verena Moritz and Hannes Leidinger (eds.), *Die Nacht des Kirpitschnikow. Eine andere Geschichte des Ersten Weltkrieges* (Vienna, 2006), pp. 66–96, here pp. 82–3.

100. Fellner, 'Die Mission "Hoyos"', pp. 119, 125, 115–16.

101. For an astute discussion of Berchtold's intentions, to which the preceding is indebted, see Williamson, *Austria-Hungary*, pp. 195–6; on the Hoyos mission, see also Manfred Rauchensteiner, *Der Tod des Doppeladlers*.

Österreich-Ungarn und der Erste Weltkrieg (Graz, 1994), pp. 70–73; Hantsch, *Berchtold*, vol. 2, pp. 567–73.

102. Berchtold, report on a conversation with the German ambassador, Vienna, 3 July 1914, *ÖUAP*, vol. 8, doc. 1006, pp. 277–8.
103. Conversation with Bratianu reported in Czernin to MFA Vienna, Sinaia, 24 July 1914, HHStA, PA I, Liasse Krieg 812, fos. 699–708.

CHAPTER 8

1. Cited in David Fromkin, *Europe's Last Summer. Who Started the Great War in 1914?* (New York, 2004), p. 138.
2. Rumbold to Grey, Berlin, 3 July 1914, *BD*, vol. 11, doc. 26, p. 18.
3. Friedrich Meinecke, *Erlebtes, 1862–1919* (Stuttgart, 1964), p. 245.
4. Akers-Douglas to Grey, Bucharest, 30 June 1914, *BD*, vol. 11, doc. 30, p. 23.
5. Poklewski-Koziell to Sazonov, 4 July 1914, *IBZI*, vol. 4, doc. 81, p. 87; Hristić to Pašić, Bucharest, 30 June 1914, AS, MID – PO, 411, fo. 689.
6. Crackanthorpe to Grey, Belgrade, 2 July, 1914, *BD*, vol. 11, doc. 27, pp. 19–20.
7. Möllwald to MFA Vienna, Cetinje, 29 June 1914, HHStA, PA I, Liasse Krieg, 810, fo. 22.
8. Note from the Ministry of War (sig. Krobatin), Vienna, 2 July 1914; Berchtold to Möllwald, *ÖUAP*, vol. 8, docs. 9996, 10040, pp. 270–71, 295–6.
9. Spalajković to Pašić, St Petersburg, 9 July 1914, AS, MID – PO, 412, fo. 28.
10. Rodd to Grey, Rome, 7 July 1914, *BD*, vol. 11, doc. 36, p. 28; Mérey to Berchtold, Rome, 2 July 1914, *ÖUAP*, vol. 8, doc. 9988, p. 263; Mikhailović to Pašić, Rome, 1 July 1914, AS, MID – PO, 411, fos. 762–5.
11. Sverbeyev to Sazonov, private letter, Rome, 30 June 1914, *IBZI*, series 3, vol. 4, doc. 29, p. 37; Mikhailović to Pašić, Rome, 1 July 1914, AS, MID – PO, 411, fols. 762–5.
12. John Keiger, *France and the Origins of the First World War* (London, 1983), pp. 139, 145.
13. Szécsen to Berchtold, Paris, 1 July 1914, *ÖUAP*, vol. 8, doc. 9970, p. 237.
14. Bosković to Pašić, London, 18 July 1914, AS, MID – PO, 411, fo. 684.
15. Mensdorff to MFA Vienna, London, 16 July 1914, HHStA, PA I, Liasse Krieg, 812, fo. 478.
16. Czernin to MFA Vienna, Bucharest, 10 July 1914, ibid., 810, fo. 369.
17. Jovanović to Pašić, Berlin, 13 July 1914, AS, MID – PO, 412, fos. 63–4; Spalajković to Pašić, St Petersburg, 12 July 1914, ibid., fos. 105–6.
18. Shebeko to Sazonov, Vienna, 30 June 1914; Vienna, 1 July 1914, Vienna, 1 July 1914, *IBZI*, series 3, vol. 8, docs. 32, 46, 47, pp. 39, 53, 54.
19. Hartwig to Sazonov, Belgrade, 30 June 1914, ibid., vol. 4, doc. 35, p. 43; on the

importance of Friedjung as a pretext for rejecting out of hand the Austrian case against Serbia, see also Manfred Rauchensteiner, *Der Tod des Doppeladlers. Österreich-Ungarn und der Erste Weltkrieg* (Graz, 1994), p. 77.

20. Bronewsky to Sazonov, Sofia, 8 July 1914, *IBZI*, series 3, vol. 4, doc. 136, p. 143.

21. Sverbeyev (ambassador to Berlin) to Sazonov, 2 July 1914, ibid., doc. 62, p. 68.

22. Benckendorff to Sazonov, London, 30 June 1914, ibid., doc. 26, p. 32.

23. Bunsen (British envoy in Vienna) to Grey, 5 July 1914, *BD*, vol. 11, doc. 40, pp. 31–2.

24. Carlotti to San Giuliano, St Petersburg, 8 July 1914, *IBZI*, series 3, vol. 4, doc. 128, p. 128; the Russian publication of this communication notes that there are no documents relating to this conversation in the Russian foreign ministry records, and the account of the same meeting by Czernin describes the conversation but does not mention this point. The reason may be that Czernin had acquired privileged information from a contact in Vienna, but wished to conceal the fact that he had divulged Austrian intentions to Sazonov. The close agreement between Czernin's disclosure and official thinking in Vienna at the time suggests, however, that the comment was indeed made and that the exchange was authentic.

25. Szapáry to Berchtold, 18 July 1914, *ÖUAP*, vol. 8, doc. 10365, p. 495.

26. Thus Shebeko verbally to Berchtold on 30 July in Vienna, see N. Shebeko, *Souvenirs. Essai historique sur les origines de la guerre de 1914* (Paris, 1936), p. 258.

27. Szécsen to Berchtold, 4 July 1914, *ÖUAP*, vol. 8, doc. 10047, p. 299.

28. Grey to Buchanan, London, 8 July 1914, *BD*, vol. 11, doc. 39, p. 31.

29. Bunsen to Grey, 5 July 1914, ibid., doc. 41, pp. 31–2.

30. Bernadotte Everly Schmitt, *Interviewing the Authors of the War* (Chicago, 1930), p. 10. Whereas Schmitt accepted Artamonov's disclaimer, Albertini was more sceptical, see Luigi Albertini, *The Origins of the War of 1914*, trans. Isabella M. Massey (3 vols., Oxford, 1953), vol. 2, pp. 81–6.

31. Wilhelm II, marginal comments on Tschirschky to Bethmann Hollweg, Vienna, 30 July 1914, in Imanuel Geiss (ed.), *Julikrise und Kriegsausbruch 1914. Eine Dokumentensammlung* (2 vols., Hanover, 1963/4), here vol. 1, doc. 2, p. 59.

32. Berchtold report of a conversation with Tschirschky, 3 July 1913, *ÖUAP*, vol. 8, doc. 10006, p. 277; Hugo Hantsch, *Leopold Graf Berchtold. Grand-seigneur und Staatsmann* (2 vols., Graz, 1963), vol. 2, pp. 566–8.

33. Szögyényi to Berchtold, Berlin, 5 July 1914, in *ÖUAP*, vol. 8, doc. 10058, pp. 306–7.

34. Hoyos memoir in Fritz Fellner, 'Die Mission "Hoyos"', in id., *Vom Dreibund zum Völkerbund. Studien zur Geschichte der Internationalen Beziehungen 1882–1919*, ed. H. Mashl and B. Mazohl-Wallnig (Vienna, 1994), p. 137.

35. Holger Afflerbach, *Falkenhayn: Politisches Denken und Handeln im Kaiserreich* (Munich, 1994), p. 151; Albertini, *Origins*, vol. 2, p. 142; Annika Mombauer, *Helmut von Moltke and the Origins of the First World War* (Cambridge, 2001), p. 190; Geiss (ed.), *Julikrise*, vol. 1, p. 79.

36. Szögyényi to Berchtold, Berlin, 6 July 1914, ÖUAP, vol. 8, doc. 10076, p. 320.

37. Imanuel Geiss, *July 1914. The Outbreak of the First World War. Selected Documents* (New York, 1974), p. 72; Albertini, *Origins*, vol. 2, pp. 137–40.

38. Albertini, *Origins*, vol. 2, p. 147; Hantsch, *Berchtold*, vol. 2, pp. 571–2.

39. Albertini, *Origins*, vol. 2, pp. 159, 137–8; Afflerbach, *Falkenhayn*, p. 151; Stevenson, *Armaments*, pp. 372, 375.

40. Geiss, *July 1914*, p. 72; David Stevenson, *Armaments and the Coming of War. Europe 1904–1915* (Oxford, 1996), p. 372; Szögyényi to Berchtold, Berlin, 28 October 1913, ÖUAP, vol. 7, doc. 8934, pp. 513–15.

41. On British concerns in the spring and summer of 1914 about the reliability of the Russians, see Thomas Otte, *The Foreign Office Mind. The Making of British Foreign Policy, 1865–1914* (Cambridge, 2001) pp. 376–8; on French concern about Sergei Witte: Stefan Schmidt, *Frankreichs Aussenpolitik in der Julikrise 1914. Ein Beitrag zur Geschichte des Ausbruchs des Ersten Weltkrieges* (Munich, 2009), pp. 266–8.

42. Konrad H. Jarausch, 'The Illusion of Limited War: Chancellor Bethmann Hollweg's Calculated Risk, July 1914', *Central European History*, 2/1 (1969), pp. 48–76; *Gian Enrico Rusconi, Rischio 1914. Come si decide una guerra* (Bologna, 1987), pp. 95–115.

43. Jarausch, 'Bethmann Hollweg's Calculated Risk', p. 48.

44. Dieter Hoffmann, *Der Sprung ins Dunkle: Oder wie der 1.Weltkrieg entfesselt wurde* (Leipzig, 2010), pp. 159–62; *Le Matin*, 4 January 1914; see also Ignatiev to Danilov (Russian Quartermaster-General), Paris, 22 January 1914, IBZI, series 3, vol. 1, 77, pp. 65–8, here p. 66. Izvolsky suspected that the article was inspired by a middle-ranking functionary of the Quai d'Orsay, see ibid., p. 66, n. 1.

45. Cited in Hermann von Kuhl, *Der deutsche Generalstab in Vorbereitung und Durchführung des Weltkrieges* (Berlin, 1920), p. 72.

46. Pourtalès to Bethmann, 13 June 1914, *DD*, vol.1, doc. 1, p. 1.

47. Wilhelm II, marginal notes to the translation of the same article, ibid., doc. 2, p. 3.

48. Bethmann to Lichnowsky, Berlin, 16 June 1914, *GP*, vol. 39, doc. 15883, pp. 628–30, esp. p. 628.

49. I. V. Bestuzhev, 'Russian Foreign Policy, February–June 1914', *Journal of Contemporary History*, 1/3 (1966), p. 96.

50. General Staff memorandum, Berlin, 27 November 1913 and 7 July 1914, PA-AA, R 11011.

51. Zara S. Steiner, *Britain and the Origins of the First World War* (London,

1977), pp. 120–24; Wolfgang J. Mommsen, 'Domestic Factors in German Foreign Policy before 1914', *Central European History*, 6 (1973), pp. 3–43, here pp. 36–9.

52. Karl Dietrich Erdmann (ed.), *Kurt Riezler. Tagebücher, Aufsätze, Dokumente* (Göttingen, 1972), diary entry 7 July 1914, pp. 182–3. The publication of the diaries triggered a long and often acrimonious debate, both over the extent of German responsibility for the outbreak of war (the 'Fischer Controversy' was still smouldering) and over the authenticity of the diaries (especially the pre-war sections). Bernd Sösemann in particular accused Erdmann of misdescribing the manuscript, which consisted of heavily edited, partly truncated loose leaves with a combination of what appear to be original diary entries and later interpolations, as a 'diary' granting the reader a contemporary window on events. See Bernd Sösemann, 'Die Erforderlichkeit des Unmöglichen. Kritische Bemerkungen zu der Edition: Kurt Riezler, Tagebücher, Aufsätze, Dokumente', *Blätter für deutsche Landesgeschichte*, 110 (1974); id., 'Die Tagebücher Kurt Riezlers. Untersuchungen zu ihrer Echtheit und Edition', *Historische Zeitschrift*, 236 (1983), pp. 327–69, and Erdmann's detailed reply: Karl Dietrich Erdmann, 'Zur Echtheit der Tagebücher Kurt Riezlers. Eine Antikritik', *Historische Zeitschrift*, 236 (1983), pp. 371–402. On the abiding value of the edition and of Riezler's notes despite the complex character of the source, see Holger Afflerbach's introduction to the reprint edition of Erdmann's edition (Göttingen, 2008).

53. Erdmann, *Riezler*, diary entry 7 July 1914, p. 182.

54. Ibid., diary entry 8 July 1914, p. 184; on the importance of this argument to German policy, see also Jürgen Angelow, *Der Weg in die Urkatastrophe. Der Zerfall des alten Europa 1900–1914* (Berlin, 2010), pp. 25–6.

55. A. Hoyos, 'Meine Mission nach Berlin', in Fellner, 'Die Mission "Hoyos"', p. 137.

56. 'Protocol of the Ministerial Council for Joint Affairs convened on 7 July 1914', *ÖUAP*, vol. 8, doc. 10118, pp. 343–51, here pp. 343–5.

57. Ibid., p. 349.

58. Gunther E. Rothenberg, *The Army of Francis Joseph* (Lafayette, 1976), pp. 177–9; Rauchensteiner, *Tod des Doppeladlers*, pp. 74–5; Roberto Segre, *Vienna e Belgrado 1876–1914* (Milan, [1935]), p. 61.

59. Samuel R. Williamson, *Austria-Hungary and the Origins of the First World War* (Houndmills, 1991), p. 199.

60. Conrad von Hötzendorf, *Aus meiner Dienstzeit, 1906–1918* (5 vols., Vienna, 1921–5), vol. 4, p. 33.

61. Berchtold, Report to the Emperor, 14 July 1914, *ÖUAP*, vol. 8, doc. 10272, pp. 447–8.

62. Conrad to Berchtold, Vienna, 10 July 1914, ibid., doc. 10226, pp. 414–15.

63. Shebeko, *Souvenirs*, p. 214; Sidney Bradshaw Fay, *The Origins of the First World War* (2 vols., New York), vol. 2, pp. 243–8.

64. The Austrian ambassador Count Mérey informed Vienna of German indiscretions in an exasperated telegram of 18 July; in his reply, Berchtold indicated that he had learned through 'secret secure sources' – a coded reference to information from intercepts – of Rome's instructions to the envoys in Bucharest and St Petersburg, see Mérey to Berchtold, Rome, 18 July 1914 and Berchtold to Mérey, Vienna, 20 July 1914, *ÖUAP*, vol. 8, docs. 10364, 10418, pp. 494, 538. On the implications of the breach of secrecy, see Williamson, *Austria-Hungary and the Origins*, p. 201; id., 'Confrontation with Serbia: The Consequences of Vienna's Failure to Achieve Surprise in July 1914', *Mitteilungen des Österreichischen Staatsarchivs*, 43 (1993), pp. 168–77; id., 'The Origins of the First World War', *Journal of Interdisciplinary History*, 18 (1988), pp. 795–818, here pp. 811–12. On all this see also: San Giuliano to Berlin, St Petersburg, Vienna and Belgrade, 16 July 1914, in Italian Foreign Ministry (ed.), *I Documenti Diplomatici Italiani*, 4th series, 1908–1914 (12 vols., Rome, 1964), vol. 12 doc. 272; R. J. B. Bosworth, *Italy, the Least of the Great Powers: Italian Foreign Policy before the First World War* (Cambridge, 1979), pp. 380–86.

65. See Shebeko, *Souvenirs*, p. 213.

66. Crackanthorpe to Grey, Belgrade, 17 July 1914, *BD*, vol. 11, doc. 53, p. 41.

67. Pašić to Serbian legations, Belgrade, 19 July, AS, MID – PO 412, fo. 138.

68. Albertini, *Origins*, vol. 2, pp. 254–7, with further details.

69. Robin Okey, *The Habsburg Monarch, c. 1765–1918. From Enlightenment to Eclipse* (London, 2001), p. 377.

70. William Jannen, 'The Austro-Hungarian Decision for War in July 1914', in Samuel R. Williamson and Peter Pastor (eds.), *Essays on World War I: Origins and Prisoners of War* (New York, 1983), esp. pp. 58–60.

71. On Vienna's confidence in deterrence, see Segre, *Vienna e Belgrado*, p. 69.

72. Memorandum composed between 28 June and 7 July 1914 by Berthold Molden, journalist and freelancer for the press department of the Foreign Ministry in Vienna, cited in Solomon Wank, 'Desperate Counsel in Vienna in July 1914: Berthold Molden's Unpublished Memorandum', *Central European History*, 26/3 (1993), pp. 281–310, here p. 292.

73. Molden memorandum, cited in ibid., p. 293.

74. Edna Ullmann-Margalit, 'Big Decisions: Opting, Converting, Drifting', Hebrew University of Jerusalem, Centre for the Study of Rationality, Discussion Paper # 409, accessed online at *http://www.ratio.huji.ac.il/*. See also: Edna Ullmann-Margalit and Sidney Morgenbesser, 'Picking and Choosing', *Social Research*, 44/4 (1977), pp. 758–85. I am grateful to Ira Katznelson for drawing my attention to these articles.

75. Ullmann-Margalit, 'Big Decisions', p. 11.

76. Storck to MFA Vienna, Belgrade, telegram, 6 July 1914, HHStA, PA I, Liasse Krieg 810, fo. 223; according to this report, the British envoy Crack-

anthorpe had confided to Storck that he found the behaviour of his 'colleagues of the Triple Entente more than strange'.

77. Thus the suspicion of the Italian minister Cora, who had been present at various occasions (including the famous bridge party) on which Hartwig had ridiculed the dead archduke; see Storck to Berchtold, Belgrade, 13 July 1914, ibid., fo. 422.

78. Giesl to Berchtold, Belgrade, 11 July 1914, *ÖUAP*, vol. 8, doc. 10193, pp. 396–8; there is a further full report of the envoy's death in Strandmann to Sazonov, Belgrade, 11 July 1914, *IBZI*, series 1, vol. 4, doc. 164, p. 163.

79. Cited in Albertini, *Origins*, vol. 2, p. 277.

80. Sazonov to Strandmann, St Petersburg, 13 July 1914, *IBZI*, series 1, vol. 4, doc. 192, p. 179.

81. Descos to Viviani, Belgrade, 11 July 1914, *DDF*, 3rd series, vol. 10, doc. 499, pp. 719–21, here p. 721.

CHAPTER 9

1. Louis de Robien, 'Arrivée en Russie', Louis de Robien MSS, AN 427, AP 1, vol. 2, fos. 1–2.

2. Ibid., fos. 3–4.

3. Ibid., fos. 6–7.

4. Ibid., fos. 8–9.

5. Ibid., fo. 13.

6. Ibid., fo. 12.

7. M. B. Hayne, *The French Foreign Office and the Origins of the First World War, 1898–1914* (Oxford, 1993), pp. 117–18.

8. Maurice Paléologue, *Cavour*, trans. I. F. D. and M. M. Morrow (London, 1927), p. 69.

9. Daeschner to Doulcet, Paris, 25 May 1914, AMAE, PA-AP, 240 Doulcet, vol. 21.

10. Izvolsky to Sazonov, Paris, 15 January 1914, *IBZI*, series 3, vol. 1, doc. 13, pp. 14–16; Bertie to Grey, Paris, 26 January and 15 June 1912; see Bertie to Nicolson, 26 January 1912, TNA FO 800/165, fos. 133–4.

11. De Robien, 'Arrivée', fo. 10.

12. Bertie to Nicolson, 26 January 1912, TNA FO 800/165, fos. 133–4; 'lamentable choix': Gérard, ambassador to Japan, comments of 18 June 1914, reported in Georges Louis, *Les Carnets de Georges Louis* (2 vols., Paris, 1926), vol. 2, p. 125.

13. Crowe, marginal comment on Bertie to Grey, Paris, 26 January 1912, cited in John Keiger, *France and the Origins of the First World War* (London, 1983), p. 5.

14. Ibid., p. 51.

15. Hayne, *French Foreign Office*, pp. 253–4, 133.

16. Izvolsky to Sazonov, Paris, 15 January 1914, *IBZI*, series 3, vol. 1, doc. 13, pp. 14–16.

17. Report on a conversation with Paléologue, early January 1914, in V. N. Strandmann, *Balkanske Uspomene*, trans. from the Russian into Serbian by Jovan Kachaki (Belgrade, 2009), p. 240.

18. On Margerie's reputation for loyalty to Poincaré, see Sevastopulo (Russian chargé d'affaires, Paris) to Sazonov, Paris, 15 January 1914, *IBZI*, series 3, vol. 1, doc. 16, p. 19; on Margerie's affection and loyalty to Poincaré, see Bernard Auffray, *Pierre de Margerie, 1861–1942 et la vie diplomatique de son temps* (Paris, 1976), pp. 243–4; Keiger, *France and the Origins*, p. 51.

19. 'The French Army', *The Times*, 14 July 1914, p. 8, col. D; 'French Military Deficiencies', 'No Cause for Alarm', *The Times*, 15 July 1914, p. 7, col. A.; Gerd Krumeich, *Armaments and Politics in France on the Eve of the First World War. The Introduction of the Three-Year Conscription 1913–1914*, trans. Stephen Conn (Leamington Spa, 1984), p. 214; Keiger, *France and the Origins*, p. 149.

20. Poincaré, diary entry 15 July 1914, Notes journaliéres, BNF 16027.

21. Poincaré, diary entry 11 July 1914, ibid.

22. Poincaré, diary entry 18 July 1914, ibid.

23. Poincaré, diary entry 16 July 1914, ibid.

24. Poincaré, diary entry 20 July 1914, ibid.

25. Maurice Paléologue, *An Ambassador's Memoirs 1914–1917*, trans. Frederick A. Holt (London, 1973), p. 5.

26. Luigi Albertini, *The Origins of the War of 1914*, trans, Isabella M. Massey (3 vols., Oxford, 1953), vol. 2, p. 189.

27. Paléologue, *An Ambassador's Memoirs*, p. 4.

28. Ibid., p. 5.

29. Poincaré, diary entry 20 June 1914, Notes journalières, BNF 16027.

30. Poincaré, diary entry 21 June 1914, ibid.

31. Paléologue, *An Ambassador's Memoirs*, p. 10; Szapáry also reported an 'indirect reference to the "Prochaska Affair"', see Szapáry to Berchtold, St Petersburg, 21 July 1914, *ÖUAP*, vol. 8, doc. 10461, pp. 567–8; Friedrich Würthle, *Die Spur führt nach Belgrad* (Vienna, 1975), pp. 207, 330–31.

32. Poincaré, diary entry 21 June 1914, Notes journalières, BNF 16027.

33. Paléologue, *An Ambassador's Memoirs*, p. 10.

34. Louis de Robien, 'Voyage de Poincaré', AN 427 AP 1, vol. 2, fo. 54. Robien was not present when the words were said, but learned of their effect from Russian witnesses.

35. Szapáry to Berchtold, St Petersburg, 21 July 1914, *ÖUAP*, vol. 8, doc. 10461, p. 568; cf. for a different view of this exchange, Keiger, *France and the Origins*, p. 151, who argues that Szapáry was wrong to see a threat in the president's words.

36. Poincaré, diary entry 21 June 1914, Notes journalières, BNF 16027.

37. De Robien, 'Voyage de Poincaré', fo. 55.

38. Ibid., fo. 57.

39. Poincaré, diary entry 21 June 1914, Notes journalières, BNF 16027.

40. Poincaré, diary entry 22 June 1914, ibid.

41. Christopher Andrew, 'Governments and Secret Services: A Historical Perspective', *International Journal*, 34/2 (1979), pp. 167–86, here p. 174.

42. De Robien, 'Voyage de Poincaré', fos. 56–8.

43. Paléologue, *An Ambassador's Memoirs*, p. 15.

44. This anecdote is reported in a letter from Laguiche to the French ambassador in St Petersburg (then Georges Louis) and the French ministry of war dated 25 November 1912; which can be consulted in Service Historique de la Défence, Château de Vincennes, Carton 7 N 1478. I am grateful to Professor Paul Robinson of the Graduate School of Public and International Affairs at the University of Ottawa for drawing my attention to this document and providing me with the reference.

45. Paléologue, *An Ambassador's Memoirs*, p. 15.

46. Poincaré, diary entry 22 June 1914, Notes journalières, BNF 16027.

47. Poincaré, diary entry 23 June 1914, ibid.

48. Paléologue, *An Ambassador's Memoirs*, pp. 16–17.

49. De Robien, 'Voyage de Poincaré', fo. 62.

50. Ibid., fols. 62–3.

51. Paléologue, *Cavour*, p. 70.

CHAPTER 10

1. 'Protocols of the Ministerial Council held in Vienna on 19 July 1914', *ÖUAP*, vol. 8, doc. 10393, pp. 511–14; Conrad von Hötzendorf, *Aus meiner Dienstzeit 1906–1918* (5 vols., Vienna, 1921–5), vol. 4, pp. 87-92.

2. This question is raised in Czernin to Berchtold, 'top secret', Sinaia, 27 July 1914, HHStA, PA I, Liasse Krieg 812, fos. 193–8.

3. Szögyényi to MFA Vienna, Berlin, 14 July 1914, ibid., fo. 446.

4. Ibid., fo. 512.

5. Samuel R. Williamson, *Austria-Hungary and the Origins of the First World War* (Houndmills, 1991), p. 203.

6. Lewis Bernstein Namier, *In the Margin of History* (London, 1939), p. 247.

7. Manfred Rauchensteiner, *Der Tod des Doppeladlers. Österreich-Urgarn und der Erste Weltkrieg* (Graz, 1994), p. 78.

8. See the text of the Austrian note and ultimatum in *ÖUAP*, vol. 8, doc. 10395, pp. 515–17.

9. Wiesner to Berchtold (two telegrams), Sarajevo, 13 July 1914, *ÖUAP*, vol. 8, docs. 10252, 12253, pp. 436–7; on the impact of Wiesner's report,

see Sidney Bradshaw Fay, *The Origins of the First World War* (2 vols., New York), vol. 2, pp. 236–9.

10. Bernadotte Everly Schmitt, *Interviewing the Authors of the War* (Chicago, 1930), p. 22.

11. Luigi Albertini, *The Origins of the War of 1914*, trans. Isabella M. Massey (3 vols., Oxford, 1953), vol. 2, pp. 90–97.

12. Musulin had drafted point 6; it was revised by Berchtold, re-revised by Musulin and then reformulated by Forgách, ibid., vol. 2, pp. 255–6.

13. Grey to Bunsen (ambassador in Vienna), reporting his conversation with Lichnowsky, *BD*, vol. 11, doc. 91, pp. 73–4; Churchill cited in David Fromkin, *Europe's Last Summer. Who Started the Great War in 1914?* (New York, 2004), p. 184.

14. Rambouillet Agreement, Interim Agreement for Peace and Self-Government in Kosovo, US State Department website at *http://www.state.gov/www/regions/eur/ksvo_rambouillet_text.html*.

15. Ian Bancroft, 'Serbia's Anniversary is a Timely Reminder', Guardian Unlimited, 24 March 2009, accessed at *http://global.factiva.com/ha/default.aspx*.

16. Crackanthorpe to Grey, Belgrade, 18 July 1914, *BD*, vol. 11, doc. 80, pp. 64–5.

17. Royal Legation of Serbia, London, to Netherlands MFA, 18 October 1912, NA 2.05.3, Ministerie van Buitenlandsa Zaken, doc. 648, Correspondentie over de Balkan-oorlog.

18. Giesl to Berchtold, Belgrade, 23 July 1914, *ÖUAP*, vol. 8, doc. 10526, p. 596.

19. Albertini, *Origins*, vol. 2, p. 285.

20. Recollection of Ljuba Jovanović, cited in ibid., vol. 2, p. 347.

21. These details were recalled by Gruić, cited in ibid., p. 347.

22. Berchtold to Giesl, Vienna, 23 July 1014, *ÖUAP*, vol. 8, doc. 10519, p. 594.

23. Strandmann to Sazonov, 24 July 1914, *IBZI*, series 3, vol. 5, doc. 35, p. 38.

24. Thus the recollection of Colonel Pavlović divulged in conversations with Luciano Magrini in October 1915, during the Serbian retreat, see Magrini, *Il dramma di Seraievo. Origini i responsabilità della guerra europea* (Milan, 1929), pp. 203–5.

25. Pašić to Spalajković, Belgrade, 24 July 1914, *DSP*, vol. 7/2, doc. 501; Regent Alexander to Tsar Nicholas II, transcript in Strandmann to Sazonov, 24 July 1914, *IBZI*, series 3, vol. 5, doc. 37, p. 39.

26. Magrini, *Il dramma di Seraievo*, pp. 205–6.

27. N. Pašić to Serbian legations abroad, Belgrade, 25 July 1914, British Foreign Office (ed.), *Collected Diplomatic Documents Relating to the Outbreak of the European War* (London, 1915), pp. 389–90.

28. Crackanthorpe to Grey, Belgrade, 12.30 p.m., 25 July 1914, *BD*, vol. 11, doc. 114, pp. 87–8.

29. Spalajković to Pašić, St Petersburg, sent 6.15 p.m. 22 July 1914, *DSP*, vol. 7/2, doc. 484.

30. Albertini, *Origins*, vol. 2, p. 354.

31. Spalajković to Pašić, St Petersburg, sent midnight 24 July 1914, *DSP*, vol. 7/2, doc. 527.

32. Gale Stokes, 'The Serbian Documents from 1914: A Preview', *Journal of Modern History*, 48 (1976), pp. 69–84, here p. 72. Spalojković to Pašić, St Petersburg, sent 1.40 a.m. 25 July (wrongly given as 24 July by the editors), *DSP*, vol. 7/2, doc. 503.

33. Spalajković to Pašić, St Petersburg, 8 p.m. 25 July 1914, *DSP*, vol. 7/2, doc. 556.

34. Spalajković to Pašić, St Petersburg, 3.22 p.m. 25 July 1914, same to same, 2.55 p.m. 26 July 1914, ibid., docs. 559, 556.

35. On the impact of the telegrams from Russia, see Albertini, *Origins*, vol. 2, pp. 354–6; and specifically on Sazonov's rejection of points 5 and 6 of the ultimatum, see Magrini, *Il dramma di Seraievo*, p. 206; Stokes, 'Serbian Documents'; cf. Mark Cornwall, 'Serbia', in Keith M. Wilson (ed.), *Decisions for War 1914* (London, 1995), pp. 79–80. Cornwall, whose analysis of developments in Belgrade is unsurpassed, argues that the wording of the telegrams from St Petersburg was too vague to satisfy Pašić beyond any doubt that the Russians intended to come to Serbia's aid. It is true that Sazonov was vague – as indeed he was bound to be – on the details of what Russia would do and when, but my own view is that the steady crescendo of indications in Spalajković's cables must have sufficed to reassure the Serbian leadership that the Russians were on track to intervene. But it must be conceded that Serbian determination to resist was strong from the start, as is implied by Belgrade's handling of the crisis from the outset.

36. On telegram transit and arrival times, see the editors' note on Spalajković to Pašić, St Petersburg, sent midnight 24 July 1914, *DSP*, vol. 7/2, doc. 527, and Stokes, 'Serbian Documents'.

37. Gruić's recollection cited in Albertini, *Origins*, vol. 2, pp. 363–4.

38. Alexander Musulin von Gomirje, *Das Haus am Ballhausplatz. Erinnerungen eines österreich-ungarischen Diplomaten* (Munich, 1924), p. 241.

39. Text of the reply (in French) in 'Note der serbischen Regierung und die Belgrader Gesandtschaft', Belgrade, no date [25 July 1914], *ÖUAP*, vol. 8, doc. 10648, pp. 660–63.

40. Miloš Bogičević, *Le Procès de Salonique, Juin 1917* (Paris, 1927), p. 132; Joachim Remak, *Sarajevo. The Story of a Political Murder* (London, 1959), p. 207.

41. Text of the reply (in French) in 'Note der serbischen Regierung an die Belgrader Gesandschaft', Belgrade, no date [25 July 1947], *ÖUAP*, vol. 8, doc. 10648, pp. 660–63.

42. Roberto Segre, *Vienna e Belgrado 1876–1914* (Milan, [1935]), p. 78; see also James Joll, *The Origins of the First World War* (London, 1984), p. 13; Joachim Remak, '1914 – The Third Balkan War: Origins Reconsidered', *Journal of Modern History*, 43 (1971), pp. 353–66.

43. See 'Monarchiefeindliche Bilder im Belgrader Kriegsministerium', a note included in the dossier circulated to Austro-Hungarian legations after the receipt of the Serbian reply, *ÖUAP*, vol. 8, doc. 10654, pp. 665–704, here p. 704.

44. Military attaché Belgrade to chief of General Staff, Belgrade, 25 July 1914, Kriegsarchiv Wien, AOL Evidenzbureau, 3506, 1914, Resumés d. vertraulichen Nachrichten – Italian, Russland, Balkan, 'B' [Balkan]; N. Shebeko, *Souvenirs. Essai historique sur les origines de la guerre de 1914* (Paris, 1936), p. 231.

45. My account of Giesl's departure is heavily indebted to Albertini, *Origins*, vol. 2, p. 373.

46. Berchtold to Mensdorff, Vienna, 24 July 1914, *ÖUAP*, vol. 8, doc. 10599, p. 636.

47. Macchio to Berchtold, Vienna, 25 July 1914; Berchtold to Macchio, Lambach, 25 July 1914, ibid., vol. 8, docs. 10703, 10704, pp. 731–2.

48. Albertini, *Origins*, vol. 2, pp. 376–80.

49. Spalajković to Serbian MFA in Niš, St Petersburg, 4.10 a.m. 26 July 1914, *DSP*, vol. 7/2, doc. 584.

50. Franz Joseph, 'The Imperial Rescript and Manifesto', 28 July 1914, trans. and repr. in 'Austria-Hungary's Version of the War', *New York Times Current History of the European War*, 1/2 (1914: December 26), pp. 223–6, here p. 223, consulted online through Periodical Archives Online.

51. Rapaport to Vredenburch, Belgrade, 28 July 1914, NA, 2.05.36, 9, Consulaat-Generaal Belgrado en Gezandschap Zuid-Slavië.

52. Ernest Jones, *Sigmund Freud: Life and Work* (3 vols., London, 1953–7), vol. 2, p. 192.

CHAPTER II

1. Maurice Paléologue, diary entry 24 July 1914, *An Ambassador's Memoirs 1914–1917*, trans. Frederick A. Holt (London, 1973), p. 21.

2. De Robien, 'Copie des notes prises par Chambrun du 23 juillet au 3 août 1914', AN 427, AP 1, Louis de Robien MSS, vol. 2, fo. 2, opposite. This interesting source consists of notes appended by de Robien to the carbon copy of a typewritten account drawn up by Chambrun at the request of Viviani itemizing the ambassador's activities during the last days before the outbreak of war.

3. Buchanan to Grey, 24 July 1914, *BD*, vol. 11, doc. 101, p. 81.

4. Paléologue, diary entry 24 July 1914, *An Ambassador's Memoirs*, p. 22.

5. De Robien, 'Copie des notes prises par Chambrun', fo. 2, opposite.

6. Szapáry to Berchtold, St Petersburg, 24 July 1914, *ÖUAP*, vol. 8, docs. 10616, 10617, 10619, pp. 645, 646–7, 648.

7. Thus Yanushkevich related the conversation to General Dobrorolsky, chief

of the Russian army's Mobilization Department, see S. K. Dobrorolsky, 'La Mobilisation de l'armée russe en 1914', *Revue d'Histoire de la Guerre Mondiale*, 1 (1923), pp. 53–69, 144–59, here p. 64; on the press release, see Paléologue, diary entry 25 July 1914, *An Ambassador's Memoirs*, p. 25.

8. These citations, based on the unpublished memoirs of the minister of finance Peter Bark, are drawn from the transcriptions in D. C. B. Lieven, *Russia and the Origins of the First World War* (London, 1983), p. 142.

9. A. Yu Ariev (ed.), *Sud'ba Veka. Krivosheiny* (St Petersburg, 2002), p. 76; see also the letters from Menshikov, one of the leading columnists of *Novoye Vremya*, to Krivoshein in RGIA, esp. F. 1571, op. 1, d. 181, ll. 2–3.

10. H. H. Fisher (ed.), *Out of My Past. The Memoirs of Count Kokovtsov, Russian Minister of Finance, 1904–1914, Chairman of the Council of Ministers, 1911–1914*, trans. Laura Matveev (Stanford, 1935), p. 349.

11. See her letter to Krivoshein in RGIA, F. 1571, op. 1, d. 289, ll. 3, 7.

12. From Bark's account of the meeting cited in Lieven, *Russia and the Origins*, pp. 142–3.

13. Ibid., pp. 143–4.

14. Sonderjournal des russischen Ministerrats, 24 July 1914, *IBZI*, series 3, vol. 5, doc. 19, pp. 25–6.

15. Leonard Turner, 'Russian Mobilisation in 1914', *Journal of Contemporary History*, 3/1 (1968), pp. 75–6.

16. Lieven, *Russia and the Origins*, pp. 59–61; on the importance of the Russian decisions of 24 and 25 July, see also Jürgen Angelow, *Der Weg in die Urkatastrophe. Der Zerfall des alten Europa 1900–1914* (Berlin, 2010), p. 145.

17. Bruce W. Menning, 'Russian Military Intelligence, July 1914. What St Petersburg Perceived and Why It Mattered', unpublished typescript, p. 20: Dobrorolsky, 'La Mobilisation de l'armée russe', pp. 64–7.

18. Dobrorolsky, 'La Mobilisation de l'armée russe', passim; Sidney Bradshaw Fay, *The Origins of the First World War* (2 vols., New York), vol. 2, pp. 286–300.

19. Turner, 'Russian Mobilisation', pp. 65–88, here p. 75; A. Knox, *With the Russian Army, 1914–1917* (2 vols., New York, 1921), vol. 1, p. 42.

20. Luigi Albertini, *The Origins of the War of 1914*, trans. Isabella M. Massey (3 vols., Oxford, 1953), vol. 2, p. 558; Turner, 'Russian Mobilisation'.

21. Lieven, *Russia and the Origins*, pp. 144–5; Dobrorolsky, 'La Mobilisation de l'armée russe', p. 68; Turner, 'Russian Mobilisation', p. 76.

22. Regulation Concerning the Period Preparatory to War of 2 March 1913, paraphrased in Fay, *Origins*, vol. 2, pp. 316–18.

23. De l'Escaille to Davignon, St Petersburg, 26 and 27 July 1914, see also Buisseret to Davignon, St Petersburg, 26 July 1914, MAEB AD, Empire Russe, 34.

24. Széchényi to MFA Vienna, Copenhagen, 26 July 1914, HHStA, PA, I. Liasse Krieg, 812, fo. 63.

25. Hein to MFA Vienna, Kiev, 27 July 1914, ibid., fo. 226.

26. Andrian to MFA Vienna, 27 July 1914, Szczakowa, 27 July 1914, ibid., fo. 237.

27. Von Haydin to MFA Vienna, Moscow, 28 July 1914, ibid., fo. 3.

28. Stürghk (excerpting report from Statthalter Galicia) to MFA Vienna, Vienna, 28 July 1914, ibid., fo. 26.

29. Corossacz to MFA Vienna, Tiflis, 28 July 1914, ibid., fo. 69.

30. On these reports, see Sean McMeekin, *The Russian Origins of the First World War* (Cambridge, MA, 2011), p. 62; on alarming concentrations of horses, Dobrorolsky, 'La Mobilisation de l'armée russe', pp. 68–9.

31. Paléologue, diary entry 25 July 1914, *An Ambassador's Memoirs*, p. 25.

32. Buchanan to Grey, St Petersburg, 18 July 1914, *BD*, vol. 11, doc. 60, p. 47.

33. Fisher (ed.), *Memoirs of Count Kokovtsov*, pp. 346–7.

34. Ibid., p. 347.

35. Ignatiev to General Staff, Paris, 30 July 1914, RGVIA, Fond 15304 – Upravlenie Voennogo Agenta vo Frantsii, op. 2, d. 16, Reports and communications made with special notebooks, l. 38.

36. Guillaume to Davignon, Paris, 30 July 1914, MAEB AD, France 12, Correspondance politique – légations.

37. Paléologue to Quai d'Orsay, 6.30 p.m., 24 July 1914; 11 p.m., 24 July 1914; 4.45 p.m., 25 July 1914, all in rough copy, AMAE, PA-AP, Maurice Paléologue, Correspondance politique 1, fos. 30–32; this document is discussed in M. B. Hayne, *The French Foreign Office and the Origins of the First World War, 1898–1914* (Oxford, 1993), p. 298.

38. Laguiche to French General Staff, excerpted in Paléologue to MFA Paris, St Petersburg, 26 July 1914, cited in McMeekin, *Russian Origins*, p. 69.

39. Thus Sazonov reported the conversation to Paléologue, see Paléologue to Quai d'Orsay, 7.30 p.m., 26 July 1914, AMAE, PA-AP, Maurice Paléologue, Correspondance politique 1, fo. 35; Szapáry's report on this encounter emphasized the minister's warm and friendly tone, but closed with the suggestion that as Russian military preparations were already under way, this overture was merely an attempt to play for time, *ÖUAP*, vol. 8, doc. 10835, pp. 804–6.

40. On 8 November 1912, a secret Russian Military Commission adopted new guidelines on the measures preceding full mobilization, see Fay, *Origins*, vol. 2, p. 308.

41. Paléologue to Quai d'Orsay, 4.45 p.m. 25 July 1914, in rough copy, AMAE, PA-AP, Maurice Paléologue, Correspondance politique 1, fol. 32 verso.

42. Paléologue to Quai d'Orsay, 11.00 p.m. 24 July 1914, in rough copy, ibid., fol. 31 verso.

43. McMeekin, *Russian Origins*, p. 34.

44. Ronald Bobroff, *Roads to Glory. Late Imperial Russia and the Turkish Straits* (London, 2006), pp. 52–3.

45. Mustafa Aksakal, *The Ottoman Road to War in 1914. The Ottoman Empire and the First World War* (Cambridge, 2008), p. 43; on the Graeco-Turkish naval race, see Paul G. Halpern, *The Mediterranean Naval Situation, 1908–1914* (Cambridge, MA, 1971), pp. 314–54.

46. Grigorovich to Sazonov, 19 January 1914, *IBZI*, series 3, vol. 1, doc. 50, pp. 45–7.

47. Sazonov to Benckendorff, St Petersburg, 8 May 1914, ibid., vol. 2, doc. 384, pp. 381–2, here p. 382; Aksakal, *Ottoman Road to War*, p. 46.

48. Sazonov to Benckendorff, St Petersburg, 30 July 1914, *IBZI*, series 3, vol. 5, doc. 281, p. 195.

49. On the Straits as a theme in Russian foreign policy, see Bobroff, *Roads to Glory*, passim; for an exposition of the view that control of the Bosphorus was the crucial motivating factor in Russian policy during the July Crisis, see McMeekin, *Russian Origins*, pp. 6–40, and pp. 98–114, where McMeekin highlights the growing importance of the Straits after the outbreak of war.

50. Lieven, *Russia and the Origins*, pp. 45–7, 99–101.

51. Dobrorolsky, 'La Mobilisation de l'armée russe', p. 68.

CHAPTER 12

1. The classic account is A. T. Q. Stewart, *The Ulster Crisis* (London, 1969).

2. See Ian F. W. Beckett, *The Army and the Curragh Incident 1914* (London, 1986); James Fergusson, *The Curragh Incident* (London, 1964).

3. Zara S. Steiner, *Britain and the Origins of the First World War* (London, 1977), p. 215: Keith Jeffery, *Field Marshal Sir Henry Wilson. A Political Soldier* (Oxford, 2006), p. 126.

4. Asquith to Venetia Stanley, 30 June 1914, in Michael and Eleanor Brock (eds.), *H. H. Asquith. Letters to Venetia Stanley* (Oxford, 1985), p. 93.

5. Asquith to Venetia Stanley, 24 July 1914, in ibid., p. 122.

6. Grey to Bertie, London, 8 July 1914, Imanuel Geiss (ed,), *Julikrise und Kriegsausbruch 1914. Eine Dokumentensammlung* (2 vols., Hanover, 1934–4), vol. 1, doc. 55, p. 133; *BD*, vol. 11, doc. 38, p. 30.

7. Grey to Buchanan, London, 8 July 1914, Geiss (ed,), *Julikrise*, vol. 1, doc. 56, pp. 133–5: *BD*, vol. 11, doc. 39, pp. 30–31.

8. Conversations reported in Lichnowsky to Bethmann Hollweg, London, 9 July 1914, Geiss (ed.), *Julikrise*, vol. 1, doc. 60, pp. 136–7.

9. Mensdorff to MFA Vienna, London, 17 July 1914, *ÖUAP*, vol. 8, doc. 10337, pp. 480–81.

10. Mensdorff to MFA Vienna, London, 24 July 1914, ibid., vol. 8, doc. 10660, p. 636.

11. Steiner, *Britain and the Origins*, p. 222.

12. Cited in H. D. Lasswell, *Propaganda Technique in the World War* (New York, 1927), p. 49.

13. Adrian Gregory, 'A Clash of Cultures. The British Press and the Opening of the Great War', in Troy E. Paddock (ed.), *A Call to Arms. Propaganda, Public Opinion and Newspapers in the Great War* (Westport, 2004), pp. 15–50, here p. 20.

14. *John Bull*, 11 July 1914, p. 6; Niall Ferguson, *Pity of War* (London, 1998), p. 219; Gregory, 'A Clash of Cultures', pp. 20–21.

15. Bosković to Pašić, London, 12 July 1914, AS, MID – PO 412, fo. 36: the offending article is in *John Bull*, 11 July 1914, p. 6.

16. Winston S. Churchill, *The World Crisis* (2 vols., London, repr. 1968), vol. 1, p. 114.

17. Steiner, *Britain and the Origins*, pp. 224–5.

18. Wilson's presentation to the Committee of Imperial Defence on 23 August 1911 is excerpted in *BD*, vol. 8, doc. 314, pp. 381–2.

19. Cited in Michael Brock, 'Britain Enters the War', in R. J. W. Evans and H. Pogge von Strandmann (eds.), *The Coming of the First World War* (Oxford, 1988), pp. 145–78, here pp. 150–51.

20. See Trevor Wilson (ed.), *The Political Diaries of C. P. Scott 1911–1928* (London, 1970), pp. 96–7, 104.

21. Brock, 'Britain Enters the War', pp. 153–4.

22. Grey to Rumbold, London, 20 July 1914, *BD*, vol. 11, doc. 68, p. 54.

23. On the incoherence and impracticability of Grey's 'concert' proposal, see Sidney Bradshaw Fay, *The Origins of the First World War* (2 vols., New York), vol. 2, pp. 360–62.

24. Buchanan to Grey, St Petersburg, 26 July 1914, *BD*, vol. 11, doc. 155, p. 107.

25. Nicolson to Grey, reporting 'Communication by German Ambassador', 26 July 1914, *BD*, vol. 11, doc. 146, p. 155.

26. Benckendorff's long account of the conversation with Grey on 8 July confirms that the British foreign secretary did not contest Russia's view of the Serbian situation, but viewed the crisis exclusively in terms of the relationship between the two alliance groups, Benckendorff to Sazonov, London, 9 July 1914, *IBZI*, series 3, vol. 4, doc. 146, pp. 141–4.

27. Buchanan to Grey, St Petersburg, 24 July 1914, *BD*, vol. 11, doc. 101, pp. 80–82 (including minutes).

28. Crowe, minute dated 25 July on Buchanan to Grey, St Petersburg, 24 July 1914, *BD*, vol. 11, doc. 101, p. 81.

29. Lichnowsky to Jagow, London, 29 July 1914, in Max Montgelas and Karl Schücking (eds.), *Deutsche Dokumente zum Kriegsausbruch*, vol. 1, doc. 368, pp. 86–9, here p. 87.

30. Grey to Goschen, London, 30 July 1914, *BD*, vol. 11, doc. 303, pp. 193–4.

31. On Grey's acceptance of the Austrian case against Serbia, see Steiner, *Britain and the Origins*, pp. 220–23.

32. Poincaré, diary entry 25 July 1914, Notes journalières, BNF 16027.

33. Ibid.,

34. Ibid., emphasis added.

35. Jean-Jacques Becker, *1914. Comment les français sont entrés dans la guerre. Contribution à l'étude de l'opinion publique printemps-été 1914* (Paris, 1977), p. 140; on French passivity, see John Keiger, *France and the Origins of the First World War* (London, 1983), pp. 166, 167; also id., 'France', in Keith M. Wilson (ed.), *Decisions for War 1914* (London, 1995), pp. 121–49, esp. pp. 122–3.

36. On Swedish public opinion, which was said to 'live in fear of Russia', see Buisseret to Davignon, St Petersburg, 28 November 1913, MAEB AD, Russie 3, 1906–1914.

37. The conversation is reported in Poincaré, diary entry 23 July 1914, Notes journalières, BNF 16027.

38. Poincaré, diary entry 25 July 1914, ibid.

39. Poincaré, diary entry 25 July 1914, ibid.

40. Poincaré, diary entry 27 July 1914, ibid. The *France* was already sailing towards Copenhagen when the decision was made to return to Paris.

41. Ibid.

42. Ibid.

43. Ibid.

44. Ibid.

45. Poincaré, diary entry 28 July 1914, Notes journalières, BNF 16027.

46. Keiger, 'France', in Wilson (ed.), *Decisions*, p. 123; Schmidt, *Frankreichs Aussenpolitik*, p. 313.

47. Poincaré, diary entry 29 July 1914, Notes journalières, BNF 16027.

48. Joseph Caillaux, *Mes Mémoires* (3 vols., Paris, 1942–7), vol. 3, *Clairvoyance et force d'âme dans mes épreuves, 1912–1930*, pp. 169–70.

49. Poincaré, diary entry 29 July 1914, Notes journalières, BNF 16027.

50. Laguiche to Messimy, St Petersburg, 26 July 1914, *DDF*, 3rd series, vol. 11, doc. 89, pp. 77–8.

51. The page is missing from the manuscript at the Bibliothèque Nationale, see Poincaré, diary entry 29 July 1914, Notes journalières, BNF 16027, fo. 124. The last paragraph records that the British have asked Sazonov to express a view on the idea of convening a four-power ambassadors' conference in London to resolve the Austro-Serbian issue and closes tantalizingly with the fragment: 'Sazonoff a malheureusement' – .

52. Caillaux, *Mes Mémoires*, vol. 3, pp. 170–71.

53. Sazonov to Izvolsky, St Petersburg, 29 July 1914, *IBZI*, series 3, vol. 5, doc. 221, pp. 159–60; also Note de l'Ambassade de Russie. Communication

d'un télégramme de M. Sazonoff, 30 July 1914, *DDF*, 3rd series, vol. 11, doc. 301, pp. 257–8.

54. Stefan Schmidt, *Frankreichs Aussenpolitik in der Julikrise 1914. Ein Beitrag zur Geschichte des Ausbruchs des Ersten Weltkriegs* (Munich, 2009), p. 321.

55. Excerpted in Viviani to Paléologue and Paul Cambon, Paris, 30 July 1914, *DDF*, 3rd series, vol. 11, doc. 305, pp. 261–3; my interpretation of this document follows Schmidt's in *Frankreichs Aussenpolitik*, pp. 317–20.

56. See Keiger, 'France', in Wilson (ed.), *Decisions for War*, pp. 121–49, here p. 147.

57. Gabriel Hanotaux, *Carnets (1907–1925)*, ed. Georges Dethan, Georges-Henri Soutou and Marie-Renée Mouton (Paris, 1982), pp. 103–4.

58. Poincaré, diary entry 30 July 1914, Notes journalières, BNF 16027; on this linkage see Schmidt, *Frankreichs Aussenpolitik*, p. 322.

59. Izvolsky to Sazonov, Paris, 30 July 1914, *IBZI*, series 3, vol. 5, doc. 291, pp. 201–2, emphasis added; see also the discussions in Keiger, 'France', p. 127; Schmidt, *Frankreichs Aussenpolitik*, pp. 323–4.

60. Cited in Schmidt, *Frankreichs Aussenpolitik*, p. 326. Schmidt argues that mobilization without concentration was probably what Messimy meant when he referred to an acceleration without 'mass transports of troops'.

61. Poincaré, diary entry 30 July 1914, Notes journalières, BNF 16027.

62. Dobrorolsky, 'La Mobilization de l'armée russe', p. 147; the article 'Rossiya khochet mira, no gotova voine' appeared in the *Birzheviia Vedomosti* and was republished in the nationalist organ *Rech* on 13 March 1914.

63. Dobrorolsky, 'La Mobilization de l'armée russe', p. 147.

64. Ibid., pp. 148–9.

65. Baron M. F. Schilling (ed.), *How the War Began in 1914. Being the Diary of the Russian Foreign Office from the 3rd to the 20th (Old Style) of July, 1914*, trans. W. Cyprian Bridge (London, 1925), p. 62.

66. Sazonov, *Les Années fatales*, p. 216.

67. Ibid., pp. 217–20; there is an excellent account of these events in Fay, *Origins*, vol.2, pp. 450–81.

68. Dobrorolsky, 'La Mobilization de l'armée russe', p. 151.

69. These discrepancies are discussed in Bruce W. Menning, 'Russian Military Intelligence, July 1914. What St Petersburg Perceived and Why It Mattered', unpublished typescript, p. 23; see also Ministère des affaires étrangères (ed.), *Documents diplomatiques, 1914. La guerre européenne. Pièces relatives aux négotiations qui ont précédé la déclaration de guerre de l'Allemagne à la Russie at à la France* (Paris, 1914), doc. 118, p. 116; on other omissions and suppressions, see also Konrad G. W. Romberg, *The Falsifications of the Russian Orange Book*, trans. W. Cyprian Bridge (London, [1923]).

70. Telegram no. 1538 to London, Paris, Vienna, Berlin and Rome, 28 July 1914, cited in Schilling, *How the War Began*, p. 44.

71. Telegram no. 1539 to Berlin, Paris, London, Vienna and Rome, 28 July 1914, cited in ibid.

72. Telegram from Benckendorff to Sazonov, cited in Sazonov, *Les Années fatales*, pp. 200–201.

73. Cited in Schilling (ed.), *How the War Began*, p. 43.

74. On Sazonov's view of Bethmann's warning, see Luigi Albertini, *The Origins of the War of 1914*, trans. Isabella M. Massey (3 vols., Oxford, 1953), vol. 2, p. 491; Horst Linke, *Das Zarische Russland und der Erste Weltkrieg. Diplomatie und Kriegsziele, 1914–1917* (Munich, 1982), p. 33; on the exchange with Pourtalès, see '16/29 July', Schilling (ed.), *How the War Began*, pp. 48–9.

75. '15/28 July', ibid, p. 43.

76. De l'Escaille to Davignon, St Petersburg, 30 July 1914, MAEB AD, Empire Russe 34, 1914; this telegram, which was intercepted by the Germans and published during the war, became a well known fixture in the post-war war-guilt debate, see e.g. German Foreign Office (ed.), *Belgische Aktenstücke, 1905–1914* (Berlin, [1917]); see also Bethmann Hollweg, *Betrachtungen zum Weltkrieg* (2 vols., Berlin, 1919), vol. 1, p. 124.

77. Telegram of Kaiser Wilhelm to the Tsar, Berlin, 29 July 1914, cited in Schilling (ed.), *How the War Began*, p. 55.

78. See, for example, Herman Bernstein, 'Kaiser Unmasked as Cunning Trickster Who Plotted for War While He Prated of Peace. "Nicky" Telegrams Reveal Czar as No Better, Falling Readily into Snares that "Willy" Set', *Washington Post*, 18 September 1917, cutting in AMAE NS, Russie 45 Allemagne-Russie; Herman Bernstein, *The Willy-Nicky Correspondence. Being the Secret and Intimate Telegrams Exchanged Between the Kaiser and the Tsar* (New York, 1918); Sidney B. Fay, 'The Kaiser's Secret Negotiations with the Tsar, 1904–5', *American Historical Review*, 24 (1918), pp. 48–72; Isaac Don Levine (ed.), *The Kaiser's Letters to the Tsar. Copied from Government Archives in Petrograd and Brought from Russia by Isaac Don Levine* (London, 1920). These early editions do not include the sequence of cables exchanged by the two sovereigns in 1914, probably because the latter were not in fact personal telegrams, but diplomatic cables and thus archived separately from the personal correspondence of the monarch – I owe this insight to John Röhl, to whom warm thanks.

79. Michael S. Neiberg, *Dance of the Furies, Europe and the Outbreak of World War I* (Cambridge, MA, 2011), p. 116.

80. Sergei Dmitrievich Sazonov, *Les Années fatales* (Paris, 1927), p. 218.

81. Ibid., pp. 218–19.

82. Menning, 'Russian Military Intelligence', pp. 13–18; D. C. B. Lieven, *Russia and the Origins of the First World War* (London, 1983), pp. 148–9.

83. Tschirschky to Bethmann Hollweg, Vienna, 2 July 1910, reporting a conversation between Kulakovsky and Sukhomlinov, PA-AA, R 10894.

84. Menning, 'Russian Military Intelligence', pp. 30–31.

85. Cited in V. R. Berghahn and W. Deist, 'Kaiserliche Marine und Kriegsausbruch

1914', *Militärgeschichtliche Mitteilungen*, 1 (1970), pp. 37–58; Albert Hopman (senior official in the Imperial Naval Office), diary entries 6 and 7 July 1914, in Michael Epkenhans (ed.), *Albert Hopman. Das ereignisreiche Leben eines 'Wilhelminers'. Tagebücher, Briefe, Aufzeichnungen, 1901 bis 1920* (Oldenbourg, 2004), pp. 383, 385.

86. Biedermann (Saxon plenipotentiary in Berlin) to Vitzthum (Saxon foreign minister), Berlin, 17 July 1914, in Geiss (ed.), *Julikrise*, vol. 1, doc. 125, pp. 199–200.

87. Bethmann Hollweg to ambassadors in St Petersburg, Paris and London, Berlin, 21 July 1914, in ibid., doc. 188, pp. 264–6, here p. 265.

88. Annika Mombauer, *Helmuth von Moltke and the Origins of the First World War* (Cambridge, 2001), pp. 190–93, 196; on German confidence in German military preparedness, see Mark Hewitson, *Germany and the Causes of the First World War* (Oxford, 2006), passim.

89. Cited in L. C. F. Turner, *Origins of the First World War* (London, 1973), p. 86.

90. Cited in Ulrich Trumpener, 'War Premeditated? German Intelligence Operations in July 1914', *Central European History*, 9 (1976), pp. 58–85, here p. 64.

91. Ibid.

92. Riezler, diary entry 11 July 1914, in Karl Dietrich Erdmann (ed.), *Kurt Riezler. Tagebücher Aufsätze Dokumente* (Göttingen, 1972), p. 185.

93. Geiss (ed.), *Julikrise*, vol. 1, doc. 123, p. 198.

94. 'German View of French Disclosures', *The Times*, 17 July 1914, p. 7, col. C; 'Attitude of Germany', ibid., 25 July 1914, p. 10, col. C.

95. Mombauer, *Helmuth von Moltke*, pp. 194–5, n 44.

96. Thus the inference of Count Kageneck, German military attaché in Vienna, see ibid., p. 194. On the impact of the Humbert revelations on German thinking during the crisis, see also Theodor Wolff (editor-in-chief of the *Berliner Tageblatt*), diary entry 24 July 1914, reporting official scepticism about French readiness, in Bernd Sösemann (ed.), *Tagebücher 1914–1919: der Erste Weltkrieg und die Entstehung der Weimarer Republik in Tagebüchern, Leitartikeln und Briefen des Chefredakteurs am 'Berliner Tageblatt' und Mitbegründers der 'Deutschen Demokratischen Partei' Theodor Wolff* (Boppard, 1984), pp. 64–5; Hopman, diary entry 14 July 1914, in Epkenhans (ed.), *Tagebücher*, p. 389.

97. Risto Ropponen, *Italien als Verbündeter. Die Einstellung der politischen und militärischen Führung Deutschlands und Österreich-Ungarns zu Italien von der Niederlage von Adua 1896 bis zum Ausbruch des Weltkrieges 1914* (Helsinki, 1986), pp. 139, 141–2, 209–10.

98. Bethmann to Schoen and Bethmann to Lichnowsky, both Berlin, 27 July 1914, in Geiss (ed.), *Julikrise*, vol. 2, docs. 491, 492, p. 103.

99. Jagow to Lichnowsky (private letter), Berlin, 18 July 1914, in Karl Kautsky

(ed.), *Die deutschen Dokumente zu Kriegsausbruch* (4 vols., Berlin, 1927), vol. 1, doc. 72, pp. 99–101, here p. 100.

100. On the German confidence in 'localization', see Hopman, diary entries 8, 13, 24, 26 July 1914, pp. 386, 388, 394–5, 397–8; on Jagow's anxiety, see same 21 July, pp. 391–2; on Bethmann as 'drowning man', see Alfred von Tirpitz, *Erinnerungen* (Leipzig, 1920), p. 242; on these features of the crisis, see also Williamson and May, 'An Identity of Opinion', esp. n 107, p. 353.

101. Wilhelm II to Franz Joseph, Balholm, 14 July 1914, ÖUAP, vol. 8, doc. 10262, pp. 422–3.

102. See esp. Wilhelm's notes on Tschirschky to Jagow, Vienna, 10 July 1914, in Imanuel Geiss, *July 1914. The Outbreak of the First World War. Selected Documents* (New York, 1974), doc. 16, pp. 106–7.

103. Wilhelm II, comments on Tschirschky to Bethmann, Vienna, 14 July 1914, in ibid., doc. 21, pp. 114–15.

104. Lamar Cecil, *Wilhelm II* (2 vols., Chapel Hill, 1989 and 1996), vol. 2, *Emperor and Exile, 1900–1941*, p. 202; Jagow to Wedel (imperial entourage), Berlin, 18 July 1914, in Geiss, *July 1914*, doc. 29, p. 121.

105. David Stevenson, *Armaments and the Coming of War, Europe 1904–1914* (Oxford, 1996), p. 376.

106. See G. A. von Müller, *Regierte der Kaiser? Aus den Kriegstagebüchern des Chefs des Marinekabinettes im Ersten Weltkrieg Admiral Georg Alexander von Müller* (Göttingen, 1959); Holger Afflerbach, *Kaiser Wilhelm II. als Oberster Kriegsherr im Ersten Weltkrieg. Quellen aus der militärischen Umgebung des Kaisers* (Munich, 2005), p. 11.

107. Holger Afflerbach, *Falkenhayn: Politisches Denken und Handeln im Kaiserreich* (Munich, 1994), p. 153.

108. Wilhelm to Jagow, Neues Palais, 28 July 1914, in Geiss, *July 1914*, doc. 112, p. 256; Afflerbach, *Falkenhayn*, p. 153.

109. Cited Afflerbach, *Falkenhayn*, p. 154.

110. Cited in Volker Berghahn, *Germany and the Approach of War in 1914* (Basingstoke, 1993), pp. 202–3.

111. Albertini, *Origins*, vol. 2, p. 467; Geiss, *July 1914*, p. 222.

112. Lichnowsky to Jagow, London, 27 July 1914, Geiss, *July 1914*, doc. 97, pp. 238–9.

113. Bethmann to Tschirschky, Berlin 10.15 a.m., 28 July 1914, Geiss, *July 1914*, doc. 115, p. 259; Stevenson, *Armaments*, pp. 401–2; on the divergence between Bethmann's and Wilhelm's views on that day, see Geiss (ed.), *Julikrise*, vol. 2, pp. 164–5 (commentary by Geiss).

114. Bethmann to Wilhelm II, Berlin 10.15 p.m., 28 July 1914, in Geiss, *July 1914*, docs. 114, 117, pp. 258, 261.

115. Trumpener, 'War Premeditated?', pp. 66–7.

116. Chelius to Wilhelm II, St Petersburg, 26 July 1914, in Geiss (ed.), *Julikrise*, vol. 2, doc. 441, pp. 47–9, here p. 48.

117. Cited in Trumpener, 'War Premeditated?', p. 66.

118. Ibid.

119. General Staff, report by the Intelligence Assessment Board, 28 July 1914, cited in ibid., p. 72.

120. See, for example, Bethmann to Tschirschky, Berlin, 29 July 1914 and same to same twice on 30 July 1914, in Geiss (ed.), *Julikrise*, vol. 2, docs. 690, 695, 696, pp. 287–8, 289–90, 290.

121. Falkenhayn diary, 29 July 1914, cited in Afflerbach, *Falkenhayn*, p. 155.

122. Berghahn, *Germany and the Approach of War*, p. 215.

123. Falkenhayn diary, 31 July 1914, cited in Afflerbach, *Falkenhayn*, p. 160.

124. George V, reported by Prince Henry of Prussia, Henry to Wilhelm II, 28 July 1914, in *DD*, vol. 1, pp. 32–89.

125. Harold Nicolson, *King George the Fifth* (London, 1952), p. 245; Berghahn, *Germany and the Approach of War*, p. 219.

126. Nicolson, *King George the Fifth*, p. 246.

127. Lichnowsky to Jagow, London, 29 July 1914, in Geiss, *July 1914*, doc. 130, pp. 288–90.

128. Wilhelm II, notes on Pourtalès to Jagow, St Petersburg, 30 July 1914, Geiss, *July 1914*, doc. 135, pp. 293–5.

129. Lichnowsky to Jagow, London, 1 August 1914, *DD*, vol. 3, doc. 562, p. 66.

130. Lichnowsky to Jagow, London, 1 August 1914, ibid., doc. 570, p. 70.

131. Cited in Afflerbach, *Falkenhayn*, p. 164.

132. Falkenhayn diary, 1 August 1914, cited in ibid., pp. 165–6. Falkenhayn's version of this exchange was broadly supported by Moltke, but may not be entirely trustworthy. According to the memoirs of the aide-de-camp and eyewitness Max von Mutius, the Kaiser asked Moltke for advice on whether a breach of the borders in the west – specifically the entry of the 16th Division into Luxembourg – could still be stopped. Moltke replied that he did not know, and it was a subordinate from the Operations Department of the General Staff, Lieutenant-Colonel Tappen, who affirmed that this was still possible. By this account, the Kaiser did not directly overrule Moltke, but remained within the conventional boundaries of his position. In any case, the extant accounts agree on the traumatic effect of this episode on the chief of the General Staff, who returned obsessively to it thereafter; see Afflerbach, *Kaiser Wilhelm II als Oberster Kriegsherr im Ersten Weltkrieg. Quellen aus der militärischen Umgebung des Kaisers, 1914–1918* (Munich, 2005), p.13.

133. Cecil, *Wilhelm II*, vol. 2, p. 107.

134. Mombauer, *Helmuth von Moltke*, p. 222.

135. Wilhelm II to George V, Berlin 1 August 1914, *DD*, vol. 3 doc. 575, p. 74.

136. Bethmann to Lichnowsky, Berlin, 1 August 1914, ibid., vol. 3, doc. 578,

p. 76; Wilhelm II to George V, Berlin, 1 August 1914, ibid., vol. 3, doc. 575, p. 74.

137. Lichnowsky to Jagow, London, 1 August 1914, ibid., vol. 3, doc. 596, pp. 89–91.

138. George V to Wilhelm II, London, 1 August 1914, ibid., vol. 3, doc. 612, pp. 103–4.

139. Lichnowsky to Jagow, London, 1 August 1914, ibid., vol. 3, doc. 603, p. 95.

140. Cited Afflerbach, *Falkenhayn*, p. 167.

141. Lichnowsky to Jagow, London, 29 July 1914, *DD*, vol. 1, doc. 368, pp. 86–9.

142. Grey to Bertie, London, 31 July 1914, *BD*, vol. 11, doc. 352, p. 220.

143. Harry F. Young, 'The Misunderstanding of August 1, 1914', *Journal of Modern History*, 48/4 (1976), pp. 644–65.

144. Stephen J. Valone, ' "There Must Be Some Misunderstanding": Sir Edward Grey's Diplomacy of August 1, 1914', *Journal of British Studies*, 27/4 (1988), pp. 405–24.

145. Keith M. Wilson, 'Understanding the "Misunderstanding" of 1 August 1914', *Historical Journal*, 37/4 (1994), pp. 885–9; on the impact of international financial instability on British thinking, see Nicholas A. Lambert, *Planning Armageddon. British Economic Warfare and the First World War* (Cambridge, MA, 2012), pp. 185–231; for a discussion of Lambert's views, see Williamson, 'July 1914: Revisited and Revised', pp. 17–18; I am grateful to Sam Williamson for drawing my attention to this strand in Lambert's argument.

146. Grey to Bertie, London, 1 August 1914, *BD*, vol. 11, doc. 419, p. 250.

147. Bertie to Grey, Paris, 2 August 1914, ibid., doc. 453, p. 263; on the 'impertinence' of this reply, see Wilson, 'Understanding the "Misunderstanding"', p. 888.

148. Communication by the German embassy, London, 31 July 1914, *BD*, vol. 11, doc. 344, p. 217; the warning was repeated on the following day, see communication by the German embassy, London, 1 August 1914, ibid., doc. 397, p. 241.

149. Asquith to Venetia Stanley, London, 1 August 1913, in Brock and Brock (eds.), *Letters to Venetia Stanley*, p. 140.

150. Grey to Bertie, London, 29 July 1914, *BD*, vol. 11, doc. 283, p. 180.

151. Grey to Bertie, London, 31 July 1914, ibid., doc. 352, p. 220.

152. Grey to Bertie, London, 31 July 1914, ibid., doc. 367, pp. 226–7.

153. Grey to Bertie, London, 8.20 p.m., 1 August 1914, ibid., doc. 426, p. 426; note the time of dispatch: this was a later telegram than the one earlier cited for that day, providing the ambassador with further detail on the conversation with Cambon.

154. Keith Eubank, *Paul Cambon: Master Diplomatist* (Norman, 1960), pp. 170–71.

155. Conversation with Cambon on 24 July recalled in André Géraud, 'The Old Diplomacy and the New', *Foreign Affairs*, 23/2 (1945), pp. 256–70, here p. 260.

156. Grey to Bertie, London, 28 July 1914, *BD*, vol. 11, doc. 238, p. 156.

157. Keiger, 'France', p. 133.

158. Cambon to Viviani, London, 29 July 1914, *DDF*, 3rd series, vol. 11, doc. 281, pp. 228–9.

159. Steiner, *Britain and the Origins*, pp. 181–6.

160. On this aspect of the Entente, see John Keiger, 'Why Allies? Necessity or Folly', unpublished MS of paper given at the conference 'Forgetful Allies: Truth, Myth and Memory in the Two World Wars and After', Cambridge, 26–27 September 2011. I am grateful to John Keiger for letting me see a copy of this paper before its publication.

161. Génevieve Tabouis, *Perfidious Albion – Entente Cordiale* (London, 1938), p. 109.

162. Cited in Steiner, *Britain and the Origins*, p. 225.

163. Asquith to Stanley, London, 29 July 1914, in Brock and Brock (eds.), *Letters to Venetia Stanley*, p. 132.

164. Eyre Crowe, memorandum of 31 July 1914, *BD*, vol. 11, enclosure in doc. 369, pp. 228–9.

165. On the growing importance of cabinet: Steiner, *Britain and the Origins*, p. 228. Cambon is cited in John Keiger, 'How the Entente Cordiale Began', in Richard Mayne, Douglas Johnson and Robert Tombs (eds.), *Cross Channel Currents. 100 Years of the Entente Cordiale* (London, 2004), pp. 3–10, here p. 10.

166. Austen Chamberlain, *Down the Years* (London, [1935]), p. 94.

167. Colin Forbes Adams, *Life of Lord Lloyd* (London, 1948), pp. 59–60; Chamberlain, *Down the Years*, pp. 94–101; Ian Colvin, *The Life of Lord Carson* (3 vols., London, 1932–6), vol. 3, pp. 14–20; on Cambon's conversation with Lloyd, esp. pp. 14–15; Leopold S. Amery, *My Political Life* (3 vols., London, [1953–5]), vol. 2, pp. 17–19.

168. Keith M. Wilson, *The Policy of the Entente. Essays on the Determinants of British Foreign Policy, 1904–1914* (Cambridge, 1985), p. 135.

169. Asquith to Stanley, London, 31 July 1914, in Brock and Brock (eds.), *Letters to Venetia Stanley*, p. 138.

170. Winston S. Churchill, *The World Crisis* (London, 1931), p. 114.

171. Asquith to Stanley, London, 1 August 1914, in Brock and Brock (eds.), *Letters to Venetia Stanley*, p. 140.

172. John Morley, *Memorandum on Resignation, August 1914* (London, 1928), p. 5.

173. Cited in Wilson, *Policy of the Entente*, p. 137.

174. Lord Crewe to George V reporting on cabinet meeting of 2 August 1914, 6.30 p.m., in J. A. Spender and Cyril Asquith, *Life of Herbert Henry Asquith* (2 vols., London, 1932), vol. 2, p. 82; Morley, *Memorandum*, p. 21.

175. On Samuel's responsibility for these formulae and his success in drumming up support for them among his colleagues, see Wilson, *Policy of the Entente*,

p. 142; also Herbert Samuel to his wife, Beatrice, 2 August 1914, in C. J. Lowe and M. L. Dockrill, *The Mirage of Power* (3 vols., London, 1972), vol. 1, pp. 150–51; Cameron Hazlehurst, *Politicians at War, July 1914 to May 1915: A Prologue to the Triumph of Lloyd George* (London, 1971), pp. 93–8.

176. On Grey's words and his 'emotion', see George Allardice Riddell (owner of *News of the World*), *Lord Riddell's War Diary, 1914–1918* (London, 1933), p. 6.

177. On the place of Belgium in British pro-war opinion, see John Keiger, 'Britain's "Union Sacrée" in 1914', in Jean-Jacques Becker and Stéphane Audoin-Rouzeau (eds.), *Les Sociétés européennes et la guerre de 1914–1918* (Paris, 1990), pp. 39–52, esp. pp. 48–9.

178. Cited in Hermann Lutz, *Lord Grey and the World War*, trans. E. W. Dickes (London, 1928), p. 101.

179. C. Addison, *Four and a Half Years* (2 vols., London, 1934), vol. 1, p. 32, cited in Brock, 'Britain Enters the War', p. 161.

180. Keiger, 'Britain's "Union Sacrée"', in Becker and Audoin-Rouzeau (eds.), *Les Sociétés européennes*, pp. 39–52; Samuel R. Williamson, *The Politics of Grand Strategy. Britain and France Prepare for War, 1904–1914* (Cambridge, MA, 1969), pp. 357–60.

181. This is the argument advanced in Keith M. Wilson, 'The British Cabinet's Decision for War, 2 August 1914', *British Journal of International Studies* (1975), pp. 148–159; reprinted as chap. 8 of id., *The Policy of the Entente*.

182. Buchanan to Nicolson, St Petersburg, 16 April 1914, *BD*, vol. 10/2, doc. 538, pp. 784–5.

183. Nicolson to Goschen, 15 April 1912, ibid., vol. 6, doc. 575, p. 747; Steiner, *Foreign Office*, p. 131; see also Wilson, *The Policy of the Entente*, p. 78; Zara S. Steiner, 'The Foreign Office under Sir Edward Grey', in Francis Harry Hinsley (ed.), *British Foreign Policy under Sir Edward Grey* (Cambridge, 1977), pp. 22–69, here p. 45.

184. Williamson, *Politics of Grand Strategy*, pp. 108–14, 167–204.

185. Eyre Crowe minute to Buchanan to Grey, St Petersburg, 24 July 1914, *BD*, vol. 11, doc. 101, pp. 80–82, here p. 82.

186. Isabel V. Hull, *Absolute Destruction. Military Culture and the Practices of War in Imperial Germany* (Ithaca, 2005), pp. 160–81; Mombauer, *Helmuth von Moltke*, pp. 102, 105, 164–7, 225.

187. Alfred von Tirpitz, *Erinnerungen* (Leipzig, 1920), pp. 241–2.

188. Note presented on 2 August at 7 p.m. by M. Below Saleske to M. Davignon, [Belgian] Minister of Foreign Affairs, cutting from the Belgian 'Grey Book' in TNA, FO 371/1910 (2 August 1914) viewed online at *http://www.nationalarchives.gov.uk/pathways/firstworldwar/first_world_war/p_ultimatum.htm*.

189. Jean Stengers, 'Belgium', in Wilson (ed.), *Decisions for War*, pp. 151–74.

190. Ibid.; reply of the Belgian government to the German ultimatum, 3 August

1914 at 7 a.m., in Hugh Gibson, *A Journal from Our Legation in Belgium* (New York, 1917), p. 19.

191. Stengers, 'Belgium', pp. 161, 162.

192. Gibson, *A Journal*, p. 15.

193. Stengers, 'Belgium', p. 163.

194. Gibson, *A Journal*, p. 22.

195. Cited in Stengers, 'Belgium', p. 164.

196. Maurice Paléologue, diary entry 1 August 1914, *An Ambassador's Memoirs 1914–1917*, trans. Frederick A. Holt (London, 1973), pp. 38–9.

197. Prince Max von Lichnowsky, *My Mission to London, 1912–1914* (London, 1918), p. 28.

198. Gibson, *A Journal*, p. 21.

199. Bernd F. Schulte, 'Neue Dokumente zu Kriegsausbruch und Kriegsverlauf 1914', *Militärgeschichtliche Mitteilungen*, 25 (1979), pp. 123–85, here p. 140.

200. Report from Colonel Ignatiev, 30 July 1914, RGVIA, Fond 15304 – Upravlenie Voennogo Agenta vo Frantsii, op. 2, d. 16 – Reports and communications made with special notebooks, l. 38.

201. Cited in Hew Strachan, *The First World War* (Oxford, 2001), p. 103.

202. V. I. Gurko, *Cherty i Siluety Proshlogo, Pravitel'stvo i Obschchestvennost' v Tsarstvovanie Nikolaya II Izobrazhenii Sovremennika* (Moscow, 2000), p. 651.

203. W. Mansell Merry, *Two Months in Russia: July–September 1914* (Oxford, 1916), pp. 76–7.

204. Thus Richard Cobb's summary of the impressions recorded in Roger Martin du Gard, *L'Été 1914* (4 vols., Paris, 1936–1940), in Cobb, 'France and the Coming of War', in Evans and Pogge von Strandmann (eds.), *The Coming of the First World War*, pp. 125–44, here p. 137.

205. Strachan, *The First World War*, pp. 103–62, esp. p. 153; on draft riots in Russia, see Joshua Sanborn, 'The Mobilization of 1914 and the Question of the Russian Nation', *Slavic Review*, 59/2 (2000), pp. 267–89.

206. Neiberg, *Dance of the Furies*, p. 128.

207. Gibson, diary entry 2 August in id., *A Journal*, p. 8.

208. See Adrian Gregory, *The Last Great War. British Society and the First World War* (Cambridge, 2008), esp. pp. 9–39; id., 'British War Enthusiasm: A Reassessment', in Gail Braybon (ed.), *Evidence, History and the Great War. Historians and the Impact of 1914–18* (Oxford, 2003), pp. 67–85; for an extraordinarily textured account of reactions to the news of war in provincial France, see Becker, *1914: Comment les français*, pp. 277–309; id., *L'Année 14* (Paris, 2004), pp. 149–153; Stéphane Audoin-Rouzeau and Annette Becker, *1914–1918: Understanding the Great War,* trans. Catherine Temerson (London, 2002), p. 95; on the 'shock, sadness and consternation' with which most people greeted the news of war, see Leonard V. Smith,

Stéphane Audoin-Rouzeau and Annette Becker, *France and the Great War* (Cambridge, 2003), pp. 27–9; P. J. Flood, *France 1914–1918: Public Opinion and the War Effort* (Basingstoke, 1990), pp. 5–33; Jeffrey Verhey, *The Spirit of 1914. Militarism, Myth and Mobilization in Germany* (Cambridge, 2000), pp. 231–6.

209. Sanborn, 'Mobilization of 1914', p. 272.

210. Thus the account provided by the '*instituteur*' of the village, cited in Flood, *France 1914–1918*, p. 7.

211. Stephen Graham, *Russia and the World* (New York, 1915), pp. 2–3, cited in Leonid Heretz, *Russia on the Eve of Modernity. Popular Religion and Traditional Culture under the Last Tsars* (Cambridge, 2008), p. 195. Many Russian memoirs record confusion about the identity of the enemy, see Bertram Wolfe, 'War Comes to Russia', *Russian Review*, 22/2 (1963), esp. pp. 126–9.

CONCLUSION

1. Rebecca West, *Black Lamb and Grey Falcon. A Journey Through Yugoslavia* (London, 1955), p. 350.

2. The memoir is that of Prince B. A. Vasil'chiko, discussed in D. C. B. Lieven, 'Bureaucratic Authoritarianism in Late Imperial Russia: The Personality, Career and Opinions of P. N. Durnovo', *The Historical Journal*, 26/2 (1983), pp. 391–402.

3. See, for example, Mark Hewitson, *Germany and the Causes of the First World War* (Oxford, 2006), pp. 3–4. On Fischer's thesis as a form of personal engagement with the contaminating legacy of Nazism, see Klaus Grosse Kracht, 'Fritz Fischer und der deutsche Protestantismus', *Zeitschrift für neuere Theologiegeschichte*, 10/2 (2003), pp. 224–52; Rainer Nicolaysen, 'Rebell wider Willen? Fritz Fischer und die Geschichte eines nationalen Tabubruchs', in Rainer Nicolaysen and Axel Schildt (eds.), *100 Jahre Geschichtswissenschaft in Hamburg* (*Hamburger Beiträge zur Wissenschaftsgeschichte*, vol. 18) (Berlin/Hamburg, 2011), pp. 197–236.

4. Paul Kennedy, *The Rise of the Anglo-German Antagonism* (London, 1980), p. 467.

5. See Paul W. Schroeder, 'Embedded Counterfactuals and World War I as an Unavoidable War', p. 42; for a powerful analysis that interprets the war as the unintended outcome of errors committed by a political elite that viewed a general war as a catastrophic outcome, see Gian Enrico Rusconi, *Rischio 1914. Come si decide una guerra* (Bologna, 1987).

6. Short-war thesis: Gerhard Ritter, *Der Schlieffenplan. Kritik eines Mythos* (Munich, 1965); Lancelot Farrar, *The Short War Illusion. German Policy, Strategy and Domestic Affairs, August–December 1914* (Santa Barbara, 1973); Stephen Van Evera, 'The Cult of the Offensive and the Origins of the

First World War', *International Security*, 9 (1984), pp. 397–419; critique: Stig Förster, 'Der deutsche Generalstab und die Illusion des kurzen Krieges, 1871–1914: Metakritik eines Mythos', *Militärgeschichtliche Mitteilungen*, 54 (1995), pp. 61–95; excellent commentary on the debate: Holger H. Herwig, 'Germany and the "Short-War" Illusion: Toward a New Interpretation?', *Journal of Military History*, 66/3, pp. 681–93.

7. Cited in Herwig, 'Germany and the "Short-War" Illusion', p. 686.

8. 'Horace Blanchon' (pseud.), 'Académie de Médecine', *Le Figaro*, 5 March 1913, cutting in NA Archief, 2.05,03, doc. 648, Correspondentie over de Balkan-oorlog.

Index

and Haldane mission to Berlin
(1912) 320
on Kaiser Wilhelm 183
Morocco question 194–5, 205–6
on Poincaré 295
relations with press 232
Cambon, Paul, ambassador to Britain
190, 192–4, 310, 354
and Balkan War 300
Entente Cordiale 193–4, 538–9
on Italy 250
July 1914 crisis and outbreak of
war 491, 502, 505, 533, 536–42,
543, 544, 545
on Poincaré 295, 359, 537
relations with Grey 213–14
Cambridge Daily News 492
Cameroons 163
Campbell-Bannerman, Sir Henry
163, 202
Canal Zone, Panama 152, 161
Cape Colony 142, 145, 336
Capelle, Eduard von 416
Caprivi, Count Leo von 127,
143–4, 197
Carlsbad 517
Carnegie Foundation, Balkan Wars
inquiry 25, 45, 276
Carnot, Marie François Sadi 409
Carol I, King of Romania 278,
406–7
Caroline Islands 151, 152
Cartwright, Sir Fairfax 161
Casimir-Périer, Jean 191
Castelnau, Édouard, Vicomte de
302, 358
Catholic Church 310
Cattaro 92
Cavour, Camillo Benso, Count of
361, 436, 450
Cetinje 92, 283
Chamberlain, Sir Austen 542
Chamberlain, Joseph 146

Chambrun, Charles de 507–8,
651*n*2
Charlotte, Princess of Prussia (*later*
Empress of Russia) 173
Charykov, Nikolai Valerievich 189,
259, 260–61, 347
Chataldja line (First Balkan War
fortifications) 253, 256, 264
Chelius, Oskar von 524
China:
Boxer Rebellion (1898-1901) 137,
153, 168, 180
British interests in 130, 131, 137–8,
166, 322
German interests in 140–41, 151,
163, 168, 180
Russian interests in 131, 137–8,
144, 153, 176, 322
Sino-Japanese War (1894-95) 137,
138, 140, 158
Chotek, Countess Sophie (*later*
Duchess of Hohenberg) 396
assassination 367–76
marriage to Archduke Franz
Ferdinand 106–7, 370, 380
Churchill, Sir Winston 210, 212, 221,
456, 493, 494, 539, 541, 542–3,
549, 552
Ciganović, Milan 53–4, 56, 383,
385, 390, 455, 465, 467,
575*n*151–2
Cincar-Marković, Dimitrije 4, 14
Cisleithania 65, 67–8, 69, 70, 84
Clary-Aldringen, Prince
Alfons 377
Clausewitz, Carl von 486–7
Clemenceau, Georges 217, 310,
311, 441
Cleveland, Grover 161
code-breaking 427, 441
Cologne 433
Combes, Émile 217
Congo 207, 208, 209